Donnie Iris and the Cruisers are the best-kept secret from the golden age of FM radio.

The long-running band of brothers called the Cruisers is just one chapter in the saga of Donnie Iris, the classic-rock king of the City of Champions, Pittsburgh.

Iris wrote his way into the national spotlight with "The Rapper," the chart-topping 1969 single by the Jaggerz, whose farewell show accurately billed the group as "Pittsburgh's #1 band for ten years." Iris returned to the bigtime with the Cruisers, a band best known for its string of seven *Billboard* Hot 100 hits in the 1980s, which included "Ah! Leah!" and the MTV favorite "Love Is Like a Rock." When the Cruisers' days on a major record label ended, the group parlayed their loyal following into a continuous, ongoing career, with growing status as regional icons.

The Cruisers' steady itinerary is the most visible part of the members' broad careers onstage and off. Donnie and the Cruisers have played, written, and recorded with Gamble & Huff, Kiss, Wild Cherry, Bon Jovi, Carlos Santana, Breathless, Sonny Geraci, B.E. Taylor, LaFlavour, a young Trent Reznor (later of Nine Inch Nails fame), Mason Ruffner, The Pulse, Wolfman Jack, the James Gang, and other luminaries.

In this exhaustively researched oral history, for the first time, Donnie, the Cruisers, and friends discuss 50 years of life in the show-business middle class.

Highlights include the longest account of the Jaggerz' colorful journey from college campuses to the *Billboard* chart; behind-the-scenes drama that shaped the Cruisers' commercial fortunes; the dynamic between Donnie Iris and creative partner Mark Avsec; a long look at the WDVE comedy sketches that reinvented Donnie's public image and the very fabric of Southwestern Pennsylvania culture; thorough reflections on the band's albums, songs, and side projects; and a parade of surprising developments even the band didn't know. Packed with revealing photos, this detailed page turner is easy to read and hard to put down.

The Story of Donnie Iris and the Cruisers is result of countless conversations between the band members, witnesses, and author D.X. Ferris, a Pittsburgh native and an Ohio Society of Professional Journalists Reporter of the Year. Features a foreword by longtime *DVE Morning Show* co-host Jim Krenn.

Library of Congress Cataloging-in-Publication Data

Ferris, D.X.
p. cm – (66 2/3)
Includes index
The Story of Donnie Iris and the Cruisers / Ferris, D.X.
Includes bibliographical references.
ISBN-13: 978-0-692-99746-8 (paperback; alk. paper)
1. Donnie Iris and the Cruisers (Musical group)
2. Rock Musicians—United States—Biography
3. Rock and Roll (Musical genre)
4. Pittsburgh
5. Donnie Iris. I. Title

Credits:

All Layout and Design, including cover: Marty Lee Hoenes, MartyLeeDesigns.com
Design and production assistance: Mary Thomas
Proofreaders: Brendan Halpin, Diana Dewey
Archivist: Glenn Ratner
Cover image: Donnie Iris © by Anastasia Pantsios
Back cover image: Donnie Iris by Marcia Resnick
Edition 1.1, updated January 2018.

THE STORY OF

DONNIE IRIS
AND THE CRUISERS

BY **D.X. FERRIS**

FOREWORD BY JIM KRENN

Table of Contents

PART II: INJURED IN THE GAME

 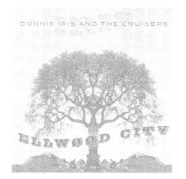 

Before you read further…

Assuming you aren't already…

Listen to Donnie Iris and the Cruisers'
"That's the Way Love Ought to Be."

Seriously.

Note Albritton's propulsive bass line.
Donnie's pumped and passionate vocals.
Kevin's smashing, crashing drums.
Listen in the dark — did you see that?
Marty's guitar and Mark's keyboards actually
shoot sparks. No, *flames*.

That's what we're talking about here.

That song is Donnie Iris and the Cruisers
at their glorious best.

Outside Pittsburgh, it was not a big song.

Here's why.

> You dance with the
> one that brung ya.

~ DARRELL ROYAL (AMONG OTHERS)

> I get by with a little help
> from my friends.

~ JOHN LENNON &
PAUL MCCARTNEY

> I was talking to
> Michael Stanley one time,
> and he told me,
> 'Rock and roll will either
> kill ya or keep ya young.'
> But that seems awfully extreme.
> I think it should be more like
> a bowling league.

~ DAVID GIFFELS

Foreword: That's Donnie.

BY JIM KRENN, THE DVE MORNING SHOW, 1988-2011

I slept out overnight to get tickets to my first Donnie Iris concert.

I'm a Pittsburgh boy, through and through. Blue-collar, hard-working family. I grew up in the Strip District, on 12th Street, in an alley. Went to St. Mary's and North Catholic High School. Then I went to IUP, Indiana University of Pennsylvania.

There's this girl I met. She loved Donnie Iris. We all love Donnie Iris. Everybody on the campus is starting to love Donnie Iris at the time — he was the hot underground thing that was breaking. He was so hot, we *knew* he was going to sell out the Fisher Auditorium. I wanted to get a ticket so I could ask that girl out. There was a line of people sleeping out overnight to buy tickets. I was one of them.

The concert was amazing. He sweats. He sings "I Can't Hear You." He says he's gonna strap on his guitar and be a big rock star. He does the rap, he gets the crowd chanting. He walks off and comes back in a yellow tux. And they play "The Rapper." It was so cool, the whole deal about him. Blew me away.

At that time, I was into Bruce Springsteen. And you could put a Donnie Iris show right next to Bruce's. The funny thing is: 30 years later, after I worked at DVE for 25 years and saw every rock performer in the world, at the end of the day, Donnie Iris and Bruce Springsteen are probably the best two live performers I've ever seen.

What makes Donnie great: the music and the songs and the attitude.

At the time, I was an aspiring performer. There was something about him: Donnie always looked like he was having the greatest time. It was fun, like he was having some sort of vacation on stage. And that's what the audience feel. It's what makes a show transcend just watching a band play: When you see a performer enjoying himself on that level, you forget everything. You have no worries, no bills, no grades, no girl trouble. Just the concert, the band on stage, *Donnie Iris*. It's still true to this day. It transcends generations, age, trends, styles. It's an intangible. It's just who Donnie is. And Mark Avsec and the whole band are part of that, the energy that they put out. They make you feel like *you're* on vacation.

With the production and arrangements that Mark created, Donnie's voice has operatic tones, believe it or not. It's got a clarity, with a rock edge. It's like Elvis meets Mick Jagger. He can go from "I Can't Hear You No More" to "Sweet Merilee" to "My Girl" — it's almost like he's three lead singers. And there's his trademark scream — it's a scratchy scream, but it's always in tune, and it's appealing. That's why I use Springsteen as a comparison: It's got the same vibe, the pride in where he's from. That's part of his swagger. And there was a bit of humor to the songs.

Pittsburgh loves rock, or classic rock, or whatever you can call Donnie. That kind of music is real. It comes from *real*. Most classic rock tells a story, whether it's the Eagles or the Stones or Donnie Iris or Springsteen. They are our storytellers. And that's why we relate to classic rock so much in our region: It's real. There's nothing fancy about it. There's nothing fancy about a Marty guitar solo. You're either great or you're not. There's nothing phony to it. And we love that. Me, being a blue-collar kid from Pittsburgh, I felt like he just tapped into that whole thing.

Donnie inspired me. I was just starting on the radio. I was a standup comedian. I loved the fact that he was a national talent who chose to live in Pittsburgh. I thought, "That's the kind of entertainer I want to be. He chooses to live in the tri-state area that he loves. He could go anywhere that he wants. But he's here, for the people here."

I met Donnie, and I got to know him. He was an inspiration. From the first moment I met him, I saw the guy treat people with respect. He has a respect for humanity that I've seen in very few performers. Fame, on any level, can be intoxicating. It can take people out of themselves. Donnie never acted like that, ever. And he could have. But he was who he was. I appreciated that. There's a transparency to any performer we love. And I don't think anyone was ever more transparent than Donnie.

Donnie is just a kind soul, a good person. That's part of his success. He never gouged anybody for money. If I ever had a charity event, I didn't have to ask twice. He'd say, "Alright, Jim. I'll be there." And he'd show up. He never said, "I need *this amount* for my fee." He never held out to be the guest of honor at a $400 black-tie gala. Never asked for anything. He's been like that with his price points, too: never gouged his audience either.

One of the reasons I love Pittsburgh: the *values* of Pittsburgh. I think we are, in general, hardworking people who are trying to do the right thing. Donnie is a reflection of all of that. There may be highs and lows, but we're going to keep striving. It's about helping out your fellow man and helping people out when they're down. And when you're down, you pick yourself up, brush yourself off, and don't complain. And that's the kind of guy he is.

I've never read an article where Donnie Iris complained. In Donnie's eyes, it was always fun, and I think he knew he was blessed. I think he'd be happy performing anywhere, if it was a little room or a stadium. He's an elite performer, because that's what performing is about. Donnie figured that out at a young age. And it shows now: It's not about money. It's about performance. That's pure. That's Donnie.

I put Donnie Iris in the Pittsburgh Mount Rushmore, with Mr. Rogers, Rick Sebak, Roberto Clemente, Mario Lemieux, Franco Harris, Rocky Bleier — all the guys who represent the Burgh. I don't think anyone would argue that he's on the Mount Rushmore of Mount Washington.

— Jim Krenn, Pittsburgh, September 2017
WDVE, 1988-2011
Co-Creator, Pants n 'Nat
Pittsburgh City Paper Readers'
Favorite Radio Personality of the Year
No Restrictions Podcast

Prologue From the Band

D.X. Ferris approached us about writing this book more than seven years ago (I think). We demurred. Not because he was not a good writer. Ferris flattered me by writing a cover story on me for *Scene Magazine* back in 2010. We knew he could write. We did not know if there was a real story about our band. And we did not know how it would get published.

Ferris (as he likes to be called) persisted and claims that he found the story. This is his book. We cooperated (tolerated?) when he called frequently for information and interviews. He had to stay on it, because we didn't always make it easy for him.

Speaking for myself (as well as for Donnie, Marty, Kevin, Albritton, and Paul), we are flattered that someone thought it was important to write a book about us.

We look forward to reading it and seeing what that story is. It has been augmented with terrific photographs taken by Anastasia Pantsios and Richard Kelly.

If you ask me, the best times for the Cruisers are happening right now. Donnie is almost 75 and singing better than ever. Our commitment to the music and to each other have been tested over time. But we have endured as best friends, full of love and respect for one another – and I think we are playing better on stage than at any point in our career. So come to a show.

It all starts with Donnie, the nicest guy in the room, who sets the tone with his love and positive outlook. And he has been lucky to be surrounded by a capable cast of musicians and technicians who are devoted to him and to this enterprise, and who set the table for him. *Donnie Iris and The Cruisers* has been a total collaborative effort over the years, with material contributions from all involved, not just one or two people.

Ferris told me he was born to write this book. I hope he has a bigger purpose ahead of him. As far as we're concerned, we're just a rock band that impacted Pittsburgh culture. I know that Donnie does not think it's a big deal. But I would agree that nobody could have written this book except for Ferris.

Besides our loved ones, there are a handful of people who motivated Donnie, myself, Marty, Kevin – and now Paul – to keep going and continuing to create through the dark years: Mike Belkin, our manager and most trusted advisor; Glenn Ratner (who created the *Parallel Time* website); Jim Markovich (our longtime sound tech); Denise Labbe at Belkin Management (who has kept us organized for years); and Mark Dvoroznak, who has been so instrumental in helping us put out albums and creative content (he has been a real friend in every sense of the word). We also extend a shout-out to drummist Tommy Rich and bass player Scott Alan, who both spent an extended period of time with us.

We appreciate that Ferris thought our story was important and that we didn't waste our time. He claims that none of us really knew the story. So we will read it too.

— Mark Avsec, December 3, 2017

What This Book Is, How It Works, and How To Use It

This is the story of Donnie Iris... and the Cruisers.

In their own words.

Mostly.

Feel free to skip the rest of this part. But it will help you understand what you're reading, where it's coming from, and how to use it.

Read the table of contents. If you don't want to hear about the band's down years, proceed directly to the chapter about how WDVE's Pants n 'Nat skits helped the Cruisers turn their career around. If numbers bore you and you want the biggest question-and-answer interview with Donnie ever, go straight to chapter 75.

This book has five parts: First, you meet the Cruisers. One at a time, you learn who the band members are and where they came from. Second is the longest, most detailed account of Donnie's first big band, the Jaggerz. It's a colorful look back at a part of America that disappeared a long time ago. Third, like never before, is the story of the Cruisers in unprecedented detail. That's most of the book. That saga breaks down into three parts: The band come together and make it big. Then the wheels come off, and things almost grind to a halt. And finally, when most groups would have fought, quit or fired everybody, the Cruisers commit to each other once and for all, and become something that is maybe less popular, but more meaningful than it ever was.

The goal for this book was to document and explain the Cruisers' largely undocumented career(s). I'm a lifelong fan. I had questions about the band. And they answered most of them, some of which I've been pondering since the 1980s.

1981. I live half an hour outside of Pittsburgh, a little town called California. I start listening to the radio, rock station 96 KX. Donnie Iris & the Cruisers are in the mix, alongside the Police, Journey, Tom Petty, Stevie Nicks, Rush, and Van Halen. I don't know Donnie's a local cat. I just know his band is as good as those other groups — and better than some. I never do buy a Rush album. But I get the entire Van Halen catalog. I like supercool frontmen.

Van Halen's David Lee Roth is a superhero, a Warner Bros cartoon, a golden god, Groucho Marx, wily Odysseus. I will never be as cool as him for one day of my life. But Donnie says he reads Spider-Man comic books. I like girls and rock 'n' roll, too. I later learn he does the best he can with what he has. Then and now, I can *relate* to Donnie Iris. By 1985, Roth and Iris are the only two artists from that list I still actively follow (though I'll come back around). But DVE — as in 102.5 FM, WDVE — doesn't play Donnie's amazing new single, "Injured in the Game of Love," nearly enough. I want *more* Donnie.

It takes some doing, but I get more Donnie. 32 years later, I know why "Injured" didn't get enough airplay. In 2017, after two years of countless questions, Donnie and the Cruisers start telling me I know more about the band than they do. I had help. But they're not wrong.

The initial idea for this book was: compile a straightforward oral history of Donnie Iris and his band of brothers, the Cruisers.

It wasn't that simple. Not even close.

It took a lot of people to tell Donnie's story.

Donnie and the band, *and* their management team, *and* their radio promoter, *and* ex-bandmates, *and* friends, *and* sound guy... not one of them knew the full story of Donnie Iris — and how his career unfolded.

Not to mention Donnie and his famously humble disposition. In two years of interviews, he steadfastly refused to claim solitary credit for a single highlight from his 50-year musical career. Not once did he frame a memory in terms of "I wrote *this*," "I rocked *that* arena" or anything to the effect of "*I* made it happen." It's all *we* and "Marty played a smokin' solo" and "Mark wrote a good song." Donnie was not the best witness to Donnie's story.

So people from Donnie's life shared pieces of the saga, as they remembered them.

Every answer created more questions. So they answered more questions, to the best of their recollection. Then they answered more. I combed through the patchy, incomplete, often incorrect historical record: articles, radio charts, books, features, reviews, fan recollections, and Glenn Ratner's invaluable online archive Parallel Time. No *way* does this book exist without Glenn, the Cruisers' biggest fan.

If you *do* know the story, your first reaction to many of the forthcoming details may be, "That's not right." Many — if not most — of the accounts and details in here contradict previous accounts and articles... and even firsthand recollections from the subjects themselves.

Prime example: For 40 years, the members of Donnie's first big band, the Jaggerz, have been saying the varsity lineup split in 1975. *That's* not right. They played their last show January 17, 1976. If Donnie confidently recalled a backwoods concert promoter pointing guns at Wild Cherry in 1978, it sure sounds reliable. But his firm recollection doesn't mean it didn't happen in 1979.

For more than four decades, a number of savvy writers have documented Donnie's career. If they were lucky, they had enough space for 500 words. Most had closer to 100. And researching his career was far easier in 2015-17 than it was in 1982 and 2009 (though still hard).

Now apply those dynamics to Donnie's 55-year career as a professional musician. Think about a time you and your wife or brother told the same story from 20 or 40 years ago. Did all the details match? Didn't think so. And, as *American Hardcore* author Steven Blush once noted for his topic, "Everything on the internet is wrong."[II.1]

Donnie and the Cruisers have not lived the typical rock and roll story: Donnie made sacrifices to be where he is, but he made them at his own expense. He was tested, and he passed. No self-destruction, addiction, or redemption. People are lost. Reconciliations are staged. But it's a story of love, not bad blood. You've been reading the short version for 37 years. We approached this volume as a unique opportunity to present the long version. If you want the full story, here it comes.

The heretofore untold saga of the Cruisers is a barrage of non-absolutes and circumstances that translate, essentially, to "Yes, *but*..." and "...mostly." The Jaggerz had a number-one single — on *one* organization's chart. The Cruisers *sort of* had a major-label record deal. Accurately presenting these matters requires a few extra words here and there. The saga defies what media people call a *narrative* — a typical arc for a story, which is often more recognizable that right.

This history features commentary from the figures who were willing to talk at the time — in case you're thinking, "Why didn't they interview this guy or that girl?" Example: Carl Maduri, the band's co-manager in their golden years, is long retired. He didn't even testify for the band's excellent 2004 documentary, *King Cool: The History of the Cruisers*. Some of the people who might have added golden commentary are no longer with us, such as sound engineer Jerry Reed, Jaggerz manager Joe Rock, and Donnie's longtime running buddy, B.E. Taylor. Some of the instrumental characters didn't want to talk. Some of the principals didn't have much to say.

Whenever possible, dates are cross-referenced between sources. If an old article or advertisement in a May 1981 issue of *Billboard* says the Fair Warning album was slated for July 1981 release, that information does not guarantee the record *was* released in July 1981. Similarly, if you have an old article that says the Cruisers were slated to play Chino Prison in December 1972, it doesn't mean the gig actually happened.

The fans and the band know the Cruisers as Donnie, Mark, Marty, Albritton, Kevin, and Paul. So that's how the book generally refers to them. Aside from that, it adheres to the convention of identifying the speakers by their last name. It's an unusual style, but it's easier to read. More important, it's a better approximation of how it feels to hear the Cruisers talk amongst themselves.

The late, great *Jerry* Reed co-founded a studio named *Jeree* Recording, often referred to as *Jerry's* studio, and often as *Jeree's*.

In Pittsburgh, music fans who listen to radio station 102.5 FM WDVE call the station "DVE," pronounced "D-V-E," no W necessary. If you know what you're talking about, that's how it is. Pittsburghers, by the way, often call the city "The Burgh." No apostrophe there either.

When astute fans react to written accounts, the most frequent comment is, "The story doesn't include this fact I know, so it's no good." Apologies if this account overlooks your favorite piece of emblematic trivia.

The use and abuse of the term "one-hit wonder" tells you everything you need to know about rock journalism, a field that is not known for professional rigor. Correctly applied, the term "one-hit wonder" refers to an act that had one — and only one — song enter the *Billboard* Top 40, the upper echelon of the magazine's Hot 100 singles chart.

Donnie Iris and the Cruisers had three Top 40 singles, so the band is not a one-hit wonder. Michael Stanley is not a one-hit wonder, because he had two Top 40 singles. The B.E. Taylor Group had two Hot 100 singles, but neither cracked the national *Billboard* Top 40. So Taylor and friends are not a one-hit wonder either, even though "Vitamin L" was *gigantic* on Pittsburgh radio.

For albums and singles, typically, the widely circulated release dates are vague or wrong. The dates in the following pages are still more detailed than ever. When they aren't precise, at least they aren't wrong.

STYLE NOTES: Punctuation is an odd and malleable thing. The transcribed dialogue is punctuated to recreate the subjects' syntax and delivery, with respect to clarity and readability. Interview portions have also been edited for clarity and concision.

Metrics like the *Billboard* charts do not necessarily reflect how *good* an album or single is, but they are significant when charting a band's trajectory. So they appear often. Capitalizing chart positions (Number 29) is a common, gratuitous convention that goes ignored here.

Properly citing previous writers' work can be clunky, and it's not a popular practice in rock writing — but it's the right thing to do.

Footnotes, endnotes, body text, and citations are formatted in A.P.E. Style. Oxford commas are useful.

Following, then, is the story of Donnie Iris. And the Cruisers. As told by the band. With a little help from his friends. A *lot*, actually. With some blanks filled in.

Thank you for reading. Enjoy.

— Ferris, November 2017

PLAYBOY'S D.J. POLL

The trouble with some contests is that they're judged by amateurs. Of course, there's good reason for doing things that way; after all, it involves the same principle that made America great. On the other hand, there are plenty of good reasons for letting the pros have their say. Experience counts. With that in mind, we asked 22 of the country's best-known radio personalities for their choices of the year's best music. Part of the point was to see just how closely their personal tastes would mirror the tastes of their audiences—you. Frankly, we didn't expect such little deviation from our readers' poll results. What this means, we suppose, is that there's some kind of uniformity out there. Quality, like the color yellow, is difficult to describe but everyone knows it when he steps in it. What follows, then, are the names of the d.j.s and their choices.

Howard Hesseman (Dr. Johnny Fever of *WKRP in Cincinnati*)
Tommy Edwards WLS, Chicago
Larry Lujack   WLS, Chicago
Steve Dahl   WLS-FM, Chicago
Garry Meier   WLS-FM, Chicago
Sky Daniels   WLUP, Chicago
John Fisher   WMET, Chicago
Kid Leo   WMMS, Cleveland
B. Mitchel Reed KLOS, Los Angeles
Jeff Gonzer   KMET, Los Angeles
Jack Snyder   KMET, Los Angeles
Mary Turner   KMET, Los Angeles
Dan Ingram   WABC, New York
Dave Herman   WNEW-FM, New York
Richard Neer   WNEW-FM, New York
Pat St. John   WPLJ, New York

Frankie Crocker WBLS, New York
Joe Bonadonna WMMR, Philadelphia
Lisa Richards   WMMR, Philadelphia
Picozzi   WYSP, Philadelphia
Jimmy Roach   WDVE, Pittsburgh
Tempie Lindsey KISS, San Antonio

D.J. POLL RESULTS:

BEST ALBUM
1. Rolling Stones / Tattoo You
2. REO Speedwagon / Hi Infidelity
3. Steve Winwood / Arc of a Diver

BEST SINGLE
1. Rolling Stones / Start Me Up
2. Donnie Iris / Ah Leah
3. The Go-Go's / Our Lips Are Sealed

BEST GROUP
1. Rolling Stones
2. Bruce Springsteen & The E Street Band
3. The Police

BEST MALE SINGER
1. Bruce Springsteen
2. Mick Jagger
3. Bob Seger

BEST FEMALE SINGER
1. Stevie Nicks
2. Chrissie Hynde
3. Pat Benatar

163

Playboy Magazine listed "Ah! Leah!" as the #2 Best Single in America in its 1982 DJ Poll.

CHAPTER 1

Donnie & the Cruisers,
Long Story Short

Donnie Iris and the Cruisers: true musical treasures, but obscure ones. If you like rock music, you should know the group and their work. So listen up.

Rock and roll was never more robust across the board than in the early 1980s. FM radio broadcast a parade of jaw-dropping talent: Veterans were hitting their peak. A quality new act arrived every week. New sounds kept coming. And the Cruisers were in the mix.

The Cruisers are a huge deal in Pittsburgh, where Donnie could run for mayor and maybe win. They're a pretty big deal in Cleveland, the nearby home of Cruisers bandleader/songwriter/producer Mark Avsec. Cleveland is a town of discriminating tastes, home of the Rock and Roll Hall of Fame — and not just because the rent is cheap.

The band still racks up regular radio spins from Tampa to San Diego. Despite over 36 years of consistent — if not overwhelming — airplay, Donnie and the Cruisers have an incorrect reputation as one-hit wonders. That dubious distinction is due to their most popular song, the immaculately produced, performance-driven, masterful slab of guitar rock that is "Ah! Leah!" It's not their biggest chart hit, but it's the song people remember. If you ever listened to real rock radio, you probably know it. If you've seen the video, you definitely remember *that*, the guy in the yellow tuxedo. That's Donnie Iris.

Donnie is not a one-hit wonder. Neither are the Cruisers. Donnie and the Cruisers landed seven singles on the *Billboard* Hot 100 singles chart between 1980 and 1985. Three of them were Top 40 singles. That's *three* hits. Three. Donnie wrote a number 1 — or number 2, depends who you're asking — single for his previous band, the Jaggerz. The long running group is best known for that jangly novelty smash, "The Rapper." Donnie and Mark had another Hot 100 song in 1988, with a different project, Cellarful of Noise.

Still, that "one-hit wonder" tag won't go away. And that's not right. It does fit a certain narrative, and people like narratives; they're easy to tell and understand, even when they're not accurate. On one superficial level, Donnie's story is a common one. Every part of the USA has a band like the Cruisers, who are exceptionally large there, but a footnote everywhere else: Crack the Sky in Baltimore. Mother's Finest in Atlanta. The Nighthawks in D.C. Oingo Boingo in Los Angeles. Michael Stanley in Cleveland. Shooting Star in Kansas City. Southside Johnny & the Asbury Jukes in Jersey.

Every city has a band like that, but Donnie and the Cruisers' careers run bigger and deeper. Donnie recorded with soul legends Gamble and Huff. Mark wrote a song for Bon Jovi. Drummer Kevin Valentine recorded with Kiss. Bassist Albritton McClain recorded with David Werner, and went on to score movies. Mark wrote an enduring disco hit. And a song for the reborn Carlos Santana. Kevin and Albritton played with a young Trent Reznor, later of Nine Inch Nails fame.

A host of other renowned artists and captains of the entertainment industry worked with Donnie and his players: Jerry Weintraub. Neil Bogart. Wild Cherry. Cinderella. The Godz. Mason Ruffner. The James Gang and Joe Walsh. Eagles manager Irving Azoff himself makes a cameo, critically wounding the band in their halcyon 1980s major-label days. The guys accomplished some things, and they kept good company. They're not the biggest names, but they were in the hunt when the game was on.

Classic rock matters. It's old, but that's the point: If you can listen to a song day in, day out for 40 years and still feel something, that's *magic*. Classic rock is modern American folk music. It has been here forever. It is not going away. Pittsburgh is the City of Champions, and Donnie is its classic-rock champion. He's the man who made it furthest in that arena, as the numbers prove.

"Donnie Iris provides a sense of community in Pittsburgh," says Jason Pettigrew, a Burgh-area native and editor-in-chief of *Alternative Press*, America's number two rock magazine. "He's like a sports team. And sports builds communities, because everybody loves a winning team. And they talk about that, and how a player performs, with a heightened sense of excitement and genuine interest. The people who are into the Cruisers probably went to see Journey and went to see the Cars. But this is the hometown team, and they're always ready to support the hometown team, even though they lost some games."

That's a great point: The Bengals are a big deal in Cincinnati; five hours away, you'd be hard-pressed to find a lot of fans. But for the people who love a team, a day built around a game is bliss. Maybe you can appreciate that franchise if you read a book about Paul Brown — but if you didn't grow up a Bengals fan, you probably don't care.

The *All Music Guide to Rock* declares: "Donnie Iris is one of the classiest rock singers who deserved widespread stardom but never achieved it. At least the public and the radio had the good sense to embrace early-'80s hits 'Ah! Leah!' and 'Love Is Like a Rock.'" [1.1]

Donnie *does* have a national audience. To name one market, he's a crowd pleaser at KFAI FM in Minneapolis.

"Whenever I put on Donnie Iris, it really gets a rise out of my listeners," says Ron Gerber, a DJ who references the band repeatedly in his book *Between the Songs*. "The kind of people who dig it are the people who like intelligent pop. They think, 'This is a good song, but it wouldn't be as good if it sold two million copies at the time. There's a lost-gem aspect to it, the same kind of *nod-wink* I get when I play 'Driver's Seat' by Sniff 'n' the Tears or 'He Can't Love You' by Michael Stanley. Here in the Midwest, we call them 'meat rock' to sum up the Cleveland-Pittsburgh kind of sound — stuff that has some *chunk* to it."

When radio was still somewhat of a meritocracy, that chunk *played*. Witness the tale of the tape: For an idea of how the Cruisers truly stack up against loosely comparable acts, look at their metrics from 1980 to 1985 — the years they were connected to prominent major labels.

SONGS ON *BILLBOARD* HOT 100 SINGLES CHART, 1980-1985

Journey:	14	Van Halen:	7
REO Speedwagon:	11	ZZ Top:	7
Foreigner:	10	**Donnie & the Cruisers:**	**7**
Billy Squier:	10	Pretenders:	6
Huey Lewis & the News:	9	John Waite:	6
The Police:	9	Asia:	5
Bruce Springsteen:	9	Cheap Trick:	5
Songs by Mark Avsec:	**9**	Corey Hart:	5
Loverboy:	8	Joan Jett:	5
Night Ranger:	8	AC/DC:	4
38 Special:	8	Bon Jovi:	4*
Thompson Twins:	7	Thomas Dolby:	3
Toto:	7	Cellarful of Noise:	1*

*Includes a song written by Cruiser Mark Avsec; all numbers from Billboard. [1.3]

In their prime, working limited promotional resources, the Cruisers still managed to be a competitive presence on national radio.

Between 1980 and 1985, Donnie, Mark Avsec and the Cruisers combined wrote as many *Billboard* Hot 100 singles as Bruce Springsteen, Huey Lewis & the News, and the Police.

In those years, Mark and the Cruisers combined wrote more charting singles than Van Halen, ZZ Top,

Toto, Loverboy, Night Ranger, Asia, the Thompson Twins, Cheap Trick, the Pretenders, John Waite, AC/DC, Corey Hart, Thomas Dolby, Joan Jett, and Bon Jovi.

Yes: Those are Hot 100 tracks. **No:** The Cruisers did not have any songs in the top 20 or Top 10. **Yes:** Bon Jovi and Bruce Springsteen grew into far larger phenomena later. No: The Cruisers weren't headlining arenas, and their sales were nowhere close. *But...*

Excluding songs Mark wrote for other groups, between 1980 and 1985, Donnie & the Cruisers scored as many Hot 100 songs as Van Halen, ZZ Top, the Thompson Twins, and Toto.

From 1980 through 1985, the Cruisers had more Hot 100 hits than Cheap Trick, the Pretenders, John Waite, AC/DC, Asia, Corey Hart, Thomas Dolby, Joan Jett, and Bon Jovi.

Donnie & the Cruisers had one fewer Hot 100 single than Night Ranger and Loverboy; two fewer than the Police and Huey Lewis.

Donnie and the Cruisers made the scene during a glorious phase when FM radio was a vital component of American life. As of this writing, the band generally exists on radio stations with the Classic Rock, Best of the Best, and Jack FM formats. In their heyday, the Cruisers were often seen as part of the AOR movement, *Album Oriented Rock*, when classic rock was evolving from the '70s style of long hair and long songs, into the '80s mode of shorter hair and shorter songs, with keyboards in the mix as often as not. In retrospect, power pop is probably a better fit.

In that milieu, Donnie and the Cruisers have their niche: Donnie is a regular guy, not a mythic figure carved from inscrutable stone. Bruce Springsteen's early theme was running until you couldn't run anymore. Hailing from a similar blue-collar world, Donnie took a different approach to life. He and Mark Avsec wrote songs about wild weekends — but they weren't fixated on escaping. Donnie sings songs about occupying his everyday world as fully as possible, doing his best to be a glowing presence, whether it's Saturday night behind Louie's bar, or a somber Tuesday morning in September 2001. Donnie has a hungry heart, but he wasn't born to run; Donnie dutifully stays where he is, does the best he can, and makes the most of it.

The Cruisers display more uncut joy than Springsteen. They have more good songs than Asia and Blue Öyster Cult. They rock harder than Toto and 38 Special. Donnie's hits have aged better than Loverboy's. He's more cosmopolitan than John Mellencamp. Ballsier than Corey Hart and John Waite. The Cruisers have more low end than Cheap Trick. They're faster than Thin Lizzy (usually). Donnie is more relatable than David Lee Roth — and he's the only other singer from this list who could have handled "Just a Gigolo."

Let's be clear: This fan is *not* claiming Donnie Iris and the Cruisers are in a league with Van Halen or Tom Petty or Led Zeppelin or Bon Jovi. But *20th Century Masters: The Millennium Collection: Best of Donnie Iris* is a must-hear compilation of tunes. They're as good as music gets, coming from mortal musicians — as opposed to certified rock gods frequently graced by the Muses.

Play the Cruisers' best tunes for a discriminating music fan, and they usually say something to the effect of, "They sound like hits," "They should have been early MTV staples," and "Donnie Iris should have been huge." Don't take my biased, Pittsburgh-native word for it.

Witness the results of *Playboy* magazine's 1982 national DJ Poll, which tallied the opinions of heavy-hitter DJs from major markets — we're talking New York, Chicago, Los Angeles.[1,2] Professionals in the know listened to everything that was on the airwaves in 1981. And they ranked "Ah! Leah!" as the number 2 single of the year, between two truly epochal tracks: the Rolling Stones' "Start Me Up" and the Go-Gos' "Our Lips Are Sealed."

But — at the risk of spoiling the story — Donnie's singles didn't always get the promotional push they deserved. His bands had the goods, though. They still do. As of this writing, Donnie is nearly 75 years old. His voice still goes as high and low as it did in the '80s (and '70s and '60s and '90s). The band rock the house live. If you can score one, get a ticket to a show at Jergel's and see for yourself.

As this book explains, there are good and bad reasons why you never heard the full tale of Donnie and the Cruisers — and maybe never heard their whole body of work. Long story short, they couldn't catch a break, even when they had some of the biggest names in the business on their team. Having a hit single was never as simple as writing and recording a good song. Life isn't fair.

And there came a time when Donnie and the band had other matters to attend to. Donnie spent 20 years as a financial professional. Mark is a respected attorney and partner in an international law firm. Guitarist Marty Lee Hoenes is a career creative professional. Original bassist Albritton McClain never stopped playing. Current bassist Paul Goll works on the cutting edge of a growing health issue. Drummer Kevin Valentine mixes sound for some of the top television shows.

Even hardcore fans don't realize how long and distinguished the Cruisers' collective creative careers are — which is reasonable; neither do most of the members. The group have over 40 years of shared history, mythology and art that they still discuss, rehash and celebrate several times a year. But even in their longest hang session, the Cruisers never connected all the different forces, people, ideas and factors that shaped their career.

Donnie's glory days were infinitely better than what happens to most would-be rockers who pick up a guitar and chase a rock-and-roll dream. When Donnie should have been down for the count, he got up and scored more hits. The Cruisers' run was better than what happens to the average band that does score a major-label deal. Donnie Iris and the Cruisers won the lottery. Donnie won it twice. They *did* it. They did it well. They did better than most.

So grab a tasty beverage. Pull up a chair. For the first time, prepare to witness the story of Donnie Iris, the Jaggerz, the Cruisers, and their friends from a golden age of rock and roll in Pittsburgh, America and — this will be news to many of you — Cleveland.

Meet The Cruisers

Donnie Iris (Photo by Anastasia Pantsios)

CHAPTER 2

Meet Donnie Iris

On the deck at Jergel's Rhythm Grille, he has them on the edge of their seats. They're crouched and waiting in the cigar bar too, three layers deep, hanging on his every word. Tonight, they're hoping to hear a story from, or maybe ask a question to, Donnie Iris.

Donnie has been singing for over 60 years — and rocking for more than 50. Now a retired businessman, the frontman floats through Southwestern Pennsylvania and Ohio on a hard-earned cloud of cigar smoke, with his integrity, friendships, voice, and smile intact.

As a recording artist, Donnie spent 19 years on the *Billboard* Hot 100 singles chart. His presence was not constant, which makes his run that much more of an accomplishment. Iris has been a bankable name and face for a full five decades, on stage and off. He hasn't been on the charts since the late '80s. But Donnie is still a commodity in this part of the country, the wooded Appalachian hills that give way to the flat Midwest.

Tonight, Donnie is in his unofficial home base, a clubhouse, the staging ground for the Cruisers. Jergel's is a sprawling hot spot 20 minutes north of Pittsburgh. It's a restaurant, concert-quality night club, and a cigar bar. Donnie draws crowds to all three parts. The Cruisers have been selling out two or more increasingly in-demand shows a year since Donnie turned 73. When the band is playing, both levels of the concert hall become a standing-room-only sweatbox.

Tonight, however, is a low-key event. Donnie is making a regularly scheduled appearance at the cigar bar, where a diverse crowd circle the singer, trying to look cool while they patiently wait for an opening to introduce themselves and hear a few words from Pittsburgh's longest-running rock star. The crowd: Immaculately attired politicians. Stylish aspiring musicians. Leather-and-denim-clad bikers. Suburbanites tipping a wine. Everybody loves Donnie Iris.

In 1969, Donnie wrote the Jaggerz' single "The Rapper." It reached number 1 or 2 on the national radio singles charts in 1970 — the number depends which organization's chart you cite. After that leftfield hit, he spent ten years in a state of Steel City renown and national obscurity, trying to write another smash single — or maybe find someone who knew what to do with him. He did.

In the 1980s, the Cruisers had a stream of successful albums and singles. Three cracked the *Billboard* Top 40, the singles chart that has always meant the most. After Donnie's biggest band slowed down, he graced the Hot 100 a third time with Cellarful of Noise, another project from Cruisers producer Mark Avsec.

Over the years, Donnie has taken the stage in starring and supporting roles. Business men and the fates tested his loyalties. At some point, the frontman decided friendship was more important than a desperate long shot to extend his chart streak into a third decade. When his days on a major record label ended, he seamlessly transitioned into a business career.

After over 20 years in the music business, Donnie spent another 20 years setting up deals, wearing a sport coat and schmoozing. He stopped wearing his trademark thick black Fortune 410s glasses. But the band never quit. Since 1981, Donnie Iris and the Cruisers haven't gone a full year without performing, even when their keyboardist became a lawyer.

"I've always been amazed," says Jimmy Roach, the Pittsburgh DJ who put Donnie on the local and national radar. "I told B.E. Taylor this once: I think Donnie made a deal with the devil when he was young, to keep his voice. You know how, when guys get old, they *sound* old? Donnie doesn't sound old. He still hits those notes, the same way he did 30 years ago. That's not *normal*."

Donnie worked with some big names over the years. He became one, too. But he always remained *Donnie*. By all accounts, the black-haired senior gentleman taking a drag from a Pardon is a refined, rehearsed version of the same guy who dropped out of college to harmonize in a rock group.

"Bands sometimes have a master plan," says James Gang founder Jimmy Fox, who was part of Donnie's management team in the early '80s. "They want to look like *this*, they want to sound like *this*. Donnie's band has always been the *absence* of that. Donnie has always been the guy standing in his dressing room in Bermuda shorts. Then he's standing on the side of the stage in Bermuda shorts. Then he walks onto stage and performs in Bermuda shorts. Donnie is who he is, and it's what you see. It's true of the other guys in the band, as well. They're very genuine. Especially when the word 'authenticity' is what appeals to people in music that is not pop Top 40."

The cigar nights are monthly, the concerts less frequent. Now Donnie's days are filled with golf, cigars and conversation. He remains as described in the WDVE morning show sketch that made him a Pittsburgh icon once and for all: curly black hair, glasses. Not tall, but a giant presence. Healthy. Upbeat. Energetic. Magnetic. Midway through his 70s, he has hair longer than ever. At his advanced age, he's still competitive in a young man's game. And he's more *Donnie Iris* with each year. It took Donnie a long time to become this Donnie.

Pittsburgh's long-reigning king of rock and rock and roll was not born Donnie Iris. He was born Dominic Ierace, February 28, 1943 — three days after George Harrison and not, contrary to his previous accounts, on the same day as Robert De Niro.

Local or national, most artists are glad to talk about themselves all day. They'll walk you through every heroic step of their self-made success. Not Donnie. If you've never heard his full story before, here's one major reason: He doesn't like talking about himself much.

"Donnie is far and away the quietest rock guy I have ever known," says Fox. "I found it very refreshing at the time, a time when bullshit seemed to rule. Donnie had none of it. Mark was not far behind. And of course, the others were not the people the writers were looking to talk to. In retrospect, it was not entirely a positive thing, as there was no one there to bear witness to the good stuff."

The rest of the Cruisers, also, are not in the habit of hyping their own career. Simply put, not one of them is a self-obsessed jerk. Their creative processes are instinctive. Most of their art resulted from a gut reaction to a fleeting feeling that happened in a shared moment. If you want to know why Albritton McClain's bass line in "That's the Way Love Ought to Be" sounds the way it does, you might as well ask Willie Stargell *why* he hit the longest home run in the history of Olympic Stadium in the particular way he did. That's where they were; that's what they did. Often, Donnie and the Cruisers don't have much to say, even when pressed.

A lot of bad information filled that void. Donnie is responsible for some of it. Mark Avsec, Donnie's longtime creative partner and friend, once circulated a bogus biography, when their band was connected to the major record label MCA. Contrary to that fake life story, Donnie did not have a second wife named Leah Iris Jones. He did not make ends meet breeding gerbils between his stints in the Jaggerz and Wild Cherry, whom he joined late. He did not sing on Wild Cherry's immortal dance-rock classic "Play That Funky Music." Donnie does get around, though.

In terms of radio play, Iris is the most successful Pittsburgh artist of his era or since. All those Top 40 and Top 100 singles put Donnie in the Pittsburgh Rock 'n Roll Legends hall of fame twice, once as a Jagger, once with the Cruisers. Iris received the Frank A. Santamaria Lifetime Achievement Award from the National Italian American Sports Hall of Fame in 2009, placing him in the elite company of WWF heavyweight champion Bruno Sammartino, Major League Baseball manager Tommy Lasorda, Hollywood actor and special effects master Tom Savini and Steel City TV icon Chilly Bill Cardille. Iris is also a 1990 inductee of the Beaver Valley Musicians Union Hall of Fame — and that's an important detail.

Donnie Iris is the kind of Pittsburgh guy who bleeds black and gold, but he's not from Pittsburgh in the strictest, downtown, zip-code-15222 sense of the term. He's a Pittsburgh guy in the sense that most proud Pittsburghers are: They're from the greater Pittsburgh area, maybe Southwestern P-A, perhaps Western Pennsylvania — *Steelers Country*, wherever you want to draw the line, when it's in Fairchance or Erie or State College. Ellwood City, 40 miles north of the Burgh, definitely counts as *Pittsburgh*. It's an outpost of the Iron City, a satellite of the Steel City, a proud part of the City of Champions. Donnie was born in New Castle, close to Ellwood City, which is where Dominic Ierace grew up. And here he became a singer, crooning the first notes in the journey toward becoming — as pronounced in a Pittsburgh accent — "*Dawnie Ahris.*"

DONNIE SAYS:

Dominic was my grandfather on Dad's side. My mum thought it was such an old name, she wanted me to have a nice, old name. Nobody called me Dominic, ever. My mother said, "Call him Donnie and not Dominic" when I was a baby. She didn't want it to be "Dommie" — she thought it sounded weird. No middle name.

I was "Donnie Iris" since I went to school. It was a matter of making it easy to pronounce. It's "eerr-OCH-ee," Italian-wise. But it's always been Americanized. Forget about the E. It's just "Iris." So I just changed it to "I-R-I-S," and I never got that question again. That would have been in the Jaggerz. Nobody called me Dominic ever, not even my dad.

I've been here all my life. I grew up in Ellwood, and I came to Beaver Falls in, I think, '68. Ellwood's smaller, but they're basically the same. All these towns around here are. I would have stayed in Ellwood, but my parents divorced, and my mom wanted to be closer to her mom, so she could be there to watch the kids.

Ellwood City's a steel town, a small steel town. A neighborhood-type place. Working-class. Small houses, small lawns. It's just this little town that's very cool, still. Both my parents are Italian. Part Abruzzi, part Calabria.

When I was a kid, my mother taught me how to sing. She played piano and taught me songs. I didn't play anything. I was just singing until I got to college and started guitar. My dad had musical people on his side too.

And his friends: A lot of his friends would come over and hang out, and I'd sing with them. One guy was a very good guitar player, and I'd sing along, songs like the Sinatra, Tony Bennett kind of stuff. I used to sing one called "Alexander's Ragtime Band." My mom had me do that one when I was probably eight or nine years old.

I was on TV when I was a kid, in Philadelphia, on the Paul Whiteman show. I was maybe nine, ten. I sang "Deed I Do," a song from that time. I sang at weddings. My mum and dad had me on the radio, local stations. I was just a kid. They used to do a lot of things like that. Back then, it was because my mother wanted me to do it. I didn't get hooked on music until my second year of college.

I didn't grow up singing in church. I wasn't an altar boy — we're not Catholic. A lot of people are amazed by that, because all the Italians were Catholic. My mother's side of the family bolted the Catholic religion. This was early on, the early '50s. I don't know if it was controversial; I was a kid, but probably was… It had to be. We went to church quite often, a Christian Missionary Alliance Church. My dad's side of the family stayed Catholic, but my dad was not a religious kind of man.

Dad was a laborer in the steel mill, Tube Mill. They made steel tubing. He worked there many years and got out of it. He became a whiskey salesman. Then, after he got out of that, he and his buddy opened a bar in Ellwood, a place called Lou's Tavern. My dad was great. He was a salesman, man. He was good at it. People loved him. Mom stayed home.

My *mum* and dad divorced when I was a junior in high school. That was unusual for the time. I stayed with my mother. My dad stayed in the house. And me, my sister, and my mother went to my aunt's house. They had room upstairs. That was very weird. I don't think I was all that affected by it, though. It wasn't all that bad. I saw my dad all the time. They were blocks away from each other. Back then, that was very unusual.

I loved my childhood. I went to grade school in Ellwood City, public schools. I did great things like playing football and basketball with all my friends. We all had dogs that would follow us around. School was something none of us really liked, but you had to go. I didn't really realize how blue-collar we were. I guess I realized that maybe one family that lives over in a different part of town, they're supposed to have a lot of money. We were semi-poor, I guess. But we had what we needed, what we wanted. Christmases were always great.

Baseball was my sport as a kid. I played third base. I was really serious about it. I wanted to be good at baseball. I wanted to keep going. I played third base when I was 11 years old. And when I turned 12, I was going to be starting third base, when I got sick. I was so frickin' bummed out.

When I was 12, I developed rheumatic fever. I was bedridden for like nine months. I was fortunate: I didn't have any ill effects after. A lot of kids develop a heart murmur. My mother had it when she was two or three, but she's 96 now.

That would have been '54, maybe. I couldn't really do anything. I used to listen to the Pirates on the radio a lot. I had the score book, and I'd keep score for the games. My dad taught me how to do that. So that's what I did. That's when the Pirates had Ralph Kiner. He was my favorite.

That was Little League. We played on a team called the Elks, sponsored by the Elks club in Elwood. I still have an old Elks' jacket — it was my dad's. It says SAM. My dad was one of the coaches. It was good. My dad and I were tight. My mum and I were tight, too. It wasn't a bitter divorce, not at all.

When I got sick, that was the end of it. I would have been going back into Pony League, and I would have been starting all over. That hurt.

I needed the glasses early, in high school. I got contacts when they first started making them, and I hated them.

I listened to so much music as a teenager. There wasn't an absolute favorite. Even with Elvis out there, I couldn't tell you he was my role model. There were so many great artists. I listened to everyone. I didn't connect to the soul artists as much until later on, when the Jaggerz were together.

Marvin Gaye was a guy I really liked, from the early days, up through the time he sang with Tammy Terrell and did duets; I loved all that material. Later on, the *What's Going On* album. I'd fall asleep with the headphones on, listening to that album. I'd do the same thing with the Beatles' White Album, listen all night long. The psychedelic thing was really something. All their songs were great, but this was a concept album that went into all kinds of stuff. I liked "Rocky Raccoon." I liked "Number 9" — like, "What the hell is this? These guys can do anything!"

My dad was a mechanic. But he got out of that because it was just too dirty and too tough. Too many knuckles being scraped. He taught me some things, how to work on cars. I used to change points and plugs, tinker with my car all the time. I used wax the hell out of my car. It was beautiful.

The *Hit Parader* article[2.1], they came out and interviewed my dad. Took pictures of me and my Buick. I had probably owned the car for a couple years at that point. It's a 1951 Buick. I bought that in Beaver Falls. It was in storage for years, in a car dealership. It was in great shape. Still had the classic seats. I bought it for like 800 bucks. I still have it.

I love cars. My first one, what my dad bought me when I turned 16, was a 1953 Chevy Bel Air, two-door hardtop. It was really a nice car. I told him I wanted an old Cadillac LaSalle, like a 1946, something like that, that they had on the lot. But he wouldn't let me get that, because it had mechanical brakes. I didn't think it was a big deal, but it was a big deal. He got me that Chevy instead. We took it out for a ride, and he said, "This is a good car, a nice, strong car."

During the mid '60s, I had a '64 Pontiac Grand Prix that I used to drag race. There were a couple drag racing places around. One was Salem, Ohio. I forget the names of the others. Me and my friends used to go to a couple. We used to drag race along River Road between Elwood City and Beaver Falls. There was a stretch that was fairly straight.

There was a drag race every night. We saw each other at a place called The Wolverine in Ellwood. It was a carhop place. We'd go there and meet up with all kind of people. Gasoline was 50 cents a gallon. We'd put $2 worth of gas in our car, and we'd be able to drive for God knows how long.

We'd try to stay in the class. I would drag race my Chevy six-cylinder against a guy with a '57 Chevy with a 348 engine, whatever it was. We'd get two of the same basic types of cars. My friend Bob Buzelli and I used to race; he had a similar car. It was friendly, no bets or pink slips or anything.

Once in a while, a car would be coming the other way. So we knew who had to back off and let the other guy pass. Whoever was behind usually had to back off a little. Nobody ever got in a crash or anything. We were lucky. Stupid, but we were lucky. I never wrote a song about that, but we wrote a song called "Dynaflow Love" — I wanted to glamorize my Buick.

I graduated from Lincoln High School, in Ellwood City, 1961. The mill was probably the biggest reason I went to school: because everybody was going to go work in the mill. My family didn't want that for me. So I went to Slippery Rock.

At that point, I was gonna be a teacher. I majored in chemistry my first year, with an English minor. Then I switched to an English major the second year. I was better at English. I did chemistry in high school, but in college, it was too difficult. I was doing real well in English. Not so much literature, but language. I was good at that. I knew about participles and all that stuff. Literature, I'd sit down to read and fall asleep. Then somewhere along the line, I knew it wasn't for me, the whole teacher thing.

I was in a band called the Tri-Vels. Tri-Vels was a trio. Me on vocals and guitar, Jim Evans on guitar, and Dave Amodie on drums. We later added Dave Reeser on bass and became Donnie and the Donnells. It was named after me. The Donnells started at Slippery Rock. We played frat parties, that kind of stuff. It was a cover band. Then I was in a band called the Fabutons.

We did material that was popular in the mid '50s, the Buddy Holly kind of stuff. We played places in Slippery Rock [State College]. It wasn't like *Animal House*. It was pretty tame, not as crazy as you might think. I remember doing one show that was held at the auditorium at Slippery Rock, maybe half an hour worth of stuff. We'd practice at the dormitory. The crowds were pretty much just standing around. There might have been some dancing going on. At the auditorium, it was people sitting. At that point, I knew that was what I wanted to do. I wanted to get out.

My second year in college, I knew I wanted to be in music, and I wanted to pursue it. I felt good about the decision. It wasn't happening for me in college. I didn't like school to begin with. But I went because it was the kind of thing you were supposed to do, or should do.

I remember going to my dad and telling him about it. You expect the worst, that you'll hear, "You gotta stay in school!" — all that.

But he was 100 percent behind me. He said, "You go ahead and do whatever you want to do, what makes you happy."

That was big. That was huge.

This was '62, maybe. That tells you a lot. My mom was the same way. My mother, I knew she would be OK. My dad, I was not sure. But he was into it.

I got into the National Guard, luckily. Otherwise, I'd have gone to Vietnam. I had a middle lottery number, but my number was coming up fairly soon. I was able to get into the guard. We started out in the quartermaster battalion. And later on, we switched to military police. So all of a sudden, I was a cop. That was awesome.

We didn't break many heads. We went to meetings. We did two-day weekend warrior things. With the Army, I never did learn to shoot a pistol. I learned to shoot a rifle, and I was good at it — very good. I did six years. Once a month, you had a weekend of National Guard Armory. And once a year, you had bivouac. That was Army National Guard. That was '65, '66.

Donnie Iris, 1961

Donnie with his '56 Fender Stratocaster and his beloved 1951 Buick

Donnie and The Donnells

I was a corporal. I never tried to do anything more than that. I knew I wanted to do six years, come out, and continue with music. Technically, I'm a veteran.

We saw some action up in Pittsburgh when the riots were going on, '68, when the cities were on fire. They took us up there in Army trucks. And they put us in front of a liquor store. It was either in the Hill District or East Liberty, one of the parts of Pittsburgh that was predominantly black. People were rioting.

Donnie (r.) served 6 years in The National Guard

They stuck us in front of the liquor store with bayonets, no bullets in our rifles, and the sheath was on the bayonet. And the two of us stood in front of this liquor store, hoping no one would loot the place. Buildings were on fire. People were in front of us, in our faces. It was scary, man. Real scary. Turns out: Two days later, these people that lived right next door to the store, they came over and said, "Man, are we glad to see you guys." They brought us coffee and donuts and stuff. There were a bunch of people out there, and they were scared as hell. The women, especially, were right in our faces, calling us "white boy," all this stuff.

At that point, race relations were terrible. There were riots everywhere. That was the year of the Democratic National Convention — it happened there. It was unbelievable. It was like the country was going through a revolution, it seemed. During that whole time in the Jaggerz, I had relatively few black friends, but I never had any kind of disrespect for them or anyone that was a different color or religion or race from me — there just weren't many around. I think it's important to respect all the different people. They're people, and they're just as good or bad as you are.

But six months into the Donnells, '64, '65, I got a call from Gary and the Jeweltones. And that turned into the Jaggers.

CHAPTER 3

Context: What You Need to Understand The Pittsburgh-Cleveland Rivalry

The longrunning blood feud between Pittsburgh and Cleveland is one of America's great intercity rivalries. Pittsburgh is nestled in the woods of Southwestern Pennsylvania. Cleveland is two hours west, in the flat outskirts of what the mythic Midwest.

Give or take a lot of hills and quite a few bridges, they're very similar cities, with similar people.

Both burgs are renowned as cities of an industrial heritage, bankrolled by titans of industry like the Andrew Carnegie. As a result of those industries, both suffered legendarily catastrophic environmental conditions: Pittsburgh ringed by burning hills of industrial waste, oppressed by fatal smog so dark that street lights were necessary at midday. Cleveland outlined by the Cuyahoga, a river once so polluted it caught fire.

Each city is in a challenged — yet evolving — economic area commonly referred to as "The Rustbelt," in honor of its dilapidated factories and disused barges. They're home to gruff people with ethnic roots on display, colorful folk with Celtic and Eastern European and Mediterranean last names that start with an *O* or end in a *-Y* sound. They work hard at tough jobs, get their hands dirty, and enjoy hearty cuisine like halushky and pierogi. They're probably Catholic, and they ain't *hoity-toity*. That's the old stereotype, anyway. It may be obsolete, but it's not fabricated.

They work hard. They play hard. Both cities have a legacy of popular *and* high culture. Uptempo music embraced by the working class. Glamorous arts subsidized by the wealthy executives.

The unpolished people in both cities exist under some economic pressure. Cities with that working-class attitude do not gladly suffer fools — or, as they call them in Pittsburgh and Chicago, "jagoffs."

And, as happens when you put two people with the same aggressive attitude in the same room: They recognize each other. They find the other's faults familiar. And they butt heads.

Before World War II, most people were too busy to travel 120 miles and brawl their way through their tribal-geographic allegiances.

But then professional football earned newfound importance. And now the Pittsburgh-Cleveland rivalry was manifest. Now it had a score card. And now, especially if you worked some overtime in your union gig at the mill, you had Sunday off, and you could drive a couple hours to hector fans from that other nearby city.

Cleveland was once a city of champions. Before the Super Bowl era, the Cleveland Browns won eight championships — before the city entered a 52-year championship drought so severe it was labeled a curse. Then the Pittsburgh Steelers, historically terrible, turned around their fortunes and won a record-setting number of Super Bowls: four, then five, then six. And the serial winners were not always gracious to their downtrodden cousins in the American Football Conference North.

For Pittsburgh, things may have been tough, but at least they could wave Super Bowl rings in their bitter rivals' faces. And for Cleveland, there was no better a disrespectful shorthand than looking at Pittsburgh's Lombardi trophies and declaring them worthless.

Perhaps a majority of people in both cities don't care. Single-minded musicians usually don't.

But it's a thing. A big thing. Pittsburgh and Cleveland do not like each other.

Mark Avsec (Photo by Anastasia Pantsios)

CHAPTER 4

Meet Mark Avsec: Cruisers Songwriter, Producer, Backup Singer, Keyboardist

They don't go out of their way to call attention to this fact on WDVE, the first station to embrace Donnie Iris, still his most reliable FM outlet, the broadcast home of the Pittsburgh Steelers:

Donnie Iris' creative partner, the man who co-wrote his signature songs, the guy with the vision for the band that became the Cruisers, Mark Avsec...

He's from Cleveland. Lifelong.

Donnie Iris as you know him was never a solo artist.

When you experience *Donnie Iris* songs, you're actually hearing the tandem work of two artists: singer-songwriter-frontman Donnie Iris, whose contributions you ***cannot*** qualify, marginalize, discount, or overvalue in any way.

And when you hear Donnie sing, you're also hearing the work of Mark Avsec, the man who wrote most of the Cruisers' material, produced all of it, played keyboards, and sang some parts that even diehard fans assume is Donnie.

It's a classic dynamic at the heart of some of the best rock music: a singer and a less-visible songwriter. Pete Townsend to the side of Roger Daltrey. Elton John and offstage Bernie Taupin. Meat Loaf and the genius sometimes-singer Jim Steinman. When the Cruisers are at their best, it's hard to tell where Donnie ends and Mark begins.

"He is definitely the driving force behind the band, always has been," says Donnie. "He loves being in the studio. We all do. But he could totally live in there. It's in his blood. He loves creating new stuff. He sits in there and puts it all together. He's a nice guy to have. As talented as he is playing keyboard and writing songs, he's also a talented producer."

"Producer" is a vague position in popular music. It can mean "the guy who sits at a giant panel, turns the knobs and tells you the album is OK, but you still haven't written a strong single." It can mean "a technically skilled quality-control agent who helps a group articulate the sounds the songwriter hears in his head." It can mean "the unseen mastermind who works behind the scenes to write songs and make beats for a good-looking young siren."

A record's producer can be someone like Rick Rubin, a student of music who doesn't have much technical ability, but who knows a lot about song structure — and can tell you when a track is getting better or worse. "Producer" can refer to a musically gifted mastermind like Bob Ezrin, who can hear an embryonic interlude, add a new beat, make some suggestions, and inspire Pink Floyd to flesh out an idea into the classic single "Another Brick in the Wall Part II." It can refer to someone like Roy Thomas Baker, who can help Queen not only develop their songs, but record them in a way that makes a 12-inch record sound big enough to fill a stadium.

In the Cruisers' case, the producer has always been always Mark Avsec. His most visible role was as the group's keyboardist and backup singer. But behind the scenes, Mark is the bedrock foundation of the band, whose labors allow Donnie to be *Donnie Iris*. Mark is the Pete Townsend to Donnie's Roger Daltrey. Most of the Cruisers' songs and their lyrics start in Mark's mind — especially since the 1980s. Mark knows what kind of sonic texture the tracks should have. Inspired by Donnie, Mark had a vision for a rock band that expressed everything Donnie's fans — and, more important, his friends — had seen in the singer over the previous 17 years, but had never been translated into a song and captured on quarter-inch master tape.

"I loved Joe Walsh," says Mark. "I loved [Glass Harp guitarist/singer] Phil Keaggy. That's what I grew up listening to. But I knew I would never be a frontman. I don't sing that well. I knew my forte was playing and writing, arranging, and being a producer. I really liked Roy Thomas Baker — the Cars, Queen. So I was doing the Roy Thomas Baker style with Donnie. I was going to make my mark as a producer, and my calling card was stacking, in the tradition of Spector's wall of sound and Roy Thomas Baker. That was my motivation."

Mark writes well over half the songs. Mark assembles the albums. And Mark leads the band.

"The quarterback, the pitcher, whatever metaphor you want to call it," says Donnie. "He's in that position, and the rest of us are the team around him. And then each guy has his part. He knows that everybody in that room is as important as the next guy. I've got to sing. Marty plays guitar, and he's got to come up with creative guitar stuff. And Kevin's got to lay the beat down. It works, when it comes down to it. And it's been relatively successful."

It's a relatively successful, average year in the Cruisers. The band are about to play the third of seven shows scheduled for the year — the second one this month, after a packed, hot scene at Jergel's. Now they're in Elyria, Ohio, playing an outside show at the Rockin' on the River concert series. It's a glorious summer afternoon, sunny, few clouds, not too hot. The Cruisers are killing time before their headlining performance, after soundcheck, where they ran through "Do You Compute?" "A Little Help From My Friends," and — for a glorious moment — a whomping take on Led Zeppelin's "Kashmir."

In the world of rock and roll, *BACKSTAGE* is a mythical and overrated destination. In reality, especially for a crew of married or romantically attached gentlemen of a certain age, backstage can be a dull downtime, with nothing to do but sit around for a few hours. But for the Cruisers, this is the good part, the hang. Moreso than the shows, the hang is what keeps them coming back. Sitting around a conference table, eating catered chicken, trading in-jokes, and laughing about ephemeral moments from 1981 — *that* is where the true essence of the Cruisers is on full display.

You get the distinct idea that Mark would be completely content if he never again had to talk about the band's history, recall recording 100 tracks to create "Ah! Leah!" and recount the ensuing lawsuit that helped derail the band's career. And if you told him he could never play "Agnes" to a screaming crowd again, he might have a momentary pause, but he'd accept it. But if you told Mark he could never have another hang session with Donnie, Marty, Paul and Kevin? Then somewhere under an iron intellectual façade, his vulnerable heart would crack, and he would be gone within a month.

Even among Cruisers fans, the depth and breadth of Mark's résumé are obscure: Before the Cruisers, he played arenas with Wild Cherry of "Play That Funky Music" renown, years before Donnie joined that band and the two bonded for life. He wrote a top-ten disco song that has enduring popularity. He's the only person alive outside Bon Jovi with a sole writing credit for that group. Far more recently, he rode shotgun on James Gang reunions, playing keyboard for Rock and Roll Hall of Fame desperado and Eagle Joe Walsh.

Mark practically hasn't stopped moving since 1976. Cruisers and friends routinely use the word "genius" and "brilliant" to describe him. Day to day, for his social and professional function, he assumes the role of the smartest guy in the room. His vision and hustle created the machine that is the Cruisers. He learned to distrust outsiders. His history of achievement has, rightfully, created an unwavering self-confidence. And when a project like the King Cool Light beer goes wrong, his Catholic guilt pounces, and he becomes his biggest critic.

Mark will always make time for the Cruisers, but other things keep him busy. Since 1995, he has been a very full-time lawyer. He is a partner at Benesch, Friedlander, Coplan & Aronoff LLP, an international law firm that is home to 56 attorneys from 2017's *The Best Lawyers in America* list. Avsec is the vice-chair of the Innovations, Information Technology & Intellectual Property Practice Group; co-chair of the Sports and Entertainment Group; and leader of the 3D Printing Legal Team. On the 23rd floor, his office overlooks Cleveland's public square, with a view of Lake Erie. If your company owns the patent on a blender, and a manufacturer in China acquired your schematics and is making bootleg appliances, attorney Mark Avsec is the man you call for justice.

And people do call him for intercession, reparations, and advice. His cooler clientele include Rock and Roll Hall of Fame musicians and small taverns. And he has a long list of bigger clients, like American Greetings, OverDrive, and Sterling Jewelers, whose business drags them into sophisticated copyright infringement litigation, licensing, celebrity endorsements – technology deals with creative content overlay.

Week to week, Avsec wears suits and shiny shoes. He's generous with his time, happy to talk through dilemmas and opportunities with local artists and small business owners, without surprising them with a walloping bill afterward. Ultimately, his second career has been in service of that most elusive of intellectual properties, the kind of thing he toiled at in his first career: a creation that becomes popular and, perhaps, generates a few dollars for its creator. His biggest rock song led him to learn, firsthand, what happens when the wrong people get bad legal advice.

The Avsec who navigates legal jet streams is not the talented, überfocused, absent-minded twenty-something bandleader who co-wrote "Ah! Leah!" and "Love Is Like a Rock." After the Cruisers' creative output sputtered, he staged a long reinvention.

"Mark was the mad scientist," recalls drummer Kevin Valentine. "He's a really smart guy who sometimes didn't operate in the reality we were in. Many times we would have a laugh about him, because he would do strange things. We'd be leaving a gig, and half his luggage would be hanging out of his suitcase, and he wouldn't know. We'd come to a hotel, and the front of the hotel was all glass. And he'd just see the front desk, through the glass. And he would walk directly at the front desk. And he'd walk into the window. His mind is always working. And many times, he's too smart to stay in the physical realm that he operates in. He operates like that. It's rare, and great for what he did."

A fan of motivational literature, Mark has three governing maxims that have guided the band through the years:

1. "Guess we have to try harder."
2. "Anything worth doing is worth overdoing."
3. "Let's create the illusion of progress."

Avsec hasn't played seven full arenas in seven days since 1982. But he's still comfortable in front of a crowd, even if it's an auditorium full of students. He's an adjunct professor of law at Case Western Reserve University. He recently gave a TED talk to a full house at Cleveland State University. He still claims to be "shy" and "weird." But backstage, when he's in the comfortable company of his longtime bandmates, he joyfully holds court for 20 minutes, transforming into characters like The Tan Man, a character that a travelling band brainstormed during a grueling tour 38 years ago.

And when Donnie floats in from his travels around the venue, Avsec is glad to surrender the spotlight. The duo at the core of the group enjoy a rare and effortless equilibrium. In the brotherhood of the Cruisers, Donnie is the king, and Mark is the boss. And seldom in the history of music has a group had such a harmonious relationship its driving figures. Mark is happy to be behind the scenes as the shot caller and creative force. And he's content to have Donnie hovering through the world as the face of the band.

All the Cruisers are here today, which is no small feat. Mark drove half an hour from the Cleveland suburbs. Donnie's commute was closer to two hours, from

By day, Mark Avsec is a partner and Vice-Chair of the Innovations, Information Technology & Intellectual Property (3iP) Practice Group of Benesch, Friedlander, Coplan & Aronoff, LLP. He's also an adjunct professor of law at Case Western Reserve University.

Beaver Falls. Marty drove nearly 90 minutes, from Canton, well south of Cleveland. Paul flew in from North Carolina. But Kevin wins. He flew in from L.A. on a red-eye. The group does well enough that it can afford a couple airline tickets every show, but not so well that they don't need to save a few hundred dollars here and there. But even if they had to, he would still be worth it. The Cruisers have a shared history over 40 years at this point, 38 together in the band. They spent 20 years trying to figure out how to field a team without a drummer who had to fly 2,300 miles to make a show. It didn't work.

Mark performing live on one of the early Cruiser tours.

The long hauls aren't a drag. They're energized and ready to go. Mark looks better than he has in years.

His hair is a touch longer than you'd expect from an internationally respected attorney and authority on copyright law. And it's a lot shorter than you'd expect for a guy who recorded with four major-label recording acts, appeared on the Grammys, and wrote eight *Billboard* Hot 100 singles.

Not only is he thinner than he was five years ago, but he's tighter and *lighter*, like a burden has been removed from his shoulders, and a dark cloud dispelled from his overworked brain. He's been working out more, his forearms taut, veins bulging, primed from years of hardcore practice on a very old-school instrument. The Cruisers are, after all, a collaboration between a guy who wrote a chart-topping single and an Ohio state accordion champion.

MARK SAYS:

I grew up in the inner city.

I'm reading Robbie Robertson's book. I don't know how I find time to read, but I do it when I travel. A lot of these guys like Springsteen and Robbie Robertson, the way they grew up, what their lives were — they had no other options. A lot of them didn't pick up their instruments and get serious until they were 17, 18, 19. Then they started playing in bands or learned as they went. They watched other people play or watched their fingers and saw what they could teach them.

I didn't learn that way. I had perfect pitch. I was a classically trained accordionist. And then I transferred to piano. I wasn't influenced by people to learn how to play. Even now, I have perfect pitch. I'll just play what I hear sometimes — I can't do it with really cool licks like Dr. John and Professor Longhair; I'd have to study or practice them. But the first band I was in, they wanted to do "Light My Fire." I listened to the album with the guys. I had my little Farfisa organ. And ten minutes later, I'm playing "Light My Fire," the whole thing, the solo and everything. I don't know where the perfect pitch came from.

Learning accordion was my idea when I was kid. I got interested in music when I was two and three. I was fascinated by notes. My uncle had these books with all music notation, and I would read them and try to understand them. I would stare at them and thought it was so cool that this was a language. I think he worked in a factory, and was a musician.

Then, because I was a Slovenian kid, I heard a lot of polkas. And I thought that's what music was. And it was. It was cultural. It wasn't mom making me learn to play. I wanted it. My grandfather, my maternal grandfather, bought me a used accordion, for a young boy. It was little, but it was a real instrument. I guess I was four. He intended to give it to me for Christmas, but he died. They had the funeral, and then they gave me the accordion.

I used to make up songs on it. I loved it. I took it to show and tell in first grade. And I took lessons, because my parents saw I was serious. I got a better accordion when I was eight. I started competing.

I wanted to play, but my parents encouraged me too. My dad took me to lessons every week, and they made sure I had good teachers. When I outgrew a teacher, they found another one. I learned the most about music theory from Walter Gauss. Light bulbs went on when I studied with him. He showed me how to break up chords and play behind a lead sheet and the keys to improvisation.

Accordion competition was not ethnic at all, as in Slovenian or Italian. That is the stereotype. This is serious accordion music written for the classical and competitive accordionist.

I had good parents. I realize now that not all kids had good parents. They did not have much money, but we lived a high quality life, with a lot of support. Dad was a mailman. Mom, great mom and housewife. She also worked part time as we got older. From time to time, like any kid, I would rather play ball than practice. On summer mornings, I played accordion for an hour around 9:00, before grabbing my glove and heading down the street for the playground the rest of the day. If I did not do it then, I might not do it.

You had to play by heart, in front of the judge panel. One year, my mind went blank during the competition. I was seven. I was disqualified. One year I practiced all year for the competition. I was going to play [Liszt]'s *Liebestraum*. I knew it backward and forward. Halfway through, the strap on my accordion broke, and I had to stop. Really crazy coincidence. I was disqualified.

At nine, I won second place in the [Cleveland Accordion Teachers Association] Ohio accordion state championship — this kid John Holodniak was real good, and confident. He was always my nemesis to try and beat. And then I got one more better accordion. And I won first place one year. I played Pietro Deiro's *Concerto in D*. This was not simple stuff.

Then, all of a sudden, I was 13. And I saw the Beatles, like everybody else, and I was enthralled. And the accordion had begun to lose its luster for me. And that's when I started getting into the best Farfisa organ, and learning things that I could do in a band.

And of course, when I hit 18, my poor parents suffered the bands practicing in our basement, and about 4:00 in the morning listening to my buddies and me haul the Hammond B-3 back into the house.

I had all this classical training. I had other options. I was a really good student. I went to a really good high school, even though I was a poor kid from a Slovenian neighborhood. But I wanted to do music, and I viewed it as a burden that I was giving up the rest of my life for this. I was just driven to succeed at this.

I consider myself a keyboardist, though I did start on an accordion. So that created its own dynamic in me. Maybe some of it's good: I learned to play with my right hand in a certain way. My left hand, in some ways, is still catching up with my right hand.

Mark Avsec playing at Thunder in the Valley, Johnstown, PA

I was always into the organ, but I couldn't afford a Hammond organ. I got into Emerson, Lake and Palmer. Then when I saw Lee Michaels at the Allen Theater. It was before Jethro Tull. I'd never heard of Michaels, didn't know who he was. He came out, and that Hammond B-3 through that PA… it sounded like *God*.

I was busy in high school. I went to a Jesuit high school, Saint Ignatius, on the West Side of Cleveland. And when you go there, you get a lot of homework. You get involved in community things. And I had jobs all through high school. I worked at an advertising agency called Meldrum-Fewsmith, in the library, stocking magazines. It was an after-school job for two hours. Then I worked at Turk's Delicatessen, which was across the street from my house on St. Clair. Then I worked for a music store in our neighborhood, where all the high school band directors came for music. I filed it. I worked mind-numbing jobs.

And then I worked in a factory after high school. The thing was: When you go to the high school I went to, you go to college. And I went to Cleveland State — for a day. Literally. I was not happy. I was very confused at 18, already. I was serious, like, "What am I going to do with my life?!"

And I overreact to everything. So whereas another guy in my shoes would be more normal and drift into it, I had read all these books about philosophy and religion… and what did I believe? I really felt empowered to make a choice as to what I wanted to do with my life. And I got pretty messed up — drugs were no part of it, but I got very depressed. And I worked in a factory for about a year, just to get that experience.

I didn't want to go to college. Everybody said, "Just do music therapy. Because you like music."

And that would have been absolutely the worst thing I could have done. So I didn't know what I wanted to do. I guess I could have been a lawyer, but I wouldn't have been happy doing that. I'm not the happiest person in the world, but deep down I'm happy now.

So I worked in a factory. And I decided I was going to do music. And I got laser-focused on it. So, yeah, when I was 21, 22, I was focused on achieving and getting from point A to point B. Sometimes other musicians looked at me like I was ruining the fun.

I'm not organized. I'm motivated. I'm motivated to be a better person. Because I'm always messing up, I suppose, I've achieved a lot in my life.

> I loved Joe Walsh.
> I loved Phil Keaggy. That's what
> I grew up listening to. But I knew
> I would never be a frontman.
> I don't sing that well. I knew my
> forte was playing and writing,
> arranging, and being a producer.
>
> ~MARK AVSEC

Marty Lee Hoenes (Photo by Anastasia Pantsios)

CHAPTER 5

Meet Marty Lee Hoenes, Cruisers Guitarist

Donnie Iris on Cruisers guitarist Marty Lee Hoenes:

"He's got style."

Marty is the last man standing, the one Cruiser who never quit, who played nearly every minute of every single gig — almost.

"Well, he missed the end of one show because he had a heart attack," says Mark. "He kind of slacked off there."

Mark is kidding about the slacking. He is serious about the heart attack.

When the group ends, Marty will retire from the team that drafted him as a rookie.

When the Cruisers' schedule thinned out in the '80s, Marty found a different application for his artistic sensibilities. With some schooling, he embarked on a new — but not entirely dissimilar — career that let him raise a family and stay in the game.

The Cruisers were his first major band. When they signed him, he was ready for a breakout season. He cut his teeth playing originals and a diverse array of cover songs with various bands. He caught Donnie's ear in promising Erie band The Pulse. His groups didn't leave behind many recordings. But on YouTube, you can find a live video for The Pulse's "Madalynn," a catchy tune worthy of Elvis Costello.

Versatile and understated, Marty plays with the efficiency of a master samurai, avoiding flashy solos and hot licks, in deceptively simple style. Marty's weapons of choice are indelible melodic riffs and lyrical hooks.

In the 1980s Cruisers videos, Marty had a thick frame and a brooding presence. The dark aura has lightened over the years, though he still prefers to let his art speak for itself. Life as a graphics and marketing professional has taught him to be deliberate, demanding, contemplative, and detail-oriented.

When Donnie suggested Marty for the Cruisers, the band's management agreed he was ready for the big show. When the Cruisers needed some hands-on development, Belkin had the band work with James Gang drummer and founder Jimmy Fox, who has played with ace axemen including Joe Walsh, Glenn Schwartz, and Tommy Bolin.

"Marty Lee, exceptionally good, under-the-radar guitar player," says Fox. "The guy can do anything, and do it brilliantly."

Hoenes hails originally from the neutral territory of Erie, Pennsylvania — two hours north of Pittsburgh, two hours east of Cleveland. He moved to the Akron/Canton, OH area along with his wife Cindy and their daughter Madison in 1996. In Erie, the big '80s haircuts never really went away, the arena holds 9,000, and sports fans are equally likely to pledge allegiance to Cleveland, the Burgh, or nearby Buffalo.

MARTY SAYS:

I was in the Pittsburgh camp, because I followed the Steelers. For me, they were right down the road. They came from Pennsylvania. And I liked the city itself. Compared to Cleveland, Pittsburgh was ahead of the curve in terms of their renaissance.

Erie, I would say it was a bit like Cleveland: The bay front area had not been developed. The parkway wasn't in place yet. That Tom Hanks movie, *That Thing You Do!*, is set in Erie — that's what it was like.

Lee is my middle name. The last name is pronounced "HAY-nuss," the way you wouldn't want to pronounce it.

The first time I heard "I Wanna Hold Your Hand," it was like nothing I'd ever heard before. It really resonated. I heard the song before *The Ed Sullivan Show*. And then I saw that, like many millions of people. I was just fascinated. At the time, I was excited to see the energy and the harmonies. I was about 12. I liked the Everly Brothers. I liked Elvis.

My mother was very musical, so I was exposed to a lot of classic and Broadway musical stuff. She was a trained soprano. So I was always around music. The Beatles made me want to *do* it. I sang, but I didn't play at that point.

My first band, I played drums. The first couple bands, I was a drummer. My first band was the Konvicts, with a K. I must have been in sixth grade or something, and I was playing drums at school. And then a dear friend of mine and another friend played in a talent show at school, a little duo. And it was great. And they knew something about me, and they wandered over to where I was working part time for my stepfather.

They said, "The Ouija board said you can play drums."

And I knew what drums were. So it wasn't not the truth. I could play a little bit on a drum pad, but not on a full kit.

They wanted me to form a band with them. They brought me down to their basement, where they had an old, beat-up set of drums. But I thought it was fantastic. They had me sit down, and I didn't know what to do. By that time, they figured they were in too deep, so they had to teach me. So I got some guidance from them, and I got my own kit, and I got better at it.

"Fireworks" (l. to r.): Mike Cooklis, John McLane, Marty Lee Hoenes. (Photo by Jerry Funk)

I don't remember what interested me in guitar, initially. I wanted one. And my parents figured out a way to get me a guitar. It was from Green Stamps. My mother saved Green Stamps, a perk that you could get at certain super markets if you buy a certain amount of food. You'd get these little stamps you could save and put into a book. And you could exchange that for merchandise later on. The concept is still in use in marketing — loyalty points. It was a big thing back in the '60s.

It was a Kay acoustic guitar. And I learned things from the other guys in my band. I was 15 years old, and I had a guitar, but I didn't really concentrate on it for awhile. I played bass for awhile. It's a good possibility that drums and bass influenced how I play guitar. I approach it from a rhythm-guitar standpoint.

My first guitar was that, and then there was another, and then another. And then I really got devoted. I practiced in my bedroom. And then I realized the more time I practiced, the better I'd get. I got an old turntable and took it to a repair man and asked him to modify it so I could play records at half speed, 16 RPM. Cream albums, Johnny Winter Live, Jimi Hendrix, *Are You Experienced*. I'd learn it slowly and speed it up until it sounded right. All those albums, I pored over them.

I was in some bands. I played in a band with some friends, called Aris. I was in a band called Fireworks, with other friends, but I played bass. We played

Music Machine and Steppenwolf and Young Rascals.

Then I started seeking out guitar teachers in Erie, PA. And I went from one to another, learning things about theory and scales, all of that — tricks of the trade, foundational stuff. I devoted a lot of time and energy to it. I can name them all. My first electric guitar teacher was a guy named Pat Talarico. Now, I could play a little, but he knew some really specific guitar tricks and moves, things I couldn't figure out myself, blues-rock type things. We're still in touch, from time to time. He plays still. Pat, after my lessons with him, asked me to join his band. He had a really successful local rock band called Red, White and Blueberry. And we played around the Erie area. By then, I'd been out of high school. I was 18, maybe 19 or 20.

After that I was in several bands, some of which included Paul Goll and Steve McConnell. After those came The Pulse, which was a blast. We did a lot of shows with the Iron City Houserockers, who used to love listening to us play "Omaha" by Moby Grape. It probably wasn't the wisest thing we could do, but we liked doing the different stuff. It was one guitar, bass, drums, keyboards. We all sang.

I had very broad taste. I listened to Mahavishnu Orchestra, Jeff Beck, Led Zeppelin. Jazz players like Joe Pass and Larry Coryell. I liked Frank Zappa. I liked all those different things.

The guys that I liked to listen to don't necessarily play in the same style that our band always has. Hendrix and Clapton and Jeff Beck. For me, I always liked Johnny Winter and Joe Walsh. Those were the guys I listened to constantly. Ritchie Blackmore.

I benefitted from being in The Pulse greatly, because of the diverse styles, because I had to learn the Steely Dan guitar parts, then Cheap Trick guitar parts, then all these different styles. I wasn't trying to impose my sound onto all this stuff.

Mark would tend to leave songs very wide open, with what the rhythm track consisted of. He would want to develop how it developed harmonically, once we got a basic rhythm going.

I think of myself as an ensemble player, part of making the song happen. So the music demands solos, and I like playing them. But I'm really excited about doing a cool rhythm part. Or the dynamics of a song interested me. So the rhythm guitar part is interesting to me.

I don't sit and wait patiently until I can take a solo. I just don't. If it's time for a solo, well, OK — but I don't think of it as more important than making the song happen. So whatever conclusion you want to draw from that. But I don't think of myself as a *Lead Guitarist*. I think of myself as a rhythm-and-lead guitarist, a guitarist — what does *the song* need? I've just always been that way. I'll fill that role when it's called for; I get that.

I related particularly to [Jeff] Beck and Walsh. There's a particular economy to their style. To me, they're saying a lot with the notes and the tone and the style, the things they're presenting to you. They're saying a lot in a very direct way. There's a lot of emotion in that one note — B.B. King would fit that description. He wouldn't play a lot of notes, but they were the right notes.

The Pulse (l. to r.) Marty Lee Hoenes, Bob Burger, Jeff Burger, Jeff "Tune" Klahr.

Marty Lee Hoenes and Rick Witkowski at Rick's Studio L in Weirton, WV.

Somebody said a long, long time ago that there's a big difference between a guitarist that plays with intention and one without. I'm not saying that a certain style doesn't have intention. But I do know that when Joe Walsh picks out a phrase, he intends to play each one of those notes in that particular phase, in that timing, with that emotion. And you can play that back or sing it or whistle along to it or sing with Beck. Clapton, he sometimes plays more notes. But when he wants to be expressive, it's all there. George Harrison would play that way, too.

As far as making a run at it, I had an idea of it while I was in The Pulse. We were playing club gigs and different types of circuits like that. I wasn't doing other work besides that.

The Pulse was a good band, and it looked like we were heading places. Bob Burger was the songwriter, and he went on to write for Styx, among other things. We recorded Bob's song "Life After Love" on one of the Cellarful of Noise records.

We were recording original music, and we had a production deal with a producer named Ed Seay, who produced some hit songs, worked with some very heavyweight artists — Brick, Paul Davis, the Commodores, Peabo Bryson, Melissa Manchester. We sent some demos out, and he called. We recorded in Atlanta. He loved The Pulse, but sadly nothing ever came of those Atlanta demo recordings. But I started to think, "Maybe there's something here. Maybe I can do this."

The Pulse had also recorded tracks in Pittsburgh with Rick Witkowski as producer — this was before he was in B.E. Taylor's band. They were the tracks that led to the Ed Seay deal. I knew Rick because years before, I'd auditioned for the second guitarist position in his previous band, Crack The Sky. This would be around 1976-ish.

Rick was given my name and a recommendation from a mutual friend. So, Paul Goll and I drove from Erie to Weirton, West Virginia, and met Rick at his home. We visited, I auditioned, I thought it went really well, but their second guitarist did not end up leaving the band. He stayed. And so I did not take that particular fork in the road.

Rick and I stayed friends. Obviously, we'll never know what would have happened had Rick and I teamed up in Crack The Sky. I almost certainly would *not* have been playing with The Pulse at Morey's Speakeasy in New Brighton that fateful night that Donnie heard me.

Marty at Reunion Arena, Dallas, TX, during one of the Cruisers' Halls & Oates tour dates.

> I don't sit and wait patiently
> until I can take a solo. I just don't.
> If it's time for a solo, well, OK
> — but I don't think of it as more
> important than making
> the song happen.

~MARTY LEE HOENES

Albritton McClain and Donnie Iris (Photo by Anastasia Pantsios)

CHAPTER 6

Meet Albritton McClain, Original Cruisers Bassist

The enigmatic Albritton McClain is the original Cruisers bassist, the band's unsung ace from the first five albums. Donnie drafted him, sight-unseen.

"I heard he was this badass bass player," says Donnie. "His reputation as a fantastic musician is why I wanted him. Then I did see him. He did not disappoint. I thought he was a monster player. Seemed like a nice guy."

When the band started, he might have been the most accomplished, seasoned, versatile recruit.

Albritton grew up in Chicago, with a nurturing family, but in a bruising environment. He sailed through the flower-power era and landed in Ohio, then Pennsylvania, where he played a series of stints — some credited, some not — with major-label bands Sweet Lightnin', Beechwood Farm (with ex-members of the Lemon Pipers), the Silencers, Roy Buchanan, and David Werner, a hotly tipped and highly funded avant garde rocker.

Along the way, Albritton played with some Donnie Iris associates past and future, including Pete Hewlett and Frank Cure. (He contributed several uncredited tracks to the Silencers' *Rock 'n' Roll Enforcers*, the 1980 debut by the Pittsburgh new wave also-rans.) By the end of the '70s, he was a known name.

"That guy is an amazing, amazing musician," says former Cruisers drummer Tommy Rich, who witnessed him in action. "I saw him years before in a local rock and roll band, and he blew me away then. He's one of those guys that you can't put a finger on why he's so good. He's like a Jimi Hendrix on the bass. Ridiculous presence. I saw him play in much harder bands, too. He could play anything, and it came straight through him. He could sing his ass off, too. That guy was just a stud."

Mark says Albritton was integral to the success of "Ah! Leah!" Live, the bassist also served as a background singer, and would take the mic when Donnie needed a brief break. Unfortunately, the digital mastering on the band's best-of album obscures his song-guiding contributions.

"Funny story," says drummer Kevin Valentine. "It was Halloween. I heard a knock on the door. I open it up, and I figure it's some kids in their costumes. But it was Albritton. He helped us pass out candy. He just showed up. He's a good guy. We fit together."

They did. The rhythm section played together after the Cruisers: Albritton and Kevin worked with a young Trent Reznor in The Innocent, a AOR band with dark wardrobe and a light sound. After Cleveland, Albritton headed West and became a capable bandleader in Albritton McClain and the Bridge of Souls, a bluesy rock outfit that kept him busy into the 21st century. He fronted the group through intricate originals and spot-on covers of Muddy Waters, Stevie Wonder and T-Bone Walker. When his rock career ramped down, he composed music for the movies *Dilemma* and *Illusion Infinity*.

In the Cruisers' glory days, he was the backing band's most virtuosic player — and the most volatile. He found some peace through his other life's work: an ongoing mission as a health and wellness advocate. He still plays daily.

ALBRITTON SAYS:

I was born March 19, 1952. In Chicago. I grew up in a great musical melting pot. And because I'm a product of so-called racially mixed marriage — my dad is African-Native American, and my mom is German-European, first-generation American — I was exposed to a wide range of music at an early age.

I started at seven years old, I'd say. Classical, soul, polka, rock and roll, country western, rockabilly, 78 RPM records — those were all on our big Motorola radio-slash-turntable console. My dad was a guitarist. My mom loved music, had a lot of records. I was exposed to everything from Rachmaninoff, Ernest Tubbs, Carl Perkins, Patti Page, Elvis — my mom was a big Elvis fan. Brook Benton, Dinah Washington. There were music TV shows: She would watch *Old American Barn Dance*, *Hit Parade* on Friday, *American Bandstand* on Saturday.

Between the ages of 9 and 10, I found an old guitar my father had played in the Army. Then I wrote a song on one string. And I played it for my little sister and my parents. And lo and behold: That Christmas, Santa brought a six-string acoustic guitar, which I probably learned a few songs on, including "Down in the Valley" and Ray Charles' "What'd I Say."

The first song I loved was Carl Perkins singing "Blue Suede Shoes" — only I thought it was Elvis on the 78. The flipside was "Honey Don't." It was explosive. And I heard Little Richard. I was around 7 or 8. I liked the energy that was early rock and roll, with Elvis, from the '50s to the '60s.

The next spring, the Beatles hit America. And that was pretty much it. When the Beatles hit, it became not only explosive, but *expansive*.

Radio changed. Now you could hear everything on one radio station: The Turtles, Sam and Dave, Petula Clark, "Downtown," Aretha Franklin, the Beach Boys, James Brown, one after another. It was an incredible time to be coming of age. My mom was a big fan. She let me grow my hair long.

I was a pretty bright kid. I had skipped a couple grades. Most of my friends were older than me. And I got an accelerated growth and learning curve, both in life and music. And that was the case during my early musical career: I was always the youngest in the band.

I had always played guitar, and continue to write on it. In my first band, the Thangg, we had three guitar players. We had to have a bass player, so I had to tune down the strings on my six-string Gibson so I could emulate the bass part.

There were a lot of great guitarists out there at the time. I thought, "Nobody's really developing the instrument, *bass guitar*. I should really take advantage of that."

Then I was hearing all this contrapuntal stuff, viola parts and cello parts, and playing them on bass. Experimental rock music bass players were given more than just the foundation parts. And my guitar knowledge translated. At that point, I said, "I'm going to be the bass player in bands."

In Chicago at that time, before there were Bloods and Crips, there were two huge gangs in Chicago, one called the Blackstone Rangers, on the South Side. One called the Devil's Disciples on the West Side — both black gangs that took over their entire region of Chicago. Blackstone had protection money paid to them from all the businesses surrounding Hyde Park High School, which is where I went to high school. They robbed, beat up, raped kids getting off the bus.

I was two years younger than everybody, so my first year in high school, I was exposed to this. I had been sheltered my entire life. I had never been outside of my square-block area without a parent, because of this low-profile regime my parents enforced. If you go out and you're a mixed kid, you get beat up by the black kids for being half-white, or by the white kids for being half-black.

So in this environment, I'm a nice, sheltered kid, not exposed to any violence. Going to school, doing the right thing. I got through the first year OK, keeping a low profile, wearing the clothes I'm supposed to wear, staying invisible.

By the second year, I got drafted into one of the branches of the gangs, called the Casanova Rangers, a branch of Black Stone Rangers. You go there and you fight the baddest cat in that gang. And if you win, you're in that gang. If you lose, you continued to get terrorized and beat up.

I had never been a fighter. I had just joined the Boy Scouts.

I had just met some great people whose parents, I guess you could call them beatniks. They had folk guitars, and Peter, Paul and Mary were on the radio.

And then I got drafted, and I thought, "What am I supposed to do? I'm supposed to go and fight this guy on Sunday."

And we opened up *Life* magazine, and saw these pictures of the love bus and hippies and flower power. And I said, "That's for me." So we hitchhiked out to San Francisco.

We went to Golden Gate Park, saw Grateful Dead and Jefferson Airplane playing for free in the park. I technically had run away from home for a month. I called my parents once I got there and said, "I'm OK." That would have been '66, '67.

That was the first thing I had ever done. It wasn't a very popular thing for whites and blacks to be married, so my family's whole attitude was, "Keep a low profile. Don't do anything wrong. Don't get in trouble with the police. Don't cause any waves." So my first step out, I go to California.

I never went back to my high school. I wound up going to a school on the West Side where we had policemen for teachers. I was the smartest kid in the school, and I wasn't learning anything. They were teaching to the dumbest kids in the class. There were tensions going on. This was just prior to the Black Power thing and the Vietnam thing. Everybody was just breaking out.

At 15, I got a gig with a seven-piece blues horn group, a Blood Sweat and Tears type of thing. I stayed in school until I was 16, old enough to leave. I had wanted to be an astronomer or chemist. When I was ten and got my guitar, I was going to be a guitar-playing chemist.

My big three influences, because of the influences and the energy and their impact, were Elvis, the Beatles, and Jimi Hendrix — because they were so different from anything that came before. And that kind of mark is what I aspired to, to do something different, to bring some light and love to the world, something other than war, something other than the same things. Bands like James Brown and Sly and the Family Stone had an influence on me, too. But it was that kind of innovation.

Then I joined my first recording group, which was a psychedelic rock group, which brought me to Ohio in 1969, called the Sacred Mushroom. They were based out of Cincinnati. When I joined the Sacred Mushroom band and started doing sessions, I thought of myself as a professional musician.

It was all original music. Very interesting time changes. We opened for Arlo Guthrie, Dr. John, early James Gang. I think our last gig was for a band whose brand new album had been released, called Grand Funk. That was in '69.

At this point, I consider myself a composer and a multiinstrumentalist. I play guitar. I play drums. I play bass. I play keyboard. Saxophone — I traded one of my 12-strings for a sax. When MIDI keyboards came along, I had enough knowledge of keyboards that I could do orchestral-type scores. When I was 17, I considered myself more of a writer. Bass gave me a lot of ideas for this and that, and I could interact with musicians.

1970, I joined two members of the Lemon Pipers — they had a hit called "Green Tambourine" back in the '60s — in Beechwood Farm. We played together for about a year. After that band broke up, that's when I met Sid McGinnis, who played in the David Letterman band later. He was originally from Pittsburgh, and that's how I got the gig with Sweet Lightnin'.

While they were getting ready to break up, we had done some gigs with a band called Freeport out of Cleveland, with Kevin Raleigh, who wound up playing with Michael Stanley. Roger Lewis from that band and Myron Grombacher, a drummer who later played with Rick Derringer and Pat Benatar, formed a band called R.M.A., out of Youngstown — "Remember Me Always" or "Roger, Myron, Albritton."

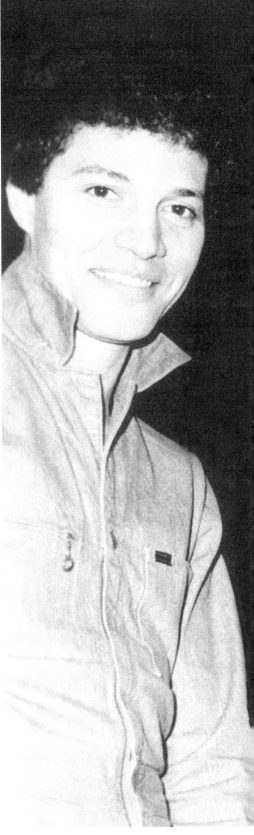

Albritton McClain, 1980's

We were together a year. We were a cover band, except for a couple songs I wrote, like "Remember Me Always." We did rock stuff. I'd do all the Jimi Hendrix lead vocals, and Roger would do all the Led Zeppelin vocals.

We were basically a three-piece. But when we were first getting together, we wanted a keyboardist. And the keyboardist that Roger knew was Herman Granati, from the Granati Brothers. We opened for bands like Rush and Ted Nugent when they'd play venues like the Agora, the Tomorrow Club.

In the 1970s, Vietnam was happening. I was a conscientious objector. I practiced Zen Buddhism, and I was into macrobiotics. And I was into a different way of eating, wasn't into Western medicine. So I couldn't work as a medic or anything in the Army. And I stood up for my Zen Buddhist beliefs. In 1972, when I joined Sweet Lightnin', my number came up.

I went to my local board interview, where you talk to the draft board, seven guys, a bunch of colonels, who don't want to hear anything about Japanese philosophy, particularly on the anniversary of Pearl Harbor. So I bring all my books and tried to convince them about a different way of eating. I got unanimously declined. I appealed, and I got my I-O status.

I had to fulfill my civilian Alternate Service gig, which was a civilian alternative non-profit organization dedicated to the welfare of the general public. And so I started doing a gig working at a drug rehabilitation program in Pittsburgh.

And I had just gotten married. And then my marriage started falling apart. My wife moved back to Cincinnati. And in order to try to pull my marriage back together, I moved back to Hamilton, Ohio, where she was living. Then I joined RMA. Then the draft board tracked me down and said, "You've got to work somewhere else, and you've got to do it now."

Then I got a gig at the Transcendental Meditation Center, T.M. Center, in Cincinnati. That was great. I wouldn't call myself a Buddhist now, but I believe in that philosophy. I meditate 20 minutes twice a day, transcendental meditation, as taught by the Maharishi Mahesh Yogi. You need that time to chill, to reenter yourself. It helps you unstress and centers you and keeps you healthy.

After Michael, my son, was born, I played with other bands. David Werner was '79. David was kind of a new-wave artist, a Bowie-esque writer. His manager, Tom Conte, with Epic Records, also managed the Silencers. [Bob] Clearmountain — he was the main engineer at the Power Station. He had done Bowie. He had done the Stones. He did Chic. He did Springsteen. They hired him to be our soundman for this tour we did. It was almost every major city in the U.S.

We had a 14-person entourage, including Clearmountain and his wife. It was a priority for the label. A lot of money was spent. We played small auditoriums like Park West in Chicago, the Stanley Theater — places we later played with Donnie. We were in great venues. At the beginning of the tour, Pat Benatar opened for us. By the time we got to DC, we were opening for her, and her first album was going gangbusters.

David Werner, when his album didn't do gangbusters, the record label pulled back. We were waiting to see what happened, and that's when I got the call to record with Donnie.

Albritton McClain, 1990's

> My big three influences,
> because of the influences and the
> energy and their impact, were
> Elvis, the Beatles,
> and Jimi Hendrix — because they
> were so different from anything
> that came before.

~ **ALBRITTON MCCLAIN**

Kevin Valentine (Photo by Anastasia Pantsios)

CHAPTER 7

Meet Kevin Valentine, Cruisers Drummer From Then and Now

The first player selected by the Donnie Iris band was a right-handed drummer out of Cleveland, who had played with Mark in EMI America recording artists Breathless. Mark's first round pick: Kevin Valentine.

"The drummer is the heart and soul of the band," says Mark. "I have a phrase I use in my non-musical life: It's called Bad Drummer Syndrome. I even use it when we hire someone at the law firm. Everybody makes mistakes. Everybody needs to learn. The question, though, is: Is he or she a bad drummer or not? Bad Drummer Syndrome is the inevitable conclusion that they'll never get it. Kevin is a good fit. All respect to everybody else, he is the *right* fit. He is the *only* fit."

After the Cruisers' major-label days, Kevin is the musician who made it furthest into the major leagues. He has the biggest body of work as a recording professional. If you don't know his music, but you watch TV, you've probably heard his handiwork this week.

Since 1998, Kevin has mixed sound for TV shows. In recent years, he has worked with some of the bigger and better ones: *Breaking Bad* spinoff *Better Call Saul*, *The Good Wife*, *Ozark*, *The Tick*, *Charmed*, *The Suite Life of Zack and Cody*, *Legion,* and *Bones*, among others. Some of it was music-related: *The Henry Rollins Show* featured some of the best televised rock performances ever.

Sound mixing was a natural extension of what made him a triple threat as a drummer: onstage, in the studio, or behind a mixing board, he consistently brings solid skills, a team attitude and a four-dimensional understanding of how to record his parts.

Most notable is Kevin's stint as a studio drummer for Kiss, the band whose makeup, costumes, and pyrotechnics redefined rock and roll showmanship. He started as a live sound man and earned a spot in the lineup — on record, at least: He played on the demos for 1989's *Hot in the Shade*, then appeared on one album track, "Love Me to Hate You." The notoriously demanding Gene Simmons and Paul Stanley kept him on deck, and he recorded one song on 1992's *Revenge*: "Take It Off," which was produced by Pink Floyd/Alice Cooper producer Bob Ezrin.

In 1996, after years without face paint, Kiss delighted its army of fans by putting the makeup on again and reuniting with original guitarist and drummer Ace Frehley and Peter Criss. The reunion sparked a phenomenal Kiss revival, and an album followed: 1998's *Psycho Circus*, which was billed as a reunion featuring all the original players. In fact, Kevin played on all but one track, to protect the "reunited classic lineup" status.

Rolling Stone bought the party line and noted, "*Psycho Circus* — an album of platform-stomping rhythms, roller-coaster guitar riffs and sing-along choruses — is far more respectable than any of the awkward flops from the no-makeup years." [6.1]

Valentine made his recording debut in 1976, with Native-American rock shaman Todd Tamanend Clark. He contributed a whomping percussion track to a dizzying cover of the Rolling Stones' "Two Thousand Light Years From Home," part of the legendary psychedelic release *A Deathguard Sampler*. From there, he moved up to the Cleveland varsity in Breathless, where he made his major-label debut. After the Cruisers, he and bassist Albritton McClain moved on to AOR squad The Innocent, which included a young Trent Reznor, long before Nine Inch Nails was a glint in the keyboard player's eyes.

From there, Kevin worked as a reliable session man and bandmate: Texas guitarist Mason Ruffner. Biker-rock band The Godz. Shadow King, a harder vehicle for Foreigner singer Lou Gramm. Metal queen Doro. Rainbow/Michael Schenker singer Graham Bonnet. Comedian Sam Kinison's live band. And occasional sessions like The Godz' Mark Chatfield and Melanie (best known for the roller-skate anthem "Brand New Key"). Valentine was never just a drummer. From a young age, he was a musician, technician and engineer.

Kevin performing live – one of the early Cruisers' tours. (Photo by Anastasia Pantsios)

KEVIN SAYS:

We live in Santa Monica now. We lived in Venice. The housing market is crazy here. If you look at the property values, I can't afford to live in my house.

I'm from Cleveland, East Side, Euclid. I met my wife, Denise, when I was 25. She's from the West Side. She lives near the airport. There was a party. I said, "I'm going out on tour. I'll call you when I get back." And we've been together since. She didn't know the band. She got to know them later.

I was just possessed from the time I was a little kid. I was beating on the table and metal garbage cans. My parents said, "He's doing that. Let's give him a shot at this."

A lot of musicians do this: I'll hear a song, and I'll sing it for hours. I hear things in nature, and I hear rhythms in them.

I started playing when I was around ten, in fifth grade. I was playing snare. One day, after a rehearsal, I went home for lunch. The concert was after lunch. I only had one pair of drum sticks, and I took them with me. And I left them at home. So I used pencils to play. It worked. Ever since that, I have to have a multitude of drumsticks.

I started the band in elementary school. In high school, which was Euclid High, the band instructor — I didn't like him.

When I was 13, I was in a polka band was called The Essence. My drum teacher recommended me. We had a bass player, two accordion players, and a saxophone player. It was great. I'm half Italian and half Slovenian, like Mark. And in Cleveland, Slovenian was the highest percentage of people. We'd do polkas and Beatles stuff and Chicago songs like "Color My World."

After the wedding band, I did a band with my brother, Gary, and another friend from high school. We were called The Maxx band. It was named after Max. He was a guy who worked at a factory or business that made tubes and amplifiers. He would steal stuff and sell it to us. I graduated 1974.

Todd Tamanend Clark may have been my first recording. Somehow my brother, Gary Kosec, got us on this recording. I don't recall *how* I got involved. This session was like a dream, because it was so long ago and bizarre. It was in a finished attic of a house in Euclid.

Breathless, they were looking for a drummer. They went to see a variety of bands. Jonah [Koslen, Breathless bandleader] said that he picked me because there were more people dancing at our show than anybody else's.

I think I was more of a showoff than anything. I started off standing when I'd play sometimes. And I took it one step further. Before Donnie and Breathless, I would do a silly-assed solo. There are some serious cats out there who can play up a storm. I'm not like that — there are much better drummers, like a Buddy Rich. Maybe it was a lack of want, but I didn't want to be that kind of player. I just focused in on the music. There are a lot of really great drummers, but they can't play *music*. To them, it's all about rudiments or that fast double-bass thing — as opposed to hearing or feeling the music and playing the appropriate part. I enjoyed that more.

I like John Bonham and Mitch Mitchell. Bonham, people think he was just boom-crash. But he was old enough to come from swing, so he had a real swing to it. Some people just have it. Not saying he didn't practice; he acted on it. And Mitch Mitchell played with Hendrix. He was basically a jazz guy. And he played jazz behind Jimi Hendrix, who was from another planet, basically. Charlie Watts, I still use one of his fills. Ringo.

With Breathless, when we toured with Kiss, after the solo, I would stand on the bass drum. I would do anything to make a connection with the audience — and that was a perfect Kiss thing to do.

"Breathless" (l. to r.): Bob Benjamin, Jonak Koslen, Rodney Psyka, Alan Greene, Kevin Valentine, Mark Avsec. Note the support act –"The Pulse", who featured Cruiser Marty Lee Hoenes on guitar.

We moved to California in '87, the year after I was married. As soon as I got here, I did Mason Ruffner. Then I was playing with The Godz. I had played with them in Ohio. I played with Randy Hansen. We did the Hendrix tribute thing. That led to me playing with Sam Kinison. Charlotte Caffey from the Go-Go's had a band called the Graces, with two other female singers; I toured with them. We played *The Arsenio Hall Show*.

My father worked for Ohio Gear, which was bought out by Caterpillar. After raising the kids, my mother worked as a secretary for a body shop. I have the ability to build things. I did the whole remodel on my back yard. I have that ability. Mark doesn't. If you're Mark, you're better off *not* operating a power saw. But you know what? Everyone contributes in one way or another. I couldn't do many of the things he does. It balanced out perfectly.

I was always a guy that wired things and put PAs together. When we did the Kiss tours, I put the PA together. When I got out of high school, I had a background in electronics, so I could have gone either way. And that turned into always reading up on things and learning things and learning what knobs do — having an interest in audio, how things sound.

I wasn't a guy recording bands at my house, because the state of the equipment at the time didn't allow that; it was a large cash outlay. I started doing some engineering in Kirk Yano's studio. [The Grammy-winning engineer has worked with Miles Davis, Public Enemy and Mariah Carey.] And when I got out here, I just started engineering in rooms. But once everything got digital, it was affordable.

I produced a couple records with Graham Bonnet, who was the singer of Ritchie Blackmore's Rainbow, out here. That was right after I was running sound for Kiss, about 20 years ago. I hired Slash to play a solo. He didn't know my work, but he was familiar with Graham. He said the studio we were in was the first recording class he ever took.

The second record I did with Graham, I took some of the budget and bought gear and built a studio. And we were able to record at his house.

I did Kiss, then Lou Gramm, then Cinderella, then more Kiss. I connected with them via Eric Singer, my drummer friend from Ohio, from Euclid High. He got here well before I did. I was maybe two years ahead of him. He must have liked me enough to recommend me.

A lot of people have said I play the *song*, not just drum parts. And that's far more important than how fast you can play or how hard you can play. It also comes into play doing sound on TV, because you're telling a story. Because if you have all the gadgets and gizmos, but your sound isn't telling the story, you're not doing your job.

There's different levels of involvement with the different bands I've worked with. But the Donnie stuff, I felt very much *involved* with. I am, perhaps, more responsible for where we got. I mean, when I played on Kiss, I was an unknown player. On the Donnie level, it was like my involvement, it seemed more like my band, like I was a full partner.

I think there's something special there. It's absolute quality stuff. It didn't have the success of some of the other, bigger acts that I played with. But you can't feel bad about that. I am, was, and am still very proud of it. And also, it's not just about chart numbers. It's the whole package. I think we did a good job. I think Mark and Donnie did a good job. Everyone is still good friends. I've played with some people out here, and some of those dudes, you don't want to have lunch with them. So it's the whole package that makes it very special. And, of course, there's a lot of years.

I feel the Cruisers should have done better than they did. But there's a combination of elements that makes a band what they are. And it could be that *one* break they didn't get.

I think it just got to a point — at least it did with me — where I was tired of working with no success. I was with the Innocent after that, and that didn't work out. And at that point, I think it was just time to move on.

My wife and I had to move to New York or California. And L.A. seemed like a better place for bands. And she's a fitness trainer, so it was better for her. We packed up everything and moved. It was just a chance we had to take. You don't want to be 50 and say, "We should have moved out here." We could have moved back to Cleveland if we fell on our faces, no harm done. But we both did rather well. And that's the way the cookie crumbles, I guess.

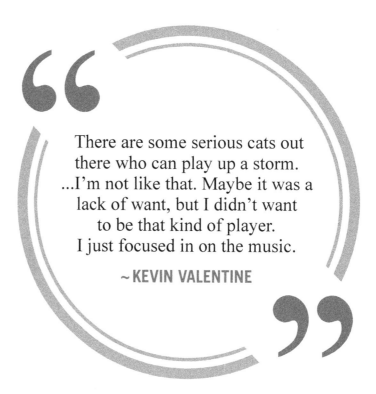

There are some serious cats out there who can play up a storm. ...I'm not like that. Maybe it was a lack of want, but I didn't want to be that kind of player. I just focused in on the music.

~KEVIN VALENTINE

Meet Mike Belkin, Cruisers Manager

The managerial muscle in Donnie Iris and the Cruisers' career is Mike Belkin, a former athlete who built the Cleveland concert industry. He and his brother Jules ran Belkin Productions — and some adjacent endeavors — through decades of sweat, savvy, luck and grind. He began managing Donnie — initially with former partner Carl Maduri — in 1979, when Iris and Mark launched the solo project, before the Cruisers were in the picture. And he has been their manager ever since.

Born in 1935, Belkin is really named Myron. More often, he's known as Michael. He's generous and unassuming, but still has the kind of presence and reputation that makes you want to call him "Mr. Belkin."

Every major city has a guy or two like the Belkin brothers: They started off small, scored some wins, took some losses, and parlayed their business into a longrunning cultural institution that, in time, was bought out by the worldwide entertainment empire that became Live Nation. But few of those regional promoters built the kind of diversified, successful machine that the Belkins did.

As promoters, the Belkins staged some of some of the bigger concerts — and, thus, some of the bigger events — in Cleveland history, including the legendary World Series of Rock shows. The World Series concerts ran from 1974 through 1980. They launched with bands like the Beach Boys and Lynyrd Skynyrd, then built to sold-out extravaganzas featuring Pink Floyd and the Rolling Stones, who sold well over 80,000 tickets each at Cleveland's Lakefront Stadium.[8.1] The 1979 lineup featured Aerosmith, Ted Nugent, Journey, Thin Lizzy, the Scorpions and AC/DC in a single show.

In his best years, Belkin ran a vast domain that spanned the country. The Belkins staged concerts in two dozen other territories from Iowa to Virginia. He narrowly avoided a role in the second-deadliest rock show in American history.[8.2] Michael booked entire tours for Johnny Carson, Liza Minnelli, and Sonny and Cher.

The Belkins' concert empire overlapped with his management team. As managers, they scored an early grand slam: Their biggest act was Wild Cherry, the band behind the indelible dance classic "Play That Funky Music." Other clients included Donnie, Michael Stanley, Mason Ruffner, Doug Sham, and the James Gang — an A-list classic rock institution whose classic lineup included Joe Walsh, who went on to greater fame as the spark plug in the peaceful, easy Eagles.

"There's a famous quote from Mick Jagger," says James Gang founder-drummer Jimmy Fox. "The quote goes, 'There are two people in the industry I'd take a personal check from. One is Bill Graham [the West Coast concert-biz legend]. One is Mike Belkin.' After a certain number of years in the industry, your reputation is either intact or it's trashed. And the artists know that they're in good hands."

Now in his 80s, Belkin still handles the careers of performers including Donnie and the Cruisers and Michael Stanley, Cleveland's record-setting rock king. Belkin still works for Live Nation. But his primary concern is Pinnacle Marketing & Distribution, a clothing and merchandise company with a warehouse full of merchandise from the Steelers, Browns, Ohio State, Penguins, Indians, Pirates, and Cavaliers.

When not at the Live Nation office, Belkin handles business for the various enterprises from the Pinnacle Warehouse, surrounded by keepsakes, trophies, and commemorations from a long, productive and varied life: His inner sanctum is decorated with famous mug shots: Elvis, Willie Nelson, Jane Fonda, Sinatra. Framed box office receipts from concerts by the Who and Johnny Carson. Commendations from charities local and international, including the Jewish National Fund. A framed calendar of Wild Cherry's racy cover art from 1978's *I Love My Music*. A gold record of *James Gang Live*.

Belkin managed Joe Walsh's solo career until a former business partner, entertainment titan Irving Azoff, turned his sights on Belkin. An apex executive, Azoff rose into uncharted heights in the entertainment business stratosphere, each role topping the next: President of the Cruisers' label, MCA. Movie producer, *Fast Times at Ridgemont High*. Chairman of Ticketmaster Entertainment. Chair of Live Nation Entertainment. CEO of Front Line Management. Over the years, he managed the Eagles, Journey, Christina Aguilera, Van Halen, Dan Fogelberg, Bon Jovi, and other superstars. And on that climb, Azoff's first documented miracle was springing Joe Walsh from his Belkin management contract — which still didn't end too badly for the Cleveland impresario.

A habitual sharp dresser, Belkin even looks fresh-pressed when he's working at the warehouse in jeans and a flannel shirt. The tall athlete's metabolism has kept him thin and durable — in full work days, he only sits for 20 minutes. In high school, he could easily palm two basketballs. But that wasn't his best sport.

MIKE BELKIN SAYS:

I did sports through the years. I started in junior high school. I played sandlot baseball in the summer, and basketball in the winter. My mother collected my clippings in a scrap book. I was just looking at them for my book. I had letters from athletic directors and scholarship offers. I had a letter from the Pirates. My wife was reading the articles, and she said, "You scored 30 points in a game?!"

I finished school at Case Western, before it was Case. At Case, my major was business administration. I started in class E and worked my way up to A. It was sort of semi-pro. We weren't supposed to be paid. I was paid. We had sponsors. I went as far as I could. I wasn't *that* good.

I went into the clothing business. My dad still had a store down on West 25th and Clark, where my brother worked. I had a discount store out in Painesville and Ashtabula. The guy who owned the building leased some space to us — my brother and I.

The guy was Leroy Anderson. He was a good promoter of his stores. He was selling major appliances and hardware. He decided, one day, to get more people in the store, he would bring in some music acts and put them down at a club called The Swallows. I think it accommodated a couple hundred people. I had absolutely no interest at all in that stuff — he brought in Louis Armstrong, Lionel Hampton, Duke Ellington. Some, he would make $300 on. Some, he would lose $300 on. It was all to get people to come into the store and buy the tickets. It was before the Beatles started.

When the Beatles started, I was still in Ashtabula. I didn't get involved in any of that. I had no interest, though I always loved music. It was an important part of my life, growing up. At a certain point I, and then my brother, said to Leroy, "Maybe we should see what's happening in Cleveland." There wasn't very much happening, contemporary-music-wise. I said, "Why don't we try and do a concert in Cleveland?"

And I always liked the Four Freshman. So they said OK.

I made a call to Capitol Records. And I spoke to someone there. And they said, "That's fine. But we don't book the group." I said, "Well, who should I be calling?" They said, "Jerry Perenchio, who had been extremely, extremely successful in the music business and radio." [Perenchio, a former Univision Chairman and CEO, died a billionaire.] So I called his agency and said, "Look, I'm from Ohio, I would like to do a concert with the Four Freshmen."

He said, "Have you done a concert before?"

I said, "No, but I'd like to start."

I asked how much it was, and he said, "$1,500." I still have the original contract and the original box-office statement for that, Jimi Hendrix, the Who, and Johnny Carson.

The next concert we did was the Mamas and the Papas at the Public Auditorium. Or we were supposed to do the Mamas and the Papas. But they canceled on us, which is one of the worst things that can happen, because you have to refund the money and pay rent for the building and pay stagehands. And the second time they canceled, also.

And so it went on like that. Hendrix, we did two shows at Music Hall that sold out, on his first tour. I was the first one to bring Bowie to town. We did all the Ohio Doors shows. I lost Jim Morrison in the Playboy mansion. But I found him. That story's in the book. A lot of good things happened. A lot of things happened that weren't so great. But that's the way of life: dealing with a lot of egos and a lot of performers you can't 100% depend upon.

The Four Freshman concert was in 1963. I went full-time as a promoter in the early '70s. We started doing concerts outside Cleveland, and those were successful. I had a good relationship with the managers and the artists.

Whenever we went into another city, I would ask them if they wanted to be partners on the date, for two reasons: One, not every concert is a winner. So when you lose money on a concert, it's nice to only lose half of the money. And it's the right thing to do, the way Jules and I did business. You can't be a pig and be a winner all the time. That's what we would do with all the big acts. But then, we had the small shows too.

The James Gang was the first band I managed. Jimmy Fox found me and said he needed some help. I said I didn't know what I was doing. But I had had some success in the business, and I was able to figure it out. After that, Michael Stanley approached me, and I started working with him. As a manager, your business depends on your product. When you have the James Gang with Joe Walsh, that makes it easier.

The Who was doing a date for us in Pittsburgh. I needed an opener for that date. I put the James Gang on. Townsend was backstage, and he heard the James Gang and Walsh playing, and he was blown away. After the show, they said, "We're going to be doing a tour, and we'd like them to open for us." It was the Who who really helped the James Gang get the notoriety they had. We became friends, and we still are today.

We were supposed to promote the Cincinnati Who concert [in 1979, which resulted in 11 deaths, 33 lawsuits, and extensive safety-code reform after the general-admission portion of the audience rushed the stadium [8.3]]. We were going to do it with an agency, Premier Talent, with Frank Barsalona, a great guy, who was the reason the British bands came to the United States. His theory was that whoever promotes a band in a city, they also get the next time they tour.

Mike Belkin

So I had done the Who prior to Cincinnati. I don't know why, to this day, may he rest in peace: He gave the concerts to another promoter out of Philadelphia, Larry Magi. Three hours before that concert, I was crazy that we didn't get that show. After, I felt horrible for what happened, but I felt differently. That changed the scene in Ohio, for the longest time. It took a long time before we were able to have general admission again.

Irving Azoff and I were partners, going back quite a few years. Lake Geneva, Wisconsin — Majestic Hills. We were partners for shows there. The Walsh lawsuit was well after.

Irving was an easy guy to get along with. He was president of MCA Records later. Irving was a good guy, a good negotiator. But sometimes when you're talking to him, you have to look outside to see if it's night or day. Sometimes he has a tendency to exaggerate. We had our ups and downs. He's a likable guy, and everybody comes out ahead. Every now and then, he'll send me an email.

I was managing Walsh. And Irving, at some point, went to L.A. and went to work for an agency. He was Walsh's agent at that time. We were on good terms. At that point, Walsh had a band which I had helped him put together, which was the "Rocky Mountain Way" band.

And then Irving went to work for a management company. He had spoken with Walsh about Walsh coming to him as his manager. It was at that point that I sued. I won the lawsuit, but Walsh continued with him. To this day, I get a percentage of his recordings, the material prior to him joining the Eagles. And I get a percentage of his percentage of the Eagles.

I also managed [subsequent James Gang guitarist] Tommy Bolin. He had some problems that have been written about. He had a habit. He didn't avoid some of the things the Cruisers did.

My goal has always been, for the bands I manage, for them to have money in the bank. The Cruisers were cooperative with that. Another artist I managed, every four, five months, I'd look out the window in the office, and they'd be driving a new Cadillac. I'd say, "You're pissing away money with a new car." The Cruisers are all bright guys. Solid.

It's the story of the team, Mark and Donnie together. They're individuals. But they're a wonderful team. They both care about people. They both care about other musicians. Mark is extremely bright. Donnie is bright. He's a likeable guy. He's a great singer. They're fortunate that they joined forces when they did.

Carl and I formed the Belkin-Maduri Organization for management.

Carl was the music guy. He would spend time in the studio. I don't spend time in the studio. I don't like to. I don't think I add anything to the music of the artists I manage. I do the business. I do the booking. We wanted to put together a stable.

We got lucky with Wild Cherry.

[Wild Cherry frontman Robert] Parissi came into the office. Carl was the music guy. Parissi spoke to Carl and played him the tape. Carl fell in love with it.

We signed him to a recording contract, which he still records under.

And the rest is history. That thing sold a zillion.

We own a certain amount of the record. We formed Sweet City so we could sign artists. We ran that through Epic. That record was a windfall. It did a lot of business. It sold a lot of copies, and was played everywhere. It's still in movies and commercials — there's a lot of money in that.

My brother and I sold the business [Belkin Productions] in 2001, to SFX, and it became Clear Channel, and now it's Live Nation. I still work for them.

We did our first Rib Cook-Off in 1987. I started selling merchandise after that. I saw all those people come in. It seemed like an opportunity. So I started buying some Indians stuff and selling it. Then I got in touch with some retail establishments. And I built upon it.

The music business has changed. It used to be important to get a lot of coverage and make sure you lots of product, records in the stores. Now it's different.

" It's the story of the team,
Mark and Donnie together.
They're individuals. But they're
a wonderful team. They both care
about people. They both care
about other musicians.
...They're fortunate that they
joined forces when they did.

~MIKE BELKIN "

Paul Goll (Photo by James Cooper)

CHAPTER 9

Meet Paul Goll,
Current Cruisers Bassist

In 1985, bassist Paul Goll was the Cruisers' first choice to replace the near-irreplaceable Albritton McClain. He turned down the offer. But he came around.

After 25 years as a Cruiser, he is still the new guy in the group, though fully accepted as a worthy brother in arms.

Goll grew up in Erie, where he played in bands with Marty. He has seen the world as much as the other Jaggerz, and he experienced the waning days of the Woodstock era in a way even the freewheelin'-but-homebound Donnie did not. Before Goll — rhymes with "Paul" — joined, he was a friend of Marty, and a witness to Cruisers history in the making.

Without original bassist Albritton McClain, the Cruisers struggled until Paul came along. Onstage, he's a subtle presence, but his bass — in tandem with the returned drummer Kevin Valentine — finally gave the band the bedrock foundation it needs.

"He's an encyclopedia," says Donnie. "You name anything, and he can play it — he knows so many songs. Great guy. Funny. Awesome bass player. Sings great background falsetto. Wouldn't trade him for anybody."

"Paul is fantastic," says Mark. "A wonderfully good, talented, nice guy. Paul is really solid."

"Paul is probably the most consistent person in the band, besides Donnie," says Kevin. "I'm calling that from recording I've done where I've had to pick performances. He's a pleasure to play with. When we play together, there's a lot of eye contact. It's enjoyable."

"As a bass player, I think Paul's greatest strength is that he is so steady and aware," says Marty. "He's very talented musically — he knows exactly what he's doing, and he knows why he's doing it. He's always been exceptional like that. And he and I go back a long, long ways. If I drift during a song, tempo-wise or arrangement-wise, he's the one — along with Kevin — that I trust to get me back on track."

Like the other Cruisers, Goll is a deep and broad talent: He fleshes out the sound with an occasional cello. He survived the trials of the rock and roll lifestyle, came out the other side, and managed to balance a satisfying musical life with a fulfilling, challenging professional career.

After a long run as a working musician, he earned a master's degree in social work. At his day job, he helps adolescent children and their families as a behavioral health therapist autism specialist. As a Cruiser, he has the band's second-longest commute: His lives in North Carolina, where he works at Mission Children's Hospital.

And, like the rest of the band, he was born again when he saw the Beatles on TV February 9, 1964

PAUL SAYS:

Paul McCartney is the guy. I love the Beatles' stuff. But also, I don't just love rock and roll. I have a history of being in orchestras and bands in my early life. I have been a lead singer, backing vocalist, and songwriter in most of the bands I have been in. Most of the songwriting happened in the band Powerglide.

My parents weren't musical. My sisters were, though. My dad's name was Paul David Goll, Senior. He was a school teacher and football coach. His area was world history and sociology. He taught at McDowell High School, in Mill Creek. He was the football coach, and then became the athletic director. Before that started, he played for the Cleveland Browns in 1946-47, as a center under Paul Brown, until his leg injury ended his career.

I was interested in music before the Beatles. I liked the Beatles and Rolling Stones, but before that, my sisters were listening to the Beach Boys and Bobbie Vinton and just a little bit of Motown stuff. So it was the British invasion and what they used to call bubblegum stuff: the Dave Clark Five. "Green Tambourine." "Red Rubber Ball" by The Cyrkle — one-hit wonders. Paul Revere and the Raiders. The Monkees, I'm a huge fan. I would watch the Monkees every Saturday and think, "That's what I want to be. I want to do that."

On the radio, a lot of the time, we could get Canadian stations. I'll never forget listening and hearing Cream and "Purple Haze" and going, "What the hell is *that*?!" It was underground, because it wasn't on the radio until it got big. You'd go to the stores, like the Boston department store and Grant's in Erie, and buy the 45 and go, "Oh, there's a *B-side*?!"

By the end of high school, I was no longer playing saxophone or baritone horn. I was playing string bass and electric bass, pretty much. And the only reason I was playing string bass was because I wanted to be in the orchestra in high school. And then after high school, I didn't do it any more. I did know how to play fretless instruments by playing the string bass. Now I play a fretless bass, but I generally don't play it with Donnie. I play five-string bass, cello, piano, and acoustic and electric bass. My wife is one of my cello teachers, and that is how we met.

I graduated in '71. From the time I was 16, I was playing clubs and concerts with various bands around town — anything from community centers to high school dances. One of the clubs was called Yogi's. You had to be 16 and join the musicians' union to play the clubs. We would do anything from Hendrix and Cream to Dave Clark Five.

My hair is probably collar length at this point, some matching outfits. By the time I graduated, I was in a band that was playing more progressive rock: Yes and Emerson, Lake & Palmer, some Glass Harp, James Gang, stuff like that. Playing Yes wasn't hard for me. We could nail it. We had a Hammond organ and a Moog synthesizer. We could do the harmonies. That band was called Anacrusis.

At that time, I was hanging out with some people that were getting motorcycles. And I got a motorcycle, and we got this plan to go to California. This was *Easy Rider*-inspired. I had a Triumph 650, and those guys had Harleys. And I rode mine from Erie to Denver, and then from Denver out to the coast.

We lived with some people in Venice Beach. That was right after Jim Morrison died, 1972, early 1973. That was a scene. Lots of drugs. Lots of crazy stuff going on. The *Whole Earth Catalog*, the Grateful Dead.

They'd have a Venice Canal jam session thing. People from Blue Cheer would show up, all sorts of people floating through. Let's just say I was experimenting with a lot of different things at that point. There were days where, well… experimenting. It was like utopia.

We stayed up late and woke up late.

The weather was wonderful, but back then, there was more pollution. So we would have days where you would go outside and you couldn't stay outside very long, because the ocean would send in cloud cover. And then that would trap all the pollutants. And it would create that smog. It was just not healthy to be out there.

But there were good days, going out on people's sailboats, the Marina del Rey, going swimming on Venice Beach, looking at all the hippies, and everybody looks stoned. And people playing music everywhere, in many forms. It was just *rich*.

I was in a couple bands out there. I was there for about a year. Too much fun, I guess, would be a way of saying it. My health was starting to suffer. I decided to leave.

I came back to Erie. This is '74, '75. That's when I met Marty. By the time I met Marty, things were changing.

We were in a bunch of bands together, playing disco in Holiday Inns, stuff like that. That's when Marty joined The Pulse. That's where Donnie heard Marty.

I was making a shift at that point: Led Zeppelin was really big, and we were playing "Houses of the Holy." I loved it. I thought that was exactly the way music was supposed to be, a natural progression. The leader in this was the Beatles, the way they evolved. Every band, I knew at least four or five of their songs.

Everything with my rock, I learned by ear. In the genres that I'm comfortable in, I can listen and know what it is. I have enough theory — I'm not a good sight reader. There weren't any limitations until I got into later progressive rock and jazz fusion, until I got up against Stanley Clarke and Jacob Pastorius. I'm still working on some of that stuff.

Right at the time Marty joined The Pulse, I moved to Florida. And that's where I joined up with a band called Powerglide, named after the transmission — I think it was a Chevy. This band was looking for a bass player. They already had a truck and a road crew and lights and sound. And they were already touring and gigging and recording. So I was psyched to be in that band. This was around 1978.

We wanted to be within shooting distance of New York City, so we settled on the outskirts of Boston. And that's about the time that the Cars and Aerosmith were taking off. So we'd see those guys around. That was around 1980. We started off more rock-jazz fusion, and then morphed through different stages of pop-rock. I was one of the songwriters and played bass, keys, and lead/backing vocals. We had three LPs and an EP. We have some songs on YouTube.

When I first saw the Cruisers live, it was '83-ish, the Paradise in Boston. Albritton was *killing* everybody. Kev and Al, like *whoa*.

There's this nonverbal communication that happens in bands, but especially a rhythm section. Without even watching the other guy, you can hear his language, his syntax, his musical vocabulary. Kevin has the musical vocabulary, how he usually does things. And if you're listening, nine times out of ten, you can follow it and play it together without saying, "You do this, and I do that."

Marty and Kevin are real monsters, so they could have gone real *progressive rock* on any of their tunes. But they didn't. They did what was needed for the band. And that's my philosophy too: You've got to lay something down that Donnie can do something with that *inspires*. Something Donnie can do something with, so Donnie can be at his best.

When I was in Boston, Marty and the band had lost the record deal, and they were independent. This is after Al left. Marty called and asked me if I was interested. And that was after we had just started doing some showcases with Powerglide in New York City. And we were starting to get some notoriety in Boston. So I said, "I think I'm going to stick with Powerglide."

Reel to Real (l. to r.): Steve McConnell, Mike Goodwin, Paul Goll, Marty Lee Hoenes.

Paul Goll

I was married. I have a son who is 37 now. He's a musician, a singer-songwriter, a multi-instrumentalist. He lives in Columbus, Ohio. I got married in 1976, and I was a family man until 1991. So there were some ongoing issues that I had some struggles with, drinking that almost got me kicked out of the band I was with. I became sober in about 1992, and I've been sober since.

I wanted to go back to school because I knew I could not sustain playing in four or five different bands and having a cleaning business on the side to make ends meet.

I went back to college in 1994, at Mercyhurst College [in Erie]. I was going for a music education major in cello, but had to drop out in 1996.

I went back to college at the University of Pittsburgh School of Social Work. I started in 2001. I got my bachelor's degree in social work, and I got my Master's of Social Work in 2006.

I realized I was a good listener, and I also got to experience family therapy first hand. I realized that I had a gift for it. I specialized in family therapy in my internships at college, and I had extensive training. I then got interested in autism after working at an autism summer camp and doing family therapy with families with children with autism.

I am a behavioral health therapist autism specialist, working at Mission Children's Hospital, in a pediatric developmental behavioral integrative practice. I work with families who have children and adolescents, one to 20 years old, with autism. And I coach parents and teach social skills to the kids. We have to solve behavioral problems associated with autism at home and in the community.

In bands, I have always been the peacemaker and mediator in between strong personalities. I work behind the scenes to facilitate change and negotiations. This requites good listening and understanding, which are essential therapist skills.

Over the years, I had stayed in touch with Marty. Before school, when I returned to Erie, he was living in there at that time. That year I moved back, Scott was playing with them, and he was playing with Humble Pie. And that was his first commitment. And he was kind of leaving Donnie high and dry. Marty asked me if I would be interested in filling in.

I was very flattered and very excited. I viewed it as a great opportunity. That started the whole thing.

> Marty and Kevin are real monsters, so they could have gone real progressive rock on any of their tunes. But they didn't. They did what was needed for the band. And that's my philosophy too: You've got to lay something down that Donnie can do something with that inspires ..so Donnie can be at his best.
>
> ~ PAUL GOLL

Opening Act

The Jaggerz (Donnie far left, in the suit he later wore for the Back on the Streets cover and "Ah! Leah!" video.) Photo courtesy of Jimmie Ross

CHAPTER 10

Opening Act: The Jaggerz, "Pittsburgh's #1 Band for 10 Years"

An ad for Jaggerz' farewell show billed the group as "Pittsburgh's #1 Band for 10 Years." It was a legitimate claim.

Donnie Iris wrote his way into the national spotlight with "The Rapper," a 1969 hit single by his first big group, the Jaggerz. The Jaggerz have gone down in history as a one-hit wonder, famous for a gold — maybe platinum — novelty song. But the band was a talented, multifaceted squad whose bread & butter was rich, expertly harmonized blue-eyed soul.

Donnie was a starter on this team of Beaver Valley all-stars as he grew from a college dropout to an accomplished artist who — for a glorious moment — competed with Simon & Garfunkel and the Beatles for the top spot on national charts.

The single is featured on a boxed set retrospective from the Jaggerz' onetime label, 1993's *The Buddha Box* compilation, alongside classic singles such as The Lovin' Spoonful's "Summer in the City," Ohio Express' "Yummy, Yummy, Yummy," Brewer & Shipley's "One Toke over the Line," Bill Withers' "Ain't No Sunshine," Curtis Mayfield's "Superfly," and Gladys Knight & the Pips' "Midnight Train to Georgia." The band repeatedly scaled the heights, but they could never quite stay there.

The Jaggerz were named to the Pittsburgh Rock 'N' Roll Legends hall of fame in 2017, on the strength of that hit, several albums, and a storied career that continues to this day. "The Rapper" was an anomaly for the Jaggerz, both as their greatest success, and as a representation of their sound. The group launched in an era where talent was mandatory and original songs were optional. As Pittsburgh rock royalty Joe Grushecky told *Rolling Stone* in 1981, the Jaggerz "were the only white guys who could do The Temptations."

During their distinguished run, the Jaggerz worked with some of the biggest names in the music business, including Gamble and Huff, the legendary songwriting-production team whose credits eventually included the Jacksons, the O'Jays, Billy Paul (best known for "Me and Mrs. Jones"), Laura Nyro, Dusty Springfield, Wilson Pickett, and Harold Melvin & the Blue Notes.

MEET THE JAGGERS

Many accounts of Jaggerz history — even recollections from the band's consistent core of stars — give the wrong beginning and end dates for the group.

Formed in 1964, the initial lineup featured Donnie on guitar and vocals, Benny "Euge" Faiella on vocals and guitar, bassist Alan George, and drummer Kenny Koodrich. The breakthrough lineup was bigger: Jim Ross on bass and vocals, Thom Davies on organ, Bill Maybray on bass and vocals, Jim Pugliano on drums, Faiella and Iris. Later lineups would feature Herm Granati of the Granati Brothers (Donnie's longtime scenemates and running buddies) and Frank Czuri (a founding member of '80s rock band the Silencers and Diamond Reo, a '70s rock act that featured Norm Nardini).

"The Jaggerz were a cover band for years," says Donnie. "Then we decided to write original songs. I learned a lot about playing guitar, singing, being able to sing night after night."

After emerging as a promising regional band, the Jaggerz connected with Joe Rock. Rock was the manager of the Skyliners, the Pittsburgh heroes best known for classic "Since I Don't Have You," which he wrote. Rock — who passed away in 2010 — guided them to high-profile record deals and colorful engagements.

The Jaggerz' three albums and 11 major-label singles are windows into the pinnacle of one era and the dawn of another. Following the band's big hit, the Jaggerz gigged hard until 1976, weathering one rock and roll sea change after another. The sharp-dressed showband didn't just nurture Donnie as a singer, songwriter, and frontman; it directly contributed a key element to the Donnie Iris iconography. Minus Iris, members of the classic lineup reconvened for an ongoing series of concerts and recordings. And their music still resurfaces as a popular hip-hop sample source. In the record business, one hit is enough.

Most Jaggerz retrospectives get the story wrong, based on a skewed, wrong, and not-unreasonable reading of the band's convoluted, largely undocumented history. Because of Donnie's later success, hasty internet profiles tend to cast Iris as the Jaggerz' leader or frontman. But that's just one of the incorrect echoes in the legend of the Jaggerz. Iris was an equal part of the group's triple-headed frontline, and definitely not the band boss.

BENNY: I'm from Aliquippa. I was raised in West Aliquippa. I started the band. Donnie and all the guys didn't want to do anything as far as the business — handling the booking, handling the paychecks, handling the band. I handled all that until Joe Rock stepped into the picture.

In 1964, I was playing a club in Geneva-on-the-Lake, Ohio, on Lake Erie. We stayed there all summer. They gave us a cabin. I was playing with a band called Gary and the Jeweltones. There were four of us in the group at the time. That summer, Donnie had come up. He was singing with these guys from New Castle called the Fabutons. I heard Donnie singing, and he had a great voice, you know?

At the end of the summer, we broke up. And the three of us wanted to continue. But we needed a singer. So I said to the drummer, "What about Donnie Iris?"

Kenny said, "He's got a great voice, but we need a guitar player, too."

I said, "I heard Donnie & the Donnells are playing down in McKees Rocks. I heard he's playing pretty good." So we went down to the club. He was playing guitar, and it was perfect for what we needed.

DONNIE: I got a call from Gary and the Jeweltones. I went and interviewed with them and did some tunes with them. And that's when we started the Jaggerz.

BENNY: We asked Donnie, and he said OK. That's when we came up with "The Jaggers."

Over the years, the Iris-Faiella-Koodrich-George lineup usually wasn't considered an official part of the band's history. Depending on how sentimental and contemplative different members are feeling at the moment, sometimes they acknowledge it. Like the lineup, the band's name would change.

BENNY: Kenny Koodrich picked up a Stones album and said, "What about the Jaggers, like Mick Jaggers, you know?" We looked up the definition, and we saw, "piercing thorn."

And the Jaggers — with an *S* — were alive and kicking. For a little while.

BENNY: The drummer was going to get drafted, because the Vietnam crisis was going on. Donnie went into the reserves for six months. We broke up.

And then I reformed, brought some more guys into the group.

We were playing bars and Geneva-on-the-Lake. And six months later, Donnie came back. Now it's '65. He gets out, he came up. We're playing. And we're so tight, he says, "Euge, I don't know if I'm good enough to come back and get in with you."

I said, "Donnie, shut up, you're fine. You've been foolin' around with that Army crap. Start rehearsing with us, you'll be fine."

His voice was *uuu-nique*. He has the quality of singing like Eddie Kendricks from the Temptations, that nice, smooth falsetto. Or he could do Smokey Robinson. He could do Joe Cocker. That's what impressed me: the quality of his voice. He had such a versatile range and a fantastic ear.

BEACH BLANKET BINGO AND THE BEAVER SCENE

Nestled midway between Erie and Cleveland, Geneva-on-the-Lake was a sun-and-fun destination for families and young adults from Ohio — where the drinking age was 18, albeit for weak 3.2% ABV beer — and nearby Pennsylvania, where the drinking age was 21. One local dubbed it "the working man's Cape Cod."

BENNY: I can't tell you how wonderful it was to play every night of the week. We played seven nights a week, and two jam sessions Saturday and Sunday, all summer, until Labor Day. Our wives and girlfriends would come up together.

In '65, times were a' changing, and the youth were getting restless. July 4th weekend, the summer hotspot was swept up in a nationwide wave of riots. Ohio's governor sent the National Guard to settle the scene.

"Police drove several hundred cursing rioters out of the town, but they returned yesterday afternoon and last night, littering the streets with broken glass, bottles, paper cups, and bonfire ashes. About 30 arrests were made," reported the Chicago *Tribune*.[10.1] Firsthand accounts aren't as dramatic or sensational, which isn't to say it was a mellow scene.

BENNY: We were there for the riots. It was a mixed crowd. Some long hair. A lot of families — they brought their kids there. So many types of people. It was motorcycle gangs that started it. There was a group from Cleveland, one from Rochester, Pennsylvania — all over, in their leather jackets and their hats and whatever. They had the streets closed off. People couldn't get into the town. A lot of arrests.

When the summer ended, the music continued.

BENNY: Then we did the club scene back here in Beaver County, a few things in Pittsburgh. In Beaver Falls, there was the Club Naturale. We played there six nights a week.

Between summer 1965 and 1966, the band solidified its lineup, adding a third frontman, Jimmie Ross. Coincidentally, Ross was the first cousin of original Jaggers bassist Allen George.

MEET THE JAGGERS?

JIMMIE: Around this area, Beaver County, it was primarily an R&B flavor. Everybody was into the Temptations and the Four Tops and Marvin Gaye and people like that. So when we got together, everybody's head was in the same place. We sang so well together.

There were four bands that came together to form the Jaggerz. Gary [Glenn] and the Jeweltones was one of them. Donnie and the Donnells was one. The Bell Boys was the third one. And the Billy Richardson Trio was the fourth. Donnie was from Donnie and the Donnells. Bennie was from Gary & the Jeweltones. [Bassist/drummer/singer] Billy Maybray was from the Billy Richardson Trio. And the drummer, Jim Pugliano, and I were from the Bell Boys. So we got together to form the original Jaggers. I had heard of them. I was flattered that they asked me.

With Ross on the squad, the Jaggers ruled the summer of '66. They scored a job as house band for Geneva-on-the-Lake's brand-new Sunken Bar — later known as Delfrate's Nite Club — a night spot with a capacity of 425.[10.2]

BENNY: College kids came. It was a dance type of scene. They came to hear us 'cuz we did the soul stuff and the R&B thing. We had the versatility in the group, with the voices. Billy could do James Brown. And we had Donnie's range. And Jimmie Ross had a high range. They would stand in line to come and see us.

In 1966, the Jaggers were surprised to learn about a record by another group called the Jaggers. This would be a recurring phenomenon. In fact, it was the work of one former Jagger: George Sabol, who had played bass in the first lineup as "Allen George." George recorded two garage rock songs, "Feel So Good" b/w "Cry." He released the 45 under the important-sounding label name Executive Records Inc., headquartered in Cleveland.

BENNY: Those are not Jaggers songs.

JIMMIE: It wasn't like a job to us, even though we were playing six or seven nights a week.

We were one of the best cover bands around. It was all covers. We played what the people wanted to hear, what was on the radio all day. But we did it better, our own way. A lot of it was the R&B — Marvin Gaye, a couple Stevie Wonder things. Any songs that fit the Jaggers' sound. Songs with vocal harmony, because we were primarily a vocal band.

We were good friends. We were all from Beaver County. We roomed together on the road. We bought motorcycles together. We even bought the same kind of cars one year, '64 Grand Prixes.

When the summer ended, the band played on.

JIMMIE: Back at home, we played a place called the Club Naturale in Beaver Falls. It was a great place, a great dance club, a local club on the main street in Beaver Falls. It was a small room. It was kinda in between and Elks and a Vegas style club. It wasn't a banquet hall. It was more elaborate. There were booths and a bar. It used to be crowded every night, six nights a week.

At that time, a lot of people did work in the mills in Beaver County and the Aliquippa area, where J&L Steel was. They were in their early 20s — it seemed like everybody was single at that time. Nobody wore suits. It was real casual. The guys, there were no longhairs in there. The girls all looked good. No more beehives. The girls, some long hair, some short, like they do today.

The best look at the band over the years is a YouTube video, "The Jaggerz ~ 2013 Slideshow," which presents pictures the Jaggerz and their forerunner groups, one photo after another in a series of coordinated formal-wear outfits, as the prom-ready slow dance number "Give a Little Love" unwinds. The site has a wealth of Jaggerz clips, from a skinny young lineup playing originals to audio of the later band covering the show tune "Old Man River."

When the Jaggerz played, the most common frontline configuration was, left to right, Donnie, Benny, Jimmie, and Billy, wearing matching outfits like shimmering dark shirts and tan slacks. Through the set, the Jaggerz would perform rudimentary dance steps that gave them a professional edge over their competition. Check YouTube for a synchronized shuffle and sway four white guys wide, with some G-rated lateral hip motion, an occasional simultaneous turn and spin, and a few kick steps to tie it together.

The band's true frontman was Jimmie Ross, a tall, burly singer with bowl-cut black hair and thick plastic glasses to match. He emceed the sets and gave the sign-off in their signature closing routine: After introducing the group, he worked the audience: "We're at the Club Naturale six nights a week — take it easy on the way home!" Ross' salutation was the band's cue: Moving like pistons, they dropped in some classical musical and pumped through one last choreographed routine.

BENNY: When I first started playing, I had to learn this waltz, "The Blue Danube." We were looking for a way to get in and out of our set for when we took our break. I said "Let's do this waltz thing I used to do." I'll go down. You guys go up. And then we'll go into this jazz then, then do some fast steps.

We'd go real fast, turn around and stop, and that would be the end of our show.

JIMMIE: At the shows, a lot of dancing, from start to finish — the jitterbug, I guess. There was no line dancing at that time. Couples dancing, slow dancing. The house wasn't that big, and there wasn't whole-house air conditioning. It could get hot. Almost every song we did was a dance song. We played the club circuit, and that's what people did at the time. They didn't sit and watch. It wasn't a concert-type thing. We played starting at maybe nine o'clock till one o'clock in the morning.

On Sunday, we would play a college. We played Edinboro. We played Slippery Rock. California State. Youngstown. They were all cool. It would be packed at every school we played. It still wasn't the hippie scene. Everybody was clean cut. But at the college gigs, it was more of a concert type deal, standing up, not so much dancing.

DONNIE: Joe Namath went to the same high school as my wife. He used to come see us at Club Naturale. I believe I met him at a place called Waite's Ice Cream.

BENNY: We didn't read music — we played by ear. We jelled together, really great. And Donnie fit great. He's a great lead singer. Jimmie Ross is a great lead singer. And I had Billy in the band. Three great singers in a band, it was great.

It was nice being a cover band for the first two years. But after that, hearing people saying how great you guys are sounding, how our songs sounded better than the records. We needed a style and identity. We needed a sound. We needed to be ourselves. We needed to be the *Jaggerz*.

COVER BAND NO MORE

DONNIE: In the late '60s, we started writing some of our own stuff. And a couple people in the band would write tunes together. We had six guys. We'd split three guys-three guys, and we wrote songs. My partners in writing were Benny Faiella and Joe Rock.

If you were a Pittsburgh rock band, Joe Rock is the man whose ear you wanted. The manager's clients included the Skyliners, and he did more than manage groups. Suffering a fresh heartbreak, Rock wrote the lyrics to "Since I Don't Have You" and gave them to the Skyliners. The haunting tune hit the *Billboard* chart in March 1959, peaked at number 12, and lives on in various forms. (The song was covered by Don McLean, Johnny Mathis, Barbara Streisand, and Art Garfunkel, among numerous others. Guns N' Roses' reverent version garnered heavy MTV rotation and peaked at 69 on the *Billboard* singles chart in 1994, a full 35 years later.)

Rock also managed soul singer Johnny Day, and landed him a deal with Stax, the famous label with a lineup starring Otis Redding, Albert King and Isaac Hayes. Rock co-wrote "Dreams to Remember" with Redding. The manager knew how to spot talent, and he knew what to do with it.

DONNIE: Joe Rock came to see us one night, and he wanted to manage us.

BENNY: He started coming around. He said, "I can do this for you guys, I can do that for you."

He'd come to Geneva-on-the-Lake. And he offered to get us a spot on a TV show in Cleveland, get us some exposure. We knew he had a career with the Skyliners. And we put our faith in him, "Joe Ross is gonna do that with us, too!"

JIMMIE: '67, we were starting to play our own stuff: "Baby I Love You," "Gotta Find My Way Back Home." And all the dance tunes, a lot of Temptations. The first original Jaggerz song was "Baby I Love You." Joe Rock wrote that.

We all worked on songs together, at the studio. We had a rehearsal space in New Brighton — we called it The Studio. It was sort of an office for the Jaggerz, with a rehearsal area in the back. Everybody put their two cents in, if somebody had an idea. People brought ideas in, and they were like a finished product. And we'd elaborate on it a little bit. "Gotta Find My Way Back Home," we played it a couple months before we recorded it.

"(That's Why) Baby I Love You" was a powerful start, a slow, slinky soul tune built around a monster piano hook, echoing chorus vocals, and smooth horn blasts. The band's sound crystalized on "Gotta Find My Way Back Home," a midtempo tune that upped the funk content *and* had another golden, stratified chorus. Rock helped refine the band's repertoire and name.

BENNY: An article came out in *Life* magazine about a band called The Jaggers. Joe said, "We have to change the name. If we change the letter to Z, it'll be fine."

The band's *Z* spelling begins appearing in Pittsburgh newspapers August 19, 1968, in an ad for their regular Wednesday night appearance at Mancini's. The "Jaggers" and "Jaggerz" variations appear in ads through September. By October, the clubs and papers had received the memo. "Jaggers" with an S last appears in the Pittsburgh papers October 2, 1968 in a Pittsburgh *Press* ad for a Thursday night show at the Psyche-Dilly in McKees Rocks, outside Pittsburgh.

JIMMIE: We knew we had something. We had huge crowds everywhere we would go in the tri-state area, and we got the recognition as one of the best bands around. Every place was packed. We never played to 25 or 50 people. It was always whatever the place would hold.

We were one of the only bands around to have three lead singers. Everybody in the band could sing, and they could sing well. So our harmony fit together like a glove. The guys were made for each other, as far as our vocal blends and what we did with the harmonies. Whenever we rehearsed, it didn't take long to get a song down. We loved it.

BENNY: We all had families. We worked a lot. That was our full-time job. We spent a lot of time together.

Donnie's personality: He's great with people. Anybody that comes up to Donnie and introduces themselves, he's very humble, and you'll get a great impression. He's down-to-earth.

Billy Maybray, he never could make his mind up about things. He wasn't sure of himself a lot of the time.

Thommy always wanted to be in control of that aspect of the business, the money.

Jimmie Ross was a worrier, worried about everything — great guy, great voice, great talent. But he's worried: He wants perfection. He wants everything to go right all the time. We called him "The Cliz." It came from "Clanton Ross" — Clanton, I don't know where *that* came from, but we called him Clanton. His name was Jimmie.

Me, I always brought my friends along. I never acted like I was on a higher level because I made it. But some of the guys got a little bit big-headed.

Pugliano… some the guys in the band wanted to do other things. So that's when I took charge.

We called Donnie the banker, "The Hunk." When we needed a loan, we'd ask Donnie.

Donnie wasn't exactly good with money — but, even more importantly, he wasn't bad with it. He didn't spend his paycheck foolishly; in fact, he often didn't spend them at all.

BENNY: Donnie lived at home. He wasn't cashing his paychecks for three months! The bank called and said, "We got a problem here, you gotta cash these." His dad was managing his money. He set up investments for him. One day we're on the road. I opened the glove compartment, and he had all this money in there, checks he never cashed.

JIMMIE: After playing six days a week in some club, driving to a college, instead of resting our voices, we would sing all the way up in the station wagon or the van. Hearing that harmony in an enclosed area like a car was unbelievable. It sent chills up your back.

There were a lot of favorites. I was a Temptations guy. They did an album called *In a Mellow Mood* that was all show tunes. We did their arrangements of "The Impossible Dream" [from *Man of La Mancha*] and [Stevie Wonder's] "For Once in My Life" off of that album. We never played any throwaway tunes. We didn't care if a song was number 1 — if it didn't fit the Jaggerz, we didn't do it. "Ain't No Big Thing" was a big song for us. "You Waited Too Long." "Pride and Joy" and "Hitchhike" by Marvin Gaye. We didn't have just *one* showstopper.

BENNY: Joe Rock knew the music industry, all the contracts, all the legal stuff. We just wanted to play. And we trusted Joe.

GAMBLE AND HUFF AND THE STEALS BROTHERS

Rock put the band on a path toward the big city: Pittsburgh. The band's first mention in the Pittsburgh newspapers was an a *Post-Gazette* nightclub ad January 6, 1968: Thursday, January 11, "THE FABULOUS JAGGERS" would headline Villa's 007 lounge, 40 minutes northeast of Pittsburgh. (The club added "fabulous" to make the new act sound more fabulous; the word was never formally part of their title.)

Rock connected them with the Pennsylvania songwriting team who would later write the Spinners' million-selling single "Could It Be I'm Falling in Love." The famous Steals twins, like Faiella and Ross, were from the Aliquippa area.

BENNY: We tried to come up with stuff, and it just wasn't making it. So Joe Rock started writing some lyrics. And we met two songwriters from Aliquippa, Mervin and Melvin Steals. They said, "Hey, there's this company in Philadelphia, Gamble Records. We're doing some stuff with them. We'll write a song for you guys."

JIMMIE: Joe and another guy — John Pergel, he was a friend of the original Skyliners guitarist; he wanted to manage us — set us up with Gamble. Kenny Gamble and Leon Huff flew in from Philadelphia to see us in Ellwood City. They were one of the biggest songwriter-producer teams at the time.

We used to hold our own dances. If we didn't go to a college on a Sunday, we would hold dances at a place called the Ellwood City Athletic Club. We would get a thousand kids, a younger crowd. It was all the kids who couldn't get into the Club Naturale — you had to be 21. It was kids right out of high school.

There were so many people in the place, I don't remember anybody dancing. It was more like a concert. We played that Ellwood Athletic Club probably once a month. That was our normal crowd on Sundays. They flew back to Philly. And in a month or two, we found ourselves in Philadelphia, recording.

GAMBLE RECORDS: *INTRODUCING THE JAGGERZ*, PART 1

When critics thoroughly look back at the Jaggerz, they remember the band fondly. AllMusic's Andrew Hamilton reviewed the band's full-length debut, *Introducing the Jaggerz*:

"The Jaggerz from Pittsburgh are rarely noted as a top-notched blue-eyed soul group because most are only aware of their one big hit 'The Rapper,' which isn't soul music…. Steeped in R&B, the Jaggerz are absolutely thrilling rehashing the Intruders' 'Together,' the Temptations' 'Ain't No Sun (Since You Been Gone),' Jackie Wilson's 'Higher and Higher,' and the Diplomats' 'Here's a Heart.' They also shine on originals ' (That's Why) Baby I Love You, ' 'Bring It Back,' and Philly sounds like 'Gotta Find My Way Back Home.'"[10.3]

DONNIE: We went to Philadelphia. We stayed there and did the record.

BENNY: We thought with what we had, our voices, we were gonna have hit records, one after another, with Gamble. Gamble and Huff were hot. They had a lot of good records. And some other band was out the same time we were, which was a white band, like we were. They were having successful R&B songs. They thought we might be able to do the same thing, because that's what we grew up on.

JIMMIE: We flew out. We stayed in a hotel. We were one of the bands that were very fortunate. We never had to live in a van and travel all over the place. We were makin' *money*. We were never a starving act that had to play dumps. We played the best places. We made the most money.

We recorded with Gamble & Huff at Sigma Sound Studios. The sessions were great.

The Intruders ["Cowboys to Girls"] were one of the biggest R&B bands out at the time. They were on Gamble. They were Gamble and Huff's protégés. They were in the studio, behind the glass, when we were doing a couple of their songs. They didn't like it.

They made the comment to Kenny Gamble, "Hey, man, they sound just like us!"

Which wasn't cool to them, but to me, that was a compliment. They were one of my favorite groups.

We were in studio B, recording. This other group was in studio B — they were the other white band with Gamble [the Soul Survivors], the ones who did "Expressway to Your Heart." The fire alarm went off. Somebody went into the bathroom and threw a cigarette into a trash can and started a fire. [The Soul Survivors] tried to say that we were trying to sabotage their session. They were pissed off.

DONNIE: Sometimes we played with our rhythm section, sometimes with Gamble and Huff's rhythm section. We were just droppin' our jaws. These cats, their rhythm section, the way they went about things — just natural-gifted. They laid it all down like it was just getting up in the morning.

JIMMIE: The Jaggerz at our best, I would say — and not just because I sang it — was "Gotta Find My Way Back Home." That's the one the Steals Brothers wrote. Fifty years later, I get emails from people saying that represented the Jaggerz.

BENNY: We had one really good song, "Gotta Find My Way Back Home." We played that with Gamble & Huff's rhythm section. Leon Huff played piano. That's a good song. It's *cool*.

DONNIE: I think they got a lot out of us, more than we thought we could do. Jimmy found a nice little thing with those guys. He sang lead, we sang background vocals. He killed it. He was always the lead singer, but I think they brought the best out in him on that song. They didn't stop us and tell us to step it up too much. We just got our parts together and went out and did it.

The album — eventually — was called *Introducing the Jaggerz*.

JIMMIE: That was recorded live. It wasn't recorded like albums are today. We were playing at the same time.

They played at the same time — when they played.

BENNY: They liked the quality of our voices, and they did what they could do for us. We could play with them. But they were so much in a hurry on some of the stuff we had. They'd change some arrangements. And they had a Philadelphia band of guys that they used to move things on quickly and get the releases out.

DONNIE: I did some leads on that album. As far as I was concerned, going into those sessions, I thought the most important thing was the *feel* those guys laid down. The songs had a certain groove that was infectious. We tried, as the Jaggerz — we did some pretty good grooving. But those guys were up there. That's what they *did*.

Gamble and Huff's house band was a famous trio: bassist Ronnie Baker, guitarist Bobby Eli, and drummer Earl Young, the percussion innovator credited with pioneering the cymbal-centric disco style, who played with the Trammps of "Disco Inferno" fame. When studio time was running short, the Jaggerz watched the pros work, and they took notes.

DONNIE: The drummer was the one who impressed me the most. He just started grooving, sat back there and killed it. I don't think he was a schooled drummer; it just came from this guy. He played his ass off. I learned that if the groove or the feel isn't there, even if you have a great lyric or great melody, if it doesn't have a certain feel to it, it's more difficult for people to like. People want to move and groove to a record. That's what I learned the most from them.

I don't remember them doing a bunch of takes or starting and stopping. They'd do one or two takes, run through a song a couple times.

BENNY: Then, in turn, we did the vocals. And when we came out and we went to perform live, we would play. People didn't know it was studio musicians on a few songs. We played on "Baby I Love You," but they added a few things.

They said, "We want you to play everything you got, so we can write for you and see what you do best." And we recorded everything we had.

In Philadelphia, the Jaggerz recorded enough prime cuts for two singles. And, with some covers in the mix, they laid down enough for an entire record. (At the time, the music business was more driven by singles than albums. And recording cover songs was a standard practice.) They headed back to the other side of the Keystone State, ready for fame and fortune.

JIMMIE: That was great. We knew how good we were, and we thought it was just a matter of time until something like that happened. I thought, "This is just the line of things that happen. You start in a little wedding band, you work your way up, you start to record."

Then I find out that's almost unheard of. That doesn't happen. We were very lucky.

DONNIE IRIS: FAMILY MAN

1968 was the band's big break. And it was a pivotal year for Donnie, too. His label relationship wouldn't last long, but he made another relationship permanent.

DONNIE: I was married through the whole ride. We were married in '68, I believe.

I met my wife at a club in the mid '60s. I was playing. She's from here, Beaver Falls. I never knew her. She went to Beaver Falls High School. I went to Ellwood City High School, totally different neighborhood, different towns. She's five or six years younger. I didn't know any of her friends. I didn't know anybody from anywhere other than Ellwood, until the Jaggerz started playing shows.

I think we kind of liked each other right off the bat. We dated a couple years before we got married. She's part German, part Irish. Us dagoes were a scourge to her dad. He hated Italian guys. And both of his daughters married Italian guys. And he was great guy, once we met him and got to know him. He was tremendous. And he loved us, too. He knew he was wrong. Or we had heard, "He don't like Italians." He wasn't that way when he was around us. I remember working with him. He was an electrician. I used to help him wire houses. I just picked up from what he taught me.

The future looked bright. Donnie figured he had enough of a career that he could put down some roots.

DONNIE: I thought that that was my gig. That was what I did, like someone else going to work at the bank. But ours was more exciting. As it related to the family, the hardest part was being away. But generally speaking, the Jaggerz was pretty much a Pittsburgh band, a local band, until "The Rapper" came along. We'd been playing nightclubs for years, but we didn't tour much. We did do some long jumps on planes, to do TV shows, things like that. But we didn't go on any extended tours like we did with the Cruisers.

SUPPER CLUB CIRCUIT

In July 1968, Gamble released the first Jaggerz single, "(That's Why) Baby I Love You." Pittsburgh's KQV, AM 1410 gave it some airplay. But it didn't register on national charts or garner any significant national press.

The Jaggerz were booking bigger and better gigs. By August 1968, the band was appearing weekly in nightclub ads in both Pittsburgh newspapers. By the fall, not a week went by without a publicized Jaggerz show, at venues like Mancini's in McKees Rocks, a historical steel city on the Ohio River, just outside of Pittsburgh proper. By the end of 1968, the Jaggerz were headlining relatively high-profile Pittsburgh gigs. One good show was a 21-34 singles' dance at the Hotel Webster Hall in Oakland, topping a bill with the Wellingtons. The beguiling ad read, "THE FUN-SEEKERS CLUB presents the Fantastic 'JAGGERZ' IN A BIG SHOW."[10.4]

As 1969 got underway, the Jaggerz were playing a regular circuit of supper clubs in and around Pittsburgh, with regular appearances at Mancini's. Every Monday and Thursday, they returned to the Staircase downtown.

BENNY: We were playing nice places. The Staircase was downstairs, on Liberty Avenue. You went down a flight of stairs, and then another flight, and then it dropped even lower. Mancini's was a big place. It held a lot of people. There were booths, some tables, dance areas. A dance area up front. People danced, people ate.

In January, they picked up steady Fridays at the Fountain Supper Club in Brentwood, on Route 51 in Pittsburgh's South Hills. The club advertised itself as a venue "for the young at heart, Pittsburgh's Greatest Soul Bands... shows & dancing Saturday night." Through the week, it hosted smaller acts like the Bell Boys, Gary Glenn Family, and the Fidels.[10.5] In that era, before live entertainment and dining was dominated by corporate interests, venues big and small often had ties to a different kind of syndicate.

JIMMIE: Back then, a lot of places were run by some… interesting people.

BENNY: I don't want to say where, but we played some gangster joints. We'd go downstairs to change, and one day they had a whole billfold of diamonds. They laid them out on the pool table and said, "Hey, do you guys want some? You want *this*? You want *that*?" They had all kinds of stuff. You'd go to some of these places, they'd have suits on racks, what must've been a whole truck full of them. "Go ahead, take some!"

DEVELOPING A REALLY BIG SHOW

In March 1969, Gamble released the highlight from the sessions, "Gotta Find My Way Back Home," as a single. Stores sold a version with "Forever Together, Together Forever" as a B-side. Radio stations received a 45 with the A-side on both sides, which eliminated any chance different stations could dilute their chart numbers by playing different tracks.

As it turned out, the concern was warranted: It outperformed the band's inaugural single, hitting on Cleveland's WIXY 1260 and Houston's KNUZ 1230. In Pittsburgh, it cracked KQV's top five, and *Record World* called it a hometown "smash."[10.6] The Pittsburgh *Press* later reported that "Gotta Find My Way Back Home" sold 100,000 copies, and earned each Steals brother around $2,000.[10.7]

The song was big enough to get the Jaggerz on the road and bump them into the big leagues.

Over spring 1969, the Jaggerz were building up steam. In addition to regular club shows, the band was playing showcases like an April 1 gig, a "So You Wanna Be a Star" day for teenagers at the downtown Kaufmann's department store. Playing the 11th floor auditorium, the Jaggerz headlined over Bimbo's Banjo Band.[10.8]

Days later, they made their first appearance at a varsity-level venue: Pittsburgh's Civic Arena, as bottom-of-the-bill support for the KQV Shower of the Stars, which starred Tommy James & the Shondells, with Tommy Roe, The Classic IV, the 1910 Fruitgum Company, the Peppermint Rainbow, the Velvet Crest, and the New Colony Six. (Tickets ran $3-$5.) Later that month, they got a taste of national touring; Gamble himself flew to Milwaukee to see the band showcase at The Attic, a classy club that hosted early rock greats like Chuck Berry and Neil Sedaka.[10.9]

The Jaggerz were earning bigger gigs, and they needed a bigger show. The band still regularly played Villa's Lounge in Aliquippa. Their local fans included an old friend of Jimmie Ross, a colorful car salesman named Bobby Meute (pronounced "mute"). Meute told the band about a friend from Detroit: Don Kelley, an ambitious and funny singer, bandleader, and choreographer. Kelley's act, the Swingin' Lads, billed themselves as a "Midwest showband." Their shows combined comedy and music. Their career highlights included appearances on the Ed Sullivan and Dean Martin shows.

Kelley sounded like the kind of help the Jaggerz needed. A few phone calls later, Faiella and Meute flew to Detroit, met Kelley, and found him agreeable. Rock cut a deal: Kelley would choreograph a full show for the band, in exchange for a royalty from every concert in which they performed it.

Between gigs, the Jaggerz flew to Detroit for two weeks, from late April through early May. The first practice left the band winded and sweaty. The Beaver boys were used to elementary footwork. Performing a full-blown, precise dance routine — as they sang — was an entirely different game. The band did their best; Kelley was not impressed.

BENNY: Don said, "You guys are *not* in shape for the kind of show I want to do." So he left. And for the next week, he had a guy working us out, doing calisthenics. The first week, all we did was get in shape and get stamina, run around the gym. We were getting pretty pissed off at first, but he was right.

The next week, Kelley's band was playing shows at the Moon Supper Club, a dim-lit night spot with a warren of rooms. As Kelley's show was winding down, the Jaggerz warmed up in the basement, bracing for long nights.

BENNY: 1:00, 1:30 in the morning, after Don was done with his set, we'd go down in the Moon Supper Club basement. We're rehearse all night. It was daylight when we were done.

Kelley and the Jaggerz would work together again.

With reinforced cardio stamina and professional moves, the group flew home and debuted their new showband routine at Indiana University of Pennsylvania, a state college 90 minutes east of Pittsburgh, tucked in the backwater midway between the Steel City and Altoona. The routine was a hit. They worked it out over the next month, squeezing proms and post-proms into their schedule of regular club appearances.

BENNY: We had a show that was an hour and fifteen minutes. Don Kelley literally choreographed every move that we did, every song while we were onstage. We became friends after that.

Don Kelley, he was playing Las Vegas. He put a *show* together. From the start to the end, there were steps — we had two spotlights that would move around. The lights would come to the middle of the stage, like a curtain coming down. Then we'd be into another tune. It was something to see. It was good enough that they wanted it in Vegas. I can't believe Joe Rock never filmed that. If there's video of that, I'd love to see it.

DONNIE: We had something like a Las Vegas act that we did, swinging microphones at each other.

By July 1969, bigger shows were the norm. The Jaggerz were picking up bigger shows, like an opening slot for José Feliciano in Canton (reserved tix $4 and $5).

Kelley's choreography was a top-flight professional production. But it was not state-of-the art. In summer 1969, silky harmonies were fading from the hit parade. Faiella and Koodrich made the pilgrimage to a big concert that was hosting some of pop music's biggest acts. Collectively, they represented not only a new breed, but a new age.

BENNY: I actually was ten miles away from Woodstock. We had tickets. I knew Sly and the Family Stone was going to be there, and Crosby, Stills and Nash — groups we wanted to see. But I didn't want to walk ten miles to get there.

Then they said the gates were down. And the weather was getting bad. It was all hippies, and we were more straight characters. These kids were more walking around with holes in their pants and fringe. Everybody was smokin' grass, and you could smell it for miles. We wanted to go for the entertainment. It was something to see all these people, all these kids.

DONNIE: I didn't know about that. He didn't invite me.

The Woodstock road trip was possible because of a medically necessary hiatus. The heartily harmonizing band had been hurting — especially Faiella.

BENNY: We were having trouble with our voices. We went to the Cleveland Clinic. Joe set something up with a doctor. I was doing all the highs. And the doctor said my vocal chords were ripped. He said, "You have a condition that sergeants and coaches have, guys that are always screaming. You've got to take off a month. And I want you guys to whisper. I went to the mountains by myself so I wouldn't talk to anybody.

The band was in flux. In 1969, their sets were beyond eclectic, flowing from hip harmonies in the Beatles' "Because," all the way over to a most unlikely show tune.

JIMMIE: Jim Pugliano, our drummer, sang lead on "Old Man River," but most of the song was all harmony sung by all of us. *That* was a show stopper for us.

With such a deep lineup, the Jaggerz didn't have one star. All the members earned time in the spotlight, and they all had their fans.

BENNY: Some people liked Donnie. Some liked Jimmy. Billy had that soulful voice; he sounded black. Donnie did stick out. He had that falsetto.

Donnie did get the last word when it was his turn to introduce the band and deliver the signoff from the first set: "We're gonna take about *20* minutes, ladies and gentlemen, and *we'll be right back*. So *please* don't go anywhere. We're here every Wednesday night, every Wednesday night, right here at *Mancini's*."

Especially after Woodstock, hip young rock crowds were not enthusiastic about the Jaggerz' classic vocal pop sound.

And, at this point, neither was the Jaggerz' label. Their modest regional success had not been enough to make the band a priority at Gamble. The band was ready to release a full album, or at least another single. Gamble disagreed. Both parties continued disagreeing.

BIG BREAK

The Jaggerz were turning some heads, though. In fall 1969, their road-tested routine won them a two-week run at the Pittsburgh area's most prestigious club, the upscale Holiday House in Monroeville, a booming suburb with a bustling strip — and the venue at the heart of it. The 900-capacity hotel-entertainment complex opened in 1955 and closed in 1988. In the days before "big show" meant "arena concert," it served as a pillar of Pittsburgh's entertainment scene, hosting acts like Frank Sinatra, the Four Seasons and Liberace.[10.10]

Initially constructed as a supper club with 18 motel rooms, the Holiday House quickly grew, taking over a neighboring motel and other properties. Soon, its lounges, restaurants, swimming club, and 200 motel rooms sprawled over 11 acres near the intersection of Northern Pike, Monroeville Boulevard and the William Penn Highway.[10.11]

BENNY: Any name act that came to Pittsburgh, that was the club they would go to. This was a scaled-down version of that Las Vegas-style room.

JIMMIE: That's when people used to dress up and take their wife or girlfriend out, to a nice place, for a great dinner and a great show. Just like we lived in the Beaver Valley area, and there used to be a place called Ciro's Top of the Mall at the Beaver Valley Mall. You walked in there, and you thought you were in a Vegas show room. There were a lot of places like that. The crowds were great. People wore suits, jackets.

The Holiday House was a good place to play. Top-notch. They brought in national acts, and they'd play there, all week, for a week, sometimes for two. And we got booked there for two weeks. It was sold out every night of the week.

The Jaggerz' two-week stand was a breakthrough. It created two big opportunities: One they didn't take. One they rode into the record books.

BENNY: After the Holiday House, we had the opportunity to go to Vegas and open for the Osmonds. And Donnie said, "I don't want to wear suits." He didn't want to do it anymore.

Donnie was making a lot of changes with what he wanted to do. He was feeling all this music out. Music was changing, with all these groups.

If he said, "Oh, that's great," Joe could have set it all up. And what would have happened with the Jaggerz if we got that exposure?

NEW LABEL: KAMA SUTRA/BUDDHA

The Jaggerz' short-lived partnership with Gamble had stalled, and Donnie and the group were in the market for a new label.

JIMMIE: We realized Gamble were not really doing much for us. Joe Rock got in touch with Neil Bogart. He got Neil to come see us at the Holiday House.

Neil Bogart was the co-president of Kama Sutra Records. Bogart would later found the era-defining Casablanca Records, sign Kiss to it, and manage a roster of '70 titans including Donna Summer and the Village People. Bogart had good taste.

JIMMIE: When Neil Bogart saw us, he told Joe Rock, "I'll give them whatever they want. I want to record them." A couple months later, we were up in New York, doing the second album, with "The Rapper" on it.

Kama Sutra Records was founded in 1965, and made a mark with "Do You Believe in Magic," the debut single from pioneering longhairs John Sebastian and the Lovin' Spoonful. Over the '60s, it picked up momentum and released rock, pop, and psychedelic acts like the Trade Winds, the Innocence, and Sopwith Camel.[10.12]

Kama Sutra was intertwined with the Buddha label. The two shared personnel and infrastructure. Pittsburgh was also the headquarters for Jack Hakim, mid-west operations director for Buddha.[10.13]

Combined, the labels were a volcano of memorable singles. They released records by the 1910 Fruit Gum Company ("Indian Giver"), the Ohio Express ("Yummy Yummy"), Captain Beefheart, Gladys Knight & the Pips, and Sha Na Na. Bogart, who also served as Buddha's vice president and general manager, was a longtime booster of the '50s throwback band. And the smooth vocal stylings of the Jaggerz were squarely in his wheelhouse.

BENNY: Kama Sutra came to Pittsburgh and saw us and wanted to sign us, even before we had written "The Rapper." Joe wanted to make an outright deal with Buddha, to go, "We want 10%, and 50% as far as publishing goes." He wanted to go in and negotiate with a finished product, and all they have to do is get behind it and promote it.

Kama Sutra wanted the band, but the Jaggerz were still technically obligated the Gamble Records. In November, Rock filed a lawsuit against Gamble Records to clear up any lingering claims.[10.14]

BENNY: I don't know about that. Joe must have filed suit. Even Donnie, we were more into the recording than what was coming out and who was in charge and the decisions.

Joe signed the agreement. We didn't even see the papers — I'm not saying it to put Joe down; I'm not sure what happened. We always wondered why we never got any [money] for "Gotta Find My Way Back Home" — we had charting records, for chrissakes. Maybe it did come in. Joe had a treasurer at the time.

Luckily, the lawsuit lasted about as long as their chart runs. The parties quickly settled: Gamble kept the rights to the recordings the Jaggerz made. And the label released the band from their contract.

BENNY: We never got paid anything from Gamble. The band didn't. The label owned the rights to that for five years after we were done with them.

It didn't feel like a defeat when we left Gamble. We were disgusted with them. We thought we could have made it. We thought they didn't do enough for us.

Gamble and Huff did fine without the Jaggerz; the two were inducted to the Rock and Roll Hall of Fame, in the Non-Performer category, in 2008. (Gamble didn't respond to invitations to talk about the Jaggerz.)

JIMMIE: I don't remember suing them at all. Joe Rock was our manager. He took care of all of the business stuff. All I know is: We were done with Gamble, and we went straight to Kama Sutra.

"THE RAPPER"

The Jaggerz were ready to move on. And they had a promising partner and product ready to go. Another heavy hitter from the record business was happy to sign the band.

Bogart came to Pittsburgh sniffing around for a group that could sing in a throwback style. And he found them. But the Jaggerz' first effort for his label featured some very contemporary social commentary. As the band's frustration with Gamble had been approaching critical mass, the band kept playing clubs. And one night, Donnie had found an idea for new song — something in a different style.

BENNY: Donnie wrote "The Rapper."

DONNIE: I was just watching guys do their thing at the clubs, going up and rappin' to chicks to get 'em up to their apartments. It was such an obvious thing to write about. The idea hit me in my sleep, and I woke up and started writing.

I brought it in to the band.

We brought stuff together in a group. We were going to go record something. Everybody was receptive to everything, and we worked hard at all the things that everybody brought in.

I wrote the riff, too. At the time, I was kind of Stones fan. And I liked the simple kind of riffs that Richards did. That's probably where I got some of the inspiration for some of the stuff on that tune.

And then the strumming guitar was probably a Creedence Clearwater kind of thing.

BENNY: We weren't even trying to write an album yet. We had the office in New Brighton. We used to meet there and go over stuff.

One day, Donnie came in and he said, "Euge, I've got a song."

I said, "Let me hear it."

He started to strum on a guitar, and played the whole thing.

And I said, "I betcha this song's called 'The Rapper.' What it called?"

And he said, "The Rapper."

When I first heard it, I thought it was a bubblegum tune that was going to appeal to a whole different audience, real young kids, and it's going to take us out of R&B. And that's the reason we went to Gamble and Huff: We were blue-eyed soul.

JIMMIE: I don't think there was an ending for the song. I kind of put the touch on the ending, the very end, the last couple chord changes and things like that, starting with the bass part. We all chipped in and did our own thing on a lot of the tunes.

The band knew they had something good on their hands. To get the song on tape, they traveled East again, past Philadelphia, to New York City's Century Sound, which had hosted sessions for the Grateful Dead, Van Morrison and Neil Diamond.

JIMMIE: We were in New York City, around Times Square somewhere. After the session, I would walk through Times Square and try not to get killed. That was in the '60s. Times Square was a mean, bad place. Since then, it's been all cleaned up.

Everybody was a hippie back then. There were head shops on every corner. Strip joints. It was a place that you had to look over your shoulder at night.

BENNY: We paid for the engineering, all the stuff on that one.

Once "The Rapper" was in the can, the Jaggerz got a crucial go-ahead vote from Marty Thau, a music biz lifer who had promoted "Yummy, Yummy, Yummy." Later, he was eyeball-deep in the classic New York punk scene, working with the Ramones, New York Dolls and Blondie. Thau knew a hit when he heard one.

BENNY: Marty Thau from Buddha records — he was the Midwestern promoter. He owed Joe big favors.

He said, "Let me hear what you've got."

We played it.

He said, "I could do good for you there. I could get stations *in*."

The commonly recycled — and incorrect — history of the Jaggerz says the band released an album on Gamble Records, *Introducing the Jaggerz*. Then the album flopped. So Gamble dropped them. Then they signed to Kama Sutra. At their new label, the Jaggerz rebounded with a smash single, "The Rapper," from the band's second album, *We Went to Different Schools Together*. That's a narrative you might reasonably assemble if you look at the band's nebulous release dates. But that's not how it happened.

Once the Jaggerz were free from Gamble, Kama Sutra signed the group and released "The Rapper" as a single — first in Pittsburgh, then in nearby markets, and soon on stations everywhere. *Then* the Jaggerz were finally headed for the charts.

Kama Sutra released "The Rapper" b/w "Born Poor" in late November 1969. The A-side was credited to Dominic Ierace, the B-side to Joe Rock and Johnny Jack, who wrote the Skyliners' 1962 single "Comes Love."

BENNY: "The Rapper" was recorded as a single. And it took off. It was selling 30,000 a day here. And the radio stations were picking up on it.

DONNIE: I'll never forget hearing myself on the radio for the first time. I was driving through Freedom, Pennsylvania. I forget which car I had. It might have been my Pontiac or my Buick. I was so into radio stations at the time. It was probably WLS. [The taste making Chicago radio station's nighttime signal reached 38 states.]

I used to listen to radio as a kid. I'd listen to WLS out of Chicago, clear as a bell, in Ellwood City. I could get WABC in New York. All these powerful AM stations. And I heard "The Rapper" on those stations that I grew up listening to.

It felt like, "I *made* it. I *made* it!"

Once I was on those stations, I really felt awesome.

BENNY: The thing that helped us with "The Rapper," too: In Pittsburgh, there was KQV, that was a big station. WLS In Chicago. KXOK in St. Louis was big. WLS in Chicago, the program director knew the program director from KQV in Pittsburgh — Chuck Brinkman and Jim McCormick both did a lot for us. McCormick said, "You guys get a record, we could help you."

We did a lot of favors for them. We did a lot of things we didn't get paid for, but it was promoting the group. And it paid off. He called the program director as soon as "The Rapper" started to hit. He got us WLS in Chicago and KXOK in St. Louis. You get on a major station, and it really starts happening.

Once we had that record, he called Chicago on it, CBS or NBC in New York, and St. Louis. Once we had three major stations playing it, the secondaries picked up, and everything took off.

JIMMIE: I remember hearing us on the radio. We were in the car somewhere. One of the guys was with me, maybe Billy Maybray. We just turned the radio up. It sounded so good.

The band's lineup was rapidly shuffling: Pugliano spent some time out of the band, and the multi talented Maybray drums on "The Rapper."

As the '60s ended, the Jaggerz were playing more big gigs, and steadily moving up the bill. They were second-from-last on a six-band card at Pittsburgh's Civic Arena: the Thanksgiving Shower of Stars, featuring JR. Walker and the All Stars, the Jaggerz, Guess Who, Steam, the Dells, and headliners Gary Puckett & the Union Gap.[10.15] And then they became headliners.

INTRODUCING THE JAGGERZ, NOT FEATURING "THE RAPPER"

The hot "Rapper" single led to the quick release of the Jaggerz' full-length debut... which did not include the song.

In December 1969, *Introducing the Jaggerz* suddenly appeared from Gamble Records. The release surprised the band, because they had barely begun writing an album worth of songs to surround "The Rapper."

The album confused the record-buying public, who were excited by "The Rapper" — then bought the album, only to find out it featured last year's singles and some soul covers. Someone, as it turned out, *did* have an album full of Jaggerz material.

JIMMIE: When Gamble saw the success of "The Rapper," they put out an album.

BENNY: When we left Gamble, we were done with them. They didn't own anything we did after that. But they owned the recordings we made for them. When we left, we went to Buddha, and "The Rapper" took off. Gamble went right into the studio, mixed down these old recordings we ran through once, put together an album, and stuck it on the market before we could get the album out with Buddha.

THE JAGGERZ, *INTRODUCING THE JAGGERZ.*
Gamble Record, December 1968

"Gotta Find My Way Back Home"
 (Lyrics by Melvin and Mervin Steals)
"(That's Why) Baby I Love You"
 (Joe Rock and the Jaggerz)
"Give a Little Love"
"What Now My Love"
"Higher and Higher" (Jackie Wilson)
"Forever Together - Together Forever"
 (Melvin and Mervin Steals)

"Let Me Be Your Man" (Gamble, Huff, Spain)
"Bring It Back" (Joe Rock and the Jaggerz)
"Here's a Heart" (The Diplomats, lyrics
 by D. Wayne and F. Stryker)
"Ain't No Sun"
"Need Your Love" (Bobby Freeman)
"Together" (The Intruders song, lyrics
 by Gamble and Huff)

Gamble had the *Introducing the Jaggerz* album in stores in time for the holidays, as "The Rapper" was breaking out of Pittsburgh and getting national traction. Their old label used some generic, vaguely psychedelic album art for the cover, wherein a giant fish sails through the air, between what might be a red sun and several interdimensional portals. The members of the group do not appear anywhere on the album, inside or out. Different Jaggerz suspect Gamble Records didn't think promoting white singers was a marketable proposition.

Back in the Burgh, the Jaggerz were working on a new full-length as fast as they could.

BENNY: Doing that writing, getting that album out, took awhile. We weren't ready with a new album, and they had an album out already. It was that soulful part of the Jaggerz, but it didn't have "The Rapper" on it. It wasn't bad, but it wasn't finished tracks. People were confused. It didn't have any pictures of us. People said, "Is that the same group?" It was too different.

Gamble had a vested interest in the album, but was content with small rewards. Without the current single or active promotion, *Introducing the Jaggerz* didn't crack the *Billboard* album chart. Still, the success of "The Rapper" made the Jaggerz' recordings something of a commodity — if not priority — for Gamble. The label began releasing singles timed around singles from the band's new label. The Jaggerz' ex-label released 45s over the next year and a half, longer than the band was signed to Gamble. Witness the release schedule for the next 17 months:

November 1969: Kama Sutra releases "The Rapper," b/w "Born Poor"
December 1969: Gamble releases the *Introducing the Jaggerz* album and the single "Let Me Be Your Man," b/w "Together"
April 1970: Kama Sutra releases "I Call My Baby Candy," b/w "Will She Believe Me?"
July 1970: Kama Sutra releases "What a Bummer," b/w "Memoirs of the Traveler"
December 1970: Gamble releases "Higher and Higher," b/w "Ain't No Sun (Since You've Been Gone)"
February 1971: Kama Sutra releases "I'll Never Forget You," b/w "Let's Talk About Love"
April 1971: Gamble releases "Here's a Heart," b/w "Need Your Love"

JIMMIE: The Gamble singles, they weren't really singles — they weren't pushing them at all. They were riding the coattails of Kama Sutra. "Here's a Heart," I probably have the only copy of that. It didn't get any airplay at all.

WE WENT TO DIFFERENT SCHOOLS TOGETHER

"The Rapper" was a single worth exploiting, though.

As 1969 drew to a close, it reached number 1 on KQV in Pittsburgh. The rest of the country caught on. Then it broke big and fast. By January 27, it was in the top 20 as far away as San Bernardino on the West Coast.[10.16]

While the hot single was burning up the charts, and the pressure was on to make a full album. The whole band felt it, especially Donnie, who was having a productive year with another partner.

DONNIE: We bought a house in Patterson Township in '67 or '68. It was a real nice, middle-class house. My wife is still in it.

We didn't actually sit down and plan kids. That's not how it worked. If you had babies, you had babies. If you didn't, you didn't.

Erin was born in November 1969. That was right about during "The Rapper." We wrote it in '69, and it became a hit in '70. That was a great year. It was special. She was unbelievably cute when she was born.

It was unbelievable, like, "I've got a *kid*, man!" And next thing I know, I've got a hit record. Things were just humming along.

BENNY: It didn't change him. We all were the same.

Now the band needed to write and record an album. In January and February 1970, the Jaggerz took two rare two-week breaks from live shows to concentrate on their first real album.

BENNY: We didn't have anything written yet in that vein of music where "The Rapper" took us. After "The Rapper" came up, Buddha was pressuring us. They said, "We need an album!" We weren't ready. We took off about a few weeks.

I stayed with Donnie for about a week and co-wrote some tunes. We were all really cramming, coming up with songs and original music. We saw the potential of what it could be if we had our own material.

Joe started writing more things for us, seeing what we could up with.

Donnie and I spent a week together. I wrote two songs with Donnie and Joe, "Memoirs of a Traveler" and "Looking Glass." We would have written more, but there was pressure.

There were other songs: Thom Davies, the keyboard player in the band, wrote "Carousel" [with Rock and Pugliano]. We titled that album *We Went to Different Schools Together*.

JIMMIE: Joe Rock gave it that title.

To bump the track list up to an even ten, the band used a time-tested strategy: they added a late-breaking cover song — in fact, a cover of a cover. Donnie was a Beatles fan, and he liked Joe Cocker's soulful arrangement of "With a Little Help From My Friends" so much, the band learned the song. It became a staple in their repertoire. The album version is not only a faithful recreation of Cocker's arrangement, but has a sonic polish lacking in both Cocker's studio version and his famous Woodstock performance. The tune is still in the Cruisers' set.

DONNIE: I knew it after *Woodstock* [the movie]. The Joe Cocker arrangement suited us a lot better, because of the background vocals. The Jaggerz could *kill* those background vocals. We looked specifically for songs that had those harmonies.

And the Jaggerz' second album, *We Went to Different Schools Together*, was ready to go:

"I Call My Baby Candy" (Lyrics by Ierace)

"Memoirs of the Traveler" (Rock, Ierace, Faiella)

"With a Little Help From My Friends" (Lennon, McCartney)

"Looking Glass" (Rock, Ierace, Faiella)

"The Rapper" (Ierace)

"At My Window" (Rock, Ierace)

"Things Gotta Get Better" (Rock, Davies, Maybray)

"Carousel" (Rock, Davies, Pugliano)

"Don't Make My Sky Cry" (Rock, Davies, Maybray)

"That's My World" (Rock, Davies)

We Went to Different Schools Together has never been released on CD for the US market. In 2009, Kama Sutra released a CD for the Canadian market, with 7 additional tracks that are now available as the digital edition. Six of them were later singles and B-sides:

"Born Poor" ("The Rapper" B-side, credited writers Joe Rock, Johnny Jack)

"Will She Believe Me" ("I Call My Baby Candy" B-side, credited writers Rock, Davies, Ierace, Ross, Maybray, Faiella, Pugliano)

"What a Bummer" (A-side of a July 1970 single with B-side "Memoirs of the Traveler," credited writer Ierace)

"Let's Talk About Love" (Ierace) and "I'll Never Forget You" (the B- and A-sides, respectively, of February 1971's single; a cover by Detroit soul group the Metros, credited writers Terry, Ashford, Lewis)

"Ain't That Sad" (the A-side of the September 1973 single, whose B-side recycled "Let's Talk About Love"; credited writers Rock and Ross)

"Wise Up! Why Dope?" (Rock and Ierace)

"Wise Up! Why Dope?" is awkward public service announcement. The 1971 anti-drug song was released as a single on Kama Sutra, in conjunction with the Pennsylvania civic organization the Jaycees — the United States Junior Chamber of Commerce, a civic leadership organization — which had a community education program of the same name.[10.17] The lead vocals were by future Silencers frontman Frank Czuri, who would replace Thom Davies after the album was out. The song starts just like "The Rapper," with a jangle riff and the lyric, "Hey..."

BENNY: Frank Czuri replaced Davies because Thom Davies played keyboard but did not sing. Frank played keys and also sang. He had been with the Igniters. He was good-looking, a great piano player. He had a terrific lead voice. He knew all the songs.

DONNIE: We had no idea. A couple of the guys in the band probably knew a little bit about drugs, but I don't think Joe did.

"Wise Up" and several other post-"Rapper" songs leaned heavily on the "Rapper" formula: jangle-and-strum riff. Singsong lyrics. Bouncy beat. None of them worked as well as the original.

March 7, 1970, "The Rapper" cracked the *Billboard* top ten. It would enjoy a six-week run in the coveted upper reaches of the singles chart.

"The Rapper" went gold on March 27, 1970, when the Recording Industry Association of American certified 500,000 copies moved.

March 20 1970, the band were flying to Los Angeles to play Dick Clark's *American Bandstand* when they got the news: Tomorrow, "The Rapper" would officially become the number 1 single in the country, as ranked by radio trade journal *Record World*.[10.18] When it hit number 1, the new top single displaced Simon & Garfunkel's "Bridge Over Troubled Water," which sank to number 3, beneath Brook Benton's "Rainy Night in Georgia." Other top-ten singles included the Tee Set's "Ma Belle Amie," John Ono Lennon's "Instant Karma (We All Shine on)," the Delfonics' "Didn't I Blow Your Mind This Time," and Santana's "Evil Ways."[10.19]

But over on the more prestigious, industry-leading *Billboard* chart, Simon & Garfunkel prevailed, holding off the boys from Beaver. Their *Billboard* run peaked at number 2, above Chairmen of the Board's "Give Me Just a Little More Time" and Lennon's "Instant Karma." The next week, its *Billboard* ranking sank to number four, below a rebounding Simon & Garfunkel, the Beatles' "Let It Be," and Lennon.

"The Rapper" still had new heights to reach. For three months now, the single had been inching toward the band's collective dream: a gold record, which represents half a million copies shipped — as opposed to actually *sold*, strictly speaking; read more about the vague math of the record business in later chapters.[10.20]

DONNIE: At my dad's bar, Lou's Tavern, he took a 45 of "The Rapper" and sprayed it with gold paint, because we wanted it to go gold. And he put it up behind the bar and drew a thermometer beside it. And he'd keep filling it in: 100,000 copies. 200,000 copies.

BENNY: When it hit 100,000, it felt great. Down at our office, we had a map of the United States. And every city, we'd pin the call letters to a flag on the map and how many copies the record was selling. St. Louis, California… all these stations were getting on it. We were getting great reviews.

When it hit 200,000 — my God.

When this record topped a million and hit number 1 over Simon & Garfunkel's "Bridge Over Troubled Water," and the Beatles' "Let It Be" and Santana — it was breathtaking, to be from Beaver County, up in Sharonville, and now you're there with artists that are established and on the charts.

I can't remember if we did have a party or not. But when the certifications came and a copy of *Record World* came — I still have that upstairs — I felt so fortunate to be part of this band. Playing on the college campuses and bars, you always wish that could be you, you know? That was my dream.

The week the single hit number 1, it went gold. March 27, 1970, the Recording Industry Association of American certified 500,000 copies moved. Donnie's dad filled in the thermometer to the top. It was a good day at Lou's Tavern.

DONNIE: It was awesome. He was so friggin' proud. It was great.

"The Rapper" stayed in the *Billboard* top ten until April 11. That week's album chart saw the Jaggerz' debut: *We Went to Schools Together* was finally out on Kama Sutra. It hit number 101, starting an 11-week run. It would peak at number 62.

ON TOUR

Now that the Jaggerz had an album they were more or less happy with, it was time to take the show on the road. Once the album was out, they headed directly to the stratosphere.

June 10, 1970, the Jaggerz played Memorial Stadium in Charlotte, North Carolina. The WAYS birthday bash drew 35,000 fans to a show featuring Bobby Sherman, Bobby Vee, Mel & Tim, Steam, the Spiral Staircase, the Dells, the Novas Nine, and the Flares.[10.21]

The shows grew bigger and better. June 14, 1970, the band played the Milwaukee County Stadium, a venue with a sports capacity of 43,000. The Beach Boys and a post-Diana Ross Supremes headlined.[10.22]

DONNIE: It was probably the biggest show I ever played. We were playing clubs, and all of a sudden, we're put in this stadium like the Beatles. It was awesome.

Not all shows were so big. And not everyone enjoyed the band. The Jaggerz were popular with music fans — critics, not so much.

Billboard's Joe Radcliffe saw them in New York City and reported on it in the August 8 issue: "The Jaggerz, a six-member rock group on the Kama Sutra label, turned in a bland, uninspiring, over-amplified concert when they appeared at Ungano's July 29. The Jaggerz' biggest problem is that they lack a sound. True, with three guitars they've got rhythm, but after a while the monotony of the beat gets to the listener. They also have an instrumental imbalance and utilize a single horn which sounds oddly out of place in the ensemble."[10.23]

Donnie doesn't remember seeing the review, but it makes him chuckle now.

DONNIE (LAUGHING): It's too bad we didn't see that review back then! We knew people in Youngstown!

Even with a passive promotion strategy, the Gamble singles managed to turn enough profit to warrant new ones. The Gamble releases consistently failed to chart nationally, but the Kama Sutra singles succeeded modestly:

"I Call My Baby Candy" was a natural choice for the next proper single: The band's second Kama Sutra single arrived in April 1970. It was the album's leadoff song, and played like a bluesy retread of "The Rapper" — minus the instructive novelty aspect. Not only was it appropriately catchy, but it was the only other song on the album written solely by Donnie, who wrote on a total of five of the album's nine original tunes. "I Call My Baby Candy," b/w "Will She Believe Me?" peaked at *Billboard* number 75 on May 23, 1970.

Kama Sutra was quick to move past the rushed album. "Memoirs of the Traveler," the album's standout performance, was recycled as the B-side of the next single, which shipped in April. "What a Bummer," also written by Donnie, was the A-side. Its prospects looked bright for a moment.

Billboard declared "Bummer" to be "a driving swinger, which should fast top the sales and chart action of the recent winner" in a column of songs "predicted to reach the top 60."[10.24]

Alas, the predictions were off. "Bummer" peaked at number 88 on August 22. In the long shadow of "The Rapper," the rest of the Jaggerz' singles truly were bummers. The band's career continued fruitfully for years, but 1970 marked their final appearance on the Hot 100.

Still, it wasn't a bad spot to be in. The band were still the undisputed kings of Pittsburgh. And being home was a much easier lifestyle than being on the road. They were able to work less, but cash bigger checks.

JIMMIE: It was great, being at home. We had the biggest radio station for music, KQV, solidly behind us, playing "Gotta Find My Way Back Home" and "The Rapper."

When the band returned home, they had already spent their first royalty checks — but they had something to show for them: a set of seven Lincoln Continentals.

"We were like 22 and 23 years old," Ross told the *Tribune-Review*'s Rex Rutkoski in 2002. "The dealer stayed open for us. The cars were all lined up, and we could pick the color."[10.25]

JIMMIE: After "The Rapper," we cut down to maybe four days a week, because we didn't have to play six days a week. We were making even more money. We wanted to live our life a little bit. We'd go to New York, play up there. I was happy to play anywhere, for people to hear the Jaggerz on the radio, and people come to see us.

DONNIE: We might have been out there for a week or two at a time. But we never jumped in the Winnebago and drove to California. It was spotty shows. We were basically still doing clubs around Pittsburgh before "The Rapper" came out. Once the song became a hit, we started doing TV shows, that kind of stuff. We started playing larger venues. My weeks were maybe four nights, playing Mancini's or this place or that place, four nights a week. We played Wednesdays, Thursdays, Fridays, Saturdays, and sometimes Sundays.

JIMMIE: Everybody knew the Jaggerz' name. We were in demand all the time. Club promoters knew if they booked us, the place would be jammed. We got the most money that bands could get at that time. And just had a great, great time.

There were a lot of girls around. When you have successful band, people are around, and half of 'em's girls. To this day, I talk to people, and they say, "We always knew if we came to see you guys at Geneva-on-the-Lake, there would be a lot of girls."

The Jaggerz were truly visible now. But after "The Rapper" peaked in March 1970, the band's commercial performance declined steadily. The national critics never did come around. As the band were playing their biggest shows — albeit as a support act — *Cash Box* gave the group a mixed accolade: Its 1970 Disc Jockey Poll named the Jaggerz the number 15 Most Promising Vocal Group, beneath the Jackson Five, Chicago, the Ides of March, Vanity Fare, Shocking Blue, Marmalade, Badfinger, and the Carpenters.[10.26]

As *Observer-Reporter* critic Terry Hazlett later noted, hitting number 1 or 2 is no small feat in any given year; but it in the environment the Jaggerz did it, the distinction was especially impressive: "In the midst of record charts swamped with psychedelic music, 'Rapper' bolted up to the [*Billboard*] number 2 position in the country."

In 1977, Benny told the *North Hill Record* "The Rapper" ultimately "hurt us more than it helped us.... If we had stayed at what we were best at doing, we could have been another Average White Band. The talent was there. Before 'The Rapper' we were known as a soul group. People who weren't familiar with us didn't know that's what we were all about."[10.27]

He was right. The band's biggest single even confused seasoned professionals. Robert Christgau, known as The Dean of American Rock Critics, dismissed the group with a devastating efficiency in his

Consumer Guide review, which gave the album a C-. He noted, "I must have gone to a different school, too — I never seem to learn that a great pop single like 'The Rapper' rarely has a half-decent album attached."[10.28]

After *Different Schools*, the Jaggerz gave it the old college try, but they never came close to matching "The Rapper."

BENNY: We did try. We really did try. That's what we needed, another hit. We did become known as a one-hit wonder. That was the only big, gold record the Jaggerz ever had. We had chart records, but we never had a number 1 after that.

The Jaggerz got used to disappointments, but they handled them well.

> "
> I was just watching guys
> do their thing at the clubs,
> going up and rappin' to chicks to get
> 'em up to their apartments. It was
> such an obvious thing to write about.
> The idea hit me in my sleep, and I
> woke up and started writing.
>
> ~ DONNIE IRIS
> "

The Jaggerz (Donnie far left).

CHAPTER 11

The Jaggerz: Encore

"THE RAPPER": OVER TWO MILLION SERVED?

BENNY: Donnie wrote "The Rapper," and we made the record as a group. We contributed to the sound of it too, from the way he wrote it. We all felt a part of "The Rapper." We changed some things. Donnie never spoke out or never once threw it in our faces that if it wasn't for him, we wouldn't be on the charts, or that we wouldn't have as much success if it wasn't for him.

DONNIE: It was just one of those things. We were hoping for the best, whatever song it was. It just happened to be "The Rapper" was the one that had the commerciality that made it a hit.

Reports vary on what kind of numbers "The Rapper" put up. The questionable RIAA certifications — the association also calls them "awards" — only have the song logged as a gold single. Benny says the record moved over a million copies. The Pittsburgh *Post-Gazette* reported it moved over 2.5 million. [11.1]

The question of how many copies the song sold intersects with how many versions of the song exist. The Jaggerz cut four versions of "The Rapper." Three are widely circulated. Late in the band's run, a different lineup re-recorded it for a K-Tel records compilation. Before that, three different versions existed. Two of them hit the airwaves and store shelves — which was another surprise to the band.

BENNY: I think in the Kama Sutra organization, there was a bootleg record on "The Rapper." When we went to New York to Century sound, we recorded three versions of "The Rapper." One we sold to Neil Bogart, as the main press. Then there were two other ones. On the other two, we did something different. We put an echo effect on one. And something different in the third one.

One day, we were signing autographs in New Castle. And the record is playing. And here's this echo effect. I said, "Oh my God, that's not the original record." So I stopped and got the record. Everything is authentic; it's on the Kama Sutra label. And that had to be somebody who was tied up either with Buddha or Neil. They got their hands on that tape.

Some fans still remember the echo mono version from AM radio, and were confused when they heard the no-echo version. (Collectors often call the popular straightforward take "the hit version" and the echo version "alternate mix.") The singles don't identify different mixes. The echo version is the sole Jaggerz selection from *The Buddha Box* compilation.

"The Rapper" became a staple selection for compilations from the era. The late William Maybray Jr., son of Bill, dug through his father's archives and estimated the song had appeared on nearly sixty collections. [11.2]

BENNY: We had a deal with Buddha that when the record went gold, we got $100,000. We got the check. I don't know if we sold more than two million — if we did, we didn't have a deal to get a second bonus check.

It was a shady business. We lost a truckload of Gamble albums from Philadelphia to Pittsburgh, 50,000 albums. Everything disappeared.

The Jaggerz didn't coast on their big breakout hit. They tried to parlay their momentum and money. They diversified.

BENNY: With "The Rapper," six of us started a publishing company, Sinuous Music Revival. We got that bonus check, and Joe said we had to incorporate. We were all involved in the publishing for the songs we wrote. Now we get performance plays, but Donnie gets publishing for "The Rapper."

We thought if we could produce some other groups that we could do the same thing that we just did, maybe with a Pittsburgh artist. Joe knew Bobby Rydell and James Darren. We put up money for sessions for them, and it never happened. And some of the money started to go out the window. When the money came like that, I thought, "Maybe I'll get $10,000 or $5,000 at one time, instead of just a paycheck all the time."

When they felt inspired, the band recorded a single at the local Jeree Recording studio. In December 1970, Gamble released the "Higher and Higher," b/w "Ain't No Sun (Since You've Been Gone)" from the vaults.

In February 1971, Kama Sutra released the new single, "I'll Never Forget You," b/w "Let's Talk About Love".

In April 1971, Gamble followed it with another single of *Introducing* tracks: "Here's a Heart," b/w "Need Your Love." At that point, the Gamble tracks were nearly three years old. And that release ended the cycle of competing Jaggerz records. It would be a while before there was another. *Introducing the Jaggerz* went out of print, and has never been reissued on CD.

None those three singles blipped on the national radar.

But the band continued, with a more-or-less unified front. They always worked in literal harmony. But the band's dress code created some discord. Donnie and the band were developing different professional goals. Their Woodstock-style Beatles cover song was emblematic of the changing times — and changing business.

DONNIE: We were always together doing shows, working on shows, and socializing.

BENNY: All those years together, we enjoyed each other's vocal harmony blend together, whether they were cover songs or our songs.

DRESS CODE

DONNIE: The Jaggerz started as an R&B band. And then when the Beatles came out, we started doing a lot of other music mixed with the R&B. We used to dress in basically the same outfits that the Beatles did. Then the '70s came along, and we started wearing other things.

Donnie's outfit from his solo highlight reel is the yellow suit from the "Ah! Leah!" video. The day-glow tux was actually a holdover from the Jaggerz days. After "The Rapper" came and went, the band returned to their roots and doubled down on their showband image. Almost a decade before the "Leah" video and MTV, the six smooth crooners took the stage in matching yellow tuxes, oversized black bowties, and spitshined shoes.

DONNIE: We were going to be looking *good*. It was like a soul group. [Laughing, he adopts his much-practiced *Scarface* voice.] "First you get the Vegas act, then you get the money. Then when you got the money, you get the power. Then when you get the power, you get the women!"

As the band were refining their '50s throwback act, Donnie was changing with the times.

DONNIE: I didn't have really long hair until the Jaggerz. I was a pseudo-hippie, I guess. Tie dyes. It was a big to-do. I got into that stuff because it was cool. Nehru jackets, I remember having those. Fringe jackets, suede vests, all that stuff. I wasn't *living* like that. We were just following the Beatles' lead. I thought it was wild. I enjoyed that stuff. But I liked the Raspberries' "I Wanna Be With You," too.

BENNY: We incorporated in 1970, when "The Rapper" went on the charts. We didn't pay corporate taxes two years in a row. And then the IRS came in. We broke up for a while around '72-'73, and there were all these changes [in the lineup] — it wasn't breaking up to break up; it was a reorganization. We wanted to play together, but we had to make changes. That's when we replaced Thommy.

After the shakeup, the band's schedule held steady: They remained regulars at Mancini's and the Staircase, packing the supper clubs and leaving a line outside. And they started picking up more gigs at rock clubs like Ohio's Aquanaut Lounge — in May, they played the same week as a new group called Wild Cherry. Closer to home, they started booking places like Caesar's House in Pittsburgh and Cecil's

C.I.C., whose ad promised "DANCING," but no mention of dinner.

The Jaggerz even played a prison. Rock booked the band two gigs in Western Penitentiary (formally named State Correctional Institution – Pittsburgh) and the United States Penitentiary, Lewisburg in Central Pennsylvania. The band was scheduled to played Chino Prison, the California Institution for Men (CIM) in Chino, California.[11.3] California in December 1972. The concert was announced. Publications from the Pittsburgh *Post-Gazette* to *Billboard* reported that it happened, which made it a permanent part of the band's lore.

BENNY: I don't even know how the hell we got booked in these prisons. Joe Rock booked us. We were supposed to play Chino, but we never actually played it.

They had other business in California.

WOLFMAN JACK

In late 1972, the Jaggerz got a call from Don Kelley, their old friend who had choreographed the stage show they still used. Kelley had successfully transplanted himself to California. And now he was managing Wolfman Jack, the gravel-voiced, hyperactive, horny, nationally syndicated radio hero and media personality. Elsewhere in the Golden State, a promising young filmmaker named George Lucas was finishing the final cut of *American Graffiti*.[11.4] Wolfman Jack was prominently featured in the movie.

Kelley was ready to capitalize on this rare Hollywood exposure — which, sure enough, completed the Wolfman's transformation from DJ to hall-of-fame American pop-culture icon. Wolfman Jack had released a self-titled rock-record on Wooden Nickel Records in 1972. But his rudimentary musical stylings proved to be far less popular than his acapella work: The single "I Ain't Never Seen a White Man" stalled out at number 106 on the *Billboard* singles chart. Kelley wanted to have another record ready to coincide with the movie. But he wanted better results, so he called a different band, who owed him a favor.

JIMMIE: We were real good friends Don Kelley. He called and said, "Hey. Wolfman's doing an album, and we want you guys to back him up." He told us he was in contact with the studio.

Benny missed a good chunk of duck-hunting season in Fall 1972, when the Jaggerz temporarily relocated to Torrance, California, where they recorded the Wolfman Jack album *Through the Ages*. The band worked at Quantum Recording Studios, with producers Dick Monda and Don Sciarrotta.

JIMMIE: Wolfman Jack wasn't a singer. He was a big radio personality. It was a novelty-type album he was doing for this company out in California. We played and sang background on his whole album. We never saw him. I didn't meet him until later. I was a guest at his house for the Academy Awards a couple years later, when I was with my own group, Cooper and Ross.

A lot of the stuff was recorded already, the band tracks — not everything. Then the other tracks, we cut ourselves and sang background. We're on every song, either singing or playing or both. We played and sang background on "My Girl." And then after we came back home, he came in and did his leads.

In summer 1973, Wooden Nickel released *Through the Ages* as part of a massive promotional blitz for the umbrella of labels distributed by RCA. In retrospect, the Summer Power campaign may have been too ambitious: The record men were spread thin, pushing 40 albums slated for a June release. Wolfman Jack received a nominal push, but took a backseat to releases by David Bowie, John Denver, Harry Nilsson, Charley Pride, and Frank Sinatra.[11.5]

The album rated the smallest of mentions in *Billboard* in August 1973[11.6], when the movie opened. And that's as far as it went. Kelley sweetened the Jaggerz' payday — and his chances of success — by including a croaky version of "The Rapper" as the B-side of the record's sole single, a wooden cover of the oldie "My Girl." Like the album, the single did not reach the *Billboard* charts.

But recording original rock albums was not Wolfman Jack's bread and butter. And the label didn't blame the band. In fact, they kept them around. And *that* was quite a deal.

JIMMIE: I don't think anybody knew about the Wolfman Jack thing. It wasn't "Wolfman Jack Featuring the Jaggerz." It was a fun thing to do.

In September 1973, Kama Sutra released its final Jaggerz single. "Ain't That Sad" recycled the B-side "Let's Talk About Love" from the previous single, "I'll Never Forget You." And that was the end of their partnership with Kama Sutra.

THIRD RECORD LABEL: WOODEN NICKEL

The three years since *We Went to Different Schools Together* had been a blur of big shows and regular bookings on the club circuit. In August 1970, "What a Bummer" barely cracked *Billboard*'s Top 100 singles. Gamble released two even-less-noticed singles. In September 1973, Kama Sutra had not released a single in two and a half years, since February 1971's "I'll Never Forget You," b/w "Let's Talk About Love."

The band self-released some invisible singles on its own Jaggerz Records, like 1974's "The Streaker," which tried to cash in on the naked trend. The band needed a new label. While recording the Wolfman Jack record, they kept the studio clean and worked hard for Sciarrotta. So they had good references with his record company.

JIMMIE: We signed with Wooden Nickel.

The Wooden Nickel deal was a good place to land. Its highest profile partner was Jerry Weintraub, who had made his bones in the music business in 1970, promoting Elvis Presley's first full-scale, headlining rock-concert tour. By the time Weintraub's label released a Jaggerz album, his credits would include the legendary Frank Sinatra comeback tour, which included the televised 1974 *The Wide World of Sports - The Main Event* special, which staged Ol' Blue Eyes on a boxing ring square in the middle of Madison Square Garden. In an HBO documentary about the raspy raconteur, Brad Pitt succinctly described Weintraub as "a force of nature."[11.7]

Weintraub later parlayed his entertainment connections into a career as a Hollywood producer and actor, with a slate of films that included *Nashville*, the original *Karate Kid* series, and the *Ocean's 11-12-13* franchise, where he played a pivotal role as high roller Denny Shields. And that was the company the Jaggerz kept during their third album. At the time the Jaggerz joined Kama Sutra, the upstart label's roster included country-fried rock singer Megan McDonough, Exile (best known for "Kiss You All Over") and a promising young rock band named Styx. The Jaggerz had a nice new home.

DONNIE: Weintraub was big time.

JIMMIE: Joe Rock or Don Kelley met him, but we never met him.

BENNY: We heard his name, and he was supposed to be someone big. That's all we knew. We didn't know he did all those things. I wish he woulda done something great for *us*. We wondered, "What the hell's happening? What's coming?" We thought we were just a tax write-off.

COME AGAIN

The Jaggerz' third album, *Come Again*, arrived in April 1975, a full five years after their previous one. The band say the time went fast; maybe they could have done more, but they definitely could have done less.

JIMMIE: It didn't seem like a long time. We were back here, working. We played a lot. Time flies, man. We didn't tour that much. We played mini things. There were opportunities, but Joe Rock was our manager, and we left it up to him, as far as the business end and bookings. And he never put us on tour. I don't remember us ever talking about it.

***Come Again* was another 10-track set:**

"I'll Be Okay in the Morning" (Granati, L. Ierace)
"Love Music" (Lambert, Potter)
"Satisfaction Guaranteed" (D. Ierace, Ross, Faiella, Czuri, Elliot)
"It's Me" (C. Sciarrotta)
"Gotta Find My Way Back Home" (M. & M. Steals)

"High Heel Rockin' Roll Shoes" (C. Sciarrotta, D. Sciarrotta)

"Shame On You" (C. Sciarrotta, D. Sciarrotta)

"Don't It Make You Wanna Dance" (D. Sciarrotta, J. Golden, L. Ierace)

"2 + 2" (M. Davis, M. James)

"It's Better to Have and Don't Need (Than to Need and Don't Have)" (D. Covay)

"L. Ierace" isn't a typo or print smudge: Two songs were co-written by Donnie's wife, Linda. Three songs were from another member of the Sciarrotta family. The adventurous set is a fascinating time capsule of rising and falling styles.

DONNIE: The album is pretty interesting. It sounds psychedelic — for that time. For me, it felt right. I listened and thought, "This is pretty dang good." One thing that nobody could take away from us is that we could sing. The harmonies were unlike anything I did with the Cruisers or anybody else. Listening to that album, those three- or four-part harmonies, without doubling it, it was amazing. No doctoring anything.

I thought that was standard fare. But nobody did that. Maybe Crosby, Stills and Nash. But they did double their vocals. We did the psychedelic harmonies, and that was being done by very few people. We didn't have to stack anything. That was all us.

For the third record, the band wrote a mere three songs. Producers Don and Engineer Tony Sciarrotta wrote as much, in addition to spitshining the band's traditional vocal pop material and adorning it with strings and layered production. The Sciarrottas' "High Heel Rockin' Roll Shoes" was a scientifically engineered boot-stomping, sing-along showstopper — but a single it was not.

The Jaggerz reached back into their catalog for a fresh take on "Gotta Find My Way Back Home," which was still one of their signature tunes, but wasn't directly earning them any cash at that point. The label and management covered their bets with a host of outside writers and wide array of cover songs. The Four Tops' "Love Music" was easy to see coming. But the album's surprising, solitary single put its Jaggerz original to the B-side. The A-side was "2 + 2," a slightly risqué narrative country-crossover ditty by Mac Davis.

JIMMIE: To this day, people say "2+2" was one of their favorite Jaggerz songs. Mac Davis was kind of a country singer, but it was a real pop tune. I guess they thought it would make a good single.

BENNY: I haven't heard that since it came out. I don't know if I even have a copy of that album.

Despite the approach of using many cooks *and* throwing in the kitchen sink, the band say the record wasn't the product of extensive calculation or discussion.

JIMMIE: We were just doing our thing. I love the strings and all. I thought that album was great. But with no promotion, it got lost. We were hoping for the best. If it happened, it happened. We had our hit, and a lot of bands can't say that.

BENNY: I think we were ahead of ourselves when we wrote that album. The timing wasn't right.

"YOUNS ARE GOIN' ON STAGE LOOKIN' LIKE HIPPIES."

For four years, the band had been playing mostly hometown gigs. Now *Come Again* re-introduced the public to a very different looking band. The mystic cover photo spans ages. It's set on sundown landscape. Staring at the camera, Pugliano and Czuri are decked out in long hair, jeans and tie-dyed T-shirts. They're standing next to an antique mirror that reflects Ross and Faiella, the pair frozen in black & white, wearing Beatlesque threads from the late '60s. Then, on the other side of the mirror, a lean Donnie angles against the mirror, barefoot and shirtless. This is not your father's Jaggerz.

Over the past two years, the classy showroom suits had given way to paisley shirts. Then the paisley shirts were replaced with T shirts, the band's hair and mustaches growing all the while. The combined weight of Donnie and the times had worn the band down.

DONNIE: I didn't dig the suit thing. It kinda felt like I was going to work or getting dressed up for school. I was getting more into the rock or pop thing.

BENNY: It was a big conversation, dropping the suits. Donnie would show for gigs in sandals. He'd wear the suits, but he didn't like it. We started changing, too.

JIMMIE: I think Donnie wanted to go a different way. We were one of the highest paid bands to ever come out of Pittsburgh. It wasn't just for the suits — it was for our image, or vocals, the show that Don Kelley choreographed for us.

BENNY: People were still coming. They were dancing when we were playing. We weren't doing the show all the time. Then we stopped doing the show, and we were doing Top 40 tunes that were big. We were doing the Stones' "[Little] Queenie." We did some by the Average White Band — "Pick Up the Pieces" and "Only a School Boy Crush." We were doing some oldie medleys. We did some Who. Whatever groups were out that were on the chart. Sly & the Family Stone, we did "Sing a Simple Song."

JIMMIE: Around 1968, we actually did play our own horns for about a year. Donnie and Thom Davies played trumpet, and I played valve trombone. Later, any horn parts that were important in the song, we would substitute with our vocals. We were the ultimate band. We did things other bands could only dream about.

BENNY: We were still doing the Staircase and Mancini's Lounge. The crowds were good. But people sent us letters and everything, saying "What are you guys doing? You were classy-act guys — and now you're going on stage looking like hippies!" We used to play a big club in Johnstown called Ace's, a big hall that held five, six hundred people. That was '72, '73, 74. We drew all the way to the end.

Late in summer 1975, the label released Styx's "Lady," which was more successful than the Jaggerz' "2+2." And that breakout didn't make the label. Instead, it broke it. Styx bolted the label for greener fields. And Wooden Nickel shuttered in short order.

So did the Jaggerz.

The new album and look didn't create new opportunities. Over the rest of 1975, the band belted it out for diminishing crowds on the Pittsburgh club circuit.

"Donnie wasn't happy to go back to playing bars after the big breakout," Joe Grushecky told Rolling Stone in 1981, when Donnie rebounded and the magazine profiled the reborn rocker. [11.8]

The band wasn't going great. But Donnie did have some things to be happy about.

DONNIE: It was exciting, very exciting to have all this happening. We didn't have another child until five years after the first. It was tough being away when Erin was young, but I wasn't away that much. It was great, having a child. I remember: She was probably six or seven years old, I would drive us to this place called Waite's Ice Cream shop.

I just looked down at the phone, and one of the girls is texting me. We're still very close. For a while there, they go off on their own. You expect them to go away for awhile. But our kids were never like that. They pretty much hung around us for a long time.

I liked everything about it. I remember people telling me, "You're married now, you have kids, it's *over*." I had a family because it's what I wanted to do. And it didn't hold me back one bit. I was encouraged, more than anything else.

But Donnie had a rock itch the Jaggerz weren't scratching. And he wasn't the only one.

BENNY: The group divided. Donnie wanted to do more rock and roll. And eventually, he said he wanted to leave the group. Jimmie was leaving. And everything fell apart.

A CLASSY FIVE-DRINK BAND FOR BOUTIQUERS

Things were good at home. But not in their hometown. Some of the factors that ended the Jaggerz' run still affect Pittsburgh, which is still often referred to as the Steel City.

JIMMIE: Probably around '74, 75, it started slowing down.

Things were changing as far as the music scene, even in Pittsburgh. The teenagers that used to come see us were not teenagers anymore. They were single. Now they're 22 or more — it's almost ten years later.

The mills closed down. The mills weren't working like they did before.

We weren't doing the thing we did best. That's like putting a fringe jacket on the Temptations. It just didn't work. We were still a vocal R&B group.

And we were competing with rock bands. There were more rock clubs than dance clubs. Bands were playing stuff by the Stones, bands like that. I'm really not a rock and roll guy, so I don't know.

That's when I got a call from Joe Rock, who also, at the time, managed Jimmy Beaumont and the Skyliners. He said one of the original guys was leaving. And that's the kind of show business I liked, doing the concerts and being on a bill with three or four traveling acts. That's when I had a chance to leave. That's when the Jaggerz broke up.

DONNIE: I didn't want to leave; Jimmy was leaving the band to join the Skyliners. And the group broke up.

The rest of us probably would have kept playing clubs. But because Jimmy was leaving, I thought, "I don't want to do this anymore."

I thought Jimmy was a hell of a talent. I think he had a lot to do with the success of the band. So at that point, I didn't care if the group broke up or not.

Mike Kalina, the Pittsburgh *Post-Gazette*'s rock beat reporter, checked in on the group from time to time.

Even when the Jaggerz brand of classy showband razzle-dazzle was going out of style, discriminating fans kept coming.

In August 27, as the band entered its final fall season, Kalina profiled scene fixture Gary "Spook" Catanese, an oversized character with a collar to match. Spook told Kalina he went to clubs five nights a week, every week. The lounge hopper described his system for rating bands: He ranked them on a scale of zero to five drinks, to measure how long he would stay and watch them. Spook ranked the Jaggerz as a five-drink act, in the elite company of Sweet Breeze and the Skyliners. "They're one of the best," he testified. Spook classified their fans as "boutiquers — people who get dressed up real fancy to hear a group." [11.9]

Donnie still gave his all on stage. But the band felt like he was losing interest. The Jaggerz' last years are the low point in his otherwise happy-go-lucky life. In two years of discussing his career, talking about this era is the only thing that makes his smile flicker. He later told writer Terry Hazlett: "After 12 years, I started asking myself 'Why?' There was just so much time I could put into a project, and 12 years was certainly enough time to put into The Jaggerz. [11.10]

"Sure, I was depressed for a while," Iris told Rolling Stone. "But I was just happy we had a hit. It was cool to know that the band was still together and had gigs to play." [11.11]

JIMMIE: Donnie got more into the rock thing than we did. I could see something happening. He didn't want to do what we had been doing for the past ten years. He was cool. It was never a problem. This was one band that never had a fight, never had an argument, in ten years. Nobody ever raised their voice to one another. We were all friends, we're still friends. Everybody wanted to do something different, I think.

THE END, A NEW BEGINNING, AND A REUNION

For 40 years, the Jaggerz have cited 1975 as the end of "the original Jaggerz" — but the band actually ended three weekends later. The Jaggerz finished out 1975 with lineup of Benny, Donnie, Jimmie, Pugliano, keyboardist Hermie Granati, and guitarist-bassist Larry Paxton.

The band played a farewell show at the Staircase Saturday, January 17, 1976. They had played the downtown club nearly every Saturday for six years. The ad plugged them as "Pgh.'s #1 Band for 10 Years." [11.12] That was a win.

The *Post-Gazette*'s Mike Kalina eulogized the band:

"The group's greatest strength was its harmonies and when they were on target it couldn't be beat. In recent years, however, the tight vocalizations began to slowly disintegrate, as did the group's popularity. There was a time when the Staircase used to draw such a crowd with the Jaggerz that you had to know somebody to get in the door. In recent months, however, the group lost many of its fans even though the members tried to constantly update its style." [11.13]

A world without the Jaggerz didn't last long.

By March, Benny assembled a new lineup, without Donnie and Jimmy. They played smaller clubs across the regional circuit for another year, gracing smaller venues in Pittsburgh and the outlying territories: the Roman Gardens in West Mifflin, Buddies in Market Square, Pogo's in Connellsville, the Jury Box in Waynesburg, and Holiday Inns in Greentree and Beaver Falls. If you still liked that kind of thing, they were still worth a drive. And when you really love a band, a small show is better.

JIMMIE: The original Jaggerz disbanded. If you want to call it the Jaggerz, Benny put together a little band to play clubs around the area, calling them the Jaggerz.

Ross went to form the Cooper and Ross group, and signed with the Cruisers' management. The co-ed adult-contemporary duo covered "Only the Lonely," by Belkin band LaFlavour, written by Mark Avsec. Its 1982 MCA-Sweet City album, *Bottom Line*, was released in association with the Cruisers' label, Carousel Records.

Jaggerz tracks have become a reliable source for hip-hop and dance samples, used by A-list groups including Curren$y and Wiz Khalifa, Dilated Peoples, Fatboy Slim and Girl Talk. The smooth soul groove from "Memoirs of a Traveler" has been rediscovered — ironically, "The Rapper" has not. In 2013, the Jaggerz had a minor legal dustup with Sony after rapper The Game used the song in his "Letter to the King" and royalties were lost in the a byzantine network of rights-holders and payments.

The music is still beloved by the old-school crowd.

RE-REUNITED

In 1989, DiCesare-Engler Productions — the concert promoters who owned Pittsburgh — called Benny and asked him if the band would play a reunion concert. Ross liked the idea. Donnie declined.

BENNY: He changed a little bit, when he started having hits on his own. I didn't get to see him that much in those years when he was in Wild Cherry. Then when he tied up with his own thing, when it was Donnie and the Cruisers, I felt he was distancing himself from us a little bit, like wanted to be recognized as Donnie Iris, and not dwell too much on his past. But we left on good terms, and we're friends today. Donnie's a great guy.

The show went well, and the band became a fixture on the reunion circuit. Not content with the nostalgia scene, they have released three albums since reforming. Maybray passed away in 2004. Pugliano followed in 2010. Thom Davies passed away shortly after the band received the 2017 Pittsburgh Rock 'N Roll Legends award. Jimmie Ross and Benny Faiella lead the current lineup, a sextet featuring old friend Hermie Granati. Their third reunion album, *The Walk*, was produced by Jay Dudt, who engineered/mixed two Grammy-winning Jazz albums. [11.14]

Donnie has returned to the Jaggerz twice: In 2015, Iris was a headliner at the Pittsburgh Rockin' Reunion concert at the Benedum Center, alongside Lou Christie, Jimmy Beaumont & The Skyliners, the Marcels, Chuck Belasco's Vogues, and the Jaggerz. He joined the band for "Gotta Find My Way Back Home" and "The Rapper." And they backed him on "Ah! Leah!" and "Love Is Like a Rock."

In 2017, the band cemented their Steel City status when voters delivered them a Pittsburgh Music Rock 'N Roll Legend award, alongside Jaggerz/Cruisers engineer and fellow Beaver boy Jerry Reed.

JIMMIE: I still see Donnie once in a great while. When we do, we talk about old times, have a couple great laughs. I didn't see him at all in the '80s. He's a level headed guy. We're still friends.

BENNY: The day we got inducted, he was sitting at the bar at Jergel's. I walked in. He came over, gave me a hug, shook my hand.

Every show, we do "The Rapper." We do that last. Jimmie sings the lead.

Part I: *Ah!*

B.E. Taylor and Donnie Iris.

CHAPTER 12

Donnie: Between Bands in the Beaver Valley

1976. January. The Jaggerz as we knew them are over. Donnie is on his own — not a solo artist yet. Just on his own. He hasn't played an arena in years.

DONNIE: I wanted to be in a band and be onstage. I wasn't thinking about being a star. I didn't see myself as a solo singer. I saw myself with a band.

The original Jaggerz play their final show January 17, 1976. After years of building tension, Donnie no longer has to choose between crooning and rocking. Now he finds some people he can rock with. So he hits the road, and he heads… 10 minutes down Route 18, to New Brighton.

The Jaggerz had recorded at Jeree Recording Studio in New Brighton. Jerry is generous with his time, and Donnie likes the vibe. It's a perfect lab to cook something up with one of the promising acts he and the Jaggerz had tried to produce: B.E. Taylor.

Donnie and Taylor have a lot in common; no wonder they click. His first major band, B.E. Taylor and the Establishment, had been regulars at Mancini's in 1970 and 1971, alongside the Jaggerz. [12.1]

After some work as a hired gun, Taylor had settled into the Youngstown-based band Coconut, with former Jagger Herman Granati. But he wanted a band to call his own.

DONNIE: He was looking for something to do. And I was looking for something to do.

Now I knew B.E., and I knew he was awesome. He was a great guy. We hit it off, and we became really good friends. I wish he was here to say when we first met up; I can't remember for sure. We had become such good friends, I thought maybe we could sound good together.

He was right. B.E. isn't quite the creative partner Donnie is looking for. But they have a blast, they form a friendship, and they establish a new base of operations for Iris.

WELCOME TO JEREE RECORDING, WHERE WE STACK IT

Jeree Recording began rolling tape in 1975, at 1469 3rd Avenue, New Brighton, PA. [12.2] After some false starts, co-founders Jerry Reed and head engineer Don Garvin bought an old Victorian house in New Brighton and set up their gear. [12.3] Garvin was an experienced musician who had played with countless musicians from Chuck Berry to the Drifters. Reed was an Air Force veteran and music fan. [12.4]

In the '70s and '80s, Jeree was a pillar of music and art in Pittsburgh and the surrounding areas. The humble studio was the foundation of Donnie Iris and the Cruisers' distinct production style. Over the years, the studio hosted sessions from the Granati Brothers, B.E. Taylor, Q, Wild Cherry, LaFlavour, Billy Price, the Silencers, Modern Man, and John Harrison, who recorded the soundtrack to George A. Romero's *Day of the Dead* there. [12.5]

STEVE NERVO, OF LAFLAVOUR/FAIR WARNING: Jeree's, it's an old house. And they had a studio in this house. What a sound they got out of it. It was all two-inch tape, not like the digital stuff they've got now. Don Garvin was the engineer — he built the board. Every now and then he'd have to go under it and hit it to get it to work, like the Fonz when he'd whack the jukebox. It was a family, home atmosphere over there. It was really cool.

B.E. Taylor and Donnie Iris.

RICK WITKOWSKI, B.E. TAYLOR BANDS: It was a professional recording studio. It was in a house, but it was a bona fide studio. It had a charm. They had a wooden drum room that had some hard surfaces in it, where we'd record hand claps and timbales, or go for that big live-room sound you heard in the '80s, like on Phil Collins' "In the Air Tonight."

DONNIE: I went down to Jeree's and started working with the board. I was an engineer, basically. I learned a lot of that electric stuff from my wife's dad. I was working for him. My wife was a hairdresser. I needed to make some money and get something going.

It was close. Jerry lived two minutes from here. I had recorded with Jerry when I was a kid. I was 15 or 16 when I first recorded there. I did an original tune called "Eileen." I wrote that tune and recorded it at Jerry's. He was a *wonderful* man, a great, great guy.

I can remember guys sometimes taking advantage of Jerry, 'cause he was nice, and a lot of times he never got paid. But Jerry was a pretty wealthy man on his own. He loved music. He loved the recording end of it.

The duo thing, that was just "Donnie Iris and B.E. Taylor." There's a tape out that we recorded at my dad's tavern. We do a bunch of Beatles tunes. That was a nice stepping stone for me. It was an acoustic thing, the two of us. We did covers, a couple originals. He was tremendous. We had crazy times together, absolutely.

BENNY: We used to play the same places as Wild Cherry. We knew Bob Parissi. Wild Cherry would come in and play the Staircase downtown. And when he went through that spell, whatever happened with Wild Cherry, that's when he called Donnie.

Donnie bought a house. Next door was a garage. Donnie was always fooling around with his motorcycle or his car. He invited me down to learn about body work. At that point, I'd have loved if we could have stayed with Donnie and have him put something together.

Donnie called me and said, "Euge, Wild Cherry called me. Rob Parissi asked me to join the band."

I said, "You know what, Don? You better do it. This could be a whole opportunity for you."

And it was. It changed his whole musical career.

CHAPTER 13

Mark in the Musical Minor Leagues

Donnie didn't know it as the famous Jaggerz were crumbling: The creative and business team that would guide him through the rest of his career was drifting toward him.

The intertwined show business careers of Wild Cherry, Mark Avsec, Carl Maduri, and Mike Belkin had been growing together in neighboring Ohio. The Buckeye State rock capital, Cleveland, was a mere two hours away from Pennsylvania — but it was a whole different world.

In 1976, Mark Avsec was a rising star on a team with a deep bench: The Belkin-Maduri Organization. Mike Belkin and his brother Jules had helped make Cleveland such a musical hot spot that it would eventually be selected as the location for the Rock and Roll Hall of Fame and Museum.

The Belkin brothers were established concert promoters and accomplished band managers at this point. They had recently joined forces with Carl Maduri. Maduri was a record company promoter who wanted to be in a different corner of the business. Over the next few years, they would come to rely on the organization's secret weapon: Mark Avsec, a classically trained musician who also wanted to conquer new realms too.

MARK: After high school, I did some recording. It would be in somebody's basement, and I would hire maybe a singer. It was reel-to-reel, a four-track setup.

I had decided to work in a factory, to try and make some money. I worked at White Motors, which was a big factory in Cleveland, for about a year and a half. I was on the labor line. I was doing all the grunt work, bringing all the guys on the assembly line what they needed. And I was shoveling whatever they told me to shovel. I was a mailman for about three months, at station B, in an urban district. It was very challenging for a 19-year-old white male to be out there.

I was making pretty good money, more than I'd ever made. I wasn't getting rich, but I could afford some studio time. I would pay two or three hundred bucks and record two or three songs.

Avsec slowly realized he wanted to be in charge of his musical destiny one day — but he knew it would take some time to get there.

MARK: Captain of the ship, that's a good way to put it. I started playing with a band in high school called Restless. I was just a kid, and the other guys were older. We didn't record at all. We just played bars.

Avsec broke into the big leagues with the popular Bluestone Union band. When the group folded, singer A.J. Robe and guitarist Al Retay moved on to Lovers Lane with fellow Clevelander Neil Giraldo. In coming years, Giraldo would become Pat Benatar's co-writer and bandleader. And for young Avsec, ability, ambition, and a couple bucks did get him noticed.

MARK: Bluestone was after high school. Al Retay started writing songs. He was a guitarist of note, a level-headed guy. He was a friend of AJ Robey's, too.

I saw AJ Robey play, and he was an intense dude. He just had this scary look in his eyes — and I don't mean that in a bad way. He had an energy.

He was a singer, a *real* singer. Most of the guys, at the time — you had your Eric Carmens once in a while. But most local bands, what was lacking was a guy who could really sing. And that's what I was watching for. I could sing background vocals, but I wasn't going to be the front guy. I was way too weird for that.

So AJ was invited to join Bluestone. I started writing the songs. I wrote this song I really wanted to record. It was not a rock and roll song at all. It was a ballad. I wrote it. I believed in it.

We recorded it at Agency Recording Studio. I thought it was going to be a Bluestone record. It sounds so dumb now — it was called "Can You See the Love You've Made?" But I thought it was a good idea. I don't think there's a tape of it.

I recorded with piano and orchestration, and I got a Mellotron, and AJ sang it. We got an acetate of it. I personally paid the studio for it. And I began to develop this relationship with AJ, because I like to work with singers, and I wanted to be behind the scenes. AJ needed me, and I needed him.

I wrote a whole musical for AJ — that's what you do when you're 19, right? It was like *Tommy*, something like that. In some ways, AJ was my first Donnie. We went into the studio and recorded a couple songs I wrote. I'm sure if you listened to them now, they weren't very good. But I was learning how to make records.

In my brain, I scored everything out that I wanted, charted it out. Of course, people couldn't read music, I learned. So then we did some things by ear. I had all these orchestrations worked out. We were in different modes. I didn't know anything about Brian Wilson at the time, but apparently, Brian Wilson charted out *Pet Sounds*. And, of course, Brian Wilson is Brian Wilson, and I'm not Brian Wilson.

Things I thought would sound good didn't. Like a French horn sound, I would put it down. And I would come home and listen to it, and it had no top end on it at all, and the whole mix sounded muddy. I really didn't know what I was doing. I was learning how to twirl the nobs, trying to make records.

This was costing me a lot of money, relatively speaking. I didn't have any money, and whatever I had, I was putting into recording. And nothing ever happened with that. And eventually, I fell in with the Belkin-Maduri organization.

THE BELKIN-MADURI ORGANIZATION

If you were in Cleveland, Belkin and Maduri were the people you wanted to be with. Belkin had been promoting concerts over a decade. And he had shepherded the James Gang to the mountaintop, guiding them from life as a standout local band to a major-label group hand-picked to open for the Who in Europe.

Once Maduri got a foot in the door at the Belkin offices, he figured out how to stay around. Maduri was another figure in the Cruisers story who astutely parlayed a novelty success into an entire career. In 1958 the Clevelander co-wrote music and lyrics to "The Hula-Hoop Song," which was a smash when recorded by Georgia Gibbs with Hugo Peretti and His Orchestra. [13.1] By the time he retired, he had producer credits with artists from Liza Minnelli to Maureen McGovern — and the Cruisers.

MARK: Carl had immense charisma. Tall, dark and handsome. Impeccably dressed. When he walked into a room, everyone looked.

BELKIN: Carl was a promotion guy for the local distributor of Warner Brothers. We would promote concerts. And he would promote the artists on Warner. He would be schmoozing with the artists and the public-relations people. He came to the office at some point and talked about getting together. At that point, I was managing Walsh and Michael Stanley and other bands. A guitarist from Texas, Doug Sham. I knew that he knew music, because he was in the music business.

He was a nice guy and a nice person. He had a good ear. There was talent there, with the music. When it came to signing artists, he would meet the guy and negotiate with the artists.

JIMMY FOX, JAMES GANG FOUNDER, BELKIN CLIENT SINCE 1969, AND UTILITY INFIELDER IN THE BELKIN-MADURI OFFICES, 1977-1982: The Belkins were more astute about how the industry runs, where Maduri was more the maverick.

The Belkins came up through concert promotions, which is a wonderful way to understand everything else in the industry. And they are brilliantly great people. They understand business. They have run successful businesses before. And they were willing to learn from the right people, because they had access to the right people. If you're working with the Stones, at some point, you're going to talk to the

Stones' agent and manager. And if you can't learn from those people, there's nobody to learn from.

Mike is very pro-artist. He's very, very loyal to his artists. I think the fact he represents Michael Stanley and Donnie how many years later — 30, 40? I think that says it all: Mike will fight for his artists. He always has, and he always will.

The Belkins were sophisticated and schooled. Maduri was the exact opposite: Maduri was a street guy — and I don't mean that in any way as a negative; it's a very big positive, because you want someone like that in your record company. Carl heard something in Donnie, and I can't say I would have, though I like to think I would.

MARK: I was trying to break into the session scene, and get into the Belkin-Maduri organization, which was the premier entity in town.

Carl wanted to make Cleveland a sort of Detroit thing. He put together a group of players called the Sweet City Band. All these guys were African-American, except for me. We were recording on things Carl would bring in, artists he had signed, like Samona Cooke, and some other people. He had had some success with "The Morning After" by Maureen McGovern. Carl Maduri was using me as the lead guy in all these sessions, sort of like a music director.

And I was doing it, man — I was making the scene. So that was really the first production work I did, even though I wasn't really the producer. I was more the musical director. There, I was working with engineers like Artie Rosenberg, who knew how to make a record. I was paying attention to what everybody was doing.

For many musicians, the fringe benefits are just as important as the art and the paycheck — if not more; not for nothing does the phrase "sex, drugs, and rock & roll" echo through eternity. As far as rock histories go, the story of Donnie Iris and the Cruisers is curiously skimpy on the first two. Mark's personal journey was a quest for music and *work*. Like Donnie, the band was his job. By the time he made the scene, he already had a girlfriend — the future Mrs. Avsec.

MARK: My first wife is a very nice person, from a good Italian family. We were very different. I knew that if I married her, we would work that way.

She was OK with the life. She had her family, and she loved the kids, and we had a very traditional relationship. I was just always thinking about the music. It was fine with her. She didn't want to work outside the home, and she accepted that I did what I had to do.

I don't know if she understood everything I was doing or what I was thinking about all the time.

I met her at a club, in a lounge band I was playing in. [Touch of Class disco [13.2].] She was there with her sister and a couple of girlfriends.

Something that affected me: I had a couple girls I was crazy about. And I didn't like that, being beholden to another person. Because there were things I wanted to accomplish in my life. Then there was this really nice girl from my old neighborhood. I really liked her a lot. And I just saw myself if I married someone like that: I'd be happy. I'd get a plain job. I wouldn't want to risk being in that relationship.

I just wanted to shore up my personal life. And I picked somebody who wouldn't control me, that I could do what I wanted to do, who was a nice person. And I had every intention of staying together forever.

I married her in 1977, just as Wild Cherry was taking off. I was a young, single guy. I could have been doing what you do on the road. But I got married instead. It gave me some stability. Instead of running around, I was always at home, writing songs and working. I liked it. I've never been one to be a partier. I'm just not. We had two beautiful daughters. And I give my first wife credit for providing me with a solid foundation.

Belkin and Maduri made the most of their young workhorse.

WILD CHERRY AND SWEET CITY RECORDS

In December 1975, Belkin and Maduri decided to form a label, synergizing Maduri's ear and Belkin's direct connection to rock audiences. Maduri combed a 300-mile radius and eventually signed the

Sweet City Band. Cincinnati funk-rock band Blaze. Cincinnati soul singer Samona Cooke, granddaughter of Sam Cooke. And Wild Cherry, a rock band from Steubenville, near the Pennsylvania border, on the Ohio side.

Sweet City stirred up the most interest from two executives tied to Epic Records: Ron Alexenberg and Steve Popovich. Popovich was from Nemacolin in Southwest Pennsylvania, and had relocated to Cleveland. The Ohio blue-collar vibe was compatible with his home culture. He found work playing rock and producing polka records. He took a job at Columbia Records and worked his way into a position of influence. When *nobody* in the business saw *any* potential in Meat Loaf's *Bat Out of Hell* album, Popovich released it on his Cleveland International Records label. Over the years, he worked with more of the 20th century's iconic rock artists, including the Jacksons, Cheap Trick, Bruce Springsteen, Bob Dylan, and Meat Loaf.

Through Popovich, Sweet City set up a "custom distribution deal." Through the deal, bands would release singles that, if successful, would be followed by albums. The first was Wild Cherry's "Play That Funky Music." The juggernaut was released as a single in April 1976. It went platinum in October, and the song moved over 2.5 million copies in its first two years of release. [13.3] The album followed in June 1976, and was platinum by December.

"Funky Music" hit number 1 on the *Billboard* Hot 100 singles chart September 18, 1976, and topped all the major US single charts — *Billboard*, *Cash Box*, and *Record World*. It also hit number 1 on *Billboard*'s Soul Singles Charts and cracked assorted top 5 singles charts around the world. In 2015, *Billboard* still ranked it the number 88 in its list of All-Time Top 100 Songs. [13.4]

Belkin and Maduri assembled a small staff that included promotion head Joe Porello, who had a musical career as the frontman and trumpet player for Joey and the Continentals, and had recorded a series of popular 45s over the '60s and early '70s. Former London Records branch manager Norm Leskiw stepped in as the national sales manager. Maduri's son Chris was only 19 years old, but he was born into the business. He admirably served as secondary markets manager. [13.5]

Over 40 years later, Sweet City is not an active label, but the name appears on Wild Cherry albums. By 1977, the label was up and running, with a sudden influx of cash — royalty checks for still-popular "Play That Funky Music" are so big they arrive on a semi truck.

BELKIN: We got lucky with Wild Cherry.

The Mark-Donnie partnership started at Jeree, but really took root in a more famous studio — a legendary one, in fact. After Wild Cherry's one-in-a-trillion startup success, Belkin's hot property required constant stoking.

Wild Cherry lived and died in the 1970s, from 1970 through 1979. Their breakout single "Play That Funky Music" gave them pop-culture immortality, though it wasn't truly their first time at bat. The group warmed up in the Pennsylvania-Ohio-West Virginia tri-state area that overlapped with Jaggerz territory. The band released early singles in 1972 ("Get Down," a 1972 virtual Sly Stone tribute) and 1973 ("Show Me Your Badge"). They went largely unnoticed.

Ohio native Rob Parissi was Wild Cherry's bandleader, the one constant through its decade-long run. The band saw 13 other members come and go over four albums and numerous tours — including Donnie Iris and Mark Avsec. The band's career took place in the glow of some of the biggest names in the business.

Accounts vary about how Wild Cherry came to the Belkin-Maduri Organization. According to a 1977 *Billboard* feature, Cleveland Recording chief engineer Ken Hamann told Maduri about the band. [13.6]

BELKIN: Parissi came into the office. Carl was the music guy. Parissi spoke to Carl and played him the tape. Carl fell in love with it. And the rest is history. We signed him to a recording contract, which he still records under.

After Parissi was hit with a lightning bolt of inspiration and created "Funky Music," he needed help to fill out an album of material. Belkin and Maduri gave a tryout to Mark, who had recently made the jump to full-time musician.

MARK: Around the same time as Sweet City Band, there was Pace — basically a lounge band — so I could quit my White Motors gig.

With a lounge band, you could make a lot more money than you could in a rock band. We played Ramada Inns, Holiday Inns, places like that. Another advantage of being in a lounge band: You would set up for maybe a week, or two weeks, or maybe even three weeks, and leave your gear there. I was making maybe $300 a week. For a musician, at the time, that's really great money. We played a lot of disco stuff, some classic stuff. Spinners, "Whenever You Want Me," stuff like that.

I didn't know Parissi. Carl said "We need a keyboard player for a session."

I came down, and that was Wild Cherry. They were doing "Funky Music."

I heard that song and said, "Man, that's a hit. Like it or not, it's a hit."

I tried a bunch of things on the song. Nothing worked. It was perfect the way it is. There's really no keyboard on the song. As far as I know, there aren't any versions with what I tried on my keyboard.

Parissi said to me that day, "If this is a hit, do you want to join our band?" I said, "Yeah. We'll see what happens."

Then I played on the rest of the album, listed as a session musician.

WILD CHERRY ON TOUR

MARK: So they called me and said they were starting a tour. I went from some Holiday Inn in Akron to the Capital Centre in Washington D.C. — the first Wild Cherry gig on the "Play That Funky Music" tour. 20,000 people. We were opening for Graham Central Station.

That show took place August 8, 1976: The crowd inside was packed to the rafters, waiting for the funk band featuring Larry Graham, formerly of Sly & the Family Stone. Outside, 2,000 unsatisfied fans who couldn't get tickets stormed the arena, trying to break down the doors. The siege led to a chain of melees, which built into a confrontation with police. A lengthy round of property damage and bottle-tossing ended in eight arrests). [13.7] Five police cars were damaged, and arrest charges included assault, tampering with a motor vehicle and possession of PCP. [13.8]

MARK: That was the first gig.

The platinum single was Wild Cherry's ticket to awards season in the new year. In January, the band split the American Music Awards' Best Soul Single trophy, in a tie with Lou Rawls' "You'll Never Find Another Love." They didn't see the win coming.

MARK: We watched the AMAs from home because it was the first year. For some reason we didn't go. We didn't think it was a big deal. We thought it was a big deal when it happened. I called Bob.

With the band home in Ohio, the award was accepted by Mark's future musical cousin-in-law: Jaggerz collaborator Wolfman Jack, who looked like he was pulled onto stage at the last minute.

"All the guys in Wild Cherry, I know they're really blown away right now," said a wide-eyed, grinning Wolfman. "Wild Cherry sends *funky love* and *great appreciation*." [13.9]

The band didn't miss the Grammys, where they were featured performers and nominees. February 19, 1977, Wild Cherry played the televised awards show, on a bill with Peter Frampton and Fleetwood Mac. The band lipsynced, but still had the swanky crowd dancing in the aisles. Bandleader Parissi, appropriately, received the most camera time. Mark was visible on the side, grooving along, resplendent in an all-white tux and a matching bowtie the size of a championship boxing belt.

Wild Cherry was nominated for Best New Artist and Best R&B Vocal Performance by a Duo, Group or Chorus. Billy Davis Jr. and Marilyn McCool took home the R&B award. Starland Vocal Band — of "Afternoon Delight" renown — won Best New Artist, beating a field that included Boston. The stars were out that night.

MARK: I was backstage in the wings with Barbra Streisand and sitting right by Ringo.

Mark didn't make any new friends in Hollywood, but other brushes with all-time icons followed.

MARK: Eventually, we did the Isley Brothers tour for six months. Then Earth, Wind & Fire. The Jacksons, with Michael Jackson.

One day, I was tapped on the shoulder: "Michael will meet you now."

We all were invited separately to meet him.

I was like, "Okay."

I think he thought it was a very polite thing to do. He was nice, and it was a sweet gesture on his part.

So one by one, we were led to the room. It was a normal, sweaty locker room. And Michael was there.

He was very nice and soft-spoken. It was kind of awkward, because we were both shy, making small talk for five minutes.

We toured with all these African-American bands, because everybody thought we were black.

Once when we were on tour with Rufus-Chaka Khan. One day after sound check in some hall, there was a piano in the back room. So I went in there to practice, and I was jamming away. And all of a sudden, Chaka Khan comes in, and she felt like singing. So the two of us jammed on Beatles songs for about a half hour. You should hear Chaka Khan sing "Maybe I'm Amazed."

Wild Cherry's commercial fortunes were all downhill after their 1976 full-length debut.

Wild Cherry's sophomore album, *Electrified Funk*, was rushed out in early 1977. It stalled after sales reached 400,000. As is so common in the industry, the number was an exceptional success *and* a dejecting disappointment. Over the next two years, four singles failed to crack the *Billboard* Top 40. A super-sexy cover photo and two Motown covers didn't lure the masses back for 1978's *I Love My Music*. The third record featured eight other songs, seven of them written solely by Parissi.

MARK: We were clearly going to be a one-hit wonder, but we didn't know it. I think Bobby was talented. He knew what he was doing. I learned a lot about how to put together records.

I Love My Music wasn't the reaffirmation of relevance Parissi wanted. But for Mark, the sessions were the beginning of a major career pivot. He met an engineer who, as fate had it, was a familiar face.

> " One day after
> sound check in some hall, there
> was a piano in the back room. So I
> went in there to practice, and I was
> jamming away. And all of a sudden,
> Chaka Khan comes in, and... the two
> of us jammed on Beatles songs for
> about a half hour. You should
> hear Chaka Khan sing
> "Maybe I'm Amazed".
>
> **~ MARK AVSEC**

Wild Cherry (Mark far left, Donnie seated front)

CHAPTER 14

Wild Cherry: When Donnie Met Mark

The Donnie Iris-Mark Avsec partnership sparked in a fabled recording studio that was the birthplace of a hundred bona-fide classics. But first, they met in a humbler studio closer to home, in Donnie's Beaver County backyard.

MARK: The third Wild Cherry album, we did at Jerry's studio. That was first time I was in Jeree's. Donnie was engineering.

I was impressed with the situation, because my first girlfriend when I was 15, Lynn Rosatti, she loved "The Rapper." So it was weird, like, "Wow! The guy who played 'The Rapper' is engineering my session!"

The Donnie-Mark friendship took some time and miles to develop.

MARK: Donnie thought I was weird that day; he'll tell you that. I was quiet, pensive.

DONNIE: I thought he was a very strange dude. Very weird. He didn't say a whole lot. A lot of the other guys in the band, especially Bobby Parissi, were really outgoing. Mark was more quiet. That was my first impression.

But in the studio, it didn't take long to realize this guy had a lot of brains, a lot of talent, a lot of ambition.

MARK: That's why Donnie and I are a good team: Donnie is the exact opposite of me. Donnie's happy-go-lucky. I have to *do* it. He's a very nice guy who's laid back. I'm weird.

This would have been '78. I'm 24-ish. I had been doing music since high school. I'm trying to figure out my life.

The title track of "I Love My Music" peaked at number 69 on *Billboard*'s singles chart April 1, 1978. It held the position for a week and slid down the rankings. But at least — unlike the album itself — the song did chart. So the band were back to the drawing board in short order.

MUSCLE SHOALS / F.A.M.E.

Many a half-assed history correctly notes that Donnie and Mark met as members of in Wild Cherry — then incorrectly says they sang or played on "Funky Music." In fact, both of them arrived after the song was ready to go, Mark very soon afterward, Donnie much later.

MARK: Wild Cherry starts falling apart. Before it did, Parissi had the idea he wanted another guitar player. He knew Donnie and knew his reputation as part of the Jaggerz.

DONNIE: It was always Parissi's thing. He was the engineer, the producer, the writer.

At this point, Donnie was 34. The veteran had been back in the minor leagues for three years now. Iris jumped at the chance to get back in a major-label band.

DONNIE: One of the guys was being let go, and they needed someone. Bobby and I got along real well. As far as what he taught me: He let me know I could do this, that I could do this again. Bobby needed somebody like me to back him up, and that's why he hired me.

Wild Cherry's fourth — and final — album was a do-or-die campaign. Belkin lined up his client with a roster full of ringers.

The band's management arranged for Parissi and the crew to record with the legendary Rick Hall at FAME (Florence Alabama Music Enterprises) Studios, more widely known as the succinct "Muscle Shoals." Hall founded and owned the Alabama studio.

Hall's endless production credits included Wilson Pickett, Clarence Carter, Etta James, Mac Davis, and Andy Williams. The magical studios had hosted sessions by Aretha Franklin ["I Never Loved a Man (The Way I Love You)"], Lynyrd Skynyrd (*Skynyrd's First*), Wilson Pickett ("Land of 1,000 Dances" and "Mustang Sally"), the Rolling Stones ("Wild Horses"), Paul Simon ("Kodachrome"), and dozens of other classic albums by bands from all over the world.

MARK: On the one hand, it's just a studio. But knowing the history, it felt like magic. What was palpable was a real music business town where publishing was active: You could write a song, and someone would give you a little advance if they liked it, and then sign it up and actively pitch it. And there was an audience of producers and A&R folks who were looking for material. So that was something.

The level of musicianship. The active scene. All the stories about how Barry Beckett and company left Rick Hall to form Muscle Shoals Sound. The fact that we were in the same studio that so many great records were made. That was something.

Parissi, in his band's desperate last gasp, was finally willing to give up the reins *and* pass the mic. For Wild Cherry's fourth album, half the songs were written by a host of outside songsmiths that Hall had corralled.

"Look at Her Dance" was penned by Russ Ballard, the former Argent frontman whose thick songbook included Ace Frehley's "New York Groove," America's "You Can Do Magic," Rainbow's "Since You Been Gone," and Kiss' "God Gave Rock and Roll to You."

"Hold on to Your Hiney" came courtesy of Tony Joe White, who had written tunes recorded by Elvis Presley, Tina Turner, and Waylon Jennings.

"All Night's All Right" was the work of W.D. Parks, who wrote the Jackson 5's "Dancing Machine," but had more credits working for artists like Dolly Parton, Dusty Springfield, and Joan Baez.

Clarence Edward Jones was a behind-the-scenes fixture at Muscle Shoals. He helped Parissi co-write the slick, sax-polished disco funk sequel "Keep on Playin' That Funky Music" with Harrison Calloway. Calloway's writing credits spanned from Bobby Womack to Roy Orbison.

Mark manages to stand out in the mix, surrounded by those high-priced pens for hire. After three years in the band, he finally places a co-write, the piano-powered disco-rock track "Take Me Back."

Donnie didn't receive any writing credits, but he is a presence in "Raindance." The midtempo country-rock stomp was written by Jeff Silbar and Larry Henley. That team later wrote Bette Midler's "The Wind Beneath My Wings."

If *that* crew couldn't get Wild Cherry back on the charts, nobody could.

That crew's collective efforts did not get Wild Cherry Back on the charts.

The album and its only single, "Try a Piece of My Love," did not chart.

MARK: Rick was fine to work with. I never thought, "Oh, man, this guy is a genius." I think luck plays a part in every person's life. I respected Rick for all he had done and we got along fine. I think the film *Muscle Shoals* is pretty accurate.

I met Walt Aldridge through these sessions, Rick Hall's assistant. And I mean: Walt would wash Rick's car if he asked him to. And then at night, Walt would record his own demos. And he was a monster songwriter, went on to write many hit songs for lots of artists.

If you're looking for early hints of Donnie and Mark's creative chemistry, don't. This time out, they're strictly sidemen, running Parissi's plays.

MARK: Donnie and I got closer down there – and that's when I really floated the idea of something he and I would do together.

DONNIE: Honestly, those days are like a whirlwind. Those records did *not* go well. I didn't like them. They weren't happening. So for me to pick out a favorite song, no *way*, man.

That was Bobby's show, and he obviously had a lot of success at it. But there's not a song in there that's really mine. I just thought, "I'm here to help."

MARK: There was not one Wild Cherry song that was a *Mark* song. And that was fine with me. I believe that's really how a band should run: Somebody's got to lead. You're not going to make good music if it's a total democracy in there. It was Bob's vision, and he deserved to have that vision — "Play That Funky Music" was a brilliant thing.

Donnie was mainly in Wild Cherry to play rhythm guitar. What he brings to the table — in our partnership, too: I tend to be not-too-cool, a little cerebral. He would bring, once in a while, a suggestion to make something more *cool*, to give something a better feel.

He would say, "Marvin Gaye would sing it like *this*,' and we would try it a certain way.

Donnie had a really good sensibility. His guitar playing is not great — but even compared to Marty, Marty will admit: If you want a simple part, a *feel* part — anything like that, he'll play it better than Marty. That's because his personality is so laid back that he's really authentic and honest. When we get excited about a project, it's really refreshing to work with him.

I liked him. It was about his ability to sing. I never thought he was represented well on record.

I watched how Bob was putting records together, and I learned a lot. I played what Bob wanted me to play. And a lot of that stuff stuck with me.

I tipped my hat to him and said, "This is his trip. That's cool. I'm going to have my own trip one day."

I always had to prove my value. Even as a lawyer. You're a sideman in a band until you can prove you can write songs. I became a producer to produce my songs because nobody else would. You can't blame people if they don't value you, because they don't know what you can do. How do you get that chance? That's what life's about.

MORE WILD CHERRY ON TOUR

Only the Wild Survive hit the streets in May 1979. Wild Cherry had to promote the record. For Donnie, the barnstorming recharged his stage persona. The group hadn't opened sold-out arena shows recently, but their smaller crowds were bigger than Donnie was used to. Since the first Jaggerz tour in 1970, he had spent most of his career singing in the cozy confines of the supper club circuit. The Wild Cherry band packed their bags, picked roommates, and hit the road.

DONNIE: Wild Cherry was the band that got out there and played large shows the entire time I was with the band. It was great to be back in front of large crowds. That made me feel great. We were in theaters. It was awesome. We had so much fun. We had a good bunch of guys, doing nice shows, flying from one place to another. Bobby flew us everywhere. He was extravagant when it came to stuff like that.

MARK: Donnie and I started rooming together.

I loved Donnie. I thought he was the nicest guy. When I'm around Donnie — this is still the case — I feel better. I feel like a better person. He *makes* me a better person. He's so happy, and I need that. He makes me laugh more. He makes me funnier. We laugh a lot.

DONNIE: We hit it off right away. We respected each other's talents and understood what we could do. Mark and I were both married. Mark definitely wasn't one to party. I was probably more of a partier.

MARK: I read books. I hauled a typewriter on my Wild Cherry tours because I was working on a novel, which is unfinished. In fact, I threw it away a long time ago.

THE TAN MEN

That last major Wild Cherry tour was the beginning of the Cruisers' chemistry. As they bonded, Donnie and Mark started developing a shtick that still brightens every interaction they have.

Donnie and Mark spawned a series of characters that resurface backstage at every show, like the Baked Crusader. (For a taste, watch the extra scenes in the excellent Cruisers documentary *King Cool — Ah! History Of Donnie Iris And The Cruisers*.) Between soundcheck and showtime, Mark becomes The

Tan Man, holding court and opining on all things manly, until the rest of the band are doubled over in laughter. With a pronounced, vaguely European accent, The Tan Man is truly the most interesting — and *manly*, and *tanned* — man alive.

DONNIE: That started in Albuquerque. We were in Albuquerque for a week, waiting to do one show with the O'Jays or somebody like that. And we'd just lay down, getting tanned. We *worked* on it.

MARK, *in a French accent:* Only a *tanned* man can be a true man. And I am *The Tan Man*. You are not truly a man unless you are tanned, man.

MARK, *no accent:* It became our mission to become as tanned as possible. We started with rules: Always wear white. White or yellow. Donnie had a karate outfit.

DONNIE: Mark was an all-business guy — but he was funnier than shit. Lots of fun with that guy.

Donnie and Mark bounced off each other with creative sparks.

MARK: I started smoking cigarettes again because of Donnie, though it's not his fault. We were rooming together, and then he was smoking. We were talking. I said, "Hey, man can I have one of those?"

It was bad for my health, but it's a great synapse connector – I know it's crazy. I felt more focused when I smoked. It was probably good for the music, though I know many would say *I'm* crazy.

At the end of the tour, Wild Cherry was nearing the end of their road. Crowds were thinning. The capital-C concerts were giving way to a series of club shows. Some of the band's late gigs were among their more memorable ones, but not because of musical highlights.

MARK: Greene County, Tennessee. We played a show at gunpoint.

DONNIE: This was later. We were back in clubs, but this was an outdoor show in the mountains of Tennessee.

A 2004 Pittsburgh Metro Guide feature[14.1] captures more dramatic details: "The band entered their dressing room. Found scurrying cockroaches. Decided to change on the bus. The thin crowd of around 'a couple hundred' made the local promoter nervous, and a posse was summoned. Donnie looked outside to see a small crew of a half-dozen bearing shotguns.

"You fixing' to leave?", one of the men asks in an accent that conjures up big screen images of Ned Beatty in the Appalachian woods.

"No," they reply.

"Well, we'll make sure you don't."

When it's time to go on, the gun-toting, good old boys escort them to the stage. As the band plays, they stand nearby, clutching their rifles.

DONNIE: I remember being on the bus. It rained or something. We couldn't finish the show.

They weren't letting us go anywhere. I don't know if they wanted us to finish the show or whatever.

I was like, "Just don't shoot me, man." One of the guys in the crew just took off and ran. Somehow, we got out of there.

After the *Only the Wild Survive* tour, Mark moved on to his next project. Before Parissi pulled the plug on Wild Cherry, he tried to hold the band together with replacement players, under a new manager. Donnie stayed on. But for once in his career, he refused to be team player. He had an allegiance to a bigger, better organization:

In this era, Pittsburgh had become known as The City of Champions. The Steelers won Super Bowl XIII in January. The University of Pittsburgh ("Pitt") had an 11-1 season. And in October, the Pirates advanced to the World Series. Things looked bad for a few days. Then the team rallied from a 3-1 deficit to defeat the Baltimore Orioles in a historic comeback. Donnie blew off work to watch a big win.

MARK: It was the last-gasp days. Donnie was still in the band after I left — except he declined to play some gigs because the Pirates were in the World Series. Which, of course, is Donnie all the way.

DONNIE: The late '70s, I was so into sports. I didn't pay much attention to what was going on, music-wise.

And one time, the manager called me and said we were doing a show during the '79 World Series, somewhere in Tennessee.

I had tickets. I told the guy, I said, "Look, I'm not doing it."

As far as I'm concerned, it was a little club, and it didn't matter. The Pirates were in the World Series, man.

The '79 Pirates were a team I got into. I liked them all: Matlock, Stargell. Mike Easler was one of my favorites. Omar. They had a lot of good players. I had the pleasure of meeting Omar Moreno for the first time about a year ago.

ERIN FUSETTI, DONNIE'S OLDER DAUGHTER: He loves baseball. When we were kids, we had this orange chair. We sat on his lap and watched the Pirates, every game, from beginning to end.

I could name every player from the '79 team. I would show him a batting stance, and he'd guess who I was. I would pretend to be Willie Stargell, Omar Moreno, Manny Sanguillén and other players. We had a lot of fun with it.

Wild Cherry was still signed to Belkin and Maduri's record company. But they handed the management reins to John Apostle, a doo-wop singer turned agent, manager, and promoter. He worked with groups like the Belmonts and Tommy James & the Shondells. [14.2]

MARK: Here's a hint at Donnie's personality: The band was going downhill. They have a new manager now. There were a lot of business breakups going on. Donnie wasn't going to go with him.

I was not going to go with John Apostle. Jonah Koslen wanted me to play keyboards in Breathless. I wanted to be in a Belkin-Maduri band. It was important to me; I was from around here.

Before Mark left Wild Cherry, he told Donnie he'd see him again. On their previous tour, Parissi would take a break and let Donnie front the band for a moment. And that moment gave Mark an idea that would sustain their careers for decades. The accordion champion finally spied an opening to launch his own rock band.

MARK: I was in Wild Cherry, and I saw how that all worked. I had this vision of songs and sounds in my head, that I wanted to realize.

I bought myself a four-track reel-to-reel and I began to write other songs. I never had a cassette; it was always reel-to-reel.

You've got to know your limitations. I was a capable musician, but I wasn't a frontperson. I'm not going to be the lead singer of a band. And that's OK. So, therefore, what's my role?

I was always looking for a great singer I could be a writer for, because I was too weird to be out front.

I heard Donnie sing a Marvin Gaye song, "Ain't That Peculiar," live in concert, with Wild Cherry. And once in a while, he would do this little scream thing. And I was like, "I think I can work with this." And so I said to him, "I want to do a project, more of a rock and roll project."

So when I approached him, I said, "I want to produce."

I saw something special in him. And more than that, I liked him.

I also realized that he would not step on me creatively. He would do anything I wanted him to do, creatively. And that is true to this day. He'll try anything. And he's very open and non-judgmental.

I was looking to work with someone I thought would be good on a team.

Breathless was Jonah's trip. And that was cool.

And *Donnie Iris* was my trip with Donnie. I think our project was more of a band than the other projects. Donnie and I were sensitive, and we realized we had great players. And for the most part, everybody was a part of everything.

DONNIE: I could tell he wasn't messing around. He was going to go for it. And seeing what he could do in the studio, he got things out of me that I didn't know I had. Or he did something with a tune that I wouldn't think of doing.

So Mark had an idea. Donnie was open to it.

But they didn't have a plan.

Not yet.

> The late '70s,
> I was so into sports.
> And one time, the manager
> called me and said we were doing
> a show during the '79 World
> Series, somewhere in Tennessee.
> I had tickets. ...I said, "Look,
> I'm not doing it."As far as I'm
> concerned, it was a little club, and
> it didn't matter. The Pirates were
> in the World Series, man.
>
> ~DONNIE IRIS

CHAPTER 15

Mark Goes Disco: LaFlavour, "Mandolay"

"LaFlavour's 'Mandolay' is a disco classic — I dare you to sit still while listening to it." — RuPaul [15.1]

Mark Avsec doesn't get enough credit. And he often gets the wrong credits.

For 20 years, newspapers and magazines have written variations on "Play That Funky Music, Lawyer Boy" as a headline for profiles of the Wild Cherry member-turned-attorney... who joined the band after the song was written and recorded.

Two of Avsec's bigger songs — his highest chart success and largest payday — are seldom if every publicly connected to him: Bon Jovi's "She Don't Know Me" and LaFlavour's "Mandolay." The latter, an international disco hit, led to the former.

In Wild Cherry, Mark played a supporting role. He only co-wrote one song. When he left, he quickly proved he could accomplish what Wild Cherry had been fruitlessly struggling to do since "Play That Funky Music": write a hit disco song.

When Wild Cherry was crumbling, Mark left. But he remained part of the group's original management stable. Belkin and Maduri still managed the hottest groups in Cleveland. One of their promising new rock bands had a spot for Mark. But first, he did what members of the Belkin-Maduri team did: Pitch in around the organization wherever it needed some help.

MARK: Carl had this artist. And he wanted me to produce them. And they didn't write songs. So I wrote all their songs.

That artist was LaFlavour, a popular local dance band from Massillon, an hour south of Cleveland. Like the Jaggerz, the future members of LaFlavour saw the Beatles on *The Ed Sullivan Show*, formed a band, and began covering soul and Motown tunes. Singer Steve Nervo is still an in-demand name in disco circles.

NERVO: In 2012, I did a show in Atlantic City, at the Taj Mahal. It was called Disco Ball at the Taj Mahal. Heatwave was on the show. The Trampps were on the show. Thelma Huston. Bonnie Pointer. Teri DeSario. That was the 35th anniversary of *Saturday Night Fever*.

My twin brother, Pete, we started when we were 16 years old, with Craig DeBock and Pete Milchak. We started in Massillon, in 1967. We were the Noblemen. Then we were the Blues Soul, that was the first name we went out with. Then it was Dry Ice, and other names. My parents had to be with us, because we were playing in bars.

Over the course of the '70s, they grew and evolved with popular dance music. Their sound and named have changed over a continuous 50-year career. They hit their stride as a sextet when the disco decade was peaking.

STEVE: Finally, we ended up as Flavour, when we started travelling. We'd do shows. We'd do Harrah's in Atlantic City about three times a year. We'd do an hour show, then a group like the Coasters would come up.

We were Flavour, then we were LaFlavour. It was the disco era. Everything was "La Freak," "La this," "La that." So we added "La."

Jules, I think — one of the Belkin brothers saw us at a festival in Solon or some place. He told his brother and Carl Maduri. And that's how we went in and started working with Carl. Carl was producing.

Avsec co-wrote both sides of the band's 1978 debut single with Wild Cherry drummer Ronald Beitle. The song was released in October 1978, on major label Mercury, through Belkin and Maduri's Midwest label. The white-bread Bee Gees homage "As Time Goes By" b/w "Sticks" didn't chart. But Maduri liked Avsec's work enough to invite him back a year later.

STEVE: Mark Avsec was from Belkin. And Mark did most of the producing. Carl came in to see what was going on. But Mark did most of the work.

"Mandolay" was the tune that got us where we were. And even today, it's being played all over the world — and it's been, what, 37 year years later? I did a show with Cynthia Johnson from Lipps, Inc., the "Funkytown" song, in Hollywood. When I got home, her road manager called me and told me to go to a website, and it was a list of the top 100 disco songs of all time. She said, "Check out number five and number 11." Number five is "Funkytown" and number 11 is "Mandolay."

In 2013, *Billboard* re-ranked and renamed its *Top 100 Dance Songs of All-Time*. "Mandolay" still rated close to the top, at number 11, between James Brown's no. 10 "Get Up… I Feel Like Being A Sex Machine" and Donna Summer's no. 12 "I Feel Love." [15.2]

Mark wasn't an active disco fan, but it was impossible to avoid. When Maduri told Mark he needed a dance song, the keyboardist gave it a try. It worked.

MARK: LaFlavour was really popular on the club scene. I listened to the radio. Disco was everywhere. So it wasn't hard to write in that style.

STEVE: We met at a place in Cleveland called the Rare Cherry. It was a big disco club. He came in one afternoon while we were rehearsing, trying to learn some new material. Carl brought him in. We started talking about what they wanted to do.

Mark was fabulous. Working with him was really cool. He was really laid back. It was a good time.

Mark wanted us to work at Jeree's. He was in there all the time, working his ass off. We had some late nights.

Mark did the whole deal. We didn't have any original material. We were a band he could work with and produce for.

MARK: I wrote the track. I was looking for a title. For some reason, "Mandolay" comes into my brain. And then, "What the hell is Mandolay?" I made it a girl's name.

STEVE: I mentioned a song that had a nice, driving beat to it — being a drummer, that was the first thing I latched onto. I got behind the drums, and I took a beat like that, and I twisted it around, played it backward. And Mark liked it, so he got on the keyboard and started playing it. And we played around.

He said, "Alright. I want you to come into the studio tomorrow, at about nine o'clock in the morning. And we'll work on that."

MARK: "Mandolay" sounds Spanish. We made it that whole kind of thing. The lyric is set in a Spanish setting. LaFlavour had three guys who could sing lead. Craig was really the frontman, master of ceremonies for the band. Rick was a really nice guy, the keyboard player, had a nice voice. And Steve, who was the drummer, ended up singing it.

STEVE: Overnight, he wrote the lyrics to this song, "Mandolay." And an hour, two hours later, we had the song recorded.

MARK: I don't remember it that way. I remember: One night, I came in with ideas for a track. We laid it down. Maybe I wrote the lyric then.

STEVE: I was surprised. He had the lyrics. It all kind of clicked. A lot of good music came out of Ohio. Wild Cherry was from here. And "Mandolay," a lot of disco has a lot of Latin feel to it, with the congas and the timbales. That was right in the ballpark.

The vocals, we started out doing soul music. Every one of us in the group were singers. I ended up singing most of the stuff, because when we did "Mandolay," we had just come off the road. Everybody in the band had a cold, a sore throat, including me. I was the only one that had enough of a voice to sing something. That's how I got to sing that song. I lucked out, and it fit me, so that's why I got to sing a lot more of the other songs.

MARK: I'll tell you the truth: I knew Steve was going to sing it, right from the start. But sometimes, I take the long way around in the studio. Because you never know. And I don't like to hurt feelings. And I want to give everybody a chance. And they all wanted to try.

So they all tried it. And Steve, when he sang it, we knew it was right. Maybe it was couched in terms of them being sick and his voice being the best on that day. But in my brain, I wanted Steve to sing it. He had the sound.

When LaFlavour worked at Jeree, Donnie wandered into some sessions and hung around. The band liked Donnie. Donnie liked the band. They would work together again.

LaFlavour's eight-song self-titled record included three six-minute disco epics. Donnie co-wrote and sang on the funkified, hi-tech, horn-infused "Can You Dance," which sounds like Steely Dan gone disco. It's a diverse set: The aggressive "Can't Kill the Beat" is a fist-pumper that wouldn't be out of place on Cruisers record — with a different beat. "Roller Shake" is a respectable bid for skating rink rotations.

During the sessions, Mark made a useful connection for "When the Whistle Blows (Anything Goes)." Avsec decided the track needed the joy of sax. Reed and Garvin recommended Kenny Blake, an acclaimed jazz artist who had recorded at Jeree. In future years, when Avsec needed a horn player for "Back on the Streets" and other tracks, Blake would be the Cruisers' go-to sax man.

Sweet City-Epic released the single "Mandolay" in December 1979. The album followed shortly, in early 1980.

Over the next three years, "Only the Lonely" and "Mandolay" landed LaFlavour on TV from Miami to Italy. As the band's outfits shifted from *Saturday Night Fever* white suits to space-age '80s outfits, a different visual contributed to "Mandalay's enduring popularity: Its unforgettable cover photo of an exquisitely made up woman, apparently wearing only a set of headphones, listening in ecstasy, her head angled up, grasping an ice cream cone, tongue on its tip, about to lower it into her ready mouth. It was shot by another future member of the Donnie Iris team: photographer Robert Holcepl.

HOLCEPL: I have a picture of the model, her last name was Ford, down in my studio. The cover, I can't remember how many ice cream cones they went through when they did that. It was quite a few, if I remember right. She said it was a lot.

"Mandolay" was, by far, the most successful single from the album. It was Avsec's highest charting single ever, and his longest running. The song hit number 77 on the *Billboard* Disco Top 100 chart just before the dance-dominated decade ended: December 15, 1979. It didn't crack the Hot 100 singles chart, but it showed amazing legs on the dance chart. The song peaked at number 7 four months later, on March 15, 1980. It held the position for a week, then began a slow slide off the charts. It held on through the week of May 24.

SEAN ROSS, *ROSS ON RADIO*: There's something a little off-kilter about all the Iris-Avsec hits, even — to the extent it counts — "Mandolay," which is the "Ah! Leah" of disco records. It's why I like them. It might be why they don't endure at radio now, although for a while in the '90s, "Mandolay" came back on WKTU New York, disproportionate to its success at the time.

The follow-up single, "Only the Lonely (Have a Reason to Be Sad)," didn't match "Mandolay" — not that it tried. Instead of spinning up another dance track, the team made a run at the regular singles chart, in a bid for a career beyond dance music.

In one small manner, the record's second single exceeded its predecessor's performance: The hot-tub-and-champagne slow jam graced *Billboard*'s Hot 100 chart June 14, 1980 — but only spent two weeks there. It debuted at 93, then inched to 91. Chicago and Detroit embraced the song, but it shortly disappeared.

Released in March 1981, "To the Boys in the Band" was an eclectic dance tour-de-force that did not chart. But it was a key development in Mark's rock repertoire. The producer also sings multiple tracks on the chorus; it's an early version of the stacked, unison backing vocals heard in signature Cruisers' songs like "Love Is Like a Rock" — moments that people assume are Donnie singing, but aren't always just him.

Mark wrote the songs, but LaFlavour picked up the ball and ran with it. The group would routinely spend 43 weeks a year on the road. Even after the smoking disco track, the band kept honing their old-school showroom revue set.

"Mandolay" proved memorable. At year's end, the song and group resurfaced for *Billboard*'s annual Number 1 Awards. The industry illuminati still tasted LaFlavour. They ranked the group the number 35 artist of the year, behind Sergio Mendes & Brazil '88 (no. 34), but ahead of Erotic Drum Machine Band (36), Blondie (38), and Kool & the Gang (43). The Audience Response poll ranked it the year's number 28 Audience Response Single/Album. [15.3]

At least 22 versions of the "Mandolay" single made their way into various markets between 1979 and 1987: Sweet City licensed it for 7" and 12" versions in America, Germany, Brazil, Italy, Mexico, the Netherlands, Venezuela, Bolivia, Canada, and France. In 1988, the DJ group Yuen Broadcasting Corporation released a limited-press proto-mashup that combined the song and "Stairway to Heaven" in a proto-mashup. Internationally, "Mandolay" reached number 1 on dance charts in the Netherlands and Australia, and number 2 in Italy. [15.4] The album was released in Greece, Spain, Italy, Brazil, the Philippines, Canada, and Venezuela. Mark says the steady spins from Spain still generate regular royalty checks.

MARK: Chris Maduri told me this story one time: He was dating his future wife, who is Mexican. And he was meeting her family in Mexico.

They were asking him what he does for a living. By that time, we had Wild Cherry, Donnie Iris, Michael Stanley. So they said, "What do you do?"

He's trying to answer in broken Spanish: "Wild Cherry."

They hadn't head of that.

"What else?"

"Michael Stanley."

"No, no, no."

"Breathless."

"No, no, no."

"'Mandolay'?"

"Oh my God, yes! But of course! 'Mand-o-lay!'"

It had been number 2 in Italy. Big deal: Five Italians bought the record. It's a funny thing. It got played. It became a cult thing. But it never made a lot of money.

LaFlavour didn't sell a lot. It was a big turntable hit. It got played on the radio once and a while. But it didn't sell records. It did well for LaFlavour's career as a club band. And a lot of people know that song.

As with many of the crew's records, the exact statistics are vague after a certain point. Nearly 40 years later, despite its enduring popularity, it hasn't been certified gold or platinum.

STEVE: The only money I get is when I go do shows, and they pay me to do the performance. We still play, and I sing it with my other group, The Originals. And I did my own recording of it down in my studio downstairs, played and sang. And I get a few bucks here and there, but that's it.

MARK: I don't own publishing on that. I did write it, so I made a few bucks off of it. It's not a lot. But it's one of those songs.

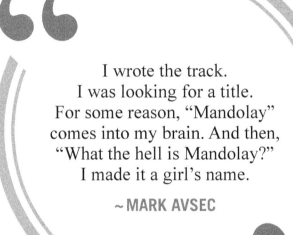

I wrote the track.
I was looking for a title.
For some reason, "Mandolay"
comes into my brain. And then,
"What the hell is Mandolay?"
I made it a girl's name.

~MARK AVSEC

"Breathless" (l. to r.): Bob Benjamin, Mark Avsec, Jonah Koslen, Rodney Psyka, Alan Greene, Kevin Valentine.

Breathless: When Mark Met Kevin

Breathless was the last stop on the road to the Cruisers. It wasn't a long layover, but it was an important one.

1979 was a whirlwind for everybody involved.

Donnie appeared on a major label album, released his solo debut single, and made a cameo on a disco sensation.

Mark was even busier: He appeared on two major-label albums, created a smash disco single — and an album to go with it. And he launched his lifelong collaboration with Donnie.

When Mark left Wild Cherry, Donnie stayed and rode out the fumes. Mark told the singer he'd be back, with material for a new band. Donnie didn't have to wait long.

But he did have to wait.

Breathless mainman Jonah Koslen is one of the great names from Cleveland rock city. The singer-songwriter-guitarist was a key part of the original Michael Stanley Band, the town's definitive group. Mark almost got in on the ground floor, too.

MARK: Michael Stanley almost hired me as a keyboard player.

I was 19 or 20, something like that. I had seen Michael with Jonah and Dan Pecchio at the Agora. And of course, I knew who Michael was: I had seen him on *Midnight Special*. I was very enamored with Michael. And I liked his *Friends and Legends* album very much. They were looking for a keyboard player.

They all came to my mother's house on 61st Street and St. Clair, and set up all their gear in my mother's living room. And I auditioned.

They said, "You have the gig." Then, later, Michael said they didn't have the budget for a keyboard player. So I was really bummed about it. That would have changed the whole course of my life. There might have been no Donnie. Michael wouldn't have been Donnie; I couldn't do my thing with Michael or Jonah. But Donnie, we were partners; he was a willing participant in hearing my ideas.

So I knew Jonah.

As Michael Stanley's lead guitarist and sometimes-singer, Koslen had written some of the band's early classics. On the landmark double live album *Stage Pass*, five of the thirteen songs are Koslen creations: "Nothing's Gonna Change My Mind," "Waste A Little Time On Me," "Pierette," "Wild Sanctuary," and "Strike Up The Band."

Koslen's next band, Breathless, launched in mid-1978. Its first major show was an opening slot for Atlanta Rhythm Section and Crack the Sky — featuring future B.E. Taylor guitarist Rick Witkowski — at Cleveland's Palace Theatre. Following shortly was a gig warming up the stage for Wild Cherry at the 4,000-capacity Mansfield Skating Coliseum. A year later, the band was still getting its act together.

MARK: Wild Cherry were splintering apart. And eventually, people were having to leave the band, because there was no more money. And I got asked to join Breathless at that time, so I did.

As a sideman in Breathless, Mark rapidly notched two more major label albums. And, more importantly, he picked up a couple key players while in the group — most notably Cruiser Kevin Valentine. Breathless carried Cleveland's rock and roll dreams on their shoulders for a bright moment.

ALAN GREENE, GUITARIST: During that era, Michael Stanley was on his way to becoming a local legend. Michael and Jonah both were great writers, really prolific. It was like Neil Young and Stephen Stills working together, two strong talents in a big band. Jonah was always seen as a real partner of Michael's. Any time that Jonah shows up at a Michael Stanley show, the place goes nuts. Not to diminish either one's status, but people loved them together. I would absolutely say they were the top of the hill of the scene. Michael in Cleveland is like Donnie Iris in Pittsburgh.

"Breathless" (l. to r.): Rodney Psyka, Alan Greene, Kevin Valentine, Jonah Koslen, Mark Avsec.

They were formed in the music of the era — bands like Foreigner, Journey, Bob Seger... what would come to be called arena rock. That's what those guys were going for, the same market Bob Seger succeeded in.

KEVIN: Joining Breathless was a big deal. My first label-recording band. First major touring. We always hoped for the best.

Koslen launched Breathless in 1978 and began developing an anthemic, infectious strain of what would soon be known as album-oriented rock, or AOR for short. The band kept the tunes simple. Koslen wrote all the songs. And he made sure crowds could sing along — and dance, thanks to some lingering disco-rock beats. Add in a new keyboardist, and they had something for everybody.

KEVIN: We rehearsed at the Shore Theatre in [Cleveland inner-ring suburb] Euclid. Big old movie theater. We had the whole building for years. It was like being at an amusement park that was abandoned. We made a bubble of visqueen plastic in the area where you would buy popcorn and where the seats were. We would just heat the bubble. It was still kind of cold in the winter.

MARK: Jonah and I got together at the bar. I said, "Look, I'll join the band. I'll be perfectly happy to support you and play keys to your songs, but I have one condition: You'll have to tolerate me having a side project. It's time for me to write songs. I need to do my writing. And Jonah said, "I have no problem with that." He knew I wanted to write and produce.

They were going to have a record deal. When Breathless got a deal, we went to Criteria [Recording] Studios in Miami, with Don Gehman producing the first record.

Once again, the story's main characters found themselves in the company of a music industry giant, but not at the right time. Breathless' self-titled debut was produced by Gehman, who would later produce a slew of John Mellencamp albums, beginning with his breakout, *American Fool*; R.E.M.'s *Life's Rich Pageant*; and Hootie & the Blowfish's 16 million-selling *Cracked Rear View*.

MARK: Don Gehman was mainly an engineer at the time. I thought he was nice. He was very laid back, and quiet. I did not think he was a real heavy producer. He went on to do very well. I did not foresee his success.

Producers come in all varieties: I am a music guy, heavy on the vision and the writing and the arrangements. Don is more laid back, more of the great engineer. But I have no idea how John Mellencamp's records were put together – Don may have been very actively involved in arrangements too. I know he's got great ears.

Some producers are really technical, and they're good for getting great sounds. Then you have other producers like a Phil Spector, who really just controls everything and writes everything. I decided I wanted to be the guy behind the scenes, who just writes a lot of songs and produces records.

The band kept good company at the studio.

MARK: I used to stand behind Barry Gibb in the morning to get coffee. They were recording the sequel to *Saturday Night Fever*.

Avsec took a liking to the drummer, Kevin Valentine. Percussionist Rodney Psyka would work with the Cruisers eventually. Mark also liked guitarist Alan Greene, one of the city's secret weapons. They had worked together before, briefly.

MARK: Before Breathless, he was in a blues band called Jimmy Ley and the Coosa River Band – Alan was great. I really admired the band and his playing. I got a chance to sit in with them during a live-on-air Agora concert. I thought I hit the big time with that. I wish I had the tape of that one. That was long before Wild Cherry.

Kevin and Mark didn't click in a big way — not that Kevin knew, anyway. Mark penciled him into a secret plan he was drafting.

KEVIN: There was no Hollywood moment when I thought, "I could work with Mark in the future!" Mark doesn't hang much, so there wasn't much chit-chat, which is where a moment like that would happen. He simply liked my playing.

Back at the office, Belkin was getting to know Mark, who entered the shop as one of Maduri's top recruits, and eventually became Belkin's star pupil. Belkin had to make some canny moves to keep Mark alive on the road — but not because of the usual lifestyle-related pitfalls other clients had encountered.

BELKIN: Mark has a lot of quirks. He sleepwalks. Kevin does, too. In Miami, they were recording. I rented a home for them. It had a pool out in the back. So they would record during the day. What we had to do at night was to tie their wrists to the bed, so they couldn't get up and sleepwalk, because we had the pool. I can tell that story. I have two other stories I can't tell.

EMI — with Belkin and Maduri's Sweet City imprint — released Breathless' self-titled debut in July 1979. Mark hoisted his Yamaha Grand, and Clavinet, and a B-3 into the truck. And the band was on the road, playing big gigs.

GREENE: Mark was wonderful to play with. He was one of the nicest guys you could ever know. He was always a great, innovative, creative, insightful, classically aware musician. I never saw him treat another musician like he was better or he knew more. He would collaborate. He knew what to put where, what sounded great.

He was fun onstage, because he'd have four banks of keyboards, and he'd wrap himself around them, one arm stretched out the left, one stretched out to the right on another keyboard. It looked cool — that was the era.

Breathless landed a primo slot opening for Kiss in 15 cities, on the tour for the controversial *Dynasty* album, which featured the disco stab "I Was Made for Lovin' You."

Audiences averaged around 6,000. [16.1] On the fly, Breathless tightened up their 50-minute set in a trial by pyro. The band had to let the music and energy do the talking. Their barebones stage production —

a handmade BREATHLESS banner stretched across Valentine's drum riser — couldn't compete with the headliners' extravaganza of smoke, lights and blood.

KEVIN: Talk about a tough audience. There's no opening for that. You can't open for a cartoon character. We were an extra 40 minutes for fans to get into their seats.

We had a percussion player, Rodney. We'd enter through his side, walking up the stairs. And we'd hear, "KISS! KISS! KISS!" The lights would come on, and I would whack a gong to make some noise to calm people down and let us get onstage. It's hard to win over a crowd like that.

On that tour, Kevin met his future boss and collaborator, Gene Simmons. They didn't connect immediately, but Simmons did provide some lessons.

KEVIN: Gene yelled at Alan Greene for wearing some other band's shirt. He's a marketing genius. What we learned from him was: Don't open for Kiss. It's not going to work out well.

The driving single "Takin' it Back" spent four weeks in the *Billboard* singles chart, but peaked at number 92 January 12, 1980. When the album's sole single sputtered, Koslen and the band bounced right back into the studio. While the album gestated, Belkin and Maduri kept the band visible with a show at Blossom, June 23, 1980. Even with all seats priced at $5, the Breathless outside summer show didn't turn into the sensation the Michael Stanley Band concerts became.

Breathless' heavier second album, *Nobody Leaves This Song Alive*, was recorded at the Sound City studios in Los Angeles, one of the great studios in worldwide rock history. It was the birthplace of a string of classic albums by artists including Neil Young (*After the Gold Rush*), Nirvana (*Nevermind*), Tom Petty (*Damn the Torpedoes*), and Metallica (*Death Magnetic*). They finished the sessions in Burbank, at the studio of producer Michael Verdict, an Eagles engineer who had a good run in the 80s: As a songwriter, producer and studio ace, his credits include Ted Nugent's *Little Miss Dangerous* and a Jay Ferguson album that doesn't have "Thunder Island."

KEVIN: The facility was a bit run down when we were there. So you think, "*This* is Sound City?!" Then you hear the sound, and you say "Oh yes, *this* is Sound City!!"

MARK: We really just did drum tracks at Sound City. I just played my parts on that record. That is why I had to do my own thing.

Koslen, again, wrote the entire album. Mark and Kevin aren't an influence, but they're a presence. Kevin's dramatic beats are the kick in opening track "Hearts in Hiding." Mark's keys serve as a call and response to the vocals and drums. Alan Greene's arena-sized riffing would earn him an initiation to Avsec's Cellarful of Noise project later.

Billboard reviewed the second Breathless album in the same issue as the first Cruisers album. A blurb declared, "Backed by a slick production, power riffs and catchy choruses, this sextet explores the back alleys of the teenage mind. The music is formulaic but well-executed and should fare well in the FM hard rock derby. Mark Avsec's keyboards add some interesting undertones and colorations." [16.2]

The Cruisers formed, recorded, and rapidly outpaced Breathless.

GREENE: Before Breathless came to a conclusion, Mark asked Jonah if he could write some songs. And Jonah rejected it. I never felt like there was any animosity, but that was a factor in him leaving.

MARK: The way Breathless worked: Jonah had left Michael Stanley so he could write all the material and be the leader of a benevolent dictatorship, like Springsteen was doing. Jonah was really modeling after that. So Jonah brought songs. Jonah writes great songs, and he's prolific. But the methodology… Breathless was like a job; they wanted to rehearse every day. I personally thought they rehearsed too much. There's a lot of yoemanship, and there's a lot to be said for that. But…

KEVIN: Even to this day, when we go into the studio with Donnie, we don't rehearse. It's a very natural, spontaneous thing.

MARK: We used to rehearse songs like crazy in Breathless. When we went into the studio, they were fully formed. And I can understand. We had strict budgets, we were at Criteria, a lot of people in the room — it maybe would have been chaotic and crazy.

Philosophically, to me, there wasn't enough room for magic to happen that way.

To me, I really believe the track tells you what it needs. My style of recording is: Go in without knowing what you're going to do, and let the magic happen. Trust your instincts. Do what the music tells you to do, what the music tells you it needs.

Breathless wasn't that much of an influence on me. But Breathless was Jonah's trip. I said, "That's fine" and told him I'd give him 100% doing that. And he was very open to any keyboard parts I wanted to play, and encouraging that. And we had the understanding I was going to work on something on the side. And that ended up being Donnie Iris.

> Any time that Jonah shows up at a Michael Stanley show, the place goes nuts. Not to diminish either one's status, but people loved them together. I would absolutely say they were the top of the hill of the scene. Michael in Cleveland is like Donnie Iris in Pittsburgh.
>
> ~ ALAN GREENE

D. X. FERRIS

"Bring on the Eighties": Donnie's Debut

1979. The story of Donnie Iris and the Cruisers truly starts. After decades of practice and preparation.

Donnie is at a critical juncture: He hasn't had a hit song for a decade.

After a lifetime of practice, Mark is running hot after a crash-course apprenticeship. He's ready to show the world what he can do.

Donnie Iris is 36.

Mark Avsec is 25.

In 1979, between the two of them, they have a full fifty years of musical experience. Both began seriously performing music shortly after they stopped wearing diapers. And they stepped into the spotlight soon thereafter, Donnie as a televised singer, Mark as a competitive accordionist.

Decades later, the duo have nine major-label albums, a platinum chart-topping single, and a top-ten dance hit under their combined belts. But none of them is a true collaboration between the two artists.

Donnie had written a number 1 single, "The Rapper," in 1969. They met as foot soldiers in a one-hit wonder band that was weathering flagging fortunes. Donnie and Mark couldn't pull Wild Cherry out of its tailspin, but they found each other.

Donnie had been a professional recording artist for 11 years, Mark for three. Mark made them count: He became a full-time musician in a bar band, in 1976, headlining Holiday Inns. Over the next few years, the rookie signed to a chart-topping band, played sold-out arenas, appeared with his victorious group at the Grammy Awards, recorded six major-label albums, and worked with a handful of big-league producers, who taught him how to make a record.

MARK: I was sick-focused. I am serious. I was so mentally focused that my brain hurt. To the exclusion of all else. And I made certain decisions in my life around that über-focus, decisions I still live with.

And now Avsec's aching brain is focused on Dominic Ierace, who for ten years had been known nationwide as Donnie Iris. Donnie was just getting started.

MARK: Once I got in Wild Cherry, Robert Parissi knew what he was doing, in terms of how you put together records and tracks. And I got it. I had been with Rick Hall down in Muscle Shoals, watched him work. So then I was ready to go really produce a record.

And Donnie knew what he was doing, too. Donnie had really good sensibilities. If I started getting too schmaltzy or too musical, Donnie had a really good connection to authentic soul music, so to speak.

So Donnie was the first thing I really did.

From the start, Mark doesn't want to simply get together and jam out some groovy tunes. He wants this project to be big. He isn't going to start without the right kind of backing.

CHRIS MADURI: Mark Avsec came to my father and myself and had an idea of producing Donnie Iris as a solo artist. We thought that was a cool idea. We were looking to grow our business with new artistry.

Donnie could sing. He wasn't a great, great singer. But he had a style. And look. And they had excellent ideas. And Mark was an excellent songwriter. So you put all those things together….

Mark had pop culture sensitivities, is the best way I can put it. He had a good idea on what teenage kids wanted to hear. I saw that and backed it. They went into the studio and did a couple songs.

FOX: Carl came in and said, "We're putting this band together, and the guy's from Beaver Falls. He's going to work with Mark." With Wild Cherry and with Breathless, Mark had gained my respect early.

One part at a time, Mark develops a secret plan. Donnie said he was interested in working with Mark. But musicians say a lot of things. Mark has to make sure Donnie is interested. Convincing Donnie to leave home, jump in his car, hit the turnpike, and drive two hours to Cleveland? It's not the most inviting proposition. If Mark wants Donnie to commit to his new project, he knows he has to make it easy. It isn't the best studio he's ever seen, not by a long shot. But Mark likes Jeree.

BELKIN: Carl had a very good relationship with Jeree's. He recorded most of his projects there. Jerry's quality was good, and he priced very reasonably.

MARK: It was a little studio. It didn't look great. But I tried it, because I was desperate to work with Donnie. And he lived near there. We made "Bring on the Eighties" there.

Mark has a plan. He has backing. But he doesn't have material. Or a name. Or a sound. Just a singer. But if Donnie is on your team, you have something to work with. Now he needs some more people to fill out the lineup.

In mid-1979, disco is still selling. Maduri wanted to make a disco track. Mark agreed. He had written a dance song. But now, if he is going to use a disco beat, it has to hit hard. Mark knows a guy: Kevin Valentine from Breathless. On the road and in the studio, Valentine has proved he is a skilled player who understands the entire process.

MARK: He was a good drummer. I liked him personally.

Kevin was always great, because he's a producer at heart. That's what he does for a living now. Kevin is not just a drummer. He is somebody who understands a record. He knows what to do with his high-hat, because he's already anticipating how the reverb will make it in the mix.

Like everybody in the story, Kevin is excited to meet *The "Rapper" Guy*. Donnie meets and exceeds his expectations.

KEVIN: Mark asked me if I wanted to play on demos for these two songs. So that's when he and Donnie and I got together.

I knew "The Rapper." Loved that song. Donnie was an easygoing nice guy. That's all there is to say. He wasn't a jerk. You couldn't hate him in a million years.

"BRING ON THE EIGHTIES"

Drafting a band, Mark and Donnie start with people they know. Mark leans on Breathless guitarist Alan Greene. Donnie taps Robert Peckman, a burly bassist who was in a late Jaggerz lineup.

MARK: I did use Alan on the first two songs. He was very gracious. When we formed the band, I just did not want to plunder Breathless. Later, Donnie did see Marty and was really high on him.

The Cruisers' beginnings are humble and unusual. At this point, the collected group of friends, strangers and secondhand associates are not The Cruisers. They are not even "Donnie Iris." They're just a few guys making some music — and connections.

Donnie's forgotten solo debut, the first full collaboration between Rustbelt brothers Iris and Avsec, is a two-song single: "Bring on the Eighties" b/w "Because of You."

MARK: "Bring on the Eighties" was basically a novelty — but I didn't see it at the time; that's how myopic I was.

In the song, some rote lyrics bring the listeners up to speed regarding the later 20th century's history of social and political upheaval. Singing Mark's words over a straightforward beat, Donnie narrates: "In the 1970s, our wounds, they needed convalescence / Watergate was the last straw, so we invented discotheques."

Mark will write better lyrics in the coming months. But Donnie delivers, showing his range on a soaring chorus. "Bring on the Eighties" is not an auspicious beginning — but it's not nothing.

"BECAUSE OF YOU"

The B side looks backward to 1978, and it sounds like a finalist for the third annual America's Whitest Disco Track competition.

MARK: When the project started, it was not rock and roll. Carl had the idea of doing a remix of Tony Bennett's "Because of You," a disco song.

So we did "Because of You," which was really weird.

We were going along with the disco thing — that kind of thing happening — but with a little more substance, a little more rocky. A little bit, not a lot. We had a so-many-beats-per-minute thing happening.

It sucked. I don't have a copy of it.

That lackluster debut yields a career-defining moment for Donnie and Mark.

MARK: That was the first time I stacked Donnie's voice. And stacking his voice was a good moment.

I was still trying to find my sound. It's not a *Donnie Iris* record at all… *except* I started stacking up his voice. I loved the way it sounded. They rubbed up really nicely. It was amazing. I was *excited*. It was awesome.

By then, I felt pretty confident that I knew how to make records.

Stacking. One vocal track, played on top of a similar — but not identical — take. Played on top of yet another. And another. All played at the same time, the overlapping sounds create a new effect, a textured echo. When the wall-of-sound vocals in "Ah! Leah!" bowl you over, the stacking is what you're reacting to, the *rub*. Mark didn't invent it. But he stumbled across it. And it put Donnie and Mark on their way to "Ah! Leah!"

FOX: I heard their first raw demos, and I thought, "Man, I *want* these guys. I want to work with them." And that was great fun.

MADURI: And we felt, at that point, we had a new artist.

As Donnie, Mark, and Kevin are cooking up this new — and as-yet-unnamed — project, Belkin and Maduri are putting arrangements in place that will guide the rest of their careers.

April 1979: Donnie signs what later legal documents will refer to as "the Donnie Iris Agreement." The contract gives the Belkin-Maduri Organization his exclusive services as a recording artist, for management. Donnie signs to Belkin and Maduri's Midwest Records as a recording artist.

August, 1979: Carl Maduri signs a production deal with Carousel Records, a California company. Now Maduri is under contract to provide finished master tapes and artwork to Carousel, which will provide production, distribution and promotion through a major label.

November 1979: The "Because of You"/"Bring on the Eighties" single arrives in the Belkin-Maduri offices. And some regional radio stations. Then on a couple airwaves. Then the disco tracks recede.

MARK: Maybe it got a couple spins in Cleveland. Without airplay, it don't happen.

Mark and Donnie don't mind much. They are ready to move on to Secret Plan Phase II. Mark doesn't love the single. But he loves the singer.

MARK: I was drawn to Donnie. I also realized that he would not step on me creatively. He would do anything I asked him to do, creatively. And that is true to this day. He'll try anything. He's very open and non-judgmental. When he does contribute, he's very cool. Because he's got a good sense of the historical context of soul music and rock and the Beatles and everything like that.

So we were a really good team. We trusted each other.

When I said, "How about if we do an album?"

We didn't know it was gonna be "Donnie Iris."

When we started the first Donnie Iris album, I did tell Donnie, "Let's do a solo album for you" – but we weren't absolutely sure.

This was my project. I decided to call it "Donnie Iris."

I made Donnie the star. We could have called it a band name. Or we could have called it "Avsec and Iris," but I thought that was gonna be stupid. So we made it *Donnie Iris*, and I would be the guy behind the scenes.

Which I got used to. If Donnie was an asshole or if I was an asshole, this thing never would have worked. But we loved each other and knew we needed each other. The whole band, really.

We all had our roles.

Since I wasn't going to be the artist, I did want to make my mark as a producer.

I really liked Roy Thomas Baker's stuff. I was looking for something. I didn't want the studio to be a place of documentation for me. I wanted it to be a place of innovation. So that was the principle implicit to me: I didn't want to set up a mic and record. Even Donnie, without working the vocals — this is not Springsteen, where you set up a mic and capture the magic.

I was trying to be like a Roy Thomas Baker. What could I do? I stacked voices, trying to create an interesting record. I felt like anybody could go in and *use* the studio. I wanted to *innovate*. I wasn't trying to sound like Queen, but I was inspired by that.

"Because of You" was the beginning of that.

Next, we recorded a song with Donnie that was supposed to be for an R&B group, called "Get It On." I wrote that for Sly, Slick and Wicked — that was a Maduri band, an R&B band.

Wiser, Mark and Donnie record a third song: "Get It On," which Cruiser fans know as "Shock Treatment," the last tune from the first Donnie album, *Back on the Streets*. It features a holdover from that pre-Cruisers moment: bassist Robert Peckman, who was also part of Belkin-Maduri band Q.

DONNIE: He played with Jaggerz. Maybray, Davies and Peckman formed a band called November after. Picky played with a lot of bands. Great musician, great singer. He sounds like Wilson Pickett.

MARK: It was not going to be a Donnie song. Maybe it was for Donnie… until we figured out what Donnie was going to be. It was a crappy song. It later became "Shock Treatment." It wasn't very good. I couldn't make it in for the session one day. Without me there, Donnie did this thing, and he recorded a vocal track. It was just too ordinary.

The sessions are creeping along. In January 1980, Mark hears something that galvanizes his creative energies, featuring another musician from Northeast Ohio: singer Chrissie Hynde.

MARK: Then we started finding our vibe. The Pretenders album came out, which I loved. I wanted to do songs that had the urgency of the Pretenders, from a rock-and-roll standpoint. But then combine it with the beauty of the stacks and the harmonies. And that's what we were starting to do. That's when we started really recording tracks for the album.

Anything I did with Donnie before what became on the album — we did before we thought about putting together *our* band for the special sessions. I was merely testing the waters with Donnie, experimenting.

> That was the first time
> I stacked Donnie's voice. And
> stacking his voice was a good
> moment. ...It's not a Donnie Iris
> record at all… except I started
> stacking up his voice. ...I loved the
> way it sounded. It was amazing.
> I was excited. It was awesome.
>
> ~MARK AVSEC

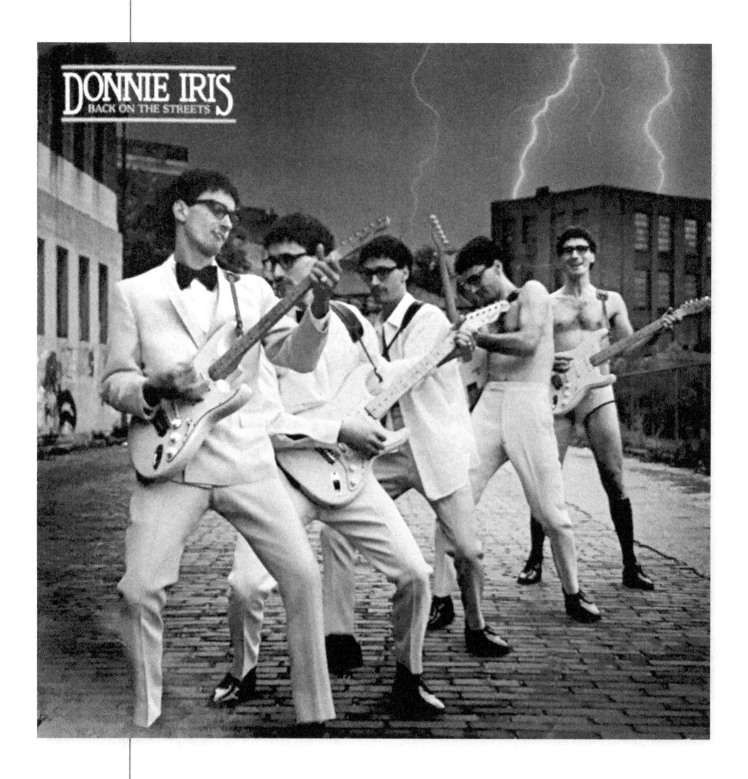

D. X. FERRIS

CHAPTER 18

Back on the Streets: The First Album, the One With "Ah! Leah!"

Back on the Streets

The first album by Donnie Iris (and the band that would, shortly, come to be known as the Cruisers). Featuring...

Side 1:
"Agnes" (Mark Avsec, Dominic Ierace) 3:30
"You're Only Dreaming" (Avsec, Ierace, McClain, Hoenes, Kevin Valentine) 4:45
"She's So Wild" (Avsec, Ierace, McClain, Hoenes, Valentine) 2:35
"Daddy Don't Live Here Anymore" (Avsec, Ierace) 3:49
"Too Young to Love" (Avsec) 5:31

Side 2:
"Ah! Leah!" (songwriting credits: Avsec, Ierace) 3:46
"I Can't Hear You" (Avsec, Ierace, McClain, Hoenes, Valentine) 3:40
"Joking" (Avsec, Ierace) 4:05
"Shock Treatment" (Avsec) 3:48
"Back on The Streets" (Avsec, Ierace) 3:36

(Versions after Midwest release switch original side 1 and side 2.)

Original release: July 1980, Midwest Records
MCA/Carousel Records national re-release: October 1980
Peak position on *Billboard* album chart: 57, December 20, 1980
Weeks on chart: 23
Top single: "Ah! Leah!" b/w "Joking"
Single's peak *Billboard* Hot 100 position: 29, February 28, 1981
Weeks on chart: 18

"*Back on the Streets* is a blend of meat-and-potatoes rock and new wave, which succeeds due to its simple nature and some infectious hooks."

— Tom Demalon, *All Music Guide to Rock*[18.1]

From the credits:
Produced by Mark Avsec for the Belkin-Maduri Organization
Executive Producer: Carl Maduri
Kevin Valentine appears courtesy of EMI records
Recording Engineer: Jerry Reed (thanks for your dedication and patience) and thanks to Don Garvin for his invaluable assistance.
Recorded at Jeree Studios, New Brighton, PA Spring 1980.

Original release: MWL1984 Midwest National Records
Re-release: MCA-3272 MCA Records
CD Release: MCA-35415 Razor & Tie/MCA Records
Out of print.

With three tracks in the can, Donnie and Mark knew they had something. And they knew what kind of thing it was going to be. And they knew what to call it — for now. But they needed a crew to *make* it.

Recording those first three tracks, Donnie gladly accepted feedback. He trusted the people around him to bring out his best.

FOX: The thing that pinches me about Donnie: It's a personality trait, rather than a music trait — and that's what leads to his music. Donnie is the most even-keeled person I've ever met. He doesn't get angry. Doesn't get upset. He just floats. He goes with it. He's got a natural-born talent for singing. He's, what, 75 this year? His voice has lost nothing. Absolutely nothing. That's nothing short of astonishing. He goes against a lot of the rules. He's not one of these guys who does a lot of vocal scales before he goes out on stage. He just has it. He can just walk out on stage, night after night after night after night, and be at his best.

I've never met anyone else who is that gracious with everything around him. Even the ones like that still have issues: "I want this," "I want that," "Why is the light in my eye?!" Nothing upsets Donnie.

And it's a brilliant way to live in this crazy rock and roll world. That's how you get to 75 years old and be able to jump around onstage like a 30-year-old. He's unflappable.

Every question I've ever asked him as a manager or an office rep, the answer 100% of the time was, "It's cool, man. Don't worry about a thing. Everything's fine."

That's a rare talent.

MARK: We said, "OK, it's going to be a rock and roll project." Our goal was to assemble the best guys we could.

I said, "I want Kevin to play. He's a freakin' monster."

At this point, Clevelanders outnumbered Pennsylvanians in the embryonic group. That was about to change. Someone caught Donnie's eye in the Beaver County backwoods, slightly closer to Youngstown than Pittsburgh.

MARK: Donnie said, "*Maaaan*, I saw this guitar player, Marty Lee. The way he plays is really *weird*" — and it is.

I love Al, but I just wanted someone a little weirder. You can tell Marty I said that.

So Donnie saw the band, The Pulse, one night.

DONNIE: I thought maybe I'd see somebody interesting. I just happened on Marty. I saw him that night, and he blew me away.

MARTY: I wasn't known, and I wasn't friends with any of those people.

We were playing a place a couple miles away from Donnie's House, called Morry's Speakeasy. That was a place we played regularly. And Donnie went out to hear some bands. I knew "The Rapper," but I didn't know Donnie.

We played a lot of different material, and we all had a chance to be featured in the set. It was everything from Cheap Trick to Steely Dan to Elvis Costello to Springsteen to Weather Report, and all kinds of odd things. There was only one guitar player in the band. And Donnie heard it, and that was enough for him, I guess.

He walked up and introduced himself.

I didn't know who he was. He was just a guy. He gave me a card. He said, "We're doing an album, and I'd like you to play guitar on it."

So I said sure.

I've met people like that numerous times — it doesn't necessarily turn into anything. You're playing in the club, somebody comes in and says, "I'm this person, I'm that person, I'm doing this." You don't expect it to necessarily be the truth.

MARK: Donnie invited Marty to Jeree's. I didn't call anybody else. I really trusted Donnie's judgment.

Then we said, "Who's going to play bass?"

Donnie said, "I heard about this badass guy, Albritton McClain."

DONNIE: I'd heard of Albritton, and he came in with a high recommendation from Hermie Granati. And B.E. Taylor might have said something about him.

At that point, Albritton McClain was a musical cousin: He had played with Jagger Frank Czuri, in promising Pittsburgh band The Silencers.

ALBRITTON: Frankie never really talked about the Jaggerz during our recording sessions, and I honestly don't think I knew Donnie was the "Rapper" guy until some time after we had formed our band. Rick Granati introduced me to Donnie.

MARK: Everybody just showed up at Jeree's studio.

ALBRITTON: I met everybody at the same time.

I met Kevin and Marty there and Mark.

Donnie was the last one to show up.

The personalities were a great combination, because we had all been exposed to other kinds of music in the last couple years, different aspects and geography. So when we talked verbally — or let the music talk — there was this instant understanding of where each of us was coming from.

My first impressions were that everybody seemed to play really well.

I didn't know them, they didn't know me — but here's the song, let's see what we can come up with.

The chemistry was good.

DONNIE: There are some good groups out there. The Cruisers always had a good chemistry together, like a good football or baseball team. Some groups might have all the best players in the world on the team, but then they can't *play* together, and it doesn't sound good. Us, it always just sounds good when we play together. I think it's 100% chemistry between the people.

Some bands are always fighting. We never really had a fight in the band. We had some disagreements, but never any fisticuffs or hard, drag-out arguments. It made for a good blend of guys.

RECORDING *BACK ON THE STREETS*: SESSION I

For all intents and purposes, Pittsburgh rock's signature album was recorded in winter and early spring of 1980, in just three sessions that summoned lightning and caught it on tape. Donnie and Mark had the blessing of their management, who knew they were doing something — but even Belkin and Maduri didn't know *what*.

The first day they met, the band didn't know what they were going to do, either. But they figured it out. Immediately.

KEVIN: Donnie and Mark had a few things prepared.

MARK: We started laying the real tracks for the album, what was going to be the album. Every session, we did a song that was going to be a jam song. And I said, "We're all going to be co-writers," even though I was going to write the lyrics and melody. Let's put the egos aside. Everybody just come up with parts. Let's see if we come up with a decent track.

That's how "I Can't Hear You" was done. "You're Only Dreaming" was like that. I'll write songs at home, and because of what wonderful musicians those guys are, it will come out a certain way.

ALBRITTON: "You're Only Dreaming" and "I Can't Hear You" started as jams — I didn't know what they were going to be called.

MARK: I laid out some song sketches. And we just cut four or five tracks, including a jam, which was "I Can't Hear You."

In the tracking and vocal phases, "Agnes" — which is still the band's staple selection for opening song at every show — was one of the first tunes to take form as Mark emerged as Donnie's bandleader and musical director.

ALBRITTON: Mark had the idea. He played it on keyboard. And we all fell into a groove with it. And he sketched out what the changes ought to be.

MARK: I thought Al was a monster player. Seemed like a nice guy.

ALBRITTON: I was used to being in the studio. I was coming off recording with David Werner.

MARK: I read a lot of articles on producers. I listened. I figured out what they were doing as far as stacking. Roy Thomas Baker. Phil Spector. I loved Bill Szymczyk [whose credits include the Eagles and Joe Walsh].

I learned from Wild Cherry a better way to make records. And I learned how all the great records were made: I learned that, generally, you don't just churn out the drums and the bass and all that; you let the players play and fall into a groove.

Many of those players cannot read music and don't rely on that. And if you need to chart out horn parts or string parts after the fact, certainly, do that.

As I came up — I wasn't a rock and roller, per se. Somebody like Donnie was more street-smart. I had to come to his way of doing things, and it was a good thing that I got more like that. I could always bring to the table when we needed a chart or a string section or weird chord changes — what I do was good. I learned that charting out every little part was not the way to make great records; you go in the studio, get some great-sounding tracks, and let some magic happen.

KEVIN: Mark's totally democratic. As we work in the studio, it's trial-and-error. Sometimes, we start with nothing. And we trot along until we find something. Mark has to hear something he can wrap his head around and write. He realizes what fits and what works.

It's a democracy — to a point: We cut the track. We have our input. Then Mark is the one that has to carry the song through and do the vocals with Donnie and write the lyrics or melody. Then it's all him. He's the producer, not just the head writer. It's all on his shoulders.

You base your future treatment of people on how you were treated in the past. And because of that, I think he wanted to have band-written songs, in part because he didn't want to exclude anyone.

MARTY: We were a little bit less inventive at that time. Mark had some songs in mind, but they weren't rehearsed. It was just "Play a guitar part" and "Fix this."

So we settled in on the basic rhythm track you hear on that song, and that's what went down on tape. They were very good players. It was all so new to me.

Through the session, everything clicked. As the Cruisers played together for the first time, Donnie and Mark exchanged approving glances. Between impromptu musical sprints, they discussed Marty and Al — and how the new guys played with Kevin. By the time the day was done, their minds were made up.

MARK: Albritton, you had to *hear* the guy – and the way he played with Kevin and Marty. We both liked the guys, but it was about the songs. Could the *songs* be good?

We knew we had a special band with all of them.

KEVIN: It felt good. In a band, there's songs, there's vibe, and there's sound. Those three elements, in that order of priority. Because there are some shitty sounding great songs that still were great.

RECORDING *BACK ON THE STREETS*: SESSION II

Happy with the vibe and sound, Donnie and Mark invited the band back for more. The songs took shape. Before Donnie screamed a note, and before he and Mark melded minds to make "Ah! Leah!," the band improvised the same recording approach they would use for the rest of their career, with this lineup and the ones that followed: 90 percent of the time, the backing band come to the studio with no songs. They jam until they have something good. The engineer records basic instrumental tracks. And then the work really starts.

At this early phase in the Cruisers' development, management still didn't know what kind of music Mark and Donnie were working on. And neither did the band.

KEVIN: At that point, it wasn't an album. It was only a three-song demo. We went back to our respective lairs. And Donnie and Mark worked on lyrics and vocals. Then they'd call us back if they needed more parts.

MARK: I was intending an album all the way. We were making masters, not demos, in my mind, from the start. I downplayed it because I did not want Kevin to think I was doing something to supersede Breathless. It was one thing to tell Kev we are doing an album, and another thing to tell Breathless I am doing just some songwriting demos, no big deal. I was in Breathless, and he was *into* Breathless. In my head, this was moving beyond Breathless. Of course, I had to prove it.

The first album was the first *my thing*. I got to engineer my own project. I got to use all my musical abilities I've had since I was five. And I got to make my own record. I'm learning how to make records. I get to make my own statement. So it was very special to me. It was *everything* to me. I think if I was a very different person, that wouldn't have happened. Everything, right or wrong, who I was as a person, it all created a climate for it.

ALBRITTON: We got called back a second time. And then we did three more songs.

KEVIN: Then we did some co-writing together. I remember being given a lot of latitude coming up with riffs and whatnot for some of the songs that would become co-writes, all of us writing together.

MARK: Everyone had latitude until I carved melodies and lyrics out of it all.

ALBRITTON: I came in with songs. We'd do one or two songs. That would be interesting. And we'd do it again.

We would learn the songs in the studios, face to face. Starting out, we were in separate rooms. I was in a big drum room. But we were playing right off the bat. We didn't need to rehearse. We met, rehearsed the songs in the studio, and laid down the tracks, right then and there. We didn't have a tape. Mark would say, "Come up with a part" or "Play this."

Mark would say, "Kevin, come up with a beat."

Or somebody would come up with an idea to go with Kevin's beat.

"You got a riff for me? Whaddaya got? Show me what you got."

"OK, Marty: Let's play the same riff, play our harmony to that, and move it up a half step or a minor third.

And Mark would come up and say, "OK, this time, let's go back to this part for the chorus" and "Let's make this change."

That's how we would come up with co-writes, right on the spot.

Donnie wasn't singing yet. But during the tracking, he did more than smoke cigarettes. While tracks were coming together, the singer voiced his approval or let the players know when they were heading into a dead end.

MARK: Donnie has a real good sense for what is cool. Donnie's got really great taste.

When the day's recording would end, the producer gave the singer homework. After the sessions, Mark would send Donnie home with a cassette of the skeletal song, structures more or less intact, as something to think about. And Donnie took the overnight writing assignments seriously.

DONNIE: Each individual album has its own life. Every album we recorded, they were done pretty much the same way, in the same studio.

We did a lot of jamming. We went in there, and we made up a lot of tracks as we went along. And we wrote the songs after the tracks were laid down. Not all of them, but a good portion were done like that.

Each album took on its own personality, depending how it felt, and what we were working on at the time. I liked working like that. I liked not having to go in with a script, so to speak. I liked having fun playing, doing the vocals and the overdubs, seeing what happens after you're done with tracks. You're going in blind. You don't really have anything ready to go. You just go in and do what you do. It makes it adventurous and fun.

I had tapes that I was writing songs to. I was putting together lyrics and arrangements in my head, "What are we going to do tonight?"

The band collaborated on songs in the studio, but that doesn't mean they were totally improvised. Mark would start the day with some fresh ideas.

DONNIE: Mark is usually the one with all the beginnings of songs. The first album and any part of the second album, we did it as a team.

It's hard for me to remember all of them, but I know Mark and I wrote a lot of the songs together, sitting around the piano. It was at my house. We had a piano in the basement. Sometimes it would start with his idea. He'd start banging around on the piano. And he'd do it until we had something.

The band still didn't have a name, but the Cruisers were headed toward the highway. Donnie watched, approving, and absorbing the music. Vocals and lyrics would come later. For now, Mark was in the driver's seat.

Between sessions, Donnie hung at Jeree and helped his father-in-law with some electrical work around town.

And now, as Mark cruised back and forth on the highway between Cleveland and Pittsburgh, the Donnie Iris band was hard at work recording an album that would soon be known as *Back on the Streets*.

RECORDING *BACK ON THE STREETS*: SESSION III

The track that became "Ah! Leah" starts with a simple drum fill, a perfect attention getter for the rest of the expertly blended band.

KEVIN: It seemed like a good way to start it. It's nothing great—just a little eighth-note tom fill. But the way it fits in with the rest of the song: the great bass, the vocal, the riff… That's what makes it good. It's not a great fill, but it's what's right for the song.

MARK: Albritton's bass part, it's not genius. He played, for the most part, eight-note bass pulses. But the fact is: Albritton *ripped* that thing. So it's genius in the way he played it.

ALBRITTON: The thing with these guys: We had all paid our dues.

And on the first album, we were generously given the opportunity to come up with our own parts and rhythms and extensions and chord changes to the songs. We were allowed to direct traffic in this new wave/punk/tongue-in-cheek direction the songs were going in.

And the music we came up with as a band was a really cool cross section of quirky new-wave verses ending in these really lush rock choruses. And the lyrics Donnie and Mark would come up with would send the songs over the top.

Going into the sessions, Mark had an idea what the record might sound like. The band didn't. Donnie didn't. But he trusted Mark.

DONNIE: Oh, *man*. We knew this was the direction we wanted. We knew they were good songs, good hooks, good chord changes, good lyrics. A lot of things that were different from the rock stuff that was happening at the time.

MARK: At some point, Marty would come back and maybe lay on a little more stuff. Kevin and Albritton would never hear anything again until the songs were done. Paul always expresses that: He plays on something, he doesn't know what's happening, and then he gets a kick out of what we've done with it, months later, when he listens to it.

ALBRITTON: And I think it was Mark that said, "A couple more songs, and we've got a whole album here." So we did four songs, maybe, the last session.

The ones I had been given the reins on and allowed to direct traffic, so to speak: "I Can't Hear You," "She's So Wild," "Joking." They had these bass riffs and these guitar riffs they were based around. It was a fun way to write, and we were feeding off each other.

The album's bass stylings still sound fine transferred to digital form for the CDs, streaming and download versions. But they're downright glorious in their original analog form, as heard on vinyl. Albritton showed up ready to play, and he emerged as the band's most virtuoso talent.

MARK: Albritton was there, on the first album, for just three or four days, sporadically. To me, he was as gifted as James Jamerson from Motown. He was a monster in his own way: tremendous technique, tremendous feel.

He played in a different way than you would imagine he would. You could say, "Albritton, do your own thing." He became this musician who was a meld of cultures. He was very gifted.

Jeree Recording Studio, New Brighton, PA.

Albritton was certainly not the only gifted Cruiser.

The songs were far from finished. Donnie still hadn't even started singing. But, after just three sessions, the band had recorded enough basic tracks for an entire album. With the music written and recorded, Donnie and Mark began to write the lyrics and build the rest of the record.

Elsewhere in the Belkin-Maduri universe, things were happening: LaFlavour's "Mandolay" was still on charts and dance floors. The second Breathless album was coming together. But it was all a warmup to get Mark ready for the Donnie sessions.

MARK: During the day, I would wake up at 11:30 or so. Go to Breathless rehearsal. Rehearse until 4:30, 5 o'clock. Hop in my car, drive to Beaver Falls, get there at 7. See good ol' Jerry there. I can't say enough good about Jerry.

DONNIE: Jerry was a sweetheart. He would help you do what you wanted to do. He would chime in with his advice, but he wouldn't do it unless he was asked.

MARK: Jerry would meet me at the studio. He'd have coffee on. Donnie would show up. I was *focused*, man. I was focused, smoking cigarettes, and drinking coffee. Marlboro Reds, in the box, with filters. Coffee with cream — which meant whatever white powder creamer Jerry had at the studio. That was it.

I felt like I was working on something really special. Donnie was into it. Jerry was into it. The three of us would be working on this imagined project all night long.

I'd get out of there at 1 or 2 o'clock, and drive home in my little Toyota Corolla. I loved the ride home every night, because I was just *juiced*. I had little money, but I was doing exactly what I wanted to do. I had a vision. I was driven.

Get home. Go to sleep. And do it again the next day. Every day.

I loved it. Best time of my life.

The interstate commute eventually inspired the band's name.

MARK: The reason the band is called "The Cruisers" was because I was a "Turnpike Cruiser" making the first record. And as Donnie pointed out, that was the name of a car in the fifties or sixties: The Turnpike Cruiser. We shortened it to Cruisers, obviously.

The company of Mark, Albritton, Kevin and Marty started using the name once the band itself was on the road. But the title didn't make its official debut until the second album, a year later.[18.2]

MARK: Jeree's is a homemade board. Don Garvin built it. And it just doesn't have typical top and bottom to its sound'. *But* limitations are good. I've always believed that.

It did have a really interesting EQ system built into the board. And with a certain compression, and Donnie's voice, and a Telefunken 251 mic, I noticed… Donnie's got a beautiful falsetto. And I'd never heard anybody sound like this, once I started stacking up his voice. Donnie's natural voice is not that unique. If we did an album with just his natural voice, nobody was going to go, "Wow!"

But he's got a beautiful falsetto voice. And we learned he's got this really great scream. And these different voices he did. Donnie, to me, is like the most wonderful vocal synthesizer you could have. And now, after we worked there for so long, we know each other so well, I just say, "Hey, use *this* voice." And he knows exactly what I'm talking about.

After eight years of failed experiments, patient observation, and improving results, Mark was fast growing into a studio ace. And he wasn't the band's only capable set of hands and ears.

MARK: I knew how to get great vocal sounds. Drums… I was lucky to work with Kevin, who is a great drummer and knew how to tune drums so they recorded well. And Marty always had a great sound on his own, just stick a microphone in front of it.

Producing, for me, became more about writing as you record, recording as you write – the iterative process. The planning logistically, to squeeze a lot of music on 24 tracks. And the order in which things needed to be done to get the stacking accomplished. I am an arranger, first and foremost.

KEVIN: We had to take advantage of what the studio had, and that was that midrange *punch*. You can hear that on the radio when the songs come on. A lot of other songs sounded full and rich and all that. But this studio just punched you in the *face*. It was great. We took advantage of that studio, what it had to offer.

But if you don't have great songs, and you go to New York and record in the best studio, you still don't have squat. Most people don't know or care that you have the best sound on guitar and drums. But they can't sing along. And "Leah," there was something special there.

Plus, we had quite a bit of involvement with the band. I felt quite a bit a part of the band. Not that I didn't with Jonah, but he came in with songs all done and an idea what he wanted to do. And I couldn't shape that as much as I did the Donnie stuff. I was more needed and valuable, I guess you could say. It's nice when you're involved and you get to put yourself in it.

> Each individual album has its own life. Every album we recorded, they were done pretty much the same way, in the same studio. We did a lot of jamming. We went in there, and we made up a lot of tracks as we went along. And we wrote the songs after the tracks were laid down.
>
> ~ DONNIE IRIS

BACK ON THE STREETS

words + music MARK AVSEC
DONNIE IRIS

CHAPTER 19

Back on the Streets:
The Band on the Songs

The individual songs from *Back on the Streets* came together in various sessions and stages. The band pounded out the basic tracks in a handful of initial sessions at the Jeree Recording studio, mere minutes from Donnie's home.

With the instrumental tracks nearly complete, Donnie and Mark would set about the much-more-time-consuming process of putting words to the music, then getting those words on tape in painstaking, elaborate, 120-track recordings.

Back on the Streets features ten original songs. Donnie co-wrote five of the songs with Mark. The entire band share credit on three. Avsec penned two by himself.

With ten tracks more or less finished, Donnie and Mark nestled into Jeree with Jerry. And they turned the rest of the recordings into fully fleshed out songs.

"AGNES"

DONNIE: "Agnes" will always be one of my favorites. That's a fun song. She's a leadoff hitter, and she always will be. We tried to switch it up a little bit, open with another song. It just doesn't work.

It was a made-up fictional story about Louie and Agnes. People ask me that a lot: 'Who was Louie?" "Who was Agnes?" Actually, so much of it was just fiction. It just so happened that "Agnes" rhymes with everything. And nobody names anybody Agnes anymore, and that pisses me off, 'cuz I love that name.

I had a piano teacher who, I thought, her name was Agnes. And I thought I told Mark, and that had something to do with writing the song.

And I checked, years later, with my sister. She said, "Her name wasn't Agnes!"

I said, "Well, what was her name?"

She said, "Her name was Irene!"

Mark was probably the guy who came up with the story. It wasn't based on anything that happened to us or we saw. I think he tried to put this whole concept of the album together, based on Agnes and Louie and Louie's Bar and fights. He should be a fiction book writer.

The whole album, really, is sort of a concept kind of a thing. That's what he wanted to do. And it brought on the persona of me.

I think we knew we were making a character. After we had the record done and we became a band, then Mark and I started figuring out how I was going to look.

Fighting Louie and having guns, hell no, that's not me. That's all made up, having fun. It's not Mark, either, no. Neither of us.

It felt great. It felt natural. It's like acting: You put yourself in a character. It was like the Superman version of me. I was probably one of these guys who wasn't a popular guy in school or anything like that.

As the songs came together, common threads developed. The definitive one was the character that fans would come to know as *Dawnie*.

Here's what makes the Cruisers record greats and timeless: Not just deft performances. Not just clever, compelling lyrics. Mark's elaborate studio wizardry involves a lot of loving attention and time. *Back on the Streets* and *King Cool* sound better than overcompressed modern radio rock because of better production and engineering. Mark, like a veteran trade worker, is both an artist and a craftsman.

"Agnes" started with a riff. Then it turned into a story. Now that Mark and Donnie had a track and lyrics, after thirty years of singing, it was time to let Donnie go all-out. For months, Mark had been holding on to a little moment from Donnie's ignored debut single, "Because of You." Now the producer was going to stack the vocals. And stack them some more. And stack them some more. And then stack them *more*.

MARK: My philosophy is: Anything that's worth doing is worth overdoing. Donnie's great about being open to anything.

DONNIE: I thought, "OK, man. Let's go for it." Whatever Mark wanted to do, basically. I was gung-ho, and so was he.

MARK: I always employed my base system: a three part harmony would consist of 27 voices, less if I want a Beatlesque sound — and Donnie is great at giving Paul or George or John. I would double Donnie's lead in that song, except for the talking part and any adlibs.

Even though it was going to take a long time to do this stuff, to stack it up like that, the end result was there. And once we heard it, we were going to do more of it. It sounded good. It sounded *big*.

Donnie had been singing and recording for decades. But when Mark played back Donnie's stacked low vocals, the singer had never heard himself like that before. This was a new Donnie, bigger, louder, badder. In that moment, Donnie bonded to Mark for life.

DONNIE: That was something I probably never would have even bothered doing. At the most, I would have double-tracked it. But to do it over and over... and then to hear how it sounded. It worked. It worked really well. It was undeniable.

I knew it sounded good. I didn't know what was gonna happen. None of us did.

(The documentary *King Cool* features striking footage of Mark playing one vocal track at a time; alone, they sound like Gregorian chants.)

Avsec was learning how to use the studio as proficiently as he played his Prophet keyboard. All the special effects in the world were empty without a solid performance as a base.

MARK: This [modern] era's going to go down for its pitch-correct and compression, the loudness wars. We used compression on the vocals, but in moderation, on individual tracks, sometimes to bizarre effect.

If you listen to the beginning of "Agnes," with Donnie talking about September and the wind, whatever it was — that's his voice, and I tried to get the sound to be a slightly over-the-top processed, so that it was eerie. But generally, it was very modest. You add in some compression so it warms it up a bit. But the loudness wars, that has to do with the overall compression of the track, so it's really loud, with zero dynamic range. It's ugly.

"I CAN'T HEAR YOU"

"I Can't Hear You" is one of the band's rare off-color moments. "Joking" fell out of the set list quickly, but "I Can't Hear You" is still in the live show. For years, it was the spot for a show-stopping monologue by Donnie, who would tell the audience a long story about his nagging girlfriend making him do chores. As the story reached a boil, Donnie would lead the crowd in a chant of "bull-shit! bull-shit!" The song's style of humor hasn't aged well, and Donnie's stage rap was long-since cut. It wasn't inspired by Donnie's home life.

DONNIE: That was Mark's idea. Some people took that as a wife, some as a girlfriend. It was so much fun.

That story, that's a completely made-up story by Mark. The whole rap we did sold it. He thought rock-and-roll guys would get a kick out of it — and they did. It's like, "We don't take nothin' from no women!"

That wasn't us, not at all. I never thought like that. My wife got a kick out of it. I don't remember getting any negative feedback. She got it. She knew we were making it up. She had fun right along with us, for sure.

ERIN FUSETTI, DONNIE'S DAUGHTER: My mom was a good sport about it, but I always felt bad for her.

Mark tells the rap's origin story one afternoon over lunch. He nervously looks around, sees tables of women, and quietly summarizes a skit he's been quoting for forty years.

MARK: It was inspired by Wildman Steve. He had this rap we used to listen to on the road in Wild Cherry. He'd call his girlfriend and lay it on thick. So I wanted to write something like that.

Looking back, of course, I don't want to glorify that. It was a caricature of a certain kind of guy and a certain kind of woman. It's not something I'm proud of. That's not me at all. It wasn't ever meant to be serious. It was to make fun of that macho kind of identity.

PAUL: "I Can't Hear You" really captures Donnie's rebellious bad-boy side.

Donnie says the "bullshit!" chant came from the crowd.

DONNIE: They would do that on their own. Our shows were always like *The Rocky Horror Picture Show*. The crowd would get into something, whether it was that or the "1-2-3-4" — they would do that every show for a long time.

JIMMY ROACH, *JIMMY AND STEVE IN THE MORNING*: Not very many singers could do that. He's got a gift for it. He's an entertainer. And it's weird, because when you're talking to him, he's more quiet and unassuming than the average guy. And then when you put the mic in front of him, something happens.

"JOKING"

MARK: That was a joke, too. Now I look back, some of these songs, in this day and age — Donnie and I are *not* like that. It's ridiculous. And Donnie could get away with things like that; Donnie is lovable.

I wrote the lyric. Donnie and I wrote the song. We didn't know what it was going to be called. All of a sudden, it emerges.

These songs speak. And they tell you, phonetically, what they say. I started hearing "joking." Now, what does that mean? And then we connive this scenario where a guy is just being a dick, telling a girl anything — and he was joking.

"SHOCK TREATMENT"

In the end, Mark decided to salvage the song that had been the pivotal point between the forgotten first single and the beloved first album. The first time around, Mark had stacked the background title vocals, a falsetto refrain of "Get it on… Get it on…" With one Donnie on one lead vocal track, the song had been relegated to the scrap heap. But with a couple dozen Donnies singing new lyrics, the tune got a new title and a new life. Most of the lyrics were already baked into the tapes, so Mark worked around them.

MARK: It was "Get It On" at first, more of an R&B type song. I had the idea to make it more urgent. I eventually went back, and we made it "Shock Treatment." And that's why there are all these "Get it on"'s in the song.

Once we got the sound and direction of the true Donnie Iris album, I changed the lyrics to the song. The lyrics have a true personal connection for me, that I do not talk about.

The hook is still there; it's a remnant of the earlier song. That was the first thing we ever recorded, before we cut tracks with anybody.

That would have been fun do to again, but the problem with that song was the 20 background vocals that need to be there.

Of this album, "Agnes," "You're Only Dreaming," "Leah," and "I Can't Hear You" are obviously my favorites. We're still doing them live. And the others were left behind.

The ten songs from the album are the only tunes the band developed to completion. The efficient sessions didn't yield any B-sides or lost tracks that are locked in an air-conditioned vault somewhere under Jeree. Donnie was the only member of the band to receive tapes of the early mixes; Mark pitched or taped over all early versions. No alternate takes exist.

MARK: There were a couple ideas we didn't use. I don't know what happened to them. But none of them are on *King Cool*. I wanted to start fresh. That was my philosophy: "If it wasn't good enough to make the record, it's not good enough." Now Springsteen, that's different: Everything he writes is great. He can put out a boxed set with his extra songs. We never will. I think I threw them all away.

And, no, Mark doesn't have any demos lying around, either. The Cruisers have never recorded a single demo.

MARK: Never. I only intended to make masters. I can't work on something if I think it's going to be a demo. Besides, most times, if it's good, you get *demo-itis*, and you cannot recreate it so it sounds as good.

"BACK ON THE STREETS"

The album's title track is a blue-collar adventure with cinematic sweep. That kind of composition was in style at the moment — but it always had been. It has echoes of the era's most high-profile producer-singer symbiosis.

MARK: If it sounds like Meat Loaf and Jim Steinman, it wasn't conscious. If it's similar, maybe it's because Steinman and Meat Loaf have a similar relationship to me and Donnie, the writer and the singer.

I was more inspired by what Springsteen was doing at the time, and thinking about Donnie being a working-class guy. I think *Back on the Streets* was a poor man's version of *Born to Run*, in a way.

I was never busted by a cop. That was fiction. I had some close calls.

Gradually, the album turns into a story and a theme. We start weaving these things together, like "Agnes" and "Back on the Streets" — I just have fun with things like that. We're trying to create a *thing* and make a great album. For lack of a better thing, you develop a story.

For us, we tried to make a piece of *art*. And whether it is or whether it's as great as we hoped it would be, I don't know. At the time we were making it, we wanted a thematic thing. Gradually, the songs began to hook together. "Back on the Streets" was later. The song is sort of weaving together the other themes from the record.

I made great use of ARP String Ensemble [keyboard], which I stacked to create an orchestra type effect. If you are hearing strings, it is the ARP, maybe layered with string sounds in the Prophet. I'd record 54 tracks of string parts to create the effect I wanted.

Back on the Streets is a state-of-the-art 1980 AOR album, but it also has some throwback flourishes, like a sax solo by Kenny Blake, who had appeared on the "Bring on the Eighties" / "Because of You" single.

MARK: We needed a '50s kind of solo. And Jerry Reed said, "Try Kenny Blake" — I think he and Don Garvin at the studio knew him. We gave him a little money. He came in. I met him. He was a very nice guy. I told him what we were looking for. We spent an hour together, crafting that solo. And that was it.

I can't remember what I had in mind, but sometimes what you have in mind, when you have a player who is skilled at a certain thing, you're better off taking what a musician could offer you, and working with that.

Back on the Wild Cherry tour, Donnie had turned Mark on to a fuel that kept his brain firing through the long sessions and longer days:

MARK: A part of me thinks I created better and differently with nicotine. That might sound stupid, but it made me focused. I may be a little healthier now, but I'm not as focused without smoking. But it's a balancing act. I'll *live* longer. And I've accomplished some good things since I quit smoking. I have to watch everything I do, or I'll go off the deep end.

I didn't want to put a lot of drugs and alcohol into my system and alter my consciousness. I am an addictive personality, so I have to watch that. But you drink a lot of coffee, you get something done.

"YOU'RE ONLY DREAMING"

DONNIE: I like "You're Only Dreaming" a lot. We've been doing that song a lot lately, and it's working out. It's an Elvis kind of slapback echo on the voice. I would go in and start singing along with the track. And Mark said, "Let's put some of the kind of echo that Elvis had on his voice." It sounded so cool. One of us would come up with an idea like that, and we'd see how it sounded. And if we liked it, we'd record it that way.

MARK: The whole band worked on it together, so we shared credit. That's the way I feel, right or wrong. I may have benefitted from it, or others may have.

The Beatles, it's widely known that McCartney wrote "Yesterday," but it's credited as Lennon-McCartney. I thought that was cool. In general, it helps art, because if somebody's worried about getting credit, they close up, or we have this tense negotiation. So if we work on a song together, and I said it's a jam, even if you didn't contribute, and I wrote the whole lyric or melody, I'm still getting as much as you. It's to those guys' benefit, too.

Sharing songwriting credits wasn't simply a generous gesture on Mark and Donnie's part. The band financially benefitted from the decision. The financial dimensions of a record deal are an impenetrable black hole: Songwriting/publishing royalties are the revenue stream most likely to emit a stream of dollars. When band members' names aren't in the songwriting credits, they make a lot less than the members whose are. The uneven cut often creates simmering tension, and it builds to fatal resentment. But when a band isn't making U2-level money, and everybody gets a piece, they realize they're all splitting a small pie... and a big piece of a little pie isn't *that* much bigger than a small piece. But the small piece *is* nice.

KEVIN: I do receive some money, mostly for "Love Is Like a Rock." It is not much, and funny how it varies so much. I'm sure Mark and Donnie get more for "Leah," but it's mostly for streaming. I believe you need a lot of plays for it to amount to something substantial.

"SHE'S SO WILD"

"She's So Wild" is one of the great lost tracks in the Cruisers catalog. The hormonal hard-rock number shows a whole different side of the band. And it gives a rare window into exactly how diverse Marty's arsenal is. Aside from some quick flashes on 1997's *Poletown* album, the pyrotechnic guitar solo is the band's most heavy metal moment. If Hoenes had the desire, he could have spent the glam decade as a shredding showboat guitarist, playing the kind of pop metal that soon came into vogue.

But the Cruisers' lead guitarist is usually content to find part of the groove and settle into the song. In this cut, however, a wild stallion solo is what the tune needs. Granted, "She's So Wild" is an oddball installment in the laid-back tales of King Cool. It's one of many deep cuts Mark does not remember fondly. In fact, he barely remembers it.

MARK: I should check it out again. I haven't heard it in a while. I don't remember how that started. It might have been Marty's lick. It probably was. It's quick. Going that high and that fast, it wasn't a challenge. It just happened that way. It's just that kind of '80s song.

MIKE PALONE, GUITARIST, SKELL (ex-WHISKEY HIGH): Fun tune. It starts off with the heavy guitar riff that sounds a little new-wave influenced to me — but it also harkens back to heavy rock of the day. I like the verse in the key of A, and how the pre-chorus goes to the relative major key of C, but then they do something very cool and modulate to the key of G sharp for the chorus, down on half step. It sounds really interesting and fresh in that key. And when that ends, it resolves back to the key of A for the verse again. It's a fun little ride of musical terrain for the listener.

Then we get to the guitar solo. Another key change for this, which is very cool. This solo is beautifully melodic. Believe it or not, it reminds me of Michael Schenker, if you could get him to slow down a little bit. Great phrasing, good note punctuation, and perfectly musical throughout. It's a great solo.

MARTY: From a guitar player's standpoint, I liked the textures, the shimmering parts, the single-note parts, constructing things. It was different. The value for me is actually because I don't relate to the whole guitar hero thing too much. I like ensemble playing. It serves the song. You don't have these long five-minute guitar solos coming from Andy Summers from the Police. It was simple, but it was song-based. For me, that's very appealing, because of how I approach the instrument.

"She's So Wild," it's not my usual style. I don't gravitate toward that. I know where to go, but I don't usually go there. That particular song, I think that might have been a riff that Albritton was playing in pieces. And then it started to change and go into different harmonic areas. And that influenced me. "OK, we've got that part now. Move it to here and here and here."

The Eddie Van Halen style is fantastic, and it was groundbreaking. And I liked hearing it, too. But Joe Walsh doesn't play like that. And Joe Walsh is a hero of mine. What Hendrix did and what Joe Walsh does, that resonates with me — I'll tell you that; I found those players very expressive and lyrical. They have a phrasing and melody. The other kind of style, I don't know if its intention is to be melodic and lyrical, as it is to create and atmosphere of fire and power.

"DADDY DON'T LIVE HERE ANYMORE"

MARK: That particular lyric didn't mean anything at the time. Sometimes, you listen to the music, and you hear a phrase. And so we went with "Daddy don't live here anymore."

And "daddy," Donnie wasn't taking it as "dad" — he meant it as a euphemism like "big daddy," something like that.

We were trying to capture that new wave renaissance style like the 60s, something like that. The Cars were big then, and we were all influenced by all that stuff.

I had a Moog synthesizer. I layered the solo a couple times, too. The sound, you just keep screwing around with the knobs, until it sounds right to you. It's modulation that creates that vibrato in the tone. As you're playing, it is a feel thing. As I'm playing it, I'm moving my left hand on the modulation. You can make it sing the way you want to, as you're feeling it.

DONNIE: To me, that's just a so-so song. You don't know what people are going to like and not like — not really, not for sure. You have an idea of the ones that are the best, but you don't know for sure.

To a man, the Cruisers like their big songs, and they don't care about the rest. If a song isn't in the set list by now, it probably never will be. And don't expect a *Best Of, Volume II*.

TAKING IT FOR A SPIN

When the tracks were complete, the producer, engineer and singer would give them a test-drive.

MARK: At Jerry's place, where we did the first albums, we had two main sets of speakers, sometimes a third: Seeburg jukebox speakers mounted in the wall. They're really loud, not studio monitors. But Ron Garvin liked them. They're not big, but we listened to them to get the low end right. Sometimes I confused myself and everybody else by cranking them up anyway.

When we mixed, we usually mixed on real cheap-assed Auratone speakers. I don't know if they make them anymore. They're little boxes. They don't sound very good, but the theory was: Maybe they sound the way a radio would. To get the proportions right, we'd mix on there, and then check it on the big speakers.

You want to get the mix right, and each speaker brings its own thing. The big speakers are great to get hyped on your work, but you get drunk on the music sometimes; you're better off playing it on a cheap little system. You're better off using the cheap speakers to cue your bass and your bottom end, but if you sound good on cheap speakers, you'll sound good on big ones. And sometimes, with

Donnie at Jeree studio. One of the big Seeburg jukebox monitors is partially visible behind him, mounted into the wall, and one of the "cheap-assed" little Auratones is sitting on the shelf next to him. (Photo by Richard Kelly)

big speakers, you can't tell if the vocals or a guitar are loud enough. And, of course, back in the day when we had songs on the radio, that might be how you sound on the radio.

For the first albums, we'd take cassettes and go home. Then we'd come back, pull a mix up, and maybe tweak it the next day. A lot of times, we'd all have a part to play: Somebody's got to ride the lead vocals, bring this down, bring this up, pan it a certain way. We'd leave the mix out so we didn't destroy it.

Stereo was big in the process. I modeled things after the Beatles a lot, that's why you will hear some vocals hard right speaker or hard left speaker – but of course the Beatles *had* to do it that way because of the layered four track recording process. They had to commit.

I just liked the way it sounded.

All the Cruisers remember the *Back on the Streets* sessions as a fun time. They were fast forging a fraternity. And now, two years after they met, the core dynamic duo were fast to cross the lines from coworkers to bandmates to family. Some nights, a tired Mark would stay in Pennsylvania and work a second shift at Donnie's house.

ERIN, DONNIE'S DAUGHTER: Addy and I would bunk together when Mark came over. Mark was a sleepwalker. When they were recording, we stayed upstairs, once in awhile we'd sneak down for a few minutes, to peek in. They would come upstairs to eat. They ate peanut butter and jelly sandwiches and chips for lunch. And drank pop.

Mark was always fun to have around. We were all like family, Mark and his wife and kids. Mark would play with us and liked to joke around.

ADDY MOLONY, DONNIE'S DAUGHTER: We would get up in the morning. My mom would make breakfast. And we would talk about Mark sleepwalking, over bacon and eggs and pancakes. Mom would make pancakes with an E or an A in them.

"TOO YOUNG TO LOVE"

MARK: I wrote the song on a grand piano. Then we laid it down. We showed it to Marty and Albritton and Kevin. Then we'd go out in the studio and do takes until we got a good-feeling take. And so then we'd overdub Marty's guitar, and he'd get his part done. And then everybody would go home. And Donnie and I would start laying stuff on there.

That was about a high school girlfriend of mine. But more than anything, it was inspired by Tom Petty's style at the time.

In that, that's an F sharp minor to an E chord, over an F sharp bass. And it may sound classical to you, because that's my training. That's the thing with me: If I'm guilty of anything, I didn't really learn songs the way Paul learned songs. Paul knows parts and all that. I studied classical, and I think a different way. But I don't learn songs the way most people do.

I have fun when I do learn songs. I was listening to "Bridge Over Troubled Water" — it's a beautiful piano part. I thought, "I should learn this." It's nice when you can play a whole part from somebody else's great song. But I don't do that.

There's a lyric to the song, a person has to follow their dreams. I think that. I believed it at the time. When I was younger, I didn't want to be in a relationship — I figured it would screw me up. I figured if I fell in love with somebody, I might just be a baker, because I'd be happy. I'd make a living, and that's it. But I really wanted, for whatever reason, to torture myself with this music industry. The same way a million other people, post-Beatles, did that. So I think that song is about that.

"Too Young to Love" — I sang a lot of the background vocals with Donnie. My voice is recognizable inasmuch as it is the "Love Is Like A Rock" unison sound, or the middle note in a harmony. All the songs had stacked vocals. That's what I was into doing.

DONNIE: Some of them, sometimes, they don't translate well on stage. "Too Young to Love" is a cool song, but it's so hard to sing. If I had to do that song night after night, I'd be done for the next gig. It'd be a couple weeks before I could sing again on a nightly basis.

MARK: I wrote a couple songs about myself, like "Too Young to Love." Then we ended up putting on the "Ah! Leah!" parts.

Donnie and Mark writing at the piano, January 1980.

Erin and Donnie, relaxing at home.

> We would get up
> in the morning. My mom would
> make breakfast. And we would talk
> about Mark sleepwalking, over bacon
> and eggs and pancakes. Mom would
> make pancakes with an E
> or an A in them.
>
> **~ADDY MOLONY**

CHAPTER 20

"Ah! Leah!"

From the official fake — **fake** — biography of Donnie circulated with 1981's *Live at the Paradise* EP:

> "Agnes" and "She's So Wild" are two hot rockers, written in honor of Iris' first wife: Agnes Iris Evans. The playing is electrifying and urgent, the vocals layered to a silky precision. The album is a classic example of beauty and the beast: tough, instrumental outbursts and desperate lead vocals encased in a commercially marketable frame of slick, sweet harmonies — all sung by Iris himself. Perhaps the greatest example of this occurs on the song "Ah! Leah!" — written with love for Donnie's second wife, Leah Iris Jones, and with whom he still has a pleasant and fulfilling relationship.

Practically nothing in that passage is true, but it's funny. The real story of "Ah! Leah!" is far more complicated than maddening passion and crazy love. In its first draft, the song was about an expensive, intractable, unwinnable Asian land war. By the time the dust settled around the tune, the Cruisers knew how *that* felt.

"Ah! Leah!" is Donnie Iris and the Cruisers' signature song. Deceptively simple and immaculately manicured, it was the band's first single. It gave them a career. It keeps them on the airwaves. In 2015, when the music supervisor of Netflix's *Wet Hot American Summer: First Day of Camp* needed to summon the quintessential and sexy sonic spirit of 1981, "Ah! Leah!" was the right choice. (As always, when song appeared, it was news to the band; MCA/Geffen signed off without consulting the Cruisers.)

Eleven years after "The Rapper" hit, "Ah! Leah!" saved Donnie Iris from the dubious distinction of being a one-hit wonder. Its prescient music video didn't break the band onto MTV — because when it was released, MTV didn't exist. The song did put the band on the map. It ultimately cost the group as much money as it made. And the single's star-crossed fate may have dealt the Cruisers fatal blow — or maybe it saved the band. Or maybe both.

With modest promotional backing, "Ah! Leah!" spent 18 weeks on the *Billboard* Hot 100 singles chart, and peaked at number 29 February 28, 1981. The chart number isn't a stunner, but major-market DJs across the country voted it the number 2 single of the year in *Playboy*'s National DJ Poll, after the Rolling Stones' "Start Me Up" and above the Go-Gos' "Our Lips Are Sealed." [20.1]

The song sold well, scored the band a label deal, thrived on FM airwaves from coast to coast. It attracted its share of glowing notices, then and later.

In 2005, website Fan Asylum asked classic Journey frontman Steve Perry...

Q: What song makes you smile whenever you hear it?

Perry: "Ah! Leah!" by Donnie Iris. [20.2]

After lengthy and careful consideration, its best review arrived in 2005, from one of the entertainment industry's top pundits. Bob Lefsetz is a lifelong music fan and music-business veteran.

"You know the kind of track that's *so* good you've got to go out and buy the album *right then*?" Lefsetz wrote in his newsletter. "Not even *caring* what the rest of the record sounds like? *That's* how good 'Ah! Leah!' is. 'Ah! Leah!' had power. And a memorable riff. And even the changes were good. But what put it over the top, what infected you, was *the chorus*! It's a modern-day wall of sound. With *endless* backup vocals sweetly singing. That's Donnie's trademark."

For Donnie and Mark, the song was the culmination of a lifetime of work, connections, technique and experience.

MARK: I realized I was getting my groove. I was thinking about *nothing* but this record. I remember mixing that thing. It was just us. Donnie and I were into it.

Once in awhile, we'd call Don Garvin in when we had technical questions. Garv built the board. We're marking things. We used to have to manually feed everything. Donnie'd have a couple faders to move, I'd have a couple, Jerry would have a couple. And we'd have to pour the mix into a two-track. And we did that with the whole record.

And then I went back to Cleveland, with the mixes in my car. I couldn't wait to get to the office to play them for everybody. I was going to blow them away.

"Ah! Leah!" is a prime example of the peculiar, circuitous, non-linear approach Avsec uses to write songs. The music arrives first, followed by an incomplete map of words. His writing process isn't what most people would recognize as *writing*: After he and the band compose and record music, he listens closely. Words, situations, plots, and characters manifest in his brain. Then they gradually make their way onto paper — often with inspiration and assistance from Donnie, who is Avsec's muse, co-writer and mouthpiece.

MARK: The way I write music, I write phonetics. I write sounds. If I could make up my own language and write in it, those might be really good songs. But the English language gets in my way.

I have great respect for Michael Stanley. He's a slogger. Every year, he comes up with a new album. Our projects are very different.

Unless I get into a Springsteen vibe, I don't write the lyrics first. And I've never worked that way with Donnie, where the lyrics really are personal to me.

I wrote "Leah!" at my parents' house, at my little upright piano. My dad had just had a heart attack in the springtime, around Easter. I really liked the background part, "*ah-lee-ah*" — it was just sounds, phonetics. And that's what I was really hearing. I wrote it as meaningless, monk-like phonetic jabber. And the real lyrics would go above it eventually, when I wrote them.

It was going to be this anti-war song, "Here We Go Again." The Russians had invaded Afghanistan in 1979, I thought, "Here we go again." That's why you hear "Here we go again" in the background.

Over the next two years, Mark would earn the reputation he sought: a tireless, innovative producer who worked endlessly, forging byzantine studio creations. He says when he's focused and running hot, the work isn't about craftsmanship — it transcends the band's interpersonal alchemy and sends him into the mystic.

MARK: It's magic.

When I wrote "Leah," there *was* a crafting. Donnie and I worked on it in his place.

I wrote it in D-flat. I like D-flat.

I wrote the hook melody. I liked it. It seemed really kind of haunting to me. And that's how I came up with the "aaaah-LEEE-aaah" — it really had nothing to do with a girl's name. It was like the Wizard of Oz chant: "oh-WEE-oh."

And so it *was* crafted.

I wrote a lyric to it that was really terrible, an anti-war lyric. And I put it down.

I took it to Jeree's, and I gave it to Donnie. We did the backgrounds in a couple of days… maybe with a day break in between, so Donnie's falsetto was clear. We did 60 voices of "Ahh-leee-AHH" — anything that's worth doing is worth overdoing.

And I listened, and I was like, "Boy, the background vocals are great, but the lyrics are dumb."

I said, "Man, I love the lick, the vocals, the background vocals. The 'Ah! AH! Ah!' part" — everything was in there. The whole background vocals were in there, but the lyrics sucked.

There's no tape of the original version. It's gone. This is before "delete."

I'd look at Jerry and go, "That's not going anywhere. Erase the lead."

Jerry would look at me like, "*Whaaat?*"

"Jerry, it's not working."

I was not a pack rat. Make decisions, move forward.

But I really loved the hook. I liked the background vocals.

And Donnie said, "Hey, what about a girl? You know, Leah is a girl's name."

I remember saying, "I knew a girl name Lee. I never knew a girl named Leah."

He said — *[relaxed, cool tone, like he's exhaling a puff of cigarette smoke]* — "I knew a girl named Leah."

I said, "Alright."

So we rearranged it.

WHO *WAS* LEAH?

In 2008, Beaver County *Times* writer Scott Tady identified who that Leah was: Leah Frankford, a Beaver Valley woman who had dated Jaggerz drummer Jimmy Pugliano in the summer of 1968. Donnie used to tell her he liked her name. In the accompanying picture, she looks like the fetching, chiseled blondes from the "Ah! Leah!" and "Do You Compute?" videos. [20.3]

But "Ah! Leah!" isn't about Ms. Frankford. And it's not about Afghanistan. In the song, Donnie is going crazy for a girl who's bad news, but he can't keep away. Donnie assumes the character of a man who might have been a rapper himself, a guy with some game who still isn't in control of the situation — or himself, and certainly not the beguiling Leah.

"Leah, it's been a long, long time," Donnie exhales, reserved and cool. "You're lookin' better than a body has a right to."

In this track, for the first time, the Cruisers fire on all cylinders. You hear all the group's trademark elements. They have other great songs, but this is perfection. Al and Kevin push along Marty's thick riff like an elevated heart rate. And by the time his story is told, Donnie has lost control, and he screams, trying to expel the doomed passion. He's a regular dude on a good day. He wants to make it. He won't. His pain is our pleasure.

MARK: One day on the way to a session, I was writing a lyric to "Leah" in the car, driving my car, hands behind the wheel.

Then we recorded it that day. I went first and recorded the lead harmony.

The magic was that it was the right stuff. That particular day. The performance.

I sang the lead, on top of Donnie. I put my voice down first, because I had the phrasing I wanted for the verses.

I would often lay down my tracks first. I wanted a certain urgency and style. I don't know if he'll remember that, but it's true. I went out there and sang "Leah," harmony.

Then Donnie went in there, and I coached him: "LEE-ah, it's been…" And those were very controlled.

And then we added Donnie as well. Donnie put his voice under. Those were doubled. Then we would do the hooks and craft it.

First we did the hooks. By the time we got to the lead vocals, I laid down this harmony part.

And Donnie goes to punch in the low part, the verses.

So I am not a great lead singer, I don't think. But I have a certain timbre to my voice. And if it's stacked within a certain range, I have an element, tonally, that was useful. And Donnie doesn't have it — it's like an F, F sharp, G, G sharp, A, above middle C. Those notes there, I used to be able to hit in a natural voice.

And then if I stacked it, it really had a nice quality. You hear it on Cellarful of Noise. So you hear my voice in the hooks. It's he and I together. It was better with me doing that G note with Donnie. That was fun. I had very limited musical range for my voice.

He liked it too. Singing with Donnie was great. He could actually sing. To find somebody that has that range! I call them falsetto or "false," voice, a scream voice, natural voice.

Donnie singing at Jeree Studio (Photo by Richard Kelly)

Even if you have to switch voices… because Donnie's voice is not that high. He can go from whatever he is low, to about, comfortably, E above middle C, maybe F. That's not that high. Then he gets into this falsetto, which he can do E above middle C, F, F sharp, G, G sharp, A, B, B flat, B above middle C. And it's not a scream then. It's a very pure choirboy type voice, like a 13-year-old. No air, it's pure voice, pitch. If he's tired, he'll get more air. So we have to be very careful. But when you stack up that pure falsetto, it's a beautiful thing.

And then he can do his natural voice, F sharp, G. That's when I want him to get rough, to display urgency and emotion. I'll make sure I write something he can reach. It almost sounds distorted, gruff. He can't really get above natural G. When he gets high, I tell him, "You gotta reach here."

In Wild Cherry, he would do "Ain't That Peculiar" by Marvin Gaye. And near the end one time, he did a scream. And I never forgot it. I may be wrong, but I don't think it was ever captured on a record before me. And the first time we did it on a record was "Ah! Leah!"

We got into the end, where he stared vamping. By then, I was real into the song.

Jerry's there, just me, him, and Donnie. We wouldn't let anybody in the studio to see how the sausage was made.

We worked on all these vocal performances together. It's not like somebody just goes in there and sings. You've got to get these emotions up. You've got to coach up. You've got to get everybody in the proper character, worked up.

I suggested at that time, "Why don't you do that scream? You've got to scream at the end."

So we stopped at the one spot about three times.

I said, "Goddammit, man, you've got to really — I just want to hear you really — " and he came out of nowhere with that big scream he did at the end, "Ahhhhh Leeeeeaaah!"

I stood up in the chair and said, "That's it! That's *it*!"

That was *it*, man.

I think we probably finished it in that day, with him doing the adlibs, the single line stuff over the chorus, and the screams at the end.

Donnie had spent years on the bench. Like a guru hitting coach, Mark adjusted his swing. And now, for the first time since the mid '70s, Donnie connected. Hard. Eight months and 60 vocals tracks after the Cruisers' inception, *this* was a new Donnie.

SEAN ROSS, *ROSS ON RADIO* **NEWSLETTER, BROADCAST INDUSTRY PUNDIT:** On "Leah," there are still traces of the Rascals-Soul Survivors-type band that the Jaggerz once were, pre-"Rapper." When "Leah" explodes at the end, that's very much a '70s R&B/disco-type ad-lib: "never/ever/ever gonna *make* it."

DONNIE: "Leah," I could definitely relate to that.

Being a cool guy — I remember dating this one girl who thought she was the shit, and let me know it for a while. And one day, I said, "I'm tired of this — later." And then I was the coolest guy ever. That was high school.

I could imagine myself being cool with the girls — not so much high school, but after, after being with the Jaggerz. I was attracted to chicks, and chicks were attracted to musicians. That was fun, playing that guy. Because I definitely was not that before.

MARK: Then Marty came back and did a lead guitar solo, and I added some keyboards. That took another couple of days.

MARTY: Going back to the first album, I was not expecting "I Can't Hear You" and "Leah" to sound like they did. That was completely unexpected.

Mark had written the "Leah" riff. But Marty made it mighty. Then Mark made it huge.

MARTY: Mark had the chord changes. I just played the chord changes, rock guitar, and gave him whatever energy I could give him. And that's it. He already had the changes.

He was playing along on piano. And I just played them.

The riff, *ba-BA-ba*… There was no song. It was just chord changes. Just *ba-BA-ba-BOM-ba-ba*.

That's what it almost always is. There was no song. It could have been any of them being scrapped because we couldn't make anything from them.

They had the whole thing pretty much mapped up, but they needed a guitar solo.

I was out with my band at the time. I left the gig and went in the studio and set up my regular rig from playing with The Pulse.

I've always played a Gibson Les Paul. They're great guitars. They have their own sound. It's very full. I love the tone, the sustain. It's always been my favorite electric guitar sound

MARTY: They said, "OK, we've got this solo section, so go for it."

I'm pretty sure that's the first take. I just played in response to what was playing. And that's what you hear.

We didn't do multiple, multiple takes. I think I tried another one, and they came back and said, "No, this is great, sounds fine, let's use it."

I like it. Very simple. I didn't quote-unquote *write* the solo. I didn't listen to the song and go home and develop the solo.

For me, as a player, if you get it in the first one, two, three takes, you've got something. And if you have to go five, six, eight takes, you don't really have anything. It's going to be like pulling teeth.

So I'm best when I just react and I'm lucky enough to get something good. It's best and it seems to fit best. Sitting down and writing something and playing it, it won't work for us.

PAUL: "Ah! Leah!" really captures Mark's creativity and angst. He really mastered the art of vocal stacking and utilizing Donnie's vocal range and abilities, with harmonic structure that made sense, not just doing it for the sake of "Let's see what happens."

Donnie's best track is "Ah! Leah!": the emotive lead vocals. The vast range he covers with all the stacked vocals.

MIKE PALONE, GUITARIST, SKELL (ex-WHISKEY HIGH): It's the definitive song — but not the only song — you think of when you think of Donnie. In 1989, I was in Los Angeles with my band, and "Ah! Leah!" came on the radio. I was like, "Wow! It's nine years after the release of the song, and you're still playing it on the radio in California!" That's when I really got the grasp of the scope of Donnie's popularity and understood that he truly was a national recording artist.

The song is heavy and tough. The solo is brilliant, and its understatement makes me think of the approach Mick Ralphs from Bad Company might take: simple, singing, big notes. No waste, no fluff. That guitar solo is perfect for the song, and that's what makes it awesome.

MARK: All-in, we probably spent about seven working days on "Leah," including basic tracks.

When Donnie writes a song, he might sit with a pen and paper and write lyrics like he's completing an essay assignment. But few Cruisers songs began with an idea, some lyrics, or a tale one of the guys wanted to tell.

MARK: We never have written like that. That would be innovative for us.

I know if I were talking to a fan or a radio station, they would like it if I had some kind of story about writing the song, where I say, 'Yeah, I wrote 'Leah': There was this girl named Leah, and I was nuts about her, and we were making out, and there was this guy, Louie…."

But that didn't happen.

Maybe I told some stories about the song a couple times. Because when I say, "We put together the track, and I had some kind of weird anti-war thing in my head, and I put in the 'oh-wee-oh / ah-lee-ah' part" — I can see their face falling.

That's not how we work. I don't work like that.

First, I would do the vocals. Because if I didn't do them right away, I would have no tracks to do them. We weren't making records the way other people were:

You're working with tape. You have a limited number of tracks. Then doing the lead vocals. First, we'd use up all those tracks, mix everything down. And then we'd get to filling in what really is the important part of the song, which is the lead vocal and lead guitar. But you have to plan that out. We made records in a different way. We put such a premium on vocals and stacking, that we had to proceed in a certain way, to leave room on the tape.

We never could have recorded the lead vocal for "Leah," the guitar tracks, and everything, and then said, "OK, now let's do the background vocals." There would have been no room for all the vocals. We needed a whole blank slate.

You couldn't sync them together. That was our limitations. And that was a good thing. Now we have no limitations on Pro Tools. So now we don't even mix down anymore. And maybe that's a good thing, but I think you lose some the attention to detail and focus. Those limitations made you arrange songs in a certain way.

Now, today, you can leave 60 vocals in, without even mixing them down. You can create some confusion, too. With tape, you're married to what you mix down. But I say, "So what? That's great. Move on. Have confidence. Make the best of the situation."

That's how we make records.

We did that for about six months.

We had three or four sessions, recording most of the music. Then Donnie and I worked together for months. The mixing took a week and a half.

We went continuously, because we could not allow anyone else in the studio, because our settings were all set on the board — so we kept going, including "Leah."

All the songs were equally labor-intensive. Everything was stacked.

I believe we spent about 500 to 600 hours on the entire record.

And so *that* was done.

KEVIN: I came back and heard Donnie singing, and I heard what Mark did with Donnie's singing

— his ability to vocally orchestrate this stuff, and to sing it. I thought, "That's pretty cool!" "Ah! Leah!" is one of *those* songs: It wasn't like anything I had heard before, definitely not anything I was ever involved in.

How do I say this without discrediting other people? "Leah" never became a number 1 single. And I know it's not as well known as some songs that made it to the top. But because it had such a unique sound, it was not generic. It means more because it was unique. It wasn't flavor-of-the-month. And I think that's kind of cool.

I remember when I heard [Yes'] "Owner of a Lonely Heart," and I heard that middle breakdown. I said, "What is *this*?" It had that *impact*. "Leah" is one of those songs that is just so different and special. Obviously, I'm biased. But it was pretty cool.

The simple, propulsive riff at the heart of "Ah! Leah!" is a distillation of the Cruisers' recordings and how they came to be: If the Cruisers were young, hard-partying kids from the Sunset Strip or a hot, happening city, they still might have written the riff. Then they might have recorded a thin version of the song and run out of the studio, ready to chase women. But with their working class hands and golden throat, Donnie and Mark took that idea, developed it, and realized its full potential by applying hours of elbow grease. "Ah! Leah!" only could have come from a town like Pittsburgh or Cleveland.

DONNIE: We were all hungry at the time. All of us wanted to do something. We thought we could write some good songs and be a good band. We were hard-working and driven to do something that we were all proud of.

MARK: We put a lot of *work* into that track, into our records. That was about what you've got going on in your life.

I had invested everything to be in that position, and I wasn't going to be denied. So it was like being an entrepreneur or the leader of a company: You're going to go through a wall to do what you need to do.

I can't do that anymore. I have achieved things in the last few years, but I have never been so laser-focused as I was back then. That was my whole life. It's hard to have relationships when you are like that. It takes a toll personally.

I liken the intensity to a movie, *Somewhere in Time*, with Christopher Reeve and Jane Seymour. It's a romantic movie. Not a bad movie. He goes back in time. And it took a thought experiment to go back in time. And then he falls in love. And that jolts him out of it.

Then he tries to go back in time, to meet his love. And he can't do it, because it's so intense, the thought, what he wants. And after that big thing, going through the whole state, I couldn't do it now. I couldn't put myself in that mode, so fixated.

You'd like to think you could. But then again, we're older. We're not relevant any more. That's why it's cool that we're older. Donnie is relevant now, culturally, to Pittsburgh, to people who love the band.

We had no other choice. We had to work our asses off to get it to sound the way we wanted it to sound, to stack them up. I think it happened, maybe, because…

I was *hungry*. I was just driving this thing. I had put all my eggs in this basket. I didn't go to college. My identity was all wrapped up into making this a success. And at the time, that intensity was really hard. It's hard on your family. You're singular.

Maybe we wouldn't have worked as hard if we were more upper-class kids. I'm more of a lower/middle-class Slovenian kid. That's what we are. We're hard workers. I believe in that. The reason work is important is because it involves effort. The lowest skill takes talent and effort. It takes effort to learn how to play piano. And then to *achieve* something in piano takes effort twice. Effort can overcome a lot of things: lack of inspiration, lack of genius, if you don't have a song.

Even today, I'll tell you: If I write a song, I need the intensity to keep staying at that song. You throw things against the wall until something works. You keep at it and keep at it, until it's the best song it can be. If you stay at it, then maybe you can write a great song. Whether anyone will care, I don't know. But in the ideal world, I believed if you wrote the ideal song, people would hear it — I don't know if I believe that any more. But I had to believe it at the time.

It might be a little crazy. But I'm a little crazy. I'll take the time to do that.

> We were all hungry at the time.
> All of us wanted to do something.
> We thought we could write some
> good songs and be a good band.
> We were hard-working and driven
> to do something that we
> were all proud of.

~DONNIE IRIS

CHAPTER 21

Looking for a Deal, Dealing for a Look

MARK: The three of us — me, Donnie and Jerry — were the real creative core. But the guys playing on the record, they added immeasurably, too.

I thought "Leah" was good. But even back then, I didn't think it would be big or popular; there's just so much luck in this business. Without hanging it all out there, I have other options in my life now. At that time, I had no other options. I had all my eggs in one basket. I was going to go for music. Driving into my future, it was my future, sink or swim. I was into it, committed.

I remember being done with the whole album. It was emotional for all three of us. We really turned that into a labor of love over time. When it was done, we listened to the whole thing, and I thought it was great. I was happy with it. We assembled the whole record, front-to-back. We all dug on it. Donnie was getting a little hypercritical, but he realized it was all good.

When Mark finally brought a *Back on the Streets* tape to the Belkin-Maduri office for a big reveal and listening party, the business team gave it an enthusiastic thumbs-up.

MARK: It wasn't a big deal. I brought it in. Chris was there. Carl was there. We were sitting in the listening room. I was sleep deprived. They liked it.

When the tape made it to the Belkin-Maduri junior executives, they liked it, too.

FOX: Between the [James] Gang and Michael [Stanley], we've worked with a lot of great producers. There are two kinds of producers: There's the kind of producer who inflects-injects himself onto you; he has a skill set that's in demand by others: He makes records in a way that will enhance the sound, the arrangements, and everything else about it. And an artist might appreciate that, because he'll benefit from the way a producer sounds.

The other kind of producer is a more kind of producer who works on bringing out the best in the artist he's working on at the time, without necessarily injecting his own sounds or arrangement into the music. Both kinds can be fantastic.

The first kind is Roy Thomas Baker — you know a Roy Thomas Baker record when you hear it, 100 times out of 100.

On the other hand, you've got a Bill Szymczyk, who can contribute to the arrangement so quietly and so passively, so that the artist almost feels their own idea coming. And what Phil does is get the most out of artists.

Mark has the ability to straddle those two styles. He has some ideas of his own, and he can make a record that sounds very Mark-ish. Or he can get an artist and bring out the best in them, like he did with Donnie. And when you're doing it for yourself, the distinction kind of blurs. But Mark is great on both sides of that. He has a wonderful ear. A great sense of arrangement.

On that first record, I think Donnie and the Cruisers were fully formed.

Sonically, the band was fully formed. But the image needed some development.

"THAT GUY LOOKS LIKE BUDDY HOLLY: CURLY HAIR, GLASSES..."

MARK: Donnie wasn't wearing the glasses then. All the imaging came later. And following "Leah" and a couple of the other tracks, we started talking about the album title. And who the artist would be. And imaging him.

It was my suggestion about glasses. Obviously, I was thinking about Elvis Costello. And Donnie, he's not a bad-looking guy, but he's not a big Adonis type guy either. I suggested glasses, and he said he had these wee little glasses — he used the word "wee" — like John Lennon had, the wire rims.

Then he said, "I had these glasses I used to wear," those 410 old '50s type frames at home. So he started wearing those, and I was like, "Yeah, that's perfect." We saw him as this "King of Cool" kind of guy, and that's how he comes off on the Blossom Music Center tape from the early eighties: Mr. Cool. With flashes of Donnie's warm personality coming through.

For Donnie, they weren't Elvis Costello glasses; they were Buddy Holly glasses.

DONNIE: They were glasses that I actually wore in high school, basically the same frame I wore through school. They were Fortune 410 glasses.

MARK: Then I wrote a stupid fake bio about his divorces and Agnes and raising gerbils. A lot of people still believe that.

BACK ON THE STREETS: THE ALBUM COVER

Once the band had a sound and image, they needed to present it to the world. To capture the new and improved Donnie Iris 2.0, Belkin-Maduri turned to Cleveland-based LaFlavour photographer Bob Holcepl.

Today, the *Back on the Streets* cover seems like leftfield kitsch. At the time, it was frugal retro-chic. Instead of hiring a stylist, Donnie rummaged through his closet. He stopped when he came to his shiniest leftover stage duds. For the shoot, he put it on — and took it off.

DONNIE: I wore that yellow prom suit in the Jaggerz. The whole group had it. We were six guys onstage in yellow suits. It was not ironic.

The cover features five versions of Donnie in progressive states, from formal dress to nigh-complete undress: On the left, he stands in the photo's forefront, holding his prized 1959 Fender Stratocaster, fully clothed in golden duds. The next iteration stands behind him, wearing no coat. The next progression has sheds his pants. In the next, he has no shirt. At the far right, Donnie stands in his underwear, grinning, proudly gripping his guitar, black socks pulled up to his knees, as lightning flashes in the dark sky above.

DONNIE: It's a Start. It has a Telecaster neck because the original neck was messed up. I still have it.

Holcepl was the house photographer for the Belkin-Maduri Organization. He had shot the eye-popping Mandolay cover for LaFlavour, and his other work includes now-obscure albums by the Chicago Gangsters and Dunn & Bruce Street. Album art was his side gig.

HOLCEPL: I was a photographer for 20 years. I've been in coffee and crepes for over 25 now. I own Crepes de Luxi in the West Side Market, in Cleveland.

The art director on the job called me. His name is Bob Rath. Bob was the contact I shot the LaFlavour album with. He was an art director at Wyse Advertising. They're the people that brought you the catchphrase, "With a name like Smucker's, it's got to be good!" Where that idea came from is Bob Rath. Conceptually, it was all him, and I was the tool.

The shoot took place on the outskirts of downtown Cleveland, in the Flats, a riverside port/industrial area chock full of smokestacks, warehouses and brick roads.

HOLCEPL: It was mostly centered there, at the North end of Old River Road. We were south of that, kind of behind where the Terminal Tower and the Sherwin-Williams headquarters are. I believe the street is still brick.

It was multiple frames that were assembled. Talking about this, there's a then-and-now problem. Now, you'd be able to take all that stuff an put it together in Photoshop in a half hour. Then, it took a long time, because you had to take original shots. And literally, each picture had to be cut apart and pasted down and airbrushed around to make it all work. That was all the work of the retoucher. He did all that. I just shot the pictures. I didn't add the rainbow, the moon, the lightning.

I still don't quite wrap my head around this concept. I personally don't feel like it was fully formed, from a conceptual standpoint. I don't know: "Skinny white boy in pimp outfits"?

I didn't understand, conceptually, what was going on. It seemed to me, "It's the '80s, we're going to throw everything at it."

MADURI: We wanted to just get some cool shots of him in the suit.

HOLCEPL: "Now you need to step back three steps and take off your jacket. Now you need to step back three steps…. Eventually, we got to the last shot, where he's in his tighties. And the little briefs that he had on literally said "Jingle balls" on them. I remember laughing at the time, and Bob and I saying, "That'll have to get airbrushed out."

Donnie was very affable, like, "Yeah, let's do this!" He was totally into it.

The Donnie Iris album, it's the only thing anybody ever talks about. I have a couple of photos in the Cleveland Museum of Art's permanent collection. You'd think people would mention *that*.

MADURI: My father had a gun in his car. So he pulled the gun out and put in in the street, next to Donnie. He put it next to his guitar, for a street look. We were laughing and loving it.

And then when MCA picked it up, they kept the same album cover, because they felt it really fit the guy.

MARK: I hated the cover. I thought it was cheesey. I wasn't around. I was in the studio, working on stuff. If people like it, that's great. All I know is: I was working on this big album. I was disappointed in the cover.

LOOKING FOR A RECORD DEAL, ROUND I

Back on the Streets was ready for the world. Donnie's team had to figure out how to get it to the world, though.

MARK: I really put the whole thing together, produced it and wrote it, and then handed it to Carl. Then later on, they signed Donnie as the record started moving up the charts.

But for now, the Belkin-Maduri organization had to interest a record label in selling the album — which is never easy or simple. Belkin and Maduri had their own label, Sweet City, which was home to the Wild Cherry catalog, featuring the phenomenal "Play That Funky Music." Sweet City distributed through EMI, which signed off on its artist signings.

EMI, however, didn't like the album. So a Sweet City record deal was not an option. Now Belkin and Maduri split up, each working their own trail, looking for record deal for the Cruisers. When he saddled up, Belkin brought one of his deputies along: James Gang founder Jimmy Fox.

FOX: I was a co-manager, in a sense, to Michael and Donnie and Mark and Breathless. I did whatever was necessary. Carl would call me if we needed to get music to a distributor. Or I'd work on music, on organization, on stage presentation, on sequencing records. Because I'd been on the artistic side of it, I was in a better position to communicate better than Mike was.

Belkin and Fox packed some Cruisers tapes and made their way to Los Angeles. In L.A., they walked *Back on the Streets* into the heart of the record business, where the two veterans were well known and highly regarded.

JIMMY FOX: I remember a frustrating lack of interest. Mike and I shopped it. It was always hard to set up meetings [to shop an unknown artist], even with Belkin being Belkin. Even from me.

I was the Sweet City A&R director. And I found that out of 100, *maybe* you could work something out with two.

They would only accept submissions that were from reliable, known sources. Once you send the tape to a record company, they can take responsibility for that tape: Let's say a Michael Jackson song comes out and they see something that might sound similar, they write Michael Jackson's people and say, "We think you stole this." And you get sued. So these people don't want any part of hearing submissions. It's much easier to take a submission from a lawyer or someone who works with MCA.

Future events would prove that Fox's note was not an unfounded concern.

FOX: Mike and I spent that week going where we could talk our way in. Most of them were cold calls. And most of them, the best thing we could get was, "Leave a tape. We'll get back to you." That was it. Even though it was Belkin and Jimmy from the James Gang.

We went into A&M Records. And at that time, a fellow named David Kershenbaum was doing their A&R. He had been a very successful producer in the late '60s and early '70s. He had done some very important work. [Kershenbaum produced or signed Joan Baez, Joe Jackson, and Supertramp, later Duran Duran and Tracy Chapman.]

So we went in and sat with David. And we were given the privilege of being able to play a couple songs from Donnie's original album.

To be honest, I thought he went nuts: "This is incredible! Tell me how this is made! Leave this with me!" and "How did you get this?!" and "How did you get that?"

He was incredulous. He kept saying, "Beaver FALLS, *Pennsylvania*."

But in the end, a real offer never came. And there are as many reasons as you can think of.

I think the song we chose was the extended tune from the album, "Too Young to Love." Maybe I made a mistake. Maybe I should have hit him between the eyes with "Leah." But I thought he was an artistic guy, and he'd appreciate the production on "Too Young to Love." So that was the kind of experience we had shopping.

We had been able to get Michael Stanley and Breathless album deals. And there's something to be said for that. But in the end, they were not successful on a national basis. We didn't make the hits.

The answer, invariably, came back kind of vague — which is what you should expect most of the time. When they want you, they're gonna go nuts and let you know right away. And that wasn't happening.

> It was my suggestion about glasses. Obviously, I was thinking about Elvis Costello. ...he said, "I had these glasses I used to wear," those 410 old '50s type frames at home. So he started wearing those, and I was like, "Yeah, that's perfect."
>
> ~ MARK AVSEC

CHAPTER 22

On the Airwaves: Donnie Meets DVE

"We are Pittsburgh. We are D-V-E."

— Fall 2017 station bumper for 102.5 FM, WDVE, Pittsburgh

Back on the Streets was dead.

After Team Donnie poured months of work into the album, nobody in the record industry wanted to touch it.

So they found a way to release it anyway. And break it. In a big way.

Belkin and Maduri reached into their pockets and released it on Midwest National, one of their record labels, which had put out Donnie's debut single.

MARK: Donnie was signed to Belkin-Maduri's production company. I signed a producer deal.

Midwest National Records released *Back on the Streets* July 15, 1980. In the corporate-dominated world of modern radio, virtually all airtime is commercial real estate that is bought and paid for. And on large stations, new independent records have no shot at serious airplay. In 1980, the gateways to radio were far more surmountable: A good song and a friendly face still had a chance. Team Donnie had a great song and a very friendly face.

At this critical point, the only people who believed in the record were on the Belkin-Maduri payroll. One of them had an even stronger connection to one of the business partners: Carl Maduri's son, Chris Maduri, Sweet City's vice president of promotion and artist relations. Like his dad, Chris was a polished smooth operator. The younger Maduri had radio contacts in the Midwest and Mid-Atlantic. One person who believes in a product can make all the difference.

MARK: Chris Maduri deserves a lot of credit for things. He broke the record. Chris got "Ah! Leah!" on Boston's WBCN and WMMS in Cleveland — of course, WDVE in Pittsburgh.

The song was also big on Cleveland's M105, which had recently begun billing itself as "Cleveland's Classic Rock."

MADURI: The phones went crazy. They started selling records.

DONNIE: DVE was the first one to play us. They were the first in the country to play "Leah." And then all the other stations started getting behind us, at least the pop stations and the rock stations.

DVE was *the* radio station, especially the morning show. They swamped everybody else, pretty much. They had good people in the morning, and they would talk about Pittsburgh.

WDVE — in Pittsburgh, commonly known simply as "D-V-E" — has been the city's unwavering rock and roll fortress on the FM dial since the days of disco, a proud purveyor of all things six-stringed, from Zeppelin to the Iron City Houserockers. Donnie was the greatest beneficiary of programmer John McGhee's "local first" strategy. [22.1]

THE DVE MORNING SHOW: *JIMMY & STEVE IN THE MORNING*

The DVE morning show, in different forms, would wax and wane over the 1980s. But it always dominated the key radio-listening audience from ages 18-34. The station would keep the Cruisers on the airwaves when Donnie's popularity and novelty evaporated. Then, in the '90s, a later version of the station's morning show would cement Donnie's position in the Pittsburgh pantheon. Through it all, every morning, DVE served classic rock, local artists, a lot of laughs, and a dash of Donnie.

The Legend of Donnie Iris generally credits the early '80s morning show *Jimmy and Steve in the Morning* — Jimmy Roach and Steven Hansen — with sparking this stage of Donnie's career. Donnie himself has often told the story of the two giving him his big break. In the early '80s, Jimmy and Steve were the Cruisers' biggest boosters — but not *yet*. The team didn't meet until September 1980, three months after *Back on the Streets* was on the street.

In July 1980, Steve Hansen was working on the West Coast. Pittsburgh veteran Jimmy Roach as also a big name nationally, as host of the syndicated radio program *The Backstage Special*. It ran on 120 stations, interspersing long-haired rock with interviews with groups like Rush, Yes, and Frank Zappa. Roach, a model of a laid-back rock dude, had good taste *and* stroke.

Website Pittsburgh Music History credits Rick Granati with introducing the Donnie album to program director Dave Lange. [22.2] The band was still billed as *Donnie Iris* at this point.

JIMMY ROACH: As far as us playing the record, a couple things run together in my head. The Granati Brothers have said Dave Lange, the program director from DVE, was at their house. And the Granatis played it for him. And he said, "If you bring it in, I'll play it on the air." And then Steve and I played it the next day.

Another version says I was at the Granatis' and heard "Ah! Leah!" and said "Jeez crimony! I've got to play this on the radio!" and played it the next day.

40 years later, I've heard so many versions, I don't know which is real.

Steve Hansen has always told me that I went out there [to the Iris house], and Donnie played it. There were so many times I went out there, and he played me stuff. I wasn't taking notes at the time.

I read an article that said Donnie said Jim and I came out to the house. And Steve said, "I love getting credit for that, but I wasn't here."

Honest to God, I don't remember.

I don't remember Donnie bringing anything to the station. He may have. I don't remember that. I remember going out to Beaver County and getting ahold of a record. I don't remember him being in the studio with me.

I'd never talked to him before that — that I remember.

The first time I heard it, I thought I'd never heard anything like that before: The layered vocals come up and slap you in the face. I remember thinking, "This is too good to be local. This is world-class stuff." And that's why I knew I had to get it on the air as soon as I could.

When we started playing it, we played it *to death*. We couldn't get over the fact it was this local guy, doing all these layers, 50 overdubs. It was unheard of.

DONNIE: People said, "We heard you on the radio!" Especially after it caught on. At the time, B.E. and I were playing softball together. I went to a softball game, and people were going up to me, telling me they heard it.

B.E. played outfield. I played infield. We had a good time.

MADURI: We worked the radio anywhere 150 miles from Cleveland. So Cleveland, Youngstown, Pittsburgh, Columbus, Wheeling West Virginal, Detroit. "Ah! Leah!" was very well received. In Pittsburgh, WDVE carried the market.

Cleveland was extremely significant, nationally. Not just with this project, but with all sorts of projects. Springsteen had broken out of Cleveland. Bowie and Todd Rundgren did, too. So it was on the heel of those successes.

STEVE HANSEN: I know Donnie gives credit to me and Jimmy Roach for playing it, but I was in San Francisco at the time. I had heard the record, and I started playing a song.

It was perfect. It was a power-pop sound. I loved everything about it. It wasn't "Ah! Leah!" or any of the hits from the album. It might have been "Joking."

I was in Pittsburgh from 1974 through 1976. And then I went out to San Francisco. So I didn't know anything about Donnie Iris at that point of time. I knew B.E. Taylor and the Establishment. I knew Diamond Reo — the guys who would go on to become a part of the Pittsburgh renaissance scene in the early 1980s.

I was working at KSAN, which was probably the most legendary station in underground radio. KSAN was one of the stations that initially championed and premiered punk rock and new wave, which initially hit on the coast.

What made punk rock beautiful was that it was a reaction to staid, boring corporate rock and boring Rod Stewarts. It was designed to, and partially did, destroy their credibility. There was an almost complete cleansing of the system. And it gave way to power pop and new wave, which was a lot more melodic. The Sex Pistols and the Clash begat the Police and Blondie. The Ramones, who initially were fairly jarring, were actually East Coast Beach Boys.

There was a lot of really good music: Nick Lowe, Elvis Costello, Dave Edmunds. I latched onto that. So I'm at a station that let you pick your own stuff. It was pretty revolutionary, especially now. I would look at all these American fly-over-state bands — the Outlaws, Stillwater, these crap bands. And being in San Francisco, I would say, "Who would play this crap?" But back in Pittsburgh, and stations like DVE, they did well.

So one day I'm at the station. And I see the first Donnie Iris album. I don't know he's from Pittsburgh. I know nothing about him. I pulled it out, and I latched onto a song.

Not very long after the album was released, I came back to Pittsburgh. And "Ah! Leah!" was already a big song on WDVE. Jimmy Roach was already playing it. WDVE had a station director named Dave Lange, who was very important. He was supportive of Pittsburgh music. After him, there was a long stretch of program directors who were not supportive of Pittsburgh music, because that's not how you make your bones.

So Jimmy and I were together, and we kept playing it.

JIMMY ROACH: Pretty soon after we started playing the tune and the reaction got so big, Donnie started coming around to hang out in the studio.

THE REVIEWS ARE IN. SOME.

Word about Donnie started spreading.

Cash Box, the music-business journal, had liked Donnie since "The Rapper." The magazine wrote up *Back on the Streets* alongside Pat Benatar's *Crimes of Passion* and Rick James' *Garden of Love*: "Big surprises come from little labels, and Donnie Iris' debut on Midwest has to be one of the year's biggest shockers. The album cover looks like the attack of the Elvis Costellos. But Iris is no clone... his sound is such a classic example of modern energized pop that

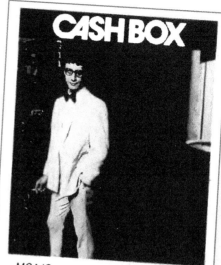

MCA/Carousel recording artist Donnie Iris delivered one of the sleeper gems of the year with his "Back On The Streets" LP. His multi-tracked wonder of a label debut was paced by the hook-ridden Top 25 single, "Ah! Leah!" And his success is as much of a surprise to him as anyone.

The Beaver Falls, Pa. native had been laying low in his basement hideout after recording an album for Cleveland-based Sweet City Records' Midwest label, when all of a sudden he found himself in the major leagues with MCA/Carousel Records.

His single was getting plenty of action in the Midwest with the tiny boutique label, but once MCA stepped in, "Ah! Leah!" seemed to take off everywhere. His sudden success isn't so surprising to pop analysts, though, as songs like "I Can't Hear You" and "Agnes" exhibit that mixture of shimmering emotion and electric energy that characterized the classic rock period of the Beatles-dominated late '60s.

In fact, Iris fronted his own classic rock period group — he was the leader of the '60s band The Jaggerz, which had a style heavily influenced by the Liverpool Four, and struck with a big hit with "The Rapper." The Jaggerz, recording for Neil Bogart's Kama Sutra label, disbanded in 1974 after recording its last fateful LP for the obscure California-based Wooden Nickel label.

Undaunted, Iris hooked up with an R&B band, Wild Cherry, in the late '70s. Invigorated by the experience, he returned to his beloved Beaver Falls to cut some fresh wax of his own.

Although it was recorded only a few doors away from his Third Ave. home, "Back On The Streets" has a brilliantly layered vocal and instrumental feeling that sounds as if it were recorded at the top 24-track studio in the country.

The brainchild of Iris and keyboardist/best friend Mark Avsec, the album became a reality via the help of local musicians Marty Lee (guitar), Albritton McClain (bass), Kevin Valentine (drums) and Kenny Blake (saxophone).

Already having hit #58 on the **Cash Box** Top 200 Albums chart, Donnie Iris looks like he's "Back On The Streets" for good.

Cashbox / April 18, 1981

one forgets the cops and just feels this refreshingly and lovably quirky sound." [22.3] A later article added declared "Ah! Leah!," "Joking" and "I Can't Hear You No More" all "sound like car radio dreams." [22.4]

STEVE HANSEN: We got calls, tons of them. Donnie was on top of the food chain, in terms of popularity and the impact of the songs.

At DVE today, "Ah! Leah!" is still a staple of the station. The other songs from the time are pretty of-their-moment.

And now there's basically two DVEs, and they're generally number 1 and number 2, or maybe 1 and 3: DVE, and 3WS [WWSW 94.5 FM] play the era of me and Jimmy. Classic rock is the common language of Pittsburgh.

All the pretty girls, back in the early '80s, were listening to [urban music mothership] WAMO and [all-things-pop station WBZZ 93.7] B-94 at the time. But the guys were listening to classic rock and DVE. And the girls, once they settled in with their guys, became DVE aficionados, as well. And they did long after other classic-rock stations faded away.

Not a lot of people leave or come into Pittsburgh, as much as other cities. Time just marches on out there. Pittsburgh, more than any other city, is stuck in a moment, a moment of music that people loved. And it's never going to change. A number of generations grew up with DVE. Everybody came through the same spin cycle. DVE owned such a large chunk of real estate.

And, to this day, no station has ever played more Donnie than DVE.

> "
> I remember thinking,
> "This is too good to be local.
> This is world-class stuff."
> And that's why I knew I had to get
> it on the air as soon as I could.
> When we started playing it, we
> played it to death. We couldn't get
> over the fact it was this local guy,
> doing all these layers, 50 overdubs.
> It was unheard of.
>
> ~ JIMMY ROACH
> "

CHAPTER 23

LEAH UNMASKED!
The Back on the Streets Video(s):
"Ah! Leah!" and "Agnes"

The saga of the *Back on the Streets* videos is one of the undocumented episodes from Cruisers history.

September 1980. "Ah! Leah!" was in stores and lighting up the FM airwaves. Carl Maduri had a novel idea. Team Donnie could jump on the latest cutting-edge, multimedia promotional trend: short films inspired by popular songs. Recording artists had been making promotional clips to match songs for decades. But the growing trend was so new that the term "music video" was not in wide use yet.

Maduri figured: Donnie didn't have a budget — or demand — to tour. But the songs were catching on. Everybody who met Donnie liked him. If they could film Donnie doing his thing, they could send it all over the country. People could see him in action. And once they saw him in action, they would want to see him in person.

Spending money to make a short film was not a slam-dunk decision. Music videos were a fresh, hot medium. But MTV would not launch until August 1981, a year in the future. On one hand, a video seemed like an unnecessary expense. But on the other hand, if it paid off, it could help break this regional release on a national scale.

BELKIN: I thought having a video was a great idea.

The video budget funded not one, but two videos: current single "Ah! Leah!" and "Agnes," which was planned as the second single. Neither video is a classic. One is infamous. One is lost to history. Both are clouded in obscurity.

WHO'S THAT GIRL? LEAH REVEALED

The "Ah! Leah!" clip stars a mystery girl; the actress' identity has been a mystery for decades, even to diehard fans and intrepid sleuths dedicated to investigating 1980s video vixens. So has the identity of the rest of the crew. Management threw out the paperwork years ago. Donnie was the only member of the band involved, and he forgot everybody's name a long time ago. The cast and crew barely have anything to say, but the truth is out there.

Maduri found an experienced pro who was willing to work relatively cheap: Kim Dumpster directed and produced the videos for both "Ah! Leah!" and "Agnes." Dempster had been at ground zero of the modern video explosion. By 1981, her body of work included producing and directing for Jefferson Starship, Iggy Pop, rocker Randy Hansen and Huey Lewis. She also directed *Rock Justice*, a live rock operetta that was the first major-label videodisc release. She had recently formed her own company, VAMP — Video And Music Productions — and agreed to shoot two videos for one check.

DEMPSTER: I directed and produced. I think the spots were done for a TV show called Videowest. I was the director for music videos and one of the producers for the show.

I moved on to [veteran music producer] David Rubinson at the Automatt Recording Studio. He had all these cool acts like Santana, the Pointer Sisters, Herbie Hancock. He said, "Why don't you start your own company, and I'll give you offices at the Automatt?" So I started my own company, VAMP. And I think I got Donnie through David. Maybe they sent me the song and I liked it.

The dubiously iconic video restages the *Back on the Streets* album cover: Donnie is back in his canary yellow Jaggerz tuxedo, working his charms on a tall blonde model, on a pure white set, with some basic digital video effects that were fairly advanced for the day.

By modern standards, the "Ah! Leah!" video looks like a no-budget affair, but it was not. Finding a stage with an all-white set is not a simple matter.

BELKIN: It was not cheap.

DEMPSTER: The video looks like we did it with no money. But it was so rare for us to shoot on a stage. And all that white was definitely on a stage. That was not cheap. We shot videos for around $50,000 then. That would have been for both videos. Until MTV existed, nobody really knew what a video was worth. And there was no MTV then. Music videos — there was no *use* for them yet. The money was really low.

I don't remember the video, in all honesty. When I watched it, I remembered Donnie was a sweetheart.

At that embryonic phase in the development of the form, there was no line between "short film" and "rock video." A 1981 *Record World* article about VAMP had to reach back six years, to Queen's 1975 "Bohemian Rhapsody" clip, to find a recognizable example of the concept. [23.1]

At the time, the two Donnie videos were considered a single piece. A *Billboard* profile of Dempster refers to the brag-worthy project as "a 6 ½-minute piece... used in-house for MCA, with possible television exposure to come." [23.2]

Dempster and a skeleton crew — cameraman Wes Dorman, no stylist, and a small cast — shot the videos in San Francisco.

The mystery video chanteuse is actress-model B.J. McAllister. [23.3] Her IMDb credits list three episodes of *The Young and the Restless* and an appearance on *Riptide*. [23.4] She didn't want to talk about it.

Based on Donnie and Dempster's best recollections, each video took a day to shoot.

"THERE'S AN 'AGNES' VIDEO?!"

Donnie returned for a leading role in the "Agnes" video, where he trades the prom tux for a leather jacket. He's one of three leads in a straightforward dramatization of the song. In the lost clip, Donnie plays the kind of garden-variety cool guy who might warrant the attention of a cocktail waitress. And who might have enough stones to brave the wrath of her pistol-packing boyfriend.

At the time, Dempster told *Billboard* reporter Jack McDonough, "Iris introduces the characters in 'Agnes' when they're young, and then they reappear... We did the video by starting with their early meetings, and if it's successful, we hope to be able to do 'Back on the Streets' and pick up the characters later on." [23.5]

It was not successful. It never saw the light of day.

MICHELE MICHAELS, WDVE *ELECTRIC LUNCH*: I worked as an entertainment reporter at [Pittsburgh TV station] KDKA-TV in the '90s, and one of my assignments was to do a story on Donnie. I went to his house for a look back at the early MTV era.

Donnie's record company made him do a music video for "Agnes," and it was damn hilarious, him describing how the director of the video wanted him to reenact the fight he sings about in the song, over this girl, Agnes, with Louie.

He was laughing so hard, because I don't think he was an Oscar contender when he tried to pull that off. He had to look like he had acting chops, and I think he found that unsettling and hilarious at the same time.

The "Agnes" video is the great lost memento from the Cruisers catalog (even moreso than the legendary album *Cruise Control*; more on that later). Dempster and her crew barely recall the "Agnes" video, and do not remember the cast. A brief clip of it appears in the documentary *King Cool*. The only known copy is in the possession of director Dave Rogant, who won't share it. It's among the Cruisers clips Avsec considers "embarrassing," so don't hold your breath for a release or leak.

DONNIE: That's a shame it disappeared. It was cool as hell, the black and white.

When the album was picked up by a bigger label, the choice for a second single changed — in America, at least. "Agnes" only met its destiny as a single on the other side of the planet, in Australia, where it was released as a single in August 1981. ("Back on the Streets" was the B-side of the Australian single.)

So it's the "Ah! Leah!" video that provides the enduring image of Donnie. In the clip, wearing the yellow suit, he dances an impromptu cha-cha with a leggy blonde, against a white background — to the continuing amusement of many an internet commenter.

Like the much-derided "Love Is a Battlefield" or "Rock Me Tonight" videos, it's a truly effective piece of art because it's memorable. As Donnie and Belkin would learn in coming years: a cheesey video is better than no video.

DONNIE: I think they're really cool, especially for the time.

BELKIN: We were happy with it.

FOX: I wasn't unhappy. But visuals are not my primary thing.

When the video did make it onto the airwaves, it surprised Donnie's former bandmates.

BENNIE FAIELLA, THE JAGGERZ: He never did like putting on the suits. And then I started seeing him on TV in that yellow suit, I thought — [*laughs*] — "That son of a bitch! He complained all the time, and now he's got that big album out, and there he is with a suit on!" He went to the rock thing. That's what he always wanted to do.

The video idea was ahead of its time. One Cruisers video did make it into the public eye, but it wouldn't arrive for over a year. For now, "Ah! Leah!" was a still just a popular radio single. The staff at their new label would find a use for the short film. In the third quarter of 1980, the video helped hit men from coast to coast understand what product they'd be pushing.

The single "Ah! Leah!" warmed up over the summer of 1980. In the fall, it got hotter.

By October, the song was in rotation at Long Island's WLIR, Detroit's WWWW, Chicago's WMET, Minneapolis' KQRS, Dallas' KZEW and KTXQ, Louisville's WLRS and Phoenix's KDKB, among others. [23.6]

MADURI: Programmers loved the layered vocals. Sixty vocals: six-zero. And then record labels began to hear about it.

(l. to r.): Kevin Valentine, Albritton McClain Donnie Iris, Marty Lee Hoenes, Mark Avsec.

CHAPTER 24

The Record Deal:
Carousel/MCA Selects the Cruisers

Here's what you need to know to understand the ups, downs, perceived shortcomings, and successes in Donnie Iris and the Cruisers' career as a major-label recording act:

Donnie Iris and the Cruisers never had a major-label record deal. Not exactly.

After the Belkin-Maduri Organization formed their own independent record label, Midwest National Records...

And after Donnie Iris' solo debut, *Back on the Streets,* was turned down by every major record company that Donnie's co-manager, Mike Belkin, could contact...

And after Midwest National independently released *Back on the Streets* in summer 1980...

And after "Ah! Leah!" found some success on rock radio...

Then the Donnie Iris team signed a deal that connected them to MCA Records, which was a major record label (and still lives on as part of the Universal Music Group, one of three surviving major-label networks).

That Cruisers recording contract was not a *record deal* with MCA, strictly speaking.

Donnie Iris & the Cruisers' "record deal" was, in fact, a production deal with a California-based company called Carousel Records. Carousel had a deal with major record label MCA Records. In *that* deal, Carousel would provide finished albums to MCA. MCA would manufacture, distribute, and promote those albums.

The Cruisers' remarkably harmonious career features a mere two sources of world-shaking drama and contention. The band's production deal with the un-prolific Carousel is one.

The group, not surprisingly, don't like talking about their record deal — which, to be fair, yielded four albums, two *Billboard* top-100 albums, two more in the top 200 albums, seven *Billboard* Hot 100 singles, an uncertain amount of music videos, and respectable rotation on MTV.

MARK: You know how involved I was in the album. I was as involved as Donnie or more. So we finally got it done. It was emotional for me: I thought it was a good piece of work, and it got passed by everybody. So then it hit the charts, finally. MCA showed some interest, maybe Chrysalis. I never heard much about Chrysalis.

Donnie ended up signing with Rick Frio and MCA.

To me, we were on the charts. He was rolling the dice. I don't think he had that much of a personal thing for it.

"The production agreement is the single most regressive and anti-artist contract introduced in the music industry," wrote *Billboard* guest columnist Bob Donnelly, a veteran attorney with Rock and Roll Hall of Fame clients, in 1999. [24.1]

Long story short: In a production deal, the artist surrenders ownership of the album, in exchange for a reduced cut of the money from the major label, which goes to the production company. The production company typically gets more money than the artist. In Donnie's case, the deal for his first two albums included an $87,500 budget apiece for recording fees, followed by a 10% royalty on singles and 12.5% for album and tape sales. [24.2]

Major label deals, while coveted, are essentially a loan from the label to the band, for a very expensive lottery ticket: Artists sign over rights to their creations, in exchange for a financial investment from the record company. If the product is profitable, and if any money remains after the project recoups its expenses, the artist is last in line to claim some of the money their work generated.

But whether or not the money matches the prestige, being a rock star is one of the most lucrative jobs in the world. And if you don't buy that lottery ticket, you can't win.

Belkin, the renowned concert promoter and successful manager, had tried to secure a record deal for Donnie Iris. And he struck out.

But Belkin's partner, Carl Maduri, had a deal in his pocket. In August 1979, Maduri had signed a production deal with Carousel Records, where under he would provide albums to Carousel, which would provide those records to a major label. And that major label would get those records to the marketplace — where the albums would fail or succeed based on their own merits, public whims, and the combined efforts of the companies' departments for distribution, sales, and promotion. And the deal with Carousel and Rick Frio was the last, best, and only deal on the table.

BELKIN: That was 100% Maduri, zero percent Belkin. Maduri had a personal relationship with a guy named Rick Frio.

Production deals were unconventional, but not uncommon. Fox, the James Gang drummer who still worked for Belkin, says it wasn't a terrible deal.

FOX: MCA, like my label ABC, was a national label, but hardly in the top five.

Rick had that independent production deal. That gives you a little more say: You have more control. Because when you sign with a record company, you turn yourself over to them.

If you have an independent production deal, you can, in theory, turn over a finished product to them. And they need to accept it the way it is. Their input is no longer part of the product chain. Rick's going to be working for the best record he could possibly get.

The difference is: When we're done as an artist, we and Rick have agreed that this is where it ends. You don't have to put up with the record company saying, "We want you to drop three songs and remix these two and re-record that one — and, by the way, we think you need a different singer."

And that happens. That happens all the time. Because the labels think they know everything. And the reality is: Very, very few record companies know everything.

And the other thing with an independent production deal: Usually there's a slightly better rate; you get an extra point or two.

During Donnie's time at MCA, several other Pittsburgh-area rock heroes would also land on MCA: the Iron City Houserockers, Norm Nardini & the Tigers, and B.E. Taylor — but their presence was largely incidental. (Taylor worked with Maduri and recorded for Belkin-Maduri's Sweet City label, but also was not signed directly to MCA.)

MARK: Belkin-Maduri, who now owned [*Back on the Streets*], did a deal with Rick Frio at Carousel, who really wanted the artist, which of course was now known as "Donnie Iris."

Frio is still in the business, as the head of Rick Frio Entertainment Management. He is the kind of music-biz figure who pops up in *Billboard* articles from time to time. In 1980, he was in the middle of a distinguished career, having worked with artists including Elton John, Neil Diamond, Olivia Newton-John, and Loretta Lynn. In 1979, he formed Carousel Productions, with an eye on film production. [24.3] In short order, Carousel diversified into music. As a label, it issued a modest catalog from 1979 through 1983. Its releases included the Cruisers and co-ed disco band Dream Express.

Carousel morphed into a subsidiary of MCA. And Frio parlayed the connection into an eight-year run with the label, where he climbed the ladder to executive vice president of marketing. Frio later managed Mavis Staples and formed New Edge Records, partnering with former Stax owner Al Bell.

FRIO: I am not going to go back from my birth into the record business, because, in fact, my father was always in it. I wanted to be involved in music. Just take me at my word: To get where I got, I must have done a great job.

In my tenure there, I hired almost every person on the staff, so we knew how to work together. There was no problem with my involvement with the careers of Elton John, Neil Diamond, Olivia Newton-John, the Who, Lynyrd Skynyrd, Johnny Rivers, Bobby Vee, Leon Russell, Cher, Sonny and Cher, Rick Nelson, Barry White…. These are only the recent artists at that time. I could go back to the '50s for Little Richard and Fats Domino as well as Chuck Berry…. Also, in my period at Universal Studios, I was involved in major movie soundtracks: *The Sting*, *Jesus Christ Superstar*, *Car Wash*, *American Graffiti* and more.

FOX: Rick Frio had connections with important people.

BELKIN: He was going to be releasing the recording on his label, through MCA. And he didn't really follow through on that. And so it got into a lawsuit. I was never a fan of his. They were both Italian, *paisan*. I never liked Rick. He was a big bullshitter.

We had a big meeting in a hotel in California, and it was like, "Where *else* can we go with The Cruisers?" We didn't have another label we could go to. It was the only deal we had.

News of the deal hit the trade magazines with one discordant detail: A blurb in *Billboard* announced that hot new artist Donnie Iris "is managed by Rick Frio [of] Los Angeles…. He is booked through the Belkin-Maduri Organization [of] Cleveland." [24.4] That small discrepancy would flare into a major situation later.

DONNIE: I always felt that [Frio] was doing a good job — up until the end. At the end, he was not doing enough to keep the band going. In the beginning, he was gung-ho. At the end, he was lukewarm.

He was real personal, outgoing kind of guy. Good guy. Very nice man.

October 9, 1980, Donnie Iris signed a recording contract with Carousel. [24.5] And, for now, he was working for MCA.

DONNIE IRIS
BACK ON THE STREETS

AH! LEAH!

CHAPTER 25

Back on the Streets:
The Reviews Are In. Also: Airplay.

In October 1980, *Back on the Streets* was back on the streets again, from a new label. On the new edition, the sides were reversed: On the first pressing, hit single "Ah! Leah!" was the first song on side two. Now it was the leadoff track, and "Agnes" now began side two. With major-label marketing and promo muscle behind the album, it would spend 23 weeks on the *Billboard* album chart, peaking at number 57, December 20, 1980.

In November, radio journal *Cash Box* rated the single in "hot" rotation at WCCM Massachusetts, WCOZ Boston, WBCN Boston, WMMS Cleveland WWWM Minnesota. It was at "medium" AT WIBZ South Carolina, WLVQ Ohio, and WABX Indiana. It wasn't on the magazine's national chart, but it was headed there, in the mix with a batch of tunes like AC/DC's "You Shook Me All Night Long," Pat Benatar's "Hit Me With Your Best Shot," and the Cars' "Touch and Go." [25.1]

The MCA push kept "Ah! Leah!" on the charts: It spun into national rotation, broke onto the *Billboard* Hot 100 singles chart December 13, stayed there 18 weeks, and peaked at number 29 February 28, 1981. A that point, it ranked 88 in *Cash Box*'s singles chart and 92 in *Record World*'s, with regular rotation on 100 stations nationwide. [25.2]

Donnie was over 37 years old when *Back on the Streets* was released, and now he had finally shed the "one-hit wonder" tag. Making a solo debut on the charts at that age was uncommon: Rock radio skewed older at the time, but similar-aged artists like the Beatles, Eric Clapton and Rolling Stones were elder statesmen, above the fray, their battle years behind them. Even Aerosmith, on the downside of their early peak, were closer to 30.

"I don't think that years matter than much in rock anymore," Iris told the *Plain Dealer*'s Jane Scott. "Look at the way that Chuck Berry keeps going. Rock 'n' roll is getting older, too." [25.3]

Even with a national push from MCA, *Back on the Streets* didn't receive reviews from any major rock magazines aimed at the general public.

Industry bible *Billboard* only reviewed albums it thought had a serious shot at its charts. It covered the record, picking up on its form and content: "Iris showcases his textured vocal within a diverse collection of hot rock tunes... His lyrics [are] conceived with a polished touch of irony and sarcasm, all encased by the intense rock rhythms of his band." [25.4]

RON GERBER, KFAI FM, *BETWEEN THE SONGS* AUTHOR: The first thing I heard by Donnie Iris was "Ah! Leah!" in 1980. It's really well produced, the way that the harmonies are put together, the backing vocals. It's singable: You can sing along in the car — but you and I could not hit the high notes that Donnie hits.

I was living in New York City at the time. So it got play on the New York City airwaves. And it sounded good. There was a circle of people that knew the kind of songs that peaked at number 30 on the chart, the equivalent of MTV hits, had MTV been around at the time. Stuff like "Ah! Leah," "Sausalito Summer Night" by Diesel, "Fantasy" by Aldo Nova, "On the Loose" by Saga. Songs that were not top hits, but sound fantastic on the radio. And the fact that we had to dig a little deeper in the bins made it that much more rewarding.

It was on *American Top 40* and on the rock stations. It crossed my path, and I had to take the extra step of hunting it down, because radio was not going to play it day and night, like they did the Police record.

It has "1980-81 CLASSIC" stamped all over it. There's a time and a place to it. It takes you back there, without being particularly trendy. If you listen to the other records from 1980, like "Whip It" by Devo, there's a new-wavey sound to them. Donnie missed that new-wave weirdness, while somehow capitalizing on it. The record has keyboards, but it's not as trendy as "Cars" by Gary Numan. It really rose above its peers.

"Ah! Leah!" turned ears at local papers nationwide, and eventually it earned some status in rock circles. Granted: Rock critics, as a demographic, tend to be cranky and wrong:

In 1983, *The New* Rolling Stone *Record Guide* book grudgingly included Donnie. It rated *Back on the Streets* and *King Cool* — the next record — both two stars (of five): "Pittsburgh rocker Donnie Iris is a terrific singer, but his brand of prepubescent pop is strictly low-grade stuff. 'Ah! Leah' from the *Streets* album and 'Love Is Like a Rock' off of *King Cool* are his best moments. Equipped with one of the more versatile voices in rock, Iris can pull off just about any style he wants." [25.5]

The album received a respectably large review (250 words) in *Boys' Life*, which ambitiously covered music and popular culture. Next to a review of Spyro Gyra's *Carnaval*, *Back on the Streets*, Ken Fulton wrote, "The title of the album sounds as hard and tough as a street hood. The music fits that description. But beneath the tough-guy posture, Donnie Iris is crying out in pain, too.... Iris's music grips you and takes you on the rollercoaster ride that has been his life." [25.6]

Donnie scored a glowing review from the Beaver County *Times*' Tom Doyle: "Local radio stations have jumped on the single 'Ah! Leah!' but unfortunately have forgotten about the rest of the songs, all of which are worthy of airplay.... The vocals on every number have a different style and are perfectly complemented by the background vocals... we have 'I Can't Hear You,' a solid, driving piece with vocals like a cross between John Lennon and Elvis Presley.... 'She's So Wild'...constantly changes style with good guitar work and is another example of how to keep the music interesting." ... The album should be a part of anyone's collection if he has any desire to sing in a band or solo." [25.7]

The record did worse in Iris's sort-of hometown newspaper. The Pittsburgh *Press*' Pete Bishop — who slightly warmed up to Donnie over the years — gave it a middling rating. The review was hidden after a gushing rave about Neil Diamond's *The Jazz Singer* soundtrack: "Local boy makes good — sort of. He has a fine voice with plenty of quality and above-average diction, basically in the Buddy Holly vein (he doesn't look unlike Holly, either) but with enough versatility to make songs sound like Bruce Springsteen and the Cars, too.

"*Back on the Streets* has its flaws, however. First, the lyrics are largely standard with less than colorful imagery, although 'Too Young to Love''s are excellent, filled with enough of the despair, pain and frustration inherent in the title to do 'The Boss' justice.

"Second, the production is so full... that the album is far more the studio than the streets.... Iris needs more work on writing compelling lyrics — and on devising a way to duplicate this mass of sound onstage if his career gets that far." [25.8]

JASON PETTIGREW, *ALTERNATIVE PRESS* EDITOR, PITTSBURGH AREA NATIVE, ex-RECORD STORE CLERK: Iris was being marketed as some sort of new wave guy, by the corporate offices at MCA. The way it was positioned to me at the National Record Mart was, "Yeah! It's great: hometown new wave! You like that stuff!" And within that context, it wasn't the Cars or the Romantics; it was a direct *rock and roll band*, rock music that had nice haircuts. It wasn't weird, it wasn't arty, and there were cool things about it. But it wasn't a pop band, per se — a pop band turned up to 10, maybe: The guitars were loud, and the vocals were always perfect. It was a working man's rock band with undeniable, *killing* hooks and great vocal melodies.

The critics came around at more humble pulpits. The Virginia Daily Press/Newport News' Mike Diana picked up on the darker, heavier side of the platter's subject matter: "Donnie Iris is a rare bird. Not only does he have catchy pop tunes that bring to mind the best of new wave, power pop and urban blues, he also has a malleable voice that brings to mind Bruce Springsteen, Freddie Mercury of Queen, and Phil Lynott of Thin Lizzy, just to name a few, aside from his own inimitable style.... The album's producer, Mark Avsec, has done a magnificent job..... Back on the Streets hails the arrival of a new star." [25.9]

Somehow, the band cultivated a loyal following in Australia. *The Age*'s Mike Daly loved the album, noting "*Back on the Streets* is worth buying for the dynamic opening track, 'Ah! Leah!' This is a song in the classic mold, with scorching guitar, strong vocals (multi-tracked, with a section reminiscent of Todd Rundgren) and an irresistible chorus.... Donnie Iris is a talent too big to ignore." [25.10]

The album had some legs. Eventually, *Cash Box* piled more praise on the disc: "*Back on the Streets*... is as contemporary and original as anything that has come out of the 'new wave'." [25.11]

"Ah! Leah!" and *Back on the Streets* got their best review a full 25 years later when, pundit Bob Lefsetz heard the name "Lea" by chance. It struck on old, fond, forgotten chord by Donnie Iris and the Cruisers. And Lefsetz wrote, "I just needed to hear them." [25.12]

In early 1981, "I needed to hear Donnie Iris" was going around.

JIMMY ROACH: The requests went through the roof. The phones lit up. It was like people were seeing an albino deer in their yard, like, "Oh, what's *this*?!" It started building, and it had its own life.

I don't know that people realized it was a local guy. Donnie didn't play out at the time. We'd mention when we played it, but after a while, you're not going so say it every time. People remembered the Jaggerz, but they weren't considered a rock-and-roll band; they were considered a Top 40 band. There was no tie-in, no overlap. I never heard anyone claiming Donnie from the old days.

Before the band hit the road, as radio play was cresting, the single "Ah! Leah!" had moved over 214,988 copies: Over 31,000 in Cleveland. Over 7,000 in Philadelphia. Nearly 29,000 in Chicago. Nearly 17,000 in Nashville. (Pittsburgh wasn't on the list.) Just under 8,000 in Miami. Over 8,000 in Dallas. [25.13]

Album sales broke 100,000, with sales over 4,000 in 11 markets. The record had moved over 12,000 copies in Cleveland, and just under 15,000 in Los Angeles. (The sheet also didn't include Pittsburgh sales.) In the first six months of 1981, the record sold 18,000 in Canada. [25.14] The Great White North was on the itinerary as Belkin made tour plans.

Donnie Iris (Photo by Anastasia Pantsios)

CHAPTER 26

The *Back on the Streets* Tour

GETTING THEIR ACT TOGETHER

January 1981. The recording act known as Donnie Iris had a hot record that was selling all over the country. Now it was time to hit the road. With co-manager Mike Belkin's contacts, booking a tour would be easy... once Donnie and Mark developed a set. And a band to play it.

The band had recorded the *Back on the Streets* tracks for sessions fees, plus the promise of future publishing royalties and other opportunities if the album was well-received. It was well-received. Now they had a steady gig if they wanted it. Mark had figured correctly: A loyal Kevin had not wanted to quit the major-label band Breathless. But when the second Breathless album, *Nobody Leaves This Song Alive*, didn't make a mark on the charts...

MARK: The Donnie album was done when we were putting finishing touches on the Breathless album.

KEVIN: Jonah called it quits, and Breathless was over. So what happened was: We did this record at the end of Breathless. Some of us were total strangers, and we said, "This feels like we've been playing together for a long, long time." Breathless broke up. "Ah! Leah!" started going up the charts. So it was a natural transition.

Mark and Donnie didn't want to do the band unless all the people were involved. And all the people were available. There's so much to be said for luck and timing and happenstance. And it all worked out. It was just a pleasure to tour.

ALBRITTON: We got a call from either Donnie or Mark, and they said they wanted us to go out and do a tour.

Belkin booked the band's first live show February 13, 1981 at the Galaxy in Canton, Ohio, a legacy industrial city an hour south of Cleveland, two hours from Pittsburgh and well within the broadcasting reach of Cleveland's WMMS, which was the band's second-biggest FM booster. The club had survived the disco era and transitioned into a happening rock club. Its illuminated disco floor attracted flipped-collar crowds straight out of an '80s movie, who danced to rock bands.

The Galaxy was the perfect place for Donnie and the band to warm up. After a year off the road, Donnie was not in fighting shape. Mark and Donnie had spent countless hours assembling the album tracks and spit-shining them, but the band had still never played a single song as a band. Even after some practice sessions, the first show was not a promising start.

MARK: It was time for us to play out.

We never practice now, but we did practice in the beginning. We had a long way to go as a live band. Donnie was just learning how to front the project.

KEVIN: We rehearsed in an old vacant movie theater in Euclid called The Shore Theatre, that I found for Breathless. We could see the large seating area and screen from where we set up. Behind us were the doors to the popcorn area. It was very cool. Kind of like being in an old amusement park after it had been closed down.

MARK: Donnie was not a natural frontman. Our first live show at the Galaxy was very awkward. He suddenly had to front this band. He had to become Donnie Iris.

Donnie had been a worthy co-star in the Jaggerz front line. But he had never carried an entire show. It's not the kind of thing you work out in a week. The Cruisers' live debut was not legendary.

MARK: The first show, we were not very good. We all sucked. We were trying to do all these vocals live. It was very difficult.

KEVIN: I just remember: It was adrenaline-filled. First show, trying to remember all the bits.

Donnie was out of breath. He didn't really have his shtick down as a frontguy. He transitioned quickly. Lucky for us, Donnie has turned out to be a really great front guy. And eventually, shortly, he got it down. And soon we had this King Cool kind of character he could do.

And then the *Back on the Streets* tour was on. King Cool was coming soon, to a town near you.

BACK ON THE STREETS: BARNSTORM

The Cruisers' career didn't build like most bands' do. Donnie and the group were never a local club band, based in one scene, playing the same circuit of clubs week after week, until record labels took notice. The band formed. They recorded a hit album. And then they went on the road.

The Cruisers didn't play Pittsburgh until they appeared, one night, as conquering heroes. By then, they had run a few laps around the Midwest and Northeast. And before they hit the road, they honed their chops in the hometown clubs Mark and Kevin knew well. So did their management. In early 1981, the Belkin-Maduri Organization was headquartered in the Cleveland area, and they tapped local connections to book a crash course in live rock and roll.

ALBRITTON: When we got together for the tour, I stayed at Mark's house the night before our first rehearsal. We stayed up all night, talking about music and Wild Cherry and my experiences and his experiences and where this thing would ultimately go. And I had a really good feeling about Donnie and Mark.

MCA/Carousel, the band's label, contributed some money for tour support. Belkin handled the booking.

FOX: I think the fact that they were able to get tours had a lot less to do with MCA and a lot more to do with Belkin's connections throughout the industry.

The Donnie Iris band — still not officially known as the Cruisers — were now in the big leagues. Belkin lined up a stellar two-month tour. Between a handful of headlining club gigs, most of the shows were opening slots for A-list hard-rock artists: Ted Nugent. UFO. The Romantics. Nazareth.

But one does not simply walk into the big show. The band needed to warm up. Belkin drew up a strategic game plan. Over the course of two and a half weeks, the Cruisers played a handful of gigs in Northeast Ohio. The *Back on the Streets* trek began in the Agora clubs.

The Cleveland Agora was the city's most storied rock club. It had changed locations over the years, but always stayed relevant. The first Agora was founded by Henry "Hank" LoConti in 1966, in the shadow of Cleveland's Case Western University.

Over the '70s and '80s, LoConti grew the Agora name into a 13-club chain that stretched from Florida to Connecticut. The Cleveland Agora helped break Belkin's James Gang. And it hosted countless landmark Cleveland gigs by groups including Springsteen, Foghat and Bad Company. After the British band Spooky Tooth split, guitarist Mick Jones spent some time working as a label talent scout before landing in Foreigner. When he needed to find a hot group, he set up camp in Cleveland. One night, LoConti was surprised to see the rocker and asked why he came to Cleveland.

"We played here a lot," Jones said to him. "And every time, you put on an opening band that kicked our ass.'" [26.1]

And now LoConti had another kick-ass band locked and loaded.

The *Back on the Streets* tour road show stepped off at the Youngstown Agora, midway between Pittsburgh and Cleveland, one of the border territories that divided in its loyalties between the Steelers and Browns. Next came a Tuesday night show at the Cleveland Agora, with Pittsburgh compadres Norm Nardini & the Tigers to warm up the building.

KEVIN: Norm Nardini was a scrappy performer.

Six days later, they played second show at the Cleveland club. Six days later, they were back in Youngstown. And two days later, they returned to Cleveland, once again with Nardini on the bill. If Cleveland embraced a band, the group had a good shot in other markets. The Cruisers passed the live test.

MIKE OLSZEWSKI, WRITER-NARRATOR, *KING COOL* DOCUMENTARY: If you went to a lot of the shows — clubs, big halls — you recognized a lot of the same faces and were pretty much part of the scene. Rock and radio were all we had to hang on to. For many years, Cleveland was like a lot of the Rust Belt, and was just crumbling.

We had expendable cash, the DUI laws weren't nearly as tough and you could still smoke in bars. People were more likely to go out, and you could see live music any night of the week. Even the hotel lounges and bars were packed. By the time a band got to the Agora level, it had to be that good. Agora crowds could be rowdy.

During that run, the Cruisers recorded an energetic set that was later partially released as a limited-run commemorative CD for the band's 2004 25th birthday concert, then later as *Live Bootleg* in 2014.

TRACK LIST FROM *LIVE BOOTLEG*

"Agnes"	"She's So Wild"	"Too Young to Love"
"Joking"	"Daddy Doesn't Live	"Ah! Leah"
"Dreaming"	Here Anymore"	"Back on the Streets"
"I Can't Hear You"	"Shock Treatment"	

Not only did the band perform a shuffled version of the entire first album, but they threw in some classic covers and — late in the set — the oldest Donnie favorite, his only top-ten single: "The Rapper."

The encore featured a triple-shot Beatles medley: "Slow Down"/"I Saw Her Standing There"/"Long Tall Sally." Depending on the night, Albritton sang lead or backup on the covers.

ALBRITTON: As a general rule of thumb, I sang all of the highest — falsetto — harmony background and chorus parts, excluding Donnie's screams, of course. I have performed and sung lead on those three songs in the Beatles medley since the '60s. I remember offering up that arrangement to fill out our time for a longer set length. In some cases, we had them in reserve.

I know Donnie was having some vocal issues that first tour, due to the grueling scheduling. We played, sometimes, three or more back-to-back one nighters. We eventually cut back to no more than two consecutive live dates to maintain his vocal health, with maybe a travel or rest day before the next batch.

THE CRUISERS PLAY *SOLID GOLD*

In between Cleveland shows, the Cruisers made a quick trip to the West Coast. A spotlight performance on the country's hottest music TV show introduced the group to its biggest national audience yet. The band's first television appearance was on the show *Solid Gold*, a weekly hourlong celebration and countdown of the day's hot hits. The group performed "Ah! Leah!" Or, more precisely, they performed *to* it.

KEVIN: That was fun. Totally lip-synced. That was all they did.

Mark rented a giant, unwieldy keytar. Marty worked his axe in black leather pants and a cutoff black t-shirt. Al shuffled back and forth. Donnie strutted, low-key, in the yellow tux. They nailed it on the second take. Host Dionne Warwick stepped onto the screen to plug the song during the guitar solo. And the show cut away shortly thereafter.

KEVIN: They shot in California. It was a rush in more than one way.

We flew out there, got in the car, got to the studio. We waited around. We didn't go to a stylist or rehearse.

The rental gear was there. We adjusted the drums so I could play them. And we had to stop once, because when Dionne Warwick did the intro, I was playing and making noise with the drums, playing too hard. So we did it again.

We did the show, stopped sweating, changed our clothes, turned around, and flew back. The record company wouldn't even pay for us to stay overnight. We got to Cleveland at five in the morning, on a red eye.

The *Solid Gold* episode aired February 20 in some markets, the 21st in others. They had played to a receptive audience. That week, "Ah! Leah!" was at number 31 on the *Billboard* chart, up from 35, headed toward a February 28 peak of 29. In newspapers, *Back on the Streets* was featured in national ads, next to Styx, the Alan Parsons Project, and Dire Straits.

The Ohio barnstorm was a success.

Eminent rock critic Jane Scott of the Cleveland *Plain Dealer* later noted that Donnie "burned up" the Agora.[26.2] At the time, she gave a positive review: "It was Iris's happy, warm smile and obvious delight in being back here and having such a good time while he performed that triggered much of the rapport with the audience.

"A skinny singer with black-rimmed glasses, short hair and a fluid tenor voice, he was a light-hearted tornado on stage. He kept up a steady stream of '60s style dance movements that fit the format.

"You could feel the tension in the capacity crowd before the group's first number, 'Agnes.' Keyboard player Mark Avsec came out and bowed to the crowd. And the five-member band started with more energy than many bands wind up with."[26.3]

Plain Dealer photographer Anastasia Pantsios captured Iris in his full skivvy glory, eyes closed, mouth open wide, mic in one hand, other arm outstretched, belting it out in striped briefs.

Scott wasn't *entirely* happy with the show. Even moreso than the "Ah! Leah!" video, the live show saw Donnie reenacted the striptease from the album cover.

"The only false note was Iris's coming back after one song dressed only in tight shorts. This was done to illustrate a photograph on his album cover, but it seemed a gimmick that was out of line."[26.4]

DONNIE: I would do it at the end of the set, during "Leah." I did it for shock value, showing we were gonna do whatever it took. We were gonna rock and roll. The band would keep doing the song. That was great. Fun. Shocking the audience was precious. I don't remember if it started as a spur-of-the-moment thing. Once we started, it wasn't something we'd do no matter what. If the audience was ready for it, we'd go ahead and do it. It had to have been the right vibe.

BACK ON THE STREETS: ON THE ROAD

The positive notices kept coming: March 9, the Cruisers planted a flag in East Lansing, Michigan. *The Lansing State Journal*'s David Winchester caught a headline gig at Dooley's in East Lansing, Michigan and raved: "a hot band with a skinny, little curly-haired, bespectacled singer worked up a sweat…. It was one of Dooley's best shows…. He wasted no time soakin' a shirt and sockin' some rock 'n' roll to a crowd."[26.5]

By now, Donnie had his wind back, and he was in his best shape since the Jaggerz showband days. On stage, he was a dancing, singing, leaping, spinning tornado. The band were part of the act, too.

Donnie in his full skivvy glory.

ALBRITTON: "Shock Treatment," we did a little skit onstage. We rolled out Donnie on a gurney. We had nurse's hats on. Mark had paddles and one of those doctor's mirrors on his forehead. It was a campy thing. I think that was Mark's idea. It was a theatrical showband kind of thing. We eventually steered clear of that.

DONNIE: Mark, he was into making something of the band, making something of us — as writers, as performers, all that stuff. Ideas like crazy, all kinds of ideas in the studio, for shows, for songs. Certain things to do with the audience.

The band would also headline clubs and theaters, including Pittsburgh's Stanley Theater and Toronto's El Mocambo. The group was still commonly billed as simply "DONNIE IRIS."

After the Ohio shows, the Donnie Iris band opened a series of Nazareth shows. The combo made a blip on *Billboard*'s Top Box Office survey. The trade magazine reported that the bands' two-night stand at the Memorial Hall in Kansas City Feb. 27 and 28 moved 6, 418 tickets at $9 apiece, grossing $56,997 for Contemporary Productions and New West Presentations.[26.6] The Nazareth opening slot was a mixed bag: great opportunity. Impatient crowds. The show didn't go over at the St. Louis Keil Opera House, where the band were booed without mercy.

KEVIN: I was a big fan of Nazareth growing up, listening to it in cars, doing God knows what.

One show, we started playing, and my drums sounded like utter rubbish, like, "What happened?!"

The back of the arena was on a very steep hill. The road crew had managed to let my drums roll down the hill. So they went out of tune.

DONNIE: St. Louis was another one where they absolutely hated us. The crowd were not being good, until we did the last song, which was "Leah." Then when they realized who we were, they started clapping for us.

KEVIN: We had done all these shows, and they were great. People were just digging us. But St. Louis, I remember Hank [McHugh, the road manager] coming up and telling us, "This crowd, I don't know. Be careful. And we stepped onstage, and they started booing us from the very first note.

MARTY: I can remember what the crowd looked like: They were camouflage. When we got to "Leah," they looked at each other, and they knew the song, and they clapped.

MARK: Albritton is biracial, and does not look Scottish. The Nazareth folks were Scottish.

And so everyone was drinking by the bar one night after a show. And Albritton tells one of the Scotsmen his name: Albritton McClain. And Albritton McClain sounds very much like a Scottish name.

And so the guys says, "No, no way, that's not your name!"

And Albritton shows him his driver's license. And the Scotsman replies, "*Well,* fook *me!*" in a loud brogue.

And everyone laughed. That is one of those lines that lived on in infamy: "*Albritton McClain, well, fook me!*"

KEVIN: They reminded me of a bunch of rough and tumble, drinking guys. It was fun to play concerts with them, since I loved many and played many of their songs growing up in a bar band.

The Indianapolis Market Square Arena show with Nazareth and April Wine went better. They think.

KEVIN: April Wine. Don't recall much on this one.

"HE HIT DONNIE IN THE HEAD WITH A ROLL OF TOILET PAPER"

March 1981 was memorable. MCA cut a recoupable tour check for $20,000, followed later by one for $28,000 — "recoupable" is a music-business gremlin that means "You can have the money now, but it comes out of your earnings later."[26.7, 26.8]

FOX: I would call it an amount "on the low side of normal" for back then. I recall working on those tour budgets. We had to fight for every dime — and that was quite typical of all but the very best of the labels.

Every penny would have been recoupable, which is the biggest load of crap in the world, but I don't think I ever knew any artist who had it any other way.

March 13, 1981, Donnie Iris opened for UFO in Chicago, at the packed Chicago International Amphitheatre, an arena with a capacity of 9,000. Depending whom you're talking to, that concert was just another show, a triumph, or an ordeal. The set was broadcast on local station WWLP, "The Loop," FM 98. The show circulates in bootleg circles, and the performance sounds fine. But there was a lot going on that night.

The atmosphere was tense. UFO's rough-and-tumble crowd tapped the long-haired heavy metal demographic. The concert had two opening acts. Their different crowds might have helped move some tickets. But the bands didn't delight the hard rock aficionados in attendance. The blog Soundaboard hosts a series of recollections.

ANONYMOUS COMMENTER 1: I saw this show.... UFO was great but for some reason they had the Romantics and Donnie Iris open for 'em. But my friend had the last laugh when he hit Iris in the head with a roll of toilet paper.[26.9]

ANONYMOUS COMMENTER 2: This was back in the day when bottles were sold, and the drummer of the Romantics was hit in the head and cursed out the crowd. UFO was great, and I remember Pete Way smashing his bass.[26.10]

JIM MARKOVICH, SOUND MAN: Chicago, no real memories.

KEVIN: Marty was getting pelted with quarters. That was a less-than-pleasant gig.

DONNIE: Chicago was one I remember.

MARTY: It was not a run-of-the-mill show. We were doing big shows at the time. UFO was big. If they're going to sell 10,000 seats, they don't need any help selling to heavy metal fans. So that might not sell out the whole place. But if you put a couple different bands on the bill, that will bring in different people, and now you've sold out the whole arena. Another heavy metal band, you're tapping the same crowd. I think that's the same thing that happened with Hall and Oates [later].

For me, the show was only memorable from the standpoint of what went on during the show. We weren't really welcomed by the heavy metal fans. And neither were the Romantics.

We went on first. Probably about halfway through the set, I could tell we weren't very well liked. At the time, our impression was, "These people hate us."

All we could see was the first 20 or 30 rows of UFO fans. The place was full, but all we could really see or hear was this black arena. All we could see was the absolute most hardcore UFO fans in the building, sitting up front. You could see their tolerance — or lack thereof — quite clearly.

Things were being thrown. I could see the looks on their faces. I could see a... lack of enthusiasm.

We got the impression we weren't that welcome there. But they didn't *despise* us. At least we had a heavy sound, especially "Leah." They tolerated us, but just barely.

Now, they *despised* the Romantics, because they didn't have a heavy sound, and they were all dressed in matching leather, and their hair was perfect. They didn't like them *at all*. They had already suffered through one band. And now they have to suffer through a second non-UFO act — torture! They might have been camped out for two days to get tickets. They have had *enough*.

Happily enough, it was being broadcast live. We thought, "We're not going to make a very good impression on Chicago. What a shame."

But the house mics that were recording the actual audience response were way deeper into the crowd, away from the hardcore UFO fans, and more into the general-metal-slash-rock crowd. So when we heard the broadcast and heard the response and the applause after the songs, the whole place was applauding after "Leah," and it sounded fine. This was a big, good, warm response. And

Donnie and Kevin backstage with The Romantics. (Photo by Anastasia Pantsios)

we got fairly high on the playlist on [Chicago rock station] WLS.

So the good news was: It really was fine. That wasn't the first time or the last time that we played on a show where we weren't appreciated that much.

KEVIN: There was a guy down front. He was just being a dick, flipping us off the whole time.

So at the end of the show, we come out to bow. And I had my drumsticks with us. And I held out the sticks to him, and said, "Do you want these?"

And all of a sudden, he turns into my friend: "Yeah, yeah! Throw me the sticks!"

And I flipped him off and threw the sticks the other way. And that was so much fun to do in front of 10,000 people.

The Romantics went on second, and *they* really got messed with. They wouldn't even stop in between songs.

INTRODUCING THE CRUISERS

The players bonded together in one trial after another. And before long, they were no longer Donnie's anonymous backing band. They were the Cruisers.

MARK: Recording the first album, there was no real band. The band was aspirational. I intended to have a hit project, but it may never have happened. Now that we had a hit, we put the band together. Kevin and Marty and Albritton wanted an identity too, so the name was "Donnie Iris and the Cruisers" based on that Turnpike Cruiser idea.

Even now, we are often billed as Donnie Iris. It's whatever people wanted to say.

When we were opening on bills for the first album, and the emcee dude would come up and say, "Please welcome Donnie Iris." Kevin would yell from the behind the drums before he kicked off "Agnes": "AND THE CRUISERS!" This was a group effort.

A few days later, the band crossed the border for one of their rare international shows, at Toronto's El Mocambo, March 19. The ad was one of many print pieces to bill the band as DONNY IRIS. This is the show that inspired a reviewer to call Donnie "the new king of cool." The coronation of King Cool didn't come from the *Globe and Mail*'s Paul McGrath, but he was there, and he had a decent time, too: "Beaver Falls, Penn., sounds like the kind of place any kid would want to break out of," McGrath wrote. "It was a fairly raucous show with four or five excellent tunes, a few so-so's and one ringer, an overblown ballad called 'Daddy Don't Live Here Anymore... Iris [is] a uniquely energetic performer, sacrificed a lot of sweat and risked a lot of permanent damage to his vocal cords to please the Toronto

Stanley Theater, Pittsburgh, PA. (Photo by Jan Gefert)

crowd..... There was plenty of heavy-metal power-chording, but the show had all the quick movement and constant beats of a good rhythm and blues show.... Marty Lee was the second focus of the evening. A quick, emotional guitarist, he managed two superb breaks, during 'I Can't Hear You No More' and 'She's So Wild.'" [26.11]

And now Donnie Iris and the Cruisers were battle-tested and ready for Pittsburgh.

PITTSBURGH: DONNIE PLAYS THE STANLEY

Donnie and the Cruisers didn't hit his hometown area — and its effective cultural capital, Pittsburgh — until they had a month of shows under their belt. Then, warm and ready, they planted their flag at the legendary Stanley Theater. The medium-sized venue now stands, renovated and renamed, as the Benedum Centre. Founded as an ornate movie house, it had hosted live music since the big-band era. In the 1960s, the Stanley began hosting shows like the Velvet Underground and the Grateful Dead. DiCesare Engler Productions — the city's reigning concert promoters, the local counterpart to the Belkins — set up shop in the building in 1977, and brought in bands like Fleetwood Mac, Van Halen, the Clash, Paul Simon, and Bob Marley (for his final live appearance).

The show was close to capacity, and the crowd were shaking the building before opening acts Norm Nardini and the Granati Brothers took the stage.

DONNIE: The place was packed. Jimmy Ross had told me he was coming. And I looked out and saw him. He was getting *into* it.

The day before, the *Pittsburgh Press*' Pete Bishop previewed the show. Three months after his lukewarm review, *Back on the Streets* had grown on him — slightly. He was still cranky and skeptical about whether the show could possibly be any good:

"Donnie Iris's 'Ah! Leah!' sounds as if the Mormon Tabernacle Choir were singing backup… So how does the Beaver Falls native… reconcile such studio chicanery with the facts that the human voice can hit only one note at a time and that he can't afford to hire a slew of singers to accompany him in concert?" [26.12]

It was a good question. And Iris answered it, with a technical assist from Mark and Markovich: The band had been using digital delay to create extra layers of vocals, in addition to the group's full frontline singing backup vocals.

JIMMY ROACH: It was one of the few acts that didn't need to be artificially pumped up in the studio. You can do 50 layers of overdub in the studio, but his voice is so good live… They absolutely pulled it off live. Of all the bands I've seen, comparing live to album, I think they were as good as anybody at transferring what they did in the studio — which is amazing, because of all the overdubbing Donnie did in the studio. I was always amazed at how they could recreate very complicated songs.

The Pittsburgh *Post-Gazette*'s Bill Stieg was considerably more excited about the show. "Ah! Leah!" still riding high at *Billboard*'s number 41. (Higher than any other Iron City bands of the era managed. Grushecky and the Iron City Houserockers, also on MCA, received glowing notices from *Rolling Stone*, the *Village Voice*, *Creem*, and the *New York Times*, but never matched Iris' national airplay or chart numbers.)

"Where is the rock 'n' roll capital of America?" wrote Stieg. "New York or Los Angeles can make legitimate claims, based on the number of clubs and big name acts who perform in those cities. But for the true spirit of rock 'n' roll, you look to the industrial heartland. Chicago, Detroit, Cleveland… and Pittsburgh. Tonight at the Stanley Theater, Pittsburgh shows its stuff. Donnie Iris, local-boy-making-good-again, returns home for a show that has the city's rock fans excited and curious." [26.13]

The show did attract some enthusiastic national press. *Rolling Stone* had heard the building buzz about the Burgh rocker. The rock journal sent reporter Lloyd Sachs, who braved the backstage mob scene — all friends and family — and wrote a piece that ran not just in the magazine, but was widely syndicated in newspapers around the country.

Wrote Sachs, "The group Iris recruited for this tour is a tight, exuberant, surprisingly tough unit that provides fresh, heavy-metal flourishes and dreamy harmonizing for Iris' craftsmanlike, hook-happy pop songs." [26.14]

DONNIE: That first Stanley show was a real feather in our cap. We did well, because it was Pittsburgh. It was an über-good feeling from playing there. You could only hear the crowd — you couldn't really see them. When you do a headline show, you're either selling it or not. It was great to play there and do fairly well.

MARK: The first time we played the Stanley Theater was a highlight. It was a big deal. It was really exciting. What we'd hoped to achieve, we achieved. That's when the whole *Donnie Mania* thing started.

The next day, *The Beaver County Times'* Tom Doyle was still swept up in the moment: "When Donnie Iris and his band took the stage, the reaction of the crowd was astonishing. They were welcomed home like champion dragon slayers, greeted with a standing ovation before their first song "Agnes" with many more rounds of applause to follow....

"Overall, the band was exceptionally tight, performing to near perfection. Considering the group has only been on the road for a little over a month, its performance was astonishing. Most touring bands take years to work up to the heights that Donnie and his band have achieved.... At age 37, he is just now starting to find his true place in the music world." [26.15]

Pittsburgh was conquered. Cleveland signed off. Now the Cruisers took on the world.

BACK ON THE STREETS: BACK ON THE ROAD

The Cruisers had an instant chemistry. On the road, they got to really know each other. They partied in moderation. Shenanigans were minor and minimal. The occasional late-night episode left a mark. From time to time, a Cruiser wound up naked in a hotel hallway, but for a reason that wasn't very rock-and-roll: The band had not one, but two sleepwalkers.

MARTY: I first saw Kevin sleepwalk while we were touring. There would be these episodes. I'll let them talk about it. I don't want to say anything embarrassing.

ADDY, DONNIE'S DAUGHTER: Mark had this super-crazy strength when he would sleepwalk. One time at the house, he picked up an armoire and threw it.

KEVIN: I think Mark and I roomed together because we could sympathize with each other, walking and talking.

One time, he wanted a room to himself, because he was writing. That's when he thought there was a lion in the room, and he walked outside, and the door clicked. And he woke up in the hallway, naked.

Had I been with him, his sleepwalking partner, I would have reeled him in. I hope he learned his lesson on that one.

I would get up and yell. Or thrash around. At home, I had an arching metal lamp that hung over the bed. And I would attack that. One time, I stood on my bed and punched out the overhead light's glass shade.

I used to stuff magazines under the door, fearing that something was coming in. My wife probably has a lot more stories than I do. I don't do that anymore.

We never sleepwalked at the same time. I woke up one morning. The room was carpeted. The ashtray was broken on the tile on the entrance way by the door. I said, "What the hell, Mark?!" He said, "That wasn't me. That was you." It's an interesting life when you have an abnormality.

MARK: Albritton, he's one of those guys, he'd have a couple drinks, and we'd say he was "peaking." He could take care of himself.

Once we were in New Jersey. We were outside, and somebody was going to pick a fight with Albritton. This guy was a big-ass dude. I told him, "I'm gonna do you a favor. That guy over there is from Chicago. You don't want to fight him. He's badass." Albritton *wasn't* some fighter. He's a very gentle guy. But I saw him get in a couple fights.

ALBRITTON: There were the highlights of the lowlights: We were at a club, on tour, and the ceiling height for the stage was like 7 feet. It was horrible. Things went horrible. The soundcheck was horrible. It was a like a cave. And when we went back to do the show, it was just a killer show, one of those great shows.

In late March, the Cruisers spent a week on the road with Ted Nugent. The Motor City Madman was professional and collegial.

KEVIN: Once again, I grew up playing his songs. Loved his guitar tone and energy. Going way back, I remember hearing "Journey to the Center of the Mind" by Amboy Dukes, driving in my parents' car, and was being impressed by its psychedelic sound and lyrics. Makes a little kid kind of nervous.

MARTY: We played with Ted Nugent — we could hear booing sometimes. Now, we usually won these crowds over, because Donnie was a very hard-working guy. But honestly, they're there to see these long-hair rock-out bands. And we come out with short-haired Donnie, with his glasses, skinny little guy. But we have power, so we would deliver that. And by the end of the show, we have a few more fans.

DONNIE: Nugent shows. Those were good. The Jaggerz played with him once, on a TV show in Cleveland. He was wild.

KEVIN: It was our first time in the Northeast, and I was taken by how beautiful it was. It was pretty standard. We got a good response, typical response for being a new band.

The last date, Nugent's crew threw donuts at us. It was hazing, but it was the opposite of hazing, because we were leaving. When we were done, we turned over the drum riser, and donuts came spilling off of it.

Nugent was cool. Nothing weird. Normal, nice treatment. It was very ordinary. He was not swinging from a vine in a leopard cloth, promoting his Republican views, or shooting guns. I didn't see any groupies backstage.

"Opening for Nugent was Pittsburgh native Donnie Iris," *The Morning Call*'s Eric Heeds added to the Nugent show review. "His set of light rock tunes went over surprisingly well." [26.16]

DONNIE: Hank, our road manager, he was from Boston, and he had that Boston accent. He was very good at being a road manager, and everything was where it needed to be when we got to the hotel. He was blusterous in ways, but a genuinely nice guy. A good-sized guy — not huge, but bigger than Mark & I. He's working for Dave Matthews now. We generally didn't have bad problems, though.

MARKOVICH: Working for Belkin-Maduri was good. Every year, Mike had a big summer party. All the office people were there, the Michael Stanley people, all the Donnie Iris people. They treat you well. They respect you. They respect what you do. I respect what they do. I've always enjoyed working for them.

It was a big deal to work for them. I don't know a lot of people from Youngstown who go on major tours. I've seen more countries than I thought I would ever see in my life. I've been to Australia three or four times, Japan at least five times. I worked for the Ramones from 1981 until their final tour. South America, they were huge. I think they thought we were the Beatles.

And travelling with Donnie, it was always fun. In the beginning, when I started travelling with them, there was the five guys in the band, the road manager, and me, so there were seven of us that travelled in Cadillacs, driving around the country.

There was the smokers' car and the non-smokers' car. Donnie and Mark smoked cigarettes. And I didn't really smoke cigarettes, but sometimes I rode with those guys. Eventually, we moved into motor homes. The gear was in a rental truck with the two stage guys — the drum tech and the lighting tech.

DONNIE: There would be times you'd get so tired, you had to switch drivers and get in the back seat. Mark was always in his own world — you knew it was bad when you let him drive. You're falling asleep, and you'd hear Mark say, "Gimme the wheel!" You pull over, let him drive, and hope for the best.

To us, the road was laughs, just a fun time. We would drive for hours. And Mark would be entertaining us the whole time, with this little keyboard he had. He'd make up songs. One time, we're driving up the East Coast in a snow storm. Mark is singing, and I'm howling. I couldn't even see, my eyes were tearing up. He had us in stitches. That's the way it was on the road, the whole time.

In March 1981, MCA had released the band's second single, "You're Only Dreaming," b/w "She's So Wild." It seemed like a sure bet: Mere weeks after "Ah! Leah!" peaked, it was a sonically adventurous throwback track, with a flipside featuring the band's heaviest moment. It couldn't miss.

It missed. The single didn't chart.

LIVE AT THE PARADISE: THE LOST EP

Afraid they had a one-hit wonder on their hands, the label brainstormed a kneejerk response that was somehow ambitious, creative, obvious, expensive, *and* aggravating.

MARK: Carl and/or MCA thought, "Oh, 'The Rapper' was a hit once, so let's do it again."

DONNIE: I did the first album. And it was suggested that we follow up "Leah" with "The Rapper"— which really was like… "No, I want to have our own career."

And we ended up at the Paradise in Boston. They recorded us live, and they recorded "The Rapper."

Nobody cared about us when we were in the studio, making the first record.

And because we had a hit, now they don't *trust* you to have a hit, so they tell you what to do.

Like, go to hell. Let me do my thing.

MCA did not go to hell. But they agreed to make it worth Donnie's while. On April 2, the blazing band recorded its first official live release at Boston club The Paradise. The rare *Live at the Paradise* EP would be released to radio stations only, in August 1981. It spawned a stopgap promotional single, "The Rapper." The rockin' live version of Donnie's biggest hit ran on both sides of a 45 aimed at nostalgic radio programmers.

MARK: I hated the idea. I thought it was a desperate, cheap idea. We just made a good album. Trust me to make another.

So it was on the *Paradise* album. I was like, "That was years ago. We are making new music now, trust me." You have to have a vision and imagination.

After the tour, Mark mixed the *Live at the Paradise* EP with help from Kevin at Jeree, with no overdubs. The 12" 33-1/3 EP arrived in July. The civilian edition of the single also followed in August, with a live "Ah! Leah!" on the B-side. Neither side created any serious radio action.

LIVE AT THE PARADISE TRACKLIST

"Agnes"	"I Can't Hear You"	"Shock Treatment"
Intro	"The Rapper"	"Ah! Leah!"

The EP featured an 8-1/2" x 11" sheet with critical blurbs and Mark's bogus Donnie biography. The live "Rapper" later surfaced on *20th Century Masters: The Millennium Collection: Best of Donnie Iris*. In the new live version, the gentle jangle is gone, and Marty reinvents the tune as a high-octane rocker with a fuel-injected central riff.

MARK: That's Marty's talent: He comes up with good stuff. That's why we asked him to be in the band.

After Boston, the band turned around and headed south, where they failed to please an impossible-to-please *New York Times*. The paper's review calls to mind a quote from Michael Wilbon, co-host of ESPN's *Pardon the Interruption*, who once said, "*The New York Times* did what *The New York Times* does: try to look smart — and get it wrong."

Critic Stephen Holden wrote, "Iris's richly layered style of hard rock echoes everyone from the Who to Gary Numan to Billy Joel. But his deftness at glossing the styles of others robs his music of identity. At the Savoy, Mr. Iris distinguished himself mainly by satirizing the typical rock-star pose with exaggerated gestures and comically savage vocal attacks. Though it made for some amusing moments, it didn't shed any new light on his songs. Eve Moon, a former New York street singer, is a hard-rock belter with plenty of vocal power but little subtlety or personal charm. Unlike Donnie Iris, she took her tough street-mama role seriously."[26.17]

KEVIN: On my dining room table, I still have a green crystal doorknob. I took it from the hotel. Because I was so taken by the city and the gig. I went inside the closet door and took it. I'm going to bring it back, I swear.

ALBRITTON: New York, the first time we played New York, I didn't go to sleep until five or six in the morning, I was so energized.

The flop single and negative notice didn't shake the label's faith in Donnie. As the tour approached its end, Donnie Iris and crew were a valued, visible member of the MCA roster. Talking to *Billboard*, label President Bob Singer was happy to pay lip service to the band. Singer explained the label's new strategy: refocusing the company on breaking new acts — and Donnie and the Cruisers were successful poster boys. The executive said new artists like Terri Gibbs and Donnie were affordable investments compared to label-stable lions like Elton John and the Who.[26.18]

While the band was still riding high, MCA formally requested a second album.[26.19]

The Back on the Streets tour ended May 6, 1981, with a headlining show at Cleveland's Front Row Theater, a ritzy in-the-round venue with a champagne bar, capacity 3200.[26.20] Jonah Koslen — who was Mark and Kevin's former boss in Breathless — opened the show. The reversed roles could have made for an awkward evening, but everyone remained cordial.

KEVIN: Funny thing is: I don't remember him opening for us at that show, so I guess no weird feelings.

MARK: I don't even remember him being at the show. It must not have been weird.

KEVIN: We didn't have a party at the end of the tour. We didn't have a period at the end of the sentence. All the way, we felt it happening. It was cool. We built it from the ground up. It was a good feeling to know we all chipped into this, and it was happening.

I don't think we've ever had a party. I think a lot of this was because Mark had a lot to do with organizing that stuff, and Mark's not into parties. He didn't even like going on the road that much.

The three-month tour had been a victory lap for "Ah! Leah!" Now that the tour was over, the band wiped off the sweat and headed home.

The next chapter was already slated to begin.

In just 12 days, Donnie, Mark, Albritton, Kevin, Marty and Jerry would reconvene in Pennsylvania, where they would record Donnie Iris and the Cruisers' sophomore album, *King Cool*.

CHAPTER 27

King Cool: Making the Album

KING COOL

The sophomore album by Donnie Iris and the Cruisers. Featuring...

Side 1:
"Sweet Merilee" (Avsec, Iris) 3:42
"The Promise" (Lee) 4:09
"Pretender" (Avsec, Iris) 5:14
"Love Is Like a Rock" (Avsec, Iris, Lee, McClain, Valentine) 3:38
"That's the Way Love Ought to Be" (Avsec, Iris) 4:22

Side 2:
"My Girl" (Avsec, Iris) 4:00
"Broken Promises" (Avsec, Iris) 4:19
"King Cool" (Avsec, Iris) 4:07
"Color Me Blue" (Avsec, Iris) 5:20
"The Last To Know" (Avsec, Ierace) 5:20

Original release: August 1981
Label: MCA/Carousel
Peak position on *Billboard* album chart: 84, November 7, 1981
Weeks on chart: 31
Recorded at Jeree Studios, New Brighton, PA, Summer 1981
Engineered by Jerry Reed
Assisted by Carl Maduri
Also thanks to Don Garvin for his invaluable assistance
Mixed at Media Sound Studios, New York, by Michael Barbiero
Mastered at Sterling Sound, Inc., New York, by Jack Skinner
Original release - MCA-5237 MCA Records
CD Release - MSD-35416 Razor & Tie/MCA Records
OUT OF PRINT

Singles:
"Merilee" b/w "Back on the Streets"
 Peak *Billboard* Hot 100 position: 80, November 21 1981
 Weeks on chart: 6
"Love Is Like a Rock" b/w "Agnes"
 Peak *Billboard* Hot 100 position: 37, February 20, 1982
 Weeks on chart: 14
"My Girl" b/w "The Last to Know"
 Peak *Billboard* Hot 100 position: 25, May 29, 1982
 Weeks on chart: 14

"King Cool toned down some of the new wave leanings of Back on the Streets and concentrated more on a classic rock sound [that] yielded rewarding results."

— *All Music Guide to Rock*. Tom Demalon

By the numbers, the cycle from 1981 to 1982 was the Cruisers' biggest and best year.

Donnie and the Cruisers avoided the sophomore jinx on their second album, which arrived a mere 13 months after the band's full-length debut. The second album is the first one with "Donnie Iris and the Cruisers" formally stamped on it — on the back. It's the highest rated Cruisers LP in the rock reference books, with five of five possible stars from the *All Music Guide to Rock*.

King Cool survived the label's erratic promotional strategy and support. It still managed to produce the group's biggest *Billboard* single. It yielded three Hot 100 singles and two Top 40 singles. It put the band on MTV. *King Cool* features the track that might be the band's best overall performance. The record contributed four of the 11 tracks on the compilation, *20th Century Masters: The Millennium Collection: Best of Donnie Iris*:

"Sweet Merilee"
"Love Is Like a Rock"
"That's the Way Love Ought to Be"
"My Girl"

When the band hit the road to support *King Cool*, they toured the country with some of the hottest bands on the planet, like Hall & Oates and Loverboy.

Pretty good year. Great album.

BACK TO THE LAB (AFTER SOME DISCUSSION)

After the leftfield success of *Back on the Streets*, the Cruisers returned to the studio less than two weeks after their first tour wrapped.

MARK: A lot was happening quickly, because there was a buzz about the band. And I was supposed to be writing new songs.

DONNIE: I thought it was a good album. I thought we had a lot of good stuff on there. In some ways, I like it better than the first one.

MARK: *King Cool* was maybe as good as *Back on the Streets*.

Donnie had launched his solo career with a contrived image, a hybrid modern man with roots in rock's distant past, strutting his stuff in black glasses from the '50s and a banana-bright suit from the '60s.

As *King Cool*'s title suggests, Donnie refined his image between albums. The cover catches Donnie in a back alley, glasses on, wearing jeans and dark gray blazer, smoking a cigarette. The campy dimension is gone. Now Donnie is a world-tested earth shaker and baby maker. He is now an accomplished sage, ready to hold court, share stories from his adventures, and issue decrees about what is good and right in life.

The writing, recording, and refining of *King Cool* unfolded much like *Back on the Streets*: Mark and Donnie had not written any complete songs before the sessions. But this time, Mark had prepared more ideas and musical pieces. Only one song came from a group jam: "Love Is Like a Rock" splits the writing credit among all five Cruisers.

Donnie and the guys had some ideas, too. The band jammed tracks into existence. Mark and Donnie took home cassettes, burned midnight oil, tinkered on their own, and collaborated. A lot. Eight of the ten songs are credited to Avsec and Iris. Marty is the sole writer for "The Promise."

MARTY: Mark and Donnie woodshedded. That's all their thing. I wouldn't expect to be part of that process, based on what it's been over the years. The two of them need to be very focused.

Mark had prepared some material on the road during the *Back on the Streets* tour. And he had composed sketches in the short vacation between the end of the *Back* tour and the start of the *King Cool* sessions, which kicked off May 15, 1981.

After some debate, the band reconvened at Jeree Recording.

MARK: I was more on a roll with second album. I wanted it to have some sort of theme. I was pumped and feeling stressed, intense but good.

I wrote a lot of the song structures at my little studio in my apartment. I had this cassette machine. I would put song ideas down. I'd go to Donnie's and we'd sit at the piano and write together.

ADDY, DONNIE'S DAUGHTER: We really looked forward to those times. It was so fun when Mark would come. A lot of laughs. Then they kind of disappeared into the basement, to work on recordings.

MARK: Kevin, right after the first album, wanted to switch studios. And I thought that was a ridiculous idea.

I remember going, "Let me get this straight: You do realize we have *a hit record* out of this studio? Do you think we were destined to have it happen? It happened because we were at Jeree's and we worked it. Something *magic* is goin' on there. We're going back."

And so we did. Jeree's had a certain sound to it. That's why I developed the stacking, to level things out.

KEVIN: Yeah, I wanted to change studios. Being the audio dweeb, I thought there were quote-unquote *better* studios. The younger me was maybe a bit foolish. Because sometimes there's magic in working in a facility. I wanted the bigger drum sound from a bigger room.

At Jeree's, I was playing in a drum room the size of a closet. That produced successful records. I picked this up later, from Bryan [Adams]: The order of importance is song, vibe, then sound.

Even though I was focused on the [legendary New York City studio] Power Station drum sound, maybe I was overlooking some of the other things. We delivered the tracks, but Mark and Donnie had to complete the records. It's more important for them to be comfortable than the band. I got over it.

King Cool took shape almost exactly like *Back on the Streets*. Donnie was the brand, but Mark led the band.

FOX: The only area that Mark asserted himself in a leadership role was in the studio. And in that, he was excellent. He was not a prick. Mark was no dictator.

But I also think he lucked out with the players. They would do anything in service of a great record. And Mark was willing to work harder than anyone. Mark had been listening to the Queen records. He liked the sound of the background singers. So he worked until he knew how that was done. And when he came to the band and said, "I would like to try to get this particular sequence to sound like that, what would you guys think?", they would say "Yes." Who wouldn't want that?

ALBRITTON: For the most part, all during my time in the band, I commuted, driving my van. First from Oxford, Ohio to Jeree's in the beginning. Then in later years, from Bloomington, Indiana. It depended on the destination. When recording at Jeree's or for gigs in the Burgh, I stayed with a good friend, John Terrier, in Pittsburgh, who opened his home to me whenever I was in town.

By now, the band had lived with each other, and they knew each other. Leading the sessions, Mark was still able to conjure the spontaneous alchemy in amazingly efficient tracking sessions.

MARTY: As I remember it, we were on a weekly payroll. I continued to be paid after we were done on tour. I was very excited. I'd never been involved in anything like that before.

MARK: The *King Cool* album was a labor of love.

KEVIN: "Love is Like a Rock" was a jam. That was actually the first track for the album.

DONNIE: Kevin layered some drum tracks, and we wanted to loop a section. This is before digital, so we had this arcane system of looping a section of the two inch tape. Once we had that down, Marty came up with the signature riff. And we were off to the races.

MARTY: It was different, because we didn't know each other on the first album. We were strangers. We all did tracks, and we disappeared. Mark just wanted rhythm tracks.

And then once they did some writing with the rhythm tracks, then they wanted us to come back — me in particular — to add things and add solos and parts. At the time, I was still playing with my band, The Pulse. I'd come in and do something. And walk out, sometimes, with half-finished songs. And they were pretty cool. I was surprised.

I remember the sessions as being very, very similar to the first sessions: We got in there. We would play some things or try some things or this and that.

Maybe Mark would have some chords, maybe not, depending on the day.

He would have some ideas, or he wouldn't.

He would mess around with things. Very experimental. That's how it felt to me: "Let's try this," "Let's try that," "Let's see how this sounds…"

When you hear the finished songs, sometimes it's sort of startling. What they chose to do, it's unexpected. They go through a process, too.

KEVIN: It's like there were two bands. Mark and Donnie worked together and made their part of it; and then they would be off planning with Belkin. And then it was me and Marty and Al. We even rode in different cars — they smoked.

MARK: Marty was a big part of the *King Cool* album.

MARTY: It would all come from everybody there, just playing things that sounded good. It wasn't as if Mark or anyone said, "This is where we're going with this" or "This is this thing we're trying to do." We would just experiment, and the thing would happen at that time.

I mean, he might make a general suggestion and say, "We want something more aggressive" or something general. But we would play around with things. The song wasn't written in most cases. Maybe there were chord changes. Mark was looking for *possibilities*.

We would play and play, and half an hour of playing would produce something.

Mark would say, "OK, that sounds like something. Let's say that's a verse, the thing you and Albritton and Kevin are playing right now."

"No, let's not play this change, let's try that one."

All of that, together.

After about 15 minutes, he might say, "I don't know about that." And he might put it on tape, and we'd listen to it and say, "What if it went here?" or "What about this chord?"

And I or Albritton would play something and Mark would say, "Let's go there."

To my way of thinking, it never was a clear path, as much as it was "Well, let's just see what we can come up with."

If we were going to do it today, we would all walk in. And we would set up. And everybody would say, "What do you want to do?"

Nobody would say, "OK, here's what we're going to do. Here's the chords. Here's the song, it's called such-and-such."

I'm not saying it never happened like that. But generally, most of the time, it got started with something like Kevin playing something. Someone would say, "That's kind of cool. Kevin, play that beat." And then *this*. And then *that*. And it would take shape, on the spot.

I think everybody would key off everybody. Mark would have some chords. Kevin would start playing something off that, sometimes. At the time, Albritton, then Paul.

Then there would be a quiet lull, and I'd play something, and Mark would say, "What's *that*?"

And I would play a couple chords, and he'd say "Do that!" And someone would follow someone and add a part to it.

Whoever had a good idea. We just wanted to make it wide open, wherever the song came from.

And keep in mind: We're just really trying to get a rhythm track, the foundation. And later, Mark and Donnie would sit with it and develop it — and, sometimes, throw it away, because nothing came from it.

I had recorded with other people before the Cruisers. The songs had been written for months before we went into the studio. And it was very well refined. If we talk to the studio engineers enough, what they tend to say is: What we do is not the norm.

KING COOL, THE SONGS: "SWEET MERILEE"

King Cool opens with… well, that's another story. The album, as it exists, begins with "Sweet Merilee." The label had high hopes for the track's mellow subtleties. The band take it slow, riding Marty's gently chiming chords.

MARTY: For me, the standout tracks are "Love Is Like a Rock," "That's the Way Love Ought to Be," and "Merilee."

On *King Cool*, my sound was the sound I had in my previous band. Although, in my previous band, this benefitted us: We played a lot of different styles of music. So when we started experimenting in the Cruisers, I had a lot of different textures and things to draw on, like the parts of "Merilee" — a lot of that came from the fact that I was doing so many different guitar parts and styles in The Pulse.

We did originals and covers. We had a very, very diverse set list. That's part of what was fun for us.

Marty, Donnie and Mark at Jeree Studio. (Photo by Richard Kelly)

We did all different kinds of stuff, everything from Elvis Costello to Steely Dan to Weather Report to Springsteen to Moby Grape. And we had a ball. There are some recordings you can hear on YouTube, but it's mostly our originals.

I listened to the Police and Costello and the Pretenders. So some of that chime-y stuff might have had roots in that. Sometimes there were layers of parts in those constructions — same with the Cars, little parts here and there. I listened to those things, and I liked those things: this part here that swims, and the part here that's more rhythmic.

When we were building songs, it comes natural to me. "Here's the chord changes, play the chord on this beat, and the next beat…"

I would play rhythmic things. And we all liked it.

So I would play around within the changes, add texture — sometimes those things happen later on. I would get called back in to do a solo.

Mark would say, "We want to make it a bit more *active* here." And I would experiment. Mark and Donnie would listen and say, "Yeah, *yeah*."

DONNIE: I knew a Merilee, but she had nothing to do with the song.

"THE PROMISE"

Marty also scored his sole solo songwriting credit on the album: "The Promise" would resurface in different forms over the years. In every arrangement, it's an emotional story about the low-key drama of blue-collar life.

MARK: "The Promise" was a song Marty brought in. It was the second album, and I did not want to bogart all of the writing. So he wrote that, and we decided to record it, and I like it. It fit in well with the *King Cool* theme.

MARTY: I demo'd it up a little bit, just a little basic demo I did with some friends. And I played it and one of two other things for Mark and Donnie. And they liked that one.

I guess, like all songs, I don't know exactly where it came from. Thoughts I had. Things I wanted to express.

I don't write a lot. I come up with ideas and throw them away. We don't record so awful much now that I can tell you how it quote-unquote works.

I come up with ideas, as we all do, and stow them away. If we were doing an album every year or so, I'd have the opportunity to get these things down. I still have ideas. I jot them down and work on them sometimes.

DONNIE: That's a great lyric, one anybody would be proud to sing. Anybody could hear that and song and think, "Good tune, man!"

"PRETENDER"

"Pretender" is a big slice of '80s new-wave keyboard bliss, with a high beats-per-minute count, topped with dollop of '60s cut-a-rug rock.

MARK: It was tough to play. It was pretty creative. I like that song. I was playing a Prophet on that.

Marty played an electric sitar. The solo was pretty involved. I wanted something like [the Beatles'] "Within You Without You," where the strings and sitar interplay. And so I layered up a big string section on an ARP string ensemble and some other synthesizers, this really fast thing that you hear on the record. I first stacked that all up, and then Marty had to learn to play with it.

It's an unusual song. It's in D flat, which is my specialty. Marty will laugh about that, because I wrote songs in flat keys, grammatically flat, like A flat, E flat — not guitar keys. And that's in D flat. It's unusual. It's an unusual riff, not a very rock-guitar-oriented riff. That's why Marty is perfect for the band: He can go off in that way, and he's not thrown off by it. It's weird stuff, and he can get weirder.

When a wave of '80s keyboard sounds came in, Mark caught it easily, despite his very traditional roots.

MARK: Everything goes in the mix. We're a product of the Beatles. There's so much Beatles in what we were doing, mainly because Donnie can do all those voices. And that was great fun, to be able to work with someone who can do all those voices.

You can hear all that stuff that was going on, and then you're trying to make your own art and your own expression. But you're influenced by what you're hearing, and you want your music to be relevant. And what sells in that market, too, because you want to do music for a living. So to accept that that was going on, I guess we were a part of that.

I'm sure at some time, the word "Pretender" suggested itself as a hook. And we laid it down and stacked the hell out of Donnie's voice, just the hook. And then we got into all this counterpoint stuff with the bell sounds.

We loved doing that, spending days doing all that stuff. We loved it. I just stacked 24 Donnies up in that nice falsetto, didn't know how it was going to sound.

And he's such a good sport. I'd say, "two more."

But in my mind, I just think, "We're gonna do *nine* of these."

You might think, "Why two more?" He'd just go, "OK."

He never gave me a hard time, never said, "Why the hell are we doing *nine*?" He just did it.

And then we'd all come in the studio — me, Jerry, and Donnie. And then, for the first time, listen to all 24 together.

And they'd all be like, "*WOW*."

And that would be the reward for the two hours of work we just did.

For the second album, Mark was a full-time Cruiser, no other band to practice for. He would hit the studio and stay there, Donnie and Jerry at his side, daylight a fading memory.

MARK: Complete studio tan.

INSIDE MARK'S MIND, INSIDE DONNIE'S BIG SOUND

The Cruisers' sonic identity is an aural manifestation of Mark's quirks. Donnie applies his voice to the producer's mental architecture.

MARK: I think our sound had something to do with the OCD I experienced when I was younger. I don't know what it is with me. I was working out this morning, I was thinking about that.

I do reps: curls, any exercise. I do sets the same way I stack vocals: I do three sets of nine. I just *do* that.

Donnie's a trooper. It seems arbitrary, but there's a logic behind it. It became nine, and I'll tell you why:

It's a three-part chord, almost always.

So there's a low, a middle, and a high.

And I would do three voices of each — that's nine.

And I would do that twice more, so it's left, right, and center. That's 27 voices.

And that was The Basic Donnie Stack: left, right, and center.

Donnie's great in that regard: I say, "We're gonna do nine. I almost always pick nine."

It's logic: There's three-part harmonies.

And doubling each voice is not enough.

So tripling each voice is nice. It has a nice sound.

And then I want to do the stereo feel. So I want it left and right.

And then, as we used to say, I want *a little in the middle*, to have this really nice chalice of background vocals, that sort of envelope the stereo spectrum.

And that's how nine comes in.

And that's how I lift weights: I don't do ten, I don't do eight. I do nine reps, three times.

Mark's obsessive attention to detail shapes the Cruisers' sound and mix.

MARK: I'm happy-crazy that way. I'm very detail-oriented when I make the record. I dwell on it. I'm fixated on it. I don't need to have everything lined up correctly or wash my hands constantly. I'm more about the way we do it.

I like to mix down during the recording process. Now we don't do that as much.

To me, limitations in the studio are a good thing. That's how *Sgt. Pepper* was recorded. When you have limitations, it forces you to make decisions. And I always used to make decisions, even on the 24-track. I would mix things down and fix them down into two tracks. I wouldn't leave them separate. Now there is no turning back.

Jerry or somebody would say, "Mark, why don't you leave them separate, so you can fix them or adjust them later?"

Maybe this is part of my OCD, but I'd say, "No. We have to make a decision now. And then we're going to move on."

And I was always comfortable with my decisions. We would mix the pianos down, mix the 18 pianos left and right. So we've got drums on maybe eight tracks. Then we've got the bass on a track, and the guitar on a track. And we usually double up the guitar right away. And you've got 13 tracks left on a 24 track. You have to be very strategic how you produce these records.

If you want to do nine vocals, you need to have nine tracks open. You do nine tracks, you mix them down to track 13, and you do that twice more. Now you've got 13, 14, 15 background vocals. It's like playing a board game: You've always got to leave tracks open.

Sometimes you know exactly where you're going. Sometimes you don't. And this is the kind of thing I got so much joy out of in the studio, what I'm describing. I love laying a track down.

You have 12, 13 tracks. And how are you going to stack the things you want to stack and create space so you have tracks left over if you needed them, if you need vocals or harmonies — or God knows what the track will tell you it needs. It's like a chess match.

"LOVE IS LIKE A ROCK"

KEVIN: Mark is generous with the songwriting credits. It's rare.

The melody, I think, is the main thing in songwriting. So I think my beat is not as important as the melody or the chord progression, because it's not something that people will sing along to.

But having said that, when we would jam on a song, you get an idea. And maybe I came up with a beat that led to everyone else coming up with another part, that maybe qualifies as songwriting. But I can't sit down at a piano and write a song. I don't have that ability. I just do what I can.

"Love Is Like a Rock" was based around a drum part. There's a perfect example. We made a drum loop. I triple-tracked a drum part. I played one part. I overdubbed on top of it. And then the third time, we wanted to come up with a jungle-type beat. And there's Mark: He's willing to do that stuff, to be creative. So we came up with "Love Is Like a Rock" as a four-bar drum loop.

We put it on a loop, and we had five minutes. And Marty came up with the chorus first, I believe. It was unique. I remember when Mark called me from the studio and played it for me. I thought, "Oh, hell: That is some really cool stuff."

We used to record on a 24-channel multitrack tape. I played this part. And then I played it over the top. I recorded ten channels of drums. And I recorded another ten channels of drums on top. And we couldn't go to 30, though I recorded close to 24 channels of drums. As they say now, we made a beat.

Mark says, "Ok, give me a beat."

And you base the song on that. So we did that. And we put it on quarter-inch tape. And we made a physical loop that was four minutes long. And we connected the tail to the head. So it was a circular piece of tape.

DONNIE: We had some weird setup in the control room with Kevin and me and Jerry, our engineer.

KEVIN: We'd all sit in the studio, and we had to guide tape. We were all holding pencils, with the tape running around them, like Pink Floyd did at Abbey Road with *Dark Side of the Moon*.

I'm not sure how long the tape was, physically, but it was big enough to fill a room. And then we reprinted that quarter-inch tape onto two channels on the multitrack.

So on the multitrack tape, which is 24 channels, we now have two channels of just drums, which was the beat. And on top of that, we overdubbed the guitar, the bass, the vocals. And that's how that song was created. Unique. It was a lot of fun to do.

Mark was very forward-thinking in the studio. You hear *Sgt. Pepper*, and you're just salivating, "This is great stuff!" And Mark, who else would create 100 vocals tracks to recreate that sound? No one *did* that.

Mark would also layer keyboard parts, as if they were MIDI'd together. It's easy to do now, but not back then.

PAUL: "Love is like a Rock" is my favorite Kevin performance from the studio. No other drummer I know can overdub drum parts like that perfectly in sync. I think he has a metronome built into his brain,

KEVIN: All that multitracking isn't easy, playing the same thing, the same way, every time.

Sometimes it's easy. Sometimes it's not.

"Love Is Like A Rock," the four-bar beat that I made, on the fourth bar, there's an inconsistency between the three drum parts playing there at the same time, all my multitrack parts. And it created a new rhythmic part, because of the inconsistency between all three parts, which was a happy accident.

You like those: In the studio, when something happens, and it's wrong or it's different than it should be, but it's pretty cool and it's a happy accident — this was a happy accident.

DONNIE: Kevin lays that beat down.

Kevin has worked with producers and engineers who worked on...

Pink Floyd, *The Wall*	Kiss, *Destroyer*
Nine Inch Nails, *The Fragile*	Lou Reed, *Berlin*
Alice Cooper, *Love It to Death*	The Rolling Stones' *Sticky Fingers*
through *The Alice Cooper Show*	and *Exile on Main St.*

He says Mark can hang with those guys.

KEVIN: Who could turn the drum loop into the song it turned out to be, "Love Is Like a Rock"?

I've worked with Andy Johns, who mixed the Rolling Stones. But his input was more technical than musical.

And you have people like Bob Ezrin, who I worked with on two of the Kiss things and one of the Lou Gramm songs for the *Highlander* soundtrack. Ezrin is very musical: If you don't come up with a drum part, he'll come up with one for you. He's talented — Pink Floyd, Alice Cooper, all the other things he's done. So many exceptional records, and he's a musical genius.

So somewhere between those two, you have to operate. I think Mark is more on the musical end, which is the more important end, because that's the stuff that hits the heart.

No one's gonna know you cut tracks in a really, really great studio and say, "Listen to those drums!" If you're not hitting the people where they feel it, it doesn't matter.

It's all about the music. And I think Mark is a genius in that area. He might not think so.

James Gang drummer Jimmy Fox says Kevin is no slouch, either.

FOX: Kevin, he's one of the greats. Very enjoyable. Very musical. He has the chops. He can play anything. But he has a sensibility about taste, what to play.

He's another guy who listens. That's why they play so well together. As long as Donnie and Mark are there, I'm gonna love them. But the original guys were my favorite version, top to bottom.

MARK: I would often lay down my vocal tracks first.

One example is "Love Is Like a Rock." Donnie's the important part, but that's all me on top, and on the hooks: "Love can rock you / Never stop you" — that's me.

And Donnie's on the bottom, doing the low octave.

I have a useful purpose to my voice. That's a color in our palette. I had one color. Donnie had 50 colors in his palette.

He has his falsetto voices, his Beatles voices — in fact, his Beatles voices can be broken down into his George voice, his John voice, and the others. And his Marvin Gaye voice. His scream. He's got all sorts of voices. That can be really fun.

MARTY: I sing live. But on the albums, no one but Donnie and Mark sang, for the most part.

DONNIE: Mark and I wrote lyrics — we could bounce things back and forth off of each other. Living a couple hundred miles away from each other, it kind of put the damper on getting together to write.

Writing is so time-consuming — at least that's how I felt about it. And the fact that lyrics come so easy to him, it just made more sense that he would concentrate on that.

And I do think we wrote some good lyrics together, bouncing things off each other, things that I didn't like that he suggested, or things that I would write that he didn't like. That's how we did "Leah," "Love Is Like a Rock," "Agnes" — those songs are pretty much co-writes.

"Love Is Like a Rock" would peak at number 37 on the *Billboard* album chart February 20, 1982. Technically, it was their highest-charting song: On *Billboard*'s Mainstream Rock Chart, it reached number 9. MTV played the video. A lot. And when the single's life was over, maybe it still had untapped potential.

SEAN ROSS, *ROSS ON RADIO*: I first heard "Love Is Like A Rock" and thought, "Okay, I know there's no new Queen record due out, so what is this?"

All three of the hits — and "The Rapper" — were songs that peaked just short of being consensus, power rotation hits for everybody. Which is too bad, because I think they hold up.

MIKE PALONE, GUITARIST, SKELL (ex-WHISKEY HIGH): "Love Is Like a Rock" is an underrated rock anthem. The riffs are classic, the chorus gigantic. No wonder it's one of Donnie's biggest songs. Guitar work is very prominent throughout, more than just a solo: little licks here and there between vocals, always tasteful and cool. Good tonality, as always, on the guitar. High energy prevails throughout, and it's contagious. It's almost impossible not to sing along.

JASON PETTIGREW, *ALTERNATIVE PRESS* EDITOR-IN-CHIEF: You've got a soccer stadium-size chant like "Love Is Like a Rock" — you just kind of wonder what people were thinking at the time, that it wasn't bigger.

I guess everybody chooses their poison, and it takes hold in ways that the already-damaged don't get it. Iris and the Cruisers were always clever dudes who made great records and had great, great songs.

To this day, the people who got it love it. The people who talk to me about music say, "Yeah, I saw this one guy, Donnie Iris. He was great. I can't understand why he didn't break out in a big way and wasn't international" or "Donnie Iris is the best local band that ever was in the 80s — that was just great!"

The song impressed the man Mark most would have wanted to impress — if he thought that way, which he does not.

Six years later, in 1987, British hard rock kings Slade — who are a footnote in American music, but a megalithic chart-topping institution in the UK — recorded the song with none other than Roy Thomas Baker, Mark Avsec's role model, the producer who made classic albums by Queen, the Cars and Foreigner. Slade's version of "Love Is Like a Rock" was released on the album *You Boyz Make Big Noize*.

Guitarist Dave Hill told the Slade International Fan Club newsletter, "Jim [Lea, bassist] suggested that it would fit in nicely to the current mold of Bon Jovi/Europe. Roy also liked the song."[27.2]

Slade fans voted it their second-favorite song on the album.[27.3]

MARK: That is definitely a high honor for me. I mean, I was imitating him, and then he produced it.

"THAT'S THE WAY LOVE OUGHT TO BE"

But the supreme *King Cool* song…

The tune that finds the group going downhill at 120, buffeted by gale-force winds, pounding in palpable harmony…

…is Donnie Iris and the Cruisers' best overall recording, "That's the Way Love Ought to Be."

If "Ah! Leah!" is the Cruisers' equivalent of the slow and methodical "Running' With the Devil," then "That's the Way Love Ought to Be" is their "Panama," a superb, unstoppable runaway ride. It's a track of magnificent momentum.

Albritton plays a propulsive bass line with perpetual-motion grace.

Kevin's drums crash like Albritton is pulling him along.

Friction from Marty's minimal chords shoot sparks ten feet in the air.

Mark's pinpoint-precise keyboard strikes are lightning overhead as Donnie grips the wheel, screaming ecstatic screams, like he might survive the ride, but probably won't — and, either way, he'll *never* feel *this* alive again.

That's the way music ought to be.

KEVIN: "That's the Way," I think that's as close to a perfect song as you can get, period. I always felt that.

MARK: "That's the Way Love Ought to Be," that is the song that best represents Donnie, who he is, what he can do. Donnie's got so many voices, and that captures all of them.

"That's the Way" had completely and utterly different versions. Different lyric, different melody, everything. I listened and listened, and I scrapped it all, and rewrote it.

I don't recall what they sounded like — they weren't as good. That's all there was to it. They had the same rhythm track, but something different on top of it. And I sat back when it was all done, and I said, "That's not it."

There were songs like "That's the Way Love Ought to Be," that went through so many iterations. It went through ten versions. And that song still isn't as good as it should have been. The *track* was that good, but I don't know if the song was.

It was all about *effort*. I kept doing it again. Then I'd do it again. And finally… it's not like I'm terribly *unhappy* with how it ended up.

That's credited to both me and Donnie. The song started, some, on my own. But it really began in Donnie's basement, I think. And then we brought it into the band.

It's in A flat. Flat key, bad guitar key. But Marty played that intro that you hear.

And then when it got to that — there are some really interesting harmonic changes. It goes from an A flat to an E natural bass, which is really weird. I love these harmonic shifts in songs, where a song starts in one harmonic area and shifts to another harmonic area.

If you can just get the music to make the right connection via chord changes, in unsuspecting surprises that are really pleasant to listen to… When I went to the E section [in the chorus] *dun-dun-dun*, I was just messing around in the studio, with the Prophet. It wasn't even layered, which is unusual for me.

The sound was so good. The guys really liked it. The whole song just had a really great feel. It was a favorite track of everybody. I thought this was going to be a great big hit. So I kept working on it and working on it.

And everything we did, I thought, wasn't as good as the track itself. And you can't have the just the track — you need the song.

It was weird: You have that synthesized melody, and you put vocals right over the melody, and it doesn't work. You have to do something that compliments it. And it ended up being what it is.

That's the track that got away. I still love that song. It's one of my favorite Donnie songs. I put an incredible amount of work in that song. I wrote and rewrote the lyric and the vocals four times.

I'd go to Jeree's, and I'd stand there with Jerry and go, "This isn't right. Just erase everything," all the vocals we had done."

And Jerry would just look at me, like, "Are you *kidding* me?!"

The reason was: The track was magical. Just the track.

It was like a song in and of itself, with the synthesizer. And then the hook, with just the synthesizer chords over Marty's guitar part. Every time we tried to put words over it, it wasn't as good as the music by itself.

Finally, I kind of gave up, and ended up with "That's the Way Love Ought to Be." But I still think it deserved a better song.

Going into the second verse, Donnie lets out a hot yelp in the grand tradition of supercharged performers like James Brown and Warren Zevon. It sounds spontaneous, but that's a studio illusion cooked up by Mark. The producer punched it in, in the same expert way Ted Templeman added prerecorded David Lee Roth asides into early Van Halen tracks, creating moments that sounded improvised, but weren't. [27.4]

MARK: It was *very* labored, and we tricked you into thinking it sounds loose. In the very end, Donnie goes in, and we coached up these little breath noises and screams. But it's a very labored environment, that one in particular.

DONNIE: The first two albums, a good deal of the songs were written in my basement, on my piano. And that was one of them.

That was a baby grand I had in my house at Beaver Falls. Me and a bunch of friends took the legs off that thing and put it on our backs and carried it down there. Somehow we did it. We had to turn it sideways and slide it down the steps.

My friend Herman Granati got his thumb or one of his fingers caught between it and one of the steps. And luckily it didn't hurt him all that bad. It was a stupid thing to do, a bunch of musicians carrying that damned thing down the basement.

MARK: "That's the Way Love Ought to Be" was a good record. That's one of my favorite songs we've done. And there were a couple other good ones on *King Cool*. But I still think the song could have been better given the great track if I had a few more months to work on it.

For all his obsessive attention to detail, Avsec says he doesn't have a *Chinese Democracy* in him, an endlessly refined album a decade in the making. *Sometimes* he feels like spending six months on a track. But generally, that's not how he likes to work.

MARK: At some point, you should just move on. Make decisions, move on, try again. I honestly think 24 tracks was enough to make a good rock record. But that's where I came from. That was the era.

"MY GIRL"

Oddly, the Cruisers' doo-woppy "My Girl" is the band's highest-reaching single on Billboard's main singles chart, the Hot 100. It peaked at number 25 during a 14-week run. As the *Best of* liner notes indicate, it — coincidentally — has a lot in common with Huey Lewis and the News, who were about to break in a big way. [27.5]

MARTY: Some people will tell you "My Girl" was a better single, but they always ask for "Love Is Like a Rock" more. So if it tracked higher, it tracked higher, but it didn't stand the test of time the way "Love Is Like a Rock" does.

MARK: Back then, the instruments that were available to me: We had a grand piano in the studio, and it was not a great grand. It was barely in tune — but if you stacked the hell out of it, it had a very interesting sound. And that was Jeree's in a nutshell: If you just went in there like a normal band recorded, you weren't going to get something that stood up to the rest of the state-of-the-art.

But if you used the studio as an instrument — "My Girl," for example, is probably 25 tracks. You'd think I'm crazy, but I *did* this stuff. I would sit there for three quarters of a day and play the "My Girl" part 25 times. I literally did that, in different octaves. That's what "My Girl" is: a grand piano in Jeree's, layered 25 times.

And then what else was available was the Prophet 5 I had. I didn't use it that much. I think I did use it on "That's the Way Love Ought to Be," the one sound in that.

Though the band's top single isn't the best representative of the Cruisers' sound, the song has much to like. Donnie's dynamic vocals are a master's class in phrasing, range, breath control, and delivery. It's a pinnacle of Donnie-Mark synergy. Mark, who co-wrote it, says the vibe isn't as retro as you might think. Mark was inspired by a new song from an old favorite. And he and Donnie strolled through the tune at a leisurely pace, until they had a hit.

MARK: I heard the John Lennon vibe — that's kind of what I was emulating. "Starting Over" had just come out.

Then we just take it line by line in the studio, and it just happens: I have something in my head, and we start shaping it.

And then Donnie does his thing with it — and if a line is cool, we keep it. And if not, then we do it again. We just throw a bunch of stuff against the wall and see what sticks.

FOX: The first album is my favorite, although I'm real strong on the second one as well.

The first one, they threw together this group of musicians, who gelled together in about 30 seconds. They were all virtuoso level musicians.

Albritton, he's played some parts that I consider to be the top of the profession. I listen to "Philadelphia Freedom" by Elton John — that's Dee Murray, a famous session player. That's an object lesson in how to play the electric bass guitar. Albritton reaches that level on "My Girl." If a fledgling bass player could listen to and master that bass track, he'd be two-thirds toward being a great bass player. It's got everything you need to learn. That's Al.

Those two albums I was involved with, I think they stand up with *anything*. They do, with no qualification. Sonics, the songs, the arrangements — everything is great. Everything is world-class.

I wish that they occupied a broader space in people's recollection of the music of the era, especially given the fact Donnie was reaching back, with some sort of taste. The James Gang was ten years old at that point; music was moving toward disco and other directions. And then Donnie was *Donnie*. It was his sensibility, and it made sense to people from the Beatles era who loved that kind of music, going forward. He was a major artist of his time, and he is very fondly remembered.

"BROKEN PROMISES"

Some of the Cruisers' most intricate interplay and explosive moments arrive in "Broken Promises." It also delivers Kevin's biggest, baddest percussion outburst. True to his style, when he gets a moment to take the spotlight, he doesn't go big or flashy; it's just awesome.

MARK: I don't think it was really a true, story, to tell you the truth. In a sense, it was true: Everybody's got a broken promises song in them.

Again, sometimes we're doing a song, and it suggests a hook. And we stack it up. And if it makes sense, I lie down with it, and I go, "What does this mean?" And I'm lying around with it for a day or two.

I suppose it is a psychoanalytical session within myself, trying to come up with lyrics. I can't remember what it was for that song.

The drum break, that was a suggestion. That was a conscious effort:

We said we're going to do a drum break. Kevin was very tuned in to where the mix placement was in the room, because we had room mics going on. Jeree's had just redone the drum room, which made me nervous, because we had just had this big hit with "Leah" from the studio. And now Garvin decided to redo the drum room and turn it from a brick and make it a lot more live.

In a way, it was disconcerting to me. But it sounded good. It was different. If you listen to it, the room just opens up there. And Kevin wanted that. He was playing stuff, imagining that happening. He would remind us: "Remember, in the big break, you've got to goose the rooms."

KEVIN: The drum break was a happy accident. It was a creative break made in the studio, and madman Mark made a thing of it. Live, Donnie would blow into the vent hole of the tom I was playing, which would change the pitch of the drum by changing the air pressure. Pretty cool.

"KING COOL"

To Mark, the title track represents the long evolution of Dominic Ierace from a fun, funny regular guy, into Donnie Iris, solo star. By the end of the second record, all the elements Donnie and Mark had tried to distill into a new character recognizable as "Donnie Iris" were now in play. The long-lost "King of Cool" review of the band's first Toronto show summarized the budding persona succinctly — and Mark made it shorter. As of this album, Donnie was officially *King Cool*.

MARK: Donnie could be cool. He was a cool guy. I'm full of angst and anxiety and nervousness. I'm not cool at all. Donnie actually is cool. What he's doing in his life now, he's a happy, cool guy. He could just hang out, smoke cigars, and play golf. When he was younger, he was cool. He was thin, laid back, he'd smoke cigarettes.

"King Cool" came from a reviewer in Toronto. We were playing at the El Mocambo show.

He called Donnie "the new king of cool."

And I can't tell you at that moment I said, "Oh, we're going to do an album called *King Cool*!" But that was right after the first album. I was writing the second album. I thought about that and wrote a song called "King Cool" about a fictitious person.

And I think what happened was: Donnie and I were writing it on a piano in his basement. And we're laying it down, and I don't think it was going to be called "King Cool." Maybe it was. We remembered it at some point. It worked with the image we were crafting for Donnie. Then we made that a theme for the record, a loose theme that we had fun with.

The song gives Marty a moment to shine. The solo isn't as splashy as Kevin's, but it's textbook Marty.

MARK: He comes up with these great little parts, Marty weirdisms. Like on "King Cool," picking things slow. "Daddy Don't Live Here Anymore," the verse on that song. Little things, not stock.

"COLOR ME BLUE"

Unlike the somewhat hybrid hip-retro single "My Girl," "Color Me Blue" is pure sock-hop material, a modulation of barebones rock, ace chops, new wave keyboards, and '50s rock, with a blues base.

MARK: That's a '50s thing. And the theme, I think Donnie came up with it, using colors as a motif. It fits Donnie. We can do our own thing with it, all those counterpoints, Beatlesque, kind of. That's really easy for us to do, 'cause Donnie can perform that.

"THE LAST TO KNOW"

After the retro '50s of "Color Me Blue," the pendulum swings back to the '80s, with an archetypal keyboard power ballad. In future albums and other projects, Mark would explore this genre in depth.

MARK: That's a song about being cheated on. At that time, it didn't mean anything to me. It's a little vignette, a soap opera thing.

And Donnie, that's one of his best performances. I really coached him up and got him into a state. His voice was just crystal clear that day.

I layered the studio grand piano like crazy, like I did on "My Girl": layers and layers of piano. I'd use Minimoog occasionally, organ occasionally.

I played the giant pipe organ at Cleveland State's facility to record for one of our records. I used to like playing pipe organs. In high school, my older buddies who were already in college used to have me come down to St. Stephen's church on the West side after they smoked pot. And they would lie in the pipes while I played.

I think that was the happiest time of my life, working on that first album and *King Cool*. I was just sitting in the studio. I didn't have much money. I was smoking cigarettes, drinking coffee. Donnie and I were very close, and laughed a lot. We loved Jerry. And the band was good. We felt we were working on really special stuff. We loved it. Doing the stacking, planning the stacking. It was a lot of fun.

And as with the rest of their albums, the *King Cool* sessions didn't produce any extra songs that resurfaced later — or didn't. Nothing remains for an expanded edition, box set or B-side. Before the sessions started, there had been some talk of one more song. And it almost reshaped the entire record. After the live "Rapper" single, management *still* wanted them to revisit the Donnie's chart-topping Jaggerz single. Again.

MARK: I remember Carl, I think, was suggesting "The Rapper" be on *King Cool*. And I was adamantly opposed.

It got serious enough where I considered doing something thematically *a la* Sgt. Pepper to make "The Rapper" fit. But I delivered the album without it, and they liked it, and the idea was dropped. I did this in secret so nobody would have input.

So the producer was happy with the album. For a moment. Mark stands by the songs. One key strategic error may have caused a misfire for the entire album, and possibly entire rest of the band's commercial career.

THE MIX-UP

As with *Back on the Streets*, *King Cool* has a track sequence fans know...

1. "Sweet Merilee"
2. "The Promise"
3. "Pretender"
4. "Love Is Like a Rock"

5. "That's the Way Love Ought to Be"
6. "My Girl"
7. "Broken Promises"

8. "King Cool"
9. "Color Me Blue"
10. "The Last to Know"

...which is not what Donnie and Mark had in mind when they crafted the album.

King Cool, the band's most successful if not best album, was done. Almost.

Mark accompanied the master tapes to New York City, for final layer of post-production gloss, to lock down the mix, balance the stereo effects, smooth out the levels and make the album sound like the recording you hear when you press play today. The songs needed to pass through two more processes: mixing and mastering. The first part went well.

King Cool received a final mix at Media sound, a prestigious Manhattan studio practically in the shadow of Carnegie Hall, which had hosted artists from Frank Sinatra to Pat Benatar. Mixing engineer Michael Barbiero had remixed Wild Cherry's "Try a Piece of My Love."

MARK: Michael Barbiero did a phenomenal job for us on *King Cool*. He's fantastic. He's a New York guy. He'd flip on one track and hear this weird stuff and look at you funny. But he saw it.

He was taking cat naps to rest his ears on the last 24-hour session. In the middle of the night, he would lie down somewhere. I could not sleep, so I would wait for him to get up — I wanted to keep working — which he would after about 30 minutes. Not sure how he slept, but he seemed to think there was a benefit in resting his ears.

Once Mark was happy with the mix, he carried the tape boxes through Hell's Kitchen, to the storied Sterling Sound studio. The high-priced facility is still one of — if not *the* — best audio mastering facilities in the industry. The biggest names in music history put final touches on some of the greatest records ever made there: Springsteen's *Born to Run*. John Coltrane's *A Love Supreme*. Later, Guns N' Roses' *Appetite for Destruction*. More recently, the *Hamilton* Original Broadway Cast Recording.

But once Mark was at Sterling Sound, something about *King Cool* changed, maybe to its detriment. It sounds great. But when you hear what, and in what order, became a profound issue. Barbiero, as it turns out, had the right idea when he stopped working and napped. A wired Mark was running in the red, and it led him to a bad judgment call he still regrets.

MARK: Sequencing. I made mistakes with that. "That's the Way" should have been first. I put it first on the second side, which is almost as good, because it was *albums* then.

It may have been fatal to our whole career. Originally, I had either "Love Is Like a Rock" or "That's the Way" first.

Mark's first choice for mastering was the man who took the final pass on the Allman Brothers Band's *Brothers and Sisters*, Stevie Wonder's *Innervsions*, and Wild Cherry's *Electrified Funk*.

MARK: I wanted George Marino. He was not available. Then I went to master it with Jack Skinner, who I thought had just done *Arc of a Diver* by Steve Winwood. I do not know for a fact that he worked on *Arc of a Diver*, but that is what he said. Jack said, "Man, you ought to put *this* song first" — "Merilee."

Skinner was not exactly a step down; in coming years, his body of work would expand to include Anthrax, the Bangles, Peabo Bryson, Cameo, Belinda Carlisle, Genesis, Rick James, Metallica, Robert Palmer, R.E.M., Soft Cell, The Talking Heads, and even Avsec's Cellarful of Noise. But this time out, Avsec regrets deferring to Skinner's expert judgment; nobody bats 1.000.

MARK: "Merilee" is a good song. But it was a weird format, not the best *rock* song. We should have gone with "Love Is Like a Rock." I had "Love Is Like a Rock" as the first single. But I completely retooled the order because I stayed up all night mixing the album with Michael Barbiero, and then Jack Skinner the mastering engineer, said "I like 'Merilee.'" So I put it first.

That set off a chain of reactions.

Everything got confused. The record company put out "Merilee" first, because somebody at the record company simply listened to the first track, I'm sure.

Maybe if George Marino mastered the record instead, "Merilee" is never inserted as side one cut one, "Love Is Like Rock" is the first single, and we are a household name.

MARTY: I don't know that I ever formed an opinion about that. "Merilee" has a huge hook, a nice chorus. I don't know. I guess, maybe.

This is the first time I've thought about it. I might have started out with "That's the Way," because it's more uptempo — that's a great song. But I don't have a strong opinion about opening the album with "Merilee."

Things turned out OK. I don't know. You can always have imagined an album doing better. That gets kind of complicated.

MARK: Looking back, I did have a say in the singles, implicitly. But I didn't exercise it. If you put something on side one, cut one, it's going to be the first single. Record company people don't even listen to the whole record. That's why "Merilee" was released. I take full blame.

One of my great regrets is "That's the Way Love Ought to Be" never was a single — that's maybe the best thing we ever did, that and "Love Is Like a Rock."

(Pittsburgh fans make note: "That's the Way Love Ought to Be" *was* played like a hot single in Pittsburgh. But the record label never released it as a 45.)

THE *KING COOL* COVER

At least Mark liked the cover. It's Paul's favorite, too.

MARK: Of all the albums, I'm not gonna say I love it, but *King Cool* is the most classy one. That's my favorite cover.

PAUL: It looks like we caught Donnie smoking a joint in the alley.

The cover photo was taken by Georgina Karvellas, whose work spanned from Ian Hunter's *You're Never Alone With A Schizophrenic* to Janis Ian's *Restless Eyes*. The rear picture is by Marcia Resnick, a New York City photographer whose staggering body of work includes a who's-who of the old-school punk rock scene, including Bad Brains, Suicide, The Talking Heads and Johnny Thunders, with additional work for the Psychedelic Furs.

The rear photo conveys a lot of personality. The band are all seated on a floor, in a huddle. Left to right: Marty looks like an archetypal '80s frontman in dark jeans and a leather jacket, his hair a tight helmet, eyebrows angled in an intense stare. Inscrutable Albritton, symbolically, is in the background. Cool Donnie presides front and center, jeans cuffed. Kevin is a mere smiling head perched on Donnie and Mark's shoulders, almost entirely obscured yet undeniably present. Hair curly, collar flipped, workaholic Mark rocks a sports coat, staring down the camera.

August 6, the Belkin-Maduri Organization delivered the master tapes for *King Cool* to Carousel.

Proofs from the 1982 photo shoot for the King Cool back cover. (Photos by Marcia Resnick. Shot at her Canal Street Studio, NYC)

CHAPTER 28

King Cool: The Tour

LIVE AT BLOSSOM

King Cool had the best possible album release party. Sort of. Within a week of the record's arrival in stores, the Cruisers opened a series record-setting concerts.

BELKIN: I was managing Donnie. I was managing Michael [Stanley]. Both were doing well with live shows. They always got together and got along. I decided to put them together. It seemed like a stretch to put them at Blossom — the last thing I want to do is not have a good-sized attendance. We were hoping for, probably, 12…15,000.

The upside of the band's production deal was a quick turnaround. Carousel stamped its name on the record and passed it to MCA, which pressed it up and shipped it out. The August 22 cover of *Billboard* magazine featured an ad for *King Cool*. And copies of it arrived in stores over the next week.

August 23, 24 and 26, the Cruisers were the opening act for *three* sold-out concerts by the Michael Stanley Band, Cleveland's equivalent of Donnie Iris & the Cruisers, a phenomenally popular hometown act with a smaller measure of success nationwide.

Stanley, also managed by the Belkin-Maduri Organization, was developing an annual tradition of headlining — and filling — Blossom Music Center, a pavilion in the woods, with a capacity of 18,000. Located outside Akron, south of Cleveland, it's Northeast Ohio's major outdoor venue — the equivalent of Pittsburgh's Coca Cola Star Lake/KeyBank Pavilion.

In 1980, Stanley had sold out *two* nights at Blossom. In 1982, with no opening act, Stanley's band drew a combined crowd of 66,377 over four nights, the highest draw of a record-setting season, which still remains a record-setting stand for the venue.[28.1]

In 1981, the Michael Stanley Band/Donnie Iris & the Cruisers shows sold out three nights, drawing 18,322 fans to each concert.[28.2]

MARK: That was a big deal. I'd played big shows before, with Wild Cherry. The Blossom shows were exciting. I didn't feel like we'd arrived — those were Michael's shows. But it felt great, playing for 20,000 people.

We did well. Donnie grew into his role. And by the Blossom thing, he'd got it down. It was his stage. It was a big deal. It was really exciting. It was great.

It was a historical stand for the Cleveland rock scene, and the MSB Blossom concerts remain legendary.

As quickly as MCA had pressed and distributed the album, the production deal's downside became apparent: MCA would push it at radio. But MCA and Carousel weren't coughing up cash for a music video. MTV launched August 1, and the cultural sea-change it set in motion was not immediately apparent through the business.

BELKIN: Money was always a problem with Frio.

Belkin had decided to film the historic Michael Stanley Band shows. And he took care of the Cruisers while he was at it. The Cruisers and Michael Stanley Band both filmed full-length concert videos, released at the *Live at Blossom* and *Live at Blossom Music Center* videotapes — and, later, DVDs.

BELKIN: I paid for the shoot.

Belkin paid a local ringer: Chuck Statler, one of the founding fathers of the music video movement, often described as "The Godfather of Music Video." The Akron native had directed *The Truth About De-Evolution*, a seminal video by multimedia new-wave figures Devo. Statler went on to work for the Cars, Elvis Costello and others. His body of work was honored in a Museum of Modern Art exhibition. On his way, he worked for Donnie.

Statler worked with Devo in the 1970s. When he talks about the arty icons, his comments are applicable to the Cruisers:

STATLER: Devo were great for the same reason the Rolling Stones were the Rolling Stones and the Beatles were the Beatles: They had that dynamic duo that brought something. And the chemistry and compatibility with those guys, they had an industrial Midwest quality. A unique personality.

There's a certain energy and spirit about Donnie. It shows in his performances.

Before the Blossom shows, the Cruisers had been off the road for a few months, though recording *King Cool* had kept them limber. The week before Blossom, the group warmed up with three shows, including the second live event held at Jeff and Flash's Monopolie$, a brand-new Cleveland club owned by WMMS morning show DJs Jeff "Jeff" Kinzbach and Ed "Flash" Ferenc, billed as a "drinking-dancing emporium."

After two more shows in the Northeast Ohio hinterlands, the Cruisers greeted capacity crowds with a show to remember. The short, tight opening sets featured half the new album. The track list from the video is:

"Agnes"	"King Cool"	"Broken Promises"
"That's The Way Love Ought To Be"	"Sweet Merilee" "I Can't Hear You"	"Love Is Like A Rock" "Ah! Leah!"

The 2006 DVD reissue features a bonus cut: The Cruisers' music video for "Little Black Dress," from the *Ellwood City* album, which was released that year. Director Tom Cummings and editor Dave Rogant — the team behind the *King Cool* documentary — made the video by cutting together a highlight reel from the Blossom footage, which was culled from all three nights.

"Little Black Dress" features the group's best 21st-century rock song, matched with corresponding concert footage of the band at its peak. This is Donnie Iris, live, in his prime: He takes the stage in black Fortune 410s and a tweedy gray sport coat, dark jeans riding high, white socks glowing in the spotlight. The coat comes off fast— the nights were hot.

The band are surging. Al and Mark occasionally headbang for emphasis. Collar flipped, Marty caresses his guitar and makes it look easy. Al shuffles in tight red pants — his dancing works *much* better when he has a stage bigger than the *Solid Gold* platform. Donnie comes and goes, shaking his upraised arms in raw, unchoreographed joy. From one wardrobe change to another, he returns in a white James Dean T-shirt and, later, the banana tux. When the songs open up, he hits the deck for spontaneous pushups and rolls on his back, butt in the air.

In one jamming moment, Donnie turns to the drum set, locks eyes with Kevin, and gives himself to the groove, shaking it for the crowd. Kevin is dressed for a set with the Scorpions, in a white T-shirt with black stripes at chaotic angles. All respect to the rest of the group's sweaty performance, it's Kevin that really pushes the show into a true arena-rock scale. The live "Ah! Leah!" video from the set starts with Kevin stomping the bass drums in a repeating rally beat, unaccompanied — except for 18,000 clapping fans. Donnie stands, legs spread, grinning beneath the glasses, one hand high, a rock and roll evangelist. This is a band that could have opened for Van Halen and won the crowd.

The "Little Black Dress" live footage is intercut with new shots of dancing Cleveland Cavaliers cheerleaders dolled up in skimpy dresses and '80s makeup and hair, taking turns sliding on Donnie's glasses. (The genius clip was the latest in a longrunning series of crossover efforts to promote the Pittsburgh icon as a Cleveland hero.)

For that show, the Iris clan sent a full caravan. As a hairdresser and Mrs. Iris, Donnie's wife enjoyed heightened status as the leader of a pack of *fully* decked out ladies — of all ages.

ADDY, DONNIE'S DAUGHTER: My mom and her friends, they all looked so hot. She and her girls would get the tightest jeans, the big hair, the earrings, major stilettos, and new outfits. Getting ready for the concert, we all went way out.

ERIN, DONNIE'S DAUGHTER: Backstage, Kevin was always sitting with his foot across his lap, drumming on his shoe. He was *the hot rock star*.

ADDY: Both of us, our first crush was Kevin.

ERIN: The rest of the band, they were younger than my dad, but they seemed like uncles to us.

ADDY: I remember Al's crazy outfits.

Dad would strip to his underwear. That was not one of our favorite parts of the show.

One show, dad split his pants. He went to do the big finish, where he hits the big note and jumps high, then lands really low in a squat. He split his black pants, and he had white underwear on.

He said to the crowd, "You're never gonna believe what happened: I just split my pants." And he bends over and shows everybody the split.

I was embarrassed about it, but now it's awesome.

MARK: *King Cool* was done, and we just received the album for the first time. We were not dealing with hectic stuff because of gear. Mike Barbiero was at the show. We were just hanging out.

The big shows were Stanley and his sextet at their finest moment — to that point, at least. The *Plain Dealer's* Jane Scott reviewed the show, with Stanley in appropriate top billing: "The excitement began before the band reached the stage… The band did two dozen songs, more than half of which could have served as a climax for other bands…. Stanley was singing and playing down on a runway, with young ladies reaching out to touch him… The Michael Stanley band is a superb, closely knit instrumental group…. This was the kind of show where the band has as much fun as the audience."

Scott thought the Cruisers were a little loud, but good: "The opening act, Donnie Iris and the Cruisers… was one of the hottest warm-up bands I've ever seen."

MIKE OLSZEWSKI, *KING COOL* DOCUMENTARY: You got the impression that each band challenged each other in a subliminal way, and that meant a lot of energy at those performances.

The live video served two purposes: Preserve the concerts for posterity. And promote the strong new album with a performance video for a new single.

The "Ah! Leah" video was receiving meager national airplay, but far less than Michael Stanley, whose "He Can't Love You" was the 47th video played on the network. The video shoot from the Blossom shows remedied that. The "Ah! Leah!" clip was an eye-catcher. But it sure didn't show the perspiring band in its full live fury like the "Love Is Like a Rock" live clip. Even without the extra hundred studio tracks, the band pulled off a live rendition that would go proto-viral.

MARK: MTV was starved for content. The played it so much, *I'd* get recognized out on the road, at McDonald's. And trust me: I *never* get recognized. That's the only time in my career people have stopped me and asked if I'm the guy from the band.

BACK IN THE PRESS: *KING COOL* REVIEWS

King Cool arrived when *Back on the Streets*' grooves were still smoking. Like Donnie's first record, it didn't receive a mountain of press, but it scored some bigger and better notices.

The Los Angeles *Times* enjoyed it: "Iris' second album is even more freewheeling, eclectic and sure-footed than his first; Iris throws a dozen styles against the wall to see what sticks, sometimes in the course of a single song.... 'Love Is Like a Rock,' for example, downshifts suddenly from thudding drumbeats to a chanted, almost Queen-style chorus to ethereal harmonies without ever sticking in a single gear for long. Those changes from street-corner soul to hard-rock to wafting harmonies are delightfully jarring, but there are also shared commercial instincts at work on this LP. Donnie Iris is probably too slippery to ever become a superstar, but he's also a thoroughly witty, fresh veteran who's too smart to be pigeon-holed." [28.4]

Rolling Stone didn't review it until two years later, when the magazine grudgingly included Iris in *The New Rolling Stone Record Guide*. The book dismissed both big Cruisers albums in as many sentences. It cited "Love Is Like a Rock" as a good song, but the record scored a lowly two-of-five stars grade. [28.5]

In Pittsburgh, both daily newspapers were curiously silent on the album. The papers covered Donnie's comings and goings, but generally treated him like a rock star who visited town from time to time — not a local musician who was a presence on the scene. In Pittsburgh, the hard-edged "Love Is Like a Rock" and "That's the Way Love Ought to Be" hit the airwaves and stayed there for years.

Cleveland had contrasting taste in unofficial singles, but the press fully embraced Donnie as an adopted son. Jane Scott wrote, "*King Cool* is sharp enough to break the group nationally." And she noted "Sweet Merilee" and "Pretender" were leading requests on WMMS. [28.6]

MIKE OLSZEWSKI, *KING COOL* DOCUMENTARY, ex-WMMS 100.7 FM CLEVELAND: The rock scene was extremely healthy thanks to A) lots of musicians playing different types of music, from punk to progressive and everything in between. B) Bars that advertised. C) Beer companies that advertised big promotions. D) Radio stations like WMMS and M105 that pushed artists and shows. And E) let's face it: People hitting the bars looking to get laid.

There were plenty of music fanatics, but a lot of folks gravitated toward live music just to be part of the event. I would still say most came for the music. I wouldn't call them yuppies by any means, but people were growing up and establishing stable lifestyles, and they wanted rock and entertainment to be part of that.

The industry press remained receptive. *Cash Box* liked the second single, "Love Is Like a Rock": "This group collaboration from the Cruisers is what you might call a pop/rock anthem. The vocal chant may remind one of Queen's 'We Will Rock You,' although the accent is on harmony and melody." [28.7]

Billboard agreed: "Iris has already proven that behind those Everyman looks lies the heart of a skilled pop-master, and this sequel to his successful debut again balances sharp melodies and soaring group harmonies with tough rock momentum. If Styx and REO made the first six months a bonanza for Midwestern rock, Iris and company could just top a fall bumper crop: like those multiplatinum peers, this band juggles rock anthems and modern romance adroitly." [28.8]

NOT COOL: THE *KING COOL* PROMO CAMPAIGN

Once *King Cool* was out, the going went from rocking to rocky.

Back on the Streets had been popular, certainly a success. It sold well under 500,000 copies, and never did go gold. Still: A Top 40 single is a great start.

Now that *King Cool* was out, the Cruisers' team were ready to mount a breakthrough campaign that that should have been a steady march toward victory.

The *King Cool* promotional cycle would run intermittently from August 1981 through June 1982. It yielded two of the band's three career Top 40 singles, including its highest-charting song. And the band played some of their biggest and best shows, in the company of some of the biggest and best bands of the day. So it's hard to see this pivotal chapter as anything but a win.

However...

The *King Cool* cycle agonizingly unfolded as a bizarrely disjointed, start-stop campaign that, in retrospect, might have done as much to harm their career as help it.

MARK: It was a series of miscues.

Even with no big-budget concept video, the *King Cool* promotional push was not entirely lacking. The band printed 1-1/2" in KING COOL / BACK TO SCHOOL / DONNIE IRIS pins. The label, again, bucked up for a front-cover ad on industry Bible *Billboard*.[28.9]

For the band, making *Back on the Streets* had been a more rapturous experience than the first album. It had the best launch party the Cruisers could have asked for. But then...

King Cool was on the streets for over a month before Carousel released a single, "Sweet Merilee."

Releasing and promoting a national single is never an easy undertaking, especially for the Cruisers.

"Ah! Leah!" had earned the band a record deal after the Cruisers' team tapped their network of regional connections and arranged some airplay. Listeners liked the song. Stations played it more. More stations heard about it. More stations played it. More listeners bought and requested the song. MCA signed the hot band.

That's the way radio oughtta be.

That's not how it works.

On a national level, getting a song on FM airwaves was not so simple. The path to radio rotation was corrupt toll road. Fredric Dannen's exhaustively researched book *Hit Men: Power Brokers and Fast Money Inside the Music Business* describes the network of palms that labels needed to grease to get their records on the radio — and, thus, keep other ones off. Dannen summarized it as "institutional payola": "After 1978, records put out by small labels began to vanish from the Top 40 airwaves[28.10].... A label might spend as much as $300,000 to promote a record."[28.11]

Radio stations, DJs, and program directors could not directly accept bribes to play records — the payola scandal of the 1950s and ensuing Congressional hearings had reined in that popular practice. But by the 1980s, radio was controlled by an expensive network of operatives called "independent promoters." Independent promoters roamed the country and convinced radio stations to play records, often armed with envelopes of cash and baggies of contraband to thank radio executives for their consideration — on behalf of whichever record company would pay for their services.

This freelance independent promoter system created a protective layer between record labels and stations. The practice was dismantled in 1986, after a prolonged investigation led to allegations of corruption and demonstrable ties to organized crime.

At the heart of the system was a core of operatives called The Network: "an informal alliance of the dozen or so top independent promotion men.... Each member had a 'territory,' a group of stations over which he claimed influence. If a record company wanted national airplay for a new single, it could choose to hire one of the Network men.... The Network was mostly a phenomenon of Top 40."[28.11]

In 1985, Warner Brothers alone would spend $6 million on independent promoters. CBS paid between $12.8 and $17 million. The combined industry spent an estimated $40 million that year. MCA wasn't big on the practice, but the label didn't hold out either. And with a roster of around 40 artists, a non-gold band like Donnie and the Cruisers, signed to a subsidiary label via a production deal, was not a top priority.[28.12]

In short, the upper reaches of the Top 40 — and, thus, the rest of the charts — were bought and paid for. A local guy who didn't have that kind of money to work with was stuck outside, on the corner, singing for his supper, hoping against hope someone would notice him and throw some money his way.

JIMMY ROACH, ex-WDVE RADIO VETERAN: Back then, you had your local regional record reps for the labels. And they'd come in and take the program director out to lunch.

And if there was a record they believed in that wasn't a major act, they would say, "If you play such-and-such, we'll give you, say, the new Stones tune three days ahead of your competition."

There were bargains cut, like the player to be named later in a baseball trade. That's what they would do. I don't know if they didn't have other acts to trade with, or if they didn't care. I didn't think Donnie was promoted well.

CHRIS MADURI: It's true that those types of actions took place, but it was nothing that we were doing [for the independent press of *Back on the Streets* and "Ah! Leah!"]. We promoted honestly, forthrightly. We knew we had a better-than-good product. And that opened the doors for the airplay.

Once we passed them on to MCA, I have no idea how they got KMET and KLOS in Los Angeles and WNEW in New York, those big powerhouse stations were playing Donnie. At that point, it was their artist, and they took the lead.

They were welcomed with open arms, the new singles, the new albums. They all did pretty well, but none of them — except for a song called "My Girl" — jumped into that top 20, 25 area.

The whole career sold less than a million albums, but more than 500,000. So it was a nice career. But it never exploded. It was a lot of exposure. We had a ton of people who liked it. It was just a matter of how the wind was blowing in those days, that it didn't go gold or platinum.

The band's labels were able to do a lot with a little. After decades in the business, Carousel President Rick Frio knew the ropes as well as anybody.

FOX: Frio, through MCA, had access to a full national promotion staff. And because he came from promotion, he had a leg up over everybody else in that regard. He could get the record to DJs, to stores, to radio stations. To make sure that they were not only provided with it, but whatever was necessary to get the work done.

Now, we're talking about an era that was beyond payola, we're beyond the era of money in a bag. It was not called payola, but it's an era of other forms of inducement. So I know that, for Donnie's records, we hired some independent promotion men that worked alongside, in addition to, the MCA promotion men. It wasn't unusual to supplement if the artists' people were willing to spend a little extra money.

The MCA people might have great ins with three out of four of the key radio stations. But maybe they were struggling with the fourth station. But if you had a relationship with a promotion man who had a relationship with the station, who would say to you, "I can get that station"… Well, you might say to that guy, "Bring me the station, twenty-five hundred bucks." And you try not to ask how he got the station. When [Carl] Maduri was around, this was a game he played well.

JIMMY ROACH: For the second record, I remember lying on the floor in Donnie's living room, trying to figure out what song to pick for a single. He was playing me these tunes, and I was saying, "That would be a good single. *That* would be a good single. *That* would be a good single."

As Maduri said, a competitive product helped. But when it came to singles, the label made the picks. And the label's first up was a big whiff.

"Sweet Merilee" was *not* a good way to start the album — and, especially, not the radio campaign. The leadoff single was released in October 1981. It peaked at number 90. ("Ah! Leah!," the band's best outing so far, had reached 29 and spent 18 weeks on the singles chart.)

MARK: We thought we made a good record. The wrong single was released. And that was *it*.

I'm not saying it was inappropriate, but it was all business. I accept the blame. By coming out of the box with the wrong single — in my opinion — we lost a chance to come out with maybe the best single candidate, "Love Is Like A Rock." When you are on a major label, you get one real chance. "Merilee" was it.

DONNIE: I heard there was another band that the label wanted to give a push, and they didn't put any money into it.

BELKIN: That's somewhat common. Not necessarily because we weren't directly on MCA. But we never had any sources at MCA. We were never able to go to the source, because we were signed with

Frio. So it was a point of contention, certainly, for me. We could have called MCA, but they would have said, "Look, you're signed to Carousel. You should be talking to Rick Frio."

And he's not into spending any money. And he's just into seeing what happens, and not really working. Frio was just waiting to get lucky. It's a whole process of trying to promote an album.

Times have changed now. You had to have those independent promoters in place to go in and promote it. And there was a lot of stuff that was going on with those guys. There were certain… situations. The Cruisers and Michael Stanley didn't do that. I never really got close to it. It's not my thing.

By October 1981, MTV was the new hotness, beloved by cool kids of all ages. "Sweet Merilee" did not receive a concept video to accompany the radio single.

MARK: We wanted to do one, but the record company didn't want to spend the money. They were probably seeing if the first single took off. And it didn't.

If it looks like you have something going, the company will throw more resources on it. But if it looks like it is losing momentum or does not have a chance, then the company will pull all resources and attach those resources to another record.

The first *King Cool* single spent six weeks on the *Billboard* Hot 100 singles chart. It peaked at number 80, November 21, 1981.

After a soft single, *King Cool* looked like a loss. With a roster of 40 bands, MCA knew how this kind of thing tended to play out. As far as the label suits were concerned, the album was done, and it was time to move on.

MCA/Carousel picked up the band's option for a third album.

The Cruisers booked studio time to start working on a new record.

Already. After three months and one single.

MARK: It's no skin off their butts if we go back in the studio — "Yeah, go make another one!" It's not like we're getting paid to make these records. It's an ordeal.

But the record business changed in 1981.

Now radio wasn't the only game in town. MTV had launched in August, and it immediately changed how fans experienced — and discovered — music.

After a flop leadoff single, MCA was definitely not paying for a cinematic music video.

The Cruisers didn't need one.

Belkin's side investment from the Michael Stanley Band/Cruisers concerts paid off.

At this point, the label was *entirely* disinterested in the band's video career. After Carousel/MCA passed on paying for the live concert shoot in the summer, they declined the opportunity to press and sell the video. The band's label signed off on the concert tape, and Sony released the *Live at Blossom* VHS in early November, 1981.

King Cool's second swing connected: MCA released "Love Is Like a Rock" in December. Boosted by steady MTV rotation, it peaked at number 37 two months later: February 20, 1982. The song spent 14 weeks on the *Billboard* chart, and could have lasted longer — more about that in a minute.

After the first single flopped, the label had been slow to commit money for tour support. Donnie made the scene anyway. In November, he and Maduri flew to Los Angeles to talk business, press the flesh, and get word out. The whirlwind tour stops included syndicated radio show *Rockline*, where he talked up the album and "Merilee" single, creating a photo opportunity in the process. The picture landed Donnie in the pages of *Cash Box* again. [28.13]

Donnie was in his prime, but programmers were increasingly tuned to a different look. As Bret Adams noted in *All Music Guide to Rock*, "...the early 1980s marked the beginning of the youth-and-image-based MTV era, and it was not the best time to be a diminutive, bespectacled Italian guy pushing age 40, no matter how great your songs and voice were." [28.14]

Over the fall, as *King Cool* found its legs, the Cruisers played just over a dozen regional shows. Now the band were headlining big clubs and small theaters like Toronto's El Mocambo, Des Moines' Civic Center, and Erie's Erie County Fieldhouse. The bigger venues had an average capacity over 2,000.

But for the most part, the band stayed home and worked on other things.

MARTY: At the beginning of the band, I lived briefly in Cleveland, in Euclid. I lived with Kevin Valentine. We were busy rehearsing. There was a lot going on.

Cleveland then was quite a bit different. This was before all the revitalization downtown, before the Rock Hall. Cleveland was a Rustbelt city, like many others. It wasn't great. Storefronts boarded up, downtown in decline, that sort of thing. There were nice areas, but the city itself had not started to dig its way out.

It was great. Kevin and I were great friends. He's a great guy, so hanging out with him was the best. A lot revolves around music, us rehearsing or going to hear somebody play. Our friendship, especially at the beginning, revolved around the band. We all liked each other and got along really well.

KEVIN CONSIDERS LEAVING

During the down time, Kevin almost got poached. The siren sound of a big drum room was still calling his name.

KEVIN: I was in love with Bryan Adams' drum sound from the Power Station.

It went so far as Bryan inviting me to his house, and I auditioned.

Someone at Belkin — I won't name names, because it's water under the bridge — had recommended me to him. Mickey Curry, I believe, was going to do the Hall and Oates thing and not continue with the Bryan Adams thing. That's how it came about.

We were about to start a tour. We had just finished the second album. I asked when he needed me, and he said, "We go on tour next week" or something.

And I didn't feel right just leaving the band.

As much as it was flattering, I knew I would mean more to Donnie. And it actually meant more to me, even though I was a massive fan of Bryan Adams.

But I wasn't sure if I was going to play on the *records* after that. As you can tell, I like to do band things. I like to have a group of fellas and-or ladies, and really go *at* something and *change* something. And that would be far less continuous with Bryan; he's the driving force, he's the writer.

It went great. I knew his songs. I didn't have to really learn them. I loved what Mickey played on the records. It went well.

Bryan said, "What do you think?"

I said, "Give me a day to think on this, at least."

And I turned him down.

It was flattering. But I probably would have been divorced by now — Bryan is a total workaholic. They play everywhere. That could have been a good thing. You're getting paid a fortune — when I say "a fortune," I mean "not a side wage." And you're on the road all the time. That's fun.

Part of the reason I got out of music full-time is: After I ran sound for Kiss, my daughter is two weeks, old, and I have to go on the road. To me, it became not-worth-it to work for a wage. It was a good wage. But if they wanted to expand the tour, I'dve had to do it. You miss a lot of events.

When you're younger, you're driven, and you've got blinders on. But when you get older, you recalibrate and you realize life doesn't go on forever. These friends-and-family things are really important, especially when you have kids. If you're a big band and you come home with $500,000, you can fly the family out to see you. But if you're not… there's always a tradeoff.

Some people said that would have been a great idea. But I wanted to be part of a *band*. And Bryan and the rest of the guys, I'm sure he treats his people well, but Donnie's a real band, and I enjoyed that.

BIG SHOWS, MAJOR AWARDS

As 1981 ended, Donnie and the band stayed close to home. Donnie had kept in touch with DVE. And Jimmy Roach auctioned off the bowtie from the *Back on the Streets* cover, among other Pittsburgh rock artifacts, in a benefit for Toys for Tots. [28.15] Then the band closed their second year together with some accolades and a big show.

In Cleveland, the *Plain Dealer*'s Jane Scott recognized Donnie in her annual achievement awards, granting him the Joe Frazier Comeback Award: "Jaggerz band singer Donnie Iris...proved you can be even better the second time around." [28.16]

Things were looking up at the end of the 1981. *Cash Box* hadn't exactly raved about the album, but the staff kept Donnie in mind during its year-end pop awards. Donnie placed at number 3 Top Male Vocalist, behind Phil Collins and Ozzy Osbourne, and above Jim Steinman (Meatloaf's writing partner, whose work outsold the Cruisers — but as a frontman, he was no Mark). [28.17]

Donnie also landed as the awards' number seven New Male performer, on a curious list:

1. Joe Scarbury	3. Phil Collins	5. Lindsey Buckingham	6. Luther Vandross
2. Marty Ballin	4. Billy Squier		7. Donnie Iris [28.18]

Then the Cruisers headlined the Stanley Theater's first New Year's Eve bash. In a preview, the Pittsburgh *Press*' Pete Bishop remained noncommittal about the new album. He gave Donnie a major spotlight interview without commenting on *King Cool* itself. [28.19]

JIMMY ROACH: That was fun. We were dressed up: I was the old year leaving, the old guy with the beard. Steve Hansen came down from the rafters. He was Baby New Year, in a diaper, with about a six-foot joint, being lowered from the ceiling. And the guys kept slipping, and he kept flopping. I thought he was going to die. And he finally got lowered down to the stage, so we could sing "Auld Lang Syne." That was a great show.

The concert was a blur.

DONNIE: I don't really remember anything from that. It was a long time ago.

KEVIN: Norman opened up? I didn't even know that.

In the new year, Donnie posed to capture a moment in 'Burgh rock history, with photographer Barbara Freeman. Freeman shot the Pride of Pittsburgh poster, an exclusive memento for the National Record Mart chain — the Pittsburgh-area retailer of choice. The 23-by-30-inch black and white keepsake was a fundraiser for the March of Dimes, and featured Billie Price, Donnie, Joe Grushecky, Norm Nardini, Bob Corbin & Dave Hanner, Rich Granati (now of G-Force), former-Jagger-turned Silencer Frank Czuri, and Pete Hewlett — all posed together like a well dressed pack of gunslingers. At that point, Donnie and the Houserockers were both pushing to be the face of Pittsburgh on the national scene.

DONNIE: I didn't know the Houserockers well, but I knew the noise they were making. We were so wrapped up in our own stuff. Grushecky was younger, but I knew who he was, and I knew he was good at what he did. A few years later, I looked forward to doing gigs together.

Following the release of *King Cool*, the third quarter of 1981 had been a fizzle. As the Cruisers eased into 1982, things looked like they were turning around.

KILLING THE SINGLE

1982 was a dizzying, rapid succession of peaks and valleys for Donnie and the Cruisers.

For an agonizing minute, the band's second album had looked like an artistic success and commercial flop. The label told the band to start working on the next album. And they planned to.

But before the Cruisers could get to work on album number three, two things happened:

The "Love Is Like a Rock" single found traction on MTV — and, then, on radio.

Then the record company killed it.

And somewhere along the way, the band booked its best tour.

Against the odds, *King Cool* got a third wind — one that nobody in the band wanted.

Over January 1982, the Cruisers recovered from the holidays. Mark and Donnie sketched ideas for new songs. The band watched, pleasantly surprised, as "Love Is Like a Rock" climbed into the *Billboard* Hot 100. The group and their handlers crossed their fingers, wondering how the Cruisers career would unfold. Would they be one-hit wonders?

"Ah! Leah!" spent 18 weeks on the chart and cracked the Top 40.

Then "You're Only Dreaming" didn't chart.

Their remake of "The Rapper," specially recorded to be resuscitating single, went unnoticed, too.

King Cool's first single, "Sweet Merilee," stalled out at number 80. It spent a mere six weeks on the Hot 100.

"Love Is Like a Rock" steadily rose up the chart, over Christmas break, into the new year, through the winter, and even as the Cruisers returned to Jeree Recording February 1, where they started working on a third album, which would become *The High and the Mighty*.

"Love Is Like a Rock" seemed bound for the rare air of the *Billboard* Top 40. Then the band received some baffling news from the label.

MARK: We were in the studio. We got a call, and they said, "They're pulling 'Love Is Like a Rock.'" They stopped supporting it.

They pulled it because suddenly someone at MCA thought we should release the softer, pop-sounding "My Girl," which made a dent on the charts, but was by no means a hit. So "Love Is Like a Rock" was aborted.

MCA gave "Love Is Like a Rock" enough chain to reach the Top 40. It peaked at number 37 February 20, 1982. And it was official: Donnie Iris and the Cruisers were not a one-hit wonder. But MCA/Carousel's radio support was done. And the song slid down the chart over the next five weeks. March 27, 1982 it bade farewell at number 98.

The next week, it was immediately replaced with "My Girl." The peppy new single entered at number 88 and ultimately climbed to number 25, which made it the highest-charting *Billboard* Hot 100 single in the Cruisers' career. But the band's best wasn't good enough to keep MCA interested in the record. And the third single was *King Cool*'s last.

MARK: We never did get a chance to release, as a single, the track which might have been the very best on the record — at least I thought: "That's The Way Love Ought To Be."

The Cruisers did, however, have the live video for the hard-hitting "Love Is Like a Rock" to represent them on televisions tuned to MTV across the country. When MCA pulled the plug on "Love Is Like a Rock," they were about to take that show on the road.

KINGS OF THE ROAD

February 1982. When it finally started, the *King Cool* tour was a parade of career highlights.

In the four months since *King Cool* came out, the Cruisers had hardly played any live shows. As "Love Is Like a Rock" steadily rolled uphill, Mike Belkin flexed his managerial might. He booked two perfect national tours for the band: a week with Loverboy, followed by six weeks with Hall and Oates. The showcases were worth pressing pause on the sessions for the new record.

BELKIN: I was booking them back then. I didn't need to pay an agent. My goal has always been, for the bands I manage, for them to have money in the bank.

Management, financially, was a small part of my business. Most of the money came from the concert [promotion] side. It was important that we had money coming it. It allowed us to do the right thing for our artists.

The Cruisers were booked to make their Los Angeles debut February 3, 1982 at the super-cool Country Club in Los Angeles. The show appears on some Cruisers histories, but they didn't actually make it there.

KEVIN: I don't remember playing L.A. with Donnie. Breathless played the Starwood, one of Van Halen's earliest venues. We kind of sucked about playing out here.

People ask me about playing out here. When I put up videos now, and I look at the plays it's a tie between Pittsburgh and Cleveland. And then, usually, third in line, it's California.

The Cruisers warmed up with a series of Ohio shows, from Columbus to Cleveland. After gigs in the Midwest, they headed south in March and connected with Hall and Oates. The smokin' duo was a future Rock and Roll Hall of Fame group, with a running streak of *Billboard* Top Ten singles, three number 1 songs in the previous year, and more on the way. [28.20]

State Journal reporter David Winkelstern had seen the light during a Cruisers club show the previous year. He returned for Donnie's set, ready to rock. The band delivered: "Donnie Iris was still something special. He wasted no time soakin' a shirt and sockin' some rock 'n' roll to a crowd crammed into Dooley's lower level.... Last March, the crowd had been much smaller. Actually, Iris and his talented crew of Cruisers deserved more of an arena audience than a barroom bunch.... Somehow, the tiny fellow can bellow out imaginative songs that are far from mellow. Iris could out-yell a yellow lion with a megaphone." [21.21]

The Cruisers held their own opening for one of the biggest bands in America. The show got good notices from Mark and Kevin's hometown crowd.

Plain Dealer reporter Anastasia Pantsios wrote, "Donnie Iris from Pittsburgh has become a special favorite here through his many cheerful shows in the last year.... Iris, with his band the Cruisers, delivered a short hot opening set that hit the high points of his two-album repertoire.... If Hall and Oates trade on their contrasting good looks and the romantic implications thereof, Iris has made much of his appearance as a skinny bespectacled dork. He doesn't fight it; he uses it, inviting the audience to identify with him and like him. As a result, he comes across upbeat, uninhibited and slightly wacky." [28.22]

The tour did well. *Billboard*'s *Boxscore* column kept an eye on it: April 2, they drew 7,714 fans to a 9, 422 capacity Summit in Houston, selling $81,455 worth of $10.75 tickets. [28.23]

And as the arena shows continued, the Cruisers were still enjoying new buzz about an old song. The April 1982 issue of *Playboy* arrived, declaring "Ah! Leah!" the number 2 single of 1981.

Donnie Iris, as heard on the radio, as seen in *Playboy*, as featured on MTV, was part of the national conversation. And he was on the road, live, in front of your naked, steaming eyeballs.

DONNIE: Wake up. Get on that tour bus. Or wake up, get in that Lincoln and drive. We always had a blast. I didn't mind the downtime, being in Des Moines on a Tuesday. We'd find something to do, play cards. We always had fun.

The hotel life was alright. It is what it is. During the days, I don't remember hanging out that much. We didn't swim in the pools much. We'd check in and check out. It was comfortable, because we always stayed in nice places. But I don't miss it.

In April, the Cruisers hit the city that never sleeps, returning to vanguard rock spot the Ritz.

KEVIN: The Ritz was a cool place. It was a typical big city show. They've seen everything, all acts, all genres come through the city, the best of the best. I think we did OK.

I met Bobby Chouinard there, the drummer for Billy Squier, after the show. He said, "We're from this band called Billy Squier, and we've got this really big drum sound. Check it out!" It was a smash.

The Cruisers were playing big tours, but they lived frugally. At first, a tour bus was too much of an extravagance. When they did upgrade to a motor home, it felt like a downgrade. They preferred the intimate luxury they had early in their touring career, when the Cruisers hit the highway in two Lincoln Continental Town Cars, with a truck and a small crew.

DONNIE: It was usually Mark and I in the same car. Kevin, Marty, and Albritton rode in one car. Me, Mark and the road manager rode in the other.

Juice, when Hank left, came on as our road manager. Juice was funnier. I don't think he had quite the experience, but he did a great job, as well. He was an organizer, although to look at him and talk to him you wouldn't think so. He was one of those guys you could kid around with a lot. He was a good dude.

Shows were beginning to evolve into the ritual Donnie Iris concertgoing experience that fans keep coming back to see, like the ceremonial crowd chant "1 / 2 / 1-2-3-4!" — as captured on the band's later *Ah! Live!* album.

DONNIE: I don't remember how the "1-2…" was thrown in. It when we were playing clubs, and the audience would get into "Love Is Like a Rock."

Kevin dialed up his performance, then dialed it back down.

KEVIN: I would flip the cymbal off my kit. During a song, I had one of my friend's cymbals, and the nut was off. And at the end, I would put two sticks underneath and launch it. And then when the cymbal hit the ground, that was the end of the song. I think one time, I took it too far and hit somebody. No serious injuries.

One time, I broke a stick, and it bounced off the stage and whacked a girl in the front row in her forehead. She had a horrible look on her face until she saw she was hit with a drumstick. She grabbed the drumstick, and she was happy. Launching drumsticks into the audience is a really bad idea; I stopped doing that a long time ago.

I didn't feel good about doing that — like I don't like singing songs about getting drunk and racing down the highway. A lot of people look up to the band, and I don't want to be responsible for that.

The Loverboy segment of the trek was the high point of the band's touring career.

KEVIN: Loverboy, nonstop great pop and image. [Frontman Mike] Reno had a killer voice. Fun to play South Dakota with them, where I think we both had top-five records. People were camping out for an indoor show like it was Woodstock.

DONNIE: The most memorable tour, for me, was the tour we did for Loverboy. That was all through the Midwest and towns like Lincoln, Nebraska. They were just *itching* for rock concerts. They were packed with people that were so happy that people were there, entertaining them — not like the big cities like Chicago, Boston, places like that, where everybody was into acting cool. Secondary markets were always great, to me.

The [Syria] Mosque shows with Michael [Stanley] were always great. But overall, the best crowds were the Loverboy shows. It was Iowa, the middle of the Midwest. Ames, Iowa. Lincoln, Nebraska. Nice outdoor venues. Those was the most enthusiastic crowds I can remember, outside the Michael Stanley shows in Cleveland and our own shows in Cleveland and Pittsburgh, the Stanley Theater. They were just crazy, all these great towns, with 10, 15,000 people coming to see us, just starving for entertainment. And we rocked the shit out of them.

Loverboy liked Donnie, too. For his birthday, they bought him a special gift to keep him company on those chilly Indiana nights.

KEVIN: Loverboy gave him the inflatable love doll. You can see it in the documentary: Someone is dancing with it. As far as I know, it went no further than the dance. She left the tour with her honor intact.

DONNIE: We did a show not to long ago. I didn't get to talk to Mike, but the drummer Matt and I started to talk about old times, how we got together. They were a good bunch of guys. Like us, they're just going out and having good times, playing in a band. We never hung out at the bars or anything, just hung out after the shows.

Donnie kept busy on the tour, and the label kept his name out there. MCA volunteered him to participate in the Radio Organized for Solar Energy — ROSE — campaign. In the push, 35 varsity-level AOR artists cut 20-second pro-solar energy public service announcements for 50 radio stations. The roster included members of Journey, Bryan Adams, Huey Lewis & the News, and Tommy Tutone. [28.24]

The Hall and Oates shows were good, too.

KEVIN: Hall and Oates, I didn't listen to any of their songs, but what a great R&B-ish band. That was a really great band with G.E. Smith [later of the Saturday Night Live and Roger Waters bands], Charlie [DeChant] on sax, and Mickey Curry, who I became friends with.

The band were having a blast, but it wasn't the kind of powder-fueled decadence that became infamous in the '80s. The fun was fun, but the band were there to work. Especially Mark.

MARK: I was never like that. I ended up getting divorced later on. But when I was in the band, I was on the straight-and-narrow. All I wanted to do was sit in my hotel room and practice. That's just how I am.

JIM MARKOVICH, LIVE SOUND: I never did any of that. I never did cocaine or whatever other kind of drugs there are. I never saw Mark and Donnie do any kind of drugs, either one of them.

The band weren't into that big '80s partying, for the most part. Even the Ramones weren't — there might have been one bassist who was into that kind of thing. For the Cruisers, they were more straight-laced guys. I think the partying was more a stereotype. I think addictive behavior is a personality trait, and I think this band loved playing in front of people. They got off on that. Donnie had been in bands for a long time before — they all had — and he wasn't wide-eyed for groupies.

The Hall and Oates tour played arenas from Austin to Baltimore. The Cruisers also played a series of solo shows at clubs like Boston's Paradise and auditoriums like the Steele at Pennsylvania's California State College.

RICK WITKOWSKI, B.E. TAYLOR GROUP: We were the opening act for them a lot. We were test driving a lot of our material. "Vitamin L" was getting a good reaction. We opened for Donnie at Westminster College, in Northern P-A. We got the whole crowd throwing their hands up in the air. We thought, "This is pretty cool."

The *King Cool* tour wrapped in late April 1982. The lubricated band played a handful of shows in May, including a triumphant return to Donnie's true hometown crowd, at Community College Of Beaver County. Fellow local B.E. Taylor opened. It was the biggest show ever for a capacity crowd at the 3,800 seat auditorium. A review described a wild crowd who were "posing, posturing, bouncing, diving, jumping, handshaking, shouting, screaming and singing." [28.25]

DONNIE: The day after a show, I take the kids to [Pittsburgh amusement park] Kennywood, and all these people had Donnie Iris T-shirts. All these people were stopping us at every step. It was tremendous. I think the kids were more excited to go on the rides.

ERIN, DONNIE'S DAUGHTER: The Kennywood thing was a big deal for us , because we didn't go every year. It was a surprise, he had been travelling and we finally had time with him. We were pretty sad when the fans kept stopping us to talk to him. It was like, "Why is this happening?"

ADDY, DONNIE'S DAUGHTER: It's the same person, my dad and *Donnie Iris*. We never knew how special he was and how fortunate we were until we went away to college. And Kennywood — that was a big one. You think, "OK, this is different than what happens to my friends."

He was always getting stopped and asked for autographs. One big thing I learned from him: He took time for every single person, and he treated people so nicely and made them feel special.

STOLEN GEAR REPORT / THE SOAPER INCIDENT

The triumphant *King Cool* cycle formally ended with two of the band's bigger starring shows. June 5, 1982, the band headlined the Blossom Music Center, south of Cleveland and outside Akron. Hot radio act Franke and the Knockouts opening the show.

The *Plain Dealer*'s Anastasia Pantsios reviewed the concert: "Iris, while firmly in the mainstream, is doing something a little unusual. While his tunes are basically production rock, he separates himself from the rank of the Loverboys, Prisms and Survivors with his light-hearted attitude and wild sense of humor."

But prime-era Donnie did grate on a critic from time to time, especially the women. On earlier tours, he had made the Cleveland writers cringe with his "I Can't Hear You" rap. Pantsios liked a new stage story about youth: Donnie told as story about his dad making him learn to play kazoo because all the rock instruments made too much of a racket. [28.26]

DONNIE: I don't remember that. That's not a true story. We must have made that up.

MARK: I made that up.

It was the band's biggest headlining show in the Cleveland area. And it was almost a disaster.

It was reported as a disaster — inaccurately. A story from the concert later reached Cash Box, which wrote, "When Donny [sic] Iris played the Blossom Music Festival [sic] in Cleveland, Ohio, a short while back, his truck and equipment valued at approximately 80 grand were ripped off." [28.27]

That report wasn't quite the fact of the matter, but the Cruisers' loaded truck had gone missing. Cross-referencing a police report and insurance claim would be a lot less entertaining than watching the band try to recall what happened when.

MARTY: It was the night before the Franke and The Knockouts show. That was our headlining debut at Blossom. And to be clear: We headlined, they opened — that's important. The gear went missing the night before the show. I remember this very clearly.

MARK: One roadie took too many soapers [sedative pills, downers, commonly known by the brand name Sopor or Quaaludes], and too soon after the show — he liked to time them so he would get off the minute he was done with his duties. But he was completely tanked, and was driving the truck by himself. Thank God he didn't injure someone. Then he parked it on a side street. And he forgot he did that.

He thought he parked it in his driveway.

When he woke up and did not see it, he freaked. He called us and said the truck and the gear was stolen.

KEVIN: "Soapers"! I do have to tell you: I slept like a baby when I took these. No crazy yelling or doing bizarre things in my sleep. Mark and I should have had a prescription for these.

MARK: You know, I have really settled down in my sleep, I am told. I quit drinking coffee.

MARTY: I received a phone call early in the morning, in a hotel in Cleveland. I was stunned.

KEVIN: We were worried about playing rented gear.

MARTY: My mom drove from Erie with a backup amp. Franke and his band, along with other friends, including MSB, helped us cobble together enough gear to do the show.

KEVIN: We did use our own gear for the show.

MARK: Are you sure we used our own gear? I sort of remember that the gear was *found* after the show ended?

KEVIN: We found our gear, because I was fearing playing the show with rented drums. You had your keytar in the video.

MARTY: We found the truck and recovered the gear, yes. But it wasn't until after the show and several days later.

In the meantime, I went to the NAMM show in Atlanta and ended up buying the black Les Paul style guitar I still use, which is a prototype made by Fernandes — and literally one of only a handful made. I thought I needed a guitar because, as far as I knew, mine was gone forever.

I love that black Fernandes. And as fate would have it, I'd never have felt such a need to buy it, had our truck not been *lost* by our crew.

I played it, along with the '75 Gibson I bought brand new at Manny's in New York City, on every recording since that fateful event.

Cleveland had pulled the plug on Belkin's World Series of Rock festivals after 1980. Later that month — June 26, 1982 — Belkin staged a massive a massive blowout, the Toledo Speedway Jam, with some of the top names in rock: Foreigner, Loverboy, and Triumph. The Cruisers opened.

KEVIN: Foreigner! Another one of my favorite singers, and I ended up being in a band with him. It was a thrill to be on this bill. Lou [Gramm] had a voice like a Marshall amp.

BILL KORECKY, ENGINEER FOR THE CRUISERS' 21ST CENTURY ALBUMS: When I see that band at the casino opening for Michael Stanley, and they play the 45-minute set, that's the same show I saw that day at the Toledo Speedway Jam, the same power and focus. They go into "Agnes," and there it is. Still.

DONNIE: It's been a great run.

NOT A SINGLE: "THAT'S THE WAY LOVE OUGHT TO BE"

King Cool was released in late August 1981. It spawned three successful singles — two of them Top 40 hits, including their best Hot 100 position. But in the subsequent seven months, the album peaked early, in November, when it hit number 84 on *Billboard*'s album chart. Even if *King Cool* was their biggest commercial success, Avsec believes in his heart it underachieved.

Pittsburghers may be surprised to learn the transcendent "That's the Way Love Ought to Be" was never a single, technically; it charged many an FM signal across the Steel City — from 96.1 WXKX's ("96 Kicks") night tracks to the DVE morning show.

STEVE HANSEN: We played "That's the Way Love Ought to Be" like a single, and I don't know that it was ever released as a single.

WDVE was a tightly formatted radio station that just played the new cuts off of an album. Compared to WMMS in Cleveland, it was a sad sack of a little sister. But 'MMS, its time passed. And DVE, by staying the course, has become a behemoth by outlasting everybody.

Ask yourself how many bands it has really broken since the early '80s period with David Lange. Pittsburgh radio has not been that supportive of local artists, save for that one period. It was a magical time for Pittsburgh rock and roll. It really was. The music was really good. And Lange didn't get in the way. He was supportive of the Houserockers. And he didn't yell at us when Jimmy and I and were four, five cuts deep on the first Donnie Iris album, then on the second Donnie Iris album.

Dave Lange left shortly after I arrived. Following him was a dickwad, followed by a bigger dickwad. And they were not supportive of Pittsburgh music. But we knew they were lazy, and they didn't get up until late in the morning. So we would play Pittsburgh music up until 7:30, 8:00, whatever time they rolled out of bed. Then we'd go back to the playlist.

Donnie was getting sporadic airplay around the country on the hippest stations. But the era of freeform stations was dying off.

The tour was over. And so was the record — outside Pittsburgh.

King Cool had a decent run. But not decent enough.

What nags away at the Cruisers' group psyche, to this day, is the strategy and content in the *King Cool* promotional campaign. The following albums didn't come close to matching the first two. And they could deal with that. But *King Cool*'s qualified successes *hurt*. Still.

MARK: The real disappointment was the *second* album.

Nobody cares. People say, "Mark, you're *pessimistic*." I'm not pessimistic; that's the way it is. You do this album, and that's it. We put hundreds of hours into our second record. And MCA released "Sweet Merilee" first, which was my fault. And that was it. It did whatever it did, got to 80 on the charts.

They never got to "That's the Way Love Ought to Be." That and "Love Is Like a Rock" were the two best songs on that record. If "Love Is Like a Rock" was the first single, maybe things would have been different.

But here's what MCA expects: They put it out. I get it. It's just like any other business. The market doesn't react right away. Now they've got to push something else. And they tell radio, "Don't play Donnie now." And they save it for some other band.

There's no reason "Love Is Like a Rock" or "That's the Way Love Ought to Be" shouldn't have been hit records. I've done a lot of crap, but those two were *good*.

Donnie and I have this Little Rascals thing:

Imagine the scene of the Little Rascals where Spanky and Alfalfa are dejected from some bad luck. When we were in the studio and we got the call that they were pulling the single, I literally looked at Donnie.

"Well, Donnie," I said in my best idiot voice. "I guess we have to try harder."

And he laughed at me.

But you know, it's basically not, "You need to do something better." *No.* You did something good. And it just didn't have a chance.

We had made some good records. The record company didn't do a damned thing with them.

The sacrilege is that "That's the Way Love Ought to Be" — my favorite — never ever saw the light of day.

JIMMY ROACH: "That's the Way Love Ought to Be" would have been a monster hit.

MARK: If "Love Is Like a Rock" bolts out of the gate with the full might of MCA… maybe it's a big hit and everything is different, our whole career.

So 1982 was only halfway over, but *King Cool* was done.

MCA wanted a new album sooner rather than later. It was time for the Cruisers to get back to that record they started in February.

Part II: Injured in the Game…

The High and the Mighty:
The Album

The High and the Mighty

The third album by Donnie Iris and the Cruisers. Featuring...

Side 1:
"Tough World" (Avsec, Iris, Lee) 3:48
"I Wanna Tell Her" (Avsec, Iris) 4:18
"Parallel Time" (Avsec, Iris) 4:15
"The High and the Mighty"
 (Avsec, Iris, Lee, McClain) 4:08

Side 2:
"This Time It Must Be Love"
 (Avsec, Iris, Lee) 4:19
"Love Is Magic" (McClain) 3:59
"You're Gonna Miss Me"
 (Avsec) 3:35

Original Release: September 1982
Label: MCA/CAROUSEL
Peak position on Billboard album chart: 180, December 4, 1982
Weeks on chart: 4
Singles:
"Tough World" b/w "You're Gonna Miss Me"
Released: October 1982
Peak Billboard Hot 100 position: 57
Weeks on chart: 6
"This Time It Must Be Love" b/w "You're Gonna Miss Me"
Released January 1983
Weeks on chart: Did not chart

From the credits:
Produced by Mark Avsec for the Belkin-Maduri Organization,
in association with Carousel Records
Executive Producer – Carl Maduri
Recorded at Jeree Studios, New Brighton, PA, Summer 1982
Engineered by Jerry Reed
Additional engineering by Carl Maduri III, Rex Burk
Mastered by George Marino at Sterling Sound.
Original release: MCA-5358 MCA Records
CD Release: Not Available on CD

"We play Donnie Iris and we play Van Halen."
> **— B-94 93.7 FM Pittsburgh program director Dan Vallie in Billboard 29.1**

Coming off his second album, Donnie was a recognizable name nationally, for radio listeners and MTV watchers. For Pittsburgh radio, he was a marquee-level act.

Donnie and the Cruisers struck again, while they were hot, while it lasted. The album was released just four months after the band's highest-charting single peaked.

In the first half of 1982, Donnie, the Cruisers, and their team gave everything they had to snatch a victory from a looming defeat. But when the *King Cool* cycle was over, it still felt like a loss. The second half of the year would deliver a sound, demoralizing defeat, leaving them feeling like *The High and the Mighty* title was wishful thinking.

If nothing, the third Cruisers album contributed the definitive piece of Donnie Iris iconography, which would be revisited and recycled in different packages the years: On *The High and the Mighty* album cover, a cheery Donnie smiles bright and wide under curly hair and Fortune 410 glasses, hands cocked on his hips, superimposed over an aerial view of New York City. Half Iron City folk hero and half Godzilla, Donnie Iris stands tall, ready to take on the world. A doctored version now graces the best-of collection.

The photo was taken by Allen Messer, renowned for his work with artists including Bob Dylan, David Allan Coe, George Thorogood, Johnny Cash, Roseanne Cash, June Carter Cash, Lucinda Williams, Townes Van Zandt, and Waylon Jennings. Donnie treated photo shoots like the live show: He didn't overthink them; he just hammed around, compellingly, until he came through with something good.

DONNIE: I can't remember exactly how it happened, but I took the guitar and slung it over me like a Robin Hood bow & arrow. It just kinda happened.

And the rest of *The High and the Mighty*... Well... They completed the album, and they survived it.

The third Cruisers record kicks off with "It's a Tough World." And, man, it sure was. This album yielded just two songs for the band's best-of collection. But technically, that's a solid .286 batting average, because the brief set features only seven Cruisers tunes. *The High and the Mighty* brought the band low. Despite their best efforts, nothing went right with the album. The band lost some friends, a lot of momentum, and — as always — a big chunk of time.

The album radio and sales numbers were disappointing, too.

But considering what a horrorshow the sessions were, fans are lucky it exists at all.

That nightmare was a problem recording the album itself, the kind of incident every artist fears. The Cruisers were still friends and brothers, harmonious partners onstage and off.

KEVIN: Marty and I bought three houses in Erie when we were living there. You figure, "You do a record, you tour, you have time off. So let's invest in real estate!" I'd stay in Marty's place, and we'd buy these HUD houses — houses Housing and Urban Development would sell us.

The band had begun recording *The High and the Mighty* in February 1982, when it looked like the *King Cool* album might tank. When it caught a second wind, they put the sessions on hold and toured the country. Five months later, they were back in Beaver, at Jeree. But there's a fine line between running hot and overheated.

MARK: The albums get progressively worse. Even the Beatles have some bad songs — not many. But if you don't have a good song, it's not a good record.

When we used to write songs, I'd say, "I'm going to write 30 songs, the sketches for *King Cool*. I'm a professional."

I'd say, "If I'm in professional baseball, I've got to go one for three. So I'm going to write 30. And that will give me ten good ones. And all those other songs, I'd just throw them away. Some guys keep all their tapes. But me, if I wrote a song and it didn't make *King Cool*, it wasn't good enough. I didn't want to hear it again. "

This time at bat, Donnie and Mark slugged "Tough World" and "This Time It Must Be Love" onto the best-of record and set list.

The problems with *The High and the Mighty* were not internal. After "The Rapper," Donnie had gone a decade without a hit single. In two years of writing with Mark and the band, he had landed five songs on the *Billboard* Hot 100.

DONNIE: It was amazing. Mark is a prolific songwriter. It's what he does. It's in his head. He comes home, he writes it down.

Back then, I probably wrote more. And I was better at it, because I wasn't so lazy. I was doing it because I wanted to do it, and I wanted to do the best I could at it. As I got further on with Mark, I thought, "I don't have to *do* this anymore. I don't have to friggin' write."

For *The High and the Mighty*, Donnie wrote plenty; he has a writing credit on five of the seven new songs. Albritton wrote one, "Love Is Magic." And Mark penned one alone, "You're Gonna Miss Me."

DONNIE: I suppose I could sit down and make something happen, but I don't want to. I'm not cut out to be a songwriter. I like to entertain people and sing and jump around on stage, stuff like that. And I do like it when we come up with a good song and I have a part of it. It's fulfilling to me. But it doesn't happen to me all that often.

Before the CD era, albums commonly ran between 30 and 40 minutes; 28 was not unheard of. The previous two albums had 10 songs apiece. *The High and the Mighty* clocks in at 32 minutes. Mark says fans are lucky it's as long as it is.

MARK: I ran out of gas. It was just not a fun album. There are some pieces of crap on there. There's "It's a Tough World." And "This Time It Must Be Love" was good. But beyond that… there's really nothing.

The album credits say the record was "Recorded at Jeree Studios, New Brighton, PA, Summer 1982" — which was mostly true. For once, working at the small studio worked against them.

DONNIE: *The High and the Mighty* album was tough on us. We had problems with some technical issues in the studio. We had to struggle with that the entire time we made that album.

Back then, we recorded on eight-track tape. And the batch of tape that we got at the studio, there was an issue with the quality of the tape.

MARK: *Everybody* knew that Scotch had put out the bad batch of tape — except Jeree's never found out, because we were a small studio.

The band were working fast, making up for lost time. And nobody knew about the bad tape until the album was well underway. In classic dramatic fashion, a random happenstance deprived the heroes of their greatest weapon, the skill they had come to rely on.

MARK: So they recalled all the tape, but we were using it. We were almost done.

It was a disaster.

So all the stacking ideas were ruined, because the oxide from the tape was coming off each time we played it. What we had to do was take it to be transferred.

We had to go to New York to mix. And before we mixed, we had to transfer the tapes, which you could almost see through at that point — because the oxide was burning off — to another set of two-inch tapes so we could begin the long process of mixing and replaying them over the heads. Otherwise, they would have just ripped apart.

We had never experienced anything like that. It was a nightmare.

It almost shredded, the tape. We lost a lot of fidelity on that record because of that. The tape was degrading before my eyes. It *disintegrated*.

DONNIE: We had to go back and redo some tunes, and work with what we had. It's a nightmare. That was definitely a bad experience.

MARK: We lost sound quality, which we had to put back with EQ.

Bad tape. Bad morale.

That was a tired-slog album. I wish it could be a redo. But that's not the way life works.

The less The Cruisers like an album, the less they have to say about it. They don't have much to say about *The High and the Mighty*. They have less to say about later albums.

THE HIGH & THE MIGHTY, THE SONGS: "TOUGH WORLD"

"Tough World," the album's hard-hitting anthem, has the makings of a classic Cruisers track. It's all guitar, rhythm and shout-along vocals. But without stacks to stand on, Marty's chords and Mark's massive chorus don't cast a long shadow. Even the rhythm section's solid tracks sound anemic.

MARK: There's not much to say. I don't think these songs are that special. I love that the fans do, and they love to talk about them. But I don't. I don't know what to say about them. We just did these tracks. I had to write a lyric. I probably had other titles for that track. But I came in there with Donnie and said, "I've got an idea. Let's try it." And we started layering it up.

On "Tough World," I wanted tubular bells. Again, this was before digital. So I went down to the local college, Geneva College, and rented some tubular bells. We were pushing these huge bells down the street and carrying them into Jerry's studio for that song. That's the way I remember it, unless it was a dream. And the sound of the bells never approached what I was hearing I my head.

DONNIE: I love that song. I don't know why we don't do it more. That's a great song. A lot of people tell me they like it.

I saw that song as being tough, the way it is in relationships.

"I WANNA TELL HER"

This tune is a stab at a vocal-powered new wave rave-up. The harmonies are nice.

MARK: "I Wanna Tell Her" is not so bad. That's one that's not terrible. The rest of them on that album are just sucky.

It was heartbreaking. It was just a bad album, bad vibe.

We were burned out. And sometimes you develop a learned helplessness, and you feel like you're an idiot in the studio.

"PARALLEL TIME"

"Parallel Time" is another oldies throwback. It starts with Donnie delivering a monologue about wandering into a mystic bowling alley, where rock and roll is there to stay.

MARK: The guys will tell you it's interesting. The guys always liked that song.

Like "That's the Way," I was playing it on a Prophet. We were recording it, and Kevin and Marty and I were all hearing the "1" on the rhythm in a different place. Kevin was hearing "1" and Marty was hearing "2."

We started recording, and it was the way it sounds, which is really weird. And we started laughing. One of us said, "You know, we're in parallel time here." So we learned it all strange like that. That became that song.

DONNIE: You're on the road. You're bored. You eat, and you hang out together, and you make jokes. That's pretty much your life. We used to say stuff like [in the voice of Tony Montana from *Scarface*]: "Yeah, man, we came to this town! We ate. We played…. And then we went bowling."

And bowling made its way into that song.

"THE HIGH AND THE MIGHTY"

If the album isn't great, it's not for a lack of effort. The album's title track swung for the fences. After years of studying Queen's studio technique, Mark finally had the chance to assemble an ambitious anthem on a military scale, with a row of snare drums rolling in lock-step precision, ready to make you stand and salute. That was the idea, anyway.

KEVIN: We started with multi-tracking snare drums to create the marching band intro. I believe I might have brought in a deep marching snare as one of the many snare drums recorded. I also remember trying to record in different areas of the studio, the staircase being one of them.

And I believe I recorded the drum set last. The band recorded to a click track of some sort. Or maybe I recorded the marching snare drum track for the full song's length. The drums sounded freshly recorded — that's the reason I recall me adding drums at the end of the recording.

On the set of the photo shoot for The High and The Mighty cover.

Some people have recorded basic tracks and then transferred a comp mix of those tracks to two channels of another 24 track tape, thereby saving the quality of the original tape and basic track instrument. Two 24 track machines were needed to play in sync together to do this. We only had one machine.

It was odd playing to the complete band. Multi-track recording is viewed somewhat like building a house. You start with the foundation — drums, bass, guitar — then add walls, ceiling, carpet and drapes: solos, lead vocals, mix etc. So I came in when the house was finished and slipped the foundation under the house. In the end, I guess it works.

MARK: That song was not called "The High and the Mighty" to start out. It was called "The Power and the Glory." So I wrote the song.

I drive this stuff. I wrote the song. I help Donnie out — I sit with him. And I'm the prime writer.

Donnie was friends with a couple artists out of Pittsburgh. And by this time, we had been through this lawsuit with "Leah." So he plays the track for these guys.

And one says, "Don't you remember, Donnie — you were over at our house, and we had a song called 'The Power of Love'?" And they threatened to sue us because we had a song called "The Power and the Glory."

And back then, I was not sophisticated. Now, I'd say, "Fine, sue me. I never heard your song."

But back then, I didn't want to go through another lawsuit.

He wanted to play it for us. And I said, "I don't even want to hear it. And Donnie had nothing to do with "The Power and the Glory" at the time.

So as much as I didn't want to do it, I wiped it, started over, and called it "The High and the Mighty."

DONNIE: I remember doing a show at Pitt. We brought the drum corps out to do that song. It was great. It was a nice part of the show. It was different from anything we've ever done.

When we'd do that live, we all had drums we strapped on and played the breakdown of the song. All the front four were out there with snare drums.

MARK: That was Kevin's idea. Sounds like something he would think of.

"THIS TIME IT MUST BE LOVE"

It wasn't a successful single, but "This Time It Must Be Love" is another rhythm track of pure perfection, layered over a tough horn section and some of Donnie and Mark's trademark words of wisdom.

MARK: You're always thinking so many things. I know Toto wasn't that respected in terms of being legitimate rock artists, because they were such great players. I always liked their songs. And that isn't as good as anything Toto made. But it was kind of inspired by them. I wanted horns on that. I don't know if it came out exactly as I was hearing it.

MARTY: If you're there when Mark is writing a song, he gives you part of the songwriting. There are different ways to contribute. He might play something, and you look at him say, "Ummm, yeah," nod your head, and that sends it in a direction.

MARK: If you're there when we work on the song, you're part of it, and you get credit. I don't do that, where I say, "You were there, but you didn't really contribute, so the other two of us deserve the *real* credit for it." I'm believe in being fair about things. You're there, you're part of it.

That started with something Marty used to do at sound check. And we recorded it. And we needed a lyric. I was scratching my head and trying to write a lyric. And that's what I came up with. And that's it. Simple as that. There's no deep thing to it. No rhyme or reason to it.

I never sat on my dad's knee like that. It's all just made up.

We're trying to write songs. You write about love. We got this track. And it was a good track. It didn't mean that much.

KEVIN: Al complimented my playing because he was a little busier than some players, and I was more a *boom-cha-boom-cha* basic player. And I think the two helped each other.

Plus, he was a very soulful bass player. His stuff was just dripping with soul. I grew up on Motown; my brothers exposed me to it, and I love that stuff, to this day. He was a really creative player, very energetic.

"LOVE IS MAGIC"

MARK: I can't remember the lyrics. Albritton wrote that.

DONNIE: Yeah, that's true. Love is magic.

"YOU'RE GONNA MISS ME"

MARK: Terrible, terrible song. Terrible. It shows you: You need a good song. That is a bad song.

It was terrible, this album, the slog album.

Funny story: I had this idea: I wanted *stomps*. And we had this drum room. We had these wooden things in there. We're mic'ing. We're trying to stomp our feet. We're all in there with headphones on.

We had gone to Arthur Treacher's and got fish and chips for lunch. And now we all have these cardboard pirate hats on from the restaurant, and we're stomping in the studio. We stacked the hell out of it, for three hours.

And it didn't work.

You can't stack just anything and make it sound great. Garbage in, garbage out.

I don't know what else to tell you about it.

Carousel/MCA were hot to get *The High and the Mighty*. They released it quickly. But once again, they didn't pour much money into it.

The band now had released two major-label albums, and had three videos under their belt: "Ah! Leah!," "Agnes," and "Love Is Like a Rock." Mike Belkin, the band's co-manager, had paid for all three of them. Now he paid for another.

As with "Agnes," "Parallel Time" did not become a single, and the video has disappeared into the static of time. No footage is in circulation.

DONNIE: We did a video, and that's the last I heard of it. I have no idea what happened to it.

I might have seen it once or twice. It was a bunch of people in a little bar, dancing to the song. I think it was '80s kids, doing all the dances from the song. It was a fun video. It was cool as hell. It would be nice to find that thing.

MARK: I shot the "Parallel Time" video on my Super 8 camera. I think I got some money from Mike Belkin for the film. I thought we would make a low budget video. One of my not-greatest ideas.

Mark isn't a big fan of the album cover. Once again, he was working on other aspects of the package.

MARK: The record company came in with the cover. They made him look like Superman or something. It's not like I *hated* it.

THE HIGH AND THE MIGHTY VS. THE CRITICS: THE REVIEWS

The High and the Mighty album was released in September 1982, with little fanfare.

Reviews were not kind to the record.

But at least *Rolling Stone* finally granted the band a first-run review… which was short and non-committal. David Marsh gave it three of a possible five stars: "Whole-hearted heartland rock…. Iris' originals are tough, metallic and sustain interest more effectively than better known hard rock bands." [29.2]

The Logansport, Indiana *Pharos-Tribune* — small step down in the pop-culture conversation — only took notice long enough to throw some stones in its direction. Bill Missett wrote, "Donnie Iris' second came and went, and his third, *The High and the Mighty*, may do the same. Although it's more together than the unimpressive *King Cool*… little here stands out from the pack…. 'You're Gonna Miss Me' is most likely the best of a weak eight-tune program." [29.3]

The fans at the *All Music Guide to Rock* give it a cursory mention, rating it three of five stars, with no review blurb. [29.4]

Radio journals gave enthusiastic notices, as is their custom.

Record World went out of business earlier in the year.

Cash Box wrote, "*The High and the Mighty* features a gaggle of original songs inked by his band… Palatable and highly melodic pop, Iris' material may be heavy on hooks yet rarely traverses into simplistic bubble-gum-type-music AOR [radio] might want to check out 'The High and the Mighty' for its anthem-like qualities and 'Love Is Magic' for its upbeat, catchy chorus." [29.5]

Billboard concurred: "This heartland band [continues] its canny balancing act between melodic pop and hard-hitting rock…. Iris brings both romance and wit to the proceedings…. That mix applies to new songs like 'Tough World' and the title track, arguing quick AOR pickup and good crossover prospects." [29.6]

Cleveland *Scene*, the city's free weekly tabloid, had a better time with it. In a cover story, Mark Holan wrote, "*The High and the Mighty*…brings all of the promise of the first two albums into one piece of vinyl. Songs like 'Tough World' and the title track speak directly to hardcore rock audiences, and indeed, one can just imagine 'The High and the Mighty' is the definitive Donnie Iris and the Cruisers anthem. While, on the other hand, the lighter side of the band is expressed in such songs as the Albritton McClain-penned 'Love Is Magic' and the Iris-Avsec-Lee composition 'This Time It Must Be Love,' the latter of which is as funky as Wild Cherry ever was…. The most consistently strong Donnie Iris album thus far." [29.7]

The High and the Mighty was sluggish at radio. MCA looked like it had learned its lesson from the previous album. It served up the album's hardest rocking track as a leadoff single. "Tough World" b/w "You're Gonna Miss Me," was released in October. The song peaked at number 57 on the *Billboard* singles chart, November 20, 1982. "Tough World" was the first American single with a picture sleeve, a 7" scale crop of a chipper Donnie, from the record's cover.

The slick sleeve barely helped: The lackluster leadoff single barely pushed the album onto the *Billboard* top 200. *The High and the Mighty* peaked at number 180 December 4, 1982, in the highlight of a four-week stint on the album chart, two weeks after its only successful single peaked.

The album did have qualified success out of the gate, in some circles:

"Tough World" and the title track never did light up the *Billboard* singles chart, but they did bound into the upper reaches of the magazine's *Rock Albums & Top Tracks* survey, a survey of album-oriented radio stations. By early October, "Tough World" was getting spins from Texas's KEGL to Minnesota's WLOL. In late October, they both cracked the top 40, and hung around through November.

"Tough World" spent six weeks on the singles chart — the same as the underperforming "Merilee," but far short of "Ah! Leah!" (18 weeks) and "Love Is Like a Rock" (14). The percussive tune's performance looked even better by comparison come January: The album's second and final single, "This Time It Must Be Love" b/w "You're Gonna Miss Me," was released and did not chart.

Donnie and the Cruisers were still the reigning chart kings from the Pittsburgh and Cleveland scenes — Michael Stanley wouldn't crack the top 40 that year, but returned in in 1983, for the second of his two Top 40 songs. The B.E. Taylor Group was building toward something big, but the best they did that year was number 54 at *Billboard*'s Mainstream Rock Tracks, with "Never Hold Back" from *Innermission*.

At that point, the Cruisers were a priority for their management and label: Donnie's name was featured in MCA's Galaxy of Stars holiday promo campaign, where he was prominently listed among artists like Olivia Newton-John and Tom Petty & the Heartbreakers.

Before the tour launched, Donnie, Mark, and Belkin logged a lot of miles in a series of trips to Michigan and back, as part of the unfolding, ongoing "Ah! Leah!" lawsuit, which was beginning to eat a lot of time, money and energy, at a time when the band had other pressing matters to attend to. The suit would drain the group's collective resources during the band's golden years. (See chapter 39 for the full story.)

In October, with court out of the way — for now — the band hit the road. A little bit.

CHAPTER 30

The High and the Mighty:
The Tour

The High and the Mighty tour was not a big one.

Without a hot single, MCA/Carousel were stingy with the tour support, once again. The road campaign for the third Cruisers album was more a series of short road trips during the fall.

The Cruisers played surges in late 1982 and early 1983, most of them in November and December '82. And unlike the bifurcated *King Cool* tour, the *High* tour didn't get a stellar second leg.

The tour hit a lot of colleges. In October, Donnie returned back to the Morrow Field House at Slippery Rock, where he had traded a career as a teacher for a life in rock.

As the Cruiser tours were downsizing, life on the road was settling down, too. As a group of individuals, the band were never completely out of control. That was a good bottom line. But the tour was a bad time for bassist Albritton McClain, who was wrestling with his own demons.

KEVIN: A lot of nights, we don't know where he went. He just took off, God knows where. But he was there the next morning, every time we needed to get him on the bus. I don't ever remember once, us having to go look for him. It was amazing, him coming up to the bus at the last minute in the morning or afternoon, whenever we were going to leave.

No matter what was on his mind, Albritton performed like a pro.

PAUL: I saw them play at the Paradise club in Boston when I was living there and playing with my band, Powerglide. Albritton's stage presence and in-the-pocket playing blew me away. "Ah! Leah!" is my favorite Albritton performance.

DONNIE: Kevin and Mart, I had to reel those two guys in all the time. They were like kids, they really were, especially Kevin. But Kevin settled down a lot.

KEVIN: I think everyone had their fair share of having fun. But Al, I think he had the chemistry where if he drank too much, he switched over to being another person for a little bit.

I never saw him get into a fight, but I saw him get in that zone. He could do things that were confrontational. He could get in your face, very intense in your face. And if you didn't know him, you could read that the wrong way. But we knew better. He would switch gears — great guy, sweetheart of a guy. But when he would go *this* way, it was kind of strange.

On the road, you are capable of what you want to do. It depends on how much you *want* to do. In school, you can hang with the good guys, or you can hang with the bad guys. You can find the people who want to party, who have the drugs. Those people know the after-hours bars. It's whatever path you would like to go down.

Marty and I did have some fun. One time, we went out before soundcheck to see *Raging Bull*. And there were about three people in there. And one kept standing up and shadowboxing. And he'd sit down and get up and do it again. Then we went out and got this cinnamon ice cream that we thought was insane. It was like we took acid, but we didn't take acid.

The now-closed Minneapolis restaurant that served great cinnamon ice cream.

Then we went to this bar that had this liqueur. And we came back, and I know we were saying really stupid things about this ice cream and liqueur. So I can see Donnie looking at us and thinking we were like children.

DONNIE: Everybody has been, in their own kind of way, dependable. Even now, if Kevin's flying in for a show from Los Angeles. He has to come in and get there in time for soundcheck. I never worry about them. Everybody knows what they need to do.

Conventional wisdom — and Belkin agrees — says a band has to tour a lot to accumulate fans and break big. In the grand scheme of things, the Cruisers did not tour much. Mark didn't like it, and the rest of the band didn't love it. They were all closer to 30 than 25, Donnie closer to 40. The Cruisers toured as much as they wanted to.

DONNIE: I don't think we ever had that mentality, being road dogs. I think we always were wanting to go in and do new stuff, to stay fresh and relevant.

Without actually going into detail, women were always around. It was cool. I don't know if I had a technique for getting rid of them, but there were certain times I didn't want to be bothered. It's hard to resist something like that.

Groupies were always around. But it was never a thing where some guys were getting chicks all the time and orgies and drugs and this and that. I never did that. It does weigh on you. The temptations are always there.

During this frustrating period, on the road and at home, the group remained calm. Even after a soft single or bad show, the Cruisers never had a screaming match, fist fight or the kind of passive-aggressive grudge that sinks so many rock bands.

KEVIN: Our biggest fight? There wasn't one. There have never even been heated words. A lot of it was to do with Mark, Donnie, and Belkin running the show. But there's never been an after-the-show where someone throws a guitar and yells, "YOU SCREWED THAT UP!" No.

And when the money wasn't great, at least it was even.

KEVIN: When I was in Cinderella and there were seven million records sold, and Tom was the sole writer, that was probably a tough one for the band members. But it wasn't a problem in this band.

MARK: Nobody gets in a band to be rich. We want to be the Beatles. Our payoff is the gigs we do now and the fact we know we impacted Pittsburgh culture in a big way. Culture is what rules, money is just currency. Bob Lefsetz said something like that.

That fact, that there is love and respect, that's worth more than the money we never made.

CHAPTER 31

Pittsburgh Rock City

Fall 1982. Back in the Burgh, a scene of sorts was bubbling up. If the tour wasn't great, good things were still happening at home.

RON GERBER, KFAI FM, *BETWEEN THE SONGS* AUTHOR: The Pittsburgh sound is hard to pin down. You associate Lynyrd Skynyrd as a Southern band, for sure. You associate a lot of the disco records with New York or Miami or Philly. But what does Cleveland-Pittsburgh sound like? To me, it's that quintessential Donnie Iris sound: There's a *muscle* to the songwriting. There's a *muscle* to the arrangement. And not terribly trendy in either aspect.

It's not totally blues-based rock, but it's not totally quirky either. There's a sensibility to it that has both feet on the ground. In some respects, that has held up better than if those records had leaned more toward those trends, or Southern rock, where they relied on four guitarists, that kind of thing. It comes across as sensible and thoughtful.

JIMMY ROACH, WDVE'S *JIMMY AND STEVE IN THE MORNING*: There was no Pittsburgh sound, not in the least. It's just good music. The common thread was that every band was different. Norm Nardini was as different from Donnie as you could get. Everybody was a talented guy who was going in his own direction.

People don't remember that DVE, in its early days, had a broad playlist. We played "Papa Was a Rolling Stone" by the Temptations. Gilbert O'Sullivan, "Get Down." We played *John Denver* to death. I mean, *a lot*. Right when Jim and I started doing mornings, in '80, was when we got a focus and weeded out that stuff that kinda didn't fit. That's when we started playing local everything. I bet we had seven or eight local bands on the air, at one time.

I came to Pittsburgh in 1973. Nobody in town played any local music at all. It was all consultants' national playlists. The first time we got local at all was that giant influx of local people: Donnie, the Granatis, B.E., Grushecky, Norm Nardini, the Silencers.

We got a great response. It wasn't like we were playing a bunch of crap. It was all as good as anything else we were playing. We weren't stretching the format to fit in local guys. It was all good and well produced. It fit in with the Rolling Stones and Stevie Ray Vaughn and everybody else.

STEVE HANSEN, OF JIMMY AND STEVE: The Silencers were a band that could have had a hit. They were a great power pop band. And the Granati Brothers had a couple of songs — they toured with Van Halen twice, and A&M put out an album of their songs. At the time, a label could afford to woodshed a band. They did that with the Police, and the Police took off. David Werner had an album that was hit-laden, but CBS was having an issue with the record stores at the time, and the album never got stocked, but he was a significant artist. But I've never seen anything like that again.

I was out at least four nights a week, because I introduced these guys at the VIP clubs — there was one in Beaver, one in Richfield, and one in Hampton. And Sunday night, I used to go to 2001 in the Northside. I saw all these guys a lot. And it was magical, the shows and the albums.

JIMMY ROACH: 2001 is a parking lot now. It was a big room. And every Sunday night, we had a rotation of bands: The Houserockers, B.E., the Granatis, Silencers, and Norman occasionally. We had them on a six-week loop. And Donnie wasn't in that. He never played it. Everybody else that had a record label played it. He didn't come hang out.

RICK: We were always working and playing, and a lot of us never crossed paths. But we'd see Donnie and open or co-headline. That's the only time I'd see the other bands. We were all trying to do our thing, trying to go national. Donnie had the most success.

STEVE HANSEN: The shows were huge. The Houserockers, the line snaked around the building out in White Oak, at the White Elephant. We did a famous concert at IUP, and it was B.E. Taylor, and then Donnie Iris. The place was jammed, packed to the ceiling.

JIMMY ROACH: Due to Donnie's attitude, he was one of the guys. He didn't try to elevate himself over the other local acts. Each of them had their own niche. Grushecky hung with Springsteen. Norman was tight with Bon Jovi. B.E. had his own national hit. It was more or less equal footing.

I did 45 years in radio. And that was the most exciting time, from '79 to '84. Everything seemed possible: Pittsburgh was going to be the hub of the new musical universe. And we weren't going to have *one* big band; we were going to have four or five. And then, one by one, they didn't get the promotion — they got MCA'd. It was tough. But for a while, everything looked positive, everything looked good.

Donnie ended 1982 with his first Christmas song, a high-tech collaboration with DVE's *Jimmy and Steve in the Morning* show.

STEVE: We did everything that we could to create an aura around Donnie, to talk about him as much as we could, in as many ways as we could. In fact, one time we went in and did a Christmas song, "HAL the Computer."

That was a score. That was part of our mission, to be with Donnie and the Cruisers, to meld us to them, them to us, and make it seem as though we were all part of a scene. WDVE was in a competition with WYDD at the time, but it quickly became not much of a competition.

1982 turned to 1983 with some bangs and a crash.

Billboard's Talent in Action rankings largely ignored *The High and the Mighty*, but squeezed Donnie in as the no. 25 Male Singles Artist.

John Cougar, Rick Springfield, and Dan Fogelberg took the top three slots, in that order. Donnie landed just under Glenn Frey, Paul McCartney, and Eddie Money. Still: The magazine's calculations had him tied for third in number of singles on its various charts for the year: behind Springfield's six and Kenny Rogers' five. But his four tied him with Neil Diamond, Barry Manilow, and Ronnie Milsap. [31.1]

New Year's Eve, the Cruisers were scheduled to headline the Coliseum in Richfield, just north of Akron, closer to Blossom. Belkin announced that McClain fractured his wrist in a fall in his home town of Cincinatti. [31.2]

KEVIN: Knowing Al, it was possibly not a fall in his home.

The band saved Albritton's limited digital limberness for a big hometown show the next day, one of the transformative Pittsburgh concerts of the era.

"THE MOST FAMOUS PITTSBURGH CONCERT"

RICK WITKOWSKI, B.E. TAYLOR BANDS: The most famous Pittsburgh concert was probably us and Donnie Iris on New Year's Day. That was a great, great, great, great, great show. That was at the peak. We had a lot of people there.

I run into people still: "Yeah, I was there at the New Year's Day Donnie Iris show!" It has a legendary status.

DONNIE: All the shows we did with B.E. were really good. They were good bands.

The Stanley Theater, the only place bigger was Heinz Hall, but that was classy. The Civic Arena would be next step up. The Stanley had theatrical acoustics. That's where Bob Marley's last gig was. David Bowie, when he came to Pittsburgh, he played the Stanley. Big deal.

STEVE HANSEN: One of the nights that Pittsburgh music arrived, one of the best, warmest experiences that I had, was the year B.E.'s "Vitamin L" went to number 1 on B-94. Rich Engler the concert promoter and Belkin, who was managing Donnie, they arranged it so New Year's Eve, Michael Stanley would play the Stanley Theater. And the next day, they swapped and played the other venues, and B.E. and Donnie came home.

I didn't get there until halfway through B.E.'s set, who was opening. And Donnie treated B.E. like a co-headliner, with all the lights.

I walk in, I open the doors. I'll never forget: The *warmth* of the crowd hit me. And it's packed. And the place is going *nuts* for B.E. Taylor. And I just thought, "Oh my God, I'm *home*, this is it! This is what music is about!"

So I go in, and Donnie comes on, and the place is just *rockin'*. That was the epitome, to me, of that whole experience.

In January, 1983, the "This Time It Must Be Love" b/w "You're Gonna Miss Me" single came and went without charting. The Cruisers played a handful of regional shows, mostly in Ohio, in early '83.

That triumphant New Year's Day was essentially the end of the *High and the Mighty* tour.

MARK: The whole album was a big disappointment commercially.

After "Tough World" only spent six weeks on the *Billboard* singles chart, Carousel/MCA formally exercised their option for a fourth album, anyway.

For the Cruisers, 1983 was a big step down from 1982. But their New Year's Day bash was a party that kept the band — and their friends — in the spotlight all year.

B.E. Taylor and Donnie Iris. (Photo by Richard Kelly)

CHAPTER 32

The Donnie Iris - B.E. Taylor - Cruisers Connections

Take all the factors and influences that added up into Donnie Iris. Drop them in a rock box. Shake it up. Open it. And you'll get something like B.E. Taylor.

A golden voice. Beatles-informed, classic-styled rock songwriting. Thick '80s guitars, which a strong backbone of a beat. Enough synths to make his band relevant, but not enough to date them. All followed by an unpredictable, bold departure. And a big bowtied box of Christmas spirit.

Taylor was one of the great names in Pittsburgh and West Virginia's rock history. He was one of Donnie's two best friends. From one band to another, their careers overlapped time and again, for over 40 years.

Donnie and the Cruisers headlined the Burgh-shaking New Year's Day 1983 show at the Stanley Theater. But the concert also marked the coronation of more Pittsburgh rock royalty: the opening band, the B.E. Taylor Group.

After years grinding on the Pittsburgh-West Virginia-Ohio rock circuit, William Edward Taylor fully arrived at the New Year's Day show. A year later, Taylor and crew shot into the national spotlight with the single "Vitamin L" from the album *Love Won the Fight*. The song entered the *Billboard* singles chart January 28, 1984. In an eight-week stint on the Hot 100, it peaked at number 66.

"Vitamin L"'s low-budget video received modest MTV rotation, but was a full-blown crossover sensation on Pittsburgh radio. In coming years, Taylor made himself as a mainstay of Pittsburgh culture, on many musical strata.

Donnie Iris was a longtime collaborator, benefactor and literal teammate as B.E. built his own amazing apparatus.

DONNIE: Sometimes I called him "Bill," sometimes, "B.E." Mostly, I called him "B." He always had time for whoever was going to be around. I learned, from him, to be that way. When people want to come up to me and take a picture or this and that, I'll take some time and talk to them. I don't care who it is. Bill was like that.

Donnie and B.E. Taylor could have been brothers. They had remarkably similar careers and lives: Like Donnie, Taylor was born and raised in Beaver County, Pennsylvania — and is a member of the Beaver Valley Musicians Union Hall of Fame. [32.2] He hailed from Aliquippa, home of two Jaggerz frontmen. At age 11, he was also struck with a temporarily debilitating illness, which pushed him into music as a refuge. Donnie and his fellow Jaggerz produced some recordings for his early group, B.E. Taylor and the Establishment. But Donnie and B.E. never found the creative spark that made their friendship and live shows as a duo so enjoyable. And the Steel City claimed him as one of its marquee rockers, even though Taylor wasn't homegrown in Pittsburgh, like Donnie wasn't. Midway through his career, Taylor made a major shift. And his repertoire followed.

STEVE HANSEN, ex-WDVE: I saw Journey and B.E. Taylor back-to-back [May 28 and 29, 1983], and I thought B.E. Taylor had the much better voice, better than Steve Perry at his height, at his most gifted.

DONNIE: I knew him early on as this cocky guy, like, "I can sing like *hell*." Arrogant. But he was different after I got to know him, especially after he became a Christian. He was never preachy, never like, "You're gonna go to hell if you don't believe." Once he did became Christian, he became this guy who you wanted to be around, the greatest guy you'd ever want to meet.

In 1991, Taylor launched a phenomenal series of traditional Christmas albums and concerts. Donnie helped spark that phase of Taylor's career, and later sang backup vocals on 1994's *B.E. Taylor Christmas* album. The holiday shows became a reliable multi-night series of sold-out events in Pennsylvania and West Virginia. Taylor died in August 2016, after a protracted struggle with brain cancer. By then, PBS was regularly airing his concert video *B.E. Taylor Christmas Live At Heinz Hall* on over 150 stations.

Taylor didn't coast on the popular and profitable Christmas gigs. His acclaim and body of work only grew. In 2008, the Pittsburgh Ballet staged a work based on his love songs. In 2010, he collaborated with Emmy-Grammy-Oscar-Tony award-winner Marvin Hamlisch for performance based on Taylor's *One Nation Under God* album. In 2008, Duquesne University awarded him its Lifetime Achievement Award. [32.3] And he was presented the Distinguished West Virginian Award by Bob Wise, governor of the state where he had long since settled down. [32.4]

One common thread through Taylor's more successful projects was guitarist-producer Rick Witkowski, who first joined him in the B.E. Taylor group in 1980. Witkowski broke into the bigtime with the prog rock band Crack the Sky in the 1970s.

Crack the Sky earned a cult following for a series of albums made with world-class talent, recording for the Lifesong label, home to Jim Croce and Dion. In *Rolling Stone* declared the group's self-titled debut its 1975 Debut Album of the Year. [32.5] The magazine stayed hot for the album, declaring it "an outright classic" and ranking the platter its number 47 prog-rock LP of all time 40 years later, in 2015. [32.6]

Crack the Sky recorded 1976's *Animal Notes* album with engineer Shelly Yakus (John Lennon, the Raspberries, Alice Cooper, Frank Sinatra) and some assistance from Jimmy Iovine, who was the star engineer on Springsteen's *Born to Run* album, and has a crisp hall of fame body of work as a producer, including U2's *Rattle and Hum* and Stevie Nicks' *Bella Donna*. Three Crack the Sky members joined Taylor to become the players in B.E. Taylor and Innermission, later known as the B.E. Taylor Group.

Witkowski has seen the inner workings of the Cruisers and the Belkin-Maduri Organization like few others. The B.E. Taylor Group's debut, 1982's *Innermission*, was produced by Donnie Iris and Mark Avsec. Witkowski has played Cruisers tunes with Donnie countless times. They recorded together on Donnie's 1999 album, *Together Alone*, which also featured Taylor. And Witkowski serves as Donnie's live bandleader on the rare occasions Mark can't make it to a performance. As the producer of the Cruisers' 2009 *Ah! Live!*, Witkowski mixed the live songs with Mark and Donnie at his Studio L facility in Weirton.

RICK WITKOWSKI: I'm in Weirton, West Virginia now. I grew up here. I was born in Steubenville, right across the river, home of Dean Martin. We were a Steelers family.

From 1975 to 1980, I lived in New York City, with my group Crack the Sky. I loved, loved, loved it. It was a fantastic time. I got to see the Ramones live at CBGB's. I used to hang down there.

I wanted to be a record producer. That's why I was living in New York. I was hesitant even to be in a band. But I came back to work with B.E.

THE BEAVER VALLEY GUYS

RICK WITKOWSKI: Donnie was a fan of us. We had steady gigs in the area, at a place called Morry's Speakeasy. And Donnie would show up to those gigs. And then we had a gig at the VIP Baden after Morry's shut down. They were rock clubs, a little bigger than a local bar. Morry's had a stage in the back. You had to bring your own sound system. There was a built-in crowd. They were rockers. There were a few dolled-up people, but it was more a blue-collar rock-and-roll kind of people.

B.E. had a steady following; Thursdays were his night. We'd do originals and covers. Bill did "Take Me to the River," the Talking Heads version. We'd stay current, do Journey, bands like that. We had a good draw. Girls liked us, and guys followed. Donnie liked the band. He'd sit in, come up and sing songs.

Their two voices were unique, but they fit together so nicely.

JIMMY ROACH: That was pretty amazing. You had two of the most amazing vocal instruments in music at the same time, at the same place. That was something to hear. They were great together, to hear those voices blend together.

STEVE HANSEN, OF JIMMY AND STEVE: Donnie and B.E. would *kill* on Marvin Gaye songs.

DONNIE: We did a lot of Beatles, a lot of the Lennon-McCartney melodies. He'd do McCartney, I'd do Lennon. We did a few Bee Gees tunes, the early Bee Gees. B.E. and I never got to the place where we had the inkling to get together, write songs, and do an album. I don't know that he and I were that good at writing tunes at that point.

ADDY, DONNIE'S DAUGHTER: Every year, my mom and dad had a very big Christmas Eve party. And everybody, *everybody*, would be there. B.E. was there, and the Granatis. That was our thing where everybody got together.

JIMMY ROACH, OF JIMMY AND STEVE: Donnie and B.E. were funny, absolutely. You put the two of them together, and it's just two regular, very, very nice people. Good energy. You didn't have to worry about what you said, to have any pretense about you. Just be yourself. That's why you played ball with them. You're not going to play ball with a big star. *These* guys were always looking for a game, always.

We had this ongoing thing where we would play basketball and softball against all the Beaver County guys. They were like a little fraternity.

I was at the Granatis' one time, and Donnie showed up with his ball bat and his glove stuck on it, like a little kid. It was really weird: We're there, eating spaghetti. And then there's Donnie: "Can youns come *aut* and play some ball?"

Donnie and B.E. Taylor never did collaborate on a full album, but they were an act people wanted to get in on. As with "Ah! Leah!," "Vitamin L" got its first airplay on the WDVE morning show, in the Jimmy and Steve era.

STEVE HANSEN: Every rock act came through San Francisco. And you made your bones by being the station that stars would stop in and almost hang out at — either come in or call in. And you could go backstage. And the listeners, the public, knew who had access.

We would also play softball with the bands. You had all the stars: The Eagles, whoever. Pittsburgh was not at all like that. Cleveland was like that. Tours staged themselves out of Cleveland: They went to these periphery markets like Pittsburgh, and booked back out of Cleveland.

In Pittsburgh, we didn't have access to any of the stars. But I wanted to create that kind of scene with the local talent, and make it like we owned the local talent. So we — Jimmy and I — were trying to make it seem as if we were cool rock-and-roll guys, in a cool rock-and-roll station, and there was a cool rock-and-roll scene. And we did it with the sports teams, softball and basketball specifically.

Softball, Donnie was OK. We played one game, and he pulled both quad muscles. Both, one at a time. He stayed in. He couldn't move very well. But he didn't come out. We only had nine guys, so he stayed in as a stationary second baseman.

The fundraiser fun included in the Granati Brothers' charity basketball game against WDVE at the Civic Arena for the Pittsburgh Food Bank; DVE's longrunning Annual Toys for Tots Drive; and the 1982-1983 Stanley Theater concerts to benefit unemployed steelworkers. [32.7]

RICK WITKOWSKI: Donnie was into playing ball. We were on the same team: me, him, B.E. We had a great game up in his area. After the game, we went over to his place. He had all the mixes done from *King Cool*. And we had a listening party. Top to bottom, we listened to the whole thing.

I was so knocked out by what a great record it was. It sounded as good as Journey. It sounded as good as the Police. I thought, "They've got some magic happening here. Let's go for it!"

This is before we signed to MCA, before we did the project with him. I was so excited to hear his record. I said, "I want you to produce us, you and Mark."

I think I had three Crack the Sky albums under our belt. And they were done in major recording studios. Our first album was done at CBS Studios in New York [City]. The second record was done in Hit City Studios with Shelly Yakus and Jimmy Iovine, the guys who did Tom Petty. This was 1976. And then our third record, we did it in a studio in Quebec where the Police [later] did *Ghost in the Machine* and Rush did *Moving Pictures*, a real high-end studio.

I was never happy with how any of our records sounded. I heard Donnie's record, and I was like, "Oh my God, this is so good. *Please* produce us."

They were into it.

Donnie got us signed to Belkin-Maduri, as a production deal through Sweet City. Maduri had a white disco-soul band called Q, and they needed some help. Donnie brought B.E. to work them, and Belkin-Maduri liked him. And they, in turn, got us signed to MCA. We had a manager, Gus Socrates. Later, Belkin and Maduri split up. Belkin took Donnie, and Maduri took us.

Sweet City/MCA released the B.E. Taylor Group's debut album, *Innermission*, in August 1982. [32.8] Donnie, B.E., and their friends cut the eclectic rock album at Jeree in September 1981, before the national *King Cool* tour began. The final credits would read, "Produced by Mark Avsec and Donnie Iris for the Belkin/Maduri Organization, in association with Carousel Records. Executive Producer — Carl Maduri." When they recorded, B.E. and Witkowski spent more time in Jeree's inner sanctum than most of the Cruisers.

INNERMISSION: PRODUCED BY DONNIE AND MARK

RICK WITKOWSKI: My memories of doing that first record: It was great, but… good atmosphere, but hard to breathe. Mark, Don, and Jerry, they were all coffee-drinking chainsmokers. They had that studio tan. We'd get up there and start at 11 in the morning, maybe. And then we wouldn't get out until two or three in the morning, just working all day.

It was painstaking, a lot of work, a lot of man hours. They were workaholics, constantly in that studio, smoking one cigarette after another, drinking one cup of coffee after another. All that coffee and nicotine and go, go, go.

I got to do records with the masters, but now I was back here, with Donnie. And Donnie and Mark were right in there, in the same league.

Working with Shelly Yakus and Jimmy Iovine: They were primarily involved in the sonics of the record. They were engineers. They didn't get production credits. Jerry was more laid-back. Shelly Yakus and Jimmy Iovine had that New York energy: "Time is money, let's move." They weren't as into experimentation or taking time. It was more *"Bang bang bang bang — let's get this done!"*

Mark and Donnie were more hands-on: "Try this guitar part," "Try this harmony," "Try that part," "Try a secondary rhythm…"

They got involved in the arrangements. Mark had the ear and the brain. Jerry did all the technical engineering. They had the goods. Jerry and Donnie Garvin's stuff sounded good.

Donnie's role, he was a producer. He was the artist. He was there every session. He would smoke cigarettes and drink the coffee and say, "Yeah, yeah, that's cool!"

He would hear something vocal, or he'd have ideas for the melody — "Instead of going to this note, go to that," or "Try this harmony part."

He was the in-between guy, between us and Jerry and Mark. They were more hands-on. Donnie would give his opinion: If something wasn't sitting right, he'd interject. He sang on it, too.

As a producer, I learned so much from Mark about being open-minded. He always wanted your opinion. He was always open to trying things. He said that's part of being a good producer. He'd say, "That idea's better than mine," and we'd do it. He was a great musician. He wanted to get the best out of who he was producing. And he wanted to give his best.

Donnie was trying to mentor us. So we were Donnie's find. He got us signed, but he didn't take anything from it or take any of our publishing. Just producer's points for the work he did.

MARK: We made nothing on the record. There were *not* sales.

RICK WITKOWSKI: I wasn't with Mark and Donnie all the time, but I never saw them get too mad about it. They never got a chip on their shoulder, not to my knowledge. Donnie is so unassuming. I saw Donnie last night. He's so laid back. He's so chill.

I wanted to get into production. We were making our own demos. Mark was asking *us* how we were doing stuff. We were all hungry, wanting to make hit records. So by the time our second album came around, we wanted to produce it. And Mark and Donnie said, "This stuff sounds great. Why don't *you* do it?"

We ended up with Maduri: Chris Maduri's son, Carl Junior, took a liking to our band. We just kind of bonded with him.

Our record, the second one [*Love Won the Fight*], we went to Beachwood. The lines were being drawn between the Belkins and Maduri. Carl Jr. went to school for engineering. He started working at studios closer to home. That's how we got involved in Beachwood.

I didn't have that much interaction with Belkin. I don't think he cared for us that much.

Carl was a song guy. He wanted to push us to have a hit song. He came from that angle. He wasn't hands-on. His son Chris was more about the concept, trying to help us come up with a brand and an image. They wanted a hit record, and Carl was really trying to get us to write a hit song. He would say what he liked and wouldn't like.

LOVE LOST THE FIGHT

The Maduris provided some useful guidance. Sweet City/MCA released *Love Won the Fight*, the group's big album, in December 1983.[32.9] The record took them places. But not often.

RICK WITKOWSKI: B-94, "Vitamin L" was number 1 on *The Top 8 at 8*. We were constantly showing up at the radio station. We were the house band, every other Saturday, in this place at Weirton, West Virginia — you only had to be 18 years old to drink. So Pittsburgh people would come down.

Carl Maduri really didn't do that much for us. Our manager did most of our booking. We never got signed to a national booking agency or anything. We never got hooked up with any tours, other than Donnie Iris.

Carl Maduri's biggest feather in his cap for us was getting us to open for Boy George in the Columbus arena. And that was the pinnacle. [The show was April 5, 1984, at the Ohio Center Battelle Hall in Ohio.[32.10]]

We had the one gig opening for Boy George [Culture Club], and they were hot. Columbus is a two-and-a-half hour drive. So we go. We got a 40-minute set. We got over. We could have done an encore, but they're strict about your time. There were 7,000 people there.

So we do the show, we drive home to Weirton. It's three in the morning. I pull in, put on my TV, pop it on MTV.

And just as I turn it on, there's Mark Goodman the VJ, saying, "There's a new band out of Pittsburgh making some noise. This is their brand-new video, 'Vitamin L.'"

I got to see our video live on MTV. Like, "We're on our way, baby!"

That was the only time I got to see it.

It got added, it was in light rotation, but the week they started playing our video, we lost our bullet on the *Billboard* chart. We got to like number 66 in the country. We were on MTV for a couple weeks. [The song peaked March 10, 1984.[32.11] Its final week on the chart was March 17, 1984.[32.12]

Four other records came out on MCA the same week, and we were fifth priority. They had their independent producers working the other records. They put us out and serviced the record because they had to, but there was nobody *working* it.

It was very frustrating. *Frustrating* is the best thing I can say.

It's like, "*We have this hit record here!*" And you don't have the people in charge of that record doing all they can do. You want to throw your hands up in the air, like, "What can we do?" We were working and making money, and we had a following. I know B.E. wasn't happy.

Then [MCA President] Irv Azoff came in and crashed the whole thing. And all the momentum we were starting to build got wiped away. After MCA stood us up, Carl got us a one-album deal with Epic.

Labels would sign a slew of bands, and the one that hit would pay for the ones that didn't. That was their theory. That's why there's no record industry anymore. It was a bad business model. You think, "We're as good as this guy or that guy, why not us?"

Epic released *Our World* in July 1986.[32.13] The album reprised half of the 1984 EP *Life Goes On,* which was released on the short-lived label First String Records. One of the recycled tracks, "Karen," briefly bounced Taylor back onto the *Billboard* Hot 100 in May 1986. It spent a week at number 94 [32.14], followed by a last gasp one-week stand at number 100. [32.15] Taylor's major-label run was over, but his legacy had barely begun. Without a label, Taylor, Witkowski, and their team figured out how to fill seats on their own.

In 1991, Pittsburgh vintage station 3WS recruited Taylor to appear on its holiday compilation, *Home for the Holidays*. To collaborate on "Silent Night" and "God Rest Ye Merry Gentlemen," Taylor pulled in Donnie and Pete Hewlett. Hewlett was a Pittsburgh native who sang on the Ohio anthem "There's No Surf in Cleveland" and later played guitar with Billy Joel, Elton John, Carly Simon and others. The trio recorded as the Hit Men.

RICK WITKOWSKI: The two songs Donnie and B.E. Taylor did became the foundation for B.E. Taylor as a group. The tracks were very well received. B.E. tried to talk Donnie & Pete into doing a full-length project, but neither were interested enough, due to scheduling and them both working on their own projects. So then B.E. decided to go it alone. And that was the start of B.E. Taylor Christmas cottage industry that flourished in our area for the last 20 years.

When Donnie was inducted to the Pittsburgh rock hall of fame [Rock 'N Roll Legends Awards, 2015], B.E. introduced him. He said something like, "I still like you. I still love you." They were great fans of each other.

ERIN, DONNIE'S DAUGHTER: Dad and B.E., it wasn't a "together all the time" friendship, but they definitely loved each other and had a special bond.

B.E. Taylor, Donnie Iris, Nat Kerr, Mark Avsec (Photo by Richard Kelly)

Interlude:
Ten of Marty's Favorite Albums

Marty *hates* comparing, ranking, and rating art.

But he agreed to list his ten favorite albums.

Or ten of his favorite albums.

MARTY: After my top 5, I could have named any of 20 others in the remaining 5 slots. Here's my top ten:

10
Peter Gabriel, *So*

9
Woodstock 1, Various Artists

8
Rolling Stones, *Rolled Gold* and *The Very Best of the Rolling Stones*

7
Jimi Hendrix Experience, *Are You Experienced?*

6
Jeff Beck, *Blow By Blow*

5
Bruce Springsteen, *Born To Run*

4
Led Zeppelin, *Led Zeppelin I*

3
Led Zeppelin, *Led Zeppelin II*

2
Beatles, *White Album*

1
Beatles, *Revolver*

MCA Headquarters in Los Angeles (Photo by Marty)

Changes. Roster Shakeups. Badness.

1983 was a transitional year of seismic shifts in the Cruisers organization.

MCA/Carousel had released The Cruisers' troubled third album, *The High and the Mighty*, in September 1982.

The record didn't do gangbusters business, but MCA/Carousel picked up the band's contract anyway, in October 1982. [33.1]

January 1983 began with what might have been the best local concert ever staged in Pittsburgh — to that point, at least.

Later that month, MCA/Carousel released the second and final single from *The High and the Mighty*, "This Time It Must Be Love" b/w "You're Gonna Miss Me." It didn't chart. The album's title track wasn't released as a single, but the song poked its head into *Billboard's* Mainstream Rock chart for a minute, peaking at number 39 in a five-week stand.

The album's road campaign limped to an end in early February, after around 30 shows over the course of four months.

Donnie had made better runs at the charts, but he was still Pittsburgh's king of FM airwaves, locally and nationally. At home, however, he made it a point not to live like a king. As a group, the band didn't have any expensive bad habits. And as for Donnie, he was content in Beaver County. The Ierace family never considered buying a chateau in a ritzy Burgh suburb like Upper St. Clair.

DONNIE: We didn't do anything extravagant. Of course, I don't think we made as much money as Wild Cherry did.

I already had a house. I bought a house when we were with the Jaggerz. We didn't buy second homes or anything like that. We didn't make that much money. Patterson Township was considered the suburbs. It's a nice place. Both my kids went to Blackhawk High School, which had great basketball teams when John Miller was their coach.

I never felt like I needed to live better. That wasn't me, that wasn't Mark, that wasn't anybody else in the band.

We didn't make that much money. The lawsuit screwed it up, too.

The band never really hindered the family. We didn't go out on the road for a long period of time, never a year or even six months. Maybe a couple of months. I was always able to spend time with my family. Some bands just toured constantly. We never did that. I think we could have, but none of us were into those long, drawn-out tours. I think we'd have stayed on the road if we were all single or whatever. But we wanted to get back to the families.

I never thought about moving to Upper St. Clair. I never could afford it. I guess we could have done Wexford. But the house my kids grew up in, we bought, probably, in '68. We made enough money to get by comfortably.

But Donnie *was* human. He would indulge in a big-ticket item… every 15 years or so. And when he did, he made them last.

DONNIE: I bought a brand-new car. I bought a Buick Riviera, 1968. It was the first brand-new car I ever bought. That was with the Jaggerz. With the Cruisers, I bought an '83 Cadillac. It's in storage. I bought a lot of things for myself, but nothing big like Bobby [Parissi of Wild Cherry] did. That was nuts.

I bought Erin and Addy cars. I bought Erin a used Volkswagen Rabbit. I bought Addy a Toyota Tercel for maybe 500 bucks. I remember trying to teach her to drive stick. She just couldn't get it. We didn't take big vacations. We went to Kennywood and stuff.

Over spring 1983, the Cruisers played a handful of shows, mostly in Northeast Ohio. May 29, the band staged a road trip to Peoria, Illinois for a show with the Elvis Brothers and Joan Jett.

KEVIN: I liked her vibe and band, but really liked her later on when I was in LA mixing a TV show called *The Henry Rollins Show*, and she was the guest. She told the story of how she couldn't get signed to a record deal and eventually licensed her music to a label, so she could retain the ownership of it. And we know what happened after that. She's a smart woman.

The Cruisers were sputtering. Behind the scenes, gears were shifting in a big way.

In April, MCA appointed a new president: Irving Azoff, one of the biggest names in the history of the music business. Manager of the Eagles and others. Mike Belkin's former partner-turned-adversary. Unlike Belkin, Azoff left the Midwest. He headed to the West Coast, where he become an unstoppable, golden success. His first documented show-business miracle was springing Joe Walsh from his management contract with Belkin. A familiar face could have been good news or bad news for a Belkin band.

Back in Ohio, the Belkin-Maduri Organization was a house divided.

After years of friendship and successful partnership, Carl Maduri called Carousel Records President Rick Frio, who held Donnie's recording contract. Maduri gave his West Coast affiliate a warning: Belkin didn't think Frio's Carousel Records was doing a good job pushing Donnie Iris into the pop-culture landscape.

As Frio would state in a 1987 deposition, Maduri warned him "Belkin was going to attempt to make some sort of an end run" to get Iris out of his contract, via a buyout or other skullduggerous machinations.

At the deposition, Frio explained his reaction to the offer: No. Because he "had worked with Donnie... and felt... Iris was one record away from being the superstar that he deserved to be... due to my input and input of several other people. I think we should all have benefited from his great success, which was in the offing. That I didn't think it was a good idea for me to sell off my portion of the contract." [33.2]

Belkin, Donnie, Maduri, and Frio/Carousel began angling toward a tense standoff. The shifting alliances and legal entanglements would take years to resolve. Through the drama, Donnie and the band found ways to work.

CHAPTER 34

Cruising Without Donnie: The Peter Emmett Story

Peter Emmett

The Peter Emmett Story

An album featuring the Cruisers. With...

Side 1:
"There Goes My Heart" (Mark Avsec, Marty Lee)
"Don't Lie to Me Laina" (Reece Kirk)
"Sleep With Me" (Eric Carmen)
"Knee Deep In Love" (Robert Peckman)
"Never Gonna Fall In Love" (Emmett, Barbra McFaul)

Side 2:
"Inside Story" (Eric Carmen)
"She Don't Know Me" (Mark Avsec)
"Don't Say You're Sorry" (Kevin Raleigh)
"Why Can't She" (Gary Jones)

Mark Avsec: piano, organ, synthesizers and background vocals
Marty Lee: guitars and background vocals
Albritton McClain: bass
Kevin Valentine: drums and percussion
Rick Bell: saxophone
Carl Maduri III: background vocals
Peter Emmett (Sonny Geraci): lead and background vocals
Produced by Mark Avsec and Carl Maduri for the Belkin-Maduri Organization, in association with Carousel Records
Recorded at Jeree Studios, New Brighton, PA
Engineered by Carl Maduri III
Mixed by Carl Maduri III at The Recording Connection, Cleveland, Ohio
Special Thanks To: The Belkin/Maduri Organization and Sweet City Records for making us a part of their family/Carl Maduri III, Don Garvin
Original release: MCA-5388 MCA Records/Sweet City
CD Release: JRR 1998 Japan Rock Reissues (Not official)

MEET PETER EMMETT; HIS FRIENDS CALL HIM SONNY

In February 1983, Sweet City/MCA released a new album by Mark Avsec and the Cruisers — not Donnie.

Singer Sonny Geraci was the star of *The Peter Emmett Story*. The album was a misguided bid to reboot the career of the Clevelander whose had fronted the Outsiders ("Time Won't Let Me") and Climax ("Precious and Few"). Geraci's website quotes *Cash Box* calling him "the Frank Sinatra of the '70s."[34.1] He passed away in February 2017.

But by the '80s, Geraci was out of hits. He needed some help. Geraci signed to Belkin-Maduri, and Maduri did what he could for him. Maduri tapped his go-to guy, Mark Avsec. Mark and the Cruisers had their finger on the pulse, so they made a record with Geraci. They banged it out at Jeree.

MARK: Once I had some success, Carl wanted to do some more things with me — some of them, things I wasn't really hip to. It's got to be something I really want to do, if I'm going to be into it. But I liked Carl, and if he wanted me to do something, I wanted to do it for him.

I knew Sonny — "Precious and Few" and "Time Won't Let Me." So we tried it.

We used my band. That decision was probably me. They probably needed money, so we got some money for everybody. So Carl paid some session fees. And it was going to be easier that way. They're such great players, so quick. So I wrote a bunch of songs. They cut the tracks.

The sessions moved even more briskly than a Cruisers recording: The songs were already written and arranged.

KEVIN: I can't remember if we got the rough songs in advance or learned them in the studio. I believe the latter. We had the Cruiser chemistry, so it was good thing.

MARK: I worked with Sonny the way I worked with Donnie. But, of course, Sonny sings in a totally different way. It was not intimidating at all. He was a nice guy.

Making that album, I did not feel the way I felt making Donnie records. It was a little bit of a slog to get it done. I was being worked pretty hard those days, between B.E. and Donnie and LaFlavour and Sonny and....

It was an odd decision, taking a known, proven veteran and reinventing with as a new name. Peter Emmett — for the brief moment he existed — was the kind of styling, profiling '80s rocker who was comfortable posing in front of a brick wall, wearing a white sport coat. If the description doesn't sound compelling, then rest assured: It wasn't.

MARK: The concept did not come from me. I don't even know why they did that. To me, it seems silly, in retrospect. And I think it seemed silly to me at the time, because he was *Sonny Geraci*. He had had success. Maybe they thought they were going to reinvent him as somebody new. I had nothing to do with that.

Peter Emmett, as it turns out, was not exactly a stage name: Geraci was born Emmett Peter Geraci, and Sonny was a family nickname. Sonny had a lot of friends. The Michael Stanley band's Kevin Raleigh, who penned and sang the breakout track "He Can't Love You," wrote "Don't Say You're Sorry," the leadoff single. Two songs — "Sleep With Me" and "Inside Story" were covers of songs by Eric Carmen, Clevelander and former lead singer of the Raspberries. Geraci only penned one song, a co-write with Barbara McFaul. Mark and Marty co-wrote album opener "There Goes My Heart." Avsec had already written "She Don't Know Me," a song that he never loved, but wouldn't stay dead. [34.2]

"She Don't Know Me" was later recorded by a young band for their debut album: Bon Jovi. And at this point, it had already been recorded by the group formerly known as LaFlavour — see chapter 41 for the full story. It could have been a Cruisers song, but Donnie didn't like it.

MARK: I forgot we even did "She Don't Know Me" with Sonny. I don't even know why we did that. Probably Carl suggested it. It would make sense if it was after Fair Warning was dropped, but before Bon Jovi had recorded it, and we didn't know they were planning to.

I don't remember whose idea it was to use it. I never thought about using it for the Cruisers. I don't think Donnie was really into the tune that much. And it really wasn't a Donnie song. Like, when I write for Donnie, I have Donnie in mind. We never really recorded it. I guess maybe we could one day, if he'd be into it. I don't think it was a great song.

Billboard politely previewed the record as "well-produced, punchy, guitar-dominated power pop" [34.3] — but wasn't so enthusiastic when it reviewed it a week later:

"Familiar production and synthesizer touches from Mark Avsec's work with Donny (sic) Iris abound on such AOR cuts as 'There Goes My Heart' and 'Inside Story.' Emmett's voice doesn't have Iris' bite, however, and the arrangements barely sustain interest. He looks like Ric Ocasek, if that helps." [34.4]

The Logansport, Indiana *Pharos-Tribune* — which was developing a surprisingly hip entertainment section — liked it better, and predicted, "A classic album of pop rock... almost certain to produce a winner." [34.5]

It did not.

MCA released the album, but didn't push it. With no official single, *The Peter Emmett Story* didn't chart, and only scored some obligatory regional FM rotation.

When the album hit the shelves, packaging was an odd mix: The credits listed the Cruisers as the band... on the bottom of the album. The top-line credit went to a crew of burly gentlemen called North Coast, who were pictured individually, in their immaculately bemulleted glory. Dave Garlic, Chris Kafka, Terry Manfredi and Billy Smith formed Geraci's live backing band, named North Coast as an Ohio reference. The group learned the material without Mark's help and played some regional shows over the next two years.

MARTY: I met some of the [North Coast] guys at a concert in a club somewhere, one night. I introduced myself and told them who I was. It was tense for a minute. I think they thought we would be mad at them. But I told them it was cool. I liked seeing the songs out there.

The Peter Emmett album fizzled. North Coast went south. Sonny reverted to being Sonny. And "She Don't Know Me" sat on the shelf. Again. That version. For now. Unbeknownst to everybody involved, the song was still working its way toward rock's permanent record.

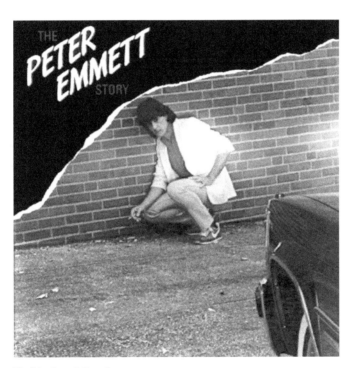

The Peter Emmett Story album.

CHAPTER 35

Fortune 410: The Album

Fortune 410

The fourth album by Donnie Iris and the Cruisers. Featuring...

Side 1:
"Human Evolution" (By Avsec, Iris,
Lee, McClain, Valentine) 3:15
"Stagedoor Johnny" (Avsec,
Lee, Iris) 3:49
"Cry (If You Want To)" (Avsec, Iris) 3:15
"Tell Me What You Want" (Avsec,
Lee, Iris) 3:22
"I Belong" (Avsec) 5:01

Side 2:
"She's So European" (Avsec, Iris) 3:28
"I'm a User" (Avsec, Iris) 2:38
"Never Did I" (McClain) 3:59
"Somebody" (Avsec, Iris) 3:53
"Do You Compute?" (Avsec, Iris) 3:40

Original release: May 1983, Carousel/MCA
Peak position on *Billboard* album chart: #127, August 6 1983
Weeks on chart: 12

Singles:
Single released June 1983: "Do You Compute?"/ "I Belong"
Weeks on chart: 7
Peak position: #64, July 30, 1983
(Only single from *Fortune 410*)
Original release: MCA-5427 MCA Records
Never pressed on CD
Out of print

"Under the trendy computers and synthesizers of 'She's So European' and 'Do You Compute,' one of the country's best rockers still isn't getting his due."

— Gary Graff, the Detroit Free Press 35.7

Summer 1983. *Fortune 410* marked the middle of the end.

The Cruisers' biggest and best years spanned from 1980 through 1985. The fourth album was the group's last true major-label release.

Fortune 410 is, thoroughly, a stylistic departure from the classic Cruisers sound. Mark moves beyond the stacked, rhythmic rock tracks and commits to a more new wave-y 1980s synthesizer sound. Two of the record's ten tracks made the best-of compilation: "She's So European" and "Do You Compute?"

Even though the group abandoned the tough, rough life, *Fortune 410* still has its share of high-energy tracks, including "She's So European" and the band's highest-beats-per-minute record, "Never Did I," which was written by Albritton. "Tell Me What You Want" and "European" are the only real holdovers of the suave and worldly Donnie — songwriter Mark had rebooted and found some new obsessions.

The band were running out of ideas and leaning into the Donnie image hard. The title sounds like the make and model of a forgotten personal computer, but it's taken from the name of Donnie's glasses, a style that was also worn by Nixon crony Henry Kissinger.

Even fewer critics devoted time and space to the record. The *All Music Guide to Rock* wrote, "During Donnie Iris and the Cruisers' 1980s prime, Avsec and Iris generally co-wrote the songs, although there was occasional input from the others. That's what makes the infectiously quirky McClain-penned 'Never Did I' such a pleasant surprise. *Fortune 410* closes with the astonishingly powerful and tuneful 'Do You Compute?' As a single it reached the Top 60, but it deserved a much better fate. Avsec's sustained synthesizer chords and McClain's driving bass set the foundation for Lee's resonant, thundering power chords and Iris' unbelievable vocals. The chorus is amazing, and so are Iris' falsetto screams." [35.1]

MARK: I wanted to make an album. As a holiday gift, the Belkin-Maduri office gave me a real little computer that I got real into, and I started programming it. And I saw *Tron* in theaters. I got so into computers that all my writing was about them. And, with me, anything that's worth doing is worth overdoing. And that album is *Fortune 410*.

Mark's first child — daughter Danna, a future Cruisers guest drummer — was born shortly before the record was released.

ERIN, DONNIE'S DAUGHTER: We always felt close to all of them, like a family. When their kids were born, it was like we had new cousins. It was the same with Marty, as well. We'd get excited when he was coming to stay with us.

ADDY, DONNIE'S DAUGHTER: There's a lot of love. Marty has had us in tears a few times, telling us how much we mean to him.

A pregnant wife and small apartment helped Mark drop his favorite vice. The band also changed their base of operations.

MARK: I was quitting smoking, so I started jogging, living a really clean life. I did not smoke around my wife when she was pregnant, but I really never finally quit until I started college at 32.

Kevin and Marty didn't smoke, those poor guys. I feel bad for them now, because I don't smoke anymore. I couldn't imagine what they had to endure, with Donnie and me and Jerry in this little unclean room with smoke and ashes all over the place — that's how we made our first three records.

Fortune 410 was a break. We switched studios. Nothing was wrong with Jeree. The third album was such a slog. We wanted to make a change, just to change.

For Mark, the new generation of synthesizers opened profound new possibilities.

MARK: This keyboard, the Chroma, has certain sounds. And that's why the album has certain sounds. That whole album, there's not a lot of stacking.

The whole concept of the synthesizer excited me, because it gave me control over my own orchestra. And, of course, it was all the rage, the synthesizer and the MIDI thing. Oddly enough, in the records that I made with Donnie, we didn't rely on that stuff.

SEAN ROSS, *ROSS ON RADIO*: AOR really peaks in 1980-81. And then in 1982, Human League/Soft Cell starts to kick in with help from — but not entirely because of — MTV. Plus, R&B music starts to cross over again — Ray Parker's "The Other Woman," "Sexual Healing," "Billie Jean," etc.). By 1984, Top 40 is soaring, WMMS is playing the Pointer Sisters and Lionel Richie, and rock radio is still not sure what to do next when [the format] Classic Rock comes along.

Fortune 410 came together in a new studio, Cleveland's Recording Connection. And a new engineer. The new engineer had actually been on site for the previous two albums. But it took some time to get his foot in the studio door.

MARK: We wanted to go to a clean studio that was more high-tech, in concert with that theme. So that's why we switched there: Recording Connection. It was in [Cleveland inner suburb] Beachwood. It was near our homes, except Donnie.

Carl did engineer that album. This is Carl Maduri III, Carl's son. He always wanted to be an engineer. He's still an engineer in Atlanta. He ended up being the real deal. He built a life doing it. I wasn't sure at first.

He came into the picture after we did the first album. His father wanted Carl to work on our second album. And I didn't want to do that. We had success. I felt it was magic going on. I didn't want that disturbed. I wanted Jerry to engineer with me. So I said, "No. We're doing it the way we've been doing it." Call me superstitious, whatever.

Well, Carl was coming down there, anyway. He would have to sit in the lobby.

Donnie, the way we work in the studio, it's like sex. It's very intimate. We don't want people to watch what we're doing. If you're there and you don't say anything, I still hear you. And I feel your presence. And I don't want to feel anybody's presence, because it's me, Jerry and Donnie, and it's really intense.

So Carl played along. He was out in the lobby. But gradually, he wore me down. He was a nice kid — he was only 19 or 20 then. So, near the end of *King Cool*, he did come in and help. He did the engineering on *Fortune 410*. He did the whole record.

DONNIE: I was adamant that when Mark and I were in the studio, nobody would be in there but us and the engineer. Especially when we were working with Jerry, it was the three of us, and that would be it. And that was because if I screwed up, it wouldn't be embarrassing to me. Things worked better when we worked alone.

LOYALTY TESTED

The label, however, wanted a much bigger new presence in the record: a new producer.

Mark wrote most of the music and more than half of the songs. Mark had the idea for the Cruisers sound. Mark made the records.

And now that the records weren't putting up great numbers, the label — more than ever — was not interested in the man who served the songs for Donnie to sing. The label was interested in Donnie, who was the voice of the band, and its public face.

Dominic "Donnie Iris" Ierace was the only artist on the contract between Carousel Records and the Belkin-Maduri Organization. From a cynical label perspective, the singer was the one true commodity in the endeavor collectively recognized as Donnie Iris and the Cruisers. He was just another face whose track record made him visible enough to shove into the spotlight. And, to the label, everything and everybody else was subject to change.

MARK: Donnie signed to Carousel. I never even did. Then when the whole thing went to MCA.

[After Donnie signed the contract] Rick Frio or MCA or somebody wanted to have a coming out party in Los Angeles. And so they wanted Donnie to go out there. At the time, in the office, it was thought of as my project with Donnie.

So they said, "You should bring out Mark Avsec, too — he's really the guy behind all this."

And Rick's like, "No, no, no. I've been through that Elton John-Bernie Taupin thing. I'm not doing that again." That's what I was told.

I realized then: I gave this to the world; I gave it to Donnie. And that's what it is: It's "Donnie Iris." And I have to get used to that.

It's been cool, because Donnie's not an asshole.

That's what I remember about Rick.

I mean, I *got* it. It was a Donnie project. That's what I wanted. [Frio] didn't even know me. I'm not saying he treated me bad. I don't think he knew Donnie much, either. I don't feel like Rick Frio gave me any thought whatsoever.

Three years and three records later, the label *had* given Mark some thought. And they thought it was time for Donnie to move on — and work with a new producer.

DONNIE: I think the suggestion might have come from the label. Somebody had talked about getting John Mellencamp to produce.

I remember going to a meeting. I can't remember who was there, even. The idea was brought up by an MCA guy. They brought up the fact that they could get him to produce my next record.

John "Cougar" Mellencamp producing an MCA-affiliated artist seems like a stretch: The label released his fizzle of a debut album, *Chestnut Street Incident*, in 1976, then dropped him. But the offer wouldn't be the first time in history a label exec offered something he couldn't deliver. Donnie didn't take the bait.

DONNIE: Although I was flattered, I just didn't see that happening — because what's going to happen?

Mark, of course he did not like the idea. I didn't like it. Nobody in the organization liked it. I do know it was out of the question.

I know how it is in the studio: When I'm in the studio, I have to feel comfortable. I wasn't going to take an outside chance of rolling with somebody else, because I feel that I work my best in the studio with people I can trust and people I can open up to — and not have to hold anything back.

And if that would have happened, if you had somebody like [Mellencamp] producing, I think I would have been beside myself, especially if something when wrong and I could do this or hit that note. I didn't want to take that chance.

I knew what it was like with Mark. I knew that we'd had success together. I knew we could have continued success together. And we didn't need another producer. We had everything we needed.

I knew how I felt at the time. I knew it wouldn't work. I know my limitations in the studio. And Mark does too. I know what I can do. And a lot of the songs are put together with that in mind. So there was no chance that I was gonna go anywhere else.

And it's great. With Mark, I'm almost 75 years old, and we're still together.

MARK: Here is the way I remember it.

Donnie was put into this position where he had to decide not to have me produce anymore. I knew he was in a tough spot. The last thing I wanted to do was be a drag on his career.

But I did want to be treated fairly. I started this band with him. It was just as much my baby as it was his. So I went to the Maduris. I said, fine, get a new producer – but someone has to give me some equity in the project, some points. Because I know I am the functional leader of this band, and my heart is not going to be in it otherwise. I drive the thing.

I may act in a naïve manner sometimes, but I'm not naïve. I'm a pretty sharp lawyer now. I have to have some incentive to continue working on the project I gave birth to.

But there was nothing in response. Nobody said "OK, we'll give you two points out of our end. Work with the new producer."

I was expected to be a sideman in my own band — for what? For nothing? So I withdrew. And I lost interest. I was not obstructing. I mentally checked out. I could not help it.

Donnie sensed that: I was not actively engaged anymore. And I believe his wife, Linda, had something to say about it too. And one day Donnie came to me and said — very emphatically — it's you and me, Spark. Which made me feel good. I would have absolutely done the same for him.

But understand: All someone had to do was give me a fair deal, and I would have enthusiastically accepted a new non-producer role. Nobody offered that. Donnie and I are now lifelong friends. I am grateful that never got between us.

When *Fortune 410* was released, it included an inscription from Donnie to Mark: "This album is dedicated to my best friend 'Spark.'"

DONNIE: He needed to know that's how I felt about him. He was the guy that I was going to continue to do music with, and that's just the way it was. I thought he might like that.

MARK: I didn't even know that dedication was in there. Donnie must have called someone and had them add it. That was nice. That was *Donnie*.

He would call me Spark. And I would call him Spyke — Marty would do it too. He still calls me Spark.

BELKIN: Donnie without Mark, and Mark without Donnie, they don't have a band that's going to last very long. Between the solidarity and the fact that they're such close friends… they respect what each other does, musically. It's like a dream come true. They're able to bring out the best in each other. It's a manager's dream.

Some people can go 99 for 100 because they practice a lot. But some are the one in a million person who has that talent, and they're able to pick up a guitar and play it and transcend with lyrics. Mark's a very good writer and a keyboard player. Donnie's a very good guitar player, but a different kind. Joe Walsh is *way* up there. But Donnie and Mark are definitely major-league talents.

JIMMY ROACH: Three records into a major-label deal, struggling, how many people would stay loyal? They'd probably look for another direction, jump on some trend. But that personal loyalty, that's what Donnie is. He's like the neighborhood guy: I don't think he'd have liked himself if he ditched them.

He could have changed directions, changed producers, moved to New York. But it wouldn't have fit him. Out of 100 artists, probably two or three would do what he did.

NEW DIGS

The new studio did not provide the extra spark that Spark had hoped for. When Mark went to work, he stayed at his station, maintaining a laser-like focus until his lights flickered. During the *Fortune 410* sessions, he set a record.

MARK: I think I went 24 hours once. And then the new LinnDrum came in, and I unpacked the box and wouldn't leave the studio because I started programming it. They had to conduct an intervention and put me to bed.

DONNIE: I wasn't real crazy about the studio. We had worked at Jeree's studio in New Brighton for years, and we loved the vibe there. It was comfortable. But the studio in Cleveland, we weren't happy there, and it showed. The first album we did there was a whole lot better than the one that followed. But at that point, we had Kevin, and Albritton was there.

MARK: I still approached it the same way, yoemanlike. Getting Donnie to show up. But the magic was gone. We were just getting tired.

It's magic. I mean, why couldn't Rob Parissi come up with another hit record after "Play That Funky Music"? Trust me: He felt the pressure. He had had that big hit record.

And you think, "Well, I did that one. I can do another one."

But it's not so easy. It's like winning the lottery, winning the creative lottery.

It all came together for "Play That Funky Music." But it's not so easy to come up with that kind of lyric, that kind of groove. You can *try* to duplicate it formulaically. You start analyzing different songs. You can look at it and go, "OK, I need a hook. I need a bass line. I need *this*. I need *that*...."

It doesn't work like that. If it did, everyone could do it. There's *magic* in pop music. And that's the beauty of it, too: You can't force it. And, for whatever reason, the first couple albums... and then...

For the fourth record, the band didn't have much to say for the record.

FORTUNE 410, THE SONGS: "HUMAN EVOLUTION"

The prescient *Fortune 410* opens with a perky, quirky, energetic, high-concept keyboard romp. It's not a Donnie song so much as a snapshot of Mark's swirling mind, a mix of Catholic mythology, hip aphorisms, and trope lyrics.

MARK: It's a concept album as much as *King Cool* — it's computerland.

I don't know why we started the album with it. I was reading about it. I was interested in it.

DONNIE: As far as I remember, that was a jam.

"STAGEDOOR JOHNNY"

It's not a fan favorite, although "Stagedoor Johnny" has the most fervent screaming of any Donnie song. Like almost every other name and character in the Cruisers catalog, the people in the tune are fictitious, and not even based on any figures from the band's life.

DONNIE: I always thought that was a pretty damned good song. I thought the performance was good. I thought the idea was good. I think the vocal performance was pretty good on that one. I was pretty happy with the way I sounded.

I don't remember all the screaming I did in it, but I liked the tune, and the premise, and the way I performed.

MARK: It's not about anybody. It was just an idea for a song. It wasn't one of my favorite songs. I think Marty liked it.

We were getting gradually burned out. We had done a couple records that barely saw the light of day — the radio reaction killed the record. They're always saying, "Go back to the studio, make another record." They have no skin in the game. They're not the one spending a thousand hours making a record. And I am. It weighs on you as you keep going.

And then the pressures of life, all of us, at this point: We're married, we're having families, money.... We're really not making much money in music. All these pressures are convoluting themselves. And we're approaching the point where Marty and Kevin are finding other things to do. And Kevin's going to move to L.A. And Donnie's finding something else to do. And at that point, I'm still doing music.

"CRY (IF YOU WANT TO)"

This earnest track could have been big on adult-contemporary radio in 1980.

DONNIE: I don't even remember that. It must not be that good.

MARK: I didn't even write that. I think that's one of the few from outside writers.

It says Avsec and Iris? We must have written it, then.

"TELL ME WHAT YOU WANT"

Marty's subdued lead and Kevin's insistent cowbell give a much-needed rocky edge to Donnie's labored vocals and Mark's layered, popping keyboards.

DONNIE: That's another song that's just… It's a stinker, like a lot of the other ones.

You're always doing your best, waiting for something to happen for it to be good. But it turns out, for whatever reason, just not that good.

MARK, after listening to it: I don't know. I don't remember the song.

"I BELONG"

The '80s saw a steady stream of rock songs that doubled as anthemic motivational pamphlets. And this tune, crafted to be a rousing singalong, fits that tradition. Mark's programmed keyboards push Marty's beefy, chugging riff into the background, and the tune isn't quite a rock song or a dance track. Kevin shares percussion duties with a drum machine. It's the first major step toward the sound Mark would develop on his *very* '80s side project, Cellarful of Noise.

DONNIE: I thought that was alright. A decent tune. It's a *ra-ra*, "I'm alright, man! Let me go out and conquer the world!"

MARK: This is a period, it's not even interesting for me to talk about the tunes, such are the doldrums.

Marty and Kevin creating a tape loop of Kevin's drum track for "Human Evolution" at Beachwood studio.

Marty's Fortune 410 guitar rig at Beachwood studio; his treasured Paul Rivera-modified 50-watt Marshall and Fender amps, and his Gibson Les Pauls and Fernandes guitars.

"SHE'S SO EUROPEAN"

All the coffee Mark drank finally kicks in on this track, which is where *Fortune 410* comes alive. The band turned a running joke into an enduring tune, and Donnie returns to form as cosmopolitan playboy. In this character sketch, Avsec and Donnie work together as lyricists, spinning some great blue-collar poetry. The tune opens with a couple of devastating couplets: "She was an army brat / She surfed in Waikiki / She told me she was French / But she's from Tennessee."

MARK: We used to have a joke on the road — that's my recollection — about a certain type of girl we met who was sort of a Valley girl type, but thought of herself as very *European*. And we used to say something like "She's so European." And so I wrote that.

DONNIE: There's some French in there. Mark gave me the way you're supposed to pronounce it.

That's pretty good. It's a good tune, has a nice feel. You get that feeling with some chicks from Europe, like they think theirs don't stink. They've got these cute accents.

"I'M A USER"

This look at addictive technology was ahead of its time. It's a sketch of a blue-collar man effectively enslaved by computers. Once again, Marty's sharp solo is buried in the mix. The guitarist is turning in some fine work, but this is not a guitar album.

DONNIE: I don't even remember that, how it goes or anything

MARK: The computer theme. "I'm a computer user."

"NEVER DID I"

The bassist's pogo-worthy pop track is an unusual Cruisers tune. Albritton's last solo Cruisers writing credit would have been perfect on the soundtrack to a thoughtful romantic comedy.

DONNIE: I thought it was pretty good. Al wrote a nice tune. Had a nice little hook to it. I didn't think it was a great song, but we tried to get the other guys involved, writing in the album. Both Mark and I definitely thought that it was something we could put on a record.

MARK: I never really heard it as a Donnie song, but wanted to record it out of respect for Albritton. I remember it was a struggle for me getting it to a Donnie style. But I know people like the song.

"SOMEBODY"

"Somebody" is all soft, Toto-style keyboards, drum machines, and harmonies.

DONNIE: I remember most when we get in the studio, and we're doing a "Love Is Like a Rock" kind of thing, where we're doing the same part, but I'll be in falsetto or an octave lower. That's what I remember about singing with Mark.

We track 'em and track 'em and track 'em. And eventually, you look up at each other and bust out laughing, like, "We've gotta do this *again*?!"

But it's fun. The final product comes out, and it's so big, it's worth it. It's fun, always.

"DO YOU COMPUTE?"

With hard-hitting electronic drums at its core, the steady midtempo "Do You Compute?" is still on the set list. It's a good chance for the band to catch their wind, and it still packs a poignant wallop. Donnie's late-song screams are as powerful as ever — but, once again, the keyboards push the voice and Marty's processed leads into the background. Donnie says the gradual transition from doo-wop to synth pop didn't mess with his head.

DONNIE: "Do You Compute," I think, is still a good song. It's fun to do live, too.

I never really felt like I was getting old. Mark drew me into the material. I didn't understand much of it then, like I do now. But it's very cool stuff, and I got into it.

MARK: "Do You Compute" is OK. But the whole album lacks the energy of Jeree's. Our best work was with Kevin and the band, at Jeree's, with the limitations imposed by that studio.

"Do You Compute?" contains a curious irony: Mark, the band's chief songwriter, writes the lyrics, "I ain't no good with words." He's not channeling a character. He's wrong, but he believes he's right.

MARK: I'm also a good writer. I can write memos, letters, legal documents. But I've never been able to write great *lyrics* — certainly not on the level of a Dylan or Springsteen, or a Michael Stanley. I'm reading Springsteen's book now, and I feel like I might be able to write better if I put a premium on the lyrics over the music.

But I've always approached the Donnie thing as first extracting melody and getting harmony and having this beauty-and-the-beast thing with the band and adding the rock and roll element. And *then* I'm extracting a lyric. I'm doing the best with what I've created myself.

And Springsteen — look, Springsteen's a rock-and-roller. I'm not. I wish I was. Springsteen comes from pure rock and roll.

If you read the book, he could barely play guitar when he first got his guitar at 9-10-11, whatever age he was. That's not where I was coming from. Me, by that age, I was playing concertos. So, in a way, I'm not coming from as pure a place in rock and roll.

Even Joe Grushecky, he comes from a place that Springsteen does, which is 1-4-5, three-chord rock. And then putting a premium on the lyrics, working up these stories and these wonderful characters.

I create these weird chord changes and all this chord stuff, and the words are the last thing to come in, and sometimes they get short shrift. I'd have to change my writing style. And I think about it.

I think about making one more record with Donnie, where lyrics are a premium. And I should be able to do that. But I'd have to come from a different place to do it. Don't even think I'm equating myself with Springsteen — I'm not; he's a special guy. Dylan's a special guy. Some artists are just weird and messed up. And that's OK.

THE "DO YOU COMPUTE?" VIDEO

"Do You Compute" was the only single from *Fortune 410*. The album was released in summer 1983. MTV had been on the air for two years. Now everybody understood the importance of music videos. The Cruisers shot their first concept video since before the band signed to Carousel/MCA. Donnie's management — not the label — had paid for all three of his previous videos. The label didn't suddenly loose its purse strings; the promo clip was subsidized through a partnership with Atari, the first name in electronic home entertainment.

When the label caught wind of Mark's computer concept, marketing representatives started reaching out to electronics companies. They connected with Atari — which, at that critical juncture, needed all the help it could to maintain its subsiding cultural relevance. The electronics giant liked "Do You Compute." And *Fortune 410*'s lead single was set.

Next came the video and its retail/radio promo campaign. The two companies partnered to shoot a clip for "Do You Compute?," which prominently featured the Atari 800 home computer. The companies ran a sweepstakes, with Donnie as its poster boy: For two to four weeks in each market, Atari gave away one prize pack per market, with additional valuable major awards. [35.2]

Belkin called the organization's go-to video professional: Chuck Statler, the Akronite director-producer who shot videos for Devo, Michael Stanley, Madness, the Cars, and the Cruisers.

STATLER: The Belkins — Mike, his son, the rest of the organization — were very hospitable and treated me very well. Mike was interested in working with this company, Video Replay from Ohio, because it sounded like they were giving him the production [for a good price].

We had a few days of pre-production. They had the full video blocked out. It's not a video that I'm boastful about. I directed them on set. The company had already created a storyline, so it was not dissimilar from my work with an ad agency: You're presented with a [story]board, and how are you going to make it better? All the other aspects of design and production were cast by the time I got there.

The "Do You Compute?" video hangs on the thinnest thread of a narrative, echoed in the later *Weird Science*, with a dark sci-fi twist: The clip stars a blonde who looks a lot like Leah and Agnes from the previous videos, but is played by a different, forgotten actress. She lies on a slab, wired to a computer, wearing a white outfit, sharp high heels, and liberal amounts of blush on her prominent cheekbones.

STATLER: We shot maybe a day in their studio. They really wanted to have this as a demo of all their gadgetry and hardware and software. There was a lot of Chroma Keying [green screen computer graphics] with it, putting them in this other environment. I didn't do any of the Chroma Key effects.

Donnie sings, "What does it take to open up your eyes?" And the answer is: an Atari 800 computer, an affordable sequel to the 1200XL model. As Donnie works his magic on a computer keyboard, the band play in an emerald cyberspace, shuffling, signing, and riffing along. Brought to life by the cyber vibes, the girl opens her eyes, zaps Donnie into the computer, then walks off in a stiff robotic gait. *Yinz have now entered the Twilight Zone!*

STATLER: Donnie was great to work with. He's a regular guy, a great guy, no pretense. I've worked with bands, and they didn't even want to be bothered with doing a video. They were really uncooperative and difficult to work with. But Donnie, he was going to do the best he could and commit 100%.

ART ATTACK/"MANDOLAY" II

In 1983, Mark had some additional techomancy up his sleeve, too: Maduri talked him into re-recording LaFlavour's "Mandolay," the international disco hit he wrote in 1979, for BMO, a new dance-label enterprise from the Belkin-Maduri Organization, distributed through Columbia's network. Mark recorded the tune and a B-side, "In Living Stereo," a midtempo keyboard workout that sounded like a synthesizer's test drive. BMO released the single under the name Art Attack, banking on the tried and true music business maxim: "It worked last time, so let's try it again."

MARK: That was a desperate attempt at a suggestion. "Mandolay" had already been a club hit. And it was suggested it could be a hit all over again. It was done electronically. Art Attack was just me. I played everything on there.

Released in July 1983, the Art Attack single spent nine weeks on *Billboard*'s Dance/Disco Top 80 chart. It peaked at number 33 October 29, 1983.

Fortune 410 fared better.

FORTUNE 410 REVIEWS

MCA/Carousel once again bucked up for *Billboard* cover ad. [35.3] But the Cruisers' fourth record garnered less press than *The High and the Mighty*.

Radio journal *Cash Box* barely blurbed it: The magazine took a look at the computer-inspired graphics and asked, "Could it be true that pop-rocker Iris has gone the trendy way of U.K. techno-dance? Naaah.... For the most part Iris is still churning out furious rock 'n' roll laced with the potent hooks he's known for." [35.4]

The synths made fans panic on general principle. The album's longest review wasn't from a big outlet, and the review wasn't a good one.

The Fond Du Lac *Commonwealth* reporter Joe Kowalski opened up, "Somewhere between *King Cool* and the new *Fortune 410*, Donnie Iris has slipped a floppy disk." [35.5]

Cleveland *Plain Dealer* critic Anastasia Pantsios called it "a perfect example of an artist trying to make his style conform on the surface to the prevailing trends without — luckily — tampering with it too much…. Some of the material… is so typically strong that it will doubtless outlive the trendy trappings it has been given…. That special sound has been toned down somewhat through most of the album with less emphasis on fat chords and fat vocals — on a fat sound in general. That probably is more 'modern,' although that doesn't make it better by definition." [35.6]

The Detroit *Free Press* didn't have much to say, but liked what they heard: Ace rock writer Gary Graff wrote, "Under the trendy computers and synthesizers of 'She's So European' and 'Do You Compute,' one of the country's best rockers still isn't getting his due." [35.7]

FORTUNE 410 ON YOUR FM DIAL

The *Fortune 410* radio campaign was rough, too.

MADURI: Airplay condensed itself back to this region, then ended.

Fortune 410, Irving Azoff took over MCA. He was interested. He was really behind the project. He thought "Do You Compute?" was a Top 10 record. He was behind it, but it just didn't happen. And then a band called The Fixx came out.

Released in June, "Do You Compute" spent seven weeks on the *Billboard* singles chart, peaking at number 64, July 30, 1983. On the Mainstream/Album Rock chart, it climbed to number 20 on July 16, and it hung on for ten weeks. August wasn't kind: MCA released the Fixx's "One Thing Leads To Another" in August. It spent 19 weeks on the *Billboard* singles chart and peaked at number 4.

MADURI: And MCA leaned toward that band, then other bands. And it was pretty much over.

The "Do You Compute?" video garnered some airplay, but didn't stand out in a tough field where video production value was rapidly escalating. The Cruisers had to compete with clips for the Police's "King of Pain," the Eurythmics' "Sweet Dreams," the Talking Heads' "Burning Down the House," and Spandau Ballet's "True." AOR acts without a competitive video — like the Cruisers and Asia — were outgunned.

The music held its own, though. *Fortune 410* had a good run: 12 weeks on the *Billboard* album chart, which was still a big step down from *Back on the Streets* (23 weeks, peaking position 57) and *King Cool* (31 weeks, peak position 84). But it was a significant improvement on *The High and the Mighty* (4 weeks, peaking at 180). The new album peaked early, though: It hit number 127 on the album chart, August 6.

Over four albums, the Cruisers would learn Carousel/MCA could have done more for them — and they could have done less. The promotional pushes may have been misguided, but at least they existed.

FOX: I would have to say it wasn't lacking. And, yes, that's a disappointment to me, when I can say that with good faith, and we didn't have the success that we wanted to.

The tour didn't save *Fortune 410*. The band worked their preferred promo outlets: WMMS in Cleveland. A DVE in-store at National Record Mart in Pittsburgh. And once "Do You Compute" was on FM airwaves, the Cruisers headed back toward the turnpike, fingers crossed.

> Donnie without Mark, and Mark without Donnie, they don't have a band that's going to last very long. Between the solidarity and the fact that they're such close friends… they respect what each other does, musically.
>
> ~ **MIKE BELKIN**

Marty, Donnie, Albritton, Kevin (Photo by Richard Kelly)

CHAPTER 36

Fortune 410: The Tour

Summer 1983. The *Fortune 410* tour was an improvement on *The High and the Mighty's* campaign. After a late-May album release, the Cruisers played around 50 shows between the summer and New Year's Eve. The band cruised through the Southeast, Midwest, Mid-Atlantic, and East Coast. The tour climaxed with four California shows in late August, followed by a handful of gigs over the rest of the year. For a minute, the band had their first international show on the books.

MARK: It wasn't as much fun anymore. We couldn't get back to where we were with the gigs. Nobody was making as much money. People were getting on with their lives. It was the last gasp.

As was the band's habit, they warmed up with Ohio gigs, which culminated in a headlining show at Blossom, the forest amphitheater south of Cleveland. The Cruisers were still brainstorming new ideas to keep the show fresh.

A review by the *Plain Dealer's* Anastasia Pantsios conveyed some of the action: "Donnie moved smoothly from the swingy Motownish 'My Girl' to the pretty 'Somebody' with all five musicians lined up along the front of the stage and singing while a tape took over from drummer Kevin Valentine.... He and the band add quirky, personal touches that have the warmth and wit the group is noted for: things like Valentine's bizarre drum solo that ends with him racing around the stage playing on speakers and audience members' hands."

During "Love is Like a Rock," the band shared the stage with a group of contest winners in uniform WMMS tees. Everyone except Kevin returned to the stage wearing marching-band snare drums strapped over their shoulders. On his fourth tour, however, Iris was testing her patience with the "I Can't Hear You" rap, though she did note, "Iris' solid, happy, unpretentious music is largely a delight." [36.1]

The group followed that big headlining gig with one of the biggest shows of its career: Ohio's Legend Valley minifestival, where the Cruisers warmed up the stage for Journey, Foghat, and Bryan Adams.

KEVIN: Journey watched our set, and they were talking to us after. Steve liked Donnie, and they were talking about how good Albritton was. We knew they needed a bassist, and we were afraid they were going to offer him the job.

The Cruisers buzzed the Southwest, worked the Midwest, circled around the Mid-Atlantic, and zoomed through the Northeast, going as far as Toronto.

The *Fortune 410* tour is remembered particularly well among the diehards at fan site Parallel Time, the unofficial online hub of the Cruisers community. User AstroJim posted the set list from the Dallas show July 3:

1. "Tough World"
2. "The Rapper"
3. "She's So European"
4. "Do You Compute"
5. "My Girl"

Donnie stage rap intro to...
6. "I Can't Hear You"
7. "Somebody"
8. "That's the Way Love Oughta Be"

9. "This Time it Must Be Love"
10. "Stagedoor Johnny"
Guitar Solo

Drum Solo
11. "Love is Like A Rock"
Encore:
12. "The High and The Mighty"
13. "Ah! Leah!" [36.2]

The Westwood One radio network — a syndicate renowned for prestigious radio concerts, which were a huge deal in the 1980s — recorded the July 9 show at Harpo's in Detroit and aired a truncated best-of set in September.

As the summer sun hit its zenith, Donnie and the Cruisers rocked the beach capital of the '80s, Ft. Lauderdale in Florida. August 13, they headlined the club Summers on the Beach, where they played a supersized set with no opening act. Parallel Time poster EdBu1 archived a set list:

1. "Tough World"
2. "The Rapper"
3. "She's So European"
4. "Do You Compute?"
5. "My Girl"
6. "I Can't Hear You"
7. "Somebody"
8. "That's the Way Love Oughta Be"
9. "This Time It Must Be Love"
10. "King Cool"
    Extended drum solo: drummer played everything (drums, speakers, chairs, floor, walls, etc.) while everybody else left the stage.
11. "Love is Like A Rock"
12. "The High and the Mighty"
13. "Ah! Leah! "
14. "Agnes" [36.3]

BIG CITY NIGHTS

It was the only tour where "Agnes" was consistently not the opener.

In Los Angeles, Donnie was in the spotlight for a glorious moment. He caught the big newspaper's eye. And the boss showed up. The Cruisers played late-night hot spot Club Lingerie on the Sunset Strip. The *Times*' Terry Atkinson had a good time through most of the set: "Donnie Iris is one of those semi obscure rock singers who just keep going, despite light sales and a lack of critical attention…. He makes fairly satisfying albums and puts on a good show. Well, it was a good show, at least, until two-thirds of the way, when the set descended into stadium-rock bombast — right down to a drum solo and a Hendrix-style guitar solo of 'When You Wish Upon a Star.'" [36.4]

MADURI: I was at Club Lingerie. A big black limousine pulled up to the front door. And out from the back came 5-foot-five Irving Azoff, to listen to the band. He got there for maybe songs 3 through 7, and then disappeared. But it was a lot for him to come out, because at that point he was involved in the Eagles and Linda Ronstadt and Dan Fogelberg. He came out because he liked the band.

As summer wound down, "Do You Compute?" had been hanging on in the lower reaches of *Billboard*'s Hot 100. By September, it was done. In its September 3 issue, Cash Box's *Rock Album Radio Report* ranked the album at number 158 with a bullet, with no new station adds. The single was in hot rotation on two stations, medium rotation on four, with a small but far-flung following from Connecticut to Denver. The report ended with a sad, lonely count of new adds: none.

September fizzled with two big cancellations:

The band was announced as low-card talent for Tennessee's Electric Cowboy Festival, a dicey three-day inaugural event slated for the vast 200-acre Webster Farm venue and campsite in Columbia. It was to be headlined by Joan Jett & the Blackhearts, Cheap Trick, Joe Walsh, Molly Hatchet, and Quarterflash — and hosted by Wolfman Jack.

September 7, the Cruisers were scheduled to play the Marquee Club in London. The show was advertised, but the band remained on the other side of the Atlantic Ocean, which is where they forever remained.

MARK: We were never in London. But the band never really played outside of the U.S.

KEVIN: I don't think anyone ever thought of Europe. I don't think we had any activity there that meant anything.

The tour was over. As usual, a trickle of live shows kept the cash coming in. After a series of homecoming season college concerts, Donnie headlined a sold out show at the Stanley on Oct 5, 1983 with B.E. Taylor.

Fortune 410 had cooled rapidly, but the Cruisers and friends still brought the heat at home. The show sold out. And *that* show was an unqualified success in front of a friendly, familiar crowd.

B.E. Taylor set the bar high, with a set that earned a standing ovation. Then the Cruisers sprang over the bar. Larry O'Reilly from the *Pittsburgh Press* witnessed it, and he didn't calm down for a while: "The 3,154 in attendance rose to their feet last night when Iris and the Cruisers opened with 'Tough World' and continued standing through encores of 'The High and the Mighty,' 'Agnes,' and the group's smash hit, 'Ah! Leah!'" [36.5]

After a tour and some rest time, the band had the show down. Donnie wailed in harmony as Marty and Mark traded solos in "She's So European," which had transcended its dubious synth-song single status: Live, they had turned it into a reliable barnburner. "The Rapper" drew the fans off their seats and into the aisles, dancing. The dancing didn't stop for "This Time It Must Be Love," which also turned into massive singalong, led by Donnie in black pants and a white sleeveless tuxedo jacket — a rock and roll update of his original stage outfit he wore in his juvenile appearance on *The Paul White Show*.

Marty's solo also wowed the crowd, but Valentine had the showstopper moment for the night: After a pounding five-minute solo, he bolted from behind the kit and took his drumsticks to the stage floor, then the amps, then the microphone stand — and *then* to the seats in the orchestra pit. "Strange guy," wrote O'Reilly. "But the audience loved it." [36.6]

Audiences all over the country were still stumbling across Donnie. Radio airplay was flagging. But the video worked. "Do You Compute?" scored two moments on the ultra-hip late-night national showcase *Night Flight*, in September and October.

Despite mixed results from the *Fortune 410* cycle, Donnie and the Cruisers were still the biggest Pittsburgh band — and outpacing the phenomenally popular Michael Stanley Band on national charts.

Things looked good.

But things were changing.

> I use the term "MCA"
> as a verb. I refer to those bands
> being "MCA'd": All these local
> guys, they were all excited when
> they got label deals. And almost
> uniformly, they got screwed.
> I never got the feeling MCA
> promoted them the right way.
> I never did.
>
> ~JIMMY ROACH

CHAPTER 37

Meet the New Boss

Late Summer 1983. Donnie and the Cruisers had a single on the charts. The president of MCA seemed to be in their corner.

It was nice while it lasted.

MCA president Irving Azoff saw the band play in Los Angeles, but he didn't stay for the full set. To be fair, the label executive and Eagles manager was a busy guy. And MCA had a lot of bands — roughly 45. Most MCA bands didn't get an opportunity to impress their new boss. And most didn't impress him.

Azoff took the big chair in April 1983. The new executive had a tough task ahead: turn around MCA's fortunes. When he later left the company, MCA would note: In 1982, the year before his arrival, its music operations had earned $24.2 million on revenues of $141.7 million.

In 1988, his final year, the operation earned $60.5 million on revenues of $661 million.

In his farewell letter, Azoff did more math: The MCA label group had shipped 35 million units in 1983 — and 120 million in 1988.

Also, by his count, MCA artists had won eight Grammy Awards in 1983 — and 22 in 1988. [37.1]

That turnaround began with a major bloodletting.

Azoff brought a blockbuster mentality to the label. Like a Hollywood movie studio, he decided managing five big projects would be easier than funding and promoting 40 small ones.

As it turned out, Azoff agreed with B.E. Taylor guitarist Rick Witkowski: Signing 45 bands and hoping five turned a profit *was* a bad business model. Unfortunately, putting a better strategy in place did not help the B.E. Taylor Group — or his many Pittsburgh labelmates.

As September 1983 began, that big roster featured three Pittsburgh bands: Donnie and the Cruisers, the Houserockers, and B.E. Taylor. That was about to change. The Houserockers had changed their name from the *Iron City* Houserockers in a last-ditch attempt to ditch the Steel City bar band image, which hadn't played on a national level. The rebranding didn't work. MCA cut them first. [37.2]

JIMMY ROACH: I use the term "MCA" as a verb. I refer to those bands being "MCA'd": All these local guys, they were all excited when they got label deals. And almost uniformly, they got screwed. I never got the feeling MCA promoted them the right way. I *never* did.

JASON PETTIGREW, *ALTERNATIVE PRESS* EDITOR-IN-CHIEF: MCA — Music Cemetery of America. If they were on Sony or Warner Brothers, maybe they'd have had a chance. I don't know if some jerk in a $3,000 white linen suit running A&R at a major label didn't know what to do with them because they weren't *L.A.* or *New York* enough.

The Cruisers don't really wear that blue collar kind of vibe on their sleeve. They didn't build their band on the precipice of Working Man's Rock. It's more "show up, plug in, do the gig, break a sweat, and make people feel good," in the best way possible. It makes rock and roll *fun*, without the stupid gestures.

Among major labels, MCA was at the back of the pack. Azoff's new master plan was not good news for the Cruisers, either.

Ultimately, savvy Cruisers co-manager Mike Belkin was able to turn the timing to the band's advantage. To recap, have another look at the intricate timeline:

OCTOBER 1982: Carousel/MCA formally exercised its option for a fourth album, which would be *Fortune 410*.

Carousel and MCA often acted in unison. But they were not the same entity, and did not always have the same interests, priorities or fiscal calendar. The Cruisers signed a contract with Carousel Records. Carousel, as a requirement of the deal with Donnie — just Donnie — had to deliver his records to a major label. The major label would produce, distribute and promote the albums. Donnie's contract did not specify which label. For the first four Cruisers records, that label was MCA.

And here's how Cruisers records would get a green light, album to album:

MCA would tell Carousel it wanted a new Donnie Iris record.

Carousel would tell Donnie to make a record. Carousel would give Donnie's management money to start a new record.

And Donnie would make a record, with Mark and the Cruisers, who — as far as Carousel/MCA was concerned — were incidental if not *detrimental* to the product.

JUNE 1983: Carousel notifies the band: As per its contract with MCA, MCA has until September 26, 1983 to renew its agreement with Donnie. And Carousel has until September 30 to think about it, then let the band know. [37.3]

AUGUST 30, 1983: The *Fortune 410* tour ends.

SEPTEMBER 13, 1983: Carousel notifies the Belkin-Maduri Organization:

Carousel exercises its option on its agreement with Donnie; Carousel wants a fifth Donnie Iris album, even if MCA does not request one.

And even if MCA does not want another Donnie Iris album, Donnie's contract with Carousel will remain in full force for another year, through October 1984. [37.4]

MID-LATE 1983: MCA slashes its roster, dropping nearly 90% of its acts. It reduces its stable from approximately 45 to 7. [37.5, 37.6] These cuts include Donnie Iris and the Cruisers.

OCTOBER 1983: Since Frio had exercised his option, Belkin requests — via lawyers — that Frio pony up $43,750 to start album #5. [37.7] "Inasmuch as your MCA/Carousel Agreement was in full force and effect at the time that you exercised your option, we expect to receive payment pursuant to the terms and conditions of said agreement, namely" $87,5000, half when the band starts recording, half when they deliver the album.

OCTOBER 31, 1983: The Cruisers return to Beachwood Studios in Cleveland, to begin recording their fifth album. [37.8]

And so, in the fall of 1983, Mark Avsec was holed up in his new, unfinished suburban basement, writing the Cruisers' make-or-break fifth album, which will — one faraway day — be known as *No Muss No Fuss*.

The Cruisers carried on, unaware of the fluctuating contracts or imminent chaos.

MARK: I honestly had no real knowledge of all of this stuff. By then I realized I pretty much gave the whole franchise away – neither MCA nor Carousel nor Rick Frio cared about me or what I thought. It wasn't the Mark Avsec album. So I was not paying attention to the MCA thing, because I'd rather not think about it.

I did care about the "Leah" lawsuit, because I took that personally.

It was a frustrating time.

> It wasn't the Mark Avsec album.
> So I was not paying attention to
> the MCA thing, because I'd
> rather not think about it.
> I did care about the "Leah"
> lawsuit, because I took that
> personally.
> It was a frustrating time.
>
> ~MARK AVSEC

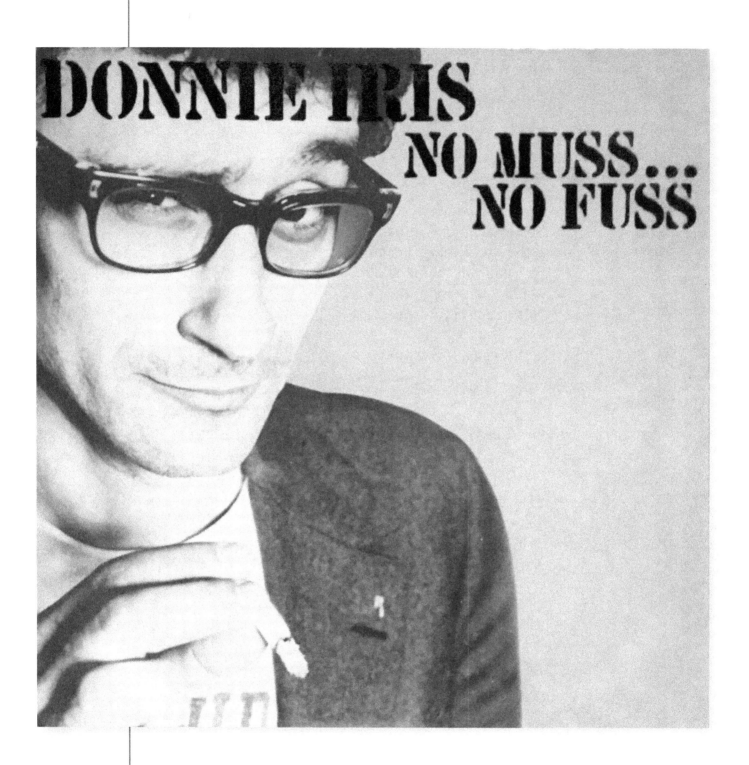

No Muss… No Fuss: The Album

No Muss… No Fuss

The fifth album by Donnie Iris and the Cruisers. Featuring…

Side 1:
"Injured in the Game of Love"
  (Avsec, Iris)
"10th Street" (Avsec, Iris)
"Ridin' Thunder" (Avsec, Iris)
"You're My Serenity" (Avsec, Iris)
"L.O.V.E." (Avsec, Iris)

Side 2:
"Follow That Car" (Avsec, Iris)
"Don't Cry Baby" (Gary Jones)
"State of the Heart" (Avsec, Iris)
"Headed for a Breakdown" (Avsec, Iris)
"I Want You Back" (Avsec, Iris)

From the credits:
Produced by Mark Avsec for Belkin-Maduri Organization
Executive Producer: Carl Maduri
Recorded at Beachwood Studios - Beachwood, Ohio
Recording and mixing engineer - Carl Maduri Iii
Mastered By George Marino At Sterling Sound
Cover Photo Of Donnie Iris By Marcia Resnick

Thanks To Chris Maduri For Your Input And Assistance In Making This Record.
Thanks To Carl Maduri For Everything And All Your Years Of Support.
Thanks To Mike Belkin For Pulling Us Through.

Original release: BFW 39949 HME Records (vinyl)
CD Release: PRI411 Primary Records (1999)
Digitally remastered and released on CD with slightly altered cover.

"Iris's strength is being what he is…. His songs are about the little guy trying to win the girl or hanging out with old friends; his character has no special advantages in life, but he's getting by and having a pretty good time." — Anastasia Pantsios, the Cleveland Plain Dealer[44.9]

The final '80s album featuring the classic Cruisers lineup was *No Muss… No Fuss*. The underrated record was released January 30, 1985. But it was written and recorded in the fourth quarter of 1983.

Fortune 410, 1983's keyboard-powered fourth album, had underperformed.

For the fifth Cruisers record, Avsec returned to a straightforward, stripped-down rock sound.

Mark had started working on the material in his apartment in Willoughby Hills — alluded to in the credits as "Jeree's West" — where he lived with his wife and newborn daughter, in the outer reaches of what could be considered the Cleveland area. In the fall, the growing Avsec clan bought a house in the 'burbs, midway between Cleveland and Akron.

Now Mark had some space to stretch out, and it looked like the band had a clear lane to make their fifth record.

They did not.

MARK: I wrote *No Muss… No Fuss* in the Twinsburg house – when I just moved in. I remember my unfinished basement.

Nine out of ten songs on the album are credited to Avsec-Iris. Far in the future, Danna Avsec, Mark's first daughter, would be the band's guest drummer from time to time. In this gestational period for the record, she was present more than the band.

MARK: She was extremely precocious as a child. She was into music, really early. When she was six months, a year old, she was already into it: She wanted to come into my studio and play stuff. She started lessons on the piano when she was five. All the guys knew her. She loved hanging out.

I hate to say it, but… my wife wanted children, so I wanted children. It was good for me. I'm certainly glad I had kids. But it was a lot of pressure. I was the only one making money. My wife wasn't working outside the home. And I wasn't making that much money as a working-class songwriter. I needed to make some money. It changed me. It changed things.

Here I am, 62 now. I feel like I'm just getting mature now. In another 3 years, I think I'd make a great dad.

I'll be honest: I don't know if I was the greatest father. I was there. I wasn't a bad father. I took her to lessons. I went to ballgames. But I was so consumed by music that I was not exactly *present*.

If you work a normal job, you come home, and you're there. But I was always like, "I eat what I kill." I remember being in amusement parks, thinking, "I've got to make money. Time is running out."

My brother's a great dad. His whole life is about his son. That's fantastic. That wasn't how I did it.

Different kinds of distractions were worming their way into the Cruisers' world. They affected the product. Making the first two albums, Mark felt like he was channeling magic. But the fifth record felt like *work*.

MARK: Then we were all pretty tired. I think Marty and Kevin were doing other things. By the time we got to "Injured [in the Game of Love]"… there was litigation. It impacted our career. And then the career was gone.

"INJURED"

MARK: *No Muss… No Fuss* – it was a slog at that point. The songs embarrassed me. They're just bad.

Avsec rightly believes "That's the Way Love Ought to Be," *from King Cool*, is the Cruisers' best overall performance. But he still thinks the song's lyrics were underbaked, and the glimmering tracks deserved a better song. Maybe it's a classic example of an artist being uniquely privy to perceived flaws in his own work — after all, John Lennon himself was dissatisfied with many Beatles classics.

But when the magnificent "Injured in the Game of Love" sputters, mid-verse, for a fleeting moment, you get a small taste of how Avsec feels when he talks about songs that, despite his best efforts, he could never quite hammer into shape. If *No Muss'* "Riding Thunder" isn't as good as "Ah! Leah!," it's not from a lack of effort.

MARK: Sometimes *effort* doesn't matter. My intensity was waning. It's magic. Magic. The gods. What's interesting about pop music is… these are pop songs. I don't know that much of pop music is going to last.

Lately, I've been listening to the *Time-Life* series and collections of the great popular music of the '60s and '70s and '80s. There's *magic* in those three minutes. It's not all effort. And sometimes magic is with you in the studio. And I would agree that "Leah" is a magical tune. But you can't do that all the time. The gods smile on you somehow.

But later, the later albums — it's got to start with good song.

I was pretty burned out. The first album, I was really intent and full of energy. That was a labor of love. Second album was also very labor-of-love. The third album, by then, we had made a couple good records.

And we were already getting this learned helplessness, almost. We were like putzes, making these records. And the label just decide, "Ah, we're going to push something else."

For the second album in a row, Donnie — not Mark — was the turnpike cruiser. The singer drive from Beaver Falls to Cleveland, playing away games, logging long late-night sessions at the studio. Some nights he stayed in a hotel. Some nights, Mark returned the favor and let Donnie crash at this place.

Donnie doesn't love *No Muss... No Fuss*, but he definitely likes it more than Mark does.

DONNIE: It just amazes me that he can take a track, have me come in, and show me a sheet of paper with a lyric he has — it would take me months and months to come up with something like that.

And it never fails: He'll come in with something for me to sing. It's a gift. We never had that kind of thing with the Jaggerz — we had some good tunes, but it was *difficult*. With Mark, we won't take a piece of literature like that and say, "We're not going to do this."

We've always given everything a chance, and then listened to it. If it seemed stupid or we didn't like it, then and only then would we get rid of it. For the most part. They each become pretty much what we're hoping they should be.

There's always surprises. Certain things that we start out with can be canned. There's always surprises that come up during the session. Things come to you in moment. And you go for it, because it sounds good.

MARK: Fred Franchi and his crew did crew duties for Wild Cherry. He had a warehouse. So we rehearsed there for Donnie.

ALBRITTON: In later years, I commuted from Bloomington, Indiana, where my son & former wife lived. That's where I also lived when not on the road or recording, in order to be near, and spend time with, my young son.

When recording or coming in for meetings or pre-touring rehearsals in Cleveland, I was put up in a hotel most of the time. Although I do seem to remember staying at [road manager] Juice's house in Chagrin Falls for at least one or two nights during *No Muss... No Fuss*. But mostly hotels when the budget allowed — and my daily presence was required.

KEVIN: Marty and I had finished our housing empire by then.

MARK: I never liked Beachwood for our stuff.

DONNIE: When Jerry was gone... I enjoyed all the sessions. But without Jerry, all the sessions, it wasn't the same. Each guy brings his own vibe. We missed him. Then the *Poletown* sessions, back to Jeree's.

Mark, he was not happy [at Beachwood]. It was nice. Mark told me he could never could *hear* right in there. Something about the sound.

KEVIN: We did *No Muss* our normal, typical way, with or without options. Marty and I and Al went in and banged out basic tracks.

I think it sounded more Midwestern, more along the lines of John Cougar, a Midwestern rock and roll. I think some of the other albums sounded more East Coast, had more of a sonic imprint on them.

NO MUSS... NO FUSS, THE SONGS: "INJURED IN THE GAME OF LOVE"

The leadoff *No Muss... No Fuss* track is "Injured in the Game of Love." It's the a greatest hit that isn't on the best of album. *The Millennium Collection* compiles the most popular songs from the first four albums, when the Cruisers were signed MCA/Carousel. By the time *No Muss... No Fuss* was released, Donnie and the Cruisers had a new label. So "Injured" isn't eligible for the official best-of collection. But it's worthy.

In a parallel reality, Mark sold the song to Bon Jovi, and it was a giant hit for them. In this universe, however, "Injured" unjustly remains out of print — if you find it on YouTube, Mark suggests you find the audio and skip the official video.

It's an infectious feel-good tune with a monster hook that speaks a timeless rock and roll truth: Donnie declares, "I like girls / And rock and roll." Even without stacking 120 tracks, when Donnie's feeling fine, he's contagious.

DONNIE: I thought it was pretty much straightforward. I don't think we did tons and tons and tons of layering, like we did with the other ones. But we had some good songs on there, for sure. That one and *Poletown*.

MARK: A lot of our fans like "Injured." I just think it's stupid. I wrote it because I had to write it. I just think it's dumb. It's *dumb*.

I just gave up on it. In another alternative universe, I probably would have worked on it more, and if I couldn't have got it there, I would have thrown it away.

I hate it live, too. I don't like the song. We do it. But I don't like it. I don't like that whole album.

Most of the best songs, the songs I think are good, are on the best-of record. And then probably the rest of them aren't that good.

DONNIE: To him, if it's not a big song, a big hit, it's nothing.

I think it's a good song. I remember playing Stratocaster on that song, the lick at the beginning. The guitar lick would have been from Marty or Mark, but that's me playing at the beginning.

KEVIN: "Injured" I don't think it's to the level of "That's the Way." Mark has a harder job, because we provide him with the track, and he's got to make a really great track out of it. That takes a lot of energy.

I could see where he was not having that feeling at that time. So I'm sure he views some of those songs through those eyes. And that probably affected the outcome, too. It's hard doing this stuff, and it's harder if you're not fully into it.

When pressed Mark will reevaluate the song. But his opinion fluctuates wildly.

MARK: It could have been really great if I had hung with it. But under that reasoning, anything would be almost a great song – if the lyrics were different, if the music was 40% better, etc.

I don't think it's a great song, but that's just me.

I think it was 50% there.

"That's the Way" was 90% there.

"10TH STREET"

The second track on *No Muss... No Fuss* is a last look at the *American Graffiti* world Donnie lived in when he was young, living for weekends, driving around, listening to the radio, and looking for fun. It pulls characters and landmarks from Donnie the Ellwood City of Yesteryear, like Lou's bar and 10th Street, the neighborhood that surrounded it.

This look at Ellwood City is an idealized version where Donnie and his guys were always at the heart of the action, everything was simple, good times were had, and nobody got hurt. The tune dovetails into "Ridin' Thunder," a midtempo cruising tune. The one-two punch is an upbeat depiction of the fading old-school USA, a time and place that was being torn down, thrown away, and paved over.

MARK: Donnie and I wrote that lyric together. We drew on the names of real people.

Maryanne was a cute little girl who worked at the studio. Nobody had a physical relationship with her. But she was cute. And I'd write her into the songs.

DONNIE: That was a real person, Pooch. Pooch De Fonde. He was a character from Ellwood City. He was that guy, driving around a '32 Ford Roaster, a souped-up old car. It was *gorgeous*. He's ride around town. That was Pooch. And Ricky, all these were just names we threw in. One or two of them were actual people.

That one happened. I went to school right across from where my house was, the West End School elementary. They tore the school down. My sister called me a week or two ago, and they tore down this house that was next to the school, to make room for more parking lot. It was a great house. We used to go steal tomatoes out of their garden. Now it's gone. And now they're talking about tearing down the Polish Club by my house. We used to go there as kids. All us kids would go, and they'd put on old cartoons. That's the way it goes: progress, I guess.

MARK: "God bless America" was just something to say, but we meant it. It was a character who believed in that kind of thing.

KEVIN: The personal thing that bothers me about that record, that's my fault: I wanted to have a bigger drum sound on that record.

I wanted to sound more like Bryan Adams from the Power Station. And could have joined that band, and I didn't do it. So I had a big bug up my ass where I suggested....

I'd read that some other people were taking drums and playing them through a speaker into a room, and then mic'ing the room. And I think it made the sound way worse. And that was my doing. You may not notice it, but I hear it.

Jeree's was a very live room, but small. Beachwood was a bigger room, but dead. If you listen to "10th Street" and all that, there's a lot of what I call "bullshit room sound."

"RIDIN' THUNDER"

No Muss starts strong: The Cruisers still play its first three songs in a typical show. In this cruising anthem, Mark's urban landscape starts to blur into Donnie's world.

DONNIE: I knew what the Flats was, the happenin' part of Cleveland. Like the South Side, but in Cleveland.

MARK: I didn't hang out in the Flats, because I was busy. But Donnie was aware of it. It was very popular. I was married. I had a kid. I was making records all the time, or I was staying home.

Bobby Jo was not real.

"YOU'RE MY SERENITY"

After the third track, the album drops into unfamiliar, erratic territory. Donnie and Mark try a little bit of everything. Avsec began this hybrid electronic/unplugged piece as a personal story.

The tune isn't slow enough to qualify as a ballad. It's largely synth-powered, with chirping keyboards and electronic drums. Then Avsec caps Albritton's live bass with a harmonica solo.

MARK: I may practice that more. I like to play it.

KEVIN: Is that a sweet song or what? Mark had his way with an "eggbeater" — a drum machine. I overdubbed real drums latter in the song. Albritton did play bass.

MARK: I sort of wrote it about the birth of my first daughter. She turned out to be a wonderful daughter.

DONNIE: When I sing in the studio or anywhere, I try to get across what his lyric is. It's coming from in here, inside. It's not just a vocal thing or me putting myself in Mark's shoes. It just comes out of me that way. I'm a very emotional guy. I find it inside; I can *feel* the lyric.

Sometimes, I get in the studio, and I try to hide what I'm feeling. But my eyes will swell up, and I start crying. I lose it. That's part of why I need to be with people I can trust in the studio. And maybe part of it comes from lack of confidence in certain things.

As *No Muss... No Fuss* goes on, the Cruisers have very little say about the songs — sometimes nothing. **The good:** The remainder of the songs are immaculate, state-of-the-art mid-'80s studio creations. **The ugly:** They're full of rote lyrics and subjects, covering the kind of thing a fella might write about if he *had* to fill a rock album, but was all out of things to say.

"L.O.V.E."

In "L.O.V.E." Donnie spells out "love."

"FOLLOW THAT CAR"

The track is the kind of peppy tune that plays over montages in '80s movies. It's another motivational anthem of a pop song, with lyrics like "Reach / For your star / You gotta believe." The album gradually drifts away from the Cruisers' rough-and-tumble Rustbelt tales, into the kind of slick keyboard pop that would fill Avsec's two Cellarful of Noise albums. Donnie rides along, and he's comfortable in the new mode.

DONNIE: None of that feels alien to me. I love all kinds of music. That's just not a good song. It's one of those things that doesn't really happen.

MARK: We wrote that for a movie. A movie was presented to us, *Spaceballs*, the Mel Brooks movie. The producers of the movie were looking for original songs. I received a script. I read the script. I wrote "Follow That Car" because there was a scene in the movie that it fit. We submitted it for use in the movie. But it was not in the movie.

"DON'T CRY BABY"

Donnie is free to cut loose for some of his best screaming, now that he doesn't have to record 60 vocal tracks for future stacking. The rest of the band chime in on sweet '50s-retro harmonies. It's the only Cruisers original not written by a member of the band. More on him later.

MARK: That's by Gary Jones. That was an outside writer. I think somebody in the band liked it, so I thought, "Let's just do it."

DONNIE: I don't remember that one.

I liked working without all the stacking, because doing that, it's so much less tedious. You just let it come out of you, don't worry about having to do it all those times.

"STATE OF THE HEART"

In this dance-rock track, Mark's keyboard is firmly in the spotlight — but when Marty steps in for an occasional lick, it's a blast from the darkness. It's so ready for a big dance floor and booming system that it was released as a 12" dance single, with some extra sonic *oommph* in a mix by James Gang bassist Dale Peters. With lyrics like "I'm a hopeless romantic," the song is also one of the few Cruisers songs that is clearly about Mark, not Donnie.

MARK: I don't know. I don't know. I wouldn't read into that too much. I don't know what the hell I am.

That period, for me…. This album, it disintegrated into the doldrums. It's not fun for me to talk about. The songs are crap. The music was crap. The business was crap. The money was crap. It was all coming apart. It just wasn't fun.

DONNIE: I thought it was OK.

MARK: I always write for Donnie. My job is to make him shine.

"HEADED FOR A BREAKDOWN"

Not for nothing does this title grace this song. Avsec has run out of lyrics. The band lean hard on Marty's riff, while Mark reaches deep for something to say, but comes up with "Whoa-oh / Yeah-ah / Oooh." Donnie chuckles about the lyrics that rhyme "physical attraction" and "reaction."

DONNIE: That's another one of those *menzamenz* kind of songs. It's a borderline song.

MARK: I can't even comment on this stuff. Ask the other guys. To me, it's not something that's interesting. To me what's interesting is that we went into the doldrums, found ourselves again, and got back together with Kevin. We came back. And now we're a really good band.

A couple more tracks in the can, and *No Muss… No Fuss* was done. But it wouldn't see the light of day for a long, long time

CHAPTER 39

The "Ah! Leah!" Lawsuit

January 1984. Donnie and Mark won their biggest battle. But it took a few years. And a lot of money.

1984 was practically The Year Without the Cruisers. But it was still an eventful, pivotal period in the band's continuous lifespan.

At the beginning of 1984, the *No Muss... No Fuss* album — the Cruisers' fifth record — was finished and ready for release. It stayed on the shelf for another year.

As the year started, the Cruisers' singer-songwriters finally saw the resolution of an expensive, draining ongoing legal issue that had ruthlessly hectored Donnie, Mark and the Belkins since the band broke big. The lawsuit rewired Mark's brain, and he never got over it. After 1984, nothing was ever the same for the band.

Donnie and the Cruisers' signature song became their greatest hassle. It diverted time, money and energy from the band — especially in 1983 and 1984, when the group could have used the resources to help reverse its flagging fortunes.

"Ah! Leah!" was the Cruisers' first single. It put the band on the map. It's their second-highest charting tune. It remains their best-known song. It gets the most airplay and streams, by far. And, in the end, they didn't make any money from it. None that they got to keep, anyway.

The painful, protracted legal proceedings shaped the band's art and commercial fortunes. The lawsuit certainly redirected Mark's life — and, hence, the Cruisers' career.

The lawsuit may have been a fatal blow to the Cruisers' career momentum. Or it might have stopped the band from being a short-lived '80s group and put the Cruisers on a path that made them a longrunning institution.

The lawsuit saw a heroic defense and another qualified victory, with an ironic resolution worthy of Hemingway.

It's hard to say how the "Ah! Leah!" lawsuit shaped the band's history. But one's thing for sure: Nothing brings out the vultures like success.

A BRIEF HISTORY OF "AH! LEAH!"

Mark and Donnie wrote "Ah! Leah!" in spring 1980, as the sessions for the group's first record were picking up steam.

Mark wrote the melody on a piano at his parents' house. He composed a set of lyrics about war, Russia, history, and Afghanistan.

The band recorded some great music, and Mark polished it to perfection.

Mark didn't like the lyrics, and he erased the vocals. Most of them. But he kept the Gregorian, stacked backing vocals, which sounded out a meaningless melody: "ahh/lee/aaahhh." And he kept a throwaway vocal, a reference to the repeating nature of history: "Here go again."

Then Donnie had an idea. The song could be about a girl. He once knew a girl named Leah....

So Mark wrote new lyrics. And the Cruisers were headed for the Top 40, with a layover in the studio to record some new vocals.

Late that spring, co-manager Mike Belkin and his employee, James Gang drummer Jimmy Fox, flew to Los Angeles, where they tried to interest major record labels in releasing the *Back on the Streets* album, which contained "Ah! Leah!" No label wanted it.

So "Ah! Leah!" was first released as a single in July 1980, on Midwest National Records, an independent label owned by co-managers Mike Belkin and Carl Maduri.

Over the summer of 1980, the single found a foothold on regional radio. The activity generated some label interest.

In October 1980, the Cruisers signed a production deal with Carousel Records, a label that had a deal to provide finished records to major-label MCA. MCA was a major label with an office in — among other places — Los Angeles.

MCA/Carousel re-released "Ah! Leah!" as a national single in November 1980. The song entered the *Billboard* Hot 100 singles chart at number 90, December 13, 1980.

The single sold over 214,000 copies by early February, 1981. It peaked at number 29 on the *Billboard* singles chart February 28, 1981.

Then things took a turn for the worse. And they stayed there.

THE CHARGES

In April 1981, a Michigan songwriter sued MCA, Donnie, Mark, and the Belkin-Maduri Organization, seeking a $2 million penalty for alleged copyright infringement.

The plaintiff claimed he had submitted a demo recording of his song "Here I Go Again" to MCA Records rep Rodney Lignum, in California, in spring 1980 — likely after the song was recorded, certainly months before MCA heard it. The plaintiff's song featured the phrase "Ahh. Here I go again."

MCA executive Lignum told the Associated Press, "There's absolutely no way Iris could have heard that tape." [39.1]

DONNIE: We couldn't believe it. We almost passed it off as something that was a nuisance.

But it kept developing.

It took a while for the thing to go into court. We hoped that would never happen, but it did. For a while, I didn't worry about it too much.

MARK: This is the kind of case that gets my blood boiling. That was a bad lawsuit. It never should have gone as far as it did. But the judge let it proceed beyond summary judgment.

Over the next few years, Donnie, Mark, MCA and the Belkin-Maduri Organization burned through money and time, traveling to Michigan and back.

Time and again, Donnie and Mark recounted the story and timeline of how the song came to be.

The Michigan contingent poured cash into musicologists who testified as expert witnesses, affirming that devious, hidden similarities existed between the two dissimilar songs.

DONNIE: It's not like he even had a lyric about somebody named Leah. I think maybe they saw something in the fact that his background vocals, from what I remember, his background vocals sang the same words, "Here we go again." It had nothing to do with "Leah," nothing except those words. It's ridiculous.

The Cruisers and company might have settled, made the matter go away by throwing $25,000 at the plaintiff and his lawyers. But settling was never a serious option. For Mark and Donnie, the lawsuit wasn't just a claim against the hit song; it was a claim against their character. The easy way out was not an option. They had written a great song. They were going to defend it.

DONNIE: *No. Huh-uh.* That wasn't going to happen. That was *not* a consideration. We knew what we did. We knew what we had. We knew it was just a pain in our ass… for a long time. It drained I-don't-know-how-many thousands of dollars, all the "Leah" money. We gave it to the lawyers, the expert witnesses, that kind of crap. But at least we didn't give it to those guys.

MARK: A lot of lawsuits are bad lawsuits, shakedowns.

I was dead opposed to paying anything. I knew I hadn't done anything wrong. More than anything else, I knew how the song was written, and I'd never heard their song.

COURTROOM DRAMA… AND COMEDY

After years of distractions, headaches, and lawyer fees, Donnie, Mark and their managers had a trial by jury, in Detroit, in 1984, after the band had wrapped *No Muss… No Fuss*. The final confrontation was an episode worthy of a Hollywood legal drama.

DONNIE: The jury was in Detroit. We were there a couple weeks. Oh, my God. It's something you don't want to go through. It's so unpleasant, the situation. Somebody thinks you stole something from somebody that cost him millions of dollars. It was more than unpleasant.

MARK: The lawyer was really going after Donnie, trying to push him around.

DONNIE: Mark always said we did well because of how I handled myself.

The jury liked me. I don't think they saw us as the kind of people who would actually rip someone off like that.

I just told it like it was: We wrote that song in my frickin' basement. And that's what I was trying to get across to them. I guess they felt that when the evidence was in — or lack of evidence.

Mark still brims with anger, face flushed red, at the memory of being grilled by "expert witness" musicologists who knew less about music than he did.

MARK: The whole thing made me mad. I felt like I was being raped by everybody in the process: lawyers, expert witnesses, everybody.

We heard the songs at the trial. They sounded nothing alike. There were a lot of songs called "Here I Go Again."

I hated it, the whole thing. I would do it differently today.

There was a piano in the courtroom. It was there for one of his music experts to demonstrate something.

I didn't appreciate how everybody was trying to control this case. Even though I wasn't a lawyer back then, I had this urge to really show that I wrote that song.

I know exactly how I wrote it: I was studying composition techniques with [jazz musician] Phil Rizzo at the time — he taught Josef Zawinul and Robert Lamm from Chicago and arranged for Stan Kenton. It's a simple song, but I wrote it based on composition techniques — transposition, reverse order: *da da da DA DA da*. I wrote the melody around certain things.

Now I'm on the stand. And they're asking me some questions. And I said to my lawyer, "Do you want me to show you what I'm talking about?" And I pointed at the piano.

My lawyer didn't even know what to say. And all of a sudden, they asked for a short recess.

There was a break in the action.

We came back, and that piano was gone.

I should have gotten up and gone to the piano and shown them how I wrote that song.

I really believe a big part of us winning was because the jury liked Donnie. He made them laugh. He's such a likable guy. The attorney was really trying to rough him up.

DONNIE: That attorney was questioning me hard. I nailed him good. It came down to the album cover, where I'm wearing the underwear.

He held the album cover up to the jury, and said, "What are you doing in this picture, in your underwear?" Trying to make me look bad.

That's when Jim Palmer, the pitcher for the Orioles, was in all these ads, TV ads, in his underwear. I said, off the cuff, "Jim Palmer did it!"

The jury cracked up. The place erupted.

The judge was banging the gavel, "Order! Order!"

He was trying to win the case for this kid. He was going after me hard.

It was like a boxing match. I don't think he landed anything on me. There was nothing to land.

We thought, all along, it was a stupid lawsuit. The way I looked at it was I was on the stand was: Just give honest answers.

I remember seeing him out in the hall, on a break. He said, "You got me on that one."

"Yeah, I kinda did."

The trial lasted ten days. It ended Thursday, Feb. 16. The six-person jury concluded that Donnie and Mark had no access to the plaintiff song. The trial completely exonerated the "Ah! Leah!" parties — Donnie, Mark, MCA, the Belkin-Maduri Organization — of any wrongdoing.

KEVIN: I never talked to Mike Belkin about anything. I wasn't a part. I heard what was going on. But I wasn't privy to a lot of that stuff. No one knows the story. I know nothing about the lawsuitThe dismissal removed any kind of asterisk from the Cruisers' record. It did eat into the band's all-time bottom line. They say it was worth it.

DONNIE: It wasn't that much money. We didn't *make* that much money.

It slowed us down a lot. Mark was probably the most affected of all of us. I think it affected his output and took his energy. All of us were, but Mark the most. His demeanor was different after. The rest of us were, too. Mark lives for the studio, lives for creating things, getting things done.

AVENGING ATTORNEY

Avsec didn't take a dark turn, turn to the bottle, or vent his frustration on his friends. But he definitely did not take it lightly.

MARTY: He was justifiably angry. He was irritated. They lost a lot of money, and there was lot of heartbreak. And it probably hurt their career. He said something to me at one point, like, "I'm going to make sure this doesn't happen to me again."

MARK: We won in a jury trial. However, it was a pyrrhic victory. The lawsuit cost about $150,000, which is way more than the song made. So I had my royalties recouped for many years.

And I overreacted: I went to law school. Anything worth doing is overdoing.

Before the questionable lawsuit, Mark Avsec was a mild-mannered and absent-minded songwriter. After the costly victory, he became an agent of legal vengeance: Mark Avsec, attorney at law, partner at Benesch, Friedlander, Coplan & Aronoff, LLP; vice-chair of the Innovations, Information Technology & Intellectual Property Practice Group.

MARK: I was motivated because of the lawsuit.

I said, "Never again."

I had this idea that I could defend other people enduring meritless infringement suits like I had endured.

What seemed like a bad thing at the time was actually a good thing.

As a lawyer, he has created educational videos about the frivolous legal application of musical knowledge. He travels the country, holding seminars for attorneys and judges, explaining how art and the law work.

MARK: I know now: That lawsuit never should have gone to trial. It was without merit: The songs sounded nothing the same. These sorts of litigations happen too much.

In fact, I just spoke to about 120 federal judges in San Francisco, about frivolous copyright infringement litigation. So now I've accomplished what I set out to do: educate future lawyers and federal judges about this topic, by teaching.

We won, but we lost because we had to pay our lawyers.

But it all turned out great, because I became a lawyer, and I am glad I did.

MARTY: He and Donnie carried a chip on their shoulders, and rightfully so. It was a motivating factor for Mark, without any doubt. That's the music biz.

MARK: So it is a cloud over your creative efforts.

When you go through a lawsuit, you feel unsettled, and it's emotional. Especially if you're being accused of something you did not do. It is a mixture of feeling that life is not fair, really being angered with the lawyers on the other side who were taking a shot – except this time middle-class people who could not afford it were footing the bill.

I always remember it. For certain clients I represent, I never forget it's personal to them.

It was an overarching concern. I'm sure even very successful songwriters like Pharrell felt the same way and Jimmy Page as well as they went through their lawsuits.

DONNIE: Although we were always trying to get better at everything — songwriting, producing, playing, singing, *everything* — the lawsuit was like a cloud blocking the sunshine.

Donnie Iris innocent in copyright lawsuit

Donnie Iris, Mark Avsec, the Belkin-Maduri Organization and MCA Records were found innocent in a music copyright infringement action by a six-person jury in Detroit.

the jury's finding that composing defendants, Iris Avsec, had no access Talkington's song before writing and recording "/ Leah!"

> I thought, and Mark
> also thought, that Mike would be
> able to handle the band's career —
> that's what we needed at that point.
> As far as records were concerned,
> we felt we could really handle
> anything we needed in the studio
> for ourselves.
>
> **~DONNIE IRIS**

Big Breakup: Leaving the Label

February 1984. With one multi-year lawsuit in the rearview mirror, Cruisers manager Mike Belkin rolls up his sleeves and navigates into another one.

In Fall 1983, the Cruisers had recorded their fifth album, *No Muss... No Fuss*. It doesn't come out this year.

Now the Cruisers have no record label — an assertion hotly contested by their record label, Carousel, who had signed Donnie Iris to a production deal in 1980.

MCA DROPS EVERYBODY

By the end of 1983, the Cruisers had released four albums for Carousel/MCA. And they had seen better days.

The first Donnie Iris album, *Back on the Streets*, was released in 1980. It spent 23 weeks on the *Billboard* 200 album chart, and peaked at number 57. It spawned two singles, one of which cracked the Top 40, landing at number 29.

The second album, *King Cool*, was released in 1981. It spent 31 weeks on the album chart, but peaked at number 84. It launched three singles. Two singles charted on top 100, and one broke the Top 40, peaking at number 25.

The third album, *The High and the Mighty*, was released in 1982. It spent a mere four weeks on the *Billboard* albums chart — barely — where it peaked at number 180. Of its two singles, only one cracked the top 100, and it peaked at number 57. Technical complications affected the band's creative output.

In April 1983, based on the Cruisers' downward trending numbers, co-manager Belkin was dissatisfied with Carousel/MCA's efforts on behalf of his client, the Cruisers. Belkin sent an offer via his partner, Carl Maduri, to Carousel president Rick Frio. Belkin didn't care for Frio, and had signed with him as a last resort. Maduri, however, was friendly with the Carousel president. Maduri conveyed Belkin's message: The Belkin-Maduri Organization wanted to buy out Donnie's contact. Frio declined.

Maduri warned him: One way or the other, Belkin planned to get Donnie out of the contract.

The Cruisers' fourth album, *Fortune 410*, was released in May 1983. It spent 12 weeks on the *Billboard* album chart. Its only single was accompanied by the band's first proper video in years. And it peaked at a relatively low number 64.

Over the course of 1983, MCA slashed its roster, reducing its number of acts from roughly 45 to 7, cutting the Cruisers in the process. MCA jettisoned dozens of also-ran acts and kept a handful of established superstars and bankable, hot young acts: Olivia Newton-John, Tom Petty & the Heartbreakers, Jimmy Buffett, Men Without Hats, Joe Ely, the Fixx and Musical Youth.

MCA President Irving Azoff would later tell *Billboard*, "We were looking for artists where we felt careers could be developed. We ran into a lot of situations with artists like Donnie Iris and B.E. Taylor who had records that made a little noise, but nothing more." (*Billboard* continued, somewhat contradictorily: "Azoff says the focus at MCA is on breaking acts rather than buying superstars.") [40.1]

In June 1983, Carousel informed Donnie and the Belkin-Maduri Organization it wanted to release a fifth album — even though it had no major label ready to produce, distribute and promote it. And the Carousel-Donnie-Belkin/Maduri Organization contract specified that Carousel must release Donnie's albums via a major label.

In September and October 1983, since Frio had exercised his option, Belkin requested — via lawyers — that Frio deliver $43,750 so the band can record its fifth album, later known as *No Muss... No Fuss*.

October 31, 1983, Donnie and the Cruisers had started recording *No Muss... No Fuss*.

And that is where we last witnessed the saga of the Cruisers' label lawsuit.

MCA'S GONE. AND NOW IT'S ON.

In November 1983, Belkin's lawyers advise Belkin that, in their opinion, Frio is in breach of contract [40.2], because he has not delivered money for recording, or connected the band with a new major label.

So Belkin sets into action a lawsuit that will formally end the band's relationship with Carousel and its president, Rick Frio.

BELKIN: He didn't follow the terms of the agreement. So I took him to court, sued him.

Ultimately, it was for breach of contract.

This was after [*Fortune 410*]. The problem was that he wasn't putting enough records into the stores, that he didn't promote the record the way he should have promoted it. It's not an easy thing.

I mean, you have to be a pain in the ass when you have a label. We had Sweet City Records. When you're dealing with a major, you have to be a pain in the ass and push it and say, "Look, you need to so-and-so, have a billboard."

You have to knock on the door all the time, "Why didn't you do this?" and "Why did you do that?"

You say 'What's happening? *Donnie Iris* is what's happening."

It's not an easy situation.

So that's part of the job of the manager's job to do, getting the artist out there to the public, getting the airplay. And the other big thing was getting the independent promoters. That was a big thing back then. It wasn't cheap. You had to hire these guys to go to radio stations. Rick didn't.

The lawsuit was a way to get him off his ass and live up to the contract.

In 1984, Belkin has a choice:

He can deliver *No Muss... No Fuss* — a solid record with three songs still in the set list — to Carousel... and hope the label makes something worthy happen to it.

Instead, Belkin keeps the album in the Midwest National vault. And he serves Frio papers instead.

BELKIN: I don't recall holding out an album, but it sounds like the kind of thing I would do.

After Maduri's friendly warning, the lawsuit does not catch Frio off-guard. During the discovery phase of legal proceedings, Frio will produce 671 pages of typed, double-spaced notes from related telephone conversations that took place from May 1983 through June 1985. During a 1987 deposition, Frio will admit he had compiled the notes via handwriting, dictation, and some tape-recorded conversations between him, Maduri, Belkin, Iris and possibly Azoff.

Eventually, Frio cross-complains, seeking damages arising from what Frio claims is a breach of contract. [40.3]

These developments put the Cruisers in a legal limbo. The band play very few shows in this period: around 20 performances between November 1983 and March 1985.

Donnie cools his heels and coaches his daughters' softball teams.

Mark writes and records the first Cellarful of Noise album.

Belkin shops Donnie, the Cruisers and *No Muss... No Fuss* to other record labels. With faltering chart performance and questionable legal status, Donnie is not an easy sell.

In November 1984, Belkin arranges a contract between Donnie and HME Records, a small label with distribution via CBS. But the lawsuit between the Belkin-Maduri Organization, Donnie and Carousel/Frio will not resolve for years. The label lawsuit lasts even longer than the "Ah! Leah!" suit.

As with the "Ah! Leah!" suit, neither side will settle. The lawsuit culminates in a trial.

BELKIN: That went to a jury. We spent a lot of time and money on that lawsuit, in California.

Belkin now says at the time, he was unaware of Maduri's tip-off.

BELKIN: Carl and I were friends. I sat with Carl at the trial. I don't think I would have sat with him if [I had known] he had done that.

The trial wraps in March 1988. Ensuing complications will take years to play out. The protracted affair is expensive, but isn't as draining as the "Ah! Leah!" lawsuit had been — not for the band, anyway.

BELKIN: As managers, we were paying for that. Prior to that, I had good luck with litigation. We had won a lawsuit for the James Gang, against ABC Records, some years before that. And it was quite a bit of money for the management company.

That was a successful lawsuit, but this one wasn't as big or successful. We didn't win the civil lawsuit.

Frio didn't win much — it was $5,000, something like that.

I've been in litigation that lasts a lot longer.

I felt that this was something that I had to do.

With the principal business of the lawsuit resolved, the Belkin-Maduri Organization's union dissolves by summer 1985. Belkin's autobiography, *Socks, Sports, Rock and Art*, says Belkin and Maduri "parted ways over [the] lawsuit with Carousel." [40.4]

The partnership — and friendship — between Belkin and Maduri was long, productive and harmonious. And now it's over.

BELKIN: After the Rick Frio thing, we decided to remain friends, but not be in business with one another, because we had different views on different topics. We split up the company. We had X amount of artists that were signed. And we divided them up.

Few in the Belkin-Maduri stable saw the split coming. With the principals of the business breaking up, their clients have to choose sides, like mature kids in a divorce.

Some of them make surprising choices.

Carl Maduri had signed the Cruisers.

Maduri had been the direct pipeline to record deals for Donnie, B.E. Taylor, and others.

Belkin felt Maduri and Frio's mutual Italian background helped bond the two. Donnie was also Italian. And he liked Frio.

Maduri had recognized Mark's talents. And banked on them. And given Mark opportunities, work and cash.

Maduri had been the first to back Donnie and Mark as leaders of a new band.

It seemed like an obvious choice: Donnie and Mark would probably go with Frio.

Belkin hadn't become the concert king of Cleveland by rolling over and taking losses. Things look bad. He makes his pitch anyway.

Mark and Donnie huddle up to talk about who they will choose to manage their respective careers: Maduri or Belkin.

B.E. Taylor chooses Maduri.

Michael Stanley stays with Belkin.

By the time Donnie and Mark talk, they have both already made their decision.

MARK: We touched bases. We both reached the same conclusion independently.

Bottom line for me: I thought it was in my — and my family's — best interests to throw in with Mike going forward. And I never regretted it. I have the closest relationship with Mike, and have for many, many years.

I had a relationship with Carl and Chris [Maduri]. I was not notified in advance of the divorce, and I think there was an assumption I would go with Carl. I had some personal reasons that drove things.

The most positive thing I could say is that Mike called me immediately and wanted to have lunch.

We spent several hours talking.

And the things I wanted, he said, "You got it."

Chris [Maduri] is a great guy, and we still see each other. Carl and I have not seen each other in years, but that's just because he lives in Florida. I still think of him fondly.

DONNIE: I thought, and Mark also thought, that Mike would be able to handle the band's *career* — that's what we needed at that point. As far as records were concerned, we felt we could really handle anything we needed in the studio for ourselves. We didn't really need Carl for that — or anybody else, for that matter.

But we needed somebody like Mike to handle the career and the affairs of the band. He had done it before. He was good at it. So that's why we went with Mike.

It never crossed my mind to go leave him.

I thought we'd be better off with him.

It was a tough decision. Because we had camaraderie with both guys. Everybody was behind us. It was a tough thing.

There were no hard feelings, not that I ever experienced. It was a great breakup, as far as I saw. It went very well, but it was a difficult thing, because he was such a good friend. It shocked the hell out of us. It was like a divorce. I don't know what caused it or any of that. I think we made the right decision. We're still buddies, all of us.

We never thought about changing managers or moving to Los Angeles.

We did when I was in the Jaggerz. We had Joe Rock as our manager. When things weren't going right, we went to California and found Don Kelley [the Wolfman Jack manager who had choreographed the Jaggerz showroom set]. For a while there, we were going back and forth between the two.

I think that did teach a lesson about loyalty. With Mike, I think we had a good team.

I think some things went wrong for us, as far as bad luck. But a lot of things went right for us. We had some good tunes. We were making good records. We had our stinkers, like everybody else does.

Donnie is comfortable where he is. In the short reorganization period, no suits sweep in from the coast and try to poach him. After sixteen years in the majors, he has learned it's better to be a top priority in a small shop than a low-priority prospect in a bigger stable.

BELKIN: I've been really lucky. Michael and Donnie and Mark are wonderful guys. They're a pleasure to do business with — and not even business, but just as family and friends.

Maduri carries on. He moves to Florida, where he founds the Oceana label, which distributes through BMG, the remains of the RCA music empire. He signs R&B and hard rock acts and buys a radio station, WLQY, that specializes in ethnic music. [40.5]

By spring 1985, even with the Carousel lawsuit looming, a new label is in place, and a record is ready to go.

Donnie and Mark have a firm alliance with Belkin, one that will last for decades, for the remainder of the Cruisers' career.

The Cruisers finally have a new label. The band, their management and label are unified and ready to go.

It's nice while it lasts.

> "I've been really lucky. Michael and Donnie and Mark are wonderful guys. They're a pleasure to do business with — and not even business, but just as family and friends.
>
> ~MIKE BELKIN

CHAPTER 41

The Saga of "She Don't Know Me"

"She Don't Know Me" is a real earworm, the kind of song that sticks in your head for hours once you've heard it. It's a dynamic vocal showcase, expertly engineered for big harmonies and bigger sing-alongs. The flexible composition is a good guitar song, and a catchy keyboard tune, and it has been both. It wasn't a giant single, but it sure made the rounds in hard rock circles in the early-mid 1980s. It's not a Cruisers song. Though the band recorded it. So did Bon Jovi. And LaFlavour, working under a different name. And the Grass Roots. And Sonny Geraci of the Outsiders and Climax. Mark wrote it.

With the time-burning "Ah! Leah!" lawsuit ending and the MCA lawsuit beginning, 1984 is a year of very little Cruisers activity. The band average less than one show a month. The *No Muss... No Fuss* tapes sit on the shelf, unreleased.

Mark notches a career high anyway.

While the Cruisers languish, the band's chief songwriter starts receiving unexpected paychecks from an old project he had all but forgotten.

January 21, 1984: A new rock band called Bon Jovi release their debut album, when the "Ah! Leah!" lawsuit is reaching its satisfying climax. Over the next four years, Bon Jovi will grow from hard-rock hopefuls into enduring superstars. In 2006, Vh1 will rank their "Livin' on a Prayer" the number 1 song of the 1980s. [41.1]

Bon Jovi have help laying that foundation: Their second single is a song called "She Don't Know Me," written by Mark Avsec. Over 30 years later, he's still the only person to write an original Bon Jovi tune with no credited input from the band.

Well, it's sort of an original tune. By the time "She Don't Know Me" lands on the now-platinum album, the song has already been recorded three times, once by the Cruisers, without Donnie. And the other two were also released on major-label albums.

In January 1984, Mercury Records releases Bon Jovi's self-titled debut album. When it takes off, it will spend 86 weeks the *Billboard* Top 200 album chart. (The album will be certified platinum in 1987.)

"Runaway" is its first single. The song spends 13 weeks on the singles chart and peaks at number 39 April 21, 1984.

"She Don't Know Me," the record's second and final single, follows in May. It spends 11 weeks on the singles chart. The song peaks at number 48, July 14, 1984, when the album is at number 53, on the way to a chart high of 43. The Cruisers connection goes largely unnoticed, but checks are on the way. For the previous three years, Avsec had assumed the song was a bust. And it was. On the way to the Hot 100, the song survived some dead-end roads.

MARK: I wrote it for Fair Warning. I was on the road with Donnie during our tour for the first album. And I was supposed to go back into the studio with LaFlavour — who later became the band Fair Warning — for an album. I was going to write the songs and produce the album. So I wrote this on the road in a hotel room.

I generally write music first, and that's what I did for this song. I don't think the lyric is anything to write home about, but it's a basic story of when you really have fallen for someone and that person does not know you exist. I felt that in my life. I think probably everyone has. [41.2]

FAIR WARNING (LAFLAVOUR, MK. II)

Fair Warning is the band previously — and currently — known as LaFlavour, the disco variety act that scored an international dance hit with the song "Mandolay," which Avsec wrote and produced for the Belkin-Maduri band. In Spring 1981, when the Jeree tape heads were still smoking from *King Cool,* Avsec reunited with them for a dramatic departure of a sophomore album. It's a solid slab of polite album-oriented rock, with all of Mark's trademark sounds: crunchy guitar, stacked vocals and even Donnie himself.

The Fair Warning chapter of LaFlavour's longrunning history shows how whimsical, arbitrary and capricious the music business can be. We rejoin LaFlavour in August 1980, just over two months after "Mandolay"'s six-month chart run ended.

STEVE NERVO, SINGER-DRUMMER OF LAFLAVOUR/FAIR WARNING: When we were still LaFlavour, we used to play in Ocean City Maryland, in a place called the Fontainebleau, in the Sheraton. It was right on the beach. It was a showroom. We'd play the whole month of May. We'd open the season. Then we'd come back and close the season, for the whole month of August.

We were there, and Maduri came down. He said they wanted to do a second album. They were going to go with MCA. And they wanted to change the name of the group, because all of a sudden, disco was taboo. Nobody wanted to hear it.

We went around and around and around with all these different names. And we had to pick one immediately, because they wanted to do this. So someone came up with the name Fair Warning.

We didn't really want to change the name or the music. But it wasn't up to us. We were already established. But they wanted more rock. That's how "She Don't Know Me" came to be. That second album was from Mark, too. That's how the whole thing switched.

MARK: Carl thought he'd done it with "Mandolay," maybe he could do it again. He was looking for acts to sign to MCA. He couldn't sign them to MCA as a disco thing.

At the time, my philosophy was, "I'll write more, work more — maybe something will happen. Make some money, make some music."

NERVO: All this stuff, we did it in the studio. We didn't bring in any tapes or anything. We created this stuff. He just talked us through it.

He said, "I'd like you to do this, this, this."

We did it.

It was a great working relationship. We figured, "This guy knows what he's doing."

It's like you're working with anybody: They have the product, you want to do well for them, so you do what you're told to do.

Mark's pretty laid back. He's not the kind of guy who came in grumpy and said, "I demand this!" and "That's not right!" He just came in. We joked around and had a good time. The stuff just flowed. It was great.

He would work with you through the whole thing. He's say, "This is what I'd like to hear, but if you have something better along those lines, do it, but this is what I'm thinking."

Avsec receives sole writing credit for all nine songs, but the band help.

When we did the "[Just Send an] S.O.S." tune on the Fair Warning album, I started out with the beat, and we built it from there, and other people had ideas. They wanted a more rock-type album.

It was weird, because "Mandolay" is what started the whole thing.

MARK: So I wrote a rock record. It wasn't really good. But it did have "She Don't Know Me" on it.

NERVO: The second album, we did it at Jeree's. Donnie was close by, so he'd come in a lot. Donnie was on both albums. He did background vocals.

We had bills to pay. I said, "We have to go back on the road — I'm going to lose my house." So Donnie helped finish the album while we were out on the road.

He's a nice guy. Really down-home. Super-talented. What a voice.

We didn't know what he'd be like. I was thinking "The Rapper." And I'm thinking, "OK, that was a big, big super hit for them. And it's cool, but I don't know if this guy's gonna be freaky or what."

He came in: no attitude, a regular guy, really cool guy. We joked around, laughed.

At Jeree, Don Garvin plays bass on "Just Send an S.O.S." With Mark and Donnie in the studio, the sessions deploy one of Mark's favorite tactics: stacking vocals.

NERVO: That was cool. I still do that. It was neat. Mark and Donnie were stack-crazy. We called them The Stackmasters. Some of our songs, like "She Don't Know Me" with the "ah-ah's" in the background. We'd do four-part harmonies. Then we'd go in and we'd double it. Then we'd double it again. And that's how you get that really fat sound. It sounded like a choir, but not a choir.

Mark was like a partner and a captain. It was his idea, but we were free to elaborate, jump in, opinionate. We were free to say whatever we want. It was always, "What do you think?"

You can probably hear Donnie the most on "When the Whistle Blows." I sing the lead on that. That was one of the songs they finished while we were on the road. Then they came in and added strings and winds and whatever. The really high part, *"When the whistle blows!"* — he's in there.

Mark simply pulls out a chair, sits down, and whips up a rock record. The sessions come together in short order, but he can't help turning the project into a full-blown Mark Avsec studio production, stacked tracks on hot wax. On the other side of the country, unbeknownst to Belkin-Maduri and everybody who counted at MCA, rock gods Van Halen title their fourth album *Fair Warning* and release it in April 1981.

Fair Warning's self-titled album is set for release in July 1981. MCA releases a sure-shot promo single with "She Don't Know Me" on both sides. [41.3]

MCA releases Fair Warning's *Fair Warning* in late August 1981. It's featured in company ads until September. And then it isn't. The band suddenly drop from MCA's "hot new faces" list — alongside Bad Manners, Joe Dolce, Terri Gibbs, Donnie Iris, and Klique [41.4] — to the label's pay-no-mind list. Before the Burgh bands, Fair Warning have been MCA'd.

NERVO: This is the story I heard, I don't know how factual it is: Maduri told us that MCA had a shakeup, from the VP on down. And that's the reason our project was shelved, and so was everybody else's from that time period.

MCA's death stroke to Fair Warning leaves a big scar on Mark. It's the kind of soul-bruising hit you can only take so many times.

MARK: I spent months making the Fair Warning Record. And then in two days, it was dead on arrival. It's like, "Well, great, I just wasted a thousand hours of my life."

I think I probably spend about a thousand hours, something like that, for each album.

There are like 8,700 hours in a year. If you are awake half that time, that's like 4,200 hours or something. So, all-in, I probably spent three to five solid years of my life just making records of one form or another — at least.

We were all just working our asses off. Nobody was making any money.

Fair Warning shake off the hit and revert to the LaFlavour name and act. They still do gangbusters on the nostalgia circuit. But that's another story.

For now, "She Don't Know Me" is dead and buried.

But somebody always knows where the bodies are buried.

THE GRASS ROOTS VERSION

In 1982, "She Don't Know Me" resurfaces as a flop single from the album *Power of the Night* by the Grass Roots, best known for 1967's top-ten single "Let's Live for Today." In the 1960s and '70s, the folk-rock band had a string of hits and two gold albums, under the guidance of Lou Adler, the music-biz hero who produced Carole King's *Tapestry* and the Mamas & the Papas' "California Dreaming." In 1982, the lineup reshuffles. They return to the scene, looking like refugees from Billy Joel's *Glass Houses* band, decked out in mullets and black button-down shirts.

Now they are under the charge of producer Evan Pace (whose other big credit for the year is Chubby Checker's comeback album *The Change Has Come,* with songwriting work R&B up-and-comer Jermaine Stewart) and Leon Tsilis (the MCA executive whose credits include work for Lynyrd Skynyrd, Wishbone Ash, Catholic Girls, and the *Conan the Barbarian* soundtrack). He needs a sound that reflects a measure of new hotness. The crew reach into the MCA vault, pull out "She Don't Know Me," record and release it. The single sinks, uncharting, without a trace.

THE PETER EMMETT VERSION

A year later, in 1983, the Cruisers record "She Don't Know Me" without Donnie. They're the backing band for Sonny Geraci. Maduri is guiding the ex-Outsiders/Climax singer through an attempt at a rockin' reboot, as the stylish Peter Emmett. That record doesn't take off, either. (Geraci will later perform as Grass Roots fill-in singer.) Mark has played the song for Donnie, who wasn't interested at all.

MARK: We never seriously worked on it.

Somebody somewhere else *has* seriously worked on it: Lennie Petze, a multitalented A&R legend and executive, who had worked with the Roundels, Aldo Nova and Cyndi Lauper. Petze has worked with some of the same labels as the Belkin-Maduri bands, and he knows the tune. It stuck with him.

MARK: So there's a good lesson in life: To get lucky, you've got to put yourself in a position to get lucky.

The Fair Warning album barely sees the light of day. Petze remembers "She Don't Know Me." He was with Epic, a record guy there, a respected guy. He had something to do with Wild Cherry.

He knew Tony Bongiovi [owner of the famous Power Station recording studio and noted producer of Bon Jovi, the Ramones, the Talking Heads, and numerous others] who was Bon Jovi's cousin. So he set it up. And when Jon was in there, recording their first record, Lenny suggested they record this song. Tony had respect for Lenny, so he listened.

GAIL PARENTEAU, PUBLICIST FOR TONY BONGIOVI: Tony was working with Columbia Records. They were in the studio a lot. They were developing Jon as an artist, trying to get him signed. Tony has something like 90 rejection letters. Petze came across the song. And he told Tony, "Here's a suggestion for your cousin."

Tony recorded it. He made a lot of recordings with Jon. But Columbia — it was Epic/Columbia back then — they never signed him. That was the extent of it. He never met Donnie Iris and the Cruisers.

But "She Don't Know Me" stays in the primordial Bon Jovi mix, even when Jon Bon Jovi signs to the Polygram label, who smell a single. He records a demo version in 1982, as John Bongiovi And The Wild Ones. Then the Bon Jovi band spit-shine it during the album sessions.

Once the song is a single, the label ponies up for a moderately ambitious video, a clip split between a narrative concept footage and performance, with most of the budget apparently spent on hairspray, denim and wind machines.

The band never include the single on any high-profile American greatest hits/best-of collections — but it does appear on *Hard & Hot (Best of Bon Jovi)*, a collection released exclusively in Australia in 1991.

In 2010, Jon Bon Jovi passes on a request to discuss the song. He has long felt the label twisted his arm into recording it. And it was the last time he used another writer's tune. But in 1995, the singer did discuss it in an interview with Gwyneth Paltrow, the star of a movie he acted in, *Moonlight and Valentino*:

PALTROW: Are there songs that you would rather kill yourself than have to play again?

BON JOVI: Everybody's got those skeletons.

PALTROW: Like what ones?

BON JOVI: Oh God! There was a song that a record company guy convinced me to do on our first album, called "She Don't Know Me," and it's the only song that I've ever recorded that I didn't write.

PALTROW: Wow.

BON JOVI: I did it because the guy said, "This is how you're going to get a record deal; you need a song like this." I said, "Oh Christ," and I did it. Never played the song live, hated it, and would rather be skinned alive than have to do it now. [41.5]

Bon Jovi lipsynced the song on *American Bandstand* in April 1984. [41.6] Then played it live in concert until 1986, shortly before the release of their ascension album, *Slippery When Wet*. The live version was sometimes the spot for a drum solo during the *7800° Fahrenheit* tour. [41.7]

Bon Jovi and the Cruisers will play together twice the next year, in 1985. (See the *No Muss… No Fuss* tour chapter for details.)

MARK: I was a shy guy. I didn't get to know those guys. They don't play the song now. It's not on any [major] compilations. I think I did mention it, and they were like… they just exchanged pleasantries.

By the time I talked to them about it, they were already a big thing, and I think their view was that they did me a favor by recording it. I remember talking to Tico, the drummer. But they wouldn't remember me now.

THE VERSIONS: HOW THEY STACK UP

For an expert ranking of the various versions: Glenn Ratner, webmaster of Parallel Time, the biggest Cruisers fan on the planet.

RATNER:

1. Peter Emmett. It's a great song that benefits from the Cruisers' sound. It has an energy the other versions don't have. Kevin really drives the song with his fills and transitions. The Avsec backing vocals are a nice counter to Geraci's good lead vocal. I once lobbied Mark to redo this with Donnie. But he wasn't interested.

2. Fair Warning. It's more simplistic, musically, than the Emmett version. And the lead vocal is pretty vanilla. But the production and background vocals are good. It sounds like the backing track is all synth-generated, so it misses the energy of the Emmett version.

3. Bon Jovi. Solid, but also missing some energy. Bon Jovi is a very good vocalist, though he's a bit reserved here. Good production, but other than the added breakdown in the middle, it's more basic musically than the Emmett version.

4. Grass Roots. This one doesn't do much for me. Nothing particularly gels here, and it's too fast, losing some of its impact.

MARK: I'm grateful [Bon Jovi] recorded it. They didn't need to. In retrospect, they probably wish they didn't. It wasn't that big a hit for them. And they became a huge band.

It's not like I made a bunch of money off it. I really don't. I made a little when I was in law school — it was "help pay the rent" money. It definitely wasn't just beer money. It helped support my family when it was first out. But that dwindles out.

NERVO: They ended up giving that song to Bon Jovi. And the rest is history with him. We never made any money on it, because we didn't write it.

MARK: I didn't know they were going to use it, either. We were in Donnie, and somebody told me this band Bon Jovi recorded it. Nobody made a big deal about it. But all of a sudden, it was on the charts. I thought, "Oh, cool."

I do not, for one second, think that "She Don't Know Me" is the reason Bon Jovi blew up. Obviously not. It was a minor hit for them. *Slippery When Wet* cemented Bon Jovi's legacy and Jon Bon Jovi's stage presence.

NERVO: When they dropped us, I didn't know they were taking the song for Bon Jovi. I found out when I saw the video on MTV. That's like going to this restaurant and there's your wife, sitting there with somebody else, and nobody told you anything. There was nothing we could do. It was a time in my life when I really had a ball. It's what I always wanted to do. And thank the Lord that I had the opportunity. How many people can say they love what they do for a living? I can say I did that. I wouldn't change the outcome — we didn't get to reap the rewards, financially. But I had the opportunity.

> I think I probably spend about a thousand hours, something like that, for each album. There are like 8,700 hours in a year. If you are awake half that time, that's like 4,200 hours or something. So, all-in, I probably spent three to five solid years of my life just making records of one form or another — at least.
>
> **~DONNIE IRIS**

CHAPTER 42

Cellarful of Noise I

"DONNIE IRIS IS MY DAD"

The Cruisers barely played in 1984. Donnie and Mark kept busy anyway. Mark made a lot of music. Donnie hung out at home.

DONNIE: 1984, what the hell *was* I doing? With the lawsuits, I couldn't really do anything. I didn't have another vocation. I was OK, financially, to get through all of that. Not much was going on, musically. I was a dad.

I was hanging out with the kids, doing regular stuff any dad would normally be doing.

ERIN, DONNIE'S OLDER DAUGHTER: He played catch with us outside. I can't remember exactly how often he was gone, but you'd think he would have been on tour more often. I know my mom felt like he was away more than we did, because she was the one dealing with things at home.

ADDY, DONNIE'S YOUNGER DAUGHTER: He was a family guy. He coached our softball teams and was very involved with our activities.

DONNIE: I didn't sleep in all that much. I was up and around when they were going off to school. We ate together most of the time.

I was very laid back with the kids. My wife was the disciplinarian. Once in a while I had to put my foot down, but not very often. I never grounded them; my wife did that. I was the easy-going dad — as long as they were home at a certain time, and they were nice and polite.

ERIN: At that time, I remember feeling there was some tension in the house, but we were protected from it. He was never bitter or angry. Our parents told us more about it as we got older.

Our life was always normal. He enjoyed his music career, but there was no superstar stuff going on.

ADDY: We had Plymouth Horizons. Dad loves those. I remember someone saying, "Most rock stars pull up in a limo; Donnie Iris pulls up in a Plymo."

We were raised to not focus on material things. We always had what we needed. Being humble and simple was important to him. He didn't do music to have big things or to be famous or for the money. He did it for his love of doing it.

Nothing that has ever happened in his career has changed him, even a little bit. A question Erin and I get a lot is, "What was it like to be Donnie Iris' daughter?"

And the answer is: We didn't know there was anything different about it, because our lifestyle was always the same.

Nothing that has ever happened in his career has changed him, even a little bit. A question Erin and I get a lot is, "What was it like to be Donnie Iris' daughter?"

And the answer is: We didn't know there was anything different about us, because our lifestyle was always the simple and normal.

Even during those times, he never turned dark or bitter or anything thing. The thing I always say about my dad is: What you see, that's how it is: a nice guy who's always smiling. That's who he is. I've never heard him say a bad word about anybody, ever.

ERIN: One day, the Granati brothers called dad and said Eddie Van Halen was at the house. He went to meet him, and he brought us. That was one of those things where you did realize it's not normal, meeting Eddie Van Halen on the random day of the week.

My dad kept it really low key: "It's Eddie Van Halen, but he's just a regular guy." And that was great, to be able to go into school the next day and say, "Guess who *I* met?"

DONNIE: We were still doing gigs. We still spent a lot of time in Mark's house, in his basement, doing things in his little studio.

MARK GOES SOLO, WITH KEVIN: CELLARFUL OF NOISE

Cellarful of Noise, *Cellarful of Noise*

A solo album by Mark Avsec, with some of the Cruisers. Featuring...

"I'd Walk the Line" (Lyrics by Avsec)
"Can't Squeeze Blood From Rock" (Avsec)
"The Price of Love" (Avsec)
"Everyday I Fall in Love With Someone" (Avsec)
"You'll Never Break My Heart Again" (Avsec)

"Something Goin' On With Us" (Avsec)
"Heartwrecker" (Avsec)
"Easier Said Than Done" (Avsec)
"Gonna Act Like a Man" (Avsec)
"Can't Put a Leash On Love" (Avsec)

From the credits:
Produced and engineered by Kevin Valentine and Mark Avsec
Recorded and mixed in The Cellar, Twinsburg, Ohio
Mastered by Jack Skinner at Sterling Sound, NY
Mark Avsec: lead & background vocals, synthesizers, drum computer, and bass
Alan Greene: guitar
Kevin Valentine: (live) drums
All words and music by Avsec
CBS ASSOCIATED: BFZ 40134 / BL 40134
Never released on CD.
Out of Print.

With Cruisers locked in legal limbo, 1984 was a lean year. Donnie and the band didn't play a dozen shows. But true to form, Mark made it a productive year. Avsec and a couple Cruisers recorded the first, self-titled Cellarful of Noise album in 1984. It was released in 1985.

While *No Muss... No Fuss* sat on the shelf, Mark holed up in his basement and recorded a solo album that turned into a Cruisers side-project. Cellarful would release two major-label records and yield Mark and Donnie's final Hot 100 *Billboard* single. From one record to another, Cellarful would recruit many familiar faces.

The first Cellarful album is a fascinating, respectable and obscure rock record with a high-powered synth under the hood. It occupies a poignant, but tougher, middle ground somewhere between '80s singer-songwriters John Waite and Corey Hart.

Kevin Valentine gets a co-producer credit on the record. He plays live drums in his and Mark's final collaboration of the '80s. Former Breathless bandmate Alan Greene tops off the tracks, playing an insistent, flashy, yet melodic lead guitar. The credits list Mark as the man who did the rest.

The album proves that Mark could have been capable frontman — though he was never interested in that role. The project existed off and on for four years, but never played live.

MARK: I was feeling the pressure. The first Cellarful album, I thought, "I'd better do something." And that was all me throwing myself into that project.

We moved into a house in Twinsburg. The basement was pretty new. This was before I even built the studio. It was all block.

The basement connection doubled, with a reference to *A Cellarful of Noise*, the autobiography by Beatles manager Brian Epstein. Avsec remains a big Beatles fan.

MARK: I also recorded Cellarful with a Shure 57 mike and TASCAM eight track, an elementary drum machine and a couple of elementary keyboards. Maybe the Chroma, I think. I worked on that diligently throughout one summer.

The record picks up the personal, technically evolved sound from later *No Muss... No Fuss* tracks like "State of the Heart." But the project didn't begin manifesting in Mark's mind until the Cruisers album was done.

MARK: I would never work parallel. It was always one band, one project at a time. We were sort of on hiatus. There was some litigation more involving Donnie, because Donnie was the one who signed with the label.

I had this idea I was going to be a producer and produce other artists. I always thought I could do it again, better. My bona fides were there. We had been through some things.

I put a lot of work into Cellarful. I literally did that in my basement. That's a lot of effort.

I used to wake up every morning, scared, thinking about how to support my family. I was married. I just had a baby. And I had to get a house. It was a reasonable house. I took the basement, and it was going to be my personal studio. It was me in a basement with a sink, a hot water tank, and an eight-track recorder.

So I bought some gear for the studio down there. That was the eight-track tape. I set up everything. And I began to make the first Cellarful of Noise album. It was my job. I spent a whole six months just every day going down there, singing by myself, playing by myself, playing, just working on it all the time.

I was still really focused on music. I could never do that today. It was an intense effort.

That was made on very primitive gear. Very unsophisticated reverb gear and compression technology. I didn't even have a decent mic.

And when I got all the songs written and laid down, I asked Kevin to help me, because I didn't like the drum machine. So Kevin came in. He's got great ears, too. He played drums, electronic drums, on all of it.

And then Alan Greene came down and played some guitar. That album was a labor of love.

GREENE: He called me up and said, "I need some rock guitar over this." The tracks were there, but no vocals yet. I think Mark is a fine singer.

The first Cellarful album is worth a look and listen, even for fans who only like Donnie and the Cruisers' harder rock. The Peter Emmett record is a full-on Cruisers album without Donnie. But Cellarful is Mark, on his own, without Donnie, and without the Cruisers sound. It's a rare glance at the guy who wrote and co-wrote the majority of the Cruisers songbook. When Mark isn't channeling Donnie's voice and repurposing stories from Ellwood City, he has a serious romantic streak. In tracks like "Heartwrecker" and "I'd Walk the Line," there's whole lot of unrequited yearning going on.

The songwriter behind the authorial voice of *Donnie Iris* was a married husband and father, but he was still plugged in to his feelings. On the first Cellarful album, Avsec expresses an adventurous, imagined parallel life. He writes using the curious dialect of '80s popular culture, topping the tracks with lyrics like "When we make love..." Donnie says the songs were a window into the mind of a friend he loves, but doesn't entirely understand.

DONNIE: I don't know what was going on in his head. I don't know if he wanted something else. But possibly he was thinking about it. You're out there [on the road], you see all these things and these people.

I don't know if [Mark's first wife] got him, or if anybody can understand a guy like Mark. Me, it's easy. I'm easily understood. He's a hard guy to understand anyway. I can imagine a guy like he is, as smart as he is, as dedicated as he is... I can understand how a chick would have a hard time getting him.

The lyrics don't read like a record written by a family guy. As a lyricist, Mark comes off as a romantic Walter Mitty. The guy in the songs spins detailed scenarios about passionate, exotic affairs. And, to Mark's credit: Unlike many an artist, after he became a father, he never started writing sappy lyrics about his kids and the miracle of fatherhood.

MARK: All the songs about love and longing on Cellarful of Noise, etc. – well, there was something going on there. I didn't *do* anything. I wrote about it.

I admit I didn't write mature songs about family and things like that. I honestly should have been able to write better lyrics. I can come up with music all day long. But I'm not a frontman.

The album also marked a turning point in Kevin's career. Mark had always admired the drummer's sonic savvy. Now he let him take the wheel.

"I'm the artist working on the thing," Avsec told Cleveland Scene at the time. "And then he can come in there, and I really need his input and opinion." [42.1]

The album has aged well — better than second Cellarful record, which was more popular. But it's very much a record of its moment.

MARK: Technology drives a lot of the records. And I use that term loosely. You don't realize it when you're sitting in it. But ten years from now, when you hear all this pitch-corrected stuff, you're going to say, "Yeah, that was this era."

I got a keyboard called a Rhodes Chroma, made by Fender Rhodes. It's a very different sounding thing, And I got very turned on by it.

And you're influenced by what's on the radio. And you're reacting to it. And you're using keyboards that other people are using. So *somebody's* going to sound the same.

The trick is — Springsteen did a good job of it: *Born in the USA*, which was about that time, sounded *of* the time. And then he did things like "Dancing in the Dark," which is totally a drum machine. And the keyboard is a very '80s thing. But Springsteen still has a voice. So that song definitely is a Springsteen song. Maybe [the timely sound] is subconscious. Right now, I'm thinking of buying a new keyboard. And I'm sure it's going to affect future writing.

Cellarful also got Mark back on a major label, at a time when the Cruisers didn't have one. Belkin scored Mark a deal for an album, with an option for a second, at CBS Associated. The excellent CBS imprint was home to Ozzy Osbourne, Joan Jett, and the Fabulous Thunderbirds. And, for once, Mark's name was on a record contract.

BELKIN: Clive Davis was there at the time. And I had signed Michael [Stanley] to Clive's label.

The label put some money into the record. For all his constant self-deprecation, Mark has always been a stylish dresser. On the album sleeve, it's his turn to sport a dark take on *Miami Vice* '80s fashion: dark button down shirt, sprayed hair, sport coat. He had some help on that outfit.

MARK: Those were not my clothes. That was the one instance of them styling me. I was in New York for the photo shoot. They took one look at me, and they said, "We've got to style you."

So they took me out with some lady, a stylist. We went down to St. Mark's place, and she bought those clothes. That was the look at the time.

Cellarful kept Mark busy through the fall.

It gave Kevin something to do, too. But not enough.

CHAPTER 43

Albritton and Kevin Join The Innocent.
Big Cameo Here, Folks.

Since the Cruisers were idling, some of the other guys built their own vehicle, too: The Innocent was a short-lived AOR band that combined the talents of the Cruisers rhythm section, Cleveland all-stars, and one of the great musical figures to emerge in the following decade: Trent Reznor, the visionary behind Nine Inch Nails.

The Innocent's lineup overlapped with Cellarful: Alan Greene played guitar. And Albritton joined Kevin in the group.

The bandleader and mastermind was Rodney Psyka (offstage, Rodney Cajka), a Cleveland luminary who became a fixture with Michael Stanley, after playing with Breathless and the Iron City Houserockers. (He sang on two tracks from 1979's *Love's So Tough* album). He was also part of the extended Cruisers family, having recorded additional percussion on *No Muss*' "L.O.V.E." For a mercifully brief time, Psyka was the new band's namesake, too: The Innocent formed with the name Hot Rodney. [43.1]

GREENE: Rodney, he's been one of my favorite people since I met him. He's funny as hell. And he has a phenomenal work ethic. It's no accident that people tend to depend on him and dump responsibilities on him. I don't know of anyone who doesn't like or respect him. A very positive doer.

Psyka's partner was the group's principal keyboardist, Gary (Lee) Jones, a Cleveland mover and shaker who had worked with the Cruisers too: He wrote "Don't Cry Baby" from *No Muss... No Fuss* and "Why Can't She," the last track on the Peter Emmett album.

MARK: He was a nice guy. I liked the songs. He also ended up being a lawyer at Weston Hurd.

KEVIN: Gary and Rodney were friends. I only knew Gary a bit at that time. Gary got us the deal. I thought Gary was a good writer.

GREENE: It's sort of misleading to think of the Innocent as either Rodney *or* Gary's group. As close friends — both musically and socially — we strived to be equals in every way possible. With the exception of Trent, we all had worked with each other, previously, in one band or another. So the natural impulse was to share literally everything, right down to songwriting credits.

LIVIN' IN THE STREET

Having said this, I will tell you that Rodney, just by his nature, was the most instrumental in pushing things ahead, just by his drive to coordinate things and make them happen. Gary's songwriting and production skills, in addition to his longtime friendship with Rodney, were paramount in giving the band credibility. Also, it was Gary's connection that eventually got the band signed to a label.

The band scored a record deal with Chicago's Red Label, which would release the Chicago Bears Shufflin' Crew's "The Super Bowl Shuffle." The label offered Jones a steady gig as a staff writer and producer, to be their in-house, full-time Mark Avsec. So the band needed a replacement keyboardist.

To complete the live lineup, the Innocent drafted a young Pennsylvanian transplant who was just starting to make a name for himself in Cleveland: Trent Reznor, future mainman of Nine Inch Nails, one of the era-defining superstars of the 1990s. In coming years, he grew into a singer, songwriter, producer and Grammy-winning-composer. As of this writing, he is a Rock and Roll Hall of Fame nominee. At the time, he was just some kid with a good look.

MARK: Trent Reznor worked at a music store I used to shop at, PI. He was quiet. I didn't really know him. Nobody knew what was inside that boy.

ALBRITTON: Gary wasn't able to go on the road. So we hired this young blond, Trent Reznor, as the road keyboardist. Real young. He had the whole Depeche Mode look about him.

KEVIN: We went to see a band called The Urge. They were playing a big rock club in Painesville, something like that. The keyboard player was Trent.

Nobody knew who he was, but he had a presence about him. He had a single keyboard on a stand, but it pivoted. He'd be playing toward the band, but then, when it was time for his solo, he'd spin around and play toward the audience. We thought it was the coolest thing. He was good.

He had a persona and a stage presence — but *within* the band; he wasn't hot-dogging it for himself. He was going for it, and he had a visual take on things. He was aware how he looked.

His dad would walk around, following him with a video camera, the old-style big one you'd put on your shoulder. And Trent was always playing toward that camera. This was in the mid-'80s, when MTV and video were taking off. He was good, he was sharp, and we had a potential record deal.

He didn't live near us, so we didn't hang out. Alan and Rodney and I were from the same area, so Trent would drive in. We were old friends, and Trent was not. So we weren't operating with him on that level.

He didn't seem like a star in the making early on, because he was conforming to our bands. We thought he was a great keyboard player, and that's why we hired him. But we knew he was not a garden-variety keyboard player.

Later on, after he left the band, I would run into him downtown, when he was recording material for his first album. It was really different and special. He obviously made the right move, and he had that stuff in him, so playing with us was definitely not for Trent Reznor. And I think he realized the deal we had with Red Label was not MCA and it wasn't Atlantic. Trent quit right before we were to record. He saw the writing on the wall.

GREENE: The Red label had a lot of money and a lot of people behind them, suggesting that they could be a real national-level label.

Jones — not Reznor, contrary to numerous accounts — plays the keys on the album *Livin' in the Street*. Reznor is not on the record, but does appear on the album cover.

The Innocent represents the fashion lowpoint for all Cruisers-related projects: On the cover, the group look like the vampires from *The Lost Boys* robbed an Aqua Net truck, picked up some hair stylists, formed a metal band and went shopping at the Pants N' Nat rock department. They wear all-black outfits — aside from some gray accessories, a silver-studded belt and Albritton's vertically striped pants. The photo is set in a seedy alley. Sleeves hiked up, Reznor stares, looking mean, with the highest net hair volume of the group. (Left to right, the album cover features Kevin, Psyka, Albritton, Greene, and Reznor.)

Don't blame look on the group for the Goth N 'Nat look.

KEVIN: The record company decided the cover. They wanted to rename the band Shakers and Movers. Really, a corporate saying for a band name?

The curiously inappropriate cover photo in no way matches the music inside. *Livin' in the Street* is apex album-oriented rock. The songs are lively '80s bar fare about living in the streets and partying all night, each cut accented by keyboard flourishes. Some, you can dance to. More of them, you can pump your fist in the air. "Freeway Ride" sounds like Foreigner in a cheap leather jacket. The band are fine, but the record shows what a service Mark did for Albritton and Kevin by rescuing them from the genre's middle tier.

The Innocent

The Innocent made their live debut Saturday, April 27, 1985, at Cleveland club Monk-E-Bizness, a short-lived rock joint on East 200th St. The band lasted another year and a half, but didn't play much. [43.2]

KEVIN: The Innocent played and even practiced at Monk-E-Bizness club, which my brother owned. We also played another club in Painesville. So, yes, we did not play much. We did go out of town for three or so dates over a weekend, but left after the first night, because the payment was for all three nights and we thought it was per night. Fluster cluck!

The band wanted to do covers at that point, and play more, but I didn't. It was not what I wanted to do. I moved to L.A. a short time after.

MIKE OLSZEWSKI: The Innocent made little impact. Great musicians, but there was no real place to hear the music outside of clubs, and there was a lot of competition on the club level. Some college stations played them, but those were the days when big league radio was still the medium to break if you had a band.

The Innocent's only album was released in June 1985. Red Label distributed through Capitol Records, which didn't help make the group a household name in Cleveland or parts beyond. [43.3]

By then, the Cruisers' fifth album, *No Muss… No Fuss*, was out. When Albritton and Kevin recorded their parts for the Innocent album, they were Cruisers. When *Livin' in the Street* hit the street, they were not.

No Muss... No Fuss, Part II:
New Lineup for the *No Muss* Tour

January 1985. Donnie returns to the ring, still ranked as an all-time Pittsburgh great.

January 20, the *Pittsburgh Press*' Jim Davidson composed a list of the all-time ten musical figures from the Pittsburgh area. Donnie was one of two recent-vintage Top 40 artists, alongside crossover jazz sensation George Benson, a Hill District native best known for "Give Me the Night" and "Turn Your Love Around."

Alphabetically arranged, the list also included the Skyliners' Jimmy Beaumont, oldies crooner Lou Christie, Perry Como, '50s singer Jill Corey, World War II era singer Billy Eckstine, jazz singer Dakota Staton, Maxine Sullivan, and Bobby Vinton.

For Donnie, a boilerplate biography paragraph spoke about his career in the past tense, citing his "three moderate hits: 'Ah! Leah!' 'Love Is Like a Rock,' and 'My Girl.'" [44.1]

THE NEW DEAL

After a year of debilitating legal rigmarole, Belkin had shopped the Cruisers. And once again, only one label was interested in Donnie: H.M.E. Records, a CBS-distributed label that looked like it had a bright future. The new one-album contract even specified the label had to pay for "a promotional video suitable in all respects for use on Music Television and similar types of programming" — which, in four records, MCA/Carousel had never done without outside underwriting. [44.2]

BELKIN: That was the only offer. That's all there was.

Technically H.M.E. had been around since 1980, but 1985 was its only big year.

At the end of 1984, a *Cash Box* column devoted a blurb to H.M.E.'s rosy future: "H.M.E. Records has increased its staff and is preparing a regular monthly schedule of major releases as a result of its recent public offering. The CBS-distributed label will be releasing albums by Robin Clark, John Palumbo, Donnie Iris, and the Fabulous Thunderbirds after the first of the year, at which time it will, according to president Chuck Gregory [an industry marketing veteran], announce 'several major artists signing and special projects which are now in negotiation.'" [44.3]

H.M.E. did not. The Thunderbirds album was released via CBS Associated, but H.M.E. did manage to pick up Canadian dance crooner Gino Vanelli. Before folding, they also signed some fellow Cannucks, the speed metal also-rans Piledriver.

But for now, after a yearlong layover, the *No Muss... No Fuss* album was released, on H.M.E., January 30, 1985.

In the album credits, the Cruisers sincerely thank both factions of their fracturing management company:

"Thanks to Chris Maduri for your input and assistance in making this record.

Thanks to Carl Maduri for everything and all your years of support.

Thanks to Mike Belkin for pulling us through."

CHRIS MADURI: We worked the four albums on MCA, and then we did a label deal with a CBS custom label. And at that point, we phased out of it. During that, the Belkin-Maduri partnership started to break up.

So had the band.

After 1983, through 1984, the Cruisers downshifted from a steady paycheck to a part-time gig. And nobody in the band had a trust fund or rich wife to keep them afloat.

ALAN GREENE: We had a potential situation where, if the Innocent had succeeded, they could have been better off, like how Mark and Donnie wrote all the songs with their other band. They came aboard because they were friends — and musically, they liked us.

ALBRITTON: We lost the label deal. I think the band had run its course.

Kevin and I recorded our parts on the [Innocent] album when we were still with Donnie.

Then the [Innocent] label wanted to make moves, and Kevin and I wanted to continue to make a living.

The Cruisers' classic lineup played their last show together — for the time being — September 30, 1984, at the Star Theatre in Youngstown.

The lineup's last concert wasn't a big production, or a formal goodbye show. It was just another gig. When the show was over and everybody said bye, as far as they knew, everyone thought they would see each other again.

But after just under five years, the lineup that made the first five Cruisers record was done.

DONNIE: I understood. I wasn't bitter. If that's what they felt they had to do, God bless 'em. Hopefully, everything works out for everybody. I never felt anything bad for them.

ALBRITTON: I had always been a writer, always wanted to do my own music, my own albums. Up until David [Werner] and Donnie, I had always been satisfied to be in a group, part of a group, not my name out front — part of an entity where everybody would write and co-write and be part of this cohesive entity. In a supporting role.

Albritton and Kevin were gone, but they were still on the band's new album. And it was just getting out into the world.

The front cover once again just read DONNIE IRIS, with AND THE CRUISERS listed on the back. The cover photo is by Marcia Resnick, a New York City ace who had shot Andy Warhol, William Burroughs John Belushi and Mick Jagger. It's another simple but revealing photo, a close-up of Donnie's face, glasses on. He holds a lit cigarette, eyebrows furrowed at an ascending angle, like he's in on a joke that's not entirely funny.

NO MUSS, THE PRESS: REVIEWS

No Muss... No Fuss received a relative lot of reviews — albeit small ones. The better notices were neutral and noncommittal. At least *Rolling Stone* took notice.

"If this entire album were up to the standard of the opening cut ('Injured in the Game of Love') and the closing cut ('I Want You Back'), it would be a pop-rock gem," wrote James Henke. "Unfortunately, it's not." [44.4]

The *Pittsburgh Press*' Pete Bishop was warming up to Donnie, and he preferred side two: "The Cruisers themselves are becoming a very solid band.... Iris usually stays in his natural range rather than playing 'The Man of 1,000 Voices'.... His lyric themes often are the same as Bruce Springsteen's, although his imagery is less vivid, striking and poetic.... But the music on *No Muss... No Fuss*, a well-produced and well-performed LP, usually makes up for them." [44.5]

[In the 1980s, more than ever, local rock critics had five go-to moves when reviewing a band: **1)** Blast the group because it was playing in a style comparable to something the writer recognized. **2)** Criticize the act for updating its sound and playing a popular new style. Or **3)** blast the group for *not* updating its sound and playing a popular new style. And/or **4)** criticize the act for doing the same thing it always does (without citing the hot new style). Rock writers also **5)** specialized in comparing the band at hand to famous popular acts, without describing the similarities.]

Billboard remained loyal when it blurbed the record and its single. David Lee Roth's *Crazy From the Heat* was the spotlight review — but next to it, an anonymous paragraph called *No Muss* "ebullient power pop…. As with earlier albums, the main suit is urgent but good-humored, melodic rock." [44.6] Earlier, the magazine had called leadoff single "Injured" "brash, raucous pop [that] reintroduces the former Jaggerz leader as a male counterpart to Joan Jett." [44.7]

Cash Box was even skimpier on space, but generous — and optimistic — with praise: "Tremendous effort from hit maker Iris which could break his career wide open." [44.8]

Even Cleveland bemoaned the relative commercial shortcomings of the nebulous "Pittsburgh Sound." Donnie Iris beat reporter Anastasia Pantsios wrote, "Iris and Avsec have let up a little on the too-thick-to-slice density of some of their earlier productions." [44.9]

THE "INJURED IN THE GAME OF LOVE" VIDEO

Donnie's contract required the label pay for an MTV-worthy video. The Cruisers knew a pro they might get a friendly rate from.

Belkin opened his Rolodex and called Chuck Statler, the respected director who had shot the Cruisers' popular live clip for "Love Is Like a Rock."

STATLER: "Injured," I drew that storyboard. I plotted it out with Donnie. We talked about different scenarios. We had a telephone conversation, then we fleshed it out when we got together.

Then Belkin offered it to [Browns defensive tackle Bob] Golic, who was a big fan and friends with Belkin. Belkin offered it to him, and then he was in it. It's not a departure from the narrative of the song. It was the love triangle and the competition and the mismatch between this monster of a guy and Donnie, who was no match. That was the genesis of it. They scouted the location. They had given me some information about the elements that were available, and I proceeded to plot it out, with a storyboard.

Statler had directed Michael Stanley's "He Can't Love You" video, which was shot on film and better conveys his capabilities. The "Injured" clip was shot on video, and it does not look great in a third-generation copy posted on YouTube 22 years later.

STATLER: When we did the "Injured" video, Belkin hired me to produce and direct it, but it was really low-budget. It was maybe a quarter of the budget of Michael Stanley; it might have been less.

Belkin recruited some other big athletes for the promotional campaign.

Two of the history's greatest fighters were about to collide: Marvelous Marvin Hagler and Thomas "Hitman" Hearns were fast approaching an April matchup that was billed as The Fight. The two sluggers staged a photo shoot in Las Vegas in February, and Belkin slid Donnie between them for a quick photo opportunity.

Cleveland photographer Bob Farrell took great shots of Donnie dressed like Italian Stallion Rocky Balboa, in Everlast trunks, black-and-white gloves, and — of course — Fortune 410 glasses.

Three images from the shoot circulated: In one, Donnie mugs a scowl upward for a hovering camera. In the other two, Donnie is dressed for the ring, standing between Hagler and Hearns, each fighter in a suit. In the first pose, Donnie's fists are raised high, as if in victory. In the other, his dukes are up, and he's ready for a fight. [44.10]

Statler, his crew, and the remaining Cruisers shot the "Injured" video over one snow-stormy day in Cleveland, in spring 1985. Donnie brought his wife and kids along to Blade's Gym, a second-floor workout facility on Cleveland's West Side.

The "Injured in the Game of Love" video popped onto MTV the week of March 18, 1985. The

Hagler-Hearns photos appear at its beginning, as part of a newscast. Seated at his desk, a sports anchor delivers a story about a surprising development at a Hagler-Hearns press conference.

"It seems a young upstart named Donnie Iris stepped between the fighters and brashly challenged the winner," the anchor says. "This wiry would-be contender raised his gloved fist and shouted, 'Nobody can defeat me, because I simply cannot be hurt!'"

Then the action begins.

Just like Rocky, Donnie chugs a glass of raw eggs and hits the gym, wearing his Beaver Falls High sweatshirt and a borrowed Royalton starter jacket.

At the gym, Mark and Marty are suiting up in the dressing room. Donnie wistfully looks into his locker, at a glamour photo of a buxom, big-haired, Spandex-clad brunette. Then he hits the gym, where he works up a sweat and takes some lumps. Donnie suffers as a big, bad jock holds the lady's attention.

Half naked in the sauna, Mark and Marty sing along, as Donnie works one station after another. In the video's third act, the brute — played by the behemoth Golic — and Donnie square off in a boxing match. Belkin's driver, a gruff-looking but likable old hand named Angelo Crimi — plays Donnie's corner man. The size advantage proves insurmountable, and an injured Donnie has to settle with a massage from masseuse who isn't so cute.

The clip scored Donnie a couple blurbs in the Cleveland press. Nobody in Pittsburgh seemed to recognize the Brown.

MARK: Over the years, Donnie got into this Rocky thing. I don't know where that came from.

DONNIE: That was based on the movie. It made its way into the stage show. I'd jump around onstage. It fit.

The eggs were one of many unhappy memories from the "Injured" video. The song makes Mark uncomfortable, but he literally winces when he talks about the bargain video.

DONNIE: I think there were at least two [eggs in the glass]. We did probably three takes. So I drank at least six eggs, maybe nine.

ERIN: I was so worried about my dad drinking all those raw eggs.

MARK: Those videos were torture. We never had any good videos. None of the videos were well-made. They looked like television. I liked videos that looked like film. A lot of videos were just stupid. Let's be honest: It was just a fad. There was no point to them.

The video only features Donnie, Mark and Marty. Because at that point, there were only three Cruisers.

NO MUSS... NO FUSS: THE TOUR

Manager Mike Belkin booked a modest tour for *No Muss... No Fuss*: two dozen shows over the next four months. And now Mark, Marty, and Donnie needed two replacement Cruisers.

Open tryouts left them with bassist Scott Alan Williamson — sometimes known as Scott Williamson, more often known as Scott Alan. The new bassist was a Bostonian who attended famous conservatory Berklee College of Music. He had been playing with Humble Pie, and came highly recommended.

DONNIE: It was a decision from all of us. He was the best guy available. He did a nice job. He'd been around a while, and he played guitar, too. And he sang. We thought he'd be a good addition, and he was.

The new rhythm section brought a flashier rock-and-roll look — an early press picture featured the new bassist *and* drummer wearing bandanas around their neck. Williamson became a footnote in the band's history; drummer Tommy Rich was around longer. In Cruiser credits, Rich bills himself as "drummist" as a nod to his hero, Keith Moon.

MEET TOMMY RICH, THE NEW DRUMMER

MARK: Tommy is a great rock and roll drummer. When he auditioned, he got the gig, that was it. He's got a great rock and roll feel. Nobody plays "Injured" as well as Tommy. He's just got the right sloppy — *good* sloppy — feel for it.

Kevin, of course, is a brilliant drummer, all the way around. Each of our drummers had a song they could really play a great version of.

JOHN GORMAN, ex-WMMS: Tommy used to be in a popular Cleveland band American Noise, which we still play on oWOW today. When Rich joined the band, he was well-enough known to draw his American Noise fans over to Donnie Iris.

Born in 1954, Tommy is another Cleveland drummer. And another Beatles baby.

TOMMY SAYS:

I saw the Beatles, and it was all over. The world went from black-and-white to color. I was already aware of rock and roll. My parents were Hungarian immigrants. But my dad was hip to the news that his band was going to be on Ed Sullivan. And we watched that.

I sat between my dad and my mom, with the TV on, and each of them in my ears going, "Look at this crap! This is horrible! Look at that hair! These are a bunch of monkeys in the jungle screaming!" I'm just laser-focused, mostly on Ringo, like, "I'm going to do what *that* guy is doing. No if's, and's, or's, or but's."

He's underrated. He has a great sense of time. And the swing he puts into it. That generation of English drummers, they *swung*. And it's almost impossible to teach. And his fills, the way he plays. He's a left-handed person playing right-handed on a right-handed set — which, incidentally, so do I. It's the feel and the time. That's what, technically, makes him.

And his personality is in the playing. I've had the good fortune to be seven, eight feet away from him on his solo tours, watching him play. That's when you go, "Man, he really is as good as that."

Rich was never quite in sync with the Cruisers' creative chemistry — but he was certainly no slouch.

The high point of his previous career was a run with American Noise, a band that straddled '70s hard rock and the leaner AOR genre. The band had a record deal with Planet Records, an Elektra sub label. He wrote fan favorite "Statutory Sue."

Between tours of duty with the Cruisers, he absolutely crushed his kit on the album *Everybody Has One*, released on major label ATCO, by the Youngstown-area hair metal band Noisy Mama — who got their deal just in time be washed away by the grunge wave.

Since playing with the Cruisers, Rich has kept busy playing around Cleveland. His résumé includes Eric Carmen and the Burnt River Band. He produces, engineers, and plays bass, keyboards and guitar. And he teaches, leading the Cleveland School of Rock, which shows aspiring youth how to play lively tunes in a concert-worthy manner. His main original project is Rumbling Spires, a fun crew with diverse roots in metal punk and indie, which lets Rich flex his wild side. [44.11]

Tommy served two stints as a Cruiser: from 1985 to 1990, then 1994 through 2003 — though not constantly. He appears on 1992's *Out of the Blue* album, which featured old songs and new tunes culled from the doomed *Cruise Control* sessions. He plays on 1998's *Live at Nick's Fat City*, a best-of set recorded in 1997. And he's on 1999's *Together Alone*, which is technically a Donnie-and-Mark solo album, though Marty and Paul appear, too.

MARK: When Tommy got the gig, we went through a whole day or two of auditioning drummers. And we're polite people, so we budgeted an hour for each drummer to set up their kit, then run through three or four songs.

But as soon as they set up their kit and started playing, literally ten seconds into the song, everybody in the band had reached their conclusion. Because you're either a good drummer or a bad drummer. And it's not about what cymbals you hit or where the fills go or the fact that you copied Kevin's fills from "Do You Compute?" It's the space between the kick and the snare that is the feel.

Road manager Tom "Juice" Simpson called and invited Tommy to an audition. He brought a friend.

TOMMY: I loved Donnie from the minute I met him, at the audition.

I walk in there, and he's just hanging out, smoking a cigarette. He's got a black leather jacket on. And it's like running into a fellow rock-and-roller at the bar.

I sat behind the drums, playing at that audition. He turned around, and he was looking at me. I don't play to any of the other guys in the band — I play to the singer, exclusively. There was a connection, which is why I probably got the gig.

My friend, Dwight Krueger, played with Eric Carmen. We both auditioned, back to back.

Steve, this guy from Erie, auditioned right after us. He nailed it. He played every lick and everything Kevin had done on those records.

Dwight and I looked at each other and said goodnight.

"Let's get out of here. Let's go have some fun."

And we went out and got completely obliterated. So when Donnie called me the next morning, I had just gotten to bed. I told him to call me back several hours later, because I couldn't even speak. My brain was pea soup. Somehow I got the gig. I still don't know what they heard.

MARK: We auditioned drummers through Tommy. It took us ten seconds to realize, when he played "Injured in the Game of Love," that Tommy was a *rock and roll drummer*. And that was it, for all of us. Tommy got the gig.

THE *NO MUSS... NO FUSS* TOUR

February 1985. Tommy got the gig. And then Tommy was on the road, supporting *No Muss... No Fuss*, in the first Cruisers show without the original rhythm section.

TOMMY: The album was done. The first gigs I played was a run in March, opening for the Kinks; Hara Arena [in Dayton, Ohio], then Richfield [NBA arena the Coliseum].

I felt good, like I just made a lateral move to a band that had a stronger track record of hits than mine did.

They let me play the way I played. I would have had a hard time fitting the manic way I play into the way Kevin did those tracks.

The Cruisers Mk. II lineup made their hometown-ish debut in the Richfield/Akron Coliseum, March 14, 1985. The group opened for the Kinks, whose resurgence was fading — "Do It Again" was wonderful, but not as popular as "Come Dancing" from the previous album. The draw was down to a respectable 9,000 from 1983's crowd of 14,000. The *Plain Dealer*'s Jane Scott also found Donnie more agreeable since his rap had toned down and moved from "I Can't Hear You" to "Injured."

"The slight, wiry singer with black-rimmed glasses has a warmth, a humorous touch and an energy that wins as much as his strong voice... This was the Cruisers' second gig with new members Tommy Rich of Cleveland on drums and Scott Williamson of Boston on bass. There was a time or two when the band almost drowned him out, but Iris rallied with a rouser, 'Love Is Like a Rock.' It was the kind of show that made you wish your best friends were with you.'" [44.12]

The new lineup had a steep learning curve.

TOMMY: Being new, I looked at the set list, read a song, and saw the wrong song. So I start playing, and they looked at me like, "Mother—."

"Injured in the Game of Love" had gathered dust for a year, but it sounded fresh in the last good year for AOR. *No Muss'* first single was strong out of the box, for a minute. It wasn't on the Hot 100 yet, but it was on its way.

The tour really got going with an intimate club show in Cleveland. The small room was *not* a downgrade. The gig was a WMMS Coffee Break Concert, part of a series of daytime matinees broadcast on the city's premier FM station. The shows were a Cleveland institution, and the station welcomed quality bands big and small: INXS. Some new group called U2. John Mellencamp. Bryan Adams. The Fixx. Foghat. Breaker. Kenny Loggins (whose acoustic set helped inspire MTV's *Unplugged* series). [44.13] And — one Wednesday morning — Donnie Iris and the Cruisers.

TOMMY: So I'd been hittin with 'em about a month, counting rehearsals.

Playing, I felt more closely connected to Donnie, because I'm self-taught. I was uneducated — experienced, but just a complete feel-and-ear-player. And that's what Donnie is. I was playing with a guitarist who is obviously super-melodic. Marty knows his shit. Mark knows his shit. Scott was a Berklee type. But Donnie was just a pure rock-and-roller.

MARK: That was a big deal to me. Since you are young, you listen to the Coffee Break concerts. WMMS definitely was the Cleveland station that supported us the most.

MIKE OLSZEWSKI, *KING COOL* DOCUMENTARY: WMMS had some great music with live shows in the middle of the day, but for a lot of people it was like opening day for the Indians. You wanted to take off and be part of the event and have a few drinks instead of going to work.

This might sound crazy, but I don't believe a lot of folks in Northeast Ohio knew Donnie Iris and the Cruisers were based in Pittsburgh. That may have helped them — that football thing that runs deep. B.E Taylor was a great talent, but "Pittsburgh favorite B.E. Taylor" in an ad didn't help him.

Plus, the nod from WMMS meant a lot. If you had 100.7 in your corner playing your records and you were willing to do them favors — appearances, Coffee Breaks, on-air interviews, record premieres — they would look after you, too. You couldn't ignore "Ah! Leah!," "King Cool," "I Can't Hear You" and all the others, so stations like WGCL, WLYT and the rest played Donnie's records.

Audio recordings of the show still circulate in unofficial channels. It's standard best-of set, close to what you're likely to hear today, with three new tunes in the mix.

1. "Tough World"	6. "That's The Way Love Ought To Be"
2. "The Rapper"	7. "Ridin' Thunder"
3. "Do You Compute? "	8. "This Time It Must Be Love"
4. "Injured In The Game Of Love"	9. "Love Is Like A Rock"
5. "10th Street"	10. "Ah! Leah!"

The Coffee Break Concert was the first time Tommy got a full dose of Donnie:

TOMMY: It was packed, a pretty electric atmosphere. It amazed me. It was probably the first time I felt comfortable to just throw what I had out there. I was really blown away. Donnie sounded great.

I was listening to an old live "That's the Way Love Ought to Be," and I'm thinking "Damn, man — I wonder where that drummer's coming from. It has no *feel*. And it's rushed. And the drummer sounds like *shit*."

And then it gets to the breaks at the end. And there's only one drummer on the planet who does the breaks like that. And it's me. So I went back and listened again. "Oh, yeah. The Coffee Break Concert in Cleveland."

I'd only been in the band for a month. That half-explains it — the rest just being that I was a crappy drummer in those days. That wasn't an off night; that was an off *morning*.

Tommy has a critical ear; the set sounds good.

OLSZEWSKI: Donnie's Coffee Break Concert appearance had an energy level all its own. You could hear it on the radio. I think Donnie and the band fed off that energy, too, because you couldn't turn off the radio when they were on. They were that good.

THE PITTSBURGH-CLEVELAND RIVALRY (OR LACK THEREOF)

The Coffee Break Concert publicly aired the band's often-downplayed secret, which was well-known in Cleveland, yet never seemed to get much mention in Pittsburgh: Half the band was from Cleveland; Donnie Iris was the only Cruiser from the Burgh.

Aside from some genial ribbing about accents and sports franchises, the Pittsburgh-Cleveland feud was never a subject of contention for the Cruisers.

DONNIE: Cleveland, even today, we play there once or twice a year. The place is packed, and it's mayhem. They're great. I don't ever remember a bad gig in Pittsburgh or Cleveland.

Mark was from Cleveland. I was from Pittsburgh. Most of the people we picked up were from Cleveland or Erie. That *is* kind of odd: Most of the bands you hear are from Pittsburgh came *out of* Pittsburgh, the entire band. But not us.

We used to get together to watch the game. They'd come to my house when the Steelers-Browns games would be blacked out in Cleveland. The rivalry was *something*. The Steelers were winning all those games, for the most part. I basked in it, but I didn't want to get on Mike and Mark too hard.

Both cities are a lot alike. Cleveland is great right now, the basketball and the baseball. It's good for that city. I love it. I feel good for all my buddies who spent so many years getting beat down and hearing Cleveland jokes, left and right. It's a great city.

They're two similar towns. And, therefore, the people are very similar. Mark and I recognize that in each other. It's not like one of us came from Hollywood and had a totally different upbringing. We all came from the same blue-collar, hardworking type of town.

MARK: I'm not so provincial. I couldn't care less about the rivalry between the Steelers and the Browns. I don't waste my time with that. The Pittsburghers, they're just people. It's definitely a colorful culture that's kind of interesting. I don't know if we're that different.

We're all hardworking. They came out of the coal mines. We came out of factories. Same thing. We're all salt-of-the-earth people, for the most part. Working class people. You don't have a trust fund funding what you're doing. You're trying to make your own way. You're trying to be a little better off that what your parents were. I think it's very much the same in both cities.

Donnie will mock me because of the way I say, "Where did you park your car?" He'll say, "*Caaar!*"

MARTY: I moved from Erie to North Canton in 1994, with my amazing girls, my wife Cindy and my daughter Madison, converting from Pennsylvania residents to Ohio residents. We do sense a sort of straddle-the-fence unofficial dual citizenship.

We are diehard, lifelong Steelers fans, yet we live in Ohio, home of the Browns. And we root for the Cavs and Ohio State. Consequently, we have a lot of fun with our Ohio friends, who try to remain civil, if slightly confused.

KEVIN: My head got wrapped around music at a young age, so I wasn't a "*PITTSBURGH STEELERS SUCK!*" kind of guy. The rivalry didn't mean anything to me.

Something that was refreshing was: It seemed like in Cleveland, bands would bad-rap each other, say, "Oh, they suck!" In Pittsburgh and Erie, they were united behind these other bands. I said, "What is *this* about?!" But that's what they did. I certainly adopted that way of thinking. It was refreshing.

OLSZEWSKI: I have to believe that Clevelanders accepted Donnie and the Cruisers their own in part because Mark Avsec and Tommy Rich were local guys, but also because Donnie looked and acted like a blue-collar guy from your neighborhood. When Donnie and the Cruisers started getting play on early MTV it was like the band at your high school dance getting its big break. Another factor that drew us close to Donnie Iris and the band was the association with the Michael Stanley Band.

BELKIN: Donnie is to Pittsburgh what Michael Stanley is to Cleveland. I think the cities are very similar. I never looked at a Cleveland band and thought, "That wouldn't play in Pittsburgh."

After the Coffee Break concert, "Injured in the Game of Love" bound onto the *Billboard* Hot 100 singles chart, at number 93, March 23. It stayed on the chart for just one more week. WDVE gave "Injured" some airplay, but not much.

"INJURED" ON THE AIRWAVES. OR NOT.

JIMMY ROACH: After a certain point, I wasn't in a position to really play him. Nobody was really talking about him. So they just kind of played the old stuff and didn't acknowledge the new stuff.

The first album, you had "Ah! Leah!" You had "I Can't Hear You." You had "Agnes." And you had "That's the Way Love Ought to Be." Those four tunes stayed in what I would call a hot rotation forever. The other songs came and went — "Do You Compute?," stuff like that.

But those four songs stayed hot. They were not official singles.

When "Injured" went south, so did the band. The song peaked at number 91 March 30, but the tour kept going. In April, H.M.E. released "State of the Heart" b/w "You're My Serenity" as a single. It did not chart.

REALLY BIG SHOWS

April on the road was a blast, though. The band hit a string of Florida hot spots: Cocoa Beach, Tampa, Ft. Lauderdale, and Orlando.

TOMMY: There was some real fun stuff on that first little tour down in Florida. The bass player and I got into some crazy stuff, like roommates do. He was another troublemaker, like I was.

We got into some shit on the road. I think that got more nuts over time. That run in Florida was just the beginning. Some serious drunkage — but on a debauch scale, barely a 5. My touring with Noisy Mama in the '90s was way crazier, the hair band era.

I don't think Scott and I meshed well at all. He came from a jazz and prog-rock background. It didn't suit the kind of playing I did. We never played together too well, but we were two peas in a pod when it came to debauching.

As the tour went on, Tommy got a better grip on the music — and more appreciation for it.

TOMMY: Kevin's a super-fine player, great feel for the song. He played the right stuff. He meshed really well on the records.

I did the fills that I thought were iconic to the record, that I thought people wanted to hear. But those guys were happy with the way I chose to do the songs. And they said, "Yeah, we love what you're doing. You never play it the same way twice. Go ahead."

As I got into the nuts and bolts of the songs and had to learn them, I became more of a fan. The songs are great.

Donnie is so distinctive. The other thing I loved was playing with Marty. As soon as he plugs in the guitar and plays a note, you know it's Marty. His concept of leads and soloing was unique to him. He was super-musical, really lyrical. When the vocal stopped and the guitar starts, I'm always telling people *that* should be taking over — you shouldn't just be throwing a bunch of notes out there. Marty is super fine in that respect: great chord voicings, all that stuff.

In May 1985, the Cruisers staged a weeklong excursion through the Midwest, followed by some short bursts around the country. In Chicago, they hit the 1,400-capacity Vic Theatre. The crowd was huge at the Red Mile race track in Lexington, Kentucky. The harness racing track hosted bands like REO Speedwagon, Cheap Trick and 38 Special on the infield, and the Cruisers scored a plum gig: Headlining the WKQQ Memorial Stakes Day blowout, which drew over 22,000 fans to the venue. [44.14]

The *No Muss… No Fuss* tour essentially ended in mid-May. But come summer, Belkin added more gigs. And those were great shows.

DONNIE GOES HEAD TO HEAD WITH BON JOVI

In June, the Cruisers played two concerts with Bon Jovi, who were now on their second album, growing, and fast on their way toward headlining arenas. June 16, the bands were equally billed in a "star double header" at Youngstown's Star Theatre with "special guest" Bon Jovi. Bon Jovi opened, as they had three days earlier, on June 13 in Pittsburgh. [44.15]

JIM KRENN, ex-WDVE: The Syria Mosque, I worked there when I was just starting out. Rich Engler and Ed Traversari were nice enough to let me open for some bands. I go to this sold-out show. And *Bon Jovi* is Donnie's opening act.

I don't know who Bon Jovi is. And I'm watching them. And I'm telling you: They shook the walls. They tore the room apart. People are standing and screaming, sweating. They ripped the room apart. And I'm a performer, and since Donnie is one of my favorite acts of all time, I'm thinking, "Wow, *how is Donnie gonna follow this?!*"

And I'm not kidding: Donnie walked up like he owned the room.

He took it up another level, ripped it up. And Donnie blew *them* off the stage. He saw it, and he knew he had to take it up to the next gear. As I say: He's a national act, but he decided to live here. And I've seen that many times.

Donnie brought along the family for the concert — for local shows, he usually did.

ERIN: I remember doing the big hair — I wanted to look older. As a 15 year old, I wanted to look like I belonged there, like I was cool.

ADDY: Mum was telling me a story: Of course, there are older men at these shows — and these young girls from Erin's group, they looked prime. A big, burly guy grabbed Erin's friend's butt.

ERIN: Mom was beating on this big, burly man. She stopped in her tracks, turned around, and grabbed this guy. She was in his face, hitting him, shouting, "Don't you touch these girls!"

ADDY: Meeting all the other rock stars, that was great. Even as young as I was.

ERIN: It definitely added to my popularity at the time, to be able to say, "Do you want to come to my dad's concert? He's playing with Bon Jovi, and we get to meet him." I had several friends who came, and we watched the show from the side of the stage. We weren't in the crowd — he was very protective of us. Bon Jovi was just hanging out backstage. Dad introduced us to him. He was very friendly.

When Krenn says Donnie outrocked a well-received Bon Jovi, it's a true story.

In a review, The *Pittsburgh Press*' Pete B. King grudginlgy noted the crowd's enthusiasm. He mistakenly credited the 42-year-old singer for drawing the young crowd.

In his last major article about the Cruisers, the skeptical veteran critic sounds like he's going to snap if he has to hear one more "Ah." The critic didn't have a great grip on where he was or what he was witnessing.

"Judging from the crowd at the Syria Mosque last night, [Donnie's] audience has a median age of about 16, tops. Pre-teens abounded."

King interpreted the Cruisers' *American Graffiti* stories as a shameful attempt to pander to bobbysoxers in the crowd.

"Iris's rich voice bounded effortlessly from bass notes all the way up to his patented, treble shriek. But his voice, as well as his appealing stage presence, contended with weaknesses in other parts of the act…. Most of all, the songs struck me (admittedly a few years on the high side of 16) as relentlessly shallow. Musically, they have their moments…"

King also blasted "opening act Bon Jovi, whose second album is racing up the charts, dragged out every heavy metal cliché on the books — obligatory pouts, struts and innuendos with guitar and microphone stand in hand." [44.16]

A look at King's old review makes King Cool chuckle.

DONNIE: He wasn't too crazy about Bon Jovi either. By the way, the 16 year olds were there for Jon, not me! Peter wasn't able to figure that out.

And that was the end of the band's summer tour.

And that was the end of the band's last big tour.

TOMMY: At first, I was on a salary. Then there were not a ton of shows. We tried to do little jaunts.

That was quite a good time, but when things slowed down, and the road work was really grinding to a halt, we went off salary. I think Scott had a young kid, and we were less available when Donnie did come up with dates for us to play.

At least Donnie was easy to work with.

TOMMY: I loved Donnie, because of his personality: There is no other Donnie except that, the guy you meet. There's no phoniness, nothing fake. Everything about him, talking to him face-to-face, is the same as talking to him onstage. The stage persona is himself. He doesn't wear it like a hat. He is everything that I love about a real performer and a rock and roller. He was such a gas to work with.

I think that is rare — especially being the singer. The singers are the divas. He isn't that, and he never was that.

The band's July itinerary had just two penciled commitments — "STUDIO" and "DEPOSITIONS."

The Cruisers did squeeze in a couple good shows before the weather changed.

TOMMY: We played a one-off show. I think it was in Lorain, Ohio. The radio station was throwing a party for us. And we all — we had a few *medicines* before we hit the stage. We had a lot of medicine, actually.

That song "Riding Thunder" — we used to do a pretty long intro to it. So we start the intro, and Donnie sits down at the front of the drum riser. And he's got a Strat in his hands. And he's playing in rhythm. And I'm playing. The band's playing.

He's just moving his head back and forth, looking down, shaking his head. A couple minutes into this, he's not starting the song.

So while I'm still playing, I stand up and reach over with one stick and tap him on the shoulder.

I say, "DONNIE! What are you doing?"

And he looks back down, and he looks up, and he says, "I'm getting *into* it."

And I started laughing. I could barely play, I was laughing so hard. So he gets up, and very *slooowly* walks to the mic.

And we're *five minutes* into this one-chord intro by then. It was hilarious.

Marty's laughing his head off, and everybody's crying, we're laughing so hard.

The band returned to Blossom August 8, opening for former Babys frontman John Waite, whose solo career was going supernova. Jane Scott once again praised Donnie's skinny frame, high energy and energetic demeanor: "You could call it 'throb rock.' If the beat doesn't get you, the melody will hook you…. We all rocked the rafters with his 'Love Is Like a Rock.'" [44.17]

As always, the Cruisers didn't take time to lament their latest record's fate. They kept the band cruising. Or they tried.

> I did the best I could with it.
> And anything I do in life, I put my
> heart and soul in it. I'm sure
> while I was making it, I wasn't
> doing a half-assed thing.
>
> ~MARK AVSEC

CHAPTER 45

Cellarful of Noise, Part 1.5

1985. September. *No Muss... No Fuss* had a short shelf life and tour. Then Mark released *Cellarful of Noise*, the solo album he recorded a year earlier, after the *No Muss* album, with Kevin and former Breathless guitarist Alan Greene. Now the band's self-titled debut was out.

Rolling Stone noticed the record and gave it a review the size of two large thumb prints, a neutral three (of five) stars. Cleveland's *Plain Dealer* didn't review the disc, but reran the magazine's blurb: "This album is chockfull of pleasant Top 40 rock that draws equally from '60s-style pop and the more recent techno-pop," wrote James Henke. "The problem, though, is the LP's lyrics — a more clichéd set would be hard to find." [45.1]

The album's only single was the layered, poignant and kinetic "I'd Walk the Line," a repetitive earworm in which Mark trades vocals with himself, while his synth and Greene's guitar pulse in the background. The more danceable B-side "Something Goin' On With Us" didn't catch on either. With little airplay, less press and no live shows, the record didn't chart.

The record probably deserved a better shake, arriving in a radio landscape where synthesizer-oriented singer-songwriter Corey Hart scored two top-ten singles and two more top-thirty singles in the 12 months surrounding *Cellarful of Noise*. [45.2]

Slathered in digital reverb, Mark's synth-rock record lives in a curious midground, with no hardcore dance tracks or slow jams. There's not a bad song on the record, but ballad "You'll Never Break My Heart Again" was too sparse to catch on radio, nor was it a feel-good anthem. A fuming Mark spits, "There's a new me, baby / I'm telling you where it's at / And I'll never, ever hurt so bad again."

Even after legal hassles and frustrating record labels, Donnie and Mark never documented their frustration on Cruisers records. Donnie doesn't *do* mad. And when Mark feels righteous anger, he uses it as fuel. On the first Cellarful album, though, he felt like venting.

MARK: Personal stuff is where the songs came from.

Ultimately, it's an unfairly forgotten record — another one Mark poured sweat and hours into. But even he doesn't revisit to it.

MARK: I never listen to it. I wouldn't want to. I did the best I could with it. And anything I do in life, I put my heart and soul in it. I'm sure while I was making it, I wasn't doing a half-assed thing.

It's a situation where, when you're a writer and producer coming up... artists are at a disadvantage, because they're willing to do anything for their art, so they're underpaid. That's just the way it is. It doesn't take much to incent them. They're there doing it. So when you just throw it out there and nothing happens, the business people move on.

C.A.R.E.

Fortunately, as always, Mark and the guys had other things going on.

Avsec ended 1985 with another freelance philanthropic credit: He helped polish "The Eyes of the Children," a benefit record for USA for Africa, a "We Are The World"-style effort from C.A.R.E. (Cleveland Artists Recording for Ethiopia).

The record was collaboration by 40 Rustbelt all-stars, including Donnie, Michael Stanley, and Skip Martin and Kenny Pettus of the Dazz Band (the Cleveland funk band best known for the astounding *Billboard* R&B chart number 1 single "Let It Whip"). Half the proceeds went to USA for Africa, half to Cleveland Interchurch Council's Hunger Task Force. [45.3]

The song was written by Michael Stanley; Stanley band members Kevin Raleigh, Danny Powers and Bob Pelander; and Avsec.

MARK: I actually drove the chord changes for that song, I sculpted them out on the piano, with everyone surrounding me. Then Michael wrote the lyric and everyone had input. I went into this with a very collaborative mindset, as did everyone. I thought it turned out well.

CHAPTER 46

Lost Album Found:
Cruise Control / Out of the Blue

Out of the Blue The first CD release by Donnie Iris and the Cruisers. Featuring...

"Ah! Leah!" (Avsec, Ierace)
"Love Whispers" (Avsec, Ierace, Lee)
"That's the Way" (Love Oughta Be)
  (Avsec, Ierace)
"Injured in the Game of Love"
  (Avsec, Ierace)
"On Our Way to Paradise"
  (Avsec, Ierace, Lee)
"Be Still My Heart" (Avsec, Ierace)

"10th Street" (Avsec, Ierace)
"Stray Cat" (Avsec, Ierace, Lee)
"The Mad Siberian" (Avsec, Ierace, Lee)
"Ridin' Thunder" (Avsec, Ierace, Lee)
"Temptation" (Avsec, Ierace, Lee)
"Love Is Like a Rock" (Avsec, Ierace,
  Lee, McClain, Valentine)
"I Want You Back" (Avsec, Ierace)

From the credits:
Produced By Mark Avsec
Mastered At Frankford/Wayne By Rick Essig
Avsec, Ierace, Lee, McClain, Valentine; Bema (ASCAP)
Track 12
"Ah! Leah!", "Love Is Like A Rock", and "That's The Way
Love Ought To Be"
Courtesy Of MCA Records, Inc.
Thanks to Mike Belkin, Susan Anton, Joe Woronka, Jim
Markovich, Jerry Reed,
and for always being there, Linda, Lenora, Cindy, and
Mindy.
CD Release: DICD101 Seathru Records
Out of print.

Diehard Cruisers fans know the group recorded a legendary unreleased album that nobody but the band has heard. The legend is half true: The Cruisers did record an album — or most of an album — that they didn't release. At the time.

Fall 1985. The Cruisers ground to a half. The new lineup had hit the road, ready to take on the world and break *No Muss... No Fuss*, their fifth album and first for their new label, H.M.E. Only one single charted, and barely. So Donnie and Mark headed back to the lab.

MARK: We've got a whole album nobody's ever heard; it's called *Cruise Control*. It's not good. I've probably got it in my house somewhere. The sessions disintegrated. It wasn't fun anymore.

In 2012, Avsec told *Classic Rock* magazine that *Cruise Control* had never been released: "The songs were not up to scratch. I would actually oppose releasing that stuff."

Loyal fans who stayed with the band through the '90s know the songs.

Cruise Control is an unusual record from its origins to its sound. The new lineup was trying to learn how to work in the studio. The sessions and material didn't come together in one continuous slog. Mark started working on an ambitious track called "The Mad Siberian" early in the summer, at Marty's house in Erie. The band returned to the Beachwood Studio in Cleveland in July 1985, then went back in December. Carl Maduri III engineered the sessions. But he never fuel-injected Mark's soul the way Jerry had.

TOMMY: We went into the studio that summer, to cut another album. It never came out, except for bits and pieces, years later.

I think those guys were kind of poking and hoping at the time. The core group was still there. But I know they missed the input of Kevin and Albritton. They had a vibe going with those guys. They're hard to replace.

They were pretty much looking forward to a new beginning, from what I could tell. We were having fun and making some pretty explosive rock and roll. My sound was quite a bit different than Kevin's. And for maybe five minutes, they liked it.

It did feel like the band was sputtering. The writing starts with those guys. And those guys were struggling in terms of being inspired to come up with cool new songs or germs of songs that would blossom when you gave them to the band — and maybe they felt the same thing from the band, like, "You know, we've got these cool ideas for songs, and the band isn't giving anything back."

I didn't see any negative vibes or bad attitudes from them.

MARK: We just couldn't cut good tracks. The songs stank. We didn't have the budget. I was out of gas. I was burned out. I really hated the tracks. Tommy could *wail* in a major-label hair metal band. But the Cruisers didn't have another "She's So Wild" in them.

TOMMY: Mark was the producer, the bandleader. I wasn't really invited to that party, to the writing thing. I wasn't even around. I was just called in to cut a drum track.

DONNIE: We were going to stick together and keep playing as a band. I knew we were never going to get to the point where we were the Rolling Stones. But I knew we were all still wanting to stay together and play shows, and people were still going to want to see us. And I still feel that way: As long as people want to see us, no matter how old I am, we're gonna keep going out there.

Nobody talked about quitting. But Mark's spirit was clearly sagging.

DONNIE: Those sessions, that's like poison to him.

The rhythm tracks were *not* happening. Tommy was in the band. Scott was in the band. And I think the studio had something to do with it. Mark and I, working at the board, listening to the speakers, it didn't have the vibe.

We just kept forging ahead in hopes that something good would happen. It just didn't. It wasn't in the cards.

MARK: The studio at Beachwood, I did not like, really, for what I do. And then the songs were not great because of all of this. And it just was not what we do.

In December, Mark and Donnie hammered the tracks the best they could, until they couldn't hammer them any more.

The band took a break for the holidays.

And they never came back.

DONNIE: I could tell Mark wasn't real excited about it. But the way he is, he'll work until the wheels fall off. You could tell the happiness wasn't there. We all put everything we had into it. I'm pretty sure he felt, deep down inside, that because of everything that wasn't happening, this album wasn't going to do *anything* for us.

I don't remember one conversation saying we should quit. There was no real sit-down and soul-searching. We didn't say, "This is bullshit, we shouldn't be doing it." We finished up as best we could and checked it out, hoping for the best. We still went through with it, and made it sound as best as it could.

MARK: I can't remember whether we finished the album. It may have gone the distance and then petered out.

The story has changed over the years, regarding whether the Cruisers completed an album called *Cruise Control*.

In December '85, Donnie told the *Latrobe Bulletin* that the band had finished the album, complete with a cover photo: Donnie dressed as a mechanic, working on a car at Taylor's Pennzoil on Ross Hill, Patterson. The *Bulletin* paraphrased Donnie: "The album gets back to the straight-on rock 'n' roll of the Cruisers' first two albums."[46.1]

DONNIE: It ended up with nine or ten songs. But nothing happened. I don't think any of the songs ended up being played live.

MARK: There might be a cassette [of *Cruise Control*] somewhere. If I could find that tape, I would burn it. The album should never see the light of day.

But *Cruise Control* is also the most of unusual of Cruisers recordings: Once Mark decided to pull the plug on the album, he kept the tapes.

Cruise Control tracks did make it into the world.

THE TRUTH IS OUT THERE: *OUT OF THE BLUE*

Years later, a batch of *Cruise Control* tracks turned up on the Cruisers' 1992 album, *Out of the Blue*, undisclosed. After the Cruisers and MCA parted ways in 1984, MCA/Carousel had never issued any of the band's music on CD. So Belkin pulled together six of the band's better tracks for the Cruisers' longer-overdue compact disc debut:

Out of the Blue features two greatest hits: "Ah! Leah!" and "Love Is Like a Rock."

And one best-of: "That's the Way Love Ought to Be."

And three songs from HME Records' *No Muss... No Fuss*: "Injured in the Game of Love," "10th Street," and "I Want You Back."

GLENN RATNER, PARALLEL TIME FAN SITE : "I Want You Back" ends *No Muss* and I think it's a one frickin' great song.

But licensing those radio hits back from MCA/Carousel, who owned the recordings, was not cheap — hence a mere two singles and one deep cut from the first four albums. A CD single wasn't exactly a seductive offer. So Belkin decided to include six brand new, never-before-released Cruisers songs:

"Love Whispers"	"Stray Cat"
"On Our Way to Paradise"	"The Mad Siberian"
"Be Still My Heart"	"Temptation"

The album does not identify when the songs were recorded, where, or with whom. But the fall 1985 sessions produced the only complete recordings with Scott Williamson and Tommy Rich. And Williamson and Rich are the rhythm section listed for *Out of the Blue*'s new tracks.

The writing credits for the new songs are all equal, alphabetical splits for the three remaining original Cruisers: Avsec, Ierace, Lee.

The CD was released by Belkin, on his own Seathru Records, which kept LaFlavour and Avsec's "Mandolay" in print — the disco hit had *serious* staying power.

After the Cruise control sessions stalled, Belkin had shopped the record, with no interest. Now he did what he had to do to recover the investment of time and money.

Mark reluctantly carved out the usable tracks from the *Cruise Control* tapes, like he was scooping the green parts from a browning avocado.

MARK: Mike was putting this record together, and that was part of the *Cruise Control* sessions.

I hated that. Yes, I went along. But I hated it.

And there is most of the lost *Cruise Control* album, hiding in plain sight, as the new songs on *Out of the Blue*.

Mark put in some extra hours to polish the lackluster tracks.

The tracks from previous albums were not remastered for the digital release, which is an essential step for quality reissues. The physical vinyl format inherently has a deeper, more resonant low end than CDs.

But some digital Donnie was better than no digital Donnie.

OUT OF THE BLUE

And Donnie and the Cruisers finally had a CD. The new songs are a subdued set without a single real rocker. The tracks don't begin to gel with the high-energy classics. A bluesy vibe dominates the proceedings. It starts with Marty's leads in opening cut "Love Whispers." Then it continues in a lead saxophone — yes, lead saxophone — in "On Our Way to Paradise."

MARK: I don't even know at this point. We were trying to make a living at this stuff. We had some success. It was on a downward spiral. We were trying to somehow hang in there. And it was going to be impossible at that point; we were *past* it at that point.

They songs aren't terrible, but they're not very *Cruisers*. They all have their moments.

Donnie's high vocals in "Love Whispers" are as heroic as any single track he ever cut.

In "Paradise," the *Donnie Iris* authorial voice is dissipating. Mark's theological background creeps in as his poetic faculties falter: "You cannot walk before you crawl / Over and over, we must fall / On our way to paradise." And once again, Donnie sounds like he's singing lyrics by Mark — as opposed to Mark lyrics that expertly channel Donnie's persona.

"I Want You Back," from *No Muss...No Fuss*, also sounds like a Mark confession, not a Donnie story: "Maybe I spent too much time on my work / And maybe I left you all alone at home..."

"Temptation" is a heartland rocker from the intersection of Bryan Adams Street and John Cougar Avenue — at about 3 a.m., after the bars have closed.

Nothing new hits hard. Tommy is simply out of his element. Scott is never a real presence, even on the sudden smooth-funk flourishes of the awkward "Stray Cat."

It's a gleaming production, but all classic-style Cruisers content is conspicuously absent. No stacked vocals. No monster riffs. No stomping drums. No muscular-but-deft bass lines. At the height of the grunge era, the new tunes were echoes of the '80s, all electronic tones and spit-shined digital reverb. Most of the new songs sound like they should be playing in the background of a Bruce Willis comedy.

MARK: These were all throwaway stuff. I don't know. I don't care. They didn't have a vibe.

TOMMY: Lookin' at the *Blue* titles, I can only even remember five. Somewhere I have a cassette of all the tracks, and maybe there were one or two more. So, likely the whole finished thing was eight or so.

One song that didn't make it is "Dynaflow Love." Donnie only remembers it was an attempt at an "I love my car" anthem. Mark doesn't remember much more.

MARK: I think it sucked too.

The only *Out of the Blue* original the band have anything to say about is "The Mad Siberian." It's an oddly happy song ever about an infamous Russian mystic.

TOMMY: "The Mad Siberian" was originally called "The Mad Hungarian." I was dicking around with some groove, and the guys in the control room started playing along with it.

MARK: I was into *Nicholas and Alexandra*, that book [about the Russian czar and his wife]. I had had a teacher in freshman history or something, who really dwelled on that story. I read it and thought it was really interesting about Rasputin. We were in Erie, at Marty's house. We tried to write some tunes, and that's what came out of it.

DONNIE: Some of the songs are pretty good. There's nothing really, really good on there, but it's OK. I think we just wanted to give something new and get those other songs out on CD.

In the *All Music Guide to Rock*, faithful Cruisers fan Bret Adams gave *Out of the Blue* four of five stars, largely on the strength of Donnie's old tunes; the seven new songs go unremarked upon.[46.2]

MARK: *Out of the Blue*, I hated, hated, hated, *hated* — have I said "hated" enough? — that whole concept. I was never into the cheap stuff, like "Let's put out some stuff we licensed!" I mean, give me a break. "Leah" was on it, on CD, but it wasn't good.

DONNIE: Once in a while, you'll have something that doesn't work. We still wanted to keep recording and playing. It just wasn't our day, and wasn't our year. It was *not* happenin'.

> "My family is definitely my biggest thing. I feel I'm doing it not only for myself, but for my family. I want them to be comfortable spiritually and monetarily.
>
> ~ DONNIE IRIS

CHAPTER 47

"Succeeding at a Slower Pace."

1986. A record-setting year for the Cruisers. Not in a good way. The band played their fewest shows yet. Life was going on.

The Cruisers had regrouped with a new lineup. In the studio, they ran into insurmountable difficulties. But outside, the legend was growing. Rock radio kept Donnie in rotation. And now — even in smaller venues, playing fewer shows — Donnie Ierace began a transition from "Donnie Iris, local also-ran rocker" to "Donnie Iris, regional icon."

By 1986, Donnie had a 20-year history as a headliner in Pennsylvania and Ohio. He had given people reason to remember him. And, more important, he had never given fans any cause to rejoice in his diminishing fortunes. Donnie was quick to let go of the few show-business trappings he had ever put on.

But it wasn't a totally painless process. The year 1986 was humbling.

The band played under a dozen shows, but the scarcity made the events more of a commodity. The Cruisers' average per-gig payday held steady from the past few years. The band played more colleges and clubs than big-venue concerts.

A BRIEF REUNION

In May, the new Cruisers lineup played with sorely missed friends at Canton, Ohio's small Palace Theater. The opening act was the Innocent, featuring the former rhythm section of Albritton McClain and Kevin Valentine, in addition to Cellarful of Noise guitarist Alan Greene. Booze provided a social lubricant, and the after party got rowdy.

GREENE: That was a little awkward. Nobody *made* it awkward. Everybody was happy to see each other.

Albritton's a monster player, monster *monster* player, and a very complex personality. A very sweet guy. But if he was drunk, one of his other sides would become a little more dominant, shall we say?

In July, Donnie and the Cruisers played their biggest show of the year, in a supporting slot for a festival at Flint, Michigan's Proving Grounds. The band warmed up the stage for Rick Derringer, the Michael Stanley Band, and headliner Night Ranger.

The other big show for the summer was a headlining gig at the Lake County Fair, east of Cleveland, August 29. The Cruisers were the first rock band to earn the distinction. While fairs aren't the most prestigious gig, far bigger bands have kept their careers afloat playing the circuit.

MARK: At the beginning, the show was all structured and staged: Wear the yellow suit. I scripted the rap before "I Can't Hear You" for him. We put together this weird persona when he was 35, 36.

Then he went through that adult period, the middle-age period, and we didn't know *what* we were.

Then we went through this carnival/county fair period, where Donnie starts showing up like he was mowing the lawn. He dropped the persona, like, "I don't care about that anymore." And we just played.

Donnie with his daughters and some friends at Ricky Granati's home. (l-to-r): Addy, Donnie, Eddie Van Halen, Erin, Kim Palko, Ricky Granati

HOME LIFE

But Donnie always had been *Donnie*. At the end of 1985, he talked to a reporter in, as the writer described it, his "attractive brick-and-cedar home. The man who once appeared on stage wearing nothing but his briefs leads the life of a middle-class father." [47.1]

In '86, he spent a lot of time there.

"My family is definitely my biggest thing," Donnie said. "I feel I'm doing it not only for myself, but for my family. I want them to be comfortable spiritually and monetarily.

"It's not real important for me to be rich and famous. It used to be, but now I look at it more realistically. Things could be better, but they could be worse. I'm succeeding at a slow pace." [47.2]

DONNIE: I never thought it was over. We had something as a band, and as long as Marty and me and Mark as long as the three of us could stay together and keep doing things, I knew we could always go out and do nice gigs. Mike was still booking us in some really cool places.

Donnie had always lived within his means. The frugal approach came in handy when the Cruisers' concert scheduled dropped dramatically. In 1985 and 1986, the band didn't play a total of 30 concerts.

DONNIE: I never had a money issue. There were some leaner times than others. But I never felt, "What am I gonna *do*?!" I was able to sustain, making as much as I needed, doing whatever I needed to do.

Early on, when I was in the Jaggerz, a friend of my dad's, maybe in the late '60s, had told me to invest some money in stocks, stuff like that. I thought, "OK, I'll do it." I put away, I don't know how much it was, in stocks. Stocks like British Petroleum and Rockwell and Boeing, stuff like that. All good stuff; it wasn't cheap. I'm glad I did it, or I'd have been on the verge of going broke.

CHAPTER 48

Lipstick

1986. AOR was out, but hard rock was evolving. Mark plants a flag in big-hair radio-friendly pop rock. Then he walks away.

The Cruisers weren't doing much, but Donnie's creative partner was still making a mark on his local scene. Pittsburgh saw Donnie as the face of a monolithic organization. Mark's contributions were obscure in in the City of Champions. In Cleveland, Mark received more recognition for his role in Donnie's music.

Cleveland musicians knew Mark was the one who had crafted that crackling rock sound and propelled the Donnie Iris band onto 'MMS. The savvy ones wanted a piece of it. Avsec's experience producing Fair Warning and B.E. Taylor had been remarkably unrewarding, financially. So when groups asked him to produce, he would say no. Then he'd say no again. One band wore him down.

YVETTE "JET" WILLIAMS, FRONTWOMAN, LIPSTICK: I needed someone who was going to *produce*. And Mark was an achiever. I loved his songs. Our band wrote really good songs, and I knew Mark was the only guy in the region who could arrange our good, catchy tunes into something meaningful that would get them on the air.

Lipstick was a promising hard rock group with an all-woman front line. Jet could shred with the best metal axemen and write sharp pop hooks. The band was managed by Mitch Karczewski, a Cleveland promoter who spent his career trying to launch an all-woman band into the stratosphere. Lipstick were in it to win it.

MARK: She was bound and determined for me to produce Lipstick. I think I asked for like $1,000. They got the money. They hired me.

Mark listened to their set and made time to record a single with his two favorites: "I Want To Be With You Tonight" and "Put-In-Bay," the band's a contribution to a small genre: Ohio beach anthems.

MARK: She's a pretty badass guitarist. I thought she was talented. They wrote the songs. I recorded them.

The songs have the faintest whiff of that magical Mark Avsec touch.

MARK: I played the keys on that. I played the castanet on my [Yamaha] DX7. Jet and Donna [Coss-Bernsdorf, keyboards] wrote the songs, and I just added parts — I don't consider that *writing*.

JET: One of the great things about Mark is: He stays true to the song. He heard the emotion in the song and felt the vibe of the emotion in the band. We were young and full of hope and freedom. And he stayed true to that. He heard the song as a big orchestrated sound. He did his Mark-stacked vocals, stacked keys, and big analog sound all the way through it, and the raw guitars. Originally, there was a third verse. Mark took it out, and he was right. And what was really great was: Whatever creative idea I wanted in the song, he kept it.

He also kept the true nature of my voice at the time. I had a very young sounding yet powerful voice in my mid-twenties. He didn't try to fatten it up, or mature it, or enhance it, which is what any other producer would have done.

The A-side was on the radio in the fall: Fans made it a popular request on WMMS. The flagship rock station remembered it at end of the year, ranking the song number 88 in its top 100 singles of 1986.

Lipstick: From left: Lyndia Ferns, Yvette "Jet" Williams, Donna Coss

It received spins in Michigan and Pennsylvania, and made some national inroads on college radio. In time, it developed a cult following in England, Germany and China. Jet still receives occasional checks for the tune. After lineup shakeups, she rebooted as a solo bandleader, then made a run at the burgeoning rock scene in the Los Angeles Sunset strip. She fit in: The band the Sheilas snapped her up, and she started a new group called First Kiss.

JET: Mark changed my life forever. He gave me hope back then.

For her moment, Jet was very much the rock queen of Cleveland: not just a smokin' singer and guitar vixen, but a talented achiever who made the city stand up and take notice. Jet liked Mark as a producer. She liked Mark *a lot*.

JET: I hoped he would record our album, but he shied away from us after the initial song. I was heartbroken over it.

I never told him how much I was in love with him.

There was no way I would ever get involved with a married man. So I would just sit and stare at him in the studio and admire him from afar.

I thought I covered up my crush.

I guess he picked up on it.

CHAPTER 49

Rocking Lake Erie,
From the Rock Hall to Erie

June 1987. Donnie And The Cruisers helped consecrate the future site of the Rock And Roll Hall Of Fame and Museum. The band headlined Cleveland's Party in the Park, a prestigious, longrunning outdoor series outdoor summertime celebrations. On their week, the sprawling show doubled as a Rock Hall fundraiser. The concert was held where the lakeside shrine would be built in coming years.

That was a rare highlight in the second consecutive lean year for the Cruisers. This year, the band played fewer than a dozen shows. Now the college gigs were drying up. The itinerary for the year began at the Holiday Inn Metroplex in Ohio and ended at the Rainbows nightclub in Columbus.

One highlight of the year was WDVE's Charity Jam and Auction in Pittsburgh, a benefit for the United States Marine Corps' Toys for Tots program. That year, the lineup was the Violators, Jimmy Krenn, Hector in Paris, and B.E. Taylor with Rick Witkowski.[49.1]

In between Cleveland and the Burgh, Donnie and the Cruisers didn't play a lot of shows, but — as always — they played some good ones. Cruisers fan Stanley Crane recounted an epic Erie show for fan site Parallel Time:

CRANE: Donnie Iris and the Cruisers played the Peninsula Inn closing. The P.I. was a restaurant-bar at the entrance to Presque Isle, just below Waldameer Amusement Park. It was Erie's most popular summer nightspot when it operated, from 1983 to 1987. The back of the bar faced the lake and had a huge sandy beach. It was the only place in the state licensed to serve alcohol up to the water's edge, enabling customers to drink on the beach.

PI had seven bars in all, including two outdoors, plus a boardwalk. Live bands played four nights a week in summer, including local favorites Donnie Iris and the Cruisers. People lined up, waiting for the restaurant to close, then rushed in to drink and hear more lively music. On a typical weekend night, anywhere from 2,000 to 3,000 people might hang out at PI. By the time PI had become successful, a multi-tiered development plan for condos was under way. It was decided that on July 19th a huge blowout would be planned for the bar, then it would close.

Heavy traffic jammed Peninsula Drive. People parked up and down Peninsula Drive, way beyond West 12th Street, about a mile away, and all over Presque Isle, including the bike path. By late afternoon police wouldn't let cars through to Peninsula — it was too crowded.

A mighty bonfire roared, fueled by driftwood. Bands rocked all weekend long, including the Other Half, Character, Friction, and Donnie Iris and the Cruisers. An estimated crowd of more than 15,000 people visited the PI during the course of that last day and night. It was just so jammed. They made such a big deal about it, when it was going to close, on the radio stations in town.

With demolition looming, the P.I. served every last drop of beer, wine and liquor. Bottles of beer sold so quickly that some waitresses and bartenders upped the price to $10 to slow it down. Driftwood fueled the last bonfire initially, but when they ran out of booze, people started tossing in PI furniture and chunks of the boardwalk. I bet you could see the fire in Canada. The fire had to be 20 to 25 feet in diameter and at least twenty feet high.

It is still today the greatest Donnie Iris and the Cruisers show I have ever seen! Especially since I snuck up and assisted in setting up the equipment.

But that was the last big show of the year. And for the 1988, the itinerary was even shorter — for several good reasons.[49.2]

TOMMY: I don't think they ever ramped it back up in a major way. It became, "We're going to do a few dates here, a few dates there." It was more of a part-time thing in the year after I started with them.

It became, "We're going to get as much work as we can, and you're on your own the rest of the time, to do whatever you did." I had other bands I played with. I went back to my part-time job at the record store, Record Theatre.

We'd do a week here and a week there. And there would be paychecks again. Then nothing for a month and a half. Then there would be another week. I know they were trying.

NEW ALBUM? NO? *NO.*

After the soggy *Cruise Control* sessions, the Tommy-Scott lineup tried to record again. Like *Cruise Control*, it went nowhere. Unlike the previous sessions, it went nowhere *fast*.

TOMMY: In 1987, I moved to New York City. Donnie decided: Instead of going through the pain of getting another guy in, they'd fly me in — they were one-off shows.

I was really fried, and I had other work I needed to get back to. I came there, and I wasn't in a good attitude. And when you go into the studio, you have to be happy and loose to create.

Their style in the studio is, "We don't necessarily have a song. Let's create some grooves." And I wasn't vibing, and that was totally my fault. I don't think they got anything good. I was hearing what they were playing, and I'm like, "Eh, this isn't great."

It wasn't a great session. So I went back to New York.

Everybody was starting to search. Donnie was finding his way with his real estate gig. Marty was finding a day gig. Mark was going to school.

Donnie and Mark didn't pull the plug on the Cruisers. But the band's golden years were definitely over.

Fortunately, they had other things to do. Mark and Kevin had some big things brewing. And Donnie was in the mix.

CHAPTER 50

On Top of the World with Mason Ruffner: Rock Gods, Gypsy Blood and Angel Love

BOB DYLAN ON MASON RUFFNER, FROM *CHRONICLES: VOLUME ONE:*

> "Ruffner played in Bourbon Street clubs like the Old Absinthe Bar. He was a regional star, had a high pompadour, a gold tooth smile with a tiny guitar inlaid. He had a few records out and some explosive licks with funky edges, rockabilly tremolo-influenced, wrote songs, too, said that he'd hung around libraries reading Rimbaud and Baudelaire to get his language down."[50.1]

1987 was not a big year for Donnie Iris and the Cruisers. But a couple Cruisers logged some quality work that led to Mark's most prestigious placement as a working musician. Avsec could produce sophisticated pop rock. And he could write for bona fide guitar heroes.

First, Mark played a major role in shaping the sophomore album of Mason Ruffner, a blues guitarist, singer and rising star managed by Belkin. Ruffner's self-titled 1985 debut earned him a slot opening for Led Zeppelin's Jimmy Page. But he didn't quite break out, and Belkin decided he'd get the ace axe slinger some songwriting assistance.

MARK: One thing I'm proud of is that I pretty much worked with all of Mike's other artists over time — and they liked working with me.

Ruffner was living in Belkin's home. Mark invited Ruffner to his studio. Ruffner liked Avsec. They worked on demos. Ruffner gave the demos to Dave Edmunds, the album's producer, whose work from the period includes the Fabulous Thunderbirds, Nick Lowe, the Everly Brothers, and k.d. lang.[50.2]

Avsec didn't score any songwriting credits, but he helped lay the musical foundation.

MARK: I had a lot to do with Mason's album. I really pre-produced it: "Gypsy Blood" was a simple blues shuffle, and I arranged it into what it became, using a drum machine and playing the keys in my studio.

I arranged much of the first album. Mason and I spent weeks in my studio in Twinsburg, laying the foundation. Then it was decided that Dave Edmunds would produce in London. Edmunds came to Twinsburg to meet me. He listened to what we were doing in my studio, and he wanted me to bring all of my gear to London.

Instead, we rented the same-exact gear in London. And everything we had done in my studio at home, I re-recorded it there. And then musicians overlaid on top of it. And, of course, Mason did his guitar again and sang.

DANCING ON TOP OF THE WORLD, AT WTC SOUTH TOWER

The album complete, Belkin pulled off an ambitious video that, sadly, became an amazing relic: The band shot a video for the single, "Dancing on Top of the World," in New York City, on top of the World Trade Center's South Tower. As the band play, a helicopter zooms around — which was no small production, and was not cheap, even in 1987 dollars, with pre-9/11 air-traffic restrictions.

Ruffner needed a drummer after the album was recorded. Mark and Belkin knew a guy: Kevin Valentine. Ruffner liked him. A replacement keyboardist appears in the video; Avsec had to bow out of the high-profile gig. In his ongoing career as a sideman, it would happen again.

MARK: For "Dancing on Top of The World," we kept my drum machine and synth for the whole track, no live musicians, except for Mason's guitar. In the video, that's Kevin.

KEVIN: It was a very memorable experience.

We were up at 4:00 a.m.- ish, after playing the night before, because we needed to be off the top of the building before they started using the microwave dishes. The time frame is reversed: It looks like the video timeline ends at sunset, but that was actually sunrise.

The old elevator I am in is obviously from another building.

It was like being on top of the world.

Sun was coming up. View of the city: *pretty F'ing cool.*

There was railing around the top, so it felt safe. But there was the looming thought of the edge and the distance down to the ground.

Being in the video and being able to say to someone, "Check this video out!" is very cool and very sad. It is one of the coolest things I've done in my rock and roll life.

ROCKIN' MTV WITH THE BLUES

For a short but memorable time, Mark and Kevin reunited in Ruffner's live band. February 8, 1987, they played a nationally televised showcase for MTV.[50.3]

MARK: We did a short leg, down South. I played the MTV Mardi Gras special, with Steve Ray Vaughn and Dr. John and the Fabulous Thunderbirds. Played Bourbon Street with Mason, which was fun.

We played the Mississippi River Boat Queen. Dr. John was there. He was at the side of the stage while I was playing organ, checking me out when I played. I was enamored with him, but was too shy to actually talk to him. But if I met him today — hell we were all in the same room having dinner — I would try to grab him for about two hours to talk. He is the man. I have read *Under a Hoodoo Moon* a few times, the best and scariest autobiography of a musician I ever read. I am a student of Dr. John now — wish I was not so ignorant back then.

KEVIN: Stevie Ray Vaughn was playing that MTV show. And I was standing on his side of the stage, backstage. I could hear his amps, and it was like he was playing a show for me, basically solo. It was so good. That's one of those things you don't forget.

MARK: Mason wanted me to go out for the whole tour. But if I did not make enough money with our band, I surely was not going to make more money touring as an effective side man with Mason.

Mason understood that. Kevin stayed on with him for a bit.

I needed to find the next chapter of my life – and the law was calling me. So I had to get off the road and go back to school so I could support myself and my family in years to come. So that's what I did.

The gig was another bittersweet reminder that the music business is a rough place, where quality doesn't correlate with commercial success.

Rolling Stone mainstay David Fricke noted Mark's presence on the album: "Ruffner's producer on the album, Welsh rock-roots expert Dave Edmunds, gives the guitarist plenty of elbow room for his outlaw-blues tangents, heightening the singing and soloing with Mark Avsec's discreet keyboards with a crisp, airy studio resonance…. [*Gypsy Blood*] is irrefutable proof that Mason Ruffner is a guitar star waiting to happen."[50.4]

Ruffner has recorded just three more studio albums since. But he has worked steadily, gigging with Bob Dylan and others. As the Cruisers have learned: Acclaim and a good reputation don't pay the bills.

The *Gypsy Blood* album spent 16 weeks on the *Billboard* album chart, peaking at number 80.[50.5] The title track was a single, and peaked at number 11 on the *Billboard* Mainstream/Album Rock chart. Even with a spectacular video, "Dancing on Top of the World" peaked at number 42 on the Mainstream/Album Rock chart.[50.6] Neither cracked the Hot 100.

MARK: *Gypsy Blood* is the lesson that you can't make an album happen. The entire CBS label was behind that record, and they promoted it to all heaven, and it did not perform well.

KEVIN: Mason was a good guy, a Texas guy, a real performer. We played Jazz Fest, before Mardi Gras. It's just a perfect day, perfect weather, sunny, and you think, "It doesn't get better than this."

RATTLING AND HUMMING: OPENING FOR U2

It did get better than that. The band opened shows on one of history's great tours, U2's arrival party in support of *The Joshua Tree*.

KEVIN: Mason was just happy to be there. Overnight, he went from playing clubs in New Orleans to touring with bands like this.

U2 were really good, really something. We were playing arenas. It was great. We did what we could. It was like when you're opening for Kiss, like Mark and I did for Breathless: The crowd is only so interested in you. Basically, you're perhaps filling some extra seats. And you're allowing people that were late to get to their seats before U2 plays. But it was good. They were so good. Every night. They're one of those bands that gets your hair standing on end, just riles your emotions.

We didn't see much of U2. It wasn't a purposeful bad thing on their part, but we would never get a soundcheck. After soundcheck, Edge would stay up there and check his delays, because delay is such a big part of his sound. And he would use most of our soundcheck time. So we would hurry up there and get a line check to make sure all the mics and instruments were working.

We weren't having steak with Bono every night. You can't expect to. Maybe people think that, but when you're touring like that, you have very little time to spend together. Mason was spending a lot of time doing press. And the band members would maybe hang around together, like we'd hang out with Hall and Oates' band. But U2, there's four stars in that band, and they're all doing press. There's really no time to hang. You're ships passing in the night.

"ANGEL LOVE (COME FOR ME)"

MARK: Mason and I started to work on a second album for him, but Mason was not ready to record that. So it never happened.

Something happened later. Much later.

In that second set of sessions, in the early '90s, Avsec invited along Cellarful of Noise/Breathless guitarist Alan Greene. In his spare time, Greene was developing into one of Cleveland's top blues guitarists. The three collaborated on a track called "Come With Me."

Mason Ruffner and Mark Avsec

GREENE: Mark had told me he wanted to get behind me and do a blues collaboration. Mason was no part of it. It was recorded in Mark's basement during our free time. Originally, "Angel Love" had different, amateurish lyrics, thanks to me — and the fact that Mark was sweet enough to encourage me to write lyrics.

I have a cassette of the original version, but it wasn't yet titled "Angel Love." It was called "Too Much About Love," a wee bit more cynical than the uplifting lyric and title that Mason contributed. It was sung by a former bandmate of mine named Scott Dykstra, who I brought in.

When Mason heard the song, he really loved the music and asked us if we'd mind if he wrote his own lyrics to put to it. It was with those lyrics that Santana heard it and wanted to do it.

After the sessions with Avsec ended, Ruffner kept the song in his repertoire as "Angel Love (Come for Me)." Ruffner recorded it on his 1994 album, *Evolution*. The song's history didn't end there.

Ruffner's big fans include not only Bob Dylan, but Carlos Santana. Santana liked the song and recorded it during the sessions for his 1999 comeback album, *Supernatural*, which moved 15 million copies, making it the number 21-bestselling album of all time (as of August 2017).[50.7]

Santana did not use "Angel Love" on the smash album. But he played it in live sets. And when Sony released an expanded two-disc Legacy Edition of the blockbuster, the label not only included the song, but made it the single and shot a video for it.

The placement provided a random check for $300. By then, Mark had been in a new gig for well over a decade. And it paid better than being a musician and sometime-songwriter. So the payday wasn't the point.

MARK: If Carlos had put it out in 1999, I would have made a lot of money. It shows, in part, how digitization has changed the music industry. But when somebody like Santana records your song, it's worth more than money. He's a legend.

CHAPTER 51

Cellarful of Noise II

1988. The second Cellarful of Noise album is a small footnote in Donnie's overall career, but it's a significant one. A single from this now-obscure record marked the third time Donnie appeared on *Billboard*'s Hot 100 singles chart as part of a different act.

Among the reasons Mark couldn't spend more time with Ruffner, another modestly selling, highly acclaimed, MTV-bound artist: Mark was working on his own thing, a second solo album. And this time, Donnie was coming with him.

This time next year, Mark would be college student. Donnie would be a full-time, tie-wearing, golfing businessman.

But before the Cruisers backed the band into the garage, they hit one last high note to end this era.

Cellarful of Noise's 1985 self-titled debut barely happened, with no chart success, lackluster sales, and zero live shows. Despite the utterly unremarkable performance, the CBS Associated label surprised Mark by requesting a second album. By the time its sole single hit the airwaves, the Cruisers' label lawsuit was largely over. Mark and Donnie ended their first decade together with one last chart appearance.

The second Cellarful album took shape like the first one: Mark cobbled together the songs in his suburban basement — now officially listed as "The Cellar, Twinsburg Ohio." And then it turned into a full international production.

MARK: The guy who signed me, his name was Michael Kaplan. He was with CBS. I don't think he really was into it all that much. I really credit the deal to Mike Belkin.

Believe it or not, CBS picked up an option, and they wanted a second record. I don't know why they did, but they did.

I was really working on that stuff. I was trying my best to get something productive done.

I did the entire album MIDI. Then we went to England for two months. And I set it up exactly like my home studio by renting the exact same gear.

The first record featured Cruisers drummer Kevin Valentine. At the time, Mark had wanted to draw a clear line between the two bands. This time, he wasn't worried about it.

"I asked him if he wanted to be a part of this now that the Donnie & the Cruisers thing had pretty much run its course. We still enjoy being partners and still work well together…. So it was just an extension of what we always were doing. We just figured we'd keep it going. We're partners."[51.1]

Magnificent Obsession, the second Cellarful record, is a lean and mean nine-song affair.

1. "Samantha (What You Gonna Do?)"
   (Lyrics by Avsec)
2. "The Day Before They Dropped
   The Bomb" (Avsec)
3. "First Love" (Avsec)
4. "Heartzone" (Rodney Psyka,
   Alan Greene, and Gary Jones)
5. "Shake It Loose" (Avsec, Iris,
   M. L. Hoenes)
6. "Temper, Temper" (Avsec)
7. "Shuck and Jive" (Avsec)
8. "Women" (Avsec, Iris)
9. "Life After Love" (B. Burger)

From the credits:

Mark Avsec: All musical instruments. Lead and background vocals.

Donnie Iris: Lead and background vocals.

Special appearance by Marty Lee on "Women" and "Life After Love."

Guitar and DX7 Clavinet on "Temper, Temper"

Special appearance by Alan Greene: guitar on "Samantha (What You Gonna Do?)"

Produced by Mark Avsec

Engineered Mark Avsec

Present on the thanks list: Ed Avsec, Mark's father, who helped with construction for Mark's enhanced command center.

Absent on the credits: Kevin Valentine. This time out, Mark used a drum machine while Kevin stayed on the road with Mason Ruffner.

Magnificent Obsession is a totally, *totally* '80s pop album, another keyboard-era singer-songwriter set. "The Day Before They Dropped the Bomb" is the kind of breezy, tech-forward tune that sounds so clunky on *Cruise Control/Out of the Blue*, but glides gracefully here, as Donnie and Mark trade vocals. A choir backs Donnie's wistful lead vocals on "First Love," a track that wouldn't be out of place with the '80s Beach Boys.

After a delicate start, the record's real rocker is "Heartzone," a song written by Rodney Psyka, Alan Greene, and Gary Jones. The track was previously recorded by half the Cruisers, on the Innocent album. Mark pumps his keys hard, Donnie sings high, and the two harmonize over a synth groove that builds like a gathering storm.

"Shake It Loose" and "Temper Temper" are, as billed, big-beat room shakers, with Donnie as the commanding master of ceremonies. Donnie, Mark and Marty co-wrote "Shake." Bob Burger, Marty's old bandmate from The Pulse, wrote album closer "Life After Love"; he later wrote the Styx song "Edge of the Century."

All in all, it doesn't sound like a Cruisers album. But if *Cruise Control* sounded like *Magnificent Obsession*, Mark definitely wouldn't have locked it in the vault for six years.

A HARD DAY'S NIGHT: MARK & DONNIE DO BRITAIN

Mark didn't see a vast distinction between the material he wrote for Cellarful and the Cruisers. "All that really changes is that my name is more out there," Mark told Mark Holan of Cleveland *Scene*. "With Donnie's band, I considered that my thing. It was as much my thing as I ever wanted, really."[51.1]

Mark's work as an anonymous sideman for Ruffner earned him some solid allies. Mark returned to England for the album. And this time, Donnie finally made it to the other side of the Atlantic for some musical business. They finished most of the record at the Crescent Studios in Bath, England. Ye olde studio had hosted sessions for Peter Gabriel's *Security*, the Stranglers' *Dreamtime*, and XTC's *The Big Express*. Producer Ted Hayton, a glowing presence in the UK post-punk scene, had worked with the Stranglers and Art of Noise. Avsec didn't know who Hayton was or the body of work he was assembling. He just liked him; he knew what he was doing.

MARK: I became familiar with an engineer in London from my work with Mason Ruffner and Dave Edmunds. His name was "Ted" something. So I got budget to mix in England with Ted. He was a great guy to work with as an engineer.

We had experience together reconfiguring all of my MIDI stuff live in England. He wanted to go to Bath, so we worked in a 15th century building that now housed a recording studio. As is typical when working on records, Donnie and I did not do much aside from mixing — we were in the studio most of the time. But I loved Bath.

DONNIE: We went down to London, where the Beatles worked, right outside the studio, Abbey Road. We took some pictures outside the studio. It was incredible — except the weather sucks. We visited a couple pubs, but we were mainly there to work.

The funniest thing, Mark thought: I had a problem with the food. I made him laugh a couple times. The British call their silverware "cutlery." I hated the food, and I'd sit there and go, "*Cutlery*! It's a fork and spoon over here!"

We stayed in a little apartment. It was like being back on tour. Very cool, especially because it was in England. I'd never been overseas before. All of our stuff was here and Canada.

Touring internationally, I didn't care if we did or not. A lot of people want to travel, go here or here. It really doesn't do anything for me. I like the United States. I like being here.

MARK: This was a really confused period for Donnie Iris and the Cruisers – the breather we all took. Not sure Donnie was so into the Cellarful of Noise thing, probably not – but how could he be? Our main thing was still our band.

"SAMANTHA (WHAT YOU GONNA DO?)"

After the international travel and inspiring setting, Mark and Donnie's final charting single was a last-minute addition recorded back at Jeree's. Without the last-minute addition, the entire album might have disappeared — literally.

In April 1987, Mark returned to New York City's Sterling Sound, where the Cruisers had taken a wrong turn with the *King Cool* sequencing. Avsec didn't hold a grudge against Jack Skinner, who mastered the new Cellarful. Unlike *King Cool*, this session wasn't rushed. They finished far in advance of the record's slated January release date.

Donnie sings on half the album, but fully owns the single "Samantha (What You Gonna Do?)."

Six months after mastering, Mark had an idea. He wrote "Samantha," a dance floor-ready pop tune that gives his synthesizer a real workout. Mark's arty manipulations create a hook with physical and aural force. Donnie yodels a chorus that plays like a mashup of music from the 19th and 21st centuries: Mark warps Donnie's lead vocal, harmonizes, grinds it all together on his keyboard, and pours it into your ear.

The new song felt like a winner. The album was only eight tracks, and another strong candidate for a single never hurts.

Mark had Belkin call Sterling to find if it was too late to add the song.

The good news: No, it was not too late.

The bad news: There was nothing to add it to.

In New York, the techs checked the master tape. They played it.

Out came nothing.

The master tape was housed on primitive digital equipment. Mark recalled the situation as explained to him: "One of the machines was slightly out."

The album had disappeared.

Nobody had noticed.

Which left the Sterling staff scrambling to find the record.

After a tense search, the staff located a backup.[51.2]

A relieved Donnie and Marked tracked the vocals at Jeree.

Mark pulled in Greene, the guitarist from the previous Cellarful album, to record the guitar part at Beachwood in Cleveland.

The whole episode — almost losing an entire record — is just one more slice of history that is news to the people it happened to.

MARK: I forgot all of that, but it must be true. Some memories I had to let go of, to make room for all of the stuff I had to know to pass the bar exam.

DONNIE: I thought that was a good one. A lot of that stuff really does happen in the studio. The way the notes are set up, it's set up for my vocal to be like a yodel. I didn't write for those; I was just there for Mark. There wasn't much collaboration going on, as far as writing.

MARK: One of the reasons I wanted to work with Donnie in the first place: He will try anything I suggest to him. He will never *not* try it.

I'll say, "This sounds weird, but let's try like a yodel."

He'll say, "Well, Spark, let's try it!"

Even now, I'm embarrassed to say it, I'm shy. I'll write a melody, and I want to show him how it goes, and I don't sing that well. I'll have to sing a guide vocal, and I'll work up my courage — even though we're so close, and we're good friends.

DONNIE: I think Mark could have gone into the studio and just turned out project after project, like Nine Inch Nails. He's a good singer. He's very creative with the lyrical end and the music. So I think he could have been a good frontman, for sure.

CBS released *Magnificent Obsession* in March 1988. Mark had high hopes for the record — and reasonably so. But the possibilities remained plans.

"We're going to wait and see what happens with the record," Avsec told Holan. "If the record does well, we probably will put a band together, call it Cellarful of Noise and just continue things."[51.3]

"Samantha" spent seven weeks on the *Billboard* Hot 100 singles chart, peaking at number 69 April 9, 1988 — better than "Merilee" (peak position number 80), but not quite as good as "Do You Compute?" (number 64). The record wasn't a blip on the Top 200 album chart, but the single has a loyal cult to this day.

STEVE HANSEN, ex-WDVE: I've listened to every Donnie iris, and it's all killer stuff. He and Mark, even though a lot of them haven't sold that well, a lot of them are awesome. "Just Go Tango" and "Samantha" — that was so close to being a hit. I loved that song.

The single garnered airplay on nearly 100 stations. Even the *Pittsburgh Press*, which covered Donnie and the Cruisers less than its Cleveland counterpart, took notice and gave Donnie a healthy chunk of ink.

Discussing the album, Donnie contrasted the rival cities and their respective scenes with the *Press*' Peter B. King: "In Cleveland, for some reason, a lot of the smaller rock clubs will let bands go in there and play their own music," Donnie explained. "They (bands) need the support of the local clubs so these kids have a place to showcase their stuff. Otherwise, they spend years and years like I did with the Jaggerz working out other people's songs."[51.4]

"Samantha" even passed the smell test with hipper-than-thou rock fans who thought AOR bands were yesterday's news.

SEAN ROSS, *ROSS ON RADIO*: I was at was WDRE, the successor to WLIR Long Island. I took Cellarful of Noise's "Samantha" into an alternative radio music meeting without telling anybody who it was, to see what would happen. I don't think other people liked it. But nobody said, "Hey, isn't that Donnie Iris? He's not alternative."

Alan Greene recalls some later sessions that could have turned into a third Cellarful album. But Mark pulled the plug and tossed the tapes.

MARK: I've thought about, with Donnie, rerecording those things. But I'm not a pack rat. Rodney Psyka, I think he's got every tape he ever recorded. That can be beneficial. I never did that.

THE PROM SHOW

Donnie and the Cruisers played some important shows in 1988. Not many, though. The year had *another* record-low itinerary.

April 29, the Cruisers played a set a Blackhawk High School in Beaver Falls, for Donnie's older daughter's prom. The band played their standard set, with no special slow-dance selections.

"He's a fine gentleman," Principal Art Cornell told the *Beaver County Times*' Jack Atzinger. "And I think it will make a special evening for the kids."[515]

ERIN: I don't remember who came up with the idea, but I remember loving every minute of it. My high school boyfriend, Brian Jones, got up on stage. Some of my other friends were up there.

I felt really special. I felt the love.

The band were all over the country then, so getting everybody to come to a high school prom was not easy.

It was exciting, definitely a big thing in my high school. People still talk about it.

A November 10 Cruisers show wasn't quite a passing of the torch for Pittsburgh rock and roll — but the Cruisers *did* lend a spark to a new band. Donnie played Fisher Auditorium at Indiana University of Pennsylvania again, in the eastern outskirts of Steeler Country. The opening act was the Clarks, who would become the Steel City's omnipresent rock heroes over the '90s.

SCOTT BLASEY, CLARKS FRONTMAN: I remember that gig well. It stands out among the thousands for a couple reasons.

The main thing that I remember about the show was the chant "*DONNIE!! DONNIE!! DONNIE!!*" that broke out before our last song. I didn't mind at all. I felt the same way.

BACK TO SCHOOL

The real pivotal show for 1988 was a September 3 gig at the Meadows, a racetrack south of Pittsburgh. After that concert, the band was officially a *very* part-time gig for the Cruisers. Donnie was a financial professional. And Mark, like the Cruisers fans at IUP, was now an undergraduate college student.

Fall 1988. The Cruisers weren't over. But they were done, pretty much. For now. Mark and Donnie moved on.

MARK: We weren't signed to a major label anymore. *No Muss… No Fuss*, I didn't think it was a great album. Then we did Cellarful of Noise. And around that time, I said, "This ain't workin' for me anymore. Donnie was already doing mortgages. I thought, "I'm ready to go back to school." I was *ready*.

Mark says he never even considered following Kevin to L.A. and making a run as a producer — or even setting up a shingle in Cleveland or New Brighton, luring touring bands to come record where the studio rates and rent are cheap.

MARK: I tried to produce B.E. Taylor. It didn't work. He's not like Donnie — he was talented and great, but he had his own ideas. I liked Bill a lot, and we still work with Rick — he's one of my favorite people.

But I don't know if I could produce anybody else. With Donnie, it's very intimate. I couldn't get into that space with B.E. — he had preconceived notions, of course. He's an artist. I'm not such a good producer with artists who have their own notion about what they want to do.

I did produce a couple of things. But then I decided I wanted to do something else like law. By the time I started seriously producing other people, I was 30, 31, 32. I had a young family. I thought, "How am I going to support my family?" I was sick of the business.

KEVIN: I think, had Mark moved to California like I did, and was exposed to more invitations to do things with high caliber bands, he would have probably done quite well. And I'm sure he would have done as well as I did.

MARK: I guess you could say there is a Cruisers I and a Cruisers II and a Cruisers III, to put it very generally. Cruisers era I is the prime period, where we were making music that was relevant in the market.

I was the last one to not get a full-time job. So I was still trying to hang in there. But I was very frustrated. I could sense that when Kevin left — that was all good, by the way. Kevin left. Then Albritton left. I *got* it. I thought it was probably over. And it was.

JOHN GORMAN, OWOW RADIO, ex-WMMS and WNCX: I was with some people last night, who were involved in the music biz, that brought up Donnie Iris. They gave their opinions why he never broke nationally. All the cards were in place, the label was behind them — then the Cleveland curse hit.

JIMMY FOX, JAMES GANG, ex-BELKIN MADURI ORGANIZATION: I don't think Donnie could have done much more to make them successful. He did everything that was ever asked of him, without bitching.

They had good producers.

They had a good record company.

They had a good booking company, a good agent.

I would like to think the Belkin organization did everything expected.

And sometimes, those answers are not easy.

CHAPTER 52

Donnie Iris: Suit and Tie Guy

JESSICATANDYBERTHAMARIEMARIJUANANAOMIIRIS R.I.P.

1988. A bittersweet year for the House of Donnie. The Ierace family took a few extra spins around the circle of life. In the story of the Cruisers, you don't get downers and tragic self-destruction. To this point, Donnie's experience with loss was limited.

ADDY: We used to have this orange van. It was this old Scooby-Doo van with a round window and shag carpet inside. We'd put a mattress in the back and go to the drive-in movie theater. The door didn't close properly, so dad had a Bungee Cord for it.

ERIN: I believe it rested peacefully in our driveway — much to mom's dismay — until my dad was finally ready to let go.

ADDY: The day they took the van out of the driveway, it was like my dad lost a family remember. He would get attached to cool vehicles. To this day, we joke that he hoards. His famous line is, "It ain't hoarding if your stuff is cool."

That year, the Iris family lost the longtime dog — which, any pet owner will tell you, truly does count as a family member.

ADDY: He was really passionate about our dog, Jessie.

She was half collie, half German shepherd. Her full name is JessicaTandyBerthaMarieMarijuana NaomiIris — all in one breath, and you say it fast.

ERIN: We got her when Addy was a baby.

ADDY: Jessie had a voice. Jessie had a lisp, and he would talk to us all the time, in the Jessie voice, like he was Jessie. He would make her dance and sing. She would get down on her back, and my dad would tickle her belly, and she would go crazy. It was The Wannathang dance.

ERIN: It was supposed to be like that "Just like Ronnie sang" song — Eddie Money, the "take me home tonight, be my little baby" one. She sang "Jesse yikes da Wannathang" to the song. Jesse would do it as soon as she heard the song. Dad was famous for making random things hysterical, and making up random things like that.

With the Cruisers off the turnpike, Donnie's professional life took an unpredictable turn. Life took a lot of turns that year.

DONNIE: Erin graduated. I remember that pretty well. As parents, the two toughest days were when Erin went off to college, and then when my daughter Addy went to college. They leave the proverbial nest, and it's friggin' sad. My wife and I couldn't even speak on the way home, dropping Erin off.

At that point, I thought it might be good to try this mortgage thing.

ADDY: That was hard to get used to, him having a so-called "real job." Him having to go to work kind of sucked. We were used to him always being around.

He was the same guy, but it was different, seeing him in sport jacket. He didn't wear suits, but he wore suit jackets. He'd go do mortgage applications in the evening. He'd say, "I gotta go take an app."

DONNIE: We never toured that much, but it was an adjustment. The big adjustment was: What they hell was I gonna do? That's when the fella came to me about doing this thing with the mortgages. And I thought that was crazy. I didn't know anything about doing that kind of thing. That was an experience there, I'll tell ya.

A friend, Greg Best, who had played for the Steelers and the Browns, was a neighbor of mine. He went to Kansas State, then the Steelers, then to the Browns, then to Canada.

This guy called us about a mortgage company he was starting up in Beaver County. Neither one of us knew a thing about mortgages. But he thought our name recognition would be good in sales for his new company, the Pennsylvania Reserve Fund.

So we went down, checked it out, both ended up doing it. Worked for this guy, maybe a year or so. We were hired as representatives. He and I were like the face of it. We didn't sell houses. We did the mortgages for the houses. We solicited real estate agents, hopefully got them to bring their buyers to us to do their mortgages. We always had good rates, so we were successful, always did well.

He was right. All these people knew who we were. And that did help, Greg going through a similar thing, having him there. We had been living one kind of life, and now there was this new thing.

We had a mortgage license. I had to pass a test to be a mortgage loan originator. I studied like hell, trying to pass that test. And I did pass.

At first, it brought me back down to earth: I had to actually go out and try to do something to make a living. After a while, I got to be the owner of my own company, and I got into it. When I'd call people, they'd say, "Who is this, really?" They thought it was a friend pranking them. They couldn't believe this rock star was in a mortgage business.

We worked mainly during the day, but we did some things in the evenings, like real estate meetings, to make contacts with people. It wasn't a 9-to-5. We had suits and sport jackets, ties. I didn't have to cut my hair; my hair really wasn't that long to begin with. It was just kind of short and curly, like my hair was early on. I never really had long hair in the Cruisers. I didn't really have to spruce up too much.

That was very weird at first. But the more successful we got at it, the better I liked it — until, finally, after a while, the thing wears off. I got out a few years ago [around 2010]. It was a good second career. Made good money at it. And it just became music again.

CHAPTER 53

Life Goes On

1988. Donnie, Marty and Mark pulled the band into the garage and put a tarp over it. The Cruisers still haven't gone a full year without playing a show since 1981. But for the next few years, the band was a vintage vehicle they only took out on nice days.

The crew would play a show when a good opportunity presented itself. Tommy and Scott were still the rhythm section when the core Cruisers needed one. And as for the old rhythm section: The guys didn't talk often, but lines of communication were open. Everybody was busy. Now on his own, Albritton became a bandleader.

BETTER CALL KEVIN

More than anyone, Kevin stayed in the game. And he made it back to the big leagues: He played with recognizable names, projects big and small: Sam Kinison, Cinderella, the Godz, and Kiss, to name a few.

Kevin stepped off the stage to work for the hottest band in the land, his old Breathless tourmates, Kiss. In Kiss, he finally got that big drum-sound he always wanted.

But Kevin had his most over-the-top rock and roll experience as part of the backing band for screaming comedian Sam Kinison, one of the all-time heavyweight greats. The wildman made music part of his show, and he tapped Kevin for his live band. Kevin played live shows, but he avoided being sucked into the lifestyle.

KEVIN: I moved to California in '87. I was out here for a week, and I left for nine months with Mason. Then I was playing with Randy Hansen, the Hendrix tribute guy. It's a total blast. We're playing at the Whiskey, and Sam shows up. And typical Sam personality, he says [in a ringer Sam impression], "Hey, you wanna go on tour with me?"

We go up to Dan Aykroyd's brother's house on sunset. Then some things happen I shouldn't talk about. So we start playing with Sam.

This is 1989. We do a set of Hendrix. He comes out and does his deal. We close the set with "Wild Thing" and other songs.

So we go on tour. We're playing Vegas New Year's Eve. There are two shows, a 10 o'clock, and a midnight show. I come down from my room. I walk backstage. I see Sam slumped in a chair, with an oxygen mask on. He does the show, and he's horrible — and Sam is *never* horrible. He's whiffing. People actually booed the set. I felt bad for him.

And then, by the next show, two hours later, he had time to gather his thoughts and do whatever to get back up to speed. And he was the typical great, sharp Sam again.

Sam was definitely wild at times. He was also wild playing guitar: He would forget to turn the volume down when he wasn't playing. So every once is a while we would hear this crazy feedback, not knowing till later it was Sam.

He was around some toxic people. They'd just go off. He'd do that skit about his Corvette wanting to go somewhere. And he'd get in his car and *go*.

Good guy. Good guy. Typical comedian: He had that dark side.

It was pretty wild. I'm not the most wild guy. I'm under control, usually. That was go-all-night, go-to-clubs… I couldn't do what he did. It was an entourage.

Kiss, I never wore the makeup, but I'm on the records. I did the *Hot in the Shade* stuff. And I played on one song on *Revenge*, which is one of my favorite Kiss records. I think that [producer] Ezrin is a genius — he did "Detroit Rock City." At that time, I was starting to do post [production] stuff in TV. I got the call from either Gene [Simmons] or Tommy Thayer. And I went in an auditioned. They said, "Great."

I played on the record before the all-original band got together. Then they got back together, and they had some issues with Peter. I played on almost every song on the record. And then I had to teach Peter the drum parts. It was weird. I felt bad for him and thought, "Holy crap, will I end up like this guy later in life?!" But so far, so good.

The Kiss recordings had big rooms. The studio where we recorded *Psycho Circus* with Bruce Fairbairn, they had two 30" woofers behind me, pumping into it certain drums to jazz me up a bit, and to fill the room. Another big room was called Tone King in Hollywood. I recorded Paul Stanley songs there, and that's where I produced two Graham Bonnet records. That's where I worked with Slash.

A more technical drummer maybe would not have laid down what was necessary for Kiss — Kiss is very much like AC/DC, where it's not really difficult stuff — but it's the *part*, or the playing easy stuff, or the connecting bits are even harder. I think it was just a good fit. And I think Kiss trusted me with not blabbing. Because at that time, it was important that they were still hiding the fact not all the original guys played on the record.

Gene is a very tough person to please. But to be fair, he has gotten where has gotten because of his 100% commitment. He demands it from other people, too. He's hard on people. But he's fun to hang with — we call him Father Gene, because he always preaches like a father to you. When you have more success, you can be more demanding.

It's different, working with Gene and Mark.

Mark is producing and writing. When I worked with Kiss, they never produced their own records. Mark is totally on par with Gene. Working with Gene in the rehearsal room and working with Mark, there is no difference. They both do what they do well.

I think of Buddy Rich: Some people are just beyond human ability. It's beyond talent. You have to make the product. You have to hit the mark.

Mark has delivered hit songs. Gene has delivered hit songs. Kiss is a much bigger band. But Mark has a lot more musical ability than Gene does.

I was trying to get into engineering. I did some mixing around here. It was tough, having kids and the hours everybody wants to work: They want to start late and go late. And Denise [Mrs. Valentine] was training Candy Spelling from the Spelling family. Denise said, "He's doing these recording sessions, and it's hard because of the hours." And Candy said, "Maybe I'll talk to Aaron [Spelling, TV legend, producer of *Love Boat*, *Beverly Hills 90210*, and *Charmed*, among many other landmark shows] and see if there's some mixing work he could do."

When you're in TV, you hear people every now and then say, "I love *The Good Wife* or *Better Call Saul*" or something like that. It really means a lot that I can help some people have their happiness in their life. You don't hear those stories directly, about your music and what it means to people very often. But when you do hear these personal stories, you think, "Wow, that's wonderful, that I can help someone out like that."

Better Call Saul, it's very much like the Donnie Iris & the Cruisers material: Vince Gilligan and Peter Gould, the team leaders on *Better Call Saul*, are very collaborative. They allow you to express yourself, as long as it serves the story. And you can see how that atmosphere comes from two extremely talented people who are extremely nice and extremely encouraging. I'm so happy to be on the show, and it directly compares to Donnie and Mark: You have some great people, and you get to be involved. It's a nice combo, in TV and in music.

Cellarful of Noise's last-minute top-70 single didn't tempt Mark or Donnie back into the seedy underbelly of Rustbelt rock and roll. Mark executed his escape plan.

At the ripe old age of 34, the former state-champion accordionist who produced and co-wrote seven Hot 100 singles for Donnie Iris and the Cruisers, who penned the second Bon Jovi single, who made butts shake internationally with "Mandolay," who rubbed elbows with Barbara Streisand and Ringo Starr at the Grammy Awards, who helped Donnie Iris get his groove back... that man was now, once again, a college freshman. This time, Mark stuck with it.

The transition from studio ace to undergrad philosophy major seems like a sudden, unpredictable redirection. But Mark had seen it coming.

Donnie and Mark had spent all the money from their hit single "Ah! Leah!" on lawyers. Avsec says he never had a moment where he consciously decided he'd rather be the guy billing $400 an hour than the guy spending $400 an hour. But his career-crashing experiences with the Cruisers lawsuits did inspire his new endeavor, make no mistake.

MARK: Being an artist is a tough way to live. I had another child, Ellen — she's a nurse now — who was born in 1988. I was so burned out by the industry and eager to learn and create progress in another field. I wanted to enlarge myself and do something else.

I'm a conscientious guy. At my age, and being the sole financial support for a family of four, I was not messing around. I always, in the back of my head, had a goal of going to law school. Like when we made the first Donnie record, I did not presume rock and roll would become my life.

It was up to me to make the decision and quit. It was never about the money. I was completely frustrated doing what I was doing. It was a feeling of total pointlessness, day after day — for what? I'm really convinced I could have made *Sgt. Pepper*, and it wouldn't have made a difference. I needed to break the cycle, do something else, become a new person.

I took it one step at a time. I had no idea where I would be in four years after I graduated from undergraduate school. The only reason I majored in philosophy was because it would have been pointless for me to major in music. You can always learn more, but I wouldn't have learned as much as majoring in philosophy, which interested me, and which is a decent pre-law major. In philosophy, you study a lot of formal logic. And that logic is applicable to law.

I really threw myself into it. I went to school for seven years. Four years undergrad. Three years law school.

I'd be home with the kids, studying. I'd take a break and sit with them, and we'd watch the *Live at Blossom* videotape over and over. I'd played it for Danna once, and she loved it. She wanted to watch it all the time. She's a good drummer. So that became something we would do.

The Bon Jovi checks helped. I supported my family for many years largely through my ASCAP royalties. Mike Belkin was supportive in many ways. He advanced publishing money.

I did a Miller beer commercial, and Jim Keltner shows up on drums, who is a very awesome session player. He played on one cut on *Aja* for Steely Dan, "Josie." [In 2016, Rolling Stone ranked him the number 38 Greatest Drummer of All Time, citing his work on John Lennon's *Imagine*, Tom Petty's *Full Moon Fever*, and Bob Dylan's "Knockin' on Heaven's Door."[53.1]

I got a great education at Cleveland State. Studied philosophy, graduated summa cum laude. Did really well in law school. Graduated law school. I finished at the end of 1994, one semester early, officially with Class of 1995.

Mike Belkin, one of his lawyers was a partner at Benesch [Benesch, Friedlander, Coplan & Aronoff LLP]. He told him about me, said, "Look, this guy is gonna be a winner." So Mike helped get me an interview.

Becoming a lawyer was very weird.

I had an interview at Benesch. And I didn't own a suit to wear to it.

So Mike asked me to come in the office. I didn't know what he wanted.

He took me downstairs, to a men's store. And he bought me a suit. And that was the suit I wore to my interview. It was a sweet gesture.

My hair was still a little longer, and I could be prone to an Einstein look. So I put some heavy hairspray on it.

It was November. I drive downtown. I'm walking, and I look in a window and see myself, and I thought, "Wow."

It was profound that I had a suit on. I don't feel that way now. But I was crossing over.

So I'm walking from wherever I parked to Benesch, and there's this huge gust of wind, whoosh. I had all that hairspray on, and I never went into the bathroom to check my look.

As it turns out, the entire time, I looked like Ed Grimley, with that big horn of hair shooting off my head. I'm interviewing with a guy named Larry Bell — a real stern taskmaster — and Steve Williger. We're having a lunch, and I'm answering questions.

We have our lunch. I leave.

And I went into the bathroom and saw it. And I thought, "No, no — it wasn't like *that*?!"

Mike calls me later in the day and says, "How did the interview go?"

I said, "I thought it went pretty well."

He goes, "Well, Larry Bell called me. He said you seemed like a nice guy, really smart — but what's the deal with the hair?"

They looked past it, obviously.

I like the fun cases. But I like to know I'm on the right side, morally. I like to believe I'm on the right side. If it's just shaking someone down because you know it's a $100,000 case and you can get a $10,000 settlement, I don't do that. It's not good business.

Like his music, Avsec's law career launched with a promising start. In 1994 — at the very beginning of his legal career — he presented an early version of an article now called " 'Nonconventional' Musical Analysis and 'Disguised' Infringement: Clever Musical Tricks to Divide the Wealth of Tin Pan Alley." In it, he convincingly argued that Ravel's *Bolero* could be interpreted as a fiendishly clever ripoff of "When Irish Eyes Are Smiling." It took first place in a contest at Cleveland State's Marshall College of Law. He presented it at the national music publisher ASCAP's Nathan Burkan Competition in 1994.

The judging panel included David Nimmer, an attorney whose encyclopedic *Nimmer on Copyright* is considered the definitive secondary authority on copyright law. Avsec placed second in the competition, and Nimmer encouraged Avsec to publish his work so he could cite it in future editions of his treatise.

NIMMER: The paper was sophisticated. A bit puckish – but also rigorous and very well-done…. [Compared to other experts in the field] he has a much greater musical background. It makes him a very engaging speaker. I find his presentations delightful. He's on a very high level.

Even when Mark had the bar exam to deal with, the Cruisers kept playing. Donnie and the band played around six shows in 1989 and 1990, closer to three in 1991, about ten in 1992, under ten in 1993.

MARK: It never was dead. We never quit. Why would we? If we got a good gig offer that comes in and we could make a few bucks, we would.

Benesch has been good to me. Here we are, 22 years, I've been with the firm. I'm a partner. I'm in a position of leadership. I have a thriving practice. It's a wonderful firm.

I'm a very loyal person. I've been with Donnie forever. I've been with the same manager forever. I have this inherent loyalty. I don't bounce around a lot.

MARTY

Marty never stopped being a Cruiser. When the band slowed down, he remained an artist.

MARTY: All of us have had led pretty interesting lives and explored other parts of who we are.

I went back to school with the intention of doing something in broadcasting, because I was comfortable in the studio setting. By pure accident, I took a course in interior design. And the instructor was a really brilliant interior designer, so I took that path. And I met another instructor in graphic design, who was really terrific. Between both of those women, I was really inspired to switch my major.

I started doing the graphic design thing after we stopped touring nationally and started playing more on a regional level. And I had an interest in finishing my degree in the first place. I went back to school since I had the time. I went to Mercyhurst University. It's a dual major, in Graphic and Interior Design. I have a degree in both.

It's not a simple major. There's a lot of science involved, a lot with materials and flammabilities. It's not decoration, *per se*. I thought it was fascinating. If you're designing, let's say, a nursing home, there's a responsibility attached to that, in terms of window height, accessibility and flammability. All these things need to be suitable. People are going to use these things. It's a lot of fundamentals so that I can be responsible for somebody else's well-being. The aesthetic is there, too.

I work in advertising and marketing, all of that. I make advertising and marketing materials: catalogs, brochures. Multimedia. We have to pull together lots of things to create. I like the intricacies and problem-solving of it. If it's advertising and there's something special about it, how do we say that in a way people are going to hear, and it's going to resonate with them, and they'd be interested in buying it?

I do all of the design work for the Cruisers, as well as others. I've been designing all of Michael Stanley's CD packages for years.

I do everything from website design to display advertising to magazine advertising. I work with product designers and builders. I help create display and fixtures and systems. I was the lead designer on a recent large project for Honda Motorcycles, which will be installed in dealers all over the country. It's really fun, thinking about what happens when somebody walks into a dealership and what happens in their mind.

The language of visual arts and the language of music is pretty much the same thing: If you're looking at a visual image, an artist will talk about the harmony of the colors, the rhythm of the elements, of space, of dissonance, of contrast. And those are all musical terms.

After a while, half the time,
I showed up in a pair of jeans and
a T-shirt onstage. It just felt good
that way, and that's how
it was going to be.

~ DONNIE IRIS

CHAPTER 54

The Cruisers II

1989.

1990.

The nineties. Donnie is brokering mortgages. Mark is studying philosophy, then law. The Cruisers show counts rise and fall. So do the head counts. The band play country clubs. Rib fests. Benefits. The band stick close to home, but hit Ohio at least once a year. Steady Pittsburgh-area New Year's Eve gigs are a reliable big show.

Labor Day Weekend 1989, Donnie and the band play the Allegheny County Rib Cook-Off, on a bill between Sha Na Na and James House.

That year, they play their 10th birthday show as part of WDVE's 20th birthday bash at Community College of Beaver County's Golden Dome.

"I call our style pure rock 'n' roll," Donnie — now a hair under 50 — tells the Beaver County Times, "a simple musical form that's attracting a broader age group than ever before. Would you believe 13 and 50 could have the same music in common?... The teens and 20s can't claim rock as their own. My daughters and I have the same taste in music. That's the kind of success that makes me really proud."[54.1]

Before the holidays, the Cruisers return to Pittsburgh's Syria Mosque, where they rock the theater to its foundation again. The band are the highlight of the annual Toys for Tots Charity Jam, on a deep bill with the Clarks, Joe Grushecky, Norm Nardini, and Billy Squier.

Pittsburgh Press critic Peter B. King meets Donnie, and likes him, and the paper finally gives him a good review: "Iris unleashed his soaring, if occasionally shrill, falsetto excursions. He also offered his wonderful stage presence — in those clunky glasses, cuffed jeans and sneakers, he's the engaging opposite of show-biz glitz."[54.2]

The Cruisers end 1989 with a gig at the Liberty Center, in downtown Pittsburgh. They send New Year's Eve festivities into high gear at the "Get Ready for '90" downtown celebration at Liberty Center Plaza, where Mayor Sophie Masloff presides.

Donnie has finally worn down his biggest critic. But King's glowing notice is Donnie's last big hometown press for some time. In 1990, the *Post-Gazette* describes his career in past tense, in a short mention of his appearance at the Pittsburgh Home and Garden Show.

1990. Tommy formally resigns, and is replaced by Steve McConnell, an Erie drummer Marty knows. Rib festivals and Cleveland club shows follow. Tommy will return.

1991. Mark earns his undergraduate degree.

1992. The Cruisers grudgingly release *Out of the Blue*, their first CD, which combines old favorites and previously unreleased *Cruise Control* tracks with a new sprinkling of Mark's magic dust. With an album to promote, the band play around a dozen shows that year.

When Donnie can't convene the entire band, he plays Cruisers hits with members of B.E. Taylor's band and the Granati Brothers.

All the while, something special is happening at the Cruisers' occasional shows. Donnie isn't turning into a creaky, silver-haired singer who can't hold the notes anymore. Donnie was never a straightlaced frontman in the first place. Now that he's getting older, he's letting his hair down. And it's still black. And he's getting looser.

MARK: That's when Donnie just started being *Donnie*. And that's when he gradually became the iconic figure.

We kept on doing stuff. We had different drummers until we went back to Kevin. But The Cruisers II began with the carnival circuit, so to speak: county fair type shows, daytime shows.

Donnie would show up looking like he just finished mowing the lawn — and sometimes he still does, if it's a hot day.

DONNIE: It's true. The Butler Fair, that's the one that I mowed the lawn and went to the show. I was just letting it go, being myself.

I never paid a dollar for a hairstylist. You'd *never* see a bunch of chains hangin' off of me. I never got into that crap. After a while, half the time, I showed up in a pair of jeans and a T-shirt onstage. It just felt good that way, and that's how it was going to be.

MARK: We all were just kind of finding our way into other things. And it just felt like, "Aw, hell, this is what it is." Not that we didn't do good shows. Not that Donnie didn't value it.

Eventually the Cruisers II evolved into the full Cruisers III, which is what it is now.

CHAPTER 55

Footsoldier in the Moonlight: The Album

Footsoldier in the Moonlight

The sixth proper album by Donnie Iris and the Cruisers. Featuring...

"Kamakazi" (Lyrics by Avsec) 4:21
"Intentional Infliction of Emotional Distress" (Avsec) 3:32
"The Best Possible World" (Avsec) 5:24
"Rally With Sally" (Avsec) 5:27

"A Sword & A Shield" (Avsec) 4:38
"The Reasonable Prudent Person" (Avsec) 2:48
"The First Love" (Avsec) 5:31

Release: November 1993

From the credits:

Donnie Iris: lead, background vocals, guitars, harmonica and claps
Mark Avsec: piano, synthesizers, horn permutations, sequencer programming, synth bass, drum machine, harmony lead vocals, Hammond organ, harmonica and synth voices
Marty Lee: acoustic, rhythm, lead guitars, background vocals
Scott Alan: bass
Steve McConnell: drums
Pete Tokar: additional percussives on tracks 3 and 4
Kenny Blake: alto sax on track 4
Danna Avsec: Hammond Organ on track 3
DD-12 conga percussion on track 10
Produced by Mark Avsec
Executive Producer: Mike Belkin
Engineered by Jerry Reed
Mixed by Pete Tokar
Danna Avsec appears through the courtesy of her parents.
Midi Tracks (3,4,7,9,10) were programmed and performed by Mark Avsec at The Cellar, in Twinsburg, OH. Band Tracks and all overdubs were recorded at Jeree Recording Studio, New Brighton, PA.
Mixed at Midtown Recording Studios, Cleveland, OH
Mastered at Frankford/Wayne, NYC, by Rick Essig.

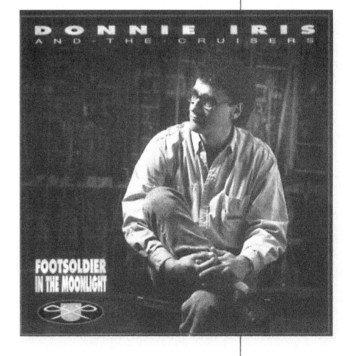

November 1993. *Footsoldier in the Moonlight* is released with little fanfare and even less attention from the tri-state media. It is universally regarded as the low point of the Cruisers' recording career.

They will gracefully rebound. Eventually.

In 1992, the release of the *Out of the Blue* collection momentarily reinvigorated the Cruisers.

With their first new release since 1985, the band played more shows than they had in years — nearly a dozen. Mark finished his undergraduate degree. The band were warmed up. Before law school started, the producer had some rare spare time. But gone were the days when Donnie and Mark can hole up in the studio for three months.

May 1, 1992: While they could, the Cruisers returned to Jeree Recording and began recording *Footsolider in the Moonlight*. The sessions spread out across 11 months.[55.1] After that much time and effort, they figured they might as well put it out.

MARK: We always ended up going back and trying a Cruisers album. The worst album we ever made was *Footsoldier in the Moonlight*.

For the Cruisers, Phase II was in effect — but not in full effect. The *new* new quintet never found their footing in the studio. Without a steady, harmonious lineup, the band still struggled to write and record.

Footsoldier in the Moonlight was the band's first new original record since 1985's *No Muss...No Fuss*, which the original Cruisers recorded in late 1983. Without Kevin and Albritton, it took them some time to find their footing.

Donnie doesn't think much of *Footsoldier* either.

Mark flat-out regrets the album. He wrote all the songs this time out. And he takes all the blame. It's not a strong set, but all the songs are well on their way to being decent tracks.

MARK: After school, before I started my law career, I tried one last gasp. And that was a terrible album.

The songs were terrible. There was no magic in the tracks. It was a terrible album. I don't think much of that period at all.

I was more interested in my legal career.

DONNIE: That was just something for us to put together. A lot of those albums, we made them to try to keep the band alive, coming up with stuff to do. But it seems like most of the songs on most of those albums, nothing stood out.

That was Mark's title. But to me, it put to mind an actual soldier out in the desert, under the moonshine.

Donnie and Mark don't have much to say about *Footsoldier*.

FOOTSOLDIER, THE SONGS: "KAMIKAZE"

The record kicks off with the kind of forced singalong designed to sound great in a live gig. If nothing else, it has a slinky groove. It's overproduced and undermixed — but Donnie and Marty are in fine form.

MARK: I remember four of these songs. I remember "Kamikaze" — that was an awful record.

"INTENTIONAL INFLICTION OF EMOTIONAL DISTRESS"

In this a sock hop barnburner, Mark mines his legal education for some rowdy lyrics. Marty's rapid-fire solo almost saves the tune. In the credits, Mark dedicates it to his study group.

MARK: "Intentional Infliction of Emotional Distress" — *that's a cool title*, right? That's an attorney thing. That's the stuff I was reading at the time.

"BEST POSSIBLE WORLD"

Gentle keyboards and piano-esque keyboard noodling match this slow ballad's poignant chorus. It's home to the title image: a foot soldier in the moonlight.

DONNIE: I don't think it's that bad of a song. I thought it was a pretty good comment on society. Lyrically, it was pretty strong.

MARK: "Best Possible World," I do remember that. I was proud of the lyric. It was based in philosophy I was reading. It was about family.

"RALLY WITH SALLY"

This rhyme-titled track is a stab at a rocking blues stomp. By the late '90s, singing about dancing was not evocative or compelling.

DONNIE: "Rally with Sally"? What the hell is that? It's a bullshit tune we came up with. [Laughs.]

MARK: "Rally With Sally," I don't remember that.

"SWORD AND THE SHIELD"

This acapella interlude appears on the record, which is news to the guys who wrote and sang it.

DONNIE: I just don't remember that.

MARK: "Sword and the Shield," I have no idea what that song sounds like.

"THE REASONABLE PRUDENT PERSON"

The band hit some powerful harmonies in the chorus — just as the album is about to end.

This crawling lament is another dramatic application of Mark's legal language. The pensive piano ballad documents the life of a dutiful, morose man who's suffering through an empty suburban existence. 95% of the Cruisers' songs are fiction. Neither Donnie nor Mark lusted after a girl named Leah. Donnie didn't slug Louie.

But if you're still poring through the catalog, looking for insights into the lyricists' lives, this one seems noteworthy. Mark had something he needed to say at the time — but now he doesn't want to talk about it.

MARK: "A Reasonable and Prudent Person," the title came from law. The lyric was OK.

DONNIE: [Laughs heartily.] That's a slow album. It did get boring. Again, it's one of those forgettable sessions.

"THE FIRST LOVE"

Footsoldier in the Moonlight fades out with this reprise of a tune from the second Cellarful of Noise album. It's the band's first attempt at a wedding theme. Stacked, Donnie accents his angelic, low backing vocals with some soaring high-pitched vocals. But high and slow aren't an ear-grabbing combination.

MARK: "The First Love," I think I remember that. I think that's a pretty decent tune.

That's a terrible album. The feel on that album is just awful, terrible.

DONNIE IRIS & B.E. TAYLOR: THE WEDDING SINGERS

Donnie and friends came through with some clutch cover songs in 1995. They weren't Cruisers tracks, though.

ADDY: Dad and B.E. [Taylor] sang together at our weddings.

ERIN: I got married in July, 1995. Dad and B.E. sang "The Wedding Song" [by Peter, Paul & Mary].

ADDY: He recorded "Daddy's Little Girl" and played it at my wedding, as a surprise for me. That was the song for our father-daughter dance. I'm getting choked up thinking about it. I was expecting it to be the regular song, and then it was his voice. Everybody at the wedding was just bawling.

ADDY: At the actual ceremony, B.E. sang. Then he and B.E. sang "Unforgettable" together at the reception. I think it was "Unforgettable."

After the lowpoint of *Footsoldier in the Moonlight*, Donnie is about to return to the spotlight and emerge bigger than ever. But not because of a new record.

Interlude:
Mark's Favorite Music

Rock:

Steely Dan, *AJA*
James Gang, the first two albums
Miles Davis, *Kind of Blue*
Peter Gabriel, *So*
Robbie Robertson, *Robbie Robertson*

Classical:

Beethoven's Ninth Symphony, conducted by Furtwangler...
1951 performance with the Bayreuth Festival Orchestra.

It is not a perfect performance. But it has so much energy,
and it teeters on the edge. It's like a great rock and roll piece that
you expect to fall apart at any instant, but it does not.
It is the best version of Beethoven's Ninth I have ever heard.

"Adagio for Strings," by Samuel Barber.
The saddest piece of music I have ever heard.

I also love the beginning of Henryk Gorecki's Symphony No. 3:
The Symphony of Sorrowful Songs

Best songs/productions:
"Bridge Over Troubled Water," Simon & Garfunkel
"You've Lost That Lovin' Feeling," Righteous Brothers
"When a Man Loves A Woman," Percy Sledge"
"Respect," Aretha Franklin
"You Keep Me Hangin' On," Vanilla Fudge

Part III: That's the Way…

Donnie at WDVE Studios, Pittsbugh, PA

CHAPTER 56

DVE n Dawnie n Pants n 'Nat

Pittsburgh has other heroes and icons — people who, strictly speaking, have *done* more for the region. Mario Lemieux, Terry Bradshaw, World Wrestling Federation champion Bruno Sammartino. But Pittsburgh has given birth to no *character* more iconic and emblematic of the regional psyche than the persona dramatized as *Dawnie Iris*. *Dawnie* is up there with the late, great Mr. Rogers, late Steelers announcer Myron Cope, and horror host/weather man Chilly Billy Cardille, with even more local flavor.

Donnie Iris first broke onto radio is the late 1960s, as part of the Jaggerz.

He truly entered the Pittsburgh area's consciousness via the WDVE 102.5 FM morning show, at the dawn of the 1980s.

1995. The latest version of the DVE morning show once again introduced Donnie to Steel City FM listeners.

And this time, once and for all, he became a true Pittsburgh icon.

A BRIEF HISTORY OF THE DVE MORNING SHOWS

In the mid '90s, *The DVE Morning Show* was enjoying a renaissance.

In 1980, Steve Hansen joined Pittsburgh veteran Jimmy Roach. Their *Jimmy and Steve in the Morning* drivetime show made WDVE's morning show a perennial winner in a competitive market.

In 1986, DVE replaced Jimmy and Steve with host Scott Paulsen. The West Virginian had worked in Knoxville, Tennessee before relocating to Pittsburgh's WHTX 96.1.[56.1] With Paulsen, the WDVE morning show became, officially, *The DVE Morning Show*.

In 1988, *The DVE Morning Show* added cohost Jim Krenn, a Pittsburgh native and standup comedian. The two enjoyed a creative spark that redefined how the city looked at itself. Paulsen and Krenn became the core of a prolific team. Before long, "*PaulsenAndKrenn*" was a single word to a loyal army of listeners. They worked together for over a decade and created a template for the station's morning drive that endures to this day.

With Paulsen and Krenn as their morning hosts, *The DVE Morning Show* became another Burgh champion team, an unbeatable institution. The station held a steady number 1 spot in the Ages 25-54 listening demographic for over 14 years. They held off all comers, including Howard Stern, the King of All Media, for his entire tenure in the Pittsburgh market, 1995 through 2005. (Stern had famously shattered the Cleveland radio market in 1994, when he unseated the city's top FM morning show, the *Buzzard Morning Zoo* at WMMS 100.7.[56.2])

A BRIEF HISTORY OF YINZING AND OTHER PITTSBURGHESE

Pittsburgh was dedicated to *The DVE Morning Show*, and DVE's morning show was uniquely focused on Pittsburgh. Like many a morning drive crew, they combined rock and talk. They celebrated and sent up local tropes, characters, institutions and icons. More than any other Iron City institution, Krenn and Paulsen reshaped and crystallized Pittsburgh's collective consciousness, by creating a funny regional self-awareness you could describe as *yinzer chic*.

Pittsburgh has long been the epicenter of a polarizing regional dialect codified as "Pittsburghese" in Sam McCool's 1982 glossary and how-to guide, *New Pittsburghese: How to Speak like a Pittsburgher*.[56.3]

Pittsburghese is the Burgh accent, variations of which are also common throughout the Appalachians, but closely echoed in nearby West Virginia and Eastern Ohio. It's a distinct hybrid of phonetic and grammatical idiosyncrasies from Scots-Irish, German, African-American, Slavic, and other cultures.[56.4]

In 2014, a national Gawker.com poll declared it America's Ugliest Accent.[56.5] If you've never heard seen yinzers in action, imagine the *Saturday Night Live* sketches "Bill Swerski's Super Fans," but with Steelers references, more of a twang, and slightly less metropolitan sophistication.

Through the 20th century, the emblematic Pittsburghese term was "youns," a contraction of "you'uns," itself slurred version of "you ones." Essentially, the term translates to "you guys," "yiz," "yiz guys," or "y'all."

In old-world Pittsburghese, it sounded like "yuunz." And, in the ears of some, it served as a verbal hallmark of un-sophistication. "Youns" was a line of cultural demarcation: *Nobody* who would *ever* attend a *fancy*-dress tea party would be *caught dead* saying "youns."

Locals who weren't worried about creating a highfalutin self-image used the word eight to ten times an hour.

Krenn and Paulsen, however, seized the word "youns" and reinvented it with a tongue-in-cheek exaggeration. As heard on the radio, "youns" now emerged as a slightly more streamlined — and eminently more palatable — "yinz."

Krenn, Paulsen, and crew created a running series of comic skits, populated by characters like Southside native Stanley P. Kachowski and nebby *maw* [mother] Shelly Kaznowski. Speaking as exaggerated archetypes, the drivetime DJs satirized the shared culture of Southwestern Pennsylvania. When Paulsen and Krenn broadcast the stereotyped characters to Burgh, they did it with warmth. The skits represented an unprecedented embrace for the marginalized, scorned dialect. It was informed, ironic, *and* loving. In no way was the shtick mean or condescending. Listeners loved it.

Paulsen and Krenn formalized a new Pittsburgh persona widely recognized as *the yinzer*. In recent years, the archetype has been further developed by Curt Wootton's YouTube phenomenon, *Pittsburgh Dad*. Yinzers may speak in a backwoods twang, but they're good, salt-of-the-earth people who are not — if you ask them — jagoffs.

For the yinzer, Burgh culture is everything. And yinzers, unlike some fair-weather fans, never grow tired of the timeless rock and roll played by Donnie Iris and the Cruisers, pronounced in Pittsburghese as "Dawnie Ahris an' tha Cruisers."

A BRIEF HISTORY OF PANTS N 'NAT, OR, *REVEALED: THE IRIS TRIPLETS*

When Donnie Iris references became a staple on *The DVE Morning Show*, his stock was at an all-time low — in the public eye, at least.

KRENN: Not to me. I was already an entertainer. I knew the ebb and flow of entertainment. I was such a fan of Donnie, as a performer and a person and role model. I started to do comedy bits. I would mention him, or use my Pittsburghese, doing Stanley P. Kachowski.

I would mention Donnie because he is, to me, the quintessential Pittsburgher: He is a hardworking guy, a good guy, a guy who has great talent. And a guy who is resilient. Because you're up and down as an entertainer. And when you're down and you brush it off and keep going forward, doing new things. I admired that. I think it reflected in the bits.

Getting to know Donnie a little bit in my early radio days, I knew he had a great sense of humor about it. I thought, "Wow, this is a fantasy for me, an entertainer I idolized."

Starting in 1995, *DVE Morning Show* skits showcased Donnie's fun-loving, friendly offstage persona in a way that no concert or newspaper feature could. They created an entire mythos around the local rock star. And they implicated him in reports that may or may not have been fake news.

The *DVE Morning Show* collected its best bits and skits into annual compilations that — like DVE's many concerts — benefited the Greater Pittsburgh Food Bank and other charities. 1995's *Wizards of Odd* album hosted the first commercial for Pants n 'Nat, "The Pittsburgh clothing store where yinz get more!"

The fake discount shop's staff are *big* yinzers, as evidenced by the store's name: "n 'nat" is a common Pittsburghese phrase that means "and such," via "and that [sort of thing]."

The next year, 1996's *Twisted* featured another Pants n 'Nat skit: A yinzer dad and his two yinzing kids need to look their best for a prestigious cultural event: a concert by Donnie Iris. A year later, 1997's *Former Alter Boys* expanded the Donnie Iris pantheon.

Donnie himself joins Paulsen and Krenn in a skit, where he plays a new character.

The bickering family revisits Pants n 'Nat, where a friendly clerk — played by Donnie — greets the family.

"Dad, dat guy looks familiar, don't he?!" says one son. "Curly black hair and Buddy Holly glasses—"

"Yeah, he looked like Donnie Iris!" says the other.

"You screwball, that ain't no Donnie Iris," the first son responds. "Ain't no *Dawnie Iris* workin' no stupid Pants 'n Nat in the middle of the stupid night! *Donnie Iris is a big rock star!*"

Later, the kid mutters, "Thanks, Mr. Iris," and the clerk responds. The family fear, for a tense moment, that Pittsburgh rock hero has been reduced to a retail gig.

"I can't believe *Dawnie Iris* is workin' at Pants 'n Nat," says the dad. "This is a sad day... I'm depressed over here.... Don't say nothin' about him bein' all *warshed* up 'n nat."

When the dad apologizes for his obnoxious kids, the courteous clerk reveals he's not Donnie Iris: He's *Lonnie* Iris, the night-shift guy at Pants 'n Nat. Lonnie, he explains, is one of the Iris triplets: Donnie, Lonnie, and Connie.

The family leave with a new black-and-gold, polka-dotted sweater, their faith in the natural order restored: *Donnie Iris is still a big rock star*.

A certain type of Burgh-area resident is aggressively anti-yinzer. Any portrayal of the stereotype drives them crazy. Mesmerized by new and shiny things, these people generally believe they should embrace more contemporary popular music, move beyond Donnie Iris. These people do not like good things, and they are not fun.

The transition from *youns* to *yinz* became a midpoint, a cultural meeting ground. Hardcore yinzers had updated their dialect. Swayable non-yinzers could embrace the spitshined term, if only on an ironic level. For both crowds, Paulsen & Krenn became their avatar, and Donnie their patron saint (when the Steelers weren't playing).

KRENN: Donnie was bringing in new music, so I was getting to know him and getting to know him as a friend. So I decided to write him in as Lonnie Iris.

Donnie brought it to a new level. People talk about it all the time. They quote it. And the fact that a guy I idolized was doing the skit with me, that was part of it too.

Over the next decade, skits would explore the Lonnie-Donnie dynamic, expand the Pants 'n Nat brand, and introduce new (fake) Donnie merchandise. These bits are *hilarious*, though they don't work as well on paper. The DVE CDs are out of print, but clips are on YouTube.

Donnie, in the meantime, grew from a bit player to a news item.

KRENN: There were Roger Waters spottings all over the Tri-State area, like he was just hanging at a bar. People would call in and say, "Yeah, I was drinkin' with Roger Waters last night."

DONNIE: Somebody called in and reported seeing me pumping gas in my car. And that was the start of the Donnie Iris sightings. It was so frickin' funny, man. It just kept going. They kept coming up with ideas.

KRENN: The Town Talk call was one of the first where people called in about him. This guy calls, just a caller, because he knows I like to talk to Donnie.

He's telling this story of how he's shopping in the supermarket, in the bread aisle. I have no idea where this guy's going with the story. He set it up perfectly.

He says he sees this guy moving up and down the bread aisle, squeezing each of the loaves, grabbing the bread.

And he says, "You know who that was? *Dawnie Ahris.*"

That was a classic piece. Comedically, it was gold.

DONNIE: [*Doubled over in laughter.*] I swear to God: Give me a Bible, and I'll put my hand on it. Believe me when I tell you: That did not happen. It was total story. I haven't bought a loaf of Town Talk for *I don't know how long.* No, hell no, I was not "moving up and down the aisle erratically."

The kid was a salesman — he pulled it *off.* He made people believe it.

Krenn admits they did not fact-check the stories.

Before cell phones and iPods and satellite radio, if you spent mornings stuck in traffic on Greentree Hill or Route 51, heading into downtown Pittsburgh, a DVE Donnie Iris skit was definitely a highlight of your month. Despite the reliance on local iconography, the skits did translate for an out-of-town audience.

RON GERBER, HOST OF KFAI FM'S *CRAP FROM THE PAST*: In the days of Napster, in '99, when it was a free-for-all and you could grab anything you wanted, I went on a rampage to find Donnie Iris stuff. I did well. I get something back called "Pants n 'Nat" from WDVE.

I thought, "What on *earth* is *this*?" the first time. "These people have really thick accents. This isn't funny."

And then I got to the end, and I thought, "Maybe I'll listen to that again; I think that might have been funny…. OK: Some people talk that way. 'Yinz' means 'y'all.' This is *very* funny."

The idea of Lonnie Iris is so great. It's nice to see that he has a good sense of humor; a lot of artists would not put up with that. He seems like the kind of a guy you want to shake his hand and buy him a beer.

DONNIE: It kept getting more popular and more popular. It was cool. People would stop me and say, "Where'd you get them pants?!"

We weren't really doing much of anything. We would just do a show once in a while. It got people talking about us again. It was great. They did us a huge favor. We hadn't had anything on the radio for a long time.

After 'DVE started talking about these Donnie Iris sightings, the band got some more momentum. It really did. We went out and played these packed clubs. People started showing up at the shows more. Even people who weren't into the group wanted to see what it was about. We were packing 'em in. It was cool.

KRENN: The reaction was huge. *Huge.* Even though his sales were at a low. But Donnie, as a personality, was still so massive. And his songs were still big.

The mere mention of Dawnie Iris makes a sketch a quotable favorite. Over the years, the *DVE Morning Show* has dropped Donnie into a Christmas carol ("Donnie Iris is comin' to town!") and placed him at the center of a mystery. In episode of *CSI: Pittsburgh*, crime scene investigators find a body outside a Cruisers concert. At the grim scene, a yinzer fan suspects the Cruisers may have *rocked the man to death.*

DONNIE: Krenn and I have become great friends. Scott Paulsen too, though I don't see him very much. [Current *DVE Morning Show* host] Randy Bauman's the same way. It's a real nice thing.

KRENN: When you see Donnie, the *transparency* is one of the appeals: He's a white light, a good person. And when you see him joking and making fun of himself in front of an audience, there's nothing more confident that an audience can see.

The live shows were so fun. We had people camped out, tailgating all night, waiting to get into a morning show. When Donnie showed up, he brought it into a frenzy. He brought it to a new level. It was crazy.

That willingness, certain performers have that. That's why they're role models. I see those people and think, "God blessed them with a gift. And that gift they're given, they're willing to share it with people — not just on a musical level, but on a *humanity* level, by acting with respect. And Donnie is like that. He treats people with respect. A lot of people get that gift, and they misuse it, "This is *my* gift!" Guys like Donnie share it.

STEVE HANSEN, WDVE MORNING SHOW, 1980-1986: He's *Donnie*. Then Jim Krenn and Scott Paulsen created *Dawnie*. And that's what it was with the people: He didn't put you off, he didn't act like a star. He's kind of slight of stature, a nice *aw-shucks* guy — everything they used to create that character, he always was. There were a couple guys in town I liked a lot, too, but they always… *believed in themselves* to a fault. Donnie was never that guy. And he was always creating the most interesting music of everybody.

DONNIE: They brought us back into the conversation! It kept us going.

BIG ROCK STARS, OF THE JAG AND NON-JAG VARIETY

1996. The Cruisers played around ten gigs. They were a special guest for two *big* ones: In Pittsburgh and Cleveland, the band opened arena shows for Rusted Root, Pittsburgh's biggest rock export of the '90s. Their major label debut, Mercury Records' *When I Woke*, went platinum that year. During their short but amazing reign, the jam band looked like they might become the next Grateful Dead-Phish-Dave Matthews Band type phenom.

DONNIE: Rusted Root, to me, that was a groove band. We opened for them at the Civic Arena. I went in the audience and checked them out. People were dancing everywhere. They were just smokin'. This great groove that was infectious. People getting lost in it!

Yeah man, I love Rusted Root. I remember my daughter talking about them when she was going to IUP.

Out on the road, another member of Team Donnie was dealing with some other platinum rock stars.

JIM MARKOVICH, CRUISERS ROAD MANAGER AND LIVE SOUND: People say, "The Ramones, three chords, big deal!" 33 songs in an hour. Great band. I tell ya.

I saw some crazy things, definitely, with the Ramones, over the different eras: The audience throwing stuff. The spinning. The slam dancing. The mosh pits. The body surfing. We used to take bets. We had to have a crash barrier at the front of the stage. We'd look at it and go, "OK… That's going to last three or four songs." Most of the time, we were right.

Joey Ramone, every year, would have a birthday party. And he would have people play. I did the gig. Ronnie Spector played. Blondie played. Debbie Harry came out during the day, and she looked good. Then she came out at the show, and she looked phenomenal. She took over the audience, like *boom*! Like Donnie.

The Ramones' final-final-final tour was in 1996: We did the Lollapalooza tour with Metallica and Soundgarden. But I was doing Donnie Iris as much as I could, because they're just great guys.

Some people out there, they treat people like shit. I don't know if treating people well is rare, but it's definitely on one end of the spectrum. Most artists, they're a bit different. Some of them are more humble that others, and some think they're the best thing ever. Some of the guys I saw in some of the big bands, I didn't like the way they treated everybody. I thought they were kind of divas.

I would say the tone was set between Mark, Donnie, and Mike Belkin. Mark makes a lot of the decisions. I think that's a personality trait: They probably treat everybody they know well.

"Dad, dat guy looks familiar, don't he?!" says one son. ... "Yeah, he looked like Donnie Iris!" says the other. "You screwball, that ain't no Donnie Iris," the first son responds. "Ain't no Dawnie Iris workin' no stupid Pants 'N Nat in the middle of the stupid night! Donnie Iris is a big rock star!"

~ WDVE
PANTS N 'NAT

CHAPTER 57

Poletown: The Album

Poletown

The seventh album by Donnie Iris and the Cruisers. Featuring...

"Poletown" (Avsec) 4:56
"How You Gonna Mend It?"
 (Avsec) 4:08
"Valerie" (Avsec) 5:52
"I Am Your Eyes" (Avsec) 4:29
"The Stalker" (Avsec) 5:16
"Don't Want to Be a Hero"
 (Avsec) 4:27

"I Lie Down" (Avsec) 4:39
"Bitter Lemons" (Avsec) 5:00
"Hey Rembrandt" (Avsec) 4:51
"Scream" (Avsec) 1:00
"Within Me + Without You"
 (Avsec) 5:59
"Come Come Come" (Avsec) 5:10
"Cross the Rubicon" (Avsec) 4:01

Original release: March 15, 1997
Label: Seathru Records, CD Release DICD103
Peak position and singles: Not applicable

From the credits:
Donnie Iris: lead and background vocals, rhythm guitars
Mark Avsec: keyboards, accordion, background vocals
Marty Lee: lead and rhythm guitars, acoustic guitars
Albritton McClain: bass guitar
Kevin Valentine: drums
Produced by Mark Avsec
Mixed by Kevin Valentine
Engineered by Jerry Reed and Kevin Valentine
Frank Vale engineered and mixed "Cross the Rubicon"
Special thanks to everyone at Belkin
Thanks, too, Jerry Reed
Donnie Iris is managed by Belkin Personal Management

1996, into 1997. The band got back together and made their best record since the early 1980s. *Poletown* reunited the classic Cruisers long enough to make a satisfying record.

The record wasn't exactly a return to form, but that was by design. It was better: something new and different, with the more energy than they had laid down on tape since Reagan's first term.

DONNIE: I think the best tunes we wrote were on the first and second albums. The ones that followed, there were a few good songs. One in particular that we did that got hardly any recognition was called *Poletown*. There were a couple things on there that I thought were really cool, alternative-sounding songs that I thought should have done better than then did.

The album was inspired by two connected, unlikely sources: a law school case study, and a young lawyer's burgeoning career.

While Donnie had been hangin' out n 'nat, Mark became Mark Avsec, Attorney at Law. He started college in fall 1988, graduated in 1992, started law school right away, finished in fall 1994, passed the bar, and started working at Benesch and associates' firm March 1, 1995.

MARK: I lost the desire to make records. And then I wanted to do *Poletown*.

I figured once I started with the law firm, I wouldn't be able to do anything — which wasn't true. And then we did *Poletown*. *Poletown* was *not* a bad album. But it was different.

Before I really got into the practice of law, I wanted to do one more album with the original band.

I discussed it with Donnie and Marty. I thought we could rekindle some of that old magic.

So I really wanted Al. And I can't remember how we afforded to do it, but we got Al back here.

Poletown is the Cruisers record that took the longest to record, but the sessions weren't continuous. The band started in summer 1994, when Avsec was nearly done with law school. When OJ Simpson and Al Cowlings were cruising around Southern California in a white Bronco, the band watched from Jeree's.

After the debacle that was *Footsolider in the Moonlight*, Donnie had faith the band could still bring the heat.

DONNIE: I was not surprised in the least to record another album. We'll keep making records till we croak.

I think Mark brought up bringing Kev and Albritton back. Mark called them.

Poletown is an album that could only have come from the Rust Belt. The title track is a true story of industrial collapse and big business' disregard for a community. For Mark, nothing sets off a slow burn like a good old legal strong-arming.

MARK: I cannot remember what came first, the song "Poletown" or the album.

I remember the song was spurred by a legal case I studied in law school, about Poletown outside Detroit. It was a Polish neighborhood. People of the community were displaced for an economic reason. Eminent domain was used to force people out and to sell their home so economic progress could be made. I saw a movie on the whole ordeal and watched these old people really get upset because this was where they had lived their whole lives, old women getting pulled out of the church they loved before the wrecking ball hit it.

It resonated with me because of where I grew up in Cleveland, my old St. Vitus neighborhood at East 61st and St. Clair.

I probably got inspired then to do a whole album.

Poletown stripped away the band's sonic calling card, the stacked-tracks production style. And without the added sonic muscle, the original Cruisers were still a formidable band with something to say.

DONNIE: We wanted to do something different than what we had done prior.

MARK: I made a conscious decision that I wasn't gonna stack. We did not stack anything. There are no real background vocals on that record, not like we generally do them.

And we went back to Jeree's. That's a weird record, but I like that record. it's creative and different. It was a concession to grunge, almost. The idea was to have a darker album. And it was.

Recording 13 simpler songs was simpler than assembling ten superstacked tracks. But it wasn't *easy*.

MARK: It always takes time. I worked when I could. Sometimes I took a day off, or went out there late afternoon or on the weekends. Inspiration comes from all things — and you have to have the *time*. When I get focused, get out of my way.

DONNIE: It was easier for me, for sure. I didn't have to stay in the studio for hours on end. And I thought it still sounded pretty damned good.

And I liked the material. Everybody has kind of a dark side. And a lot of the songs on that record are dark.

It was a great feeling being able to create music again. I believe it was a very creative session. I really like that record.

Mark wrote every song on *Poletown*, but it feels like the kind of thing Donnie might have written anyway. As Donnie and Mark say, it truly is a dark — but balanced — set of tunes about collapse and renewal, damage and recovery, dreams and screams.

The bandleader remains committed to slower songs, ponderous tracks and ballads: the organ-driven confessional "Valerie," the tentative "Come Come Come," and pensive "Rubicon," which drifts from a near-piano keyboard to a wailing organ.

Albritton — who still played daily — slides right back into the lineup and sounds at home, whether he's stirring the dirty grind "I Am Your Eyes" or gently massaging the passionate "Valerie."

Poletown is the most *Marty* album in the Cruisers catalog. Without an artificially thick sound, Marty fills the air, connects the moments, and keeps the songs moving. The album starts off with gentle pastoral strumming — and when the first chorus ends, he breaks the chain and never comes back.

Marty's has his heaviest guitar outburst since "She's So Wild" in the title track. It gives way to a sudden soft accordion solo, then roars back with a vengeance. Kevin sounds like he's trying to hammer his kit through the floor.

"The Stalker" moves through a downright evil groove that matches Donnie's creepy delivery of lyrics about an obsessive pursuit. Iris follows with a tender turn in "I Don't Want to Be a Hero." In the gentle rocker, Avsec explores the celebrity culture that never served the Cruisers, and Donnie concurs in the chorus: "I don't wanna be a hero / I'll only break your heart."

Free from the '80s zeitgeist, Mark drops the synth tones and finally explores the organ sounds that blew his young mind. After some ups and downs, the record's sole songwriter arrives at a good place in "Hey Rembrandt." Donnie delivers some loving words of support and advice: "Pick up a brush and see what you can do." Mark the lawyer opened the door for Mark the artist, and Donnie sings as well as ever. And from time to time — as in an aptly named sixty-second vocal sprint — the 53-year-old frontman proved he could still *scream* it, too.

POLETOWN, THE SONGS: "POLETOWN"

DONNIE: Mark brought it to me, and said, "This is what it's all about." It's all in the history books, right there for everybody to see. It's the kind of thing that could have happened here. I had the rhythm track, and I had this thing I was doing on the guitar. Mark brought in the vocals over the guitar thing. It worked out nice.

PAUL: That's my favorite Marty recording. He really gets out there.

"VALERIE"

DONNIE: I look at it like a guy who couldn't get this Valerie chick out of his mind; he's making love to one chick and thinking about somebody else. I know it has happened to people a lot.

"I AM YOUR EYES"

DONNIE: I love that song. I love the track, the steamy sound of the track, the darkness, the power.

We did some different tunings on the guitars. It was so cool, just to go in there and do more basic stuff, more gritty, dirty kind of stuff. It has this *gut* type of thing to it. I like the way the track sounds. I like the vocals, how the verses are and how it leads into the chorus.

These things just happen. You get a song. You don't know what it's going to be like. And at the end, "Bam — I like that one."

"DON'T WANT TO BE A HERO"

DONNIE: Mark wrote that, but that was something that could easily come out of me. That spoke to me. I was just trying to bring the lyric out, so people could relate to it.

"I LIE DOWN"

DONNIE: I could relate to that. There's so many *songs* on that one.

I think it was easier to do all those *Poletown* tracks in that style than something like *King Cool*.

"BITTER LEMONS"

DONNIE: That's not one of my favorites, but I think it was pretty good. My grandfather had a garden. That was a big part of my life. He used to show me it; he was so proud of it. He had everything: basil, tomatoes, cucumbers, peppers. It was huge, beautiful.

PAUL: That's my favorite studio performance by Albritton. I have a lot of respect for his bass playing.

"HEY REMBRANDT"

DONNIE: That's a great lyric. Mark's just good at lyrics. He always was. There's nothing wrong with that tune. When he brought it to me, I saw it like a "What's Going On" tune — "it's your world, do something with it."

"SCREAM"

DONNIE: We had fun with that. I thought it was pretty cool. We were pretty much trying to capitalize on my screams.

"ACROSS THE RUBICON"

DONNIE: I thought that was an OK tune, as far as my performance was concerned. I didn't think I killed on that.

DONNIE: It was great getting the original band back in the studio again. It felt like taking the bike out of the garage, taking the tarp off.

MARK: *Poletown* had more soul. Of course, it is all about the songs. I don't always write decent songs, that's for sure. It was good to play with Kevin and Albritton again. It reminded me how impactful Albritton was. We still had the magic.

POLETOWN: REVIEWS, REACTION AND ADAPTATIONS

Some agreed, some not.

The Pittsburgh press didn't rally behind it. The *Post-Gazette* gave it a one-star review.

"I like Donnie Iris," began *Post-Gazette* critic Ed Masley, trotting out his credibility as a longtime fan — while rolling up his sleeves and mentioning he didn't grow up in an area with an "All Donnie, All Day" radio station. "At best, it could pass for a bad Dire Straits impression. The riffs are generic, the vocals too talky." In conclusion, Masley balked at the title track's basic premise, and speculated that Joe Grushecky would have thrown it away.[57.1] Some people in the Rust Belt get tired of hearing the Rust Belt narrative.

Donnie's true hometown newspaper cut *Poletown* more slack. But writer Virginia Ross Lutz still didn't know what to make of the Cruisers in a mode that was, in every sense of the term, heavier:

"Iris has a little fun with fallen love and hopeful recovery in 'Within Me and Without You,'" wrote Times/Beaver Newspapers critic Lutz. "Note a definite highlight here, because there aren't many....

"Overall the work might come across as negative. But weaved with clever phrases, it effectively digs into and at times brings humor to life's little ironies. It offers an abundance of sin, lust, adultery, guilt, anger discouragement and cynicism. Whew! You can either listen and have some fun with it (move around a lot, that is) or really listen and get into some heavy thinking."[57.2]

The Cruisers celebrated *Poletown*'s release with a two-night stand March 14 and 15 at Nick's Fat City, Pittsburgh's reigning hot spot for original rock.[57.3] Albritton had played with them, live, while he was in town. Kevin lived in California now, and Tommy was still the live drummer.

Mark playing the "Poletown" accordion solo.

Six songs from the album made it into the live set at various points, but didn't last long: "How You Gonna Mend It?," "Valerie," "Bitter Lemons," "I Am Your Eyes," and "Cross the Rubicon." The title track made their imminent live album, *Live at Nick's Fat City* — where the band had had some trouble with the song.

GLENN RATNER, PARALLEL TIME: At Nick's during the song "Poletown," Mark put his accordion on while he was inside his keyboard section. And then right before it was his time to play the solo, he tried to step out to get to center stage — and realized he couldn't get out with the accordion on, because the gap was too small.

So then he's frantically trying to get it off so he can get out before he gets to the solo. Total Spinal Tap moment.

PAUL: Mark was trapped. That stage was *soooo* small. Marty, Donnie, and I often hit each other by accident with our guitar necks.

My favorite *Poletown* song to play was "How You Gonna Mend It." Al's bass part was fun to play.

MARK: I thought *Poletown* was a good record. I thought it had some good material. But again: Nobody gave a damn anymore.

Finishing *Poletown* ate most of the band's available time for the year. Not a lot of shows for the rest of the year. But they made the remaining ones count .

(Photo by Richard Kelly)

CHAPTER 58

Live at Nick's Fat City: The Album

Live at Nick's Fat City

The first official live album by Donnie Iris and the Cruisers. Featuring…

"Agnes" (Lyrics by Avsec, Iris) 6:05
"Do You Compute?" (Avsec, Iris) 4:52
"10th Street" (Avsec, Iris) 4:09
"Tough World" (Avsec, Iris, Hoenes) 5:29
"I Can't Hear You" (Avsec, Iris, McClain, Hoenes, Valentine) 3:45
"That's the Way Love Ought to Be" (Avsec, Iris) 4:52

"Poletown" (Avsec) 6:06
"This Time It Must Be Love" (Avsec, Iris, Hoenes) 4:39
"Injured in the Game of Love" (Avsec, Iris) 8:43
"Love Is Like a Rock" (Avsec, Iris, Hoenes, McClain, Valentine) 6:39
"Ah! Leah!" (Avsec, Iris) 7:06
"The Rapper" (Iris) 5:15

From the credits:

Release: March 16, 1998

Label: Primary Records Group

Recorded at Nick's Fat City in Pittsburgh on September 12 and 13, 1997

Produced by Mark Avsec and Rick Witkowski

Recorded LIVE! by Rick Witkowski, Lou Contumelio and Craig Maloney

Mixed at Studio L by Rick Witkowski

Concert sound: Jim Markovich

Primary Records Group, Inc.

Donnie Iris: vocals

Mark Avsec: organ, accordion, synths, piano, vocals

Marty Lee Hoenes: guitar and vocals

Paul Goll: bass guitar and vocals

Tommy Rich: drummist

"**Trust me, the ONLY place to see Donnie live is in a crowded bar. I remember this one time, Donnie had to stop talking over the 'Here we go, Steelers' cheer.**"
— **YouTube user Junkyardkid, comment from "Injured" video**[58.1]

September 1997. Through the '90s, Nick's Fat City was the best Burgh bar to catch your favorite local band — and any national artist they could book. The Clarks practically lived there. Around 1997, Donnie and the Cruisers planted a big, old yellow flag there, too.

Poletown was complete and out in the world. While the Cruisers were running hot, Donnie and the band recorded their definitive in-concert document, the album *Live at Nick's Fat City*.

Promotional shot glasses from a performance at Nick's Fat City

In the 1990s, Nick's Fat City was the best live-music venue on the South Side, a happening neighborhood across the Monongahela River from downtown. Carson Street was a congested strip of clubs, bars, record stores, coffee spots, retail and restaurants that, simply, was *the* place to be. A big square with two tiers, it didn't have one bad sightline. And the ace bar staff worked fast.

TOMMY: Nick's was a favorite place to play: great stage, good sounding room. And the whole South Side strip had a cool vibe to hang in. We usually went across the street — the restaurant there [Mario's South Side Saloon] was owned by the Nick's peeps, and they took great care of us. Lots of pre-show cocktails and food. Sometimes a lotta fans hangin' around and BS'ing with us. And usually, there was some mayhem back at the hotel afterwards, just fun partying for whoever was around. The shows at Nick's were just real good, fun, well played nights. The second night, often with a hangover.

Live at Nick's Fat City marks the Cruisers recording debut of Paul Goll, the band's current bassist, who replaced Scott Alan in 1992. The track list is the band's standard best-of set, long versions with extended jams in place, and their traditional set opener, "Agnes," in its rightful place.

The Cruisers and their fans had long since figured out how they liked their Donnie. And now it was time to document the barebones, sweaty, live-wire concert experience. As Mark explains in the liner notes:

"The songs took on another life when the band started playing them in concert. Donnie turned out, of course, to be a phenomenal live performer, and he always rocks the house. But these live recordings also showcase the rock-steady Paul Goll on bass, the reckless and rollicking drumming of Tommy Rich, often taking the band on journeys to destinations unknown, and the intelligent ferocity of guitarist Marty Lee Hoenes, one of the most inventive musicians I have ever been privileged to play with.... These recordings are a snapshot of a period in Donnie's and the band's career worth memorializing.

"People line up for the shows at Nick's, which are always sold out, hours before the doors open. The crowd knows the lines well and comes to participate in the experience of the show.... What you hear on this CD is what happened on two warm September nights, when the wind was blowing through the trees and this dude, Louie, was looking for a fight."

MARK: I got burned out on studio albums and wondered whether anyone cared about new songs. We never did a live album. We wanted to memorialize the Nick's Fat City run we were doing at the time.

We did not rehearse for *Live at Nick's*. We never rehearsed. Ever. Maybe once or twice when we were auditioning drummers, or maybe for 10 minutes after a sound check. We should probably rehearse for a whole day and redo the set. But we just don't.

TOMMY: I can't remember individual gigs really, 'cause we played there so much. We did two nights, ran the set straight through.

PAUL: On Live at *Nick's Fat City*, Mark plays accordion on "Pole Town," and it's outstanding. He is also a master on the accordion and can play polkas and do impromptu humorous performances.

DONNIE: I thought that lineup worked pretty well live. The *Nick's Fat City* album was pretty damned good.

MARK: We might re-release it.

Tommy is really good on that album. *Live at Nick's* was a great recording of us live. In the studio, we struggled to get good tracks with Tommy — and I'm not saying it was because of Tommy. Maybe because the songs were bad.

TOMMY: I'm just happy I got to do the *Live at Nick's* record. That was cool, and real. It don't suck.

MARK: Rick Witkowski was a big part of that record, he really captured it and mixed it. Wonderful person and good ears.

TOMMY: Mark gave me the roughs from each night and asked for my input on the performances of each song from one night vs. the other. I believe I got 'em, cause drums was the one thing that couldn't be fixed. That said, they didn't fix hardly anything. It's a very live-*live* record. I've produced some "live" records that the only thing live left after fixes was the crowd.

MARK: No overdubs.

MICHELLE MICHAELS, LONGTIME WDVE *ELECTRIC LUNCH* HOST: My two favorite Donnie songs are "That's the Way Love Ought to Be" and "Love is Like a Rock," recorded at Nick's Fat City. It was the audio snapshot of the definitive relationship between Donnie and his Pittsburgh fans. It was so exemplary of the love and party fun he had with all of us — and we right back at him.

The band released the *Live at Nick's Fat City* CD at another two-night stand at Nick's March 20 and 21, 1998.

Live at Nick's was the first release from Primary; the Cruisers took over their distribution from Belkin, who was still their valued mentor and manager. Distribution was spotty; one of the record's few reviews told fans they could purchase bit by sending a check to the band's Cleveland post office box.

The people who heard it got it. The *Times'* Scott Tady — the Beaver Valley's latter-day *Dawnie* beat reporter — cultivated a perspective on the record: "Halfway through the disc, Iris and the Cruisers bring the tempo to a screeching halt with last year's vastly underrated 'Poletown' from the same-named CD.... 'Poletown' offers some of the toughest guitar and most emotional singing to ever grace an Iris album."[58.2]

"AH! LIA!"

For Donnie, the overdue, well-received live gonzo was not the most important arrival in March '98.

Another family Dominic was born March 31, 1998. Donnie was now a grandfather. Erin, his older daughter, later named her second child Sammy, after Donnie's dad, who the grandchildren called "Pappy Sam." Gianna, Donnie's first granddaughter, followed in 2008.

ERIN: Dad was there when each of his grandchildren was born. When Dominic was born, the nurses were all very excited and talking about Donnie Iris being there in the hospital when his first grandson, and namesake, was born. One of them called DVE, and they announced it on the radio. Addy, Donnie's second daughter, also has three kids: Jack, Chase, and Lia. The two elder ones chose the third's name, voting for "Leah" over "Iris." Addy opted for the Italian spelling, and Lia was born in 2014.

ADDY: My dad drove to Maryland through a blizzard to be there for Jack's birth.

ERIN: Our cousins Carrie, Ryan and Jason were more musically inclined than we were. The boys have been involved in the Pittsburgh rock scene, and are still actively involved with music.

My son is in college now, and he's experiencing the same thing I did in college: He has friends who are amazed and that he is Donnie Iris' grandson. They have started to come to the concerts, and they have a blast. I would have never guessed our kids' friends would still know the music, but the love for his music has been handed down from generation to generation.

ERIN: Dad was always about playing with the kids, and still is. When we were growing up, we had parties, but he always spent time with the kids. He would get us in what he called The Trap of Doom, which was so much fun.

ADDY: We were on the ground, and he would scissor his legs around us and our cousins. We were trapped, and he would tickle us until we couldn't stand it. And now he does it to our kids too. They loved it when they were little. It's always a good time, tons of laughing.

And *that's* important to understand. Look at Donnie from the *Live at Blossom* video, when he's rocking an arena, busting one rock star move after another. And look at him now: still totally entertaining, way more than you could reasonably expect from any 75-year-old. But it's loose and freeform, nothing staged or choreographed about it. See him live now, and Donnie is having fun, with 50-plus years of experience behind how he shakes his *dupa*. What keeps Donnie on stage, unafraid to bang his head a little?

Donnie Iris is playful.

STEALING THE SHOW AT STARLAKE

So anyway: 1998 was a big year for the band at Nick's — and beyond. Things were ramping back up. 1998 was the first year since 1985 they played more than ten shows. 1999, they played nearly two dozen. Only the fans noticed. The Pittsburgh press stilled referred to Donnie in the past tense, churning out the familiar biographic rehash: "Donnie Iris was in the Jaggerz. 'Ah! Leah!.' Now he's a grandfather and a mortgage broker. He's playing with Joe Grushecky Friday."

When they took the time to watch him, they left with a better impression.

In 1999, Donnie held his own with mid-card opening slot opening for Hootie & the Blowfish and Collective Soul, at WDVE's 30th birthday bash at Star Lake Amphitheatre (the Pittsburgh Blossom), above Shawn Mullins of "Lullaby" fame" but below Collective Soul ("Shine"). They rose to the occasion, and the *Post-Gazette*'s John Young had a hoot during an all killer-no-filler 30 minute set: "Iris' yowl was strong as ever during the code of a pounding 'That the Way Love Oughtta Be.'"[58.3]

Planet Christmas: The (Mark) Album

1998. Merry Christmas. Get used to it.

Mark released another solo project, a flight of fancy from his home studio, *Planet Christmas.* The disc is a warped and experimental world-music collection of instrumental Christmas classic, not unlike *Joyeaux Mutato*, the yuletide one-off by Devo mastermind Mark Mothersbaugh. Mark says he didn't take the project seriously. But he did finish it. And release it. And, as history would prove, the theme was one he felt worth revisiting.

"God Rest Ye Merry Gentlemen (Intro)"
"Jingle Bells"
"Angels We Have Heard On High"
"God Rest Ye Merry, Gentlemen
  (Reprise)"
"O Christmas Tree"
"The First Noel"
"The Little Drummer Boy"
"Silent Night"
"We Three Kings"
"O Holy Night"
"Joy to the World!" / "Hark!
  The Herald Angels Sing"
"O Come, All Ye Faithful"
"Angels, We Have Heard
  on High (Ending) "

Primary Records
1998

MARK: *Planet Christmas* was just me and a six-pack of beer, having fun by myself. And I decided to put it out.

(Photo by Anastasia Pantsios)

Interlude:
Donnie Iris' Top Ten Albums of All Time

10
Led Zeppelin, *Led Zeppelin*

9
Beatles, *Abbey Road*

8
Derek and the Dominos, *Layla & Other Assorted Love Songs*

7
Temptations, *Greatest Hits*

6
Rolling Stones, *Sticky Fingers*

5
Pink Floyd, *Dark Side of the Moon*

4
Beatles, *Sgt. Pepper's Lonely Hearts Club Band*

3
Beatles, *Rubber Soul*

2
Beatles, White Album

1
Marvin Gaye, *What's Going On*

> I can sit down and write a song,
> but it's like pulling teeth. ...I'm too
> lazy. I don't want to sit home and
> woodshed and try to write songs.
> I'd rather go to a baseball game.
> I'd rather play golf.
> But Mark is just so good at it.
>
> ~ DONNIE IRIS

CHAPTER 60

Together Alone: The Album

An album by Donnie Iris+: Donnie and Mark Avsec, with the Cruisers. Featuring...

"Amazing Grace" (John Newton)
"The Promise" (Hoenes)
"Lay with Me" (Avsec)
"Together Alone" (Avsec)
"You're Holding My Heart
  in Your Hands" (Avsec)

"Fade Away" (Avsec)
"Ah! Leah!" (Acoustic version –
  Avsec, Iris)
"I'd Rather Go Blind" (Avsec)
"Holy Love" (Avsec)

Release: November 20, 1999
Primary Records Group

From the credits:
Donnie Iris: Vocals
Mark Avsec: Organ, piano, synthesizers, strings, voices, programming
Marty Lee Hoenes: Acoustic and electric guitar
Paul Goll: Bass and cello
Tommy Rich: Drums
Produced by Mark Avsec
("The Promise" co-produced by Mark Avsec and Rick Witkowski)
Engineered and Mixed by Greg Zydyk
Mastered by Francisco Rodriguez - Digital Dynamics Audio Inc.
Recorded and mixed at MetroSync Recording Studio, Cleveland, OH
(except "The Promise" basic track recorded at Studio L, Weirton, W. VA)
Design: Marty Lee Hoenes
The Cruisers are: Mark Avsec, Marty Lee Hoenes, Paul Goll, and Tommy Rich
November 1999. The Cruisers gave fans a deep blue holiday gift.

Right when the Cruisers were developing momentum, a new Donnie album took a sudden turn. *Together Alone* doesn't sound like a Cruisers album, and it isn't one — it's Donnie, the Cruisers, a collection of Pittsburgh all-stars, and some expert pals from the tri-state area. But the name Cruisers does not appear on the album. Technically, the record is Donnie and Mark doing their thing. And that thing, in this case, is mostly Mark's thing. The CD spine says "Donnie Iris +." It's not a Donnie solo album; it's more of a Mark solo album.

DONNIE: I didn't even realize it was called just Donnie Iris. That's a question for Mark.

On paper, it should have been a crowning achievement. It did reaffirm Donnie's role as the benevolent godfather of Pittsburgh rock. Donnie and Mark recruited a who's-who from the fertile Iron City scene

— including some leaders from a generation of musicians who grew up listening the Cruisers, formed bands, and earned major-label record deals of their own. But even though Donnie's name is on this record, it's not about Donnie.

For this record, Mark relocated to MetroSync, a well-stocked Cleveland studio. Engineering the sessions was studio co-owner Greg Zydyk, a Clevelander whose body of work included Lucky Pierre and Prick, two groups from the nexus of new wave and industrial scenes that spawned Trent Reznor and Nine Inch Nails. Also in the mix were other old friends and regional heroes. It's a delicate collection from a fragile juncture in Mark's life.

Mark didn't much care for making records at this point. But he had needed to work through some things.

MARK: All the people did good work. But that is a terrible album. That's my fault.

It was at a bad time in my life. I don't remember the sessions, how it came together. It's just a mish-mosh.

It wasn't really a Cruisers album. He's been a great friend over the years, Donnie. If I wanted to record a song or something, he'd do it. And I wanted to do a set of songs with him.

Mark's first marriage ended in 1999. The title and the lyric sheet read like a divorce album.

DONNIE: I think what Mark meant was him being with a woman, together, but actually alone.

MARK: The title, I don't know.

And that's how the mind of Mark Avsec works: intellect in the front, feelings pushed all the way to the back, swirling in his subconscious. Sometimes they leak out as art; consciously processing a negative emotion from 20 or 30 years ago is physically painful. And if he has to do it, he'll toss and turn all night, then wake up with an emotional hangover.

Mark and Donnie recorded *Together Alone* with the working title of *Postcards From Eternity*. The Pittsburgh all-stars concept, says Mark, was not a grand plan; it just worked out that way.

Together Alone is not a Cruisers album in name or form. The record is a motley mix, with many a mighty performance. But it starts with a slow electronic groove — and it does not gain momentum. If you include the hidden track, it's an hourlong dark night of the soul, a placid meditation on spiritual matters and interpersonal alimentation.

The collection begins a tri-state who's who taking turns on an electronic cover of John Newton's transcendent "Amazing Grace." Rusted Root's Jim DeSpirito programmed the unpredictable version of the spiritual standard, which connects turns by Donnie, Michael Stanley, B.E. Taylor, Clarks frontman Scott Blasey, and Kelsey Barber (now Kelsey Friday, then frontwoman of Pittsburgh alt-rock era stars Brownie Mary).

Joe Grushecky and Donnie trade verses in an earthy-yet-tender reprise of "The Promise," the Cruisers song Marty wrote for *King Cool*.

Donnie has never sounded as sad as he does in "Lay With Me," the most fully realized of Mark's piano ballads.

The title track is a showstopper of an unplugged duet between Donnie and Barber, whose textured voice, always in fine form, sounds better than ever.

Things stay somber in a piano-based arrangement of "Ah! Leah!" The original "Leah" suggests Donnie might win her one day; in the solemn version, he sounds *sure* they're never gonna make it.

The beats-per-minute count bottoms out in the hypnotic "Holy Love," in which Donnie recounts some of Mark's smoldering memories: "My love, I heard the angels sing / I heard the church bells ring / Holy love I may never feel again / But I was blessed by your holy love." For most of the song's five and a half minutes, it's all Donnie's tender voice and Mark's plaintive piano — but it ends with harmonies from Barber, a quick electric lick from Marty, and church-worthy organ from Mark.

As the *Times*' Scott Tady points out, the songs are focused on religion, and to a lesser degree, sleep.

The album opens with "Amazing Grace" and ends with a hidden track of church bells, an "allelujah" refrain, droning keyboards, and a choir.

Tady's balanced take on *Together Alone* concludes, "Obviously, the days of Iris appearing on the Top 40 charts are long gone. So, it's admirable that the Patterson Township resident has tried a dramatic change in style, rather than trying to rehash his old sound.... But for some late night, sip-a-glass-of-wine-and-ponder-your-life music, you can rely on *Together Alone*."[60.1]

The record barely rated a mention from the collective Pittsburgh and Cleveland press.

It's not what you want from a Cruisers album, but it's a coherent, touching and effective mood piece. Mark's momentary obsessions weren't enough to drive him back into a pew, and Donnie hadn't been a churchgoer for some time. But the spiritual mood is not insincere.

Mark, the record's mastermind, looks back at it like he's recalling a bloodletting.

MARK: I was morose. Not a good time in my life. Probably pondering lots of themes. That was a really bad album. I guarantee you that I will never listen to it again.

The subdued CD contributed more than its share of songs to the band's relatively static set list — for a short while. The band worked out "Lay With Me" live before the CD was out. "Amazing Grace" appeared from time to time in the album's wake. In 2006, Joe Grushecky made a surprise appearance at a Cruisers show at the Byham Theater, and the band played the *Together Alone* arrangement of Marty's "The Promise." The unplugged "Ah! Leah!" is still a staple in shows — in addition to the full electric version, not instead of it.

GLENN RATNER, PARALLEL TIME: "Lay With Me" was a change of pace from the usual fare at a Donnie Iris and the Cruisers high-octane rock and roll show. It gave Donnie a chance to show off his versatility as a singer. And with just Mark accompanying him at the piano, it was a very intimate moment in the show.

As for the uncharacteristically Donnie-free writing credits, the frontman didn't mind singing an album full songs entirely by Mark.

DONNIE: I can sit down and write a song, but it's like pulling teeth. It gets to the point where it's annoying. It's too tough. I doubt myself too much. I'm too lazy. I don't want to sit home and woodshed and try to write songs. I'd rather go to a baseball game. I'd rather play golf. But Mark is just so good at it.

PAUL: *Together Alone* was done at MetroSync, which was a nice old style studio.

We did a really cool version of Marty's song "The Promise" where Donnie and Joe Grushecky created magic singing together — my favorite.

We just knocked those tracks out with very few takes. I played my fretless bass on "The Promise" and played my cello on "Lay With Me." We did have some problems getting a decent sound on the cello, because it was not a very good instrument and I was still a beginner.

TOGETHER ALONE: DONNIE ON THE SPECIAL GUESTS

Mark and Donnie don't have anything to say about the songs from *Together Alone*. But they liked the friends who helped make it.

MARK: Were all of those people on the record? I don't even remember. Too bad it wasn't better; it's my fault I didn't write a better record. I knew they were the cream of the crop from Pittsburgh. They'd do anything for Donnie; anybody would.

DONNIE: It's like family around here: the Clarks, Joe Grushecky, B.E. Taylor, all those guys.

Everybody was easy to work with. It's not like we were all in the studio at the same time. I wasn't in the studio when Scott did his part or Kelsey did hers or Scott.

I wasn't in the studio with any of them. We laid down the tracks. Then Mark laid down their vocals over my tracks. I wish I would have been in the studio; it would have been great. But it was too hard to put something like that together.

I thought "Amazing Grace" was a sensational vocal performance. Everybody sounded so good, especially Scott. I think Scott brought that whole thing home. I don't go back and listen to stuff much at all, except the Christmas album, because it's Christmas. But I thought it was a really good performance with some really good voices.

I don't remember singing the song in church, but it's a classic song everybody knows. It's just one of those songs you've heard so many times. Rick Witkowski did a great job on that, too. He's a great player.

Scott and I are good friends, and he's a great singer, a great songwriter. We do quite a bit of benefit shows together. We all look forward to it. It's a blast, seeing everybody and being on stage together.

I don't remember it being my idea, but I was glad it happened, because I loved what Scott did with the song, with a register I had never heard before. It was with the high end of his voice, the upper limits of his notes. And it sounds just great. I thought it was one of the highlights of the record.

I know the Clarks real well. They're a great band, especially live. They rock hard. They're very, very good. I've sat in with them a couple of times, at a couple of the big shows. They asked me to come up and do "Leah" and "Love Is Like a Rock" at Station Square. I'll still sit in with them every now and then.

[Early Clarks classic] "Penny on the Floor" is a great lyric. Great, great song. He and Greg, the bass player, they write great songs. That's just a good, iconic Pittsburgh band.

They may all have been Mark's invites. I know [Kelsey] very well. Great girl. I like her voice. I like her presence on stage. Her attitude. I think she did great. Her voice sounded just right. They worked well together.

Rick's a great guy. I've known him for years, will still do shows with him every once in a while. We're going to do a show for the mayor for his inaugural party and Christmas party. I'll see Rick there and Scott there, Joe Grushecky. He's definitely a bandleader type guy. He knows everybody's songs. He knows everybody's stuff. And if I know he's there playing guitar, I know it's gonna be great.

Rusted Root, I know Michael Glabicki better than any of them. We've done some benefit shows with them. Michael is a different type of talent, one of a kind. He's like a left-hand turn off the straight rock-and-roll path. He's just a good guy. We hit it off very well.

Michael Stanley is a great songwriter. He's been a great friend since the '80s when we played together at all those gigs. And he's got a nice voice, too. It's just a pleasant, gritty but still good. I like it more than a lot of other people. He doesn't get enough credit.

We never worked together on the track. Joe [Grushecky] is a dedicated singer-songwriter-musician, even though he is a dedicated schoolteacher. You can tell he works at it a lot. That's what I like best about Joe: He is a true student of the industry. It shows. He writes some great songs. His band is a great rock-and-roll band.

There's some cool things on there. There's some cool things on all the records. It's OK.

CHAPTER 61

Parallel Time:
The Cruisers Fan Community

2000. The internet was, as they said, getting big.

When Mark's spirit was flagging, a new fan forum lifted it. Pittsburgher Glenn Ratner had launched the website Parallel Time in 1997. It became the online hub for the community of worldwide Cruisers fans well into the Facebook era. It still is the definitive resource for Cruisers history. The site hosts recollections, show dates, flyers, articles, comments, questions, answers and all kinds of ephemera documenting the band's underdocumented career.

MARK: An inspiration to me was Glenn at the Parallel Time site. At that time they were pretty active, I thought, "Wow. Somebody cared this much?"

GLENN: I first heard Donnie in the late '80s, after I had my license and was listening to WDVE a lot. They played the hits, and then some deeper tracks like "I Can't Hear You." I remember loving that song — and then finding out it was Donnie Iris and the Cruisers and being surprised. It didn't sound like Donnie.

I saw them live and saw how great of a band they were. I realized it was more than just Donnie. It wasn't really until after I started the website that I came to know how important Mark was in everything, and it wasn't a true "solo artist" situation.

I'm a big music fan, and all of my other favorite artists had great fan run sites that I loved. More often than not, these sites were better than the official band sites. I couldn't believe such a great band didn't have one. Because when you went to the shows, you could see the passion the fans had for the band. Cruisers fans are regular working class people that love rock music and like to have a good time.

In fact, in 1997 there was virtually nothing on the web about them. I contemplated it for a bit, and then *Poletown* came out. It was such a great album. It proved they were still capable of greatness. And that's pretty much when I decided to do it.

The name, I just wanted to use something related to the band. And that song title lent itself to kinda being a destination. Cool tune too.

Best Cruisers show you ever saw?

The 25th Anniversary show at the Chevy Amphitheater at Station Square. It was pretty special just because it was different. The *Ellwood City* release show at the same venue was memorable too. They've never been better than when Kevin is behind the drums.

Favorite '80s album?

No Muss… No Fuss starts off with three classic songs, and it stays strong before finishing off with two should-be classics. Donnie has never sounded better, and the songwriting is some of Mark's best.

Favorite post-'80s album?

While I love *Poletown*, my favorite later album is *Ellwood City*. It's a return to their classic sound and style. Very strong album, start to finish.

Favorite side project or related band?

Cellarful of Noise. Some great songs on both albums.

Favorite song?

"That's The Way Love Ought To Be." A great, hard-rocking, yet melodic tune. It's everything I love about this this band. The lyrics are timeless. It's never better than live, when everybody's got their fist in the air singing the "hey hey hey" parts!

THE AUDIENCE GET IN ON THE ACT

After 1999, the Cruisers kept fans happy, with an average of 15-20 shows a year. The played Nick's, clubs, colleges, regattas, fairs, and opened for an occasional national act like Eddie Money or Pat Benatar, whose bandleader is also a Cleveland guy, Neil Giraldo.

The Cruisers officially turned 20 in 2000. By then, every show was a party, and the band didn't need a birthday bash. Live sets had become a full-on Steel City ceremony. Donnie's Rocky shtick caught on with the fans, and now every Cruisers show was part *Rocky Horror*:

RATNER: There are three main audience participation parts:

The "no more" parts in "I Can't Hear You": You throw your arm in the air like you're showing your muscle, in an L shape.

The "hey hey hey!" parts in "That's The Way Love Ought To Be," fist in the air.

"Love Is Like A Rock," the "1... 2.... 1... 2... 3... 4!" counting off on your fingers raised in the air.

Very few bands have signature audience participation parts — let alone *three*.

In the millennial years, new songs had a way of working themselves out of the set list. The Cruisers' old label was about to formally commemorate the Cruisers' old-school favorites.

The Millennium Collection: Best of Donnie Iris. The Album.

20th Century Masters: The Millennium Collection: Best of Donnie Iris

Hot hits and fan favorites from the MCA years, 1980-1983. Featuring...

"Ah! Leah!" (Avsec, Ierace)

"I Can't Hear You" (Avsec, Ierace, Hoenes, McClain, Valentine)

"Agnes" (Avsec, Ierace)

"Sweet Merilee" (Avsec, Ierace)

"Love Is Like a Rock" (Avsec, Ierace, Lee, McClain, Valentine)

"That's the Way Love Ought to Be" (Avsec, Ierace)

"My Girl" (Avsec, Ierace)

"Tough World" (Avsec, Ierace, Lee)

"This Time It Must Be Love" (Avsec, Ierace, Lee)

"Do You Compute?" (Avsec, Ierace)

"She's So European" (Avsec, Ierace)

"The Rapper" (Live – Ierace)

Released: September 18, 2001
Label: Geffen
Tracks 8-12 available on CD for the first time

September 2001. Another big "...sort of" qualification in a long list of Cruisers footnotes: Donnie & the Cruisers' best-of album.

The collection is most of the better tracks from the band's first four albums, the ones released between 1980 and 1983, the MCA records. As of this writing, this collection is the only Cruisers material from the 1980s that you can legally purchase and stream. As far as best-of albums go, it's better than most.

The Millennium Collection is not unpopular: As of August 17, 2017, it was Amazon's #11-selling Power Pop album, #95 New Wave release, and #180 arena rock record. With 72 customer reviews, it averaged 4 and a half stars (of a possible five). At the iTunes store, 66 customer reviews averaged four stars. Granted: That and $1.29 will buy you an mp3 copy of "Ah! Leah!"

The *20th Century Masters: Millennium Collection* series is the Universal Music Group's preferred method of dealing with its ocean-sized catalog: issuing affordable, respectably curated best-of discs, via its Geffen label, with generous liner notes — and, often, forgetting the rest of the band's catalog.

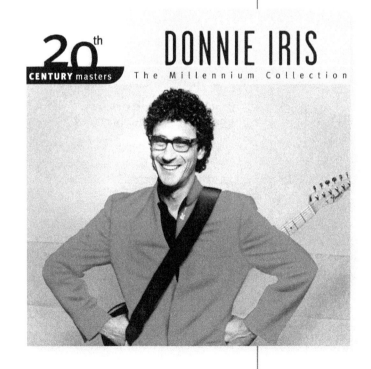

Finding the Cruisers on CD has always been a dicey proposition.

The Cruisers' 1980s albums are not commercially available in CD or digital form (as of this writing). The vinyl albums are also out of print.

("Out of print" does not mean "You can't get them anywhere"; it means "no longer being produced and sold by an authorized source.")

MCA has *never* released the band's first four albums on CD. Selling the discs — or posting them at the iTunes store — seems like a simple enough proposition. But it isn't.

Attempts to make Donnie's classic albums commercially available are complicated; when they were terminated in 1983, the Cruisers were a low-selling band at the far end of MCA's trough. Their mass-market appeal has not appreciated since.

Some '80s albums have been available on CD, for short bursts.

Belkin bought rights to *No Muss… No Fuss,* and Mark's Primary Records had it remastered and re-released on CD in 1999. It is out of print, rare and goes for a mint on eBay.

In 1993, the big indie label Razor & Tie — onetime home of the Clarks and numerous others — licensed and reissued *Back on the Streets* and *King Cool* as individual CDs. Fans say these versions sounded better than a later CD with both albums on one disc. The Razor & Tie release has no mastering information, and the albums were likely not remastered.

In 2007, American Beat Records licensed *Back on the Streets* and *King Cool*, then released both on a single CD — but removed "Too Young to Love," the final song from *Back on the Streets*, to accommodate available space. That version is out of print. This pressing has no CD mastering information, but it sounds different than the previous digital edition.

MARK: They were remastered. I was totally disrespected in the process. Nobody wanted to talk to me about the remastering.

They only wanted to talk to Donnie — "He's Donnie Iris, not you."

I said, "Fine, talk to Donnie."

Then Donnie said, "Talk to Mark."

So then they talked to me. I cannot remember that I had that much input.

Smaller labels have inquired about licensing the MCA albums, but MCA requires a sizable investment and a large number of copies.

The only legal digital source for any — not all — of Donnie's better 1980s tracks is the collection *20th Century Masters: The Millennium Collection: Best of Donnie Iris*, which is available via CD, streaming and digital download at all major sources.

In the *All Music Guide to Rock*, Stephen Thomas Erlewine gave it four of five stars, in a review full of back-handed compliments: "When it clicked, like on 'Ah! Leah!', it clicked perfectly, illustrating that the gap between power popsters and the supposed charlatans was simply a matter of style…. The best songs here will be irresistible to anyone with a serious power pop jones and no pop snobbery."[62.1]

For the best-of collection, Universal/Geffen commissioned efficient liner notes from author, journalist and music-writing veteran Bill DeYoung. The text runs about 1,000 words, the size of a full-page feature in a weekly paper, longer than most of the stories written about the Cruisers.

DeYoung on *Back on the Streets*: "Pure and honest to Holly-esque pop music, bubbly Beatles sounds and blue-eyed soul…. keyboard and synthesizer work [that run] the gamut from barrel-house boogie-woogie to New Wave riffs ripped from the ranks of the Tubeway Army." And on *King Cool*: "balanced a kind of New Wave hipness with a heartfelt appreciation for clean, straightforward rock 'n' roll, its subject matter pretty much boy/girl stuff down the line."[62.2]

MARK: The best-of for Universal, I don't think for we even knew about it. It was not remastered, and it just came out. I don't have an issue with it.

DONNIE'S BEST: NOT THE WAY YOU REMEMBERED

But, as always, it's never that simple. The tracks aren't remastered. And they're not exact transfers from the vinyl masters. Three songs on the Millennium Collection feature noteworthy differences: One is trivial. One is subtle, but significant. And one a big deal.

Subtle but different: On the digital transfers, the gloss is slick, careful, and well executed. It gives the songs a radio-quality punch. But the new treatment makes Albritton's bass less pronounced in the wall of sound.

Trivial: "My Girl" begins with an extra second of drum clicks at the beginning.

Kind of a big deal: Compared to the album version, "Love Is Like a Rock" sounds very different.

KEVIN: Hell! These versions sound totally different. Almost like two different mixes. I'm sure it's just different mastering, but that mastering made a world of difference. There is a ton more reverb on the album version. It sounds like there were two mixes. Maybe this was an alternate mix with less reverb, unlike the album version.

Unless the choice was made to go with the alternate version, it was a mistake that someone chose the other version for the *Millennium* CD. I prefer the album version: It does have that extra reverb, and it sounds more hyped, or more like what the radio compression would do to the song, even though it's maybe just the additional reverb. The *Millennium* version is dryer and more clear, but doesn't have the life and animation of the album version. The real question is why.

DJ and old-school fan Ron Gerber had similar questions. He got answers from the source. Gerber tracked down Doug Schwartz, who is listed as the mastering engineer. In an email exchange, Schwartz explained...

SCHWARTZ: In all honesty, I can't remember exactly what sources were given to me for that Donnie Iris project. I'm almost certain this was not a special remix, but the question of where that song was sourced may be irretrievable. Typically I'd get a box of tapes from the vault and would evaluate on a case-by-case basis which would yield the best results....

I did a whole slew of those Best of/20th Century Masters with Andy McKaie and the crew at Universal, and often he would have a Post-it note on the outside of a reel, saying "Song A, Song B" or whatever....

My best guess would be that the vault has several passes at that song. Oftentimes, mixes for single/45 had a narrower stage (if not downright mono). So somehow my bet is that there's a better source than what was used initially for the *King Cool* release. This brings us back to [Bill] Inglot, who used to absolutely insist on using the first generation master tape and not an EQ'd for LP copy. Guys at the vault in the dawn of the CD era were not so versed in what the differences were, and how important that could be.

GERBER: So we can conclude definitively that it was not remixed from the multi-tracks for 20th Century Masters, but was made earlier and was probably unused.[62.3]

BEST OF?

For the Cruisers, the proposition that some songs are better/best is a hot-button issue.

MARK: The best songs are there. Nobody's going to say they like "She's So Wild."

"She's So Wild" is fun song — perhaps a *tad* juvenile, but a rocker.

MARK: We don't think some of our songs are that big a deal. I don't walk around going, "'You're Gonna Miss Me,' man — that's a great song!" No. That's a tired-sounding song that made a record that shouldn't have made it. I'm not proud of it.

"You're Gonna Miss Me" is not a terrible song.

MARK: It's just not interesting to talk about these songs. I might love some James Gang song, and Joe would be, "What? *Why?*" I get that.

But to us, the band, it's about a relationship with each other. We threw a bunch of stuff against the wall and saw what stuck. And a few things stuck. And they're probably the best songs.

Most of the best songs, the songs I think are good, are on the best-of record. And then probably the rest of them aren't that good.

MARTY: I really do like most all of our recorded work for various reasons, and in various ways. And I tend to appreciate them all as examples of what we did, at those points in time. If we didn't like them, generally speaking, they didn't end up appearing on our albums.

Look, I have few favorites of ours and of other artists — but It would be difficult for me to care less how U2, for example, would rank their songs into best of groupings. Do they think "Sunday Bloody Sunday" is better than "Beautiful Day"? Really? I find it hard to imagine they see their work in those terms. But that's me.

So yeah, I see why a label would arbitrarily create a best-of album — it's business — take them out of context, like ripping separate chapters from different novels, shove them into a CD and sell 'em. But as an artist? I don't think that way.

DONNIE: Absolutely with you on this, Marty.

MARK: Those first four records aren't they online? That surprises me. I can't do it. MCA's not going to do it, because they don't care, and they won't make money on it. They're not rude, and they're not bad people; if I were them, I wouldn't care either.

Three people say they want them — but people are going to work every day, they're trying to do their job. And even *I* don't have time to call MCA about it. It's all about what you've got going on in your life. If I didn't have a whole lot going on in my life, I'd be upset about it. But the fact is: I have a whole lot going on.

The Cruisers did not sell a ton of records, so the Napster digital-bootleg download era didn't hurt their modest bottom line. The legal, streamlined iTunes store evolution didn't move the needle or swell their periodic checks, either. And Spotify's meager royalties for legal high-quality streams definitely aren't paying for Kevin and Paul's airfare.

MARK: Digital didn't change our world, because it was already done. We weren't relevant in the age of downloading. It changed our world in a slight fashion, the way we make records now. People don't think of music now as buying a piece of something — maybe that's ok, and it has evolved.

But we never really made royalties on our records. So digital didn't matter to us.

And I'm not the one signed to the record label. Donnie signed. I was the producer. I signed the BEMA publishing contract. Those records cost a certain amount and never recouped, I'm sure, technically.

We got money from writing. I get some money every three months, for writing and mechanical royalties, but it's not much. I don't drink beer, but it buys some wine — the money is appreciated, I'll say. I just read Bruce Springsteen's book. He didn't make any money when we was doing *The River*, and that was after *Born to Run*. He didn't make any money until *Born in the USA*.

Sometimes it's just a long tail: Not enough people are buying them, so they don't press them anymore. So they're out of print.

Selling the 80s albums online, apparently, is not nearly so simple as posting them and collecting the money.

MARK: Do *you* want to be on the phone with me when I call MCA? If I can even get through to the right person, here's what they're going to say: "Sure: We need a $10,000 advance, probably more. Then royalties against that."

Our fans don't buy our records now. They can say they will, and they want it. But they don't buy them.

CHAPTER 63

The James Gang Rides Again, With Joe. And Mark.

2001. It was a big year for Mark, personally and musically. He remarried. And he landed a gig with a musician who's as high-profile as it gets. One of Mark's original musical heroes saddled up his first big band again. And he roped Mark into the posse. Joe Walsh reunited with the James Gang, the band behind radio warhorses like "Funk 49" and "The Bomber," which elegantly flows from a piledriver riff, through Vince Guaraldi's jazz landmark "Cast Your Fate to the Wind," into Ravel's *Bolero*, and back again. It's one of classic rock's great visionary moments.

Then Walsh joined the Eagles, when the aerie of titans needed some extra wattage to enhance their credibility as a *rocking* rock band. It worked. With Walsh on the team, they became one of the biggest groups in the history of rock. Three of their releases moved over ten million copies (*Their Greatest Hits 1971-1975*, *Eagles Greatest Hits Volume II*, and *Hotel California*). *Their Greatest Hits*, at 29 times platinum, is the second-best selling album of all time.

Walsh nurtured a soft spot for his old band, despite an ugly breakup with their mutual manager, Mike Belkin. In 2001, Walsh reunited with bassist Dale Peters and drummer Jimmy Fox, who had worked for Belkin and helped Donnie and Mark build the Cruisers machine.

The trio reunited needed a keyboardist for classic tunes like "Tend My Garden."

Fox knew a guy. Fox knows a lot of guys.

Jimmy Fox
(Photo by Panel F Media Photography)

FOX: ["Like a Rolling Stone" keyboardist] Al Kooper is good. He's a great friend, and he's a lot of fun. But. Mark Avsec is a guy who grew up listening to the James Gang records, with a little transistor radio on his pillow at night. He was a fan. And it occurred to me, after knowing Mark, that he knew our music as well as anyone — as well as we did.

So when it came time to look for a keyboard player, I did think of Mark. I asked Joe about it. Joe didn't have a current suggestion. He was happy to take my word for it, just bringing Mark in for specific dates.

MARK: I loved polka music. Then I got infected by the Beatles. Who I really wanted to be, in high school, was Joe Walsh, even though he was a guitar player. That's why it's such a thrill to play with them. I've achieved my boyhood dreams. That's the epitome of it, to me.

Joe is a tremendous player. He's really enigmatic, a true rock star. But he's a very sweet guy, and we got along great. As a musician, he plays phenomenally. More than anybody I've ever played with, he is focused on every detail of the show. He's playing, and he'll suggest ways for me to play things, and he'll have thoughts on what gels to use for the lights.

FOX: He played with us in '01, for a benefit. We did three shows with Mark. They sold Joe on Mark's ability. Mark made it very easy.

Joe played those parts himself on the records. So live, Joe knew pretty well what he wanted. I've seen it myself, with drummers who know more about my parts I played than I do. That's what it was with Mark.

Mark Avsec, Joe Walsh, Jimmy Fox, Dale Peters

Joe's expectations are absolutely on the moon. And I share them with him. And when we got finished with that, Joe expressed how appreciative he was that Mark was that prepared. Mark is that guy. He listens, above all. He listens to whatever everybody else is playing, and reacts appropriately. That's the key to any player.

And after, I said, "How was Mark? Did he work out for you?"

Joe looked at me like I was crazy. He said, "Are you kidding? The guy's *awesome*."

In 2005, Walsh returned for two more shows. Mark got the call again. As before, the experience was like a Cruisers show: No practice. Just show up, play with the mighty Joe Walsh, and exceed expectations.

FOX: We wanted Mark for '06, for the tour. We wanted him badly. And Mark had a dilemma.

To his credit as a human being, he was a partner at the law firm. He was entangled in all business. And it was not a great time to take an extended leave of absence. He would have been gone from work for several months. And he had to turn us down. And it was very, very sad.

MARK: I had to make a decision. I had matters. I had people depending on me. And I couldn't just leave for six weeks.

When I passed it up, I was bummed, playing piano kind of morosely.

And then Joe called me, personally, rather than just Jimmy, to let me know he wanted me to come. He offered to fly me to Red Rocks, or maybe it was Sturges.

And I just couldn't.

I drank some wine then.

I felt bad. But it was the right decision. Hopefully if they do more shows, I can do those.

FOX: He was our first choice. And if we go out tomorrow, he's our first choice.

MARK: In some ways, playing with the James Gang the zenith of my career. When you dream about playing with a band and then you do it, what could be better?

CHAPTER 64

Things Donnie Does

2002. Donnie got a golf jones.

Iris cruised into the 21st century. Business was good, but he never outgrew rock and roll. And rock and roll never outgrew Donnie. As he approached 60, his voice was holding up.

Donnie never outgrew his favorite movies, either.

DONNIE: I watched *Scarface* dozens of times. That and *Tombstone*. I think I like *Tombstone* better. Scarface didn't happen until a lot later after it came out.

I started hanging around with some guys from this area. And there was a group of five or six of us that were super *Scarface* fans. We'd all watch the movie and try to get every line right. One guy just had it down. We'd have get-togethers in bars and just watch *Scarface* and have a good time.

There are so many good lines. The most famous is, "SAY HELLO TO MY LITTLE FRIEND!" My favorite is, *"Look at her: Her womb is so polluted, she cain't eefen haff kids!"*

Donnie began spending many an afternoon on his new favorite pastime: golf.

DONNIE: A friend of mine, my accountant since the Jaggerz, he got me into it.

I played pretty good today: 86. I have a 13, 14 handicap about now. Depends where I'm playing. If I'm familiar with the course, I can shoot in the high 70s. If I go to a tough, tough course I might shoot 100.

It's challenging. And I like the camaraderie with the guys. Just awesome. These guys love to take your dollar when the round is over. It's not about the money; it's about *taking* it from the other guy.

Donnie had Hot 100 hits with three bands. On the golf course, his record is even more impressive.

DONNIE: I had a 2 on a par 5 — double eagle — at Pheasant Ridge in 2015.

And three hole-in-ones: Strawberry Ridge, 2009. Beaver Valley Golf Club, 2010. Cranberry Highlands, 2017. My greatest accomplishment.

Golf made Donnie even more of an in-demand celebrity guest.

DONNIE: I like doing fundraisers. I've done some with Brett Keisel from the Steelers. I'll show up for the events.

My daughter has a lot to do with a wine event in Beaver County every August, for Cystic Fibrosis. They're getting a lot of good research on it. Erin's niece, she has it. She's 21 now. She's a beautiful girl, and she seems to get along OK. They're getting a handle on it.

Donnie pursuing his favorite pastime.

I've donated to 65 Roses and some others. It's just awful: The kids can't breathe. And being that close to home, that's what drew me to it.

ERIN: We did a walk-a-thon every year, until about eight years ago. Now we do Uncorking the Cure, which is a huge undertaking for our family. Wineries come in to supply tastings, catered food

From left, Greg Fusetti (Erin's husband), Sammy Fusetti (Donnie's grandson), Dominic Fusetti (Donnie's grandson), Mark Fusetti (Erin's brother in law), Donnie, Bill Fusetti (Erin's father in law). Photo taken at the Blackhawk Golf team's fundraiser outing, held at Blackhawk Golf Course.

and entertainment. We had close to 800 people last August. We raffle off an autographed Donnie Iris guitar every year which helps us generate a nice amount of money. He always gets a picture with the winner, which I frame and give to that person.

STEVE HANSEN, ex-WDVE: Donnie remained a nice guy, to this very day. He didn't know how to say no. He never said he was too busy. It's always nice to see him. Even when I was at KDKA later, and it wasn't selling many records, he'd still come in and make an appearance.

CHAPTER 65

The Show Stops, Nearly for Good

October 2002. Marty almost dies onstage. An old bandmate helps save his life.

That year, the band added drummer Brice Foster, a West Virginian whose credits include Running With Scissors, the Adrian Niles Band, and the Brett Cain Band. As Brice's band bio says, "Norman Nardini flat-out told Donnie that he had to hear 'Nice' Brice." Nardini was right, and Foster would shuttle to the Burgh from Nashville, where he works as a session musician, and has worked with Gretchen Wilson, Jon Nicholson, James Otto, Kid Rock, Chance, Mista D, and the Godfrey Brothers."

The band's official biography lists his joining date as 2003, but previous drummer Steve McConnell was in the audience at a late 2002 show. Even though McConnell was no longer a Cruiser, he probably saved the band's life. He very likely saved Marty's.

The Cruisers were still averaging between ten and 20 shows a year.

In 2002, Marty proved his devotion to the Cruisers in a way that few rock artists ever have. A show almost killed him. Or maybe this particular show saved his life. Probably both.

October 11, 2002. The Cruisers played Rainbow Gardens, an old ballroom in Marty and Paul's hometown, Erie, Pennsylvania, one Great Lake away from Canada.

Over the years, many of their Erie shows had been summertime outdoor gigs, with some breeze blowing from the lake to offset the heat from the crowd.

Not this show.

20 years after their last Top 40 single, the Cruisers still drew healthy crowds, especially in smaller markets that didn't draw many top-shelf touring bands. For this fall show, they came out in droves.

PAUL: We were in the pavilion, which is an old wooden structure where had big bands in the 1940s, and other society functions. Then later, they had rock concerts. Marty and I played there in various bands.

This was a hot night, and it was really hot and humid in the venue.

MARTY: It was packed. It was hot.

There was smoke. There was not very much oxygen in the air.

The conditions were not good, and I was not good.

DONNIE: I think Steve McConnell was drumming.

MARK: It was Brice. Or the Angel Gabriel.

PAUL: The sound was awful in there, and it was all echo and feedback. We had to keep stopping the show due to feedback and technical problems.

MARTY: Oddly enough, ten months before that, I had had a whole cardiac workup, and I had a clean bill of health.

PAUL: We were about four, five songs into our set, when I felt Marty leaning on my shoulder while we were in the middle of a song. And he just continued to collapse on me.

MARTY: I literally had a heart attack onstage. Dropped over. And was dying.

PAUL: The others helped me break his fall and get his guitar off so he could lie on the stage.

The band cleared the way while some medical professionals in the audience responded and an ambulance was called.

Steve McConnell, our former drummer, was in the audience and was responsible for helping save Marty's life. He found a nurse he knew in the audience, who had some nitroglycerin.

Marty was able to stabilize after the treatment, and be transported to the hospital, where he had an angioplasty treatment to clear the blockage.

MARTY: Look at where it happened: I grew up in Erie. I was born there. And it happened in Erie.

There's a heart center in Erie called Hamot Medical Center, and I was there within minutes. They took excellent care of me, as they do many other people.

We do a lot of shows out in the hinterlands. We play shows that are in the middle of nowhere, where a heart center might be an hour and a half away. It just happened there was help within minutes.

PAUL: We were all in shock, and I remember going to the hospital and waiting to hear about his condition.

Fortunately, he responded to treatment and did not have to go through any invasive procedures.

MARTY: This is all great. I don't say that in a flippant way. But it was in 2002, and time has given me a little bit of time between that and the trauma. It's all — I don't want to say borrowed time, but it's all time that I might not have had.

TOMMY: I left the band before Marty had the heart attack, so I wasn't there. But Donnie called me to bust my balls. He said, "See what you caused?!"

The Cruisers canceled a November show, but Marty was back in action in late December.

THE CRUISERS ON THE CLIPPER

The group's long run of regular Nick's Fat City shows had ended in 2001 — though Donnie's yellow tux from the Jaggerz and "Ah! Leah!" video remained a fixture, mounted on a wall until it closed in 2004.

The group replaced the event club concerts with two or three shows a year at another quintessentially Pittsburgh location: the Gateway Clipper, a riverboat that hosted floating parties on the Burgh's three rivers.

PAUL: Gateway Clipper shows were so intimate, with the crowd surrounding us in close proximity. It really brought out some of our best live performances.

Fans loved it too. The response was overwhelming at times. They really treated us well. They gave us a large section for use to use as a dressing room. We'd invite guests to eat with us. They would attach another boat to the main vessel for sold out shows.

One time we were partway through our show, when a really drunk guy jumped off of the boat. And the boat had to turn around to rescue him. I can still see him in the boat spotlight, treading water and laughing. Nick's Fat City was like that too, except the dressing room was in a dank basement that was full of graffiti.

DONNIE: Those were rocking times, getting out on the river, on the river band, the crowd going ape. We played there once or twice a year, up until maybe 2010, 2011. Once you're on the boat, you can't leave until it's over. You've got a captive audience.

CHAPTER 66

The 25th Birthday Concert

Donnie Iris and the Cruisers: 25 Years

A limited-run keepsake from the Cruisers' 25th birthday concert. Featuring...

"Bring on the Eighties"
"Agnes" (live)
"You're Only Dreaming" (live)
"I Can't Hear You" (live)
"She's So Wild" (live)
"Daddy Don't Live Here Anymore" (live)
"Shock Treatment" (live)

"Too Young to Love" (live)
"Ah! Leah!" (live)
"Back on the Streets" (live)
"Samantha (What You Gonna Do?)"
"Love Me With the Light On"
"Ellwood City"

Released: Released August 20, 2004
Label: Primary Records Group. CD Pri415

2004. To commemorate a quarter-century as a band, the Cruisers celebrated with an intimate, bonding evening for with their families, friends and a few thousand fans.

MARK: I just never thought about a 20th anniversary concert. It's a lot of planning, and I pretty much have to drive it. I had a lot going on then. So we did it for 25.

The group hastily assembled a souvenir for the concert: the limited edition *Donnie and the Cruisers: 25 Years* CD. It compiled rarities, obscurities, lost tracks and a preview of the next record.

The disc kicked off with "Bring on the Eighties," one of Donnie and Mark's two original 1979 recordings.

The next ten tracks are versions of recordings from the band's first concerts, which would later be released as *Live Bootleg* in 2014. The new version was necessary: Pressed for time, the band found old tapes of their radio show. They gave them a listen. The Cruisers were playing *really* fast. They scratched their heads and figured everybody was totally stoked that night in early 1981. They were wrong.

"These recordings contain technical imperfections and very fast tempos," Mark observed in the liner notes, momentarily unaware the two were connected: The recordings were transferred from tape at the wrong speed. On the CD, the songs play too fast. But the old band sure do sound energetic.

The disc closed with two tracks from the band's in-progress next album, which was still two years on the horizon: "Love Me With The Light On" and "Ellwood City."

Addy, Donnie, and Erin backstage after the 25th anniversary show

The birthday concert drew the band's best crowd in decades, maybe ever, to the venue formerly known as the Chevrolet Amphitheatre at Station Square, also the Tribe Total Media Amphitheatre at Station Square, formerly the I.C. Light Amphitheater.

Now closed, the venue was across the Monongahela River from downtown Pittsburgh. The giant, multisectioned tent was the best place to have medium outdoor events like concerts, the Pittsburgh Irish Festival and Tom Savini's Halloween Fright Fest. The amphitheater had a capacity around 5,000. And on the right kind of night, it was glorious.

On the right kind of night.

When the weather cooperated.

The day of the show, the Cruisers had a lot going for them. Pittsburgh Mayor Tom Murphy had proclaimed August 20, 2004 Donnie Iris Day. Tickets were priced to commemorate the band's origins: $19.79.

Like the keepsake CD, the concert was not a smooth affair. The entire endeavor had black clouds hanging over it, ready to strike.

MIKE: The Donnie Iris concert that really sticks in my mind is his 25th anniversary show in Pittsburgh. There was heavy cloud cover, and we were pretty sure there was going to be rain…we just didn't anticipate how much rain. Turns out the rain was the remnants of Hurricane Charley and the worst of it was going to hit Pittsburgh right about the time Donnie walked on stage.

DONNIE: Most of my family came. Once in a while, my nephews will come, and my sisters will come, and my daughters. But that night, all my cousins were there. It was a night for family.

I remember hanging backstage right before and after the show, talking to people about what a long career I'd had: 25 years this group was together, and also the Jaggerz, ten years prior to that.

KATRINA, PARALLEL TIME POSTER: I arrived at the Amphitheatre about 7 o'clock and walked toward the back, where the vendors are located. Who do I see dressed in a T-shirt and jeans, talking with a few people, right in the middle of everything? DONNIE! As usual, he took the time to chat for a few minutes, pose for a picture and then head backstage to change into his yellow suit coat and bow tie. What a guy!

GLENN RATNER, PARALLEL TIME FAN SITE: The boys really pulled off a unique and amazing show.

The stage setup had three full drum kits along with a smaller drum kit setup on the stage. There was also a grand piano on stage, near Mark's keyboards.

The band took the stage directly after the video clip of Donnie singing the National Anthem at the 2001 championship game. Donnie had on a yellow jacket reminiscent of his famous yellow suit from the *Back On The Streets* era.

OLZEWSKI: Let's just say the downpour was biblical in scale. We ran to the venue, just a short distance, and we were drenched by the time we got through the gate. We started making our way to the seats, stepping over cables and huge puddles of water.

The crowd was obviously ready for the show, and there were video screens showing Donnie and the band getting ready backstage. Maybe it was just me, but they looked tense. That seemed to disappear when they walked onstage to cheers that drowned out the sound of thunder.

For this gig, the band broke some traditions. They *didn't* greet the crowded venue with the traditional powderkeg "Agnes." Instead, they opened with a subdued, as-yet-unreleased song from *Ellwood City*: "River of Love."

MARK: The place was packed with between 4,000 and 4,500 people – they were stoked and screaming. When we hit the stage, the decibels were off the charts. If we had opened with "Agnes," the roof would have come off the space. Instead, I suggested "River of Love" which nobody in the crowd knew. Mistake, mistake.

The roof *would* come off, though. The two-hour set tested the will of everybody in the venue.

DONNIE 25: THE SET LIST

"River Of Love"	"King Cool"
"Joking"	"The Promise" (Marty and Donnie lead vocal)
"I Can't Hear You"	"Ellwood City"
"Agnes"	"You're My Serenity"
"Sweet Merilee"	"I Left My Heart in San Francisco"
"That's the Way Love Oughta Be"	"Tough World" (drummer: Kevin Valentine)
"Do You Compute?" (drummer: Tommy)	"Love Is Like a Rock" (all four drummers)
"This Time It Must Be Love" (Tommy)	"Ah! Leah!" (Kevin Valentine)
"Poletown" (Tommy)	"The Rapper" (all four drummers)
"10th Street" (drummer: Danna Avsec)	

RATNER: The first surprise of the night was when the band broke into "Joking." What a great tune, and awesome to hear live.

The first guest spot was when the Donnie announced Tommy Rich. He joined the band — as Brice exited — for several songs, starting with "Do You Compute?." Tommy played the normal synthesizer intro beat on the drums.

Brice was the drummer for most of the evening, but he was joined by all the other Cruiser drummers of record — plus one of their biggest fans, a young drummer who had probably watched the *Live at Blossom* videotape more than anybody alive: Mark's daughter, 21-year-old Danna Avsec.

RATNER: Mark's daughter Danna replaced Tommy, and they broke into a smoking rendition of "10th Street." Danna stayed on and played a few more tunes also.

KEVIN: Danna is a pleasure to be with. And Tommy and Brice, too. I'm always into that stuff. Danna, I love her. It would be hard for me not to love her, because she used to watch the Blossom video and play all my parts and tell people she was Kevin. And I appreciate that.

I think she has what Mark has, whatever you want to call it: a gift, the bug. Musicians, you've gotta be born with a lot of it. You have to work hard, but you have to have that base. She's a musician at heart. She really plays her ass off, and she plays in high heels, which I think is a real hoot.

OLSZEWSKI: The band sounded great. You could sense it was pretty emotional for all involved, especially the hometown crowd. Donnie pointed out the people who inspired many of his songs who were in the audience.

RATNER: Another rarity played was "You're My Serenity," with Mark on piano and Paul Goll's girlfriend on cello. Very cool.

PAUL: I felt really bad for Elizabeth Elliott, who was my girlfriend at the time, and now my wife. She brought her cello to perform a special moment in the show where we had Donnie and Mark accompanying on a medley that included part of the Beatles' "She's Leaving Home."

Elizabeth came out, and we had to escort her out under an umbrella and get her set up. When it came time for her to play, the mic was not working. and did not get fixed in time to hear anything she played. Very disappointing.

The special two-hour set included some one-time performances. To accommodate the extended show, the band broke another tried-and-true custom: Donnie and Mark *practiced* — not the entire set, but the two worked up a special rendition of "I Left My Heart in San Francisco." They performed it unplugged, just Donnie's vocals and Mark's piano, the Cruisers' core duo seated side by side.

DONNIE: That was great. I love Tony Bennett. I wanted to do something different that night, because it was a big show. It went over well. Maybe someday down the road, if Mark and I get the urge, we could do something like that.

OLSZEWSKI: True to the forecast, Charley picked up steam, and the water is rushing through the audience. The winds got heavy, and the roof started tearing off. Rain is pouring in.

Even though we were invited to the after-show party at the Hard Rock, it was time to go. We left as Donnie was singing "I Left My Heart in San Francisco." It was still worth it.

MARK: "I Left My Heart in San Francisco" which was another Avsec brainstorm that was not a good one. It did not go over.

KEVRO, PARALLEL TIME POSTER: I loved it when Donnie took the liberty to do "I Left My Heart In San Francisco." He knew that it wasn't a house-rockin' song, but he wanted to do it, so he did. It was his moment. It was a very intimate show, which normally wouldn't be the case in such a large venue. They all had such a fun time up there on stage.

The highlight might have been "Love is Like a Rock." Avsec thought of a new way to recreate the multi-track stack effect live: Use *four* drummers.

KEVIN: "Love Is Like a Rock" was three drum tracks on top of each other. It's hard to play three drum parts at the same time. When four drummers play, it's really cool.

It rained like hell. They were calling for tornadoes. It was a wet mess, but it was packed. A couple of the flaps opened up. People got wet.

We were very distracted because the water was soaking all of the cords and snake boxes and not getting signal to the mixing board. We rose above it and put on a great show in spite of all the glitches.

PAUL: The rain sucked! It soaked the crowd, but they all stayed there and grooved with us. They were really inspiring.

JTD 66, PARALLEL TIME POSTER: Amazing. That was a night that will be with me forever. I just got back in town from driving up from Orlando, and I can honestly say I would have driven another 1,000 miles to see that show.

To be a part of something like that after waiting an entire lifetime cannot be put into words. My brother and I found ourselves right up on the stage, and it was unreal. To see Donnie come out in his yellow tux was all we needed. The set list was awesome, and the lead-in from acoustic to full version "Ah! Leah!" was one of the greatest things ever.

SLIDETUBA, PARALLEL TIME POSTER: Oh my God! This was our first Donnie show. It was the best damn show I have seen in a *very* long time. As always, Donnie was fantastic! His voice is stronger than ever, and he can still rock with the best of 'em. I was at the foot of the stage for the entire show, and that is the place to be. I brought a friend who has never seen Donnie live before, and she was totally blown away.

Her exact words were "Wow, it's like a cult. I've never seen anything like it before."

My reply was, "Yes, and that's what makes Donnie's shows so awesome." It's the crowd singing all the songs and rocking out with the band!

WHITE HARD HAT, PARALLEL TIME POSTER: I have been going to see Donnie Iris since 1981 — Stanley Theater — and let me tell you: This was his *best* show ever! I heard songs that he hasn't done in years. It was great to see all the old drummers, especially Valentine. And didn't Mark's daughter play the **** outta the drums? There is no way that this man is 61 years old.

STEEL RIVER RAT, PARALLEL TIME POSTER: Afterparty at the Hard Rock Café was cool. Also, somebody won an autographed guitar signed by the whole band. Donnie also took photographs with everybody. What a perfect night of fun in the best city in the world.

DONNIE: It was something that I really enjoyed. Other than the weather, it was great. I loved that show.

2004 ended with a Christmas miracle: Kevin rejoined the band for a full set at the Rock Club in Pittsburgh. It felt good. The Cruisers left the stage hungry for more.

2005 was over in a flash: Donnie reunited with B.E. Taylor — not that they had ever been apart long. The two formally played a handful of shows together, in Pennsylvania, West Virginia, and Ohio. Some of the Cruisers' fifteen-odd shows were big, like a headlining return to the Chevrolet Amphitheater. Some bigger, opening for Dave Mason, then Blue Öyster Cult in Cleveland. Some smaller, like Denny's Bar and Banquet in Edinboro, PA.

Donnie made a rare guest appearance on *Chasing Down a Spark*, a record by rising Pittsburgh star Bill Deasy. The Clarks' Scott Blasey had introduced the two, and Donnie sang on the rousing "Levi."[66.1]

But mostly, Donnie worked on his own album, *Ellwood City*. The going was slow.

DONNIE IRIS AND THE CRUISERS

IRIS

ELLWØØD CITY

Ellwood City: The Album

Ellwood City

The eighth studio album by Donnie Iris and the Cruisers. Featuring...

"Little Black Dress" (Avsec, Goll, Hoenes, Ierace, Valentine)

"Let's Go" (Avsec, Goll, Hoenes, Ierace, Valentine)

"River of Love" (Avsec)

"Just Go Tango" (Avsec, Goll, Hoenes, Ierace, Valentine)

"Rocque Fantastique" (Avsec, Goll, Hoenes, Ierace, Valentine)

"Ellwood City" (Avsec)

"Love Me with the Light On" (Avsec, Goll, Hoenes, Ierace, Foster)

"No Rest for the Wicked" (Avsec, Goll, Hoenes, Ierace, Valentine)

"Love Messiah" (Avsec, Goll, Hoenes, Ierace, Valentine)

"You Got My Body (You Don't Have My Soul)" (Avsec, Ierace, Valentine)

"Tuesday Morning" (Avsec)

"Just Go Tango" (extended mix – Avsec)

"With This Ring" *(special bonus track)*

"Hard Spot" (Avsec)

Released May 25, 2006
Label: Primary Records Group. CD release.

From the credits:

Donnie Iris: Lead and background vocals, guitar on "Let's Go" and "You Got My Body (You Don't Have My Soul)"; Bass on "You Got My Body (You Don't Have My Soul)" and "Tuesday Morning"; Acoustic and Electric Guitar on "Let's Go"

Mark Avsec: Keyboards and vocals, pipe organ

Marty Lee: guitars

Paul Goll: bass

Kevin Valentine: drums

Brice Foster: Drums on "River Of Love," "Ellwood City," and "Love Me (With The Light On)"

Engineered by Bill Korecky

Mixed by Bill Korecky, with Donnie Iris and Mark Avsec

Mastered by Roger Lian at Masterdisk, New York

Design: Marty Lee Hoenes

June 17, 2006. Donnie's first hometown, Ellwood City, declared another Donnie Iris Day.

Ellwood City always informed Donnie's art. Now he officially made it part of the catalog, with an album and song named after the town, released in May 25, 2006.

True to form, it took Mark, with input from Donnie, to write an album about the town where the singer grew up.

Three years in the making, *Ellwood City* turned into a one-CD double album. The Cruisers' ninth record — 11th if you count *Together Alone* and *Live at Nick's* — featured 12 official tracks. Four more bonus cuts pushed the total runtime over 80 minutes. 16 songs is an unprecedented about of Donnie.

MARK: Who was our drummer then? Brice?

All of our drummers have certain styles. Brice could play "This Time It Must Be Love" better than almost anybody — he's a *funky* drummer.

We try to make a good record. But then they just weren't that good. I think *Ellwood City*, we kind of started getting back to what we did.

Jerry Reed, the engineer so essential to the best Cruisers albums, passed away in 2000. He was 78.[67.1] Filling his chair was not easy.

Seven years after Reed's departure, Mark finally found a new engineer who could his match his skills and dedication: Bill Korecky.

Korecky — who is still the band's engineer — is the proprietor of Mars Studios in rural Mantua, Ohio. He was an unlikely match for the Cruisers: He helmed sessions with metallic avant garde bands like Craw and Mushroomhead. In the 1990s, as an engineer and producer, he had set a new standard for sound quality in hardcore punk, working with bands like Integrity and Earth Crisis.

Bands from all over the country flocked to Korecky's studio, a building he built on a plot of farmland his family has owned for generations. Korecky was a longtime fan of Donnie, the Cruisers and Mark. He connected with Mark The Lawyer, but he soon came to know Mark The Musician.

MARK, FROM THE *AH! LELUJAH!* LINER NOTES: Mars has good gear. Bill has good ears.

KORECKY: It's been an honor and a pleasure to work with these guys.

MARK: I was into a band who almost had a deal with Sony. They were badass, and Bill was working with them. I liked Bill when I met him. He is *committed* to the task at hand — namely, whomever he is recording. His phone is off and nonexistent.

I used to work other places, and engineers would pick up the phone if someone called — *vibe killer*. I want to work with someone who believes we are working on something special, because that's the only way something special is made. Only one other person has the dedication that Bill Korecky has to my records, and that was Jerry Reed.

Ellwood City also marked bassist Paul Goll's true debut on an all-out Cruisers studio album, with the amps turned up. After over a decade with the band, he was ready to rip.

During the sessions, Goll was joined by some unexpected quality company. Brice had recorded four songs. And then, after some good vibes at the 25th birthday concert, Kevin rejoined the band. He would fly in for sessions and shows forevermore — when work permitted.

PAUL: This was my first experience recording original material with the band. I got to see the process of how they record the songs.

Basically, Mark came in with some sketches/chord progressions that he had some idea of what he wanted to shoot for.

KEVIN: Al is very funky. He comes from R&B more, and he wants to be more in the forefront. And Paul can be incredibly funky, but he chooses to be more in the bass position, not in the forefront.

MARTY: Kevin absolutely helped create and drive all the MCA recordings, as well as almost everything else we've ever recorded as a band. He is obviously still very important now. Paul, important to us live, and has done the bass playing on most of the latter-day studio recordings.

MARK: We hired Brice. He played with us for a while. And it just didn't work out. Brice had other gigs in Nashville — that's my recollection. It got harder for him to do gigs, and we just amicably split. And that's when we got Kevin back.

The tracks in the studio with Brice, for whatever reason, it wasn't the same. Kevin's track sounds great, because he really knows how to tune his drums — and he hits *really* hard too.

Kevin had a full, rich life in LA, a television and film career. And he was open to playing with us again. And it's absolutely worth it.

And when he's not playing with us, we're absolutely lucky that we have Mark Tirabassi, who is a friend and does a fine job when Kevin can't make it. But we love Kevin. It is like being in a mother's arms when you're playing in a band with a drummer like Kevin, who is in control of the feel, the tempo — he just has it all.

It's not cheap to fly him in, especially for him, because he gives up two days. If we can have a gig on a Friday, as bad as we all want a gig, we'll say, "No possible way." We've got to have a Saturday, because Kevin can't make it on a Friday. That's how important Kevin is. Yeah, the expenses are a little higher. It's a sacrifice. And nobody, including Donnie, is getting rich off shows. We all love seeing each other.

Kevin is more than a drummer. At this point, he is really the driver behind the live show, and making sure it stays fresh. It's beginning to have a good effect on me, because he cares so much. He's the original drummer, and now he's available to do it, and we love it.

All I can tell you is: Kevin is worth it.

PAUL: And it was also my first experience with Kevin in the studio, which is where he really shines. The rhythm section had pretty much free reign, but Mark and Donnie coached us some: "Kevin, give me this kind of groove."

After rhythm tracks were done, Marty would come back to do leads and extra guitars. Then Mark and Donnie would put the finishing touches on.

Kevin does it old-school: He plays with no click track, no headset. With Valentine back in the mix, the endless sessions finally sparked. Nine of the songs' writing credits are group jams, eight of them from the Kevin lineup.

MARK: How many songs did we do? I don't know why we did that many. We just did.

Six of the songs are credited entirely to Avsec, including the title track, "Ellwood City," a languid story of lost teenage love. It's the ultimate symbolic representation of the Donnie and Mark's synergy: Mark absorbed Donnie's stories about life in Pennsylvania. And "Ellwood City" is what he gave Donnie to sing.

MARK: That was my idea. I was channeling Donnie. I always do: I think about Donnie, and I write the songs.

PAUL: Mark would start a progression, and we would jam until we had verse, bridge, chorus. We would put down between five and seven rhythm tracks, then come back at a later time to do some more.

It was kind of interesting to hear what the songs evolved into. Some were totally different than I imagined they would be like.

There were tracks that I was not part of that were total surprises, like "You Got my Body", "Tuesday Morning," and "With This Ring."

After 22 years worth of varied and experimental records, *Ellwood City* primarily deals in the classic Cruisers approach.

The disc comes out swinging with "Little Black Dress," which has it all: Kevin's *wake-up-now* drums. Marty's sharp riffs. Donnie's cocksure attitude. His hot-and-bothered vocals. Mark's perfect-match backup vocals. Paul's bass is impenetrable back line that unifies the rest of the band's efforts.

Marty and Paul play in perfect tandem, moving along together in the relaxed groove of "River of Love." Depending on the mood, Mark tickles the ivories or pounds the keys. In "Rocque Fantastique," Marty fires flaming hot licks 30 feet in the air, and Kevin pounds away. Donnie goes high and low, fast and slow; King Cool's vocals give the distinct impression he was shaking his *badonkadonk* all through the session.

The group get their groove on and stay there: 10 of 15 non-remix tracks run 4:50 or longer, and another is close to the five-minute mark. Only one song, "With This Ring," runs under 3:50.

The album's real departure is "Let's Go Tango," a heavy dance number powered by Mark's keyboard — it documents Donnie's growing appetite for hot nights in Latin Florida. The sparse "Tuesday Morning" is a still scene from a quiet September morning. Over Kevin's bouncing, irresistible beat, "You've Got My Body (You Don't Have My Soul)" is a lively look at the hard-labor grind Donnie escaped when he headed to college. The CD version closes with a bonus track, a wedding waltz that's pure Mark. It's based on Beethoven's *Pathetique Sonata*, with new words, by the man who brought you the similarly tranquil "Holy Love."

Inside the disc is a great picture of young Donnie at service station, in his 1951 Buick Super.

Ellwood City met a cold critical reception, and it soured Mark on the record: He worked on it, and now he's done thinking about it. Donnie holds it in higher regard.

DONNIE: I thought there were some pretty cool tunes on that one.

ELLWOOD CITY, THE SONGS: "LITTLE BLACK DRESS"

DONNIE: I still think, to this day, it's a good song. A lot of people ask for it. Mark doesn't like to play it live. Alice Cooper liked that one. He put it on his radio show; he thought it was a great power-pop tune. For some reason, the song didn't transfer onstage. It was just OK live.

"LET'S GO"

DONNIE: I don't remember that.

"RIVER OF LOVE"

MARK: Don't ask me why I opened the concert with it. It was as bad a decision as me putting "Merilee" side-one-cut-one on *King Cool*. My big mistake.

"ROCQUE FANTASTIQUE"

DONNIE: That was fun, that kind of character. It was album-worthy.

"JUST GO TANGO"

DONNIE: I liked that. That was fun. I like that kind of thing — not that I can do a tango. I spent some time in Florida in the early 2000's, in those Spanish bars. I spent a lot of time on South Beach.

I didn't need Mark to coach me through the Spanish lyrics; I'm good at Spanish words. I took it in high school. My teacher loved me. She thought I was one of the few who could pronounce it.

"ELLWOOD CITY"

DONNIE: I thought that was nice. He did great writing that. We talked about me growing up in Ellwood City, and he retained a lot of that stuff. That came out of him in that song.

He's so critical about his work. Aside from a few select songs, he's just not happy with much of what he's come up with over the years. And a lot of those songs have merit.

"LOVE ME WITH THE LIGHT ON"

DONNIE: I don't remember that.

"NO REST FOR THE WICKED"

DONNIE: I like that one. It's a pretty good rocker. I thought I was digging into a part of my voice — I thought about Ray Charles when I sang it.

"YOU GOT MY BODY (YOU DON'T HAVE MY SOUL)"

DONNIE: That was a good song. Singing that, I remembered my dad working in the mill when he was a young man and I was just a kid. So that was easy, to go back and pull out of my head. But what I really like abut that is the song is the rhythm track.

"WITH THIS RING"

MARK: It was a play on Beethoven, which you are allowed to do since Beethoven was in the public domain. The words were personal.

PAUL: It was a great experience because we got to make wonderful music, but we also laughed ourselves to exhaustion at times. No booze, drugs, or babes — just good clean fun.

I know that you will not hear this from any other band member, but my favorite album is *Ellwood City*. Part of this is selfish, because I believe it is the best studio album that I played on. But also, it has some really great tracks like "River of Love," "Love Me (With the Lights on)", and "Ellwood City."

SOME PEOPLE LIKE THIS RECORD. IT'S GOOD.

Then came the broken-record part of the story: Once it was out, *Ellwood City* caught a couple good breaks. And it drifted away, into the Beaver Valley fog.

Rock god — and disc jockey — Alice Cooper played "Little Black Dress" on his syndicated radio show, *Nights With Alice Cooper*, where the Cruisers are a perennial presence, most often with "Ah! Leah!"

Reviews were scant. The Pittsburgh *Post-Gazette*'s Scott Mervis landed some haymakers in a 3-of-5-stars review: "*Ellwood City* jumps all over the map, sounding like Bowie one minute, the Beatles the next, then touching on U2, Springsteen, ELO, Nick Lowe and a lot more before wrapping it up. A newcomer to King Cool might be hard-pressed to know what Donnie Iris really sounds like. The common thread is that Iris loves a hard-driving rock song bolstered by a big clean wall of sound.... 'River of Love' is a ripoff of Rob Thomas' 'Smooth' with a local travel commercial thrown in... Iris is 62 and spends his days running a mortgage company. In light of that, he's practically stripping off the suit and wearing an *S* on his chest on some of these rockers."[67.2]

The Cleveland *Plain Dealer* liked it better, giving it a B+ letter grade: "It has been more than a quarter-century since Donnie Iris and the Cruisers parlayed their studio-crafted rock sound — defined by such hits as 'Ah! Leah!' and 'Love Is Like A Rock' — and their Buddy Holly look into the national spotlight. The outfit is alive and well, evident in the Pittsburgh band's new effort, *Ellwood City*.

"Normally, this is the place in a review where a classic-rock band is lambasted for rehashing old chords from decades ago. Amazingly, and it is amazing, considering Iris and his bandmates have been out of the public eye for a while, the band has created a well-rounded and imaginative album that rocks ('Little Black Dress') and experiments ('Just Go Tango') with David Bowie-sounding results... Steelers town affiliation aside, Iris is still cruising."[67.3]

Avsec had the idea for the "Little Black Dress" video. (See the *King Cool* tour chapter for more details on the retro clip.) And, like many a Cruisers gem, it disappeared in the dense forest of decentralized modern media.

In Cleveland, Donnie teamed up with the Cavs girls again, on billboards, to promote Armstrong Cable, who kindly underwrote the CD. The corporate sponsorship was also Avsec's forward-thinking idea for world where music is digital and CDs don't sell much. Kevin placed "Rocque Fantastique" in a Meg Ryan movie he was working on, *Serious Moonlight*. "Little Black Dress" made the set list.

MARK: I don't think it was a bad record. We really put the time in on that one. I think Glenn really liked it.

GLENN RATNER, PARALLEL TIME SITE: *Ellwood City* is a great album, and I'd put it up there with the with the first five albums. I think it's an excellent album and a real return to form. I loved *Poletown* — I think there's some brilliant stuff on there, though much of it doesn't feel like Donnie Iris and the Cruisers. *Ellwood City* was right in their wheelhouse, though.

MARK: *Ellwood City* represented a lot of work. I'm not un-proud of that. At the end of the day, I probably spent a thousand hours of my life on *Ellwood City*. And it's like, "Mom, look what I did!"

We don't do any songs from *Ellwood City* live. There's a handful of people that say, "I like *Ellwood City*. Thank you."

THE BIG FANCY BYHAM SHOW

The Cruisers closed 2006 with a show to remember. December 29, Donnie, the Cruisers and friends played the Byham Theater in downtown Pittsburgh. Formerly the Fulton, the narrow two-level upscale venue has an orchestra pit and a big staff. A special subdued holiday-season set featured new material, slow arrangements, unplugged tunes, and a guest appearance... all in a setting that some fans found classy, and some found constrictive. Joe Grushecky opened with an acoustic set to set the tone for the evening.

MARK: The venue was chosen because it was downtown and right-sized. But it was a union hall, which posed a lot of problems. Lots of rules with union halls: You can't move your own equipment, even on the stage. You have to quit at a certain time, or else you have to pay them double or triple overtime. This is why we are playing Donnie's 75th birthday concerts where we are.

RATNER: It was an unusual show and unusual crowd.

The house lights dropped, and the stage lights revealed three drum kits lined up across the rear of the stage.

Kevin couldn't make the show, so the Cruisers replaced him with Mark Tirabassi, Danna Avsec, and a returning Brice Foster. Donnie glided onto stage in a Penguins Jersey, number 67, with IRIS from shoulder to shoulder.

Donnie was, as always, loose, ready to fire a zinger.

He had some fun with the pristine room, telling the fans, "It's time to get down dirty and funky — in a smoke-free environment!"

Between songs, he had an improv exchange with the crowd.

DONNIE: That beat makes me feel so sexy.

WOMAN IN AUDIENCE: "YOU ARE SEXY, DONNIE!"

DONNIE: It makes me want to shake my *dupa*.

WOMAN IN AUDIENCE: Do it!

He did.

Reports from the show varied. Everybody seemed to enjoy the performance. The swanky crowd remained seated through most of it, and some skirmishes flared up: Excited Donnie disciples who wanted to dance incurred the wrath of fans who wanted to stay seated and enjoy some passive entertainment. Ushers officiated the exchanges, which left everybody involved aggravated.

Set list:

"Agnes"	"Ellwood City"	"Sweet Merilee"
"Do You Compute"	"The Promise" (acoustic	"This Time It Must Be Love"
"Joking"	with Joe Grushecky)	"Little Black Dress"
"I Can't Hear You No More"	"How You Gonna Mend It"	"Love Is Like a Rock"
"That's The Way Love	(slow and mellow version)	(3 drummers)
Ought to Be"	"Rocque Fantastique"	"Ah! Leah!"
"River of Love"	"Minnie the Moocher"	

TURNPIKE CRUISER, PARALLEL TIME POSTER: "The Promise" came across very well (great song written by Marty Lee). Joey G. sang the first verse, and Donnie the second verse, nicely done, with Joe and Marty both on acoustic guitar.

"How You Gonna Mend It" was done differently for the first time live (slow and mellow). It was nice to hear it done this way, but IMHO I much prefer the rockin' original version.

I like "Rocque Fantastique" in the set list, a real rocker to keep the blood flowin'. Since the entire *Ellwood City* CD is an absolute masterpiece, I would like to hear some new songs from EC added to the shows in 2007. (Hint: "Just Go Tango" is one of them.)

I believe that "The Rapper" was planned to be the closer for the set list, but it was pulled due to a 10:55 p.m. show completion time that the band was required to meet. A real bummer.

JASON PETTIGREW, *ALTERNATIVE PRESS* EDITOR-IN-CHIEF: The value of a new album from a legacy band: If you're going to do something that documents where your head is *right now*, if your aesthetic is what drew people to you in the first place — then it matters.

For a moment, it melts the amber down so that it's not frozen. And it's live, and it's vivid, and it's honest and sincere, and people react to it. And just because it didn't sell 29 million copies or whatever *Hotel California* sold, that doesn't make a song any less awesome in your head. And anybody who says otherwise is just armchair quarterbacking it, and, really, being a dick.

> We thought it would be good
> to get the old guys back together, see
> what happens. It was fun.
> It was still there. Those boys have
> the stuff, that's for sure.
>
> ~DONNIE IRIS

CHAPTER 68

You Can't Really Miss Me... The EP

You Can't Really Miss Me (If I Never Go Away)

An EP from Donnie and a lot of different Cruisers and friends. Featuring...

"Hard Spot" (Avsec)
"I Can't Really Miss You (If You Never Go Away)" (Avsec)
"Ode to Jane (Immortal Beloved)" (Avsec)
"Screamin' Boy" demo (Avsec)
"The Twelve Dawnie Days of Christmas" live (Avsec)

From the credits:
Donnie Iris: lead and background vocals
Mark Avsec: keyboards
Marty Lee Hoenes: guitars
Alan Greene: guitar, "Screamin' Boy"
Paul Goll: bass, "Hard Spot"
Albritton McClain: bass, "I Can't Really Miss You" and "Ode to Jane"
Kevin Valentine: drums, "I Can't Really Miss You" and "Ode to Jane"
Brice Foster: drums, "Hard Spot"
Tommy Rich: drums, "Screamin' Boy"
Produced By Mark Avsec
Engineered and Mixed by Bill Korecky at Mars Recording Studio
Design: Marty Lee Hoenes
CD Release: PRIMARY
Released: December 13, 2008

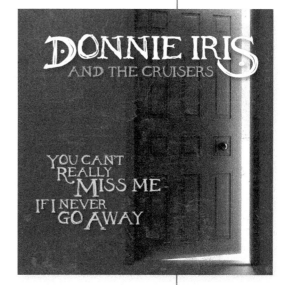

2007. By now, Donnie was a respected rock and roll dignitary. The Cruisers didn't get the press they used to, but they continued playing sold-out shows for the faithful, like the Boos Cruise, a Halloween-season three-hour tour on the Gateway Clipper, sponsored by Pittsburgh's 3WS 94.5 FM, which had reformatted to emulate vintage DVE.

Donnie remained in demand, onstage and off. From time to time, they rolled out the red carpet for him.

In Cleveland, Donnie rated a mention in the Plain Dealer's calendar section, as a featured participant in the Cleveland Botanical Garden's Iron Floral Avenger Competition.[68.1] And so it went.

2008. The band would average eight to ten shows for the next few years. Donnie sang the National Anthem before a Pirates game at Pittsburgh's PNC Park. And the band were working on a little something.

The *You Can't Really Miss Me (If I Never Go Away)* reunited the classic lineup and captured some of the DVE *Dawnie* shtick on a Cruisers record.

None of it really stuck, though. Technically, it's an all-star EP; in practical terms, it's a essentially a big single by the classic Cruisers lineup, with three bonus tracks.

A growling Donnie is cornered and determined in "Hard Spot," a hypnotic downtempo rocker left over from the *Ellwood City* sessions. Brice leads the track's start-stop dynamics, directing Marty's jackhammer riffing.

"The Twelve Dawnie Days of Christmas" was taped live and unrehearsed at a *DVE Morning Show* holiday show, in front of a rollicking crowd, who cheer Pittsburgh references in the carol.

The meat of the EP is tracks 2 and 3, "I Can't Really Miss You (If You Never Go Away)" and "Ode to Jane (Immortal Beloved)."

"Miss You" is a feel-good group singalong.

Then things take a menacing turn on the ambitious "Ode to Jane." The Cruisers' track length continues to drift: All the cuts are basically five minutes, except the rowdy — and aptly named —"Screamin' Boy," an old experiment with Tommy Rich and Alan Greene, who play epic, aggro blues.

The last track is labeled "(Demo)," and Avsec says the tracks *all* are.

MARK: We just get together, throw stuff against the wall, see what sticks.

But they're all demos, because do you think anybody's going to play them anymore? Never. Never, never.

And if you go into the studio thinking you're making a record so it gets played on the radio, you are really misleading yourself. That had better be how you like spending your time, because, number one, nobody's going to buy it — our fans don't buy our music unless Donnie signs it. And two, no radio's going to play it.

I'm not being cynical here; you've got to know your limitations, in business and in art. So they're all demos at this point. The days of selling records and radio play are over.

YOU CAN'T REALLY MISS ME: THE SONGS
"I CAN'T REALLY MISS YOU (IF YOU NEVER GO AWAY)"

Albritton accepted Mark's invitation to come back and see what happened. If he's frank — and he is — he'll admit not much happened. Mark doesn't think much of the title track.

MARK: It was a terrible song, too. Nobody noticed it. Nobody bought it.

I think we wanted to rekindle that magic and see if something was there. We gave Albritton some money and flew him in. And he came in.

DONNIE: I thought that was a pretty good tune. It's fun. It was nice having Al and Kevin back.

We didn't have to talk about that too much. We thought it would be good to get the old guys back together, see what happens. It was fun. It was still there. Those boys have the stuff, that's for sure.

KEVIN: It's a chemistry thing. It's always there. Like if you have friends you don't see for years, and when you see them again, it's like no time has passed. There's nothing awkward, nothing to get over. You're back to where you were.

Like the studio songs, the live versions were beginning to swell into jams with extended grooves. Mark says the longer track times isn't part of a grand plan; it's just how they come out.

MARK: Some of that stuff is really good. Some is really bad. And most of it is my fault when it's bad, for sure. And when it's good, I had a lot to do with it.

"HARD SPOT"

Mark pounds the keyboard on this lurching, heavy track. After it was recorded, he played with some vocal effects, which compensated for Donnie's sore vocal cords. When Marty rips a solo, he owns the spotlight.

DONNIE: That was hard to sing. I was beat up by then.

"SCREAMIN' BOY"

Donnie pushes the pedal to the metal and sees whether he can blow out his voice.

DONNIE: I had fun screaming that one out. It's a screaming anecdote: It's something I've been doing all my life, screaming my ass off, trying to get it all out there. But it's not a great song.

I think it was more *demos*. We were just having fun in the studio. We knew it wasn't going anywhere.

"12 DONNIE DAYS"

For Donnie fans who don't know the DVE skits, this track captures the Dawnie cult and caricature on disc.

MARK: That was just on one night; I just had the idea. I don't know why I did it and decided to record it, but there must have been a reason at the time.

We're not very good at marketing; we just aren't. We probably should do that every year around this time. The crowd would eat it up.

DONNIE: They just gave me the lyric, and I went up there and belted it out.

"ODE TO JANE"

The EP's standout is an odd Cruisers track, but a good one. Ominous and heavy, it might be the angriest mood Donnie and Mark ever conjured. It's gloomy and murderous, and it's a true story — but not for Mark or Donnie.

MARK: It's based on Beethoven's Ninth Symphony. I thought it was cool. I'm a big Beethoven fan. I was reading about him. It's a pretty twisted thing. The story, there was a rumor that his brother's son was really *his* son. You just try things. Some work.

DONNIE: That's weird and dark. I had fun doing that one. That one brings back pretty good memories. Mark told me was where it came from, the premise and the melodies.

Singing songs like that, it's not like acting. I don't have to go too dark to sing songs like that. The feel of the track is dark to begin with. Once the music is in my head, it just comes out. It's angry.

I guess the music brings it out of me. It's something that's in all of us; it's all down there somewhere. I had fun doing that tune.

You Can't Really Miss Me was a thoroughly independent release. It didn't receive any press notices or airplay.

Two new studio releases were carefully kept secrets for the fanbanse. Without trying, the Cruisers found a new prominence on radio: Two growing FM formats were throwbacks to the glory days of radio, when a station could go deep and wide with its playlist. The formats turned into a corporate movement, but they did open the door for relatively obscure artists from yesteryear, like a three-hit wonder form the '80s that discriminating rock-heads remembered well.

SEAN ROSS, *ROSS ON RADIO*: "Leah" was a signature record when the Jack- and Bob [B.est O.f the B.est format] FMs began signing on 15 years ago. It still gets some airplay at that format and Classic Rock. It's the kind of record radio people love because it's up and fun, and you don't hear it all the time. And still, a lot of the spins for that song — or any of his others — are in markets that are somewhere on I-76 or I-80.

Eclectic or not, they weren't touching the Cruisers' new songs. The outing left Mark dejected and Donnie wryly grinning, ready for the next at-bat.

Interlude:
Paul's Favorite Albums

Here's what I could come up with and it was hard to keep it close to 10:

The Beatles, Sgt. Pepper
Abbey Road

Jimi Hendrix
Electric Ladyland

Genesis
Foxtrot

Peter Gabriel
So

King Crimson
In the Court of the Crimson King

Yes
The Yes Album

Led Zeppelin
I-IV

Jaco Pastorius
Jaco

Jeff Beck
Wired and Blow by Blow

Crosby, Stills & Nash, *Crosby
Stills & Nash and Déjà Vu*

The Doors
L.A. Woman

CHAPTER 69

Ah! Live!: The Album

Ah! Live!

The second official full-length live album by Donnie Iris and the Cruisers. Featuring...

"Little Black Dress" (Avsec)
"Sweet Merilee" (Avsec, Iris)
"King Cool" (Avsec, Iris)
"I Can't Hear You" (Avsec, Iris, McClain, Hoenes, Valentine)
"Rocque Fantastique" (Avsec)

"I Can't Really Miss You (If You Never Go Away)" (Avsec)
"Love Is Like a Rock" (Avsec, Iris, McClain, Hoenes, Valentine)
"Ah! Leah!" (Avsec, Iris)
"The Rapper" (Iris)

Released May 24, 2009
CD Release - Pri418 PRIMARY. (P) 2009 Primary Records Group,

From the credits:

Live tracks produced by Rick Witkowski, Mark Avsec and Donnie Iris

Live tracks recorded by Rick Witkowski and mixed by Rick (with Mark and Donnie) at Studio L • Assistant Engineer: Anthony Rankin

Mastered by Roger Lian at Masterdisk

Donnie Iris: lead vocals • Mark Avsec : keyboards & background vocals

Marty Lee Hoenes: guitar & background vocals • Kevin Valentine: drums

Paul Goll – bass guitar and background vocals

2009. The Cruisers' 2008 reunion EP was a swing and a miss. A live album worked the last time.

When Albritton left town, Paul slid back in seamlessly. The band cut another concert album. *Ah! Live!* captures a mixed set of old favorites and new tunes, with a substantially different vibe than *Live at Nick's Fat City*.

Ah! Live! combines concert cuts from two shows: The first was taped July 18, 2008 at the Kittanning's Warehouse Club (in deep rural Eastern Steelers Country). The second was July 24, at Presque Isle Downs & Casino (a shiny new venue in Marty and Paul's hometown).

The band released the CD in May 2009. And by the time it was out, Donnie was surprised to find himself at the advanced age of 66.

"I look back to when I'd see Chuck Berry on TV, doing his stuff," Donnie told the Erie *Times-News*. "He was 60 at the time. And I thought to myself, 'No way I could be doing that at that age.' I never thought it'd happen. But the fact is the band still likes to play and record. I don't ever see us stopping until people stop coming to see us."[68.2]

The band's second official live gonzo is a more relaxed affair than *Live at Nick's*. The band turn in a looser, intimate performance that plays like a second set, Saturday night, at a blues bar.

Mark puts his keyboard in organ mode, leaves it there, and deftly harnesses it to keep the songs moving. With no overdubs, the band harmonize on old deep cuts ("I Can't Hear You") and new rockers ("Rocque Fantastique").

The shows seems like it was fun. But it's not one of the band's favorite releases.

KEVIN: I think it's a horrible show. It didn't sound any good onstage. It doesn't sound good on the recording. I'm not a fan.

CHAPTER 70

King Cool: The Beer

In 2009, the overworked Cruisers poured themselves a cool one. Team Donnie launched an adventurous new enterprise that left King Cool Incorporated 0 for 3 in recent outings: Donnie and company developed and released King Cool Light. The satisfying, flavorful beer was full-bodied, yet low in calories. It was a good brew.

MARK: We wanted to have our own company with our own beer with our own name. We were mistaken.

The team pooled their resources and divvied up the heavy lifting. Mark had the idea. Donnie was the face of the project. Belkin was the business guy. Marty designed the graphics. The project also brought some new players to the forefront. Mark Dvoroznak is the unsung member of the team who provides sage advice and angel capital. And he doesn't mind grunt work like shipping T-shirts.

MARK: Mark Dvoroznak is an honorary Cruiser. An angel to us. Without his work and help, aspects of what we have been able to do over the years would not have happened. He's the most humble person you will ever meet. I say he is a mensch, which is a Jewish title of the highest honor – he's not Jewish, and neither am I, but many of my friends are Jewish. I don't think we have a word as good as *mensch*.

To quarterback the effort, the Cruisers drafted Gary Medved, who lives in Cleveland, but is a longtime fan from the olde country.

MEDVED: I met Mark Avsec at a show. We became friendly. He knew I had been involved in business development for new companies and owned companies. So he tapped me and sent me the plan. The name, the idea, the concept, the packaging — they had it already. But they had no beer, no brewer, no packer, nothing but the idea.

I got involved. I thought it was going to be less involving than it was. It turned out to be a big project. I owned another company at the time.

It was a fun three-year process, developing the beer business. I'm a huge fan of the band and the individual people in the band, back to the *Back on the Streets* album. I'm from a small town in Pennsylvania, about seven miles west of Uniontown called Republic, by Brownsville.

MARK: We wanted to license the name to Iron City [Pittsburgh Brewing Company, makers of Iron City and I.C. Light]. We met with them. They were very nice. We met with a manager, and he proceeded to explain to us why we would never be successful with that beer.

And it made a lot of sense. They explained why they wouldn't be interested in licensing deal, how building a brand takes this and that.

He was right. It cost us some money and sweat equity to learn that.

King Cool Light got off to a good start. November 20, 2009, the Cruisers returned to the former Nick's Fat City — now called Diesel, and similarly rocking — for a launch party.

MEDVED: It looked like a good idea for the first month and a half.

But then the bigger brands started taking notice. Especially Coors Light, who comes into Pittsburgh with a $2 million budget and a mission to become the number one beer in the city.

"What's going on?!" It's like a movie, where you're holding your own against the local guys, and they then call in the big guns from Chicago. It got ugly.

MARK: Bud Light, Coors Light, all those beers have a ton of ads on radio and TV all the time because all the beers taste the same. You've got to promote it and build a brand with advertising. And we had no money for that. We blew $60,000 to have a commercial on Pittsburgh Pirates home games — Donnie and I made that spot.

MEDVED: We would strongly, *strongly* urge these bars to do a bartending gig with Donnie.

I would show up an hour and 45 minutes early. I'd give them a playlist of rock music with Donnie Iris in the mix, playing throughout the evening. And I'd bring a case full of apparel and table tents. Donnie would show up, always on time. He never played the rock star. He'd greet the bar owner, bartender, managers, owner. And for two hours, it was a party. He'd get behind the bar, give away T-shirts, sign autographs. He's 66, and he's still commanding this kind of crowd.

After a while, we came to the conclusion that without the deep, deep, *deep* pockets that Coors has, we're not going to make it.

The beer business busted up the Cruisers' most popular party, the Gateway Clipper river-cruise gigs in Pittsburgh.

MEDVED: The Boos Cruise, the Halloween cruise. Someone in charge refused to promote King Cool Light. And Mike Belkin got into a war of words with them. And they had I.C. Light on special that night. So our beer was more expensive. It pissed everybody off.

I don't think they've done another cruise since. It seemed like the problem was 90% beer, 10% something else.

MARK: We didn't lose a ton of money. We had a lot of fun with it.

The image shows a six-pack of KING COOL LIGHT beer.

Text visible on the packaging:

BREWED IN THE
THIS IS MY SIG...

TRADITION OF UNC...
HOPE YOU ENJOY IT.

6 *Longneck 12 fl. oz. non-returnable bottles*

WWW.KINGCOOL.COM

KING COOL LIGHT

A Light American Lager made with the finest domestic two- and six-row barley and a perfect blend of American and European hops. A touch of caramel malt gives it its brilliant amber color and rare flavor.

KING COOL LIGHT

...beer that rocks!

Donnie Iris
& the Cruisers

Ah! Leluiah!

The Christmas Album

D. X. FERRIS

CHAPTER 71

Ah! Leluiah!: The Christmas Album

Ah! Leluiah! The ninth studio album by Donnie Iris and the Cruisers. A holiday special featuring...

"Introduction"
"Angels We Have Heard on High"
"We Wish You a Merry Christmas"
"Blue Christmas"
"Emmanuel"
"O Come All Ye Faithful"
"White Christmas"
"Carol of the Bells"
"Alleluyah Sasa! (He Is Born)"

"This Child" (original song, written by Avsec)
"Ave Maria"
"We Wish You a Merry Christmas" (reprise)
"Panis Angelicus"
"The Hallelujah Chorus"
"Auld Lang Syne"
"Have Yourself a Merry Little Christmas"
"Silent Night"

Release: November 18, 2010
Label: Primary Records Group. CD: Pri419

From the credits:
Produced by Mark Avsec
Recorded by Bill Korecky
Album design by Marty Lee Hoenes
Mixed by Three Wise Men at Mars
Mastered by Roger Lian at Masterdisk, New York, New York
Selected arrangements of public domain compositions

2010. A straightforward idea turned into Donnie and Mark's most painstaking album in decades. The Cruisers got their studio mojo back, thanks to a sustained dose of Christmas magic.

STEVE HANSEN, *JIMMY AND STEVE IN THE MORNING*: Donnie has continued to make tremendous music. The Christmas album was a major undertaking, to arrange something new out of songs you've heard a million times before, and make it sound good and natural. That maybe wasn't appreciated as much as it should have been. Donnie is a tremendous artist, a tremendous singer.

MITCHELL KEZIN, DIRECTOR OF CHRISTMAS MUSIC DOCUMENTARY *JINGLE BELL ROCKS!*: I couldn't begin to hazard a guess as to when this album was recorded. It sounds equally modern and also like a treasured Christmas gem dug up from the deep sloughs of England, from the early '60s.

Donnie had dabbled in Christmas music over the years, from WDVE's "HAL the Computer" in 1982, to 2011's duet with Pittsburgh singer-pianist Nina Sainato, "Baby It's Cold Outside." In 2010, he went all-in.

Ah! Leluiah!, the Cruisers' yuletide holiday album, applies the band's trademark studio techniques to enduring holiday hits. The Cruisers adapt songs refined over centuries and revered worldwide.

MITCHELL KEZIN: As a Christmas Album, it's one of the most successful, and consistently lovely sounding, mixes of the sacred and secular that I've heard: very tastefully chosen chestnuts, interspersed by gorgeous re-imagined orchestration in each of the carols. This record surprises me at every turn. It is as inventive — or is that innovative? — as The Beach Boys' *Pet Sounds*.

The set list comprises songs written by a saint, refined by Elvis, polished by Sinatra, inspired by Jesus, and expertly embellished by a mailman. The Cruisers made a record that was designed to *not* be ignored.

MARK: I wanted Donnie to shine. I wanted this to be his, and our, legacy album.

Just because it's a Christmas record, people will play it. They probably play it more than others they have. With me, we watch Christmas movies at home is December — which probably means we watch those more than any other movie. And so I decided we were going to make a great, great record. And I stand by that record. When we don't make great records, I'll say it. That is a great record.

Did I know what I was getting into? Probably not.

But anything worth doing is worth overdoing.

When Mark had the idea, it seemed like a simple plan: record some Christmas songs. But the album immediately grew into the band's most elaborate studio work.

After decades making ambitious and eclectic popular music, Donnie and Mark built a true tour-de-force of a record that covered every aspect of their musical lives: classical, rock, jazz, blues. Loud, soft, reverent, rocking, traditional, touching. As described in thorough liner notes, *Ah! Leluiah!* tapped all 116 years of Donnie and Mark's combined musical experience. It explored new styles. And it reached around the world for material.

MARK: It really didn't have anything to do with *Planet Christmas*. I wanted to do big songs that were profound, not "Jingle Bells" and "Santa Claus Is Coming to Town." The timeless Christmas songs.

I can't remember where the idea came from, except we had never done a Christmas record. And we weren't trying to do what B.E. Taylor or T.S.O. did — and they're great, and maybe I thought of it. But they do that already. We wanted to do our own thing.

By far, the two albums I enjoyed making the most were the first Donnie Iris album and the Christmas album.

Both of these were true labors of love.

Donnie and I were the prime movers of the first album – the guys were a big part of it, too. But then it was Donnie and I and Jerry, the engineer. Donnie and I really felt we were working on something special. And that was the best time of my life. And the three of us were the team.

And then, for me, I did not have that feeling again until the Christmas album. For some reason, I really dove into that. And it was a ton of work, and I don't even care that most people will never hear it. I'm proud of it. And I listen to it every year.

The Christmas album, I put it up there with *King Cool*. And to every Donnie fan out there, I would say, "Get the Christmas album." Stream it.

Donnie and Mark started soon after Christmas, in January 2010, when snow was still on the ground. For the new Cruisers studio team, Christmas lasted all year long.

Mark, Donnie and engineer Bill Korecky started with one of the more audacious undertakings in the history of recorded music: Mark wanted to record Handel's "Hallelujah" chorus, one of the most famous and revered pieces of music in history. Handel used two full church choirs — one male, one female — to perform the piece.[71.1] And Mark wanted to do it using just one singer: Donnie Iris.

MARK: I thought we could really *Donnie Iris* that up. We spent a lot of time on that. That was a spiritual thing.

That was something I worked on with Bill Korecky. The way we approached it, I don't care what anybody says or what it sold, it was not a waste of my time. Years from now, Donnie and I will always have that record.

KEVIN: The studio we work in now, Mars, is very much like Jeree's. I like working with Bill. From the base, he gets it. For instance, drum sounds. You put a drum set in there, and he's going to capture it. It's a great room.

PAUL: Bill is a great guy, and was very creative and patient with us. He brought a lot to the sessions.

DONNIE: I enjoy Christmas with the kids. But I'm not a big decorate-the-tree guy.

Knowing Mark, I thought, "OK, this isn't gonna be a run-of-the-mill album." I knew it would be good, and it would be different.

Mark was *way* into it. He had a lot of ideas. I didn't really think it would be easy. We were really going to work our ass off and come up with something good.

MARK: The Christmas album, in *one* sense, was an easy album to make. The crapshoot with recorded music is: Are you going to write a good song? With Christmas music, you're taking tried and true songs that work. When you start there, you can be as creative as you want.

When I was a kid, I was extremely religious. And Christmas was very magical and special to me.

So we started with the "Hallelujah" chorus. I don't remember what I was doing when the idea came to me. But my ideas come to me in layers. If I get really creative early in the morning, I just get these ideas:

We stack vocals.

And I had this idea of the "Hallelujah" chorus.

What if Donnie sang the whole thing himself?

And so I approached Donnie about it.

And he said, "We'll try it, Spark."

That's what he always says.

I ordered it online, got a couple-three arrangements of it. And I created my own version, because we don't follow any of them exactly.

I would have the score we used in front of me. And we would take short phrases, eight seconds, ten seconds of the piece.

It would be soprano, alto, tenor, and bass. And we'd start with the bass — sometimes alto or tenor, definitely not soprano. I know there were 81 voices in the end. I know that there were nine soprano voices, for the most part. Those killed Donnie. In some places, we only have five or six. But in the rest of them, we have 24 or 27 tracks.

We worked on that January through March, probably five-six sessions a month, about four hours a session. That's all we worked on at first. I had the keyboard in the control room. I would play Donnie a part — soprano, alto, tenor or bass. He would sing it however many times.

Each one is a new track, a new take. And that's an example of not having limits, recording digitally. Maybe it would have been better analog, if we mixed them down — but Bill knows what he's doing.

I'm known as working in classic rock or whatever they want to call it, but I really put a lot of my training and education into that album.

By April, working on Handel for more than two months, it was an ordeal.

And that massive multi-month undertaking was just the beginning. Once Mark turned Donnie into a one-man choir, a two-take walk through "Run Run Rudolph" was off the table.

PAUL: The Christmas album was pretty much the same experience as *Ellwood City*, but we really stretched out, messing with traditional Christmas music and making it our own. Lots of "Try this" or "Try that" and "*Yeah*! That's cool!"

MARK: At some point, early, I had the idea for the *Sgt. Pepper* homage. I'm a Beatles freak, and I love *Sgt. Pepper*.

AH! LELUIAH!: THE SONGS. "INTRODUCTION"

Ah! Leluiah! warms up like a symphony, a party, and a classic Beatles album. The record starts with an attention-grabbing tease: Donnie sings a snippet of the "Hallelujah" chorus. Then follows a preview of "O Come All Ye Faithful," chased with snippets of traditional 19th century spirituals that didn't make the record.

MARK: "Mary Had a Little Baby," we recorded that whole song, and that was left over. "Go Tell It on the Mountain," I don't know how much we did.

"ANGELS WE HAVE HEARD ON HIGH"

Donnie and Mark fly this 19th century English carol into a space that's dramatic, dark and heavy — but not negative. The album's first proper song taps a controversial 21st century vocal effect: Auto-Tune, a pitch-altering effect that was popular in radio and R&B circles. Normally, engineers use it to fix singers who can't sing. Around this time, the pitch correction was commonly used as its own sound.

DONNIE: I thought I'd try it. It worked. Very cool.

MARK: We had never done that before. We did that because the song needed something. Something was missing in the way it sounded—it didn't work. Donnie sounds great, and he's got these great voices. But sometimes, if he's in a lower register, singing normal, it's not that special. I *work* his voice. It needed a little bit of an animation there. I know it was trendy, but we decided to use the Auto-Tune.

"WE WISH YOU A MERRY CHRISTMAS"

The British serenade has unclear origins, but is generally dated to the 16th century, when Christmas was transitioning from a religious festival to a community celebration. Mark's lifetime of musical training comes full circle in a joyous accordion solo.[71.2]

DONNIE: Mark playing the accordion, if you've ever seen him, it's really fun to watch. He really gets into it. He's incredible.

MARK: It's one of the few times I've really leveraged my ability to read music and write music. I usually don't feature keyboards and those kind of things on the records — it's all Donnie and Marty.

With the Christmas record, the Christmas songs, it's not like rock records, where you need a great riff for a great song. It was freeing, because you had this thing to work with, that you could do any which way. It was probably my first time playing accordion on a record.

I bought that accordion for the band. It's a newer one. It's a pretty good one. It's called an Excelsior Grand. I picked it up on eBay.

I wish I had more time to practice. For me to play accordion as well as I did, where I was a state champion, I would have to play a lot of hours. But for me to play those little parts, it was easy, not a big deal.

Pet Sounds was an influence in that way, too: Brian Wilson used accordions as a big part of the sound, the rhythm things. People don't realize he would mix two accordions with piano, like on "Wouldn't It Be Nice" and other songs. Once you know it, you'll hear it. We used it a little bit like that, too.

KEVIN: Some of it was very creative. Every song had a vibe. "We Wish You a Merry Christmas" was an ELO vibe.

"BLUE CHRISTMAS"

The song was around almost a decade before Elvis recorded it — but once the King cut a version, he owned it.[71.3]

Donnie tips his hat to Elvis without directly emulating the king. This cheerful rendition traces rock 'n' roll back to its country roots and comes up with a gem: a steel-pedal guitar solo that will make your heart glow. The song's introduction incorporates one of the most beloved traditions from the Cruisers' fan community: counting off during the band's most rhythmic track, "Love Is Like a Rock."

MITCHELL KEZIN, *JINGLE BELL ROCKS!*: A stand-out for me is Donnie Iris' version of "Blue Christmas." With the rich, syrupy steel guitar and big drums, I'm reminded a bit of Gram Parsons, who I always wished had recorded an album of his own Christmas songs.

MARK: That's when I began to take it somewhere new. I love developing these loose concepts. It feels like we're making a broader statement, like it becomes more a work of art.

It starts off with "Angels We Have Heard on High," and that's fine. Then it goes into the orchestration thing, which is like *Sgt. Pepper*. That's deliberate.

Then "We Wish You a Merry Christmas" comes in, and the accordion plays, and there's the laughter — it's deliberate, to evoke that.

And "Blue Christmas" is "With a Little Help From My Friends." We used a piece of the *Live at Nick's* album where the crowd is going "1, 2 / 1, 2, 3, 4" — I went to the CD and pulled that off there.

We made it a country song. By that time, it was "A Little Help From My Friends." It was supposed to be something different. It was my idea to do the steel guitar.

That is one instance — when we're laying down parts, all of us, rarely do we get a perfect take. We like to really work with the tracks, to coax them along. We discourage rehearsal ahead of time. But…

That said, Steely Dan Morris, who played the steel guitar on that, he's a retired postman. Bill told me about him. I called him. He's a very nice guy. I told him we'd pay him to come to the studio and play pedal steel.

He says, "I'd like to hear it in advance."

Honestly, I was thinking, "I'd prefer you didn't." But he seemed nervous, and I wanted him to do it. So we sent him our track.

He came down that day. And he set up his pedal steel. We got a level. And we started the tape.

And he played it front-to-back. And that's what you hear on the record.

We didn't stop it. It took literally three minutes, thirty seconds. He deserves all the credit for that. He just knew what to play, and it was perfect.

Donnie and I were just going, "Wow!"

It seemed silly to have him come in for three minutes. So we said, "Well, I guess do another one."

And he did another one, almost exactly the same.

And we went with the first one, because it was magical.

"EMMANUEL"

The magazine *Christian History* called "Emmanuel" "the season's most somber hymn." Popular in both Catholic and protestant traditions, the tune took its modern form as an advent hymn in 1851, but has roots in an antiphon chant codified as a metrical Latin poem in the 12th century. Its inspiration was *Luke* 1:46-55: "My soul magnifies the Lord; my spirit rejoices in God my Savior."[71.4]

A young Mark, you'll recall, heard Lee Michaels' Hammond B-3 and thought it "sounded like God." On "Emmanuel," he applies the worldly instrument to religious piece.

MARK: "Emmanuel" was a little bit of a nod to "House of the Rising Sun" by the Animals. I don't know if it's a great version, but Donnie sings his ass off on that. He sings his ass off on the whole album. But at the end of "Emmanuel," when he's crooning, he's at the top of his natural range, without screaming.

First, you cut the tracks, with them full of energy — and that's all Kevin and Paul. Kevin gives us a great, high energy track with drums. And we'll all play together, like "Emmanuel."

And once we have the great track… I think I kept most of my organ. Marty might have re-done his guitar in stereo. And Paul will repeat any bass things he missed. So the track is kind of live. Then you stack a lot of things.

I loved "Emmanuel." I went to Catholic school. During Advent, every morning, we'd have to go out in the hallway for an Advent ceremony. We'd have to sing "Emmanuel." I thought it was a really haunting, spiritual thing. Now, that's not what we captured. It was more an homage to a classic rock era. I'd love to do it again and set it without drums.

"O COME ALL YE FAITHFUL"

This hymn dates to the 18th century, and was originally written as the Latin "Adeste Fideles," which translates to "Come, all ye faithful." It was translated into English in the 1840s, then framed with its current melody in 1906.[71.5] Some arrangements are joyful. Some are dour. Donnie took a moving, meditative approach in one of his most powerful performances. Technically, it's not flawless. But it's a perfect delivery, with real emotional heft.

DONNIE: That one, I cried. That song is bad-ass. There's some tunes on there that I've seen bring other people to tears.

MARK: At Bill's place, we've been using Donnie's car to test the mixes. He's got this Cadillac, and it's got a pretty good stereo. We'll check a mix in there, if the bass and low end are right, if the lead vocal is loud enough or too loud.

DONNIE: That song almost didn't make the album.

We went out in my car and listened to it. And I was almost at the point to where I'm welling up.

And I said, "What do you think?"

Mark said, "I think it's great."

"WHITE CHRISTMAS"

"White Christmas" was written by Irving Berlin in 1939. Bing Crosby's 1942 performance in the movie *Holiday Inn* made it an instant classic. In the year 2000, it was still the most-recorded popular song in the world.[71.6]

The Cruisers' quiet, jazzy version captures another running bit on the permanent record: Donnie and Mark introduce the song like they're hosting an old-time radio special. In the dialogue, they use their nicknames for each other.

DONNIE: That's our thing, Spyke and Spark. That was a lot of fun to do, to get that in there. That one went pretty quick. That was maybe two takes.

That came from the days... I had a bunch of buddies in a bowling league, every Wednesday night at Sim's Lanes, on Route 18 between Koppel and Beaver Falls. Me and maybe ten other guys.

Somehow, it came up: A name that would totally *not* fit me would be "Spike." And then some of the guys ended up calling me that as my nickname. And they spelled it with a Y. Everybody had their name etched into their bowling ball, and somebody said, "Put a *Y* in there instead of an *I*."

KEVIN: There was one song with a drum machine, "White Christmas." I didn't play on that.

MARK: I didn't know if Marty was featured enough on the record. So I talked to him, and I said, "What would you think about doing 'White Christmas' in a real jazzy kind of way?"

And I had this keyboard that I rented, a Roland Phantom — I know it sounds like a bass, but it's really a sampled acoustic jazz bass on a keyboard. So I had that sound. And the trumpet was from the same keyboard; it has a great trumpet sound.

We put it together in an afternoon. Donnie learned to sing from his mother, and that's what that is: It's him singing the song in that style.

And then to work it into our concept, we made it like this 1940s radio special. Donnie says "Spark," and it was nice to document that on an album. A lot of thought went into that album — a lot of work, a lot of good vibes.

"CAROL OF THE BELLS"

This haunting earworm began as the Ukrainian folk chant "Shchedryk."[71.7] Composer Mykola Leontovych refashioned it as a choral composition in 1914.[71.8] Later, composer Peter Wilhousky heard a choir sing it, thought of bells, and wrote the English lyrics.[71.9]

Once again, Donnie is a one-man choir on this beloved, spiraling Christmas melody — but on a far smaller scale. One of the album's many emotional high points comes from a small improvised moment: After a late-song chorus, Donnie lets out a mournful wail that echoes through your soul.

DONNIE: That was interesting. I liked "Carol of the Bells," with the brushes. That was fun. Mark did a really good job on this.

MARK: "Carol of the Bells" was always one of my favorites. We're not Trans-Siberian Orchestra — you hear it, and you immediately think of them, because they do such a great job on it. We're us. We wanted to do our own thing.

And when you have a voice like Donnie… My favorite thing about Donnie: His voice is my favorite instrument.

Again, I got the score, because I read music. It's one of *those* compositions. It's a classic that's just magical. That's the thing about music: When you stumble across writing a hit song or whatever, it's just magical. It's just *good*.

I can *analyze* it, though: That's what you do when you adapt. I can go through the composition techniques and say, "It has the motif, *da-da-da-DA*." Then you transpose it higher. It's a textbook lesson in developing short fragments of melody through composition techniques that make a lot of sense — and that's why it lives. But that's not the only reason it lives; it just strikes the hearts of people, including myself.

The "whoa" was an ad-lib in the studio. We needed something there. I love to stack, but stacking is just setting the table. We do the stacking so he can be *himself*.

It was an ad-lib I suggested to Donnie. We were experimenting for him to do something there. And that's just his voice, solo — you hear how he can sing. That's what we wanted to do with the whole album: *contribute* something to the songs.

DONNIE: That was not hard to do, but time-consuming, and vocal-consuming. The high, quick parts — that was very weird.

"ALLELUYAH SASA! (HE IS BORN)"

The party abruptly pivots with this modern romp, which was commissioned in 2008.[71.10]

The world-music workout was written by Ben Allaway, a composer who works in a broad collection of ethnic music styles from all over the world. Allaway is a California native, and more recently of Iowa — which warrants a note because the song is an adaptation of a choral piece written in Swahili. The original version has lively percussion, but is not the aerobically demanding performance Kevin puts in.[71.11]

The title translates to "Alleluia now," not "He is born."[71.12]

This track is a unique pairing in the Cruisers catalog: It's just Donnie and Kevin.

MARK: God knows how I found it. I was on the internet. I don't know what I was looking for that I came upon that. It was a total African Swahili thing. And by that point, I was into my *Sgt. Pepper* homage, and I thought that could be my "Within You Without You," just playing this really different culture to mix in.

I found out who wrote it. And I licensed it and got the sheet music and made my own arrangement of it. It was pretty involved, the whole thing. It's a short version.

I heard from the guy who wrote it. He sent me an email. He was thrilled with it. He absolutely loved it, which felt good.

Kevin's drums were an addition. We knew what we were doing with it at that point. We asked Kevin to play a drum beat. I didn't tell him what to play. We started with that.

KEVIN: There was a really odd timing in that song. Mark knew it. We played it in the studio. And we played it in the studio, and I was having trouble getting it. In the end, I just watched Mark for the accents. He would give me the "bang the tom" symbol for the accent in the chorus. That was difficult. Cool song, though, right?

PAUL: I continued to be blown away by Kevin's ability to come up with a groove and just nail it in one or two takes. He also knows his way around a recording console, and knows how to mic drums, and get amazing sound from them. Our engineer would often consult with him about Pro Tools software questions.

DONNIE: The Swahili thing, Mark gave it to me, said, "Here's how it goes." And I worked on the phrasing in a phonetic kind of way.

MARK: I had the sheet music, and I could read the words, and there are some complex lyrics. He would stumble over it a little bit, understandably, until he learned it. And then we would stack the hell out of it.

I may have changed some of the words. At the end, we completely punted and went off on our own thing with it.

"THIS CHILD"

The album's original Cruisers song is an energizing original credited to Avsec, who deals from a deck of popular religious images. Over a jaunty riff, Donnie reminds us of the reason for the season. It's built on the structure of the public-domain "What Child Is This." (The piano version is one of the themes in Vince Guaraldi's *A Charlie Brown Christmas* score.) The lyrics were written by William Chatterton Dix, who experienced a religious renewal during a serious illness. Inspired, he wrote the poem "The Manger Throne," and set it to the music of the 14th-century British melody "Greensleeves."[71.13]

MARK: We wanted an original. I didn't even realize, in my brain, it was based on that traditional song, "What Child Is This?" It was some association in my deep unconscious.

Lyrically, it is a tune more about questioning faith, about the juxtaposition between reason and faith. That's the kind of thing I think about. That's what that record is.

Donnie had a total cold when he sang it. If you listen, maybe you can hear him being stuffed up. It was the summer, and we needed to get it done.

I brought in a sketch of the song on a keyboard. I think I heard that riff, and I asked Marty to play it.

The thing that really works on that song: I don't know where we got "Hark! The Herald Angels Sing," but it was in a different key. Maybe it was for something we were recording for the record that we didn't use. And I found that if you juxtaposed that key over the end of "This Child," it really worked.

"AVE MARIA"

This beloved tune, always a tearjerker, is one of the most ethereal melodies ever written. Donnie sings an obscure arrangement by Giulio Caccini, 17th century Italian composer widely credited with paving the way for the Baroque style and opera itself.[71.14] (Maybe overcredited, but if nothing, he was a good self-promoter; and then as now, it's an important part of the business.)

MARK: I didn't know about the version written by Caccini. I'm familiar with the Schubert one. And then I heard a version Andrea Bocelli had done, and I thought it was brilliant. I put it in Donnie's key, letting Donnie reach still. It's boring if you don't have Donnie reach. You have to set his key so he's going to be comfortable, but reaching in parts. *That's* where you get that urgency.

I never played Bocelli's version for him. I didn't want him to hear it.

It was summer. It was June. I called [Cleveland studio] MetroSync — they had a really good piano, a 1952, 1953 Steinway. I went in on a Sunday morning. They were kind enough to let me in, because I was inspired.

It didn't take long. That day, I laid the piano for "We Wish You a Merry Christmas." I played the "Ave Maria" without a click track — I just wanted the feel. And then I put the strings down that day.

Then I took the tracks to Mars Studio. Donnie showed up. I taught him the song. He sang it.

We went through, line by line., as we always do. And it's one of my favorite performances by Donnie. Donnie's a *singer*. If he gets worked up enough and you get the right setting for him, he can really croon and really sing.

DONNIE: My mom has listened to that album. I've listened to it with her. She holds it back, but you can tell she's getting emotional. I remember all of us sitting around, listening to it at my sister's house — my nephews, my mom, everybody was there. I look over at my mom, and you can tell she's on the verge of tears. She held up pretty good, though.

She doesn't have a favorite song I do. Everything I do, in her eyes, it's the best. My dad was the same way: Anything I did was great.

"WE WISH YOU A MERRY CHRISTMAS" (REPRISE)

Marty, Mark and Donnie briefly revamp this tender tune in the Cruisers' third heavy metal moment— they have one every decade or so. When you're recording Christmas songs in a corn field in the middle of July, things are bound to take some twists and turns.

MARK: We wanted to evoke that reprise of "Sgt. Pepper." The idea to go heavy, it's kind of ugly in a way. But Donnie thought it was cool. So we went that way, and Donnie, on his own, started singing it like that. And that's not at all what I was hearing. But he was so excited about it that we kept it. And then it goes into "Panis Angelicus."

I read an interview with Donnie, and he said he thought recording all year was a little odd: He's on the golf course, and then he's going in the studio to sing "Silent Night."

To me, the songs were inherently atmospheric. That was a labor of love. Bill was a big part of it, too. We went on a journey together, the three of us. The whole band did, but the reason I say "the three of us" is because that's the way it works: We cut the tracks, and we hung together for several days. We had a lot of laughs. But then everybody leaves, and it's just Donnie and me and Bill.

"PANIS ANGELICUS"

Like many other sacred pieces, the stunning "Panis Angelicus" is a hybrid adaptation of previous works, one old, one ancient. It's not a Christmas hymn, but it is very Catholic. The words are a segment from the hymn "Sacris Solemniis," written by Saint Thomas Aquinas, the eminent 13th century priest and philosopher, in commemoration of the Feast of Corpus Christi. The title means "bread of angels." The feast celebrates transubstantiation, which transforms ceremonial bread and wine into the Eucharist, the physical manifestation of the body and blood of Jesus Christ.[71.15] In the lyrics, Aquinas praises the patient poor and bows before the Holy Trinity.

Belgian-French composer Cesar Franck wrote the music in 1872, originally composing it for tenor, organ, harp, cello, and double bass; he later adapted it into a three-voice mass.[71.16] Backed by just Mark's keyboard, this version might be Donnie's finest vocal performance.

MARK: I just thought it was a classic song. We did it as a nod to "A Lighter Shade of Pale" by Procol Harum. Listen to it, and you'll get it. I was raised Catholic, so I was indoctrinated with Aquinas. I have a broader worldview now.

DONNIE: I love the way that turned out. It's beautiful. Mark didn't have to help me too much with the pronunciation on that. I remember some Latin from when I was a kid. I maybe had a Latin class in early high school or middle school. I knew the basic melody of the song.

MARK: "Panis Angelicus," that's our "A Day in the Life." That's why it has strings on the end, building to the big ending. Don't think that I'm suggesting it's as good as *Sgt. Pepper*. But it was an homage to that, to an era when albums had meaning. And it's a collective work, and meant to be listened to front-to-back.

"THE HALLELUJAH CHORUS"

This all-time-great piece of classical music is very rock and roll: The traditional response, even in the stodgiest setting, is for the audience to stand when the vocals drop.

Dejected, unheralded, and deep in debt, keyboardist and composer Frideric Handel had quit music. Then his friend Charles Jennens wrote a religious libretto about the life of Christ. Flush with cash from a commission, Handel wrote *Messiah* in 1741, working obsessively, inspired by divine visions.[71.17] The "Hallelujah" chorus is the best part.

In America, the chorus is most famously associated with the Mormon Tabernacle Choir, who know something about stacking vocals; the group uses 360 singers. Donnie and Mark pull it off with one.

KORECKY: Donnie is the real deal and always has been. He is a tracking machine, how he is able to stack and repeat himself. The "Hallelujah" chorus is an example of how he can stand there and spit out hundreds and hundreds of tracks. As fast as I can get the machine started, he's ready for another track. Everything that comes out of his mouth is good, all the time.

DONNIE: I couldn't imagine what it was going to sound like. But knowing Mark's knowledge of the song and the music, I knew it would be something. It was all in his head. I just did it, concentrating on the notes and where the melodies go.

There's some things on there that I wish I could have done better. A couple notes, I wish I could have gone higher. Some of those notes were totally out of my range, but I never really had those notes in my range.

I listen to it, and all those voices together, that's me — that feels great. It might be the best thing we've ever done, the Christmas album. The cool thing about it is: It'll go on, every Christmas. People will be talking about that thing, anybody that hears it.

Recording the "Hallelujah" chorus, we'd sing all afternoon until I couldn't go anymore. I would have to stop. I wouldn't lay off the cigars, though; the cigars don't seem to have any effect.

Maybe Queen did that kind of thing, with that kind of insight and talent. Some groups can do that.

PAUL: What Mark does with our tracks in the studio is amazing, what they build them into. I wish I got to be around for more of it.

MARK: I gave a presentation in Las Vegas: I lead our group's 3D-printing initiative. I saw some presentations. There was a presentation by Reebok, who use a robot that's analogous to 3D printing. He was talking about how many stacks they use — they keep using the term "stack." And that's the term I always use to describe Donnie's vocals. If you go to Jeree's, Jerry had a sign made, something like "We stack it," something like that. Maybe that's why 3D printing appealed to me: It's creating something layer by painstaking layer.

There was a movie studio that makes stop-motion animated movies. And they 3D print every figure. It takes them something like three years to make a movie. I forgot how many shots and setups you need to create three seconds of film. I thought, "Man, that's the way I worked on the 'Hallelujah chorus' with Donnie."

"AULD LANG SYNE"

The accordion-powered "Auld Lang Syne" isn't the flashiest performance on the record. But if you understand the album's mission statement — Mark crafting Donnie's legacy album, to honor the Cruisers' decades of collaboration — then it stands as the album's emotional core.

The popular form of the song is credited to the preeminent Scottish poet Robert Burns, circa 1788. But Burns identified it as a much older folk song about bonding, friendship, and good memories past — the title means "old times' sake."[71.18]

Mark concludes the album's liner notes with a quote from the lyrics: "We two have run about the slopes and picked the daises fine; and wandered many a weary foot, since auld lang syne."

MARK: "Auld Lang Syne" pulls at the heartstrings, it's about old friends and family and being together — I don't know if that's what it *means*, but I get that feeling. Our group has stood the test of time. We are still great friends.

"HAVE YOURSELF A MERRY LITTLE CHRISTMAS"

This countlessly covered modern classic was written by Hugh Martin and Ralph Blane, for a Christmas scene in the 1944 musical *Meet Me In St. Louis*. Over the years, singers of all stripes have recalibrated it with varying degrees of bittersweetness or — as in the hands of Frank Sinatra — majesty. Donnie splits the difference in this brief, unplugged adaptation, which floats through one verse and loops the title lyrics into a lullabye.

MARK: I imagined John Lennon singing "Have Yourself a Merry Little Christmas" – and that's the way we did it.

Mark, unlike many card-carrying Beatles fans, isn't partial to John or Paul — or Ringo *or* George.

MARK: I like them all. Without each other, it doesn't happen. Donnie can sound like John or George.

The song cuts short before Donnie has to choose between the lyrical variants "muddle through somehow" or "star upon the highest bow."

MARK: I don't know why I did that way. I had all of these songs… I saw it as an epilogue to the record, the final thing before the lonely "Silent Night." Some have asked me, "Why did you not put 'Auld Lang Syne' last?" I saw that as earlier in the queue. But then 'Auld Lang Syne,' it's over — wait, one more Christmas wish for the kiddies!

"SILENT NIGHT"

The Cruisers' Christmas ends with one more stirring performance by Donnie, unembellished, just a single track — with an assist from the album's walk-on guest star, mailman Steely Dan.

One of the more enduring, mutable, and beloved worldwide Christmas carols originated with another keyboardist who was writing material for a guitar. Its original German lyrics were written by Austrian priest Joseph Mohr in 1816. In 1818, when a church organ broke, organist Franz Gruber turned them into a song, writing a melody and playing it with a guitar.[71.19]

MARK: Lonely. Simple. One voice. One pedal steel guitar. Silent night.

"Have Yourself a Merry Little Christmas," I thought that was the end. But when Steely Dan was doing the pedal steel on "Blue Christmas," for the heck of it, I asked him if he could do it.

I said, "Can you play 'Silent Night'?"

He said, "Sure."

And he went out there, and we played it. We did it in the key of C.

He did that on the spot, too. He knew it enough to improvise it.

It was so sad. I loved it. And I thought, "*That's* the way to end the thing."

DONNIE: That was a couple takes, pretty straightforward, once or twice.

MARK: I did the second verse, I recall, because I did not want it to sound as familiar. I wanted it to be a plaintive wail, just a real lonely thing. And you put a steel guitar behind something like that, and it takes on a certain mood.

The track is a *performance*. That's what you're supposed to do. It's supposed to be a mix: You do the things that are highly produced, like the "Hallelujah" chorus. But other songs, we're really trying to get those glimmers of no-stacking, just emotion. No click track; we don't use click tracks — so you feel some heartbeat. So "Silent Night" was great for that.

I wouldn't play anybody anything until it was done.

We mixed that with great care and sent it off to mastering.

The mastering engineer really liked it; he never says all that much, but he sent me a note, and he said, "Man, that was a really ambitious thing. I really liked it. It wasn't what I expected."

In a perfect world, where time and money aren't a practical consideration, Mark would like to pour that kind of effort into every Cruisers track.

MARK: But it's a given we're not going to make money on anything we record. It just is. And you've got to have good assumptions when you go into anything; the reasonable assumption is that nobody will buy our records. Because nobody does, including our fans. They experience us live.

I spent a lot more time than I planned to. And money, at that point, we had a little money in our primary account. A real friend to the band is Mark Dvoroznak. He's got a big-time finance gig with Sherwin-Williams. We couldn't have done a lot of this stuff without him managing our finances. He has fronted the band some money to do things. He's been a friend, and he's a great guy. Besides Jim Markovich, Mark is the unsung hero. He has been a rock for our band. He's at the heart of all of our planning for our big events.

That is an album I do like. It doesn't matter that it didn't sell. The reviews I read of it, on Amazon and others, that I appreciated. And they made it worth it for me to do that record. And it was also an act of friendship among the guys, and in particular, between Donnie and me.

We're making a new record together, very slowly. But let's face it: Most of the records we will ever make together are behind us. I don't want to be morose about it. But I viewed the Christmas record as something that, as each of us begins to die — and it will happen at some point — that's still a record we'll put on around Christmas. I saw it as a heavy thing.

When I was done with that with Donnie, I kind of shed some tears. Because I felt like maybe it was the last thing we'd ever do together.

We had a listening party for the album in Gary [Medved]'s house. He has a full home theater system in his basement. And a couple of the people we invited were in tears, listening to Donnie sing "Painus Angelicus."

And sometimes a fan will tell me what it means to them — and that's gratifying. And I can tell they really heard and liked it and appreciate it.

And my kids. My daughter Ellen texts me and says, "We're putting the tree up, and your Christmas album is on. It's really good."

I'll take that at face value. I like it.

AH! LELUIAH! MADE PEOPLE HAPPY

Ah! Leluiah! didn't a lot of big reviews in the press. But, as Mark said, the right people got it.

RON GERBER, KFAI FM, *BETWEEN THE SONGS* AUTHOR: I don't like Christmas music at all, but that thing was great. Christmas music strikes me as songs you break out once a year, but never want to hear again. I like that it's *Donnie Iris*, and he's just letting go: He's all Donnie, all the time. He can do whatever he wants. And it sounds pretty good. I have a copy that I keep under my eye, with all the rest of the Donnie Iris stuff.

No Depression — the eminent music journal focused on roots music — appreciated it:

"Despite being well into his '60s, Iris's voice has held up extraordinarily well over the years, but, even more importantly, so has his creativity and artistic passion," wrote Adam Sheets. *"Ah! Leluiah!* features mostly traditional music, but it is performed in a very non-traditional manner.... This isn't just a Christmas album, it's the best Donnie Iris album in decades."[71.20]

Martin "Stubby" Johns, Christmas aficionado and blogger, took it all in: "Donnie Iris isn't a household name, but he should be. ... Just as Iris' own life is a history of rock n roll, so too is this Christmas album. Nothing sounds forced or contrived; these wonderful arrangements all sound perfectly organic.... The production is absolutely incredible.... This album features highlight after highlight. It retains a reverence for both the meaning of the holiday and for rock 'n' roll throughout — no easy task... Can I get an Amen?"[71.21]

This time out, the Pittsburgh papers stood and saluted: The *Tribune-Review*'s Behe Rege wrote, "Iris is best known as having a near-perfect rock 'n' roll voice, and that's exhibited on his versions of 'Angels We Have Heard on High' and 'This Child.' 'Have Yourself a Merry Little Christmas' and 'We Wish You a Merry Christmas' each have a Beatlesque *Rubber Soul* quality that falls well within the repertoire of his band, the Cruisers."[71.22]

And the *Post-Gazette* echoed the first reviews of "Ah! Leah!" and its byzantine production. Scott Mervis wrote, "The result is quite stunning. Picture the Mormon Tabernacle Choir meets Queen, with a little bit of rock 'n' roll grit."[71.23]

Atop the good notices and pleased fanbase, a full 30 years after the band's inception, *Ah! Leluiah!* sold very well for an independent Cruisers' record.

Then, as always, the other shoe dropped.

AND THEN...

MARK: I was *pushing* the record. When I get into something, I get into it. The album was selling well. We were moving some product that first year. We did some in-store appearances. And Borders took an order for 1,000. I personally delivered them. Mark Dvoroznak went with me. We took them to Pittsburgh — that's where it's going to sell.

And Borders went belly-up. They went bankrupt. And we never saw them or the CDs again. Good luck getting paid as a creditor. Welcome to the music industry. We didn't make money on that album — let's put it that way. The Borders deal probably sent us into the red on the album. But either way, it just isn't a lot of money involved.

It's been suggested: "Why don't you do another Christmas album?!"

Like: Right. Who bought this one? But it's one of those things that's just worth doing, because it has inherent meaning. I might not be opposed to doing another one, being super creative, and doing something else.

That Christmas album, I like it. I'm glad we did it.

CHAPTER 72

Donnie & Mark Grade the Catalog

And that, for now, is Donnie Iris and the Cruisers' discography: Nine Cruisers albums, three studio releases, and two live albums. Donnie and Mark grade the Cruisers records together:

Back on the Streets
MARK: Magic.
DONNIE: Good album.

King Cool
MARK: Magic.
DONNIE: Not too bad.

The High and the Mighty
MARK: No magic.
DONNIE: Good album.

Fortune 410
MARK: No magic really, but it has "Do You Compute?."
DONNIE: Not bad.

No Muss... No Fuss
MARK: No magic.
DONNIE: Decent.

Out of the Blue
MARK: No magic at all. Terrible.
DONNIE: Compilation, old stuff.

Foot Solider
MARK: No magic.
DONNIE: *Puh-lease*.

Poletown
MARK: Some magic. I like it.
DONNIE: Like it.

Live at Nick's Fat City
MARK: Magic, decent snapshot.
DONNIE: Sounds good. I like it.

Together Alone
MARK: Misguided, no magic.
DONNIE: Eh.

Ellwood City
MARK: I think some magic.
DONNIE: Not bad.

You Can't Really Miss Me EP
MARK: No magic.
DONNIE: Oh, I don't know...

Ah! Live!
MARK: Not magic, not terrible.
DONNIE: Don't even remember that one.

Ah! Leluiah!
MARK: A lot of magic if you ask me.
DONNIE: Now you're talkin'.

MARK: My conclusion:

"Magic" happens when you have persistence, caring, and a great work ethic to *chase down* the magic. And *then* you need the luck of great performances to intercede.

Basically, if you have any talent and you really care and you are persistent, you have a good chance to get the magic.

In *Out of the Blue*, no effort. They were throw-away songs cobbled together. I am embarrassed.

In *Fortune 410*, there was effort, but the studio was not conducive to the magic.

In *High and the Mighty*, there was effort. But there were collateral things that interrupted the magic, like bad tape and other issues. And the songs were not as good probably as a result. But I won't make excuses.

No Muss... No Fuss, there was effort — but again, it was not Jeree's, and the magic was not there.

Poletown, back at Jeree's. Some magic, and the effort was there.

Foot Soldier, the tracks were bad.

Ellwood City, a lot of effort, just like the old days. I think it's not bad.

Ah! Leluiah! I think is very good a whole lot of effort. And I thought my arrangements were imaginative. I'm as proud of that as anything. For me it's top three, along with *Back on the Streets* and *King Cool*.

But it goes to show, with *High and The Mighty* and *Fortune 410*: You can put in the effort and still not achieve the magic.

You need the right studio, the right people combination.

The right song, the right playing in the studio, the right mixes.

A lot of variables, and it's not always achievable, despite your best efforts.

CHAPTER 73

Since...

The Cruisers play shows.

They tinker with songs.

Donnie golfs.

Mark, twelve years younger than Donnie, still works. A lot.

2012. Mark survived a second divorce. In time, he shook it off and rebounded, healthy and happy.

But he was touch-and-go for a while there.

DONNIE: I think Mark can handle anything thrown at him, as far as his lawyer business is concerned. He's so smart, it's gonna wear on him, but he's gonna *do* it. But when it came to his second wife, I think that was the absolute toughest time of his life.

I don't think we did anything for a year. He would always just call me to go in the studio when he has an idea and he wants to get me started. And I didn't hear from him for a year or more.

The divorce scuttled any possibility of Donnie and Mark retiring together and recording an album every year, like Michael Stanley does.

It may lead to more producer work for Mark, though.

He has plans to record once again with Lipstick, the girl-powered rock band he helped break onto Cleveland's WMMS in 1986 — the group whose singer, Yvette "Jet" Williams, had a big crush on Mark, who was married.

YVETTE "JET" WILLIAMS: We invited him to our big show at the Hanna Theater to celebrate our hit — to celebrate not just our success, but his too.

But he did not come to the show, and we were really disappointed.

He now says he couldn't work with us more because of me.

MARK: I hadn't talked to her in 30 years. And after the divorce, I found her again through Facebook. We're a couple.

We've been together five years now, and that is a happy partnership.

Yvette, whom I love, whom I'm crazy about, she's my equal: She will challenge me. She's very creative. I say to her: I would never have accomplished what I did if I'd been with her my whole life. It's not a put-down.

After a spending his entire adult life as a suburban dad, Mark sold the house and moved to a big loft in a cool part of Cleveland. And in this House of Avsec, Mark's creative life is no longer relegated to the basement.

MARK: Where I live now, it's like an apartment, but it's a whole artist's loft. It's not a little thing. It's cool.

I love the area. It's my first time living in the city, other than when I was a kid, growing up. To be able to walk everywhere, it's cool. I don't have to worry about shoveling and all the snow. If we want to get something to eat, we can just hoof it.

Yvette and I talk music. She is very attuned to what gear is on stage when we go to concerts. She always wants to see bands. If we had the time and budget, she would want to go to the studio all the time. One day we may play together as we age — something interesting.

DONNIE: He and his girlfriend have something now: I think she understands him totally. She's a musician, so she understands where he's coming from.

FUTURE PROSPECTS

MARK: I have a long way to go in my law practice; I am not in a position to retire. I also would love to write more serious symphonic works, I go to see the Cleveland Orchestra a lot now since I live nearby. I went last night. I wonder if I could ever write a good novel. Musically, I still think the best album Donnie and I can partner on has not been written yet.

I thought about doing a covers album, but I don't want to do a bunch of covers. Unless you do something really different, you can't do a cover of a song that's better than the original.

If I'm not going in there because I'm inspired to make art, I'm an idiot. Right now, I don't have the confidence to go in there and write original songs, to make art. I could do an original thing that's a concept.

When I'm in the studio now, I don't know, frankly, how meaningful it is. For us to record a song, it's got to be fun and legitimate again.

These are all aspirational, and I don't know if I will ever have the time and intense focus to do any of this at the expense of relationships and just living life.

Because when I was in the middle of the Donnie stuff, I was focused on that, and that was it — I did not care about going to shows, going to movies, doing anything except being in that studio, and the writing was flowing. It was a great time for my life. But a life lived so intensely like that for an *entire* life… it misses a lot.

The secret of our success — in addition to the great musicianship from the band bandmates — is my drive and creativity and ideas, *with* Donnie's talent. And more than that: with his *personality*. Whereas I can get pensive and weird, Donnie is just good-natured, likable and gregarious. And friendly and warm. Put someone else out front of this band that has an opposite personality, and I tell you: This would have ended about 25 years ago.

Donnie has pretty much remained Donnie. But Donnie's image has become iconic – that's for sure. Lo and behold, what happened is Donnie truly became *Donnie Iris*, because he was himself: very gregarious, basic — in a good way. A man that every man related to.

I just read Springsteen's book, and it is good. He talks about being in a band as such a weird thing and it is true. You meet these people when you are barely adults, sometimes kids, and you go on with them for 40 or 50 years.

When does that happen? You are locked together forever. And that's the case in our band. And I have said it before, but we're all about love. We love each other and respect each other – and Donnie's warm personality sets the tone. And there is simply just love and respect.

It is the thing I am *most* proud of.

DONNIE: Our band, we've been like brothers over the years. And it's a great feeling to go in there, knowing you're with a bunch of guys who feel the same way you do. You understand what you're doing, and understand each other. You know each other's limits and what we're capable of and what we're not capable of, and you work within those boundaries. You want to go in there and do the best you can.

CHAPTER 74

The Cruisers III: Pittsburgh Made

2014.

2015.

2016.

2017.

Still.

The music continues.

In 2015, Donnie enters the Pittsburgh rock hall of fame, in the second year of the Rock 'N Roll Legends Awards, with Skyliners/Del-Vikings singer Lou Christie, and DJ Porky Chedwick. And he hasn't retired.[74.1]

The Cruisers record a new tune now and then. They drop a song here and there, like 2014's digital warbly digital single "Sing the Songs Of Summer (All Night Long)."

Mark still talks about recording another ambitious album, but he's a busy guy. They're all busy guys. When they cut a track they're happy with, they let it out into the wild, for free, as a stream and a free download.

In 2016, the Cruisers release a song Donnie and Mark had been tinkering with for years. Mark wrote the Steel City anthem with a big chorus based on things Donnie had described over the years: "Grew up here with Iron City Beer / Steelers, Buccos, music on the radio..."

"PITTSBURGH MADE"

DONNIE: I like it. I think it's perfect for Pittsburgh. Mark brought the lyric. He wrote it all.

MARK: "Pittsburgh Made," I'll be thrilled if the audience eventually learns it. And maybe by the time this book comes out, it'll be a highlight of the show. It'll be a fun tune to do live. But Donnie and I spent a lot of time in the track, and I spent more work than Donnie. We took it to 'DVE, and they're not interested in it. So it takes a while to collect yourself and go, "Oh, well…"

We do it just for the sake of doing it. For a businessman, it's easy to say, "Well, if five people like it, it's worth doing." But for me, who has a very busy life, there's an opportunity cost. Maybe it's not worth it anymore.

We're not relying at all on recorded music. It's almost like how the music industry doesn't rely on recorded music now. Our fans aren't worried about new music. They love the band. They want to see us. They want to see Donnie, as he has aged. He went through that middle-aged period at the beginning of Cruisers II.

And now the Cruisers III, fully, is just a live band. We put more energy into the live show. Now we're past the has-been period. Now we're in the legend period. Now it's fun.

DONNIE: I don't warm up before a show. I know Albritton used to. But that was him. B.E. Taylor used to do that all the time, too. I just never did. I guess you should. The show — the songs are set up so the first couple songs are a warmup.

KEVIN: He sings great. I was thinking about this the other day: I heard someone singing, and they were slightly out of tune with a live performance. And I thought, "You know what? I can't think of one single time where I heard Donnie sing out of key." It's weird. I heard Robert Plant sing out of tune, as great as he is. But I never heard Donnie do it.

PAUL: My favorite Mark: He is a master on the B-3. Very creative.

"Sweet Merilee" is my favorite Kevin song live. No other drummer that has played with this band can play that groove the way Kevin does.

I love it when Marty stretches out on solos at shows, like "Ridin' Thunder" and "Love Is Like a Rock." And when he used to do "Minnie the Moocher" with the talk box, "the bag."

KEVIN: We have a very high, good, collaborative culture in our band. A lot of talent there. At this point, everybody knows each other's talents and respects them.

MARK: The band continued to get good. And we're all comfortable. And we know we're good.

We all found other careers. Donnie's happy. Now he's a real elder statesman. Now I really enjoy playing in the band. Kevin has a lot to do with that. He's a challenge in respect to new ideas, but that's because he cares. That's good.

Mark lists the songs for each set. *Most* of the songs.

KEVIN: The hammer hit me on the head one day. I did like to have things down with the set and play the same set, so you can hone it and really deliver.

Then we were playing a show, and it's outdoors, at the Chevrolet Amphitheater in Pittsburgh. People are out there in the rain. I realize these people stood there an hour and a half in the rain, freezing cold, to see us. And after that, I got pissed off at myself and us. I thought, "We can't continue to deliver the same thing."

And since we have so much distance between our gigs, I'd like to have more difference in our sets. And then I started to take on things, because I really want to give people more. But it's difficult to do. I had that conversation, and we continue to have that conversation. We shake things up, maybe not as much as I'd like, but that's the reason why.

MARK: Paul has been the greatest bass player we could have chosen to replace Albritton. Now everybody's involved.

Kevin is a huge part of the live show. Kevin cares about the live show more than anybody. He has ideas to improve it, to do new songs. He makes the films to play before.

Right now, Marty contributes mostly onstage. He's probably the most dynamic musician on the stage, in terms of what people love to hear.

MARTY: I thank the fans. It's the fans that make this all possible.

Marty isn't the only one who collapsed on stage. Not for nothing does Donnie take the stage in a game jersey from time to time. July 1, 2017, the Cruisers play a private show in Pennsylvania. The band take the stage on a hot, muggy evening, expecting Donnie to give his all. He does, literally until he drops.

Luckily, a nurse is in the audience.

MARK: He had heat stroke, just gave everyone a scare.

The rattled band call their manager for some advice.

Belkin later recalls the conversation for Ultimate Classic Rock:

"Mark said, 'He wants to go back on for the second half!' I said, 'Let me talk to Donnie.'

"So Donnie gets on the phone. 'How are you feeling?'"

"'I feel great. I'm driving home.'"

"I said, 'Donnie, look — here's what's going to happen. If you stay there and don't drive home, I'm going to make a phone call now to a hooker and have her come down to where you're at." He started laughing and ultimately, he drove home.'"[74.2]

MARK: We got him some air. He drank some water. And we finished the show. He was fine.

And then Donnie is Donnie. He might say, "That's not cool," or "I don't want to do this." But it's a true band.

Donnie is the frontman. And he is everyman. And he represents what the band is.

The band is gonna end one of these days. But we'll be friends the rest of our lives. We'll miss the music, but the friendship and laughs will always be there.

But it would not surprise me if Donnie will be on the stage in 10 years, as an octogenarian.

YOU HAVE ENTERED DONNIE IRIS TERRITORY

A lifetime later, you can find Donnie Iris and the Cruisers at the same places: venues around Pittsburgh. And Cleveland. And 102.5 FM, DVE.

South of Cleveland, not far from Blossom, the Cruisers' new home away from home is the Northfield Park Hard Rock Rocksino. The Cruisers still open for Michael Stanley two or three times a year. And the upscale casino sells out, reliably and quickly.

JIM MARKOVICH, LIVE SOUND: Donnie Iris and Michael Stanley together, it's a great pairing. Some people like 'em both. Some like Donnie. Some like Michael. But what I always say is: We get the crowd roarin' and ready to go. The crowd is the same, but different. We're a little more upbeat, a little more drive to it. He can fill up some places. We can fill up some places.

Donnie's like Norm from *Cheers*: He knows everybody. Or they say they know him. He'll do signings at the end of the show, take pictures with people for an hour. They love him. People love him.

In 2014, the Cruisers played their first live show at Jergel's, outside Pittsburgh. With a capacity over 600, it has a full concert schedule filled with groups like Dokken, the Reverend Horton Heat, David Allan Coe, and George Clinton & P-Funk. By 2015, they were regulars at the club. By 2016, Donnie was practically part of the furniture. Every show, the tickets move a little faster. Witness the set list from Jergel's, May 2017:

"Agnes"	"Pittsburgh Made"
"Do You Compute?"	"Sweet Merilee"
"I Can't Hear You"	"This Time It Must Be Love"
"That's the Way Love Oughta Be"	"Love Is Like a Rock"
Drum Solo	"Ah! Leah!" (with slow intro)
"You're Only Dreaming"	"The Rapper"

MARK: We had a great show. It was roaring. Jimmy Krenn introduced us.

DONNIE: Jergel's is my favorite. I've made many friends there, and it's always sold out.

KEVIN: Oh my God. It was great. It was sold out. It was so. Frickin'. Loud. There. It was a great show. We played "Pittsburgh Made" for the first time, and it went over really well. I really love where the band is at right now. I see good things ahead as we move into our senior years.

MARK: Living in Cleveland, sometimes I forget what big deal Donnie is in Pittsburgh. What throws me and puts a smile on my face — all our faces — at the end of "That's the Way" and "Leah"… We're gonna go down in volume, and Donnie's gonna do his scream thing. The crowd knows what's gonna happen. To look out in the crowd and see a sea of smiling faces and, literally, love for the performer — Donnie is *beloved*.

JARROD WEEKS, A.K.A. "LORD GRUNGE," GRAND BUFFET: As a son of the 'Burgh — technically an adopted son but a son nonetheless — and somebody who has spent a substantial amount of time in the trenches of the music business, I can say without hesitation that I have always taken a reserved but fervent pride in knowing that my town was, and is, home to Donnie Iris. It's the same subtle-but-potent *amour-propre* I feel knowing that Fred Rogers and Andy Warhol are from Pittsburgh.

Pittsburgh has balls, and it has teeth. I view these as fundamentally good things, but they can create some inclement weather for the artist, both socially and metaphysically. The city's children tend to be a little rougher on their homegrown artists than a lot of other towns. The fact that Donnie made not only a major impact here but a serious dent on a national level and remains extant to this day and still revered by locals is testament to the fact that his is the stuff of legends. I've witnessed firsthand the manner in which Pittsburghers respond to his presence, and it's no joke, and it's something deeper and more purposeful than just spotting a local celebrity and reacting accordingly. It's an earnest showing of respect, and an ounce of respect in Pittsburgh is tantamount to a truckload of it in a lesser town.

MICHELE MICHAELS, WDVE'S *ELECTRIC LUNCH*: I probably get a *Lunch* request for Donnie just about every day. It's mostly transplanted Pittsburghers who either call from all over the country — or world, if they are from the military — and need a little Donnie fix. Or they are coming back to see family and are getting into listening range and want that taste of Pittsburgh they crave. Or leaving the Burgh after seeing family, and haven't had their Donnie tune yet.

"Ah! Leah!" — sometimes the live version DVE has from the *Nick's Fat City* CD. "Agnes." "That's the Way Love Ought to Be" is a biggie as well. Sometimes "Do You Compute?" and "Love is Like a Rock." I'll get a request for "Little Black Dress" every now and then.

Local artists, the requests for the Cruisers are neck-and-neck with the Clarks.

Donnie and the Cruisers certainly hold their own with all the monster bands that listeners request on DVE: They may not be up there with "Stairway to Heaven" or "Simple Man" or "You Shook Me All Night Long" — but they're scratchin' at the door.

This town has its icons who make us proud, but also make us feel anchored, and that all is right with the world. Donnie and the Cruisers are precious to us in that way.

CHAPTER 75

Donnie Iris: The Exit Interview

Donnie doesn't talk about himself much.

This might be the most he has ever spoken about his family, his life, and his career. And what it all means to him.

What was your mom like?

She's religious. She was very pretty in her day. A little thing, probably not even five foot tall. She's still alive. She was a musician, played piano. She was Catholic, but she left.

When the Jaggerz were together, she used to make dinner for the whole band. The group was always at our house.

She could set you straight. If I got out of the hand at the dinner table, my mom, you could get a backhand. But my dad, he would call me if I was out a little too late. I'd hear him, and I knew I'd better get my ass home. He wouldn't beat me, but the *threat*…

What was the first instrument you owned?

My dad bought me a Harmony guitar, acoustic. It might have been made by Sears.

What's the best instrument you ever owned?

I've got three favorite guitars. They're all basically the same. Stratocasters, 1956, 1959 and 1963. They're ones I've had over the years, never let go of them.

If you could own any instrument, what would you take?

I wouldn't mind having an old Les Paul, even though I'm not an old Les Paul player.

When you became a musician, who did you want to be?

(Without hesitation, smiling wide) Lennon.

Who was the coolest guy ever?

Steve McQueen. Coolest musician, Marvin Gaye.

What was the best concert you ever saw?

I really haven't seen a whole lot of concerts. Early on, the late '60s, I saw James Taylor open for Chicago. He kicked me in the *ass*. He was *awesome*. It was before he became famous. He was on his way up. He *killed* me. He was by himself, had his guitar and a mic in his face.

Did you like punk at all?

I really wasn't listening to those bands that much.

Did you ever like metal?

In a way I did. When I started really getting into Zeppelin, I thought, "Geez, these guys are freakin' *good*, man!" The '80s groups, not so much. I didn't have anything against them. But during the '80s, we were doing our own thing.

When did you get into the Spanish thing?

After being down there and hanging out in Miami. I ain't gonna do a tango, but I like the music.

You never take all the credit for anything, even writing the Jaggerz' biggest song. You never say, "Well, _I'm_ the one who made the Jaggerz _really_ big."

No. It didn't happen that way.

Where does that come from? How you were raised?

Yeah. My mother, she was the type of person who would want you to be a nice person. My mother had me doing entertainment things my whole life.

She took me to these dance studios when I was a little kid. My dad didn't like it at first. He thought that she's make a sissy out of me. But I did, and I guess I enjoyed it. And it worked out, because in the end, I did pursue music.

When you look back at that little boy in a tux singing "Deed I Do" — who was that kid? Do you feel like the same guy?

Man, I was just a regular kid. My mother was focusing me into music. I was like everybody else: I wanted to play outside, play baseball and football and basketball with all the kids. But she continually coaxed me to sing. And I'm glad she did, or who knows what could have happened? She's the one who made it happen.

Was there a time when you had to rededicate to music, decide this is what you wanted to do, whatever it took?

Right after college. I did a couple years at Slippery Rock. And I knew, two and a half years into it, I didn't want to do that. I wanted to do music. And I wasn't having a good time. I didn't like college at all.

So what did you want? Did you want to be the Beatles, or a working musician in a band, or...?

From when I was a kid, I knew I had some talent. I thought, "I just want to go for it and see what happens."

Why not be a plain civilian?

I guess I didn't want to be. I didn't want to be a teacher.

What did you learn from your time in the Jaggerz?

My time in the Jaggerz was my time to build calluses on your fingertips, playing guitar every night. My fingers had this bulge on them from playing. In fact, lately, I've been playing more guitar, trying to build them up again, because I can't play guitar for a very long time. Back then, I could play all night long. I guess I learned some chops. And the fact that this is what I want to do.

The Jaggerz were a cover band for years. Then we decided to write original songs. I learned a lot about playing guitar, singing, being able to sing night after night.

At the time, were they satisfying creative partners? Did you think there was more out there for you? Were you hoping for someone like Mark?

No. I had no ambitions of being a solo artist or anything like that.

Then, 11 years later, when you were back on the charts with "Ah! Leah!," how did that feel?

That was amazing. I never really thought about it.

When you were playing Morry's and doing shows with B.E. Taylor, what was your idea of success? Did you think you'd be back in arenas?

Once I was in the studio, and Mark was in there with Wild Cherry, and then I was in the band, and Mark wanted to do something together... I thought he was real talented. He had a lot of ambition.

When he said he wanted to do something together, did you think he just another guy who was all talk, saying, "Hey, man, we should do something — something big!"

No, not at all. That's what I liked about him. He was straight ahead, definitely an exception. Not a rah-rah kind of guy.

It seems that when the band is at the best, it's impossible to tell where you end and Mark begins.

I was like a vehicle for those songs for him. Together, we just… Whether he was writing a song on his own, or if I was helping him write it, it's just what we did, whether it was him pouring out what he was going through at the time. Or with *Ellwood City*, it was him writing songs about what he thinks I was like in Ellwood City. It worked. The two of us gelled together. And we still do. We're going in the studio Saturday to work on something.

Do you think Mark is jaded, maybe more critical of the catalog than he needs to be?

He is. A lot of the songs aren't *that* bad.

What are your songs *about*?

I just think of us as being two guys who wanted to write music, do our own music, and put it out there. Mark was probably thinking a little more about the songs and what they meant. I just wanted to get in there and sing them the best I could to make it more of a performance.

During the "Leah" lawsuit, did you ever feel like you were being tested?

I think both of us really felt like, "What the hell happened?! It was going so well, and now nothing was going right." I probably would have gone along with whatever happened. If Mark would have stopped and just become an attorney, I would have finished up my life doing whatever I was doing. But he would not give up, man.

Did you even think, "I want to quit"?

No. No. No. As long as Mark wanted to do something, I was always into it. Maybe not as much as he was.

Did you see the "Leah" lawsuit as a pain, or as the cost of doing business?

It was a bullshit lawsuit. That's all it was. And it drove us both crazy for awhile.

Most artists would be pretty happy with your career, even the people who put out a couple major-label albums, and definitely the people line up to talk to you and give you their CD. Jay Mohr — he's an actor, comedian, and radio host; he played Bob Sugar in *Jerry Maguire* — he quotes Martin Short and he describes his career in "the show business middle class": He lives well, but he still has to hustle and find work.

That's well-put. "Middle class show business." It fits us to a T.

Was there ever a downside to being Donnie Iris?

I really don't see a downside. There wasn't a bad time. I don't remember really being depressed. I had a family. I had kids. It was cool. We weren't ever on the road that much, and I didn't miss much of the kids' growing up.

Is there anything you would have done different?

I really don't think so. What I've done, the people I've met, who I've played with — I don't see me changing anything. I really don't.

If you never met Mark, what do you think you would have done?

I don't know what I've have done. I have no idea where I would have gone without that guy. I don't know if I'd be in music any more. I might have ended up going back and getting back together with the Jaggerz.

Out of all the people he's ever met, I'm probably the one that gets him the most. I understand where he's coming from: He's so creative, and he wants somebody to help him show it, to express it, to have it sound and feel the way he would want it to feel. But he needs help. That's where I come it. That's exactly what I needed, for sure.

If you'd met Mark when you were 25, do you think you would have handled the ride as well?

Who knows?

You were never out of control with the Jaggerz, but did that time in the wilderness between the Jaggerz and the Cruisers humble you? Did it make you appreciate the Cruisers when it happened?

Yeah. It made me realize you could be on top with a hit like "The Rapper," and nothing could happen for ten freakin' years. It did make me appreciate it more.

I think it did. When I did go into the studio, it sounded good. The songs sounded like contenders, serious music. Great musicians, with a lot of vision for what our music was going to sound like.

What did you think at that point? Did you think, "We're on the way. We're going to be back and opening for Nugent!"?

We were just making music and seeing what happened. I did think we had a real good chance something was gonna happen. I don't know if I had that feeling with the Jaggerz at the end.

In your travels, were you ever star struck? Who were you the most excited to meet?

It was a pleasure meeting some of the Steelers. I never ran into anybody like Marvin Gaye or James Brown. If I'da run into one of them, I probably would be star struck. I have a picture of me and my kids and Eddie Van Halen. That was at the Granatis' house. They were real tight with those guys. He was at their house, and he called me and said to come up. So I brought the kids up and took pictures. In front of my kids, that was cool as hell.

Is there anybody you still want to meet?

I want to meet Paul McCartney. He seems like a genuinely nice guy. You could sit down and talk to him.

If you could meet anybody ever?

I think I'd be intimidated by Lennon. I'd love to have met Marvin Gaye.

In the mid '80s, was there a single moment when you decided to drop the suits and the glasses and the show and just be you?

I thought, "This is what it is. This is who I am." All those shows, I was happy to go to the small clubs. We'd still be going crazy and all into it. I don't know if I felt exactly like getting rid of all that, but there were times when I thought, "Let's just do this gig." As long as people were watching us, I was into it.

Did you feel like you stopped playing a character onstage and just started being you?

I think it was more of a gradual thing, going from being the Buddy Holly bowtie-wearing punk to this regular guy that's going to get there and sing some songs.

What is the value of being the first priority on a smaller team with Belkin, versus being with a giant of the industry like Jerry Weintraub — but being the last guy on the roster? When the albums stopped selling and the hits stopped, you didn't try to ditch Mike Belkin or tell Mark, "Sorry, I have to find someone who can write me some hits."

No. I don't have that kind of confidence, thinking I could go out and get anybody and start over. But I liked Mike. He's valuable to me as a person, not just a manager — understanding how I feel about the business and life in general. Same as Mark. I had a chance to meet other producers, but I wasn't the kind of guy who wanted to break away from something I thought was comfortable. Without Mark, I don't trust my own abilities.

Was that an Ierace family value? Did your parents use the word "loyalty" a lot? Was it a lesson from all those years in the music business?

To a certain extent, you learn to recognize the promises from other people, and I didn't want that. It was the comfort level and how I was brought up. But how I felt about Mark and Mike, that was the entire thing. I knew how they felt about me. We were on the down side, but what the hell — we'll try it again.

What was the biggest blowup, argument, disagreement or fight the band ever had?

I don't know that there ever was one. I don't ever remember a situation where things got *tense* about something. There was none of that stuff. Maybe there were times when Albritton had a couple too many drinks, or Kevin and Marty got a little out of hand in the hotel room. But never a fight between any of us.

What's the best thing you *didn't* do in your career?

The best I didn't do was leaving Mark when MCA was trying to get me to go to someone else for production.

What is your best performance?

Of all our recordings, I think probably "Leah."

Was the Cruisers what you wanted, if you could have written the story? The long-term career, together forever?

Yeah. If I could have thought of wanted I wanted after the Jaggerz broke up, the Cruisers were perfect. And Mark just enhanced me and *made* things out of what I can do. He just kept going and going. It was the exact road I wanted to take.

What's your drink of choice?

When we're doing a gig, I'll do a shot before the show, maybe two. Either Crown or Jack.

Favorite beer?

I like the way Corona tastes, but I usually drink Heineken. They say it's a *clean* beer — it doesn't have any additives preservatives.

What's the best cigar?

There's a lot of great cigars. I can think of ten.

What do you smoke the most often?

This contradicts what I have on our contract riders: The Padron Natural, I forget the size.

What would you smoke if someone offered to buy you one, anything from anywhere?

The Exclusivo Maduro, instead of the Natural wrapper, I've learned to love the Maduro wrapper better.

Can you talk about cigars like people talk about wine, wax poetic about the "nice, oily Cameroon wrapper"?

No, no. I just know what I like.

What's the best car you ever owned?

I've had some pretty good cars. A '64 Pontiac Grand Prix comes to mind.

If you could have any car, what would you pick?

I'd probably take a '57 Chevy Bel Air convertible. I never drove a '57 Chevy. I had a '59. It was wonderful.

Do you have a favorite book?

I don't. I'm not much of a reader?

Where were you for the 1960 World Series?

I was in 11ᵗʰ grade. I remember listening in the band room.

'71 Series?

I don't remember that.

'74, the Steelers' Super Bowl?

All those '70s Steelers games: me and B.E. at a friend's house in Beaver Falls or a bar.

The '79 Pirates?

I was there when they won it at home. I was at Three Rivers [Stadium]. Decent seats. Omar Marino, I think he's the center fielder, he caught the fly ball for the last out. I don't remember what we did after.

'79, Super Bowl?

Same thing. Me, B.E., and friends watching it here.

The '91 Stanley Cup?

I was never a big hockey fan, because I never played it as a kid. Hockey was unknown to the whole city.

2005 Super Bowl?

We watched those games at local bars, for the most part. Kelly's Riverside Saloon. We watched a lot of Steeler games in that place.

2008 Super Bowl?

Same place, probably.

How would you describe your relationship with Mark?

It's hard to put a label on. Like an older brother to him — totally respectful of what he can do. Like he's younger brother, not a *kid* brother. More a friend than anything else, all the stuff we've run into. He's family to me, probably more than anybody else in my entire life.

What's the best you can describe him in the fewest words?

Sometimes introverted, sometimes outgoing.

Do you have a favorite part of being in a band?

It's just great making music with other musicians, whether it's the Cruisers or the Jaggerz. Some people don't help you to do that. But that's what we do.

When people meet you, what do they ask you about the most?

"This show, we were down in front, in 1986, don't you remember that?!" I hear that a lot. And people that are into music, they ask for advice, and I encourage them.

What do you tell them?

Things are different nowadays, but basically it's the same thing: Keep doing it. And if you end up not liking it, and you don't want to do it, stop. But if you're into it and you want to do with it, then keep doing it. And go for whatever you can go for.

You're retired. What do you do, day to day?

In the summertime, I play a lot of golf. Besides the shows we do as a group, every once in a while, I get a call to do something like the Pittsburgh All-Stars, with Joe Grushecky. Or with Rick Witkowski. We do three or four of those every year, benefit things. Summer time, I golf. Winter time, I'm not doing a whole lot of anything.

What is your happy place?

I gotta tell ya: I love being with my kids. I love being with my family. But when I'm outside on my porch, smoking a cigar. Maybe either reading the paper or having a cup of coffee, or playing golf with my buddies. But that alone time is what I truly enjoy. I just sit there and enjoy that cigar.

Is this the life you wanted?

This worked out a lot better than I thought it might. After we started going down after the first couple albums, who knew what was gonna happen? But we keep going to these clubs, we still pack 'em in. They're older like we are, but there are some younger people, too. It's great, even now. We only do a half-dozen or a dozen shows a year, but they're all really cool shows. I'm pretty satisfied where I am.

Author Interviews

ORIGINAL INTERVIEWS CONDUCTED BETWEEN SEPTEMBER 2015 AND OCTOBER 2017:

Mark Avsec. Mike Belkin. Scott Blasey. Kim Dempster. Eugene Faiella. Jimmy Fox. Rick Frio. Erin Fusetti. Ron Gerber. Paul Goll. John Gorman. Bill Korecky. Jim Krenn. Chris Maduri. Jim Markovich. Gary Medved. Addy Molony. Albritton McClain. Michele Michaels. Mike Olszewski. Steve Nervo. Mike Palone. Jason Pettigrew. Glenn Ratner. Tommy Rich. Jimmy Roach. Jimmie Ross. Sean Ross. Chuck Statler. Kevin Valentine. Yvette "Jet" Williams. Rick Witkowski.

Endnotes

All *Billboard* chart positions cited are from Billboard charts, their week cited, either online or archival issues. All websites accessed 2015-2017 and verified October 2017, unless otherwise noted.

EPIGRAPHS

Giffels quote from Ferris, D.X. "The Difficult." Cleveland *Scene*. November 16, 2005. Online: CleveScene.com.

I.   FOREWORD. BY JIM KRENN OF THE CLASSIC *DVE MORNING SHOW*.

II.   WHAT THIS BOOK IS, HOW IT WORKS, AND HOW TO USE IT

II.1: Blush, Steven. *American Hardcore*. First edition: 2001 p. 303. Los Angeles.

III.   PROLOGUE FROM THE BAND. BY MARK AVSEC.

1.   DONNIE IRIS AND THE CRUISERS, LONG STORY SHORT

1.1:   Adams, Bret. "Donnie Iris: *Fortune 410*." *All Music Guide to Rock*, Third Edition, 2002, Backstreet Books. Page 562.

1.2:   "Playboy's DJ Poll." *Playboy*. April 1982. Page 163. Poll of 22 DJs: Howard Hessman (actor, "DJ Johnny Fever" of sitcom *WKRP in Cincinnati*. Tommy Edward and Larry Lujack, WLS-AM Chicago. Steve Dahl and Garry Meier, WLF-FM Chicago. Sky Daniels, WLUP Chicago. John Fisher, WMET Chicago. Kid Leo, WMMS Cleveland. B. Mitchel Reed, KLOS Los Angeles. Jeff Gonzer, Jack Snyder and Mary Turner, KMET Los Angeles. Dan Ingram, WABC New York. Dave Herman and Richard Neer, WNEW New York. Pat St. John, WPLJ New York. Frankie Crocker, WBLS New York. Joe Bonadonna and Lisa Richards, WMMR Philadelphia. Picozzi, WYSP Philadelphia. Jimmy Roach, WDVE Pittsburgh. Temple Lindsey, KISS San Antonio.

1.3:   Whitburn, Joel. *Top Pop Singles, 1955-1996*. 1997. Wisconsin: Record Research Inc. 892 pages, compiles *Billboard* chart information. Count of bands' singles that reached peak positions from the years 1980-1985. As of this writing, *Billboard*'s online database sucks.

2.   MEET DONNIE IRIS

2.1:   Cresp, Charley. *Hit Parader*. "Roots: Donnie Iris." 1982, month unknown. Page 30.

3.   CONTEXT: THE PITTSBURGH-CLEVELAND RIVALRY

4.   MEET MARK AVSEC, CRUISERS SONGWRITER-PRODUCER-

5.   MEET MARTY LEE HOENES, CRUISERS GUITARIST

6.   MEET ALBRITTON MCCLAIN, ORIGINAL CRUISERS BASSIST

7.   MEET KEVIN VALENTINE, CRUISERS DRUMMER

7.1:   Ali, Lorraine. "Kiss: Psycho Circus." November 12, 1998. At RollingStone.com.

8.   MEET MIKE BELKIN, CRUISERS MANAGER

8.1:   Belkin, Michael and Wolff, Carlo. *Socks, Sports, Rock and Art*. Page 156. 2017: Act 3 Creative. 221 pages.

8.2:   Beaudoin, Jennifer. "The 14 Most Deadliest Concerts Ever." February 16, 2011. Q103Albany.com.

8.3:   Bishop, Lauren. "The Who Tragedy: 30 years Later." The Cincinnati *Enquirer*. December 3, 2009. Page A1.

9: PAUL GOLL, CURRENT CRUISERS BASSIST

10: THE JAGGERZ, PITTSBURGH'S #1 BAND FOR 10 YEARS

10.1: "Hoodlums Riot at Resorts; Damage Heavy; 600 Arrested." Tribune Wire Services. Chicago *Tribune*. Monday, July 5, 1965. Section 1, p. 2.

10.2: "Sunken Bar (Delfrate's Nite Club." SummerFunHeritageTrail.com.

10.3: Hamilton, Andrew: "The Jaggerz: Introducing the Jaggerz." AllMusic.com

10.4: Webster Hall ad. *Pittsburgh Press*. December 22, 1968. Section 4, p. 14.

10.5: Fountain Supper Club ad. *Pittsburgh Press*. January 23, 1969, p. 29

10.6: Rudman, Kal. "Money Music." *Record World*. May 10, 1960. Page 14.

10.7: Nelson Jones, Diana. "Sometimes You Can't Rush Love — or Love Songs." Pittsburgh *Post-Gazette*. February 14, 2004. At Old.Post-Gazette.com.

10.8: Kaufmann's ad. *Pittsburgh Press*. April 1, 1969. p 45.

10.9: Ochs, Ed. "Soul Sauce." *Billboard*. April 12, 1969. Page 36.

10.10: Lawson, Kyle. "Monroeville's Holiday House Offered Memories of Different Time." Pittsburgh *Tribune-Review*. Aug. 14, 2013. At TribLive.com

10.11: Togyer, Jason. "The Night Monroeville Almost Killed Liberace." Tube City Online. June 04, 2013. At TubeCityOnline.com.

10.12: Hyde, Bob. "Good Time Music: The Early Days of Kama Sutra." Both Sides Now Publications. 1993, updated April 11, 2000. At BSNpubs.com.

10.13: Cohen, Harold V. "At Random." Pittsburgh *Post-Gazette*. October 10, 1969. Page 10.

10.14: Jaggerz v. Gamble Records overview at Pacer. Plaintiffs Aiella [sic], Eugene B; Davies, Thomas E; Ierace, Dominic; Maybray, William R; Pugliano, James F; Rock, Joseph V; Ross, James. Defendant: Gamble Records, Inc. Filed November 6, 1969. Pennsylvania Western U.S. District Court: Pittsburgh Office. 2:69-cv-01274. Viewed 17 November 2016, via PACER.

10.15: Shower of Stars Ad. *Pittsburgh Press*. Nov 16, 1969. Section 8, page 3.

10.16: "San Bernardino's Top 20." San Bernardino County *Sun*. January 27, 1970. Page B-6.

10.17: The national organization published a 79-page booklet, "Wise Up, Why Dope?: A Programming Manual of the United States Jaycees for Community Action to Curb the Excessive Use and Misuse of Drugs. " Contributor: Smith, Kline & French Laboratories United States. Jaycees, 1973.

10.18: Ross, Jimmie. The Jaggerz Facebook page. March 19, 2014.

10.19: *Record World*. "Pull-Out Guide: 100 Top Pops." Week of March 21, 1970.

10.20: Via RIAA requirements, gold status granted to represent 500,000 copies moved — specifically, shipped, downloaded as part of a transaction, and/or, essentially, being requested politely. "RIAA And Gr&F Certification Audit Requirements. RIAA Digital Single Award. RIAA.com

10.21: "Congratulating WAYS'...." *Billboard*, July 4, 1970. Page 47.

10.22: "Bits and Pieces," *Sheboygan Press*. June 11, 1970. p34.

10.23: Radcliffe, Joe. "Jaggerz: Ungano's, New York." *Billboard*, 8 August 1970. Page 22.

10.24: *Billboard*, "Top 60 Pop Spotlight." July 18, 1970. Page 72.

10.25: Rutkoski, Rex. "'Rapper' Still Draws Applause, But Jaggerz Perform R&B." February 14, 2002. Pittsburgh *Tribune-Review*. At TribLive.com.

10.26: "*Cash Box* 1970 Disc Jockey Poll: Most Promising Vocal Groups." *Cash Box*. July 4, 1970. Page 20.

10.27: "Vibrations: Gold Record Hurt Jaggerz." *North Hills Record*. October 25, 1977. At Parallel-Time.com.

10.28: Christgau, Robert. *Consumer Guide* [database edition]. "The Jaggerz." RobertChristgau.com.

11.   THE JAGGERZ: ENCORE

11.1: Levans, Michael. "The Jaggerz Playing a Comeback Tune for 'Rapper' Reunion." *Pittsburgh Press*. June 22, 1989: p. B3.

11.2: Maybray, William Jr. "The Jaggerz — The Rapper." YouTube video compilation. March 8, 2009.

11.3: "From the Music Capitals of the World." *Billboard*, December 16, 1972. Page 13.

11.4: Hearn, Marcus. *The Cinema of George Lucas*. Pages 67-69. NYC: ABRAMS Books. 2005.

11.5: "RCA Puts Campaign on 'Summer Power.'" *Billboard*. June 16, 1973. Page 6.

11.6: Ad: "New LP/Tape Releases." *Billboard*. August 18, 1973. Page 50.

11.7: *His Way*. 2011. Director: Douglas McGrath. HBO Documentary Films, Polsky Films, Consolidated Documentaries.

11.8: Sachs, Lloyd. "Donnie Iris: the Rapper's Back." *Rolling Stone*. May 14, 1981. At Parallel Time.

11.9: Kalina, Mike. "Music Makers." Pittsburgh *Post-Gazette*. August 27, 1975. Page 22.

11.10: Hazlett, Terry. ""After 12 years, I started asking myself ..." At Parallel Time.

11.11: Sachs, Lloyd. "Donnie Iris: the Rapper's Back." *Rolling Stone*. May 14, 1981. At Parallel Time.

11.12: Staircase ad. *Pittsburgh Press*. Jan 17, 1976. Page 8.

11.13: Kalina, Mike. "Music Makers." Pittsburgh *Post-Gazette*. January 21, 1976. Page 9.

11.14: Best Jazz Vocal Album, 2004: Nancy Wilson's *R.S.V.P. Rare Songs, Very Personal*. And Best Jazz Vocal Album, 2006: *Nancy Wilson's Turned To Blue*. Not Nancy from Heart.

12.   DONNIE: BETWEEN BANDS IN THE BEAVER VALLEY

12.1: "B.E. Taylor." Pittsburgh Music History. Online:

12.2: "History." JereeRecording.com. Accessed. October 2017.

12.3: Pittsburgh Music History. "Jeree Recording."

12.4: "About Us: People." JereeRecording.com.

12.5: "About Us: Milestones." JereeRecording.com.

13.   MARK IN THE MUSICAL MINOR LEAGUES

13.1: "The Hula Hoop Song." SecondHandSongs.com. Accessed October 2017.

13.2: Scott, Jane. "Squeezes in His Own Songs." Cleveland *Plain Dealer*. July 7, 1985. Page 11-P.

13.3: "Platinum Singles Top '76–'77 Years." *Billboard*. Vol. 90, no. 34. August 26, 1978. Page 114.

13.4: "Greatest Hot 100 Singles." *Billboard*. 2015. At Billboard.com.

13.5: Sippel, John. "Sweet City Label Hits in 1 Year." *Billboard*. May 21 1977. Pages 11, 78.

13.6: "Ibid, your honor."

13.7: "Melee Leads to Arrest." Associated Press. *The Daily Times* (Salisbury, Maryland). August 9, 1976. Page 8.

13.8: "Eight Arrested at Concert." Associated Press. *The Daily Mail* (Hagerstown, Maryland). August 9, 1976. Page 3.

13.9: "Lou Rawls & Wild Cherry Tie For Favorite Soul Single - AMA 1977." Video. YouTube.com. Posted by AwardsShowNetwork Mar 12, 2012.

14. WILD CHERRY: WHEN DONNIE MET MARK

14.1: Article describes the gunpoint scene, but lists 1978 as the date, apparently citing Iris; Donnie wasn't touring with the band in 1978, but was in 1979. *Pittsburgh Metro Guide*. 2004. Page 75. Article fragment archived at Parallel Time.

14.2: Hailey, Gary. "Roget Pontbriand." At Songfacts.com.

15. MARK GOES DISCO: LAFLAVOUR, "MANDOLAY"

15.1: Fishwich, Samuel. "You're Born Naked and the Rest Is Drag." Evening *Standard*. June 29, 2015. At Standard.Co.UK.

15.2: *Billboard* re-ranked and renamed its *Top 100 Dance Songs of All-Time*. "Mandolay" still rated close to the top, at #11, between James Brown's no. 10 "Get Up... I Feel Like Being A Sex Machine" and Donna Summer's no. 12 "I Feel Love." 15.2

15.3: "Number One Awards." *Billboard*. December 20, 1980. Page TIA-38.

15.4: "LaFlavour" at 45cat.com.

16. BREATHLESS: WHEN MARK MET KEVIN

16.1: Kranstuber, Scott. "Breathless to Breeze Ballroom Stage." *Daily Kent Stater*. November 30, 1979: Volume LIII, number 50. Page 7.

16.2: "Top Album Picks." *Billboard*. November 8, 1980. Page 60.

17. BRING ON THE EIGHTIES: DONNIE'S DEBUT

18. BACK ON THE STREETS: THE FIRST ALBUM, THE ONE WITH "AH! LEAH!"

18.1: Demalon, Tom. "Donnie Iris: Back on the Streets." *All Music Guide to Rock*, Third Edition, 2002, Backstreet Books. Page 562.

18.2: Holan, Mark. "Eye to Eye With Donnie Iris." Cleveland *Scene*. February 12, 1981. Archived at Parallel Time.

19. BACK ON THE STREETS: THE BAND ON THE SONGS

20. "AH! LEAH!"

20.1: "Playboy's DJ Poll." *Playboy*. April 1982. Page 163. (See 1.2 for full voter list.)

20.2: "Steve Perry." Fan Asylum. November 15, 2015. At FanAsylum.com. Song is incorrectly transcribed as "'Alea' by Donnie Iris."

20.3: Tady, Scott. "The Ah-ha! It's Leah!." Beaver County *Times*. June 19, 2008. At TimesOnline.com.

21. LOOKING FOR A DEAL, DEALING FOR A LOOK

22. ON THE AIRWAVES: DONNIE MEETS DVE

22.1: Dragonfly. "Music: Artist Spotlight: Donnie Iris." The AV Club After Dark. 2017. At Disqus.com.

22.2: "Jimmy Roach and Steve Hansen: Revived Comedy Radio and Promoted Pittsburgh Music." Pittsburgh Music History.

22.3: "Album Reviews." *Cash Box*. August 16, 1980. Page 13.

22.4: Cetner, Mark. "Points West." *Cash Box*. November 29, 1990. Page 14.

23. LEAH UNMASKED! THE BACK ON THE STREETS VIDEO(S)

23.1: Sekuler, Eliot. "Concept Video Catching On, Says VAMP'S Kim Dempster." Record World. June 20, 1981. Page 14.

23.2: McDonough, Jack. "Dempster off to Fast Video Start." Billboard. February 28, 1981. Page 42.

23.3: Actress B.J. McAllister identified as "McAllester" in this article. Her identity was later confirmed by Dempster and two other associates. Dempster, Kim. "Creative Visual-Music." *Recoring Enginer-Producer*. April 1981 Vol 12 #2. Pages 78-92.

23.4: "B.J. McAllister." IMDb.com.

23.5: McDonough, Jack. "Dempster off to Fast Video Start." *Billboard*. February 28, 1981. Page 42.

23.6: "Air Play." *Cash Box*. October 25, 1980. Page 23.

24. THE RECORD DEAL: CAROUSEL/MCA SELECTS THE CRUISERS

24.1: Donnelly, Bob. "What's The Deal With Production Deals?" Billboard. Jul 31, 1999. Page 4.

24.2: Correspondence between MCA Records Vice President, Administration Arnold Stone, Carousel Records, and Belkin-Maduri Organization/Midwest Records, Inc. April 23, 1981.

24.3: "The Inside Track." *Billboard*. Oct 27, 1979. Page 98.

24.4: "New on the Charts: Donnie Iris." *Billboard*. December 20, 1980. Page 44.

24.5: Correspondence from Belkin-Maduri Organization attorneys to Midwest Records Inc./Belkin Maduri Organization/Mike Belkin. November 17, 1983.

25. BACK ON THE STREETS: THE REVIEWS AND AIRPLAY.

25.1: "Singles." *Cash Box*. November 8, 1980. Page 15.

25.2: Scott, Jane. "Ex-Star in Step With Hit Parade." *Plain Dealer*. December 11, 1980, pages 1-F and 3-F.

25.3: Scott, Jane. "Ex-Star in Step With Hit Parade." *Plain Dealer*. December 11, 1980, pages 1-F.

25.4: "Top Album Picks." *Billboard*. November 8, 1980. Page 60.

25.5: "Donnie Iris." *The New Rolling Stone Record Guide*. Random House/Rolling Stone Press. Oct 12, 1983. Page 242. Editors: Dave Marsh, John Swenson

25.6: Fulton, Ken. "Records: Music From the Streets: *Back on the Streets*," *Boy's Life*. February 1981. Page 18.

25.7: Doyle, Tom. "Local Singer Donnie Iris Blooms on Solo Release." *Beaver County Times*. December 3, 1980. Page 24 of 62.

25.8: Bishop, Pete. "Diamond Shines On Disc." *Pittsburgh Press*. December 28, 1980. Page G-6.

25.9: Diana, Mike. "Hear Say." *Daily Press/Newport News*. February 27, 1981.

25.10: Daly, Mike. "New Notes: Clapton Delivers." *The Age*. April 16, 1981. Page 10.

25.11: "New Faces to Watch: Donnie Iris." *Cash Box*. September 12, 1981. Page NF-10.

25.12: Lefsetz, Bob. "Ah! Leah!" The Lefsetz Letter. July 18, 2005. At Lefsetz.com.

25.13: Midwest National Records. "Ah! Leah!" sales figures sheet. Dated 2-17-1981.

25.14: Midwest Records. *Back on the Streets* sales figures sheet. Dated 2-17-1981.

26. THE BACK ON THE STREETS TOUR

26.1: Yarborough, Chuck. "Roast, Toast and Concert Pay Homage to Agora Founder Hank LoConti Sr." Cleveland *Plain Dealer*/Cleveland.com. March 22, 2013. At Cleveland.com.

26.2: Scott, Jane. "The Happening." Cleveland *Plain Dealer*. April 10, 1981. Page 43.

26.3: Scott, Jane. "Iris Proves He's No Wallflower." *Plain Dealer*. February 18, 1981. Page 7-D.

26.4: Ibid.

26.5: Winkelstern, David. "Hall, Oates Returning." Lansing *State Journal*. February 20, 1982. Page 8S.

26.6: "Top Box Office." *Billboard*. March 14, 1981. Page 39.

26.7: Correspondence from MCA Vice President, Administration Arnold Stone to Carl Maduri/Belkin-Maduri Management. March 11, 1981.

26.8: Correspondence from MCA General Counsel William R. Straw to Rick Frio/Carousel Records. March 23, 1981.

26.9: "UFO: 13th March 1981." Comment posted March 3, 2009. Soundaboard. At SoundABoard.blogspot.com.

26.10: "UFO: 13th March 1981." Comment posted January 22, 2012. Soundaboard.

26.11: McGrath, Paul. "Donnie Iris Looks Set to Make It." Toronto *The Globe and Mail*. March 21, 1981. Online archive.

26.12: Bishop, Pete. Rock: "Beaver Falls Singer Plays His Own Turf." *Pittsburgh Press*. March 19, 1981. Page D-3.

26.13: Stieg, Bill. "Donnie Iris is Back on the Stage Before Hometown Crowd." Pittsburgh *Post-Gazette*. March 20, 1981. Page 24.

26.14: Sachs, Lloyd. "Donnie Iris: the Rapper's Back." *Rolling Stone*. May 14, 1981. At Parallel Time.

26.15: Doyle, Tom. "Donnie Iris Is Back on the Stage Before Homecoming Crowd." *The Beaver County Times*. March 25, 1981. Page D-2.

26.16: Hedgedus, Eric. "Ted Nugent Unleashes His Brand of Rock 'n' Roll at Stable." The Morning Call. March 31, 1981. Page D7.

26.17: Holden, Stephen. "Donnie Iris and Eve Moon." The New York Times. April 9, 1981 [Late City Final Edition]. Section C, page 22, Column 1.

26.18: Harrison, Ed. "Singer Reports Hits, Cutbacks Aid MCA Profits." Billboard. April 4, 1981. Page 9.

26.19: Correspondence from Rick Frio to MCA Vice President of Administration Arnold Stone and Mike Belkin. Dated April 23, 1981. While the band was still riding high, MCA formally requested a second album.

26.20: Nutile, Alaina. "15 Memories from the Highland Heights Front Row Theater." Cleveland *Scene*. Jan 28, 2014. At CleveScene.com.

27. KING COOL: MAKING THE ALBUM

27.1: Demalon, Tom. "Donnie Iris: *King Cool*." All Music Guide to Rock, Third Edition, 2002, Backstreet Books. Page 561.

27.2: "Dave Hill Interview." *Slade International Fan Club Newsletter*. April-May-June 1987. March 27, 1987. Page 14. Archived at SladeFanClub.com.

27.3: "You Boyz — Opinion Poll" Slade International Fan Club newsletter. July-August-September 1987. Page 8. Archived at SladeFanClub.com.

27.4: Renoff, Greg. *Van Halen Rising: How a Southern California Backyard Party Band Saved Heavy Meta*l. Page 281. 377 pages. 2015. Toronto: ECW Press.

27.5: DeYoung, Bill. *The Millennium Collecti*on: Best Of Donnie Iris liner notes. Geffen Records. September 18, 2001.

28. KING COOL: THE TOUR

28.1: Scott, Jane. "Blossom Attendance Sets Records." *Plain Dealer*. October 14, 1982. Page 99.

28.2: Scott, Jane. "Michael Stanley Band Proves Why It's a Sellout." August 25, 1981. Cleveland *Plain Dealer*. Page 6-B.

28.3: Scott, Jane. "Michael Stanley Band Proves Why It's a Sellout." August 25, 1981. Cleveland *Plain Dealer*. Page 6-B.

28.4: Pond, Steve. "King Cool." Los Angeles *Times*. December 20, 1981. Calendar: Page 106.

28.5: *The New Rolling Stone Record Guide*. Editors: Dave Marsh, John Swenson Random House/Rolling Stone Press. Oct 12, 1983. Page 242.

28.6: Scott, Jane. "Kinks, Iris, Generators Score Well." Cleveland *Plain Dealer*. September 4, 1981. Page 36.

28.7: "Reviews: Singles." December 5, 1981. *Cash Box*. Page 9.

28.8: "*Billboard*'s Top Albums." *Billboard*. September 21, 1981. Page 74.

28.9: *Billboard* cover (page 1). King Cool ad. August 22 1981.

28.10: Dannen, Fredric. *Hit Men: Power Brokers and Fast Money Inside the Music Business*. Page 14, 5. Vintage Books. 1991. 407 pages.

28.11: Ibid. Page 11.

28.12: 28.10: Ibid. Page 264. 407 pages.

28.13: "Cooling It on the Airwaves." *Cash Box*. November 7, 1981.

28.14: Adams, Bret. "Donnie Iris: *Fortune 410*." All Music Guide to Rock, Third Edition, 2002, Backstreet Books. p. 562.

28.15: Anderson, George. "Triangle Tattler." Pittsburgh *Post-Gazette*. December 22, 1981 Page 26.

28.16: Scott, Jane. "Closing the File on 1981." *Plain Dealer*. December 27, 1981. Page D-1.

28.17: "Pop Awards." *Cash Box*. December 26, 1981. P. 18.

28.18: "Pop Awards." *Cash Box*. December 26, 1981. P. 52.

28.19: Bishop, Pete. "Donnie Iris Sings His Way Home." *Pittsburgh Press*. December 31, 1981. Page B-2.

28.20: Hall and Oates Billboard Hot 100 chart history at Billboard.com

28.21: Winkelstern, David. "Hall, Oates Returning." Lansing *State Journal*. February 20, 1982. Page 8S.

28.22: Pantsios, Anastasia. "Double Bill Pleases Rock Fans." *Plain Dealer*. March 18, 1982. Page 10-E.

28.23: "Boxscore." Billboard. April 17, 1982. Page 34.

28.24: McDonough, Jack. "Solar Energy Group Plans AOR Push." Billboard. April 17, 1982. Page 28.

28.25: Wilson, Gladys Blews. The Beaver County *Times*. November 12, 1989. Page D5.

28.26: Pantsios, Anastasia. "Iris Warms Weather-Dampened Crowd." Cleveland *Plain Dealer*. June 7, 1982. Page 5-D.

28.27: Ressner, Jeremy. "Coast to Coast." *Cash Box*. June 19, 1982. Page 14.

29. THE HIGH AND THE MIGHTY: THE ALBUM

29.1: Mehno, John. "Broad Music Mix Buoys B-94." Billboard. July 3, 1982. Page 29. *That* is Pittsburgh Rock City.

29.2: Marsh, David. "The High and the Mighty." *Rolling Stone*. Reprinted in Jackson Sun, Jackson TN. February 4, 1983. Page 30.

29.3: Missett, Bill. "Records: Pop/Rock." Pharos Tribune. Logansport, Indiana. November 7, 1982. Page 24.

29.4: Adams, Bret. "Donnie Iris: *Fortune 410*." All Music Guide to Rock, Third Edition, 2002, Backstreet Books. p. 562.

29.5: "Reviews." *Cash Box*. October 9, 1982. Page 12.

29.6: *Billboard*'s Top Album Picks." *Billboard*. October 9, 1982. Page 60.

29.7: Holan, Mark. "Donnie Iris Gets High and Mighty." Cleveland *Scene*. October 21-27, 1982. At Parallel Time.

30. THE HIGH AND THE MIGHTY: THE TOUR

31. PITTSBURGH ROCK CITY

31.1: "Talent in Action." *Billboard*. December 25, 1982. Pages TIA-3, 23.

31.2: Scott, Jane. "The Happening: Iris Out..." *Plain Dealer*. December 24, 1982..

32. THE DONNIE IRIS-B.E. TAYLOR-CRUISERS CONNECTIONS

32.1: *Billboard* Hot 100, January 28, 1984. At Billboard.com

32.2: "Beaver County Hall of Fame." Beaver Valley Musicians Union online. At www.BVmusiciansUnion.org.

32.3: Mervis, Scott. "Singer B.E. Taylor, of 'Vitamin L' and Christmas Tour Fame, Dies at 65." Pittsburgh Post-Gazette. August 8, 2016. At Post-Gazette.com.

32.4: "Biography" at BETaylor.com.

32.5: Holden, Stephen. Rolling Stone, issue 203. January 1, 1976.

32.6: Reed, Ryan. "50 Greatest Prog Rock Albums of All Time: Crack the Sky." Rolling Stone. June 17, 2015. At RollingStone.com.

32.7: "Stanley Theater - Rock Era." Pittsburgh Rock Music History.

32.8: Peaches record store ad. St. Louis *Dispatch*. August 20, 1982. Page 10A.

32.9: You'll often see the *Love Won the Fight* release date listed as January 1, 1983, but don't believe it. See Bishop, Pete. "Colour By Numbers a Tame Portrait of Culture Club." December 18, 1983. Page F6.

32.10: Radel, Cliff. "Cultural Shock Trails Boy George. Cincinnati *Enquirer*. Page B-4, *Tempo*.]

32.11: *Billboard* Hot 100, March 10, 1984. At Billboard.com

32.12: *Billboard* Hot 100, March 17, 1984. At Billboard.com

32.13: Bishop, Pete. "Sit Back and Enjoy Latest From Genesis," etc. *Pittsburgh Press*. July 13, 1986. Page J6.

32.14: *Billboard* Hot 100, June 7, 1986. At Billboard.com

32.15: *Billboard* Hot 100, May 31, 1986. At Billboard.com

33. CHANGES. ROSTER SHAKEUPS. BADNESS.

33.1: Correspondence from MCA to Carousel Records, attn: Rick Frio. October 15, 1982.

33.2: Opinion: Klein, P. J., with Arabian and Croskey, JJ., concurring. Frio v. Superior Court (Ierace) (1988). [No. B033638. Court of Appeals of California, Second Appellate District, Division Three. August 26, 1988.] Richard Frio et al., Petitioners, v. The Superior Court Of Los Angeles County, Respondent; Donald Ierace et al., Real Parties in Interest. Online at Justia.com: Justia › US Law › Case Law › California Case Law › Cal. App. 3d › Volume 203 › Frio v. Superior Court (Ierace) (1988).

34. CRUISING WITHOUT DONNIE: THE PETER EMMETT STORY

34.1: "Biography." SonnyGeracy.net.

34.2: Scott, Jane. "Back to the '60s: Emmett Geraci Says We're Ready." Cleveland *Plain Dealer*. March 11, 1983. Page 43.

34.3: "*Billboard's* Top Albums." *Billboard*. February 19, 1982. Page 60.

34.4: "*Billboard's* Top Albums." *Billboard*. February 26, 1982. Page 52.

34.5: Missett, Bill. "The Peter Emmett Story: Peter Emmett." The Logansport, Indiana *Pharos-Tribune*. February 27, 1983. Page 20.

35. FORTUNE 410: THE ALBUM

35.1: Adams, Bret. "Donnie Iris: *Fortune 410*." *All Music Guide to Rock*, Third Edition, 2002, Backstreet Books. p. 562.

35.2: Sutherland, Sam. "MCA, Atari Pushing Donnie Iris." *Billboard*. August 13, 1983. Page 56.

35.3: *Billboard* cover, June 4, 1983.

35.4: "Reviews." *Cash Box*. June 18, 1983. Page 10.

35.5: Kowalski, Joe. "Donnie Iris Cashes In on Electronic Wizardry." The Fond Du Lac *Commonwealth*. September 25, 1983. Section D, page 2.

35.6: Pantsios, Anastasia. "Is Modernizing Tinkering?" *Plain Dealer*. June 17, 1983. Pages 23, 34.

35.7: Graff, Gary. "Sound Judgment: Briefly Noted." Detroit *Free Press*. August 21, 1983. Page 7F.

36. FORTUNE 410: THE TOUR

36.1: Pantsios, Anastasia. "Iris Bands Proves Self Once More." *Plain Dealer*. June 24, 1983. Friday section: pages 11-12.

36.2: AstroJim. Parallel Time. Post: "Another 1983 Set List." Sat Jun 30, 2007.

36.3: EdBu1. Parallel Time. Post: "Re: ** Official Donnie Iris & The Cruisers Concertography **." Dec 23, 2009.

36.4: Atkinson, Terry. "Pop Review: The Donnie Iris Show Must Go On." Los Angeles *Times*. September 1, 1983. Part VII, Page 7.

36.5: O'Reilly, Larry. "Iris Leaves Audience Standing in the Aisles." *Pittsburgh Press*. October 6, 1983. Page C9.

36.6: Ibid.

37. MEET THE NEW BOSS

37.1: McNary, Dave. "Azoff resigns from MCA." UPI Business wire. September 5, 1989.

37.2: Wilson, Woody. "*Cracking Under Pressure*, The Houserockers." Phoenix Arizona *Republic*. November 9, 1983. Page 213.,

37.3: Correspondence from Carousel Records' Rick Frio to Midwest [National] Records Inc. September 13, 1983.

37.4: Ibid.

37.5: From 44 to 7, according to *Billboard* and/or ...

37.6: From 46 to 5, according to *Hit Men* book. Apparently, the numbers are subject to how MCA International artists are counted.

37.7: Correspondence from Belkin's attorney to Rick Frio of Carousel Records. October 25, 1983.

37.8: According to Cruisers 1983 tour itinerary.

38. NO MUSS... NO FUSS: THE ALBUM

39. THE "AH! LEAH!" LAWSUIT

39.1: "Songwriter's Suit Claims Tune 'Lifted.'" Associated Press. Printed in newspapers including the Indianapolis Star April 22, 1981. Page 14.

40. BIG BREAKUP: LEAVING THE LABEL

40.1: Grain, Paul. "Azoff Says MCA Ready to End Ties to NARM." *Billboard*. May 12, 1983. Page 64.

40.2: Correspondence from Belkin-Maduri Organization attorneys to Midwest Records Inc./Belkin Maduri Organization/Mike Belkin. November 17, 1983.

40.3: Opinion: Klein, P. J., with Arabian and Croskey, JJ., concurring. Frio v. Superior Court (Ierace) (1988). [No. B033638. Court of Appeals of California, Second Appellate District, Division Three. August 26, 1988.] Richard Frio et al., Petitioners, v. The Superior Court Of Los Angeles County, Respondent; Donald Ierace et al., Real Parties in Interest. Online at Justia.com: Justia › US Law › Case Law › California Case Law › Cal. App. 3d › Volume 203 › Frio v. Superior Court (Ierace) (1988).

40.4: Belkin, Michael and Wolff, Carlo. *Socks, Sports, Rock and Art*. Page 152.

40.5: Scott, Jane. "Local Vocalist Introduces New Album." *Plain Dealer*. July 7, 1990. Page 24.

41.   THE SAGA OF "SHE DON'T KNOW ME"

41.1: Vh1. *The Greatest*: 100 Greatest Songs of the 80s. Hour 5. 2006.

41.2: Wood, James. "Bon Jovi, Donnie Iris and Copyright Law: A Conversation With Mark Avsec." March 26, 2012. At Go.Jimmy.Go.net: August 2017.

41.3: "MCA Discography." Discos. Viewed August 2017. And "MCA USA Singles Discography 51000-51233 1980-1982," 45Cat.com. Viewed August 2017.

41.4: MCA ad "MCA Hot and Getting Hotter With Our New Faces." *Cash Box*. September 12, 1981. Page 33.

41.5: Patrol, Gwyneth. "From Hair to Rock Eternity - Interview With Rock Icon Jon Bon Jovi." Brant Publications. July 1995. At BonJOvi230055.free.fr.

41.6: *American Bandstand*. Season 27, episode 28: "Bon Jovi/Mr. Mister." Apr 28, 1984. ABC. Performance also included "Runaway." At TV.com.

41.7: See YouTube.

42.   CELLARFUL OF NOISE I

42.1: Holan, Mark. "Mark Avsec's Cellarful of Noise: A Gang of Two." Cleveland *Scene*. March 24-30, 1988.

43.   ALBRITTON AND KEVIN JOIN THE INNOCENT

43.1: "Grapevine." Cleveland *Scene*. Feb 14-20, 1985. Page 5.

43.2: Scott, Jane. "Patrolmen's Group Digs New Beat: Rock 'n' Roll." Plain Dealer. June 7, 1985. Page 42.

43.3: Ibid.

44.   NO MUSS... NO FUSS, PART II: NEW LINEUP FOR THE NO MUSS TOUR

44.1: Davidson, Jim. "Take Ten: Jazz, Pop Giants in Assorted Sizes." *Pittsburgh Press*. January 20, 1985. Magazine, page 10.

44.2: Distribution agreement between the Belkin-Maduri Organization Inc. and H.M.E. Records Inc. November 14, 1984.

44.3: "H.M.E. Records Plans Major Push." *Cash Box*. December 15, 1984. Page 6.

44.4: Henke, James. *Rolling Stone*, "No Muss... No Fuss." Reprinted in the Cleveland *Plain Dealer*, "No Muss... No Fuss." March 24, 1985. Page 14-P.

44.5: Bishop, Pete. "District Rock Bands Showing Their Stuff on New Albums." Pittsburgh *Press*. February 17, 1985. Page F-5.

44.6: "Donnie Iris: *No Muss... No Fuss*." *Billboard*. February 9, 1965. Page 64.

44.7: "Donnie Iris: Injured in the Game of Love." *Billboard*. January 19, 1985. Page 6.

44.8: "*No Muss... No Fuss*." *Cash Box*. February 16, 1985. Page 8.

44.9: Pantsios, Anastasia. "Pittsburgh Sound Deserves Better. "Friday, February 15, 1985. Page 46.

44.10: Grapevine." Cleveland Scene. Feb 14-20, 1985. Page 5.

44.11: Wolff, Carlo. "CJN's Jews of Interest: Tommy Rich." *Cleveland Jewish News*. May 17, 2013. At ClevelandJewishNews.com

44.12: Scott, Jane. "The Kinks from U.K. Does OK." Cleveland *Plain Dealer*. March 16, 1985. Page 4-C."

44.13: Gorman, John. "The WMMS Coffee Break Concerts." The Buzzard Book Blog. October 22, 2009. At BuzzardBook.wordpress.com.

44.14: Scott, Jane: "Double Stages Set Up for Breaker-Rapper Festival." Cleveland Plain Dealer. May 31, 1986. Page 36-37.

44.15: Cruisers-Bon Jovi flyer for June 15, 1985 show. At YoSteelStrings.com.

44.16: King, Peter B. "Donnie Iris Wows Young Crowd at Mosque." Pittsburgh *Press*. June 15, 1985. Page B9.

44.17: Scott, Jane. "A Baby Emerges as an Idol." *Plain Dealer*. August 10, 1985. Page 5-C."

45.   CELLARFUL OF NOISE, PART 1.5

45.1: Henke, James. In "Funky Guy Puts Fate on Record." Reprinted in *Plain Dealer* September 15, 1985. Page 7-B.

45.2: Ballad "Never Surrender" peaked on *Billboard* Hot 100, number 3, August 17, 1985.

45.3: Kane, Dan. "Cleveland Rockers To Fight Hunger." Canton, Ohio's *The Repository*. July 5, 1985. Archived at Parallel Time.

46.   LOST ALBUM FOUND: CRUISE CONTROL/OUT OF THE BLUE

46.1: "Iris Succeeding At A Slower Pace." Associated Press. Latrobe *Bulletin*. December 5, 1985. Archived at Parallel Time.

46.2: Adams, Bret. "Donnie Iris: *Out of the Blue*." *All Music Guide to Rock*, Third Edition, 2002, Backstreet Books. p. 562-3.

47.   "SUCCEEDING AT A SLOWER PACE."

47.1: "Iris Succeeding At A Slower Pace." Associated Press. Latrobe *Bulletin*. December 5, 1985. Archived at Parallel Time.

47.2: Ibid.

48.   LIPSTICK

49.   ROCKING LAKE ERIE, FROM THE ROCK HALL TO ERIE

49.1: Kalina, Mike. "Jam for Charity." Pittsburgh *Post-Gazette*. December 15, 1987. Page 19.

49.2: Crane, Stanley. "stanleycrane42". Post "The Peninsula Inn In Erie, Pa. Donnie Iris And The Cruisers Played The PI Closing." Jun 29, 2009.

50.   ON TOP OF THE WORLD WITH MASON RUFFNER

50.1: Dylan, Bob. *Chronicles: Volume One*. Page 182. Simon and Schuster, 2004.

50.2: Pantsios, Anastasia. "Gypsy Blood Bath." *Plain Dealer*. May 29, 1987. Page 38.

50.3: Bernade, Scott. "Enigmatic Neil Diamond... Final Note." South Florida *Sun Sentinel*: Fort Lauderdale, Florida. February 27, 1988. Page 28.

50.4: Fricke, David. "Mason Ruffner: Gypsy Blood." Rolling Stone. July 1987. Archived at MasonRuffner.com

50.5: *Billboard* Hot 100 Album chart: *Billboard*. August 8, 1987. At Billboard.com.

50.6: Album Rock Tracks chart: *Billboard*. August 22, 1987. Page 19.

50.7: List of the top-moving albums of all time: Recording Industry of Association of America, "Top 100 Albums as of 13 August 2017. The RIAA counts each disc of an album moved/shipped/given-away-under-the-right-circumstances as one record sold; so if the double album *The Wall* sells one copy, it counts as two units sold. Some double albums are higher on the list than *Supernatural*, but *you* do the math.

51. CELLARFUL OF NOISE II

51.1: Holan, Mark. "Mark Avsec's Cellarful of Noise: A Gang of Two." Cleveland Scene. March 24-30, 1988.
51.2: Ibid
51.3: Ibid
51.4: King, Peter B. "Once Again, Donnie Iris Flirts With Bright Lights of Rock 'n' Roll Stardom." *Pittsburgh Press*. Thursday, March 1988. Page C8.
51.5: Atzinger, Jack. "Rock 'n' Roller to Perform at Daughter's Senior Prom." Beaver County *Times*. April 3, 1988. Page A3.

52. DONNIE IRIS: SUIT AND TIE GUY

53. LIFE GOES ON

53.1: "*100 Greatest Drummers of All Time*: 38. Jim Keltner." Rolling Stone. March 31, 2016. At RollingStone.com.

54. THE CRUISERS II

54.1: Wilson, Gladys Blews. The Beaver County *Times*. November 12, 1989. Page D5.
54.2: King, Peter B. "Iris a Hit, but Squier Not Needed at Toys for Tots Charity Jam." Pittsburgh *Press*. November 25, 1989. B7."

55. FOOTSOLDIER IN THE MOONLIGHT: THE ALBUM

55.1: *Footsolider in the Moonlight* credits. Donnie Iris and the Cruisers. November 1993, Seathru Records.

56. DVE N DAWNIE N PANTS N 'NAT

56.1: McCoy, Adrian. "The Mourning Show: Scott Paulsen Signing off From WDVE." Pittsburgh *Post-Gazette*. December 17, 1999. At Old.Post-Gazette.com.
56.2: "Up Close with WDVE/WXDX OM John Moschitta." FMQB Staff Writers. February 1, 2007. At FMBQ.com.
56.3: McCool, Sam. *New Pittsburghese: How to Speak like a Pittsburgher*. Pittsburgh: Renaissance News Inc. 1982.
56.4: University of Pittsburgh "Pittsburgh Speech and Society" website based on the work of Barbara Johnstone, Professor of Linguistics and Rhetoric at Carnegie Mellon University, and Scott F. Kiesling, Associate Professor of Linguistics at the University of Pittsburgh. According to the site, "Johnstone and Kiesling are sociolinguists who are studying the speech of the Pittsburgh area. The research was funded in part by the U.S. National Science Foundation Collaborative Research Award nos. BCS0417684 and BCS-0417657." At PittsburghSpeech.pitt.edu/
56.5: Evans, Dayna. "Dear Jagoffs, Pittsburgh Officially Has the Ugliest Accent in America." October 20, 2014. Gawker.com. http://gawker.com/dear-jagoffs-pittsburgh-officially-has-the-ugliest-acc-1648212760

57. POLETOWN: THE ALBUM

57.1: Masley, Ed. "Donnie Iris: Poletown." Pittsburgh *Post-Gazette*. March 14, 1997. Weekend: Page 9.
57.2: Lutz, Virginia Ross. "A Nice Place To Visit But... Iris Paints Gloomy Picture With New CD, "Poletown." The *Times*/Beaver Newspapers, Inc. April 23, 1997. Online.
57.3: Mervis, Scott. "Weekend Hot List." Pittsburgh *Post-Gazette*. Weekend section, page 3.

58. LIVE AT NICK'S FAT CITY: THE ALBUM

58.1: Junkyardkid. 2008 comment From YouTube posting of "Injured in the Game of Love" video, published by kpaxfaq July 12, 2007.
58.2: Tady, Scott. "Iris Comes to Life at Nick's." April 30, 1998. The *Times*/Beaver Newspapers, Inc. Page C5.
58.3: Young, John. "Hootie, Collective Soul Rock Star Lake." *Post-Gazette*. June 29, 1999. Page 10.

59. PLANET CHRISTMAS: THE (MARK) ALBUM

60. TOGETHER ALONE: THE ALBUM

60.1: Tady, Scott. "Iris Shows Softer Side on New CD." The *Times*/Beaver Newspapers, Inc. December 2, 1999. Archived at Parallel Time.

62. THE MILLENNIUM COLLECTION: BEST OF DONNIE IRIS. THE ALBUM.

62.1: Erlewine, Stephen Thomas. "*The Millennium Collecti*on: *Best Of Donnie Iris*." *All Music Guide to Rock*, Third Edition, 2002, Backstreet Books. p. 563.
62.2: DeYoung, Bill. *The Millennium Collection: Best Of Donnie Iris* liner notes. Geffen Records. September 18, 2001.
62.3: Excerpts posted on Top40MusicOnCD.com, in forum.

63. THE JAMES GANG RIDES AGAIN, WITH JOE. AND MARK.

63.1: Eagles numbers in "Top Tallies." Recording Industry Association of America. At RIAA.com. August 17, 2017.

64. THINGS DONNIE DOES

65. THE SHOW STOPS, NEARLY FOR GOOD

66. THE 25TH BIRTHDAY CONCERT

66.1: Masley, Ed. "Creative 'Spark.'" Pittsburgh *Post-Gazette*. Thursday, July 14. Page W-17.

67. ELLWOOD CITY: THE ALBUM

67.1: "Jerry Reed and Don Garvin's Hitsville in Beaver County." Pittsburgh Music History.
67.2: Mervis, Scott. "For the Record: Donnie Iris and the Cruisers: *Ellwood City*. Pittsburgh Post-Gazette. June 8, 2006. Page W17.
67.3: Benson, John. "Ellwood City." Cleveland *Plain Dealer*. October 20, 2006. Online.

68. **YOU CAN'T REALLY MISS ME… THE EP**

68.1: Washington, Roxanne. "Cleveland Celebrities to Compete in Flower-Arranging Contest at the Botanical Garden." September 20, 2007. *Plain Dealer*. At Parallel Time.

68.2: "King of Cool." Erie *Times-News*. June 25, 2009. Online.

69. **AH! LIVE!: THE ALBUM**

70. **KING COOL: THE BEER**

71. **AH! LELUIAH!: THE CHRISTMAS ALBUM**

71.1: Green, Aaron. "A Classical Music Profile of Handel's Messiah." February 13, 2017. Thoughtco.Online at ThoughtCo.com.

71.2: Studwell, Willliam. "William Studwell's Christmas Carols of the Year Series." Updated 2010. Chicago *Tribune*. At ChicagoTribune.com.

71.3: Greene, Andy. "Readers' Poll: The Best Christmas Songs of All Time." 30 November 2011. Rolling Stone. Online.

71.4: Woodruff Tait, Jennifer. "O Come, O Come Emmanuel." Christian History Issue 103 in 2012, online at ChristianHistoryInstitute.org.

71.5: LindaJo H. McKim 1993. "The Presbyterian Hymnal Companion." p. 47. Westminster John Knox Press.

71.6: Lunden, Jeff. "The NPR 100: 'White Christmas.'" *All Things Considered*. December 25, 2000. Transcript at NPR.org.

71.7: Thompson, Matt. "The Ironic Intensity of 'Carol of the Bells.'" December 21, 2015. The Atlantic. Online.

71.8: Korchova, Olena. "Carol of the Bells: Back to the Origins." December 17, 2012. The Ukrainian Week. Online.

71.9: Thompson, Matt. "The Ironic Intensity of 'Carol of the Bells.'"

71.10: 2008 date: "Alleluyah Sasa! (He Is Born)" sheet music, page 1. Allaway, Ben. Santa Barabara Music Publishing.

71.11: "About Ben Allaway." Ben Allaway.com. 2012. At BenAllaway.com.

71.12: Fulps, Linda. "Brighten the Holiday Season With S&T Choirs." November 24, 2009. At news.mst.edu.

71.13: Montgomery, June and Renfrow, Kenon. Stories of the Great Christmas Carols. Alfred Publishing Company, 2003. Page 47-48.

71.14: Wainwright, Jonathan. *From Renaissance to Baroque: Change in Instruments and Instrumental Music in the Seventeenth Century*. See introduction. Routledge. July 28, 2005. 340 Pages.

71.15: "Sanctissimi Corpus et Sanguis Christi." Roman Missal, 2011 Latin to English translation.

71.16: Green, Aaron. "Panis Angelicus Lyrics and Text Translation." ThoughtCo. Updated July 21, 2017. Online.

71.17: "The History of 'Hallelujah' Chorus from Handel's *Messiah*." Mormon Tabernacle Choir. August 29, 2016. Online.

71.18: "The History and Words of Auld Lang Syne." Scotland.org.

71.19: "Christmas Carols." BBC. Updated August 4 2009. BBC.co.uk.

71.20: Sheets, Adam. "Adam's Mini-Reviews, Col. 7—Christmas Edition." *No Depression*. December 15, 2010. Online.

71.21: Johns, Martin, a.k.a. "Stubby." "Donnie Iris: Ah! Leluiah! The Christmas Album." Stubby's Christmas. November 17, 2010. At StubbysChristmas.com.

71.22: Behe, Rege. "Pittsburgh Rocker Donnie Iris Records First Christmas CD." Pittsburgh *Tribune-Review*. Tuesday, December 7, 2010. Online.

71.23: Mervis, Scott. "Light Up the Night: Donnie Iris is a One-Man Choir on First Holiday Record." Pittsburgh *Post-Gazette*. November 18, 2010. Page W-16._

72. **DONNIE AND MARK GRADE THE CRUISERS CATALOG**

73. **SINCE…**

74. **THE CRUISERS III: PITTSBURGH MADE**

74.1: Mervis, Scott. "Pittsburgh Rock 'N Legends Awards to Induct Donnie Iris, Lou Christie and Porky Chedwick Darrell. Pittsburgh *Post-Gazette*. March 19, 2015. Online: Post-Gazette.com.

74.2: Wardlaw, Matt. "Concert Promoter Mike Belkin Dishes on the Doors." Ultimate Classic Rock (online). 12 October 2017. UltimateClassicRock.com.

75. **DONNIE IRIS: THE EXIT INTERVIEW**

75.1: Conducted Thursday, September 7, 2017 at Z Pub & Diner, Beaver Falls, PA

Index

Acknowledgements

Ferris expresses repeating gratitude to the many people who helped and kept him going through this project, including but not limited to…

Donnie Iris. Mark Avsec. Kevin Valentine. Paul Goll. Martin Hoenes. Mike Belkin. Albritton McClain. Mark Dvoroznak.

Glenn Ratner: You are the best; this book is proof.

Everybody in these pages. **Alan Greene,** a true guitar hero. Michael Olszewski. **Jim Krenn.** Jimmy Fox. Bill Korecky. Jimmy Roach. Michele Michaels. Jimmy & Steve. Benny Faiella. Jimmie Ross. Ed Traversari. Chuck Statler. Everybody at Parallel Time. Ed Salamon. Stereotom and Sundry1 at 45.com. Ron Gerber. Sean Ross. Annie Zaleski. **Matt Wardlaw.**

Alan Natali. Vince, Tracy, Lucas and Macayla of Clan Bloom-Stigma. Tom Morrissey & Chaplain Tom Morrissey, Sr. Bob Kiefer. Jason Bracelin. Michael Gallucci. David Giffels. Tom Colaberardino, Jon Henderson, and Rich Pronesti. Steven Blush. David Konow. Greg Renoff. Steve & Leah Halpin. Master Randy Harper & family. Tony Erba. Dr. David Barker. Ken Ertel. Gerard Dominck. Dean B. Trew. Christy Carathers Carmody. John Bartolotta. Aaron, Anne, Neil & Cheryl Forsythe. Brian Bittner. James G. Lakely. Jean & James "Butch" Thompson (thank you for taking me to the Syria Mosque). Jarrod Weeks & Jackson O'Connell-Barlow (Grand Buffet). Jayson Shenk. Paul Hooper. Corey Bing. Scott Rupert. Chuck Cage. Audra Heaslip. Sean O'Hara. BJ Kramp. Dr. Jason Martin. Greg Forrest. Sean Byrnes. Svenllama. Gary Suarez. Schuler Benson. Beth Piwkowski. Kapusta Diamond. Argus. Sean Maguire. Jeff Stonehouse. Tim Minneci. Jeff Treppel. Clark Nova. Majorie Blackthorn. Joanna Wilson. Dominic Caruso. Pete Kotz. Frank Lewis. Kevin Smith & Marc Bernardin. Brian Koppelman & Six Second Screenwriting Lessons. Joe Rogan & Onnit. Jay Mohr(s). Diamond Dallas Page & DDP Yoga. Leah, Dalton, Megan, Ryan, Lily, Rich & Char Bardo. Marc Tomasik. Darren, Renee, Carly & Nelly Collins. WBs Bob Becker, George Seabeck, Ron Nockengost, and Michael Bailey. Dan LeRoy. **James, Max, Samantha, and Sumner Ferris.**

RIP: Sumner J. Ferris. Ronald Forsythe. Nora Agnes Ferris. Vera Lehane. David Moran. Gertrude & Vincent Roskovensky. Ronald & Anna Mae Nypaver. Carol & Rich Bardo. Diamond Dave Herth. Olivia Bartolotta. Tim Trunzo. Glenn Robert Traverso. Bernard DeFilippo. Lori Martin. J. Budd Grebb. Mike Hudson (The Pagans). George Stumpf/Spike LeMay (Balomai Brothers). Adam West. Grant Hart. Rik Mayall. Harold Ramis. Bill Paxton. John Hughes. George A. Romero. Fred Rogers.

This book was written to music by Brant Bjork, John Coltrane, Agnes Obel, Max Richter, Max Roach, Sinya Sugimoto, Joe Minadeo, Nine Inch Nails, Lyle Workman, DJ Shadow, Agnes Obel, and Marvin Gaye.

Rachel, Ryley, Sydney, Poppy, Nyx. You are the best. Love is like a rock

Also By D.X. Ferris

***Slayer's* Reign in Blood**
Part of Bloomsbury's *33 & 1/3* series

Slayer 66 & 2/3: The Jeff and Dave Years:
A Metal Band Biography...

The Oral History of Alternative Press

Suburban Metal Dad: Compendium One

The Successful Lodge: Best Practices in Freemasonry
with Ohio Past Grand Master James F. Easterling Jr.

The Martial Arts Parent's Frequently Asked Questions:
How to Unlock Your Child's Potential
with Grandmaster Ryan Andrachik

Donnie Iris is the classic rock/power pop/album oriented rock champion of Pittsburgh, where he has been a fan favorite since the 1960s. As a member of the blue-eyed soul band the Jaggerz, he wrote "The Rapper," which was a no. 1 or no. 2 single, depending which organization's chart you consult. In the Cruisers, he partnered with producer/bandleader Mark Avsec to record seven *Billboard* Hot 100 singles and 13 albums in a long run that kicked off with the hit single "Ah! Leah!" He placed another song on the Hot 100 with Avsec's Cellarful of Noise Project.

He is a retired mortage broker, active frontman, avid golfer, father of two, and grandfather of six. He still has plenty of gas in the tank.

D.X. Ferris grew up in California PA, where the nightly 96KX countdown introduced him to Donnie Iris & the Cruisers, Van Halen and the Police. He spent his paper route money at National Record Mart, Eide's, and the Civic Arena. He later moved to Greentree, in the shadow of Pittsburgh classic rock beacon WDVE. His cousins are from Parma.

Ferris is an Ohio Society of Professional Journalists Best Reporter of the Year. His work includes leadership/motivational/how-to books, an ongoing comic strip, and two books about heavy metal titans Slayer, one of which is part of the prestigious *33 1/3* series.

He still can't decide whether "Ah! Leah!" or "That's the Way Love Ought to Be" is the better song.

Follow him online:
Twitter.com/dxferris
SlayerBook@gmail.com
Facebook.com/SlayerBook

CPSIA information can be obtained
at www.ICGtesting.com
Printed in the USA
BVHW010129290719
554526BV00031B/225/P